The ECONOMICS of The CANADIAN FINANCIAL SYSTEM:

Theory, Policy and Institutions

DAVID E. BOND, Ph.D

Public Service of Canada

RONALD A. SHEARER, Ph.D

Professor of Economics, The University of British Columbia

PRENTICE-HALL **p⚫h** **OF CANADA, LTD.**

Scarborough, Ontario

Prentice-Hall, Inc., Englewood Cliffs, New Jersey
Prentice-Hall International, Inc., London
Prentice-Hall of Australia, Pty., Ltd., Sydney
Prentice-Hall of India, Pvt., Ltd., New Delhi
Prentice-Hall of Japan, Tokyo

Library of Congress Catalogue No. 70-157054
ISBN 0-13-229781-7

2   3   4   5   76   75   74

PRINTED IN CANADA

To

JOSEPH A. CRUMB,
Professor Emeritus, The University of British Columbia,
teacher, critic and friend,
whose passionate interest in monetary economics
attracted many students to the field

&

ROBERT E. HUKE,
Professor of Geography, Dartmouth College,
teacher, scholar, and friend,
whose inspired teaching and thirst for knowledge
are an example to all men

&

RENATE & ELIZABETH
with love

Contents

Preface

This book is intended as a textbook for undergraduate courses in money and banking at Canadian Universities. The level of the analysis presumes the mastery of at least a standard course in the principles of economics.

Over the years, a rather standard format has developed for textbooks in money and banking. With some exceptions, most of the widely used books are variations on a basic theme. The structure and content of this book reflect our dissatisfaction with the standard model. We are critical of the model in general, but feel particularly strongly that it is inappropriate for courses concerned with Canadian financial institutions and Canadian monetary policies. We have consciously departed from it in several important respects.

First, we take the view that we must be concerned with microeconomics as well as macroeconomics. Indeed, to the limited extent that it is possible, the macroeconomic analysis should build on microeconomic foundations. The standard textbook does have a microeconomic section, but we believe that the relevant microeconomics is more than just a description of banking institutions and their operations.

Institutions must be described, and we have devoted considerable space to that task, but we do so on the presumption that the proper scope of the discussion is the whole financial system, including both the chartered banks and non-bank financial intermediaries of all types, and the money and capital markets in both their domestic and their international dimensions. At the same time, we have attempted to avoid presenting a mail-order catalogue of financial institutions. It is important that the institutions be viewed as an integrated system which performs certain basic economic functions (in the spirit of Gurley and Shaw). To this end, their operations must be interpreted in terms of a systematic body of economic theory. We have attempted to do so, using as our foundation an elementary and slightly modified version of what has come to be called portfolio balance theory.

We also take the view that the purpose of economic analysis is the exposition of public policy and policy alternatives. Therefore we have devoted considerable space to the discussion of the development of public policy with respect to the structure of the financial system, both in Canada and the United States, and to the discussion of some of the major issues which have been troubling economists concerned with microeconomic policy in this area. Inevitably we have paid considerable attention to the *Report* of the Royal Commission on Banking and Finance and the subsequent revisions of the *Bank Act*.

Our second major departure from the standard model is in our treatment of historical topics. The typical textbook has major sections on the history of money and of banking institutions, and perhaps an extended discussion of the history of monetary theory. Although we recognize the value of a historical perspective on theory and institutions, these are specialized topics with an already abundant and readily accessible literature. In this book, we could only add another superficial survey. While there are many historical references scattered throughout the text, we have confined our historical chapters to the analysis of the evolution of the structure of the financial industry and the development of government policy toward the financial structure in Canada and the United States. Given the orientation of our microeconomic analysis, these are important topics and, unlike other historical topics, are less adequately developed in the literature which is readily available to undergraduate students.

Our third major point of departure from the standard textbook is in the treatment of international finance. Canada's is an open economy, and, what is more important from our present point of view, the Canadian financial system is likewise open. Canadian monetary economics, like Canadian monetary policy, must have an international orientation. In the standard textbook, international finance is discussed separately in a section at the end of the book, almost as an afterthought. It is our impression that many instructors never get to this section, or, if they do, deal with it very superficially.

We take the position that the discussion of international finance must be *fully integrated* with the discussion of monetary theory and monetary policy. There is no excuse for leaving the Canadian student with a model of monetary policy appropriate only for a closed economy. While our discussion of the macroeconomic aspects of international finance does come towards the end of the book, we have developed the analysis as an extension of the models of monetary policy developed in the previous chapters. We have attempted to adapt the familiar IS-LM model to demonstrate the balance of payments constraint on monetary policy in a regime of fixed exchange rates, and to explore the implications of a regime of flexible exchange rates. We have also explored such topics as speculation in foreign exchange markets and the international liquidity problem from the perspective of their implications for Canadian monetary policy.

Finally, as a fourth major departure, we take the view that wherever possible the conclusions of economic theory must be considered relative to the findings of empirical research. It is difficult and frustrating to attempt to interpret for undergraduate students the often conflicting findings of empirical researchers (the subtleties of methodological controversies defy explanation); however, wherever it seemed relevant, we have attempted to do so. We refer frequently to the results of empirical research, and the second to last chapter is entirely devoted to a survey of research on the effectiveness of monetary policy.

Helpful comments from a number of people helped us to catch many errors before they reached print, though undoubtedly some will remain. Those that do are our fault alone. We must acknowledge particularly useful observations from Carol Clark, Basil Moore, Philip Neher, Douglas Purvis, John Chant, Tom Maxwell, A. A. Shapiro, and John Borcich.

We have been extremely fortunate in having hard-working and imaginative research assistants and we owe a special debt of gratitude to George Temple, Richard Lewin, Tom Gusman, and John Dickenson. In addition, our typists Patricia Miller, Karen Wildie, Trish Purvin-Good, Julia Popp, Mary Shearer and Maria Rasonivic dealt effectively with often illegible manuscripts and strange spelling. They rendered loyal service indeed. Finally we owe much to our students in Economics 308, particularly in the year 1968-69. They suffered through the use of part of the manuscript in its earlier rough state and we profited from their finding our mistakes.

D. E. B.
R. A. S.

The ECONOMICS of
The
CANADIAN
FINANCIAL SYSTEM:
Theory Policy and Institutions

1
The Functions of the Financial System

To the average citizen, finance, financial activities, and the financial system have an aura of mystery. Successful practitioners of the financial arts are widely held in awe — although it is also fair to say that many people regard these financial experts with somewhat the same skepticism as they do astrologers and fortune-tellers. On the one hand, reports of fortunes created overnight, almost magically, stir the imaginations and gambling instincts of many. Likewise, reports of bankruptcies under mysterious circumstances and losses of life savings by "innocent" investors stir rumours, allegations, and public outcries for investigations of fraud and deceptive financial "manipulations". Some of these investigations, in fact, reveal practices which are either illegal or ethically suspect. Partly as a result, the financial industry is surrounded by more government rules and regulations than perhaps any other industry, and new laws are being added to the books almost every year. On the other hand, public forums on the somber issues of government economic policy are seldom considered complete unless they include the considered advice of bankers or investment analysts. Yet back-room discussion of the economic problems of our time commonly center on the theme of the conspiracy of the bankers, domestic or international.

1/THE FINANCIAL INDUSTRY

Myths about finance are embedded in our culture and an anthropologist or sociologist could undoubtedly write a fascinating analysis of the social functions performed by invocations of the financial spirits. To an economist, however, the financial system is but another industry in the economy. True, it is a particularly important industry that frequently has a far-reaching impact on society and the economy, but stripped of its occult trappings, it is, like any industry, a group of firms which combine factors of production (land, labour and capital) under the general direction of a management team, and produce a product or cluster of products for sale in financial markets. These markets have varying degrees of competition,

1

and are regulated by the forces of supply and demand within a general context set by government laws and regulations. It is not quite the same thing as the widget industry, but the general principles applied to the analysis of the widget industry in introductory principles of economics courses can also be applied to the financial industry.

The Output of the Financial Industry

The product of the financial industry is not tangible, as are automobiles, food or clothing. Rather it is an intangible service such as those produced in the barbering or laundry industry. Indeed, it is incorrect to refer to *the* product of the industry. We are not talking about a single service, but a collection of services. It is true that some financial firms specialize in the provision of a single service (or a cluster of very closely related services), but many, including some of the very largest, are complex multi-product firms. The industry as a whole, including specialized and diversified firms, produces a wide range of services, but all of these services are related directly or indirectly to assets and liabilities, i.e., *claims* on people, corporations, institutions, and governments. These are the forms in which people accumulate much of their wealth.

It is not important that we have a complete catalogue of the services offered by the industry, but it useful to identify the most important ones. Basic to almost all the activities of financial firms is the systematic collection and interpretation of *information* on almost all aspects of economic activity. Some of this information is passed on to clients in the form of *professional advice* on invesments and other personal economic problems. On the basis of such information certain financial firms will also undertake to manage the economic affairs of clients (or their estates) on a *trusteeship* basis. Comprehensive, detailed and accurate information is an essential input into almost all the activities of a financial firm, including what we call brokerage and financial intermediation. Many financial firms serve as *brokers* in the same sense that they bring borrowers and lenders together, thus arranging a transaction (for a fee) without being a party to the transaction themselves. Perhaps more familiar are the activities of financial firms as *financial intermediaries*. In this capacity they act simultaneously as borrowers and lenders together. Like a broker, a financial intermediary brings borrowers and lenders together, but unlike a broker it is a party to the transaction. The financial intermediary actually borrows from one group in society (who are often happy to trust the financial intermediary whereas they would not trust those to whom the intermediary lends) and lends to another, thus putting itself at risk should some of the loans be defaulted. The activities of a financial firm as an intermediary are sometimes confused in the popular mind with another service, the provision of *safekeeping* for valuable property. Thus, depositors in a bank frequently fail to recognize that they are creditors of the bank: they have in fact lent the bank money. Safekeeping is provided by the safety-deposit box department of the bank, not by the deposit wickets. Furthermore, safekeeping is a minor service to customers, incidental to the main business at hand. Finally, we must note that the financial system provides facilities for the *transfer of purchasing power* from individual to individual, or from firm to firm, both within the country and internationally. It thus arranges the financial side of almost all exchanges consummated in markets in the economy, and in the process provides a detailed set of *records* of transactions, both for the use of the individuals concerned and, in different forms, for government agencies and the public at large. The financial system is a primary source of statistics used in analyzing national and international economic activity.

Value Added in the Financial Industry

So much for the nature of the products of the financial industry. How important is this industry relative to the total economy?

The accepted measure of the aggregate output of the economy is the gross national product. Correspondingly, the appropriate measure of the output of any single industry is "'value added" in that industry. "Value added" is defined as the difference between the market value of the product produced and sold by the industry, and the cost of all materials purchased from other industries (e.g., raw materials, component parts, fuel, advertising services, etc.). It is thus equal to the payments for the services of all factors of production directly employed in that industry (rents, wages, interest) plus any residual profit earned by the owners of the firms. In other words, it is the value of "income originating" in the industry. Since such a calculation avoids the error of double counting – of counting as output in one industry what is in fact the output of another industry, as when you simply add up the value of sales by industry – "value added" is the best measure of the relative contribution of any industry to aggregate national output.

In attempting to measure value added in the financial industry, certain complications arise which are discussed in books on national income accounting. The problem arises in the treatment of interest. In accounting for value added in a normal industry, interest received is deducted from the income of the firms on the grounds that this does not represent payment for services of capital employed in production in that industry. If this procedure is carried out for financial intermediaries the value added by the industry is almost invariably negative. According to national income accountants this answer is "unacceptable" so they resort to imputations; that is, they assign an arbitrary value to the services provided by the financial intermediaries to their customers. The resulting estimates are severely criticised by some economists, and must be regarded as approximations only. Further complications arise in attempting to use the published estimates, since value added by the financial industry is not shown separately, but is included in the category "Finance, Insurance, and Real Estate". In recent years this category accounted for less than 10% of gross national product. The financial industry proper (excluding real estate, but including insurance) probably accounted for 3% of gross national product.

Put differently, the financial industry directly accounts for perhaps 1/30 of the gross output of goods and services produced in this nation. This clearly establishes it as a major industry. But can we take this as sufficient indication of the importance of the financial industry?

2/ECONOMIC FUNCTIONS OF THE FINANCIAL SYSTEM

The economic significance of the financial system and its operations cannot be assessed in the same way as that of the widget industry. It is not simply a matter of adding up value added and expressing that as a proportion of national output. If the widget industry were removed from the economy, perhaps by an act of Parliament, repercussions might be felt in many segments of the economy. Suppliers of materials would find that part of their market had disappeared, and hence they would have to adjust the scale of their production. Employees in the widget industry, and probably in supplying industries, would have to seek new employment. Purchasers of widgets would have to make do with substitutes, and if the widget were an essential input into some other industry perhaps that industry would be faced with impossible difficulties. Depending on the size of the industry and the nature of its relations with other industries, the repercussions could be felt over a wide circle of economic activity. In some cases, the adjustments could be painful and protracted. However, given time, the economy would adjust. Without the widget industry, economic activity would be different; but it would carry on.

If the financial industry were removed in the same way, we could not be so optimistic about the outcome. Unlike the widget industry, the financial industry provides services which are essential to every industry in the economy. In this sense, financial activities are complementary to all other economic activities. While the financial industry may not be unique in this respect, it nonetheless means that the importance of the industry transcends that indicated by the relative size of value added in the industry. It performs certain essential functions for the economy, including the maintenance of the payments system, the collection and allocation of the savings of society, and the creation of a variety of stores of wealth to suit the preferences of individual savers.

The Payments System

The payments system is the set of institutional arrangements through which purchasing power is transferred from one participant in an exchange to another, i.e., from the buyer to the seller.

Why do we consider this to be an essential economic function? Ever since the discipline of economics was established as a systematic analysis of economic activity, economists have been asserting that specialization in productive activities is a necessary (but not sufficient) condition for the achievement of a high general standard of living. Without an elaborate division of labour into specialized tasks the application of modern technology would be inconceivable. But the counterpart of specialization is exchange. The man who specializes in the activity of dog-catching must somehow obtain the variety of goods and services which he and his family wish to consume. He must exchange his services for the products of other specialized producers. Efficient exchange also implies an intermediary which we call money. Money, in a sense, is generalized purchasing power: something which all of the participants in the economy are willing to accept in payment for goods and services, not because they want to consume it, but because they know that they can exchange it with some other person, now or later, for the things which they desire. The use of money in the exchange process is quite apart from any utility which the monetary medium itself might yield as a commodity. Indeed, it is not necessary that the monetary medium be something which is desired as a commodity: it can be marks on the books of a banker as well as some finite object such as pieces of gold or paper. We will return to the concept and properties of money later in the book. Suffice it to note at this point that any number of things have been used as money under varying circumstances. But whatever the instrument, and whatever the concrete historical circumstances of its evolution as the monetary medium, confidence that others would accept it in the normal course of business has always been a necessary condition for anything to serve as money.

It is difficult, but not impossible, to conceive of an exchange economy without money. All exchange would have to involve a direct bartering of goods for goods. But barter can only be an efficient method of exchange when there occurs a *double coincidence of wants,* that is, when each party to the exchange has precisely what the other party desires, at the time required, and in quantities appropriate to the exchange. In a large, complex society this implies a remarkable coincidence of events in time and space. Under other circumstances — that is, under normal circumstances — barter must involve a series of indirect exchanges. Each individual must take payment in kind, consume what he wishes, and store or perhaps transport the excess until the time and place are right for him to exchange it for the items which he requires. Clearly, such a system would be highly wasteful of time and resources.

What we have referred to as the payments system is simply a set of institutional arrangements for the transfer of money from person to person, frequently among persons widely separated geographically, often in different countries using different monies. Our interest in the payments system is that of an economist and not that of a financial expert, an accountant, or a geographer. We are not concerned with the techniques of effecting payments or with techniques of recording payments, or even with what the patterns of payments tell us about the geographical patterns of production and trade. Granted that a payments system is essential to an exchange economy, what further questions might an economist ask about it?

The answer is two-fold: he must be concerned with the *efficiency* of the payments mechanism and with its *neutrality* with respect to the essential economic decisions of society.

As we have described it, effecting payments is essentially a mechanical activity, one increasingly performed by electronic equipment. Still it is not a costless activity: it absorbs scarce resources (labour and capital) which have alternative uses. The less the labour and capital absorbed in effecting a given value of payments, the greater the efficiency of the payments system, the greater the supply of these scarce resources available for other productive employments, and hence the greater the potential output of the economy. This, then, must be a primary interest of economists in the payments mechanism.

Although efficiency is a primary interest of the economist, it must be only part of his concern with the payments mechanism. The economic system is, at root, a social mechanism for making certain decisions: for effecting social choices relating to what is to be produced, how and where it is to be produced, and to whom it is to be distributed. As a mechanical counterpart of the exchange process the payments system is involved in this decision-making. But apart from the fact that the participants in the process must bear the cost of effecting transactions emanating from their decisions, the payments system itself should be essentially neutral as among possible outcomes. The operations of the payments mechanism should not discriminate among transactors or among types of transactions except on the basis of different marginal costs of effecting transactions. Given the pervasive involvement of the payments mechanism in the exchange processes of the economy, the economist must ask if this neutrality is in fact achieved.

Our discussion of the payments system in Chapter 2 is largely descriptive. In part this reflects the fact that description is a necessary preliminary to analysis. However, it also reflects the fact that little economic research has been done on the Canadian payments system. While we attempt to cast some light on the two important economic issues, we are perhaps doing so in the spirit of suggesting relevant fields for research rather than reporting on established research findings.

The Accumulation and Allocation of Savings

In principles of economics courses it is demonstrated that an exchange economy can be characterized as two reciprocal flows: a flow of real goods and services and a reverse flow of payments. The real flows are our ultimate concern. These are what determine our standard of economic well-being. However, the *financial flows* are not irrelevant for they *elicit and guide the real flows.*

Thus, consumer expenditures (or expectations of such expenditures) elicit production of appropriate items. Likewise, income payments from business firms elicit flows of productive services. On the real side of this scheme, households appear as consuming units with distinct preferences, and as providers of productive services with distinct characteristics. Business firms appear as producing units motivated by profits, and as units which absorb productive services to produce the goods and services demanded by households (and by other firms and government agencies). The government has an ambiguous role. In some respects it is a unit for collective consumption; in other respects it is a producer of goods and services; in still other respects it is a vehicle for the establishment and administration of public policies. Like other producing units it participates in the circular flow as an absorber of productive services. Unlike the consumer and business units, it does not normally respond to market indicators in its decisions on what to produce.

In real terms each of these groups of units has distinct functions and characteristics. However, they are all alike in that they are all *spending units;* all receive funds from various sources and spend funds for the purchase of goods and services. Each spending unit has sources of revenue: primarily the sale of productive services in the case of households; the sale of products in the case of business firms; and tax collections in the case of governments. In a general way, the expediture of any spending unit is linked to its revenue. However, revenues do not have to control expenditures on goods and services during any period of time. A spending unit's revenues may well exceed its expenditures on goods and services, and in this sense it may have a *surplus* budget. But alternatively its expenditures on goods and services may exceed its revenues, and for that period it may have a *deficit* budget.

These financial surpluses and deficits have their counterparts in real terms. A financial surplus implies that during that period the spending unit has chosen not to acquire all of the goods and services which its revenues would permit. A financial deficit implies that during that period the spending unit has been able to acquire more goods and services than its revenues would permit. Taking the two together, there is a transfer of command over resources from the surplus spending units to the deficit spending units. The transfer is arranged through the financial system; and this then is the second major function of the financial system. *It collects the surpluses of the surplus spending units and makes them available to the deficit spending units.*

Stated this way, it sounds like a mechanical process similar in effect to the payments mechanism. There is much more involved than the mechanical acts of collection and transfer. The financial surpluses (and their real equivalents) are, after all, scarce resources capable of many alternative possible uses. It is necessary to adjust the total available supply and the total demand (either by adjusting the demand or the supply, or both), and to allocate the actual supply forthcoming among all of the competing demands. That is, the financial system must act like a market — a market in which prices are formed and adjusted to variations in supply and demand so as to clear the market. This is far from the mechanical type of process described in the discussion of the payments system.

The prices which are formed in financial markets are interest rates. While they perform the same general role, they have a significance somewhat different from other prices in the economy. Interest rates indicate the market rate of exchange between dollars for present use and dollars for use at some time in the future. In this sense they reflect the opportunity cost of funds devoted to current consumption by households, and thus should affect household decisions regarding the division of income between consumption and saving. Likewise, they represent the opportunity cost to corporations of funds devoted to particular capital projects. They provide a standard against which the probable profitability of any project can be assessed to determine whether the project should be undertaken. Thus, even if the agency of the financial system is not directly involved, the information provided by the financial system should be highly relevant to a broad range of economic decisions, i.e., those relating to the balancing of future gains and present costs.

Throughout this discussion (with one exception) we have studiously avoided the terms *saving* and *investment* in describing this function of the financial system. As a result, in place of the straightforward statement that the financial system transfers command over resources from savers to investors we have had to use the cumbersome phrase "from surplus spending units to deficit spending units". While it sounds pedantic, we have chosen this expression quite deliberately and with another purpose in mind. Saving and investment are technical terms in economic analysis with important and widely recognized meanings. They are not necessarily the same as the financial surpluses and financial deficits to which we refer. Investment implies expenditures to acquire physical capital goods, to expand the productive capacity of the firm and hence of the economy. But a spending unit may be in deficit for reasons unrelated to capital formation. A household, for example, may require funds simply to support a level of consumption in excess of its current income. Likewise, a spending unit may save and yet not have a financial surplus in the sense of that term used here. This would be true, for example, of a firm which finances its capital formation (investment) out of its undistributed profits (savings).

It is true, however, that the bulk of the transfers to which we are referring are related to the process of capital formation. They involve the collection of the financial counterpart of the saving of the society and its allocation to competing demands for capital formation. This means that the operations of the financial system are vital to the pace and structure of the growth of the economy. However, we must not forget that some portion of the transfers are to households to acquire consumer goods and services and to governments for assorted purposes, including collective consumption.

What are the questions that an economist would ask about the functioning of the financial system as an allocative mechanism? The answer is quite simple: he would be concerned with its effectiveness in directing funds to uses with the highest social value at the margin, and doing so at least cost, and the mechanism's flexibility in adapting to changing patterns of demand and supply. Inevitably, as in any market, the quest for such information leads the economist to an analysis of competitive conditions in financial markets.

Again, much of our discussion must be descriptive. The financial system is incredibly complicated even in its purely domestic aspects. The fact that any student of the Canadian financial system must immerse himself in international financial arrangements as well only adds to the complications. There is no escaping the fact that an analysis of the economic efficiency of the financial system must be predicated upon a reasonably full understanding of the complex interrelationships within the system. And again, as in the discussion of the payments system, our conclusions on the efficiency of the financial system as an allocative device may seem weak by contrast to our ambitions as set out here. The reason again is the paucity of professional research on the economics of the Canadian financial system.

Financial Intermediation

Assets, liabilities, and wealth are central concepts in our analysis of the financial system. These are familiar concepts to accountants; indeed, they are the stuff of which accounts are made. The terms refer to market values (even though the market value is frequently estimated rather than determined by actual transactions) measured in terms of the unit of value, or unit of account, the dollar. Thus, one's assets are the things of value owned. Assets derive their value either from the fact that they are capable of yielding income in the future (as a factory might yield income to its owners) or from the fact that they have qualities which are prized by others who are therefore willing to pay to obtain them (as a work of art might be prized and hence valuable). One's liabilities are the value of his obligations, what he owes. Wealth is simply the difference between the value of assets and liabilities.

An individual, a family, or a nation becomes wealthy by the process of accumulating assets in excess of liabilities. This is normally done through the acts of saving and investing. If we leave aside the possibility of accumulating claims on residents of other countries, a nation can accumulate wealth in basically two forms: physical capital goods and the intangible skills, knowledge, organizational patterns, and work habits of its population (what is sometimes called human capital). These are the assets which are capable of producing output and hence income to the inhabitants of the nation in the future. However, through the financial system, any individual within the nation has a much wider range of choices open to him as to the forms in which he can accumulate wealth. He is not restricted to the accumulation of physical and human capital. He can hold financial instruments or securities which represent claims on other individuals or organizations. Hence, he can participate, directly or indirectly, in the income stream generated by the human and physical capital held by others. This indirect participation is made possible through the financial system.

You may well ask how significant is this fact? Is not our ultimate concern real income and wealth? Is it not true that, for society as a whole, income and wealth can only be produced by the underlying physical and human assets to which we referred earlier? Indeed, if we set out to measure the wealth of society, all of the complex layers of financial claims would cancel themselves out, leaving only the underlying human and physical capital assets. This follows because every claim which appears as some person's assets is simultaneously someone else's liability. When you measure the wealth of the two combined, the asset of one (positive wealth?) cancels out the liability of the other (negative wealth?). Thus, if Jones owns a $1 million claim on Smith, and Smith owns a factory worth $2 million, the wealth of the two combined is $2 million, not $3 million, i.e., it is the value of the underlying capital asset. If we say Jones' wealth is $1 million, then Smith's is only $1 million, the value of his asset less the value of Jones' claim. We can push it a step farther by noting that, if Smith and Jones could exchange promissory notes (promises to pay), each would acquire an asset, his claim on the other, and each would acquire a liability, the other's claim on him. In the extreme, they could create a truly staggering total of paper assets for each of them. Note, however, that in spite of all this financial activity no real wealth would be created. Can we not conclude, therefore, that as economists interested in the real income and wealth of society we can well afford to ignore the complex of claims and counter-claims generated through the financial system? Do they appear as a veil, obscuring the real processes of saving and investing which create the real wealth of society, but having no vital significance of their own? Perhaps we would do better to allocate our scarce analytical resources to the study of the real processes themselves.

Reverting to the Jones-Smith example, everyone would presumably agree that it is possible that without Jones' indirect participation Smith might not have had the resources to build the factory. In this sense the creation of financial claims may have some significance. But this is just another aspect of the process which we have already discussed. The financial system serves as a vehicle for collecting the surpluses of surplus spending units and transferring them to deficit spending units. The surplus unit (Jones) is given a financial instrument as evidence of its continuing command over the scarce resources of the economy. This is nothing new. This transaction simply amounts to Jones and Smith pooling their resources to achieve an objective which, at that point in time neither could achieve alone. It perhaps illustrates the point that financial instruments are *divisible* in a fashion in which real capital assets may not be, but that is about all.

The fact of *divisibility* is important, however. At a maximum it permits the pooling together of the small financial surpluses of many isolated individuals to finance a venture of considerable magnitude. Thus, divisibility is important for the efficient collection and use of the savings of society, especially where these savings occur in small, isolated quantities.

Beyond this, divisibility also permits a *diversification* of asset holdings which would not otherwise be possible. Let us refer to any individual's collection of assets as his *portfolio*. We have said nothing about the form of Jones' claim on Smith. Perhaps it takes the form of a claim to half of the profits earned by the factory. In agreeing to share in Smith's venture in this way Jones must recognize that the returns from the factory are conjectural. If they occur at all, they will occur in the future. The magnitude of the possible profits cannot be known now with any degree of certainty. Market conditions could emerge in which not profits, but rather heavy *losses,* are sustained by the venture. On the other hand, the returns could be much in excess of any expectations that the two men might have at the outset. There is some element of *risk* involved; returns may be large or small, and in the extreme the asset could become worthless. By holding only this asset in his portfolio, Jones bears the full burden of this risk. If the factory fails, his wealth is correspondingly reduced (of course, if the factory should prosper beyond all expectations, his wealth would increase correspondingly).

However, Jones does not have to commit all of his resources to Smith's venture. Even if he split his resources between two ventures which are in some sense equally risky, the total risk on his portfolio would be reduced, at least if the success of one of the ventures was not in some fashion related to the success of the other (i.e., if the risks were *independent* of each other). This follows because it is less likely that two independent ventures will fail at the same time than that either of them will fail individually. The risk on his portfolio could be reduced even farther by spreading the funds over a variety of ventures, each with risks independent of each other. The financial system makes such diversification feasible for even relatively small portfolios.

But the financial system goes even farther than that. It creates financial instruments which have properties completely unlike those of physical or human assets. It creates a variety of assets which are virtually — indeed, in the extreme, completely — free of the risks inevitably attached to the real capital assets upon which the value of the financial instruments ultimately rest.

As a step in that direction, we might again consider the claim which Jones has upon Smith, and particularly the *form* of that claim. So far, we have implicitly assumed that it took the form of a claim to a share of the potentially variable earnings of the venture. That is, we assumed that it was a *variable income security*. This is not the only form possible. The agreement between Smith and Jones might call for a specified dollar payment to Jones periodically (and perhaps a final payment on some date, after which the claim would no longer exist). Then the claim would take the form of a *fixed income security*. In the case of the variable income security, Jones bore part of the risk of fluctuation in the venture's earnings. In the case of a fixed income security, Smith bears all of this risk. Jones is entitled to a *certain* fixed payment, whether the earnings of the venture are large or small. Of course, there is a still larger risk which Jones cannot escape in this way. There is the risk that the venture will fail completely; that is, the risk that Smith will be unable to meet his commitment. This risk can only be hedged against by diversification. The certainty of payment on a fixed income security is only certainty in the small, i.e., in the absence of major catastrophes to the venture.

The financial system facilitates diversification in another way. Not only does it permit the division of real assets and income streams into smaller parcels, it also provides markets in which the financial instruments can be traded among individuals. Securities vary in *marketability* as the characteristics of the underlying concerns are or are not known to a wide circle of potential investors. However, through efficient, organized markets, millions of dollars worth of transactions in securities occur every day in Canada.

Our man Jones has wealth of $1 million at his disposal. He can obtain a considerable range of diversification among his assets, and yet have a significant sum invested in each venture. This is not true of the typical individual, who may have only a few thousand dollars at his disposal (over and above his own earning power, which is normally his major asset). However, what is possible for an individual through diversification of his portfolio is also possible for specialized financial institutions. We call such institutions *financial intermediaries*, and the function which they perform in the economy we call *financial intermediation*. These institutions hold a diversified portfolio of claims, each of which may have a substantial degree of risk, and issue their own liabilities which are largely (but not necessarily completely) devoid of such risk. Standing as an intermediary between the ultimate lender and the ultimate user of the funds, they absorb risk, and thus completely alter the range of investment opportunities open to individuals, and particularly the small investor. Financial intermediaries provide financial instruments which incorporate the advantages of portfolio diversification by being claims upon diversified portfolios.

Indeed, through the vehicle of the financial intermediary, the financial system carries the process a step farther. The system provides a variety of financial instruments — each of which is a claim on a diversified portfolio of claims — with widely varying characteristics designed to appeal to the specific preferences of very differently situated assetholders. We will have occasion to examine some of these later on, but one type of instrument requires special mention at this point. Financial intermediaries create assets which have the property of *liquidity*, or convertibility into a fixed amount of money on demand. Indeed, what we widely use as *money*, the demand deposit or chequing account, is precisely such a financial instrument. Many economists argue that this provision of liquidity is the most significant aspect of financial intermediation. While holding essentially illiquid assets themselves intermediaries are able to create liquid assets to be held by the ultimate savers in the economy.

What then is the significance of the fact that the financial system creates a wide variety of financial instruments and markets on which they can be traded efficiently? What is the economic importance of financial intermediation? Have we really answered our earlier objection that all of this financial activity is so much window dressing, a curtain obscuring our view of the true processes of saving and investing in the economy? What is the economist's interest in it all?

Underlying our analysis is the assumption that individuals have preferences as to the *form* in which they accumulate their assets. By creating a diverse range of assets the financial system permits a more complete satisfaction of these preferences, and in this sense permits an increase in economic welfare. This includes making available relatively risk-free and highly liquid assets as well as assets in which the degree of risk is accentuated and which are therefore calculated to appeal to those with gambling instincts.

Beyond this are the implications for public policy designed to influence the level of income, employment and prices in the economy. If individuals have preferences among assets, they presumably alter their portfolio choices as the characteristics of assets change, and particularly as the relative yields on assets change. Thus, a decline in the yield on a particular asset may induce many individuals to select something else. On the one hand, a general decline in the rates of reurn on financial assets may well induce the selection of non-financial (real) assets in their place. On the other hand, the decline in rates may encourage some to borrow so as to acquire a real asset. Such *substitution effects* can have important implications for the level of economic activity.

We have discovered over time that the government, primarily through the agency of the central bank, is able to alter the supply of certain types of financial instruments, particularly money and claims upon the central government. This affects the rate of return on these assets, and hence produces substitution effects of the type noted above. The end product should be change in the demand for real capital assets, and hence an effect on aggregate demand, the level of income employment, and prices in the economy. This suggests the possibility of a monetary policy, by which we mean a policy designed to use these financial linkages for constructive social purposes, particularly the stabilization of the economy. Proper policy proposals then, are a matter of major interest to the economist. How can such a policy be effected? What rules ought to guide it? How powerful will its effects be? How successful have we been in using this tool? These matters, of profound significance to every citizen, are the subject matter of the second half of this book.

3/THE SOCIAL INTEREST IN THE FINANCIAL SYSTEM: OUR APPROACH TO THE ANALYSIS

Following this rather academic discussion of the functions of the financial system, it may be well to extract the essence of what we have said about the social interest in the financial system. Why should students of economics be concerned with money, banking, and finance?

Our first proposition is that the payments mechanism is part of the financial system, and its efficiency affects the overall efficiency of the economy. Secondly, the financial system is a vehicle by which a scarce resource, savings, is allocated among alternative competing uses. The use of the flow of savings affects both the rate of growth of the economy and the structure of economic activity. It is a matter of basic importance. Thirdly, the financial system is the repository of the claims to wealth of most families in this country, who have selected financial assets partly because of their belief that these assets are safe. It is important that this not be an illusion, for the consequences of financial collapse are grave. Finally, we have suggested, the interrelationships within the financial system give rise to the possibility of monetary policy designed to influence the level of income and employment in the economy. This alone should be sufficient to create an interest in the economics of money and finance.

2

Money and the Payments System

Money is a commonplace phenomenon. It is involved in all of our personal economic activities and is so much a part of our everyday life that we tend to take it for granted. Occasionally, perhaps following a casual visit to a numismatic shop or a discussion with a coin-collecting friend, we may be bemused by the diversity of things which have been used as money in different times and places. Or we may struggle with strange coins and unfamiliar denominations in another country, and wonder at how such different "monies" can coexist in the world. But seldom do we stop and carefully consider how the "money system" works. Why can I obtain what I want at a store by handing over pieces of paper? Why will only certain pieces of paper do? How can I be sure that if I write and mail a cheque to pay a bill in a distant city (or perhaps another country) that my creditor will in fact be paid? And if he is paid, what are the mechanics of the transfer? If we give pause, these and many similar questions may occur to us.

1/THE MONEY SUPPLY

Money Defined

What is money? A suitable definition might be: *anything which is normally accepted when a transfer of purchasing power takes place.*

Long philosophical treatises have been written about the essence of "moneyness", attempting to explain why money is money — why certain objects are "normally accepted when a transfer of purchasing power takes place". Our definition, however, is pragmatic, not probing the essence of moneyness, but rather acknowledging as money anything which is in fact used as a customary and normal medium of exhange.

The words *customary* and *normal* are important. Our definition rules out things which may emerge on an occasional *ad hoc* basis as an intermediary in isolated and irregular exchange, but at the same time admitting the possibility of a wide variety of objects performing this function in different times and different places: cigarettes in prisoner of war camps; cowrie shells in the primitive native trading economies of the precolonial Pacific Islands and the coasts of Africa; tobacco or warehouse receipts for tobacco in the colony of Virginia; playing-cards in New France; gold and silver in the form of bullion, dust or coins; and paper promissory notes of governments throughout the world.

What money is, then, is a matter of customary practice. The nature of the money supply in any particular area will evolve over time as customary practices adapt to changing circumstances. A list of items to be considered money at one point in time may be inappropriate at another. Moreover, at any given point in time, such a list may seem somewhat arbitrary. Whether a particular item qualifies as money or not involves a matter of judgement: is it a "normal and customary medium of exchange"?

Commodity vs. Fiat Monies

The story of the evolution of money in different historical, geographical and cultural contexts is fascinating. Many people have sought general principles underlying this evolution, and it may be that such principles do exist. However, it is not part of our purpose to attempt to identify them, such a quest being more suited to the sociologist or anthropologist than the economist. As one scholar has noted, "Money does not exist in a vacuum. It is not a mere lifeless object, but a social institution."[1] However, we must take some interest in the form of the basic monetary medium because it affects the possibility for deliberate manipulation of the money supply as an aspect of government economic policy. The significant fact from this point of view is that while the process has been neither steady, one-directional, nor complete, the development of modern monetary systems has involved the displacement of *commodity monies* by intangible claims or *fiat monies*.

In early history, the object used as money tended to be one with intrinsic value as a commodity (as well as certain other desirable properties), or to be representative of such a commodity and freely convertible into it on demand. This commodity is normally referred to as the *standard money*. The most widely recognized monetary commodities are, of course, gold, and to a lesser extent silver, and as a result the historical literature on monetary systems abounds with references to types of gold standards, silver standards and bimetallic standards (with both metals as standard monies). Indeed, in spite of the passing of a formal gold standard, many people still regard gold as money *par excellence*.[2]

One effect of having a commodity base for the money supply was to place the size of the money supply largely (but seldom completely) beyond the control of the government. It was strongly influenced by forces governing the availability of the standard commodity. Thus, with a gold standard, the money supply would be affected by forces affecting the output of newly mined gold (including erratic discoveries of new rich deposits); the flow of gold in international trade; and the absorption of gold by industry for non-monetary purposes.

In modern times this link to a commodity has largely been broken. The coins issued by a modern state tend to be simply tokens, the value of the metal which they contain being far less than the value of the coin as a coin. Similarly, the notes which are issued as currency are generally not convertible on demand into any standard commodity (except in the sense that any holder of money can presumably purchase whatever commodities he prefers in the open market). Modern currencies are *fiat monies*. They are issued by governments, are not representative of any commodity, and are not redeemable in terms of such a commodity. By government fiat or decree, they are *legal tender*. That is, creditors are legally obligated to accept such currencies in settlement of debts. Since there is no legal link to a commodity, modern monetary systems are generally referred to as inconvertible paper standards. The possibilities for deliberate manipulation of the money supply — for good or evil — should be apparent.

There is another aspect of an inconvertible paper standard which also should be of interest to a student of economics. When the money supply is based on a commodity such as gold, an expansion of the money supply can only be accomplished by employing scarce productive resources to produce more of the commodity (or by attracting more of the commodity from alternative possible uses). A substantial economic cost is involved, equal, at the margin, to the value of the money created. With inconvertible paper money, the creation of more money is virtually (but not completely) costless. It does not absorb anywhere near the same value of scarce productive resources. As a result, by economizing on the scarce resources of the world, while performing exactly the same economic function, inconvertible paper money permits the attainment of a (slightly) higher overall standard of living.

In fact, in any modern economy, both token coins and fiat paper currencies constitute but a fraction of the money supply and account for an even smaller fraction of the total value of payments in the economy. By far the most important medium of exchange is the bank deposit which is convertible into currency on demand and is transferable among individuals by cheque. By our definition, these deposits are money, although they are not legal tender. They are "normally accepted when a transfer of purchasing power takes place." Yet they are completely intangible. They are claims on a private institution, a bank, taking the form simply of entries in a ledger book. Such money is commonly referred to as *bank money* or *credit money*, or, since it is based on trust in the soundness of the institution, *fiduciary money*.

The Canadian Money Supply

Armed with our pragmatic definition of money, what would we have to count if we set out to measure the Canadian money supply? The most obvious items, upon which we would all immediately agree, are the coins and notes used for hand to hand circulation. While the term *currency* is frequently used only with reference to the paper notes, we can properly use it to refer to both the coins and notes. In Canada, all currency is now issued by agencies of the Government of Canada.

Coins. Coins are manufactured and issued by the Royal Canadian Mint, a branch of the Department of Finance. With one exception, (a $20 gold coin minted in 1967 and 1968 and designed and sold as a collector's item rather than for actual circulation, although it is legal currency), these coins are intended to be *tokens*. That is, the face value of each coin is intended to be substantially greater than the market value of the metal contained in the coin. Since the coins are in effect sold to the public at their face value, the manufacture and issuance of coins is normally a profitable business. The difference between the face value of the coins and the value of the coins as metal is known as *seignorage*, and, after allowing for the other expenses related to the operation of the mint, it provides a (relatively minor) source of revenue for the Government. In 1970, for example, the Royal Canadian Mint reported net gains on minting coins of approximately $8 million.

While coins are *intended* to be tokens, they do contain metal which has market value as a commodity. Since that market value can change under the combined pressures of supply and demand, it can happen that the value of the metal as a commodity comes to exceed the face value of the coin. This was dramatically illustrated in 1966 when the price of silver rose sharply in the open market, making the commodity value of Canada's silver coins exceed their value as coins. This not only made it unprofitable for the Mint to manufacture the traditional silver coins, but also made it profitable for private individuals to melt down the silver coins for their metal content (this is illegal, of course). As a result, the Government reduced the silver content of new Canadian coins and in 1968 began to replace the silver coinage with pure nickel coins.

Paper Currency. The issuance of paper money in Canada is a government monopoly. It is the exclusive right and responsibility of the Bank of Canada, a crown corporation under the jurisdiction of the Minister of Finance.

The issuance of notes for circulation was not always a government monopoly in Canada. Prior to 1935, privately owned chartered banks had the right to issue paper currency. On December 31, 1934, of total currency outstanding of $252 million, $119 million, or 47%, were chartered bank notes. The balance was in coin and Dominion Notes issued by the Government of Canada. In 1935 the Bank of Canada began operations and assumed responsibility for the issuance of paper currency. (Initially privately owned, it was nationalized shortly after it was founded.) The chartered banks were required to gradually reduce the amount of their notes in circulation, and in 1950 the liability for such bank notes as were still outstanding (approximately $14 million) was assumed by the Bank of Canada in exchange for a corresponding payment to the Bank of Canada by the banks.

Bank of Canada notes are liabilities of the Bank of Canada, and until June 1970 they all bore the inscription, "The Bank of Canada will pay to the bearer on demand one dollar" (or "two dollars", or "five dollars", etc., as the case might be). This, however, was an essentially meaningless phrase, an anachronism which might have had some meaning if Canada had been on a gold standard under which the Bank was obliged to redeem all notes for an equivalent value of gold. Such is not the case today, nor has it been the case since the Bank of Canada was established.[3] If someone presents the Bank of Canada with some of its notes for payment "on demand", all he can expect to receive is a different combination of Bank of Canada notes. In June of 1970, as it began issuing a new series of notes, the Bank took the obvious step of removing this meaningless inscription. The new notes simply state "This note is legal tender".

Paper currency in Canada is thus a form of government debt, but it is non-interest bearing debt which need never be retired. Since the face value of Bank of Canada notes exceeds the value of the paper as a commodity, the Government also earns seignorage on the issuance of paper money (Bank of Canada profits automatically revert to the Government). We do not know the magnitude of this seignorage, but it is not as large as might be expected from the obvious nominal cost of a paper note. Paper currency wears out rapidly and must be continually replaced, significantly raising the costs of maintaining the outstanding volume of paper currency.

Bank Money. As in other modern economies, the bulk of the money supply in Canada is bank money, the deposit liabilities of private banks. Just as paper currency is in effect government debt, so bank money is private debt. Bank depositors have made a loan to the bank. They are creditors, the banks debtors. What happens in the payments process, therefore, is a transfer of ownership of the debts of banks.

There are many types of deposits (and we shall see later, many types of "banks"), not all of which qualify as money on our definition. That is, not all deposits are designed to be used as a medium of exchange and hence not all deposits are customarily used as such. The essential technical requirement for a deposit to be money in the narrow sense in which we have defined money is that the ownership of the deposit can be readily transferred from individual to individual, i.e., that it be chequable.

A cheque is a written order from a depositor instructing his banker to pay a specified sum to a third party. It is the instrument through which the transfer of purchasing power is effected. Not all deposits can be transferred by cheque, and indeed, by focusing attention on this property we can readily identify three categories of deposits. In one category we have deposits which can only be withdrawn on a specified date or after a minimum period of notice. We would not want to classify these *term* or *notice* deposits as money. At the opposite extreme, and unequivocally money, are those deposits which can be withdrawn on demand and which are transferable among individuals by cheque, including current account demand deposits, *personal chequing accounts* and some (but not all) *personal savings accounts*. Although banks can legally require notice prior to the withdrawal of all personal savings deposits, in fact they do not.

A third type of deposit which can be withdrawn on demand, but only "over the counter", is the *non-chequable personal savings deposit*. However, it is debatable whether such deposits should be considered money or not. On our narrow formal definition they appear to be excluded. If they cannot be transferred by cheque, they are not designed and cannot be effectively used in their existing form as a medium of exchange. At the same time, it only takes a trip to the bank to transfer the funds from such an account to a chequable account. If our concern was with the impact of the money supply on the behaviour of firms and households, we would want to think twice about excluding such deposits. If they can be so readily transformed into "money" should not the holder of such an account behave as though he had money in his hands? Certainly if such deposits are not money, they are the nearest of *near monies*. The concept of near money will play a prominent role in our analysis in later chapters, when we will define it more precisely.

In referring to these deposits we have used the expression *bank money*. We might well ask if it is necessary for the deposits to be with a bank for them to be considered money. If we mean by a bank an institution which has a charter to engage in "the business of banking", issued by the Federal Government under the terms of the *Bank Act*, (i.e. a "chartered bank"), then the answer is clearly no. There are, in Canada, a large number of institutions which accept deposits on essentially the same terms as chequable savings deposits with the chartered banks. These institutions are frequently called near banks and consist of certain trust companies, mortgage loan companies, provincial government treasury branches, credit unions, caisses populaires and Quebec savings banks. We will examine their activities in greater detail in later chapters. What is relevant at the moment is that they hold deposits which are very close substitutes for personal savings deposits (chequable and non-chequable) with chartered banks. If we are to measure the money supply of Canada on the definition of money which we have proposed, then at least chequable deposits with such institutions must be included. They are normally and customarily accepted when a transfer of purchasing power occurs. Although they are not as important as bank deposits, they are a medium of exchange.

The Canadian Money Supply. We are now in a position to answer the question with which we introduced this section: what should we count if we want to measure the Canadian money supply?

Our pragmatic definition of money says that we should include all of those items normally used when a transfer of purchasing power takes place. However, even this is a matter of degree. The items used most actively as media of exchange are currency (coins and Bank of Canada notes in circulation outside banks) and demand deposits with chartered banks. We can refer to these items as payments money in the narrowest sense (and in measuring the money supply we will include only currency and deposits held by the public). Chequable savings deposits with chartered banks and near banks are also payments money, although they are used much less intensively in the payments stream. In Table 2-1, we have set out data on the Canadian money supply at the beginning of 1970 on both definitions. As we will see later in the book, it is sometimes argued that a broader definition of money is appropriate for certain analytical purposes, including certain types of near money. Accordingly, Table 2-1 also includes data on near-money deposits with near banks.

Table 2-1
The Canadian Money Supply*, January 1, 1970

Payments Money		Millions of Dollars
Currency (coin and notes)	3,337	
Demand Deposits with Chartered Banks	7,465	
Payments Money (Narrow Definition)		10,802
Chequable Personal Savings Deposits with:		
Chartered Banks	5,695	
Trust and Loan Companies	600	
Quebec Savings Banks	494	
Caisses Populaires and Credit Unions	2,101	
	8,890	
Payments Money (Broader Definition)		19,692
Near Money Deposits		
Non-Chequable Deposits with:		
Chartered Banks	12,869	
Trust and Loan Companies	6,270	
Caisses Populaires and Credit Unions	1,677†	
Government Savings Institutions	302	
	21,118	
Money and Near Money Deposits		40,810

* Excluding deposits of banks and the federal government.
† Term Deposits and Share Capital.
SOURCE: Bank of Canada *Statistical Summary*.

The Composition of the Money Supply. There are, then, several items which can be used as money in Canada. What determines the composition of the money supply? Is the composition constant over time?

In considering these questions, the important principle to keep in mind is that while the various types of money in use in Canada are not officially convertible into any commodity like gold or silver, they are *freely convertible into each other.* Thus, the holder of a demand deposit in a bank can, at any time (at least while the bank is open) convert his deposit into currency. Likewise, a holder of Bank of Canada notes can readily convert them into coins, or into a demand deposit, or into a personal savings deposit at any of the banks or near banks which hold such deposits. This means that the *composition* of the money supply depends simply on the relative demands of the public for each type of money. (We italicize the word "composition" because this is not true of the *size* of the total money supply).

Why might the public have different demands for each type of money? A major explanation (apart from habit) must be that each type of money is efficient for different purposes.

As is evident from Table 2-1, deposits, transferable by cheque, constitute the largest part of the money supply: about 70% on the narrow definition. This refers to the stock of money held at any point in time. What is not shown on the table is the fact that the actual transfer of such deposits accounts for an even larger portion of the total value of payments made in Canada. There are no data to which we can refer, but some authorities estimate that between 85% and 90% of the value of transactions are affected by cheques.

The users of money in Canada clearly find bank money the most convenient form for most purposes. As an asset, bank money is safer than currency. It can only be withdrawn by the owner of the deposit; whereas currency can be lost through theft, fire, natural disaster, etc. So, there is much less risk of loss as long as the bank itself is sound (Note: in Canada, additional safety is provided by the fact that bank deposits are insured by government agencies up to a maximum of $20,000 per deposit). The cheque is a convenient and (at least for large transactions) relatively cheap method of making payment. It can be drawn for exactly the correct sum, and can be readily transported over long distances through the mail at very low cost. The shipment of currency, by contrast, can be very expensive, and in addition involves risk of loss. There are alternative transfer arrangements with currency, e.g., postal money orders or telegraphic transfers, but again these are relatively expensive as compared to cheques. It is also worth noting that cheques leave a very convenient record for the firm or individuals.

Bank money, then, is relatively convenient for most commercial purposes, but there is always some demand for currency from individuals who do not trust or do not understand banks. There is probably also some demand from individuals who find that the property of cheques of leaving a record of transactions is a disadvantage, e.g., persons trying to avoid income tax or persons engaged in illegal transactions.[4] Beyond that, currency is relatively convenient for relatively small, local transactions. Given a standard bank charge per cheque (regardless of the magnitude of the cheque), cheques are relatively costly for small transactions. Moreover, the person drawing a cheque may have to go through the inconvenient and time-consuming routine of identifying himself and providing evidence that he indeed has an account with the bank in question. Coins, moreover, have a particular use in automatic vending machines, which are of increasing importance in the retail trade. The active use of currency, therefore, is closely related to the retail trade, and particularly "small ticket" retail sales.

Little research has been done on the changing composition of the money supply in Canada. Research in the United States shows a relatively strong downward long-run trend in the ratio of currency to the total money supply, at least until 1930. There were major increases in the ratio in the depression of the 1930's (when there was a widespread loss of confidence in the banking system as a result of a wave of bank failures) and during World War II (perhaps because of increased foreign hoardings of U.S. dollars, and increased use of currency for illegal transactions and tax evasion), and although the long-run trend seemed to re-emerge after World War II, by the mid-1960's the ratio of currency to money was much higher than in the pre-war period (the 1920's for example).

Within each year (and each month, and each week), there are also striking patterns in the use of currency relative to deposits, following mainly the retail trade (and for shorter time periods, payroll arrangements). Thus, the ratio of currency to money systematically rises to a peak in December with the burst of retail activity related to the Christmas season, and has several minor peaks during the year also related to retail activity.

2/THE PAYMENTS SYSTEM

Payment by currency is a straightforward affair, about which little more need be said. However, as we have already pointed out, currency is a relatively inconvenient medium of exchange, except for small local transactions. In fact, transfers of currency probably account for a rather small share of the total value of transactions. The arrangements for transferring purchasing power by cheque are necessarily more complicated, although the principles involved are in fact very simple.

Payment by Cheque. To illustrate the principle underlying payment by cheque we can trace through what happens when you have purchased some major item, received the bill, and have written a cheque in payment. The cheque, you will recall, is nothing other than a written order to your banker to pay the appropriate amount to the merchant. If both you and the merchant have accounts with the same branch of the same bank all that happens is that the bank makes the appropriate entries on its books. The merchant's account is credited (increased by) the appropriate amount; your account is debited (decreased). Purchasing power is transferred with a few strokes of the bookkeeper's pen (or, more likely, a few punches on a bookkeeping machine).

If you have accounts with different branches of the same bank the transfer is only slightly more complicated. The merchant's branch credits the appropriate sum to his account and sends the cheque to your branch. After verification of the authenticity of the cheque, the appropriate sum is deducted from your account. Again, all that is involved is a series of bookkeeping entries, even though you and the merchant live in different cities.

But what if you do *not* have accounts with the same bank? The principle is just the same. If you mail a cheque from Vancouver on a Royal Bank account to a merchant in Montreal with an account at the Bank of Montreal, he will deposit it in his branch of the Bank of Montreal, which will forward it to your branch of the Royal Bank in Vancouver for verification and deduction from your account. The only important difference is that the Bank of Montreal ends up with a claim on the Royal Bank in the amount of your cheque, requiring an interbank settlement of this debt.

The Clearinghouse. The banks will not make separate interbank payments for each individual cheque. Rather, once each day in major centres across the nation representatives of each bank will meet in a central location, called the *clearinghouse*, to simultaneously exchange all of the cheques drawn on each other and received for deposit since the previous day's clearing. The claims of each bank on each of the others are totalled by the manager of the clearinghouse, and the banks then settle the *net balance* due.

In principle, the interbank settlements could be effected by payment of currency. In fact this will not be done. While the arrangements for settlement are somewhat different at the smaller clearing centres, all interbank transfers are ultimately effected through bookkeeping entries at the Bank of Canada.[5]

Each bank maintains a deposit with the Bank of Canada (in this sense the Bank of Canada is a "bankers' bank"), which is notified of the results of the daily clearings at each major clearinghouse. It then simply transfers the appropriate sums from the deposits of those banks which have lost funds in the clearings to the deposits of those banks which have gained funds.

Service Charges. Payment by cheque is more efficient than payment by currency for many types of transactions. The use of currency is frequently inconvenient, risky and costly. But we should not assume that the service provided by the bank is costless. Indeed, the costs associated with the servicing of demand deposits are among the major costs incurred by banks. In the United States it has been estimated that between 40% and 50% of all bank employees are assigned to the cheque-processing function. While we do not have comparable data for Canada, it is presumably approximately the same in this country. This should not be surprising since on an average business day millions of cheques will be written, and while the volume of activity depends on the size and location of the office, major bank offices will handle many thousands of cheques drawn on out of town branches and other banks. Thus, in the late 1960's Canadian banks handled over 900 million cheques per year, with an aggregate value in excess of $630 billion.

The costs in question arise in connection with the handling of all the documents and bookkeeping entries involved in transferring funds by cheque. This has provided fertile grounds for automation, and while there are large numbers of items, the costs involved depend more directly on the *number* of cheques handled than on the total value of payments transferred. Thus, it costs no more to handle a cheque for $1 million than it does to handle a cheque for $1 (providing it is cleared through the same channels).

The banks attempt to recover the costs of handling these payments in two ways.

They do not pay interest on current accounts. Thus, in effect the depositor makes an interest-free loan to the Bank, foregoing interest income for the privilege of writing cheques. The bank can use the money to make loans or purchase securities, using the interest income to help cover the costs of providing chequing facilities. In the case of chequable personal savings deposits, the banks do pay interest, but at a lower rate than on non-chequable accounts, and they discourage the writing of a large number of cheques.

In addition to the interest foregone, the depositor is normally assessed a *service charge* which is related to the number of cheques he writes. The exact amount of the charge depends on the type of deposit, the size of the minimum balance maintained in the deposit (which affects the interest income the bank can earn on funds deposited), and the number of cheques written each month. The service charges bear relatively more heavily on cheques drawn for small sums of money than on cheques for large sums. This is one factor making the cheque a relatively more efficient instrument for large payments than for small ones.

Near-Bank Access to the Clearing System. The network of local and regional clearinghouses is clearly a vital element in the domestic payments system. In Canada these clearinghouses are established by and operated under the jurisdiction of the Canadian Bankers Association, an association of all the chartered banks. It will be remembered that there are many other financial institutions which hold chequable deposits: institutions such as trust companies, *caisses populaires*, and credit unions, which we referred to collectively as *near banks*. These institutions are not members of the Canadian Bankers' Association, and hence are not automatically members of the clearing system. However, they are granted clearing privileges for a fee. Each near bank maintains an account with at least one chartered bank, which acts as its agent in the clearing process. Cheques drawn on the near bank and deposited in one of the chartered banks are presented to the near bank's clearing agent through the clearinghouse as though they were cheques drawn on the clearing agent itself. This bank makes payment as on its own cheques, and then arranges the appropriate settlement with the near bank.

An Alternate Clearing System: The United States

The principle of local clearinghouses is common to all banking systems. However, the arrangements for the clearing and collection of out-of-town cheques are sometimes significantly different from those which prevail in Canada. Partly because the institutions of the United States banking system have a direct and obvious importance to Canadians, and partly because the United States system contains features advocated by some economists for adoption in Canada, it is useful to briefly compare the United States system for handling out-of-town cheques.

Branch Banking versus "Fragmented" Banking. The most striking feature of the Canadian banking system is that there are only nine banks, of which five account for over 90% of all deposits. Each of these five major banks has a network of branches in every major city in every province in the nation. Out-of-town cheques deposited in any branch are collected through the facilities provided by the nation-wide network of branches. The local clearinghouses provide links between the nation-wide branch banking organizations, but the collection of out-of-town cheques is essentially internal to each branch banking organization. While the central bank is involved in settling clearing balances, no external agency is involved in the cheque collection process.

In the United States such large-scale nation-wide branch banking firms do not exist. In place of Canada's five nation-wide and four regional or specialized banking firms, the United States has some 13,700 banks. Many of these have extensive branch organizations in limited areas, but branching across state boundaries is not permitted. While the term is not fully accurate (since there are many branch-banking firms) the United States banking system is generally referred to as a *unit banking system*. Perhaps the term "fragmented" would be more descriptive.

A second distinctive feature of the United States banking system is that not all banks are required (or allowed) to maintain deposits with the central bank, i.e., the Federal Reserve System. The term "system" is quite appropriate. The central bank is in fact a network of 12 regional Federal Reserve Banks, coordinated by the Board of Governors of the Federal Reserve System in Washington, D.C. The fact that not all commercial banks belong to the Federal Reserve System is a product of the dual character of arrangements for chartering banks. Both the Federal and State governments can issue bank charters. National banks are required to be members of the Federal Reserve System and to hold deposits with the regional Federal Reserve Bank. State banks, if they meet certain minimum requirements, are permitted to join the system, but they are not required to do so.

It should be obvious that the process of clearing and collecting cheques in the United States *must* be considerably more complicated than in Canada. It is not possible to rely on the facilities of nation-wide branch-banking organizations: they do not exist. All clearings cannot be handled through the central bank: not all banks hold deposits with the central bank. Indeed, in one sense there is not one central bank, but twelve, so arrangements must be made for each Federal Reserve Bank to settle clearing balances with each of the other Federal Reserve Banks.

There are in fact two parallel systems for the collection of out-of-town cheques in the United States: through the Federal Reserve System, and through the correspondent banking system.

The Central Bank as a Cheque Collection Agency. Unlike the Bank of Canada, the Federal Reserve System is actively involved in the collection of out-of-town cheques. Each Federal Reserve Bank will accept cheques from member banks (and under some circumstances from non-member banks also) which it will then forward to the appropriate cities for collection. The bank depositing the cheques for collection will receive appropriate credit in its deposit with the Federal Reserve Bank, and the corresponding adjustment will be made in the paying bank's deposit at the other end.

The Correspondent Banking System. Although this cheque collection service is free, most out-of-town cheques are not collected through the agency of the Federal Reserve System. Indeed, a recent study revealed that while the larger banks (i.e., those with deposits of $100 million or more) collected between 55% and 60% of the value of their out-of-town cheques in this way, the smaller banks (e.g., those with deposits of $10 million or less) used the facilities of the Federal Reserve System to collect less than 10% of the value of their out-of-town cheques. The rest of the out-of-town cheques were collected through an alternate system, a network of *correspondent banks*. Thus, as the study concluded, "the Federal Reserve System only supplements — it did not supplant — the correspondent banking system."[6]

Correspondent banking relations involve banks maintaining deposits with each other and performing certain services for each other. Generally speaking, smaller banks in outlying areas maintain deposits with correspondent banks in larger cities in the region, which banks in turn hold deposits with correspondent banks in still larger cities. However, the structure of the system is not a simple pyramid. Many banks, and particularly the larger banks in larger cities, both hold deposits for other banks and maintain deposits with these same correspondents. Moreover, the larger banks will have correspondent relations with many banks, including many foreign banks. Thus, according to the study cited earlier, the large city banks (deposits of $100 million or more) on the average are correspondents for over 240 banks and on the average hold correspondent balances with over 30 banks. One large New York City bank is reported to hold correspondent balance for over 4,000 banks.

City correspondent banks provide a variety of services for their country correspondents. This includes participation in loans too large for the small bank to handle, advice on investments, assistance in trading in government securities, and sometimes assistance in the recruitment and training of personnel. But the main service, and the only one of interest to us, is the clearing and collection of out-of-town cheques. Correspondent banks act as agents for other banks in the collection of cheques. Thus, instead of using the facilities of the Federal Reserve System, a bank receiving a cheque drawn on an out-of-town bank has the option of sending it to a correspondent bank in that city for collection, and having the proceeds deposited in its account with the correspondent. Similarly, a bank having to make payment in another city can do so by drawing drafts on its correspondent balances. In the Canadian banking system this same service would be provided by distant branches of the same bank. A branch-banking firm has its own built-in correspondent system. Thus, from the point of view of cheque clearing and collection and of a whole range of banking services and operations branch banking and correspondent banking are substitutes.

Two clearing systems coexist in the United States partly because many banks do not belong to the Federal Reserve System. But even member banks make heavy use of the correspondent system. Because of the increased deposits which it provides to them, many city banks have found it profitable to compete actively for correspondent business. The result of their competition is fast, efficient service in collecting cheques (plus all of the other services that go along with correspondent relations) which many banks find preferable in some respect to the service provided by the central bank. In general, the Federal Reserve System is used most heavily to collect cheques drawn on very distant banks, and the correspondent system is used to collect cheques drawn on banks which are not so remote.

The correspondent banking principle is a universal principle in banking. While the dominance of nation-wide branch banking in Canada makes an elaborate network of correspondent relations unnecessary in domestic banking operations, the institution (although not called correspondent banking) can be seen in our description of the Canadian clearing system. It is the principle which underlies near bank access to the Canadian Bankers' Association clearinghouses. In addition, the smaller, regionally oriented Canadian banks maintain correspondent relations with their larger, nation-wide counterparts. All Canadian banks have extensive correspondent relations with banks throughout the world.

Par Clearing. The involvement of the Federal Reserve System in the cheque collection process has had another important effect on the United States payments system. The Federal Reserve System has insisted on what is called *par clearing*.

Until June 1970, Canadian banks levied a special charge, called an *exchange charge*, on all cheques cashed or deposited which were drawn on branches or banks outside the region serviced by the local clearinghouse. The charge was usually 1/8 of 1% of the face value of the cheque, with a minimum charge of 15¢. The banks justified exchange charges on out-of-town cheques on the grounds that it is more costly to handle such cheques than it is to handle local cheques. They justified a fee based on the value of the cheque (rather than on the number of cheques) on the grounds that since the customer depositing the out-of-town cheque is given immediate credit for it, even though it may take the banks several days to collect the cheque from the person who wrote it, the bank in effect makes an interest-free loan to the person who deposits the cheque (and, incidentally, the bank runs some risk that the cheque may "bounce," giving rise to additional collection costs). Thus, until very recently the Canadian system involved *non-par clearing*. Out-of-town cheques were not necessarily accepted at their face value.

Exchange charges of this type were also common in the early banking system of the United States. However, throughout its history (since 1913) the Federal Reserve System has attempted to eliminate exchange charges and hence to impose the principle of par clearing. It has done this in two ways. Initially it made par clearing compulsory for member banks of the Federal Reserve System, and when this did not achieve the desired results (because many banks chose not to join the system), it gave non-member banks access to the Federal cheque collection service on condition that they accept the par clearing principle. The Federal Reserve efforts have been largely successful. While about 6% of all banks in the United States are still non-par banks, they tend to be small, country banks, concentrated in the rural areas of the southeastern and mid-western states, and they hold only 2% of all bank deposits and account for a correspondingly small fraction of all cheque clearings.

Since, as we have already noted, the process of clearing and collecting cheques is far from costless, it can be argued that a charge for the service is both fair and economically efficient. It would be economically efficient on the grounds that those who use the scarce resources of the economy ought to pay a price equal to the value of those resources in their alternative uses, i.e., ought to pay a price equal to the marginal cost of the service. Why, then, has the Federal Reserve been so insistent on par clearing?

The Federal Reserve case rested largely on the social interest in an efficient, low-cost cheque payments system. The non-par clearing system led to circuitous routings of cheques to avoid exchange charges, with consequent delays in payments. Equally important, the exchange charges had discriminatory effects. Not all bank depositors were treated alike, and the differences were not necessarily related to costs. Banks were accused of exploiting whatever monopolistic power they had, making the charging of exchange charges a profitable activity. (It is still true that non-par banks are typically the only bank in any given town.) The principle of the recipient of a payment being required to pay the cost of the payment rather than the remitter can also be questioned. Perhaps the appropriate place to levy charges is on the deposit, with the charges related to the activity of the account.

Foreign Payments

So far we have examined how transfers of purchasing power are made possible within the confines of one nation. For a trading nation such as Canada an important number of the total transactions involve payments to or from places outside the nation's boundaries. Such payments introduce two complications: The Canadian bank may not have branches in the relevant foreign center (although Canadian banks do have agencies in many important foreign financial centers), and the payment involves another currency besides the Canadian dollar.

The first of these complications is readily solved using the correspondent banking principle already examined in the context of the United States clearing system. To illustrate, assume that you live in Winnipeg and that a bill you owe in Minneapolis is payable in United States dollars. (The bill could just as well be made payable in London, Cairo, Tokyo or Moscow.) You could use different methods to pay the bill. You could go to your local bank branch and buy United States currency in exchange for Canadian currency. The United States currency could then be mailed to Minneapolis, completing the transfer. This method involves a risk of theft or loss and would be suitable for small transactions only. More safely, you could purchase a bank draft payable in United States funds and send it to Minneapolis. This draft is in effect a check written by the

Canadian bank upon an account it holds in a United States correspondent bank. The recipient of the check in Minneapolis deposits or cashes the draft and it is then put through the clearing system just as if it were any other check written on a United States bank. The Canadian bank reduced its holdings of United States dollars (i.e., its deposits with its Minneapolis correspondent) and increased its holdings of Canadian currency or reduced its deposits liabilities by an equivalent amount. For providing this service the bank charges a fee for the draft and a fee for exchanging Canadian dollars for United States dollars.

A second question then arises: how does the Canadian bank obtain the United States dollar deposits to sell to its customers? There are two possibilities. First, corresponding to the payment by Canadians to foreigners are reverse payments by foreigners to Canadians. To the extent that the Canadian recipients of these payments are customers of the bank, it has a flow of United States dollars out of which it can meet its customers' demands. Secondly, if the demands for United States dollars exceed the funds which the bank has available, it can enter the foreign exchange market and purchase the required United States funds from other banks which have a surplus. This market is an essential part of the international payments process. We will examine it in more detail in a later chapter.

In summary, the crucial institutions involved in international payments are an international network of correspondent banks and a foreign exchange market in which foreign monies can be bought and sold just as if they were commodities like wheat or rice.

3/ECONOMIC ISSUES IN THE OPERATIONS OF THE PAYMENTS SYSTEM

So much for a description of the institutions of the payments system. What are the *economic issues* posed by the operations of this system in Canada? As noted in Chapter 1, the relevant questions are two-fold: is the system efficient and is it neutral? In raising the question of *efficiency* we mean to ask: Does the existing system accomplish its task with the minimum amount of resources required? Would some alternative system accomplish the task with fewer resources? The question of neutrality, on the other hand, is concerned with whether the existing payments arrangements induce people to discriminate in favour of one method of payment rather than another, with some consequences for the allocation of resources in the economy. In attempting to answer both of these questions the evidence is at best only circumstantial. Indeed, a search for quantitative answers to these questions is one virtually untouched field for economic research.

Efficiency of the Payments System

The Supply of Currency. Discussions of the efficiency of the payments system inevitably focus on arrangements for payment by cheque. We should not forget, however, that provision of the currency supply also absorbs real resources, and hence involves costs which should be minimized in the interests of efficiency. There are two types of costs involved, the costs of operating the institutions which produce and distribute currency and the value of the resources embodied in the currency media. We do not have data on either of these costs. However, in 1969 the production and shipment of Bank of Canada notes cost $5.0 million, and accounted for approximately one-third of the total operating costs of the Bank of Canada (and this does not include all of the costs involved in operating the Currency Division of the Bank of Canada since salaries and other expenses are not included, and it does not include costs incurred by chartered banks in handling currency). This might be a low estimate, then, of the cost of maintaining and providing for one year's increase in the supply of paper money. Furthermore, the operation of the Royal Canadian Mint cost an additional $4.4 million. This can be taken as an estimate of the cost of maintaining and providing for one year's increase in the stock of coins. The annual operating cost of this side of the payment system, then, is significant but nonetheless small. It accounts for substantially less than 1/80 of 1% of the gross national product, and even if there were evidence of substantial inefficiencies (which there is not), the total savings in the aggregate would be very small indeed (i.e., a fraction of a small fraction).

Such calculations ignore the value of metal embodied in the outstanding stock of coinage, including only the value of metal embodied in annual increases in the coinage. As we noted earlier, Canada does not have a commodity currency. The largest part of the currency supply consists of paper notes, and hence probably embodies the least amount of scarce productive resources possible, given the necessity of some type of tangible currency. The balance of the currency supply consists of coins which embody a relatively larger value of scarce resources per dollar of money in circulation. The changeover to pure nickel coinage has resulted in substantial economies in this portion of the payments system. However, the changeover to nickel coinage had complications. One of the major uses of coins is in vending machines, which must have a device to select good coins from slugs. The existing coin selectors did not work with the new coinage. The vending machine industry, therefore, was faced with a major problem and a considerable investment in adapting to the new coinage. As a result of economies in the public sector, some additional costs were incurred in the private sector.

Payment by Cheque. We have already referred to the substantial and rising costs involved in processing cheques through the banking system. Cheque processing is basically a series of mechanical activities, involving several different sortings of items and recordings of amounts. Not surprisingly this has proven to be fertile ground for the application of automated techniques. Thus, for example, the coding of relevant information on the face of each cheque in magnetic ink has permitted the processing of cheques through high-speed sorting equipment connected to an electronic computer. The cost reductions from this technological advance apparently have been dramatic. Although automation has not progressed as far in the Canadian banking system as it has in the United States, there is no evidence that it has not proceeded as rapidly as is appropriate in the Canadian context. In the absence of careful (and published) research on costs in Canadian banking it is not possible to draw any meaningful conclusions on the efficiency of these operations. Undoubtedly we can expect significant changes in these banking procedures in future years.

It is frequently suggested that the cheque is outmoded as a method of payment. The volume of paper work and sequence of mechanical handlings of the payment order can be significantly reduced, critics argue, by adopting alternative payments arrangements. Since the volume of paper work involved and the manpower requirements of the sequence of handlings of cheques gives rise to the costs we are discussing, such alternative arrangements are alleged to be cost saving.

A Giro System for Canada? One proposal for the reduction of costs involved in transferring payments by cheque involves the establishment of a publicly owned *giro* or credit transfer system. This, in fact, is not a new system. Indeed, it has a long and successful history in several European countries and in Japan. The principle underlying payment by giro is the same as that underlying payment by cheque. It involves an order to a banker to make appropriate bookkeeping transfers among accounts. What is different is the order of events. With transfers by cheque you mail the cheque to your creditor who then deposits it in his account with his bank, which then directly or indirectly sends the cheque back to your bank to be deducted from your account (with appropriate settlements among the banks) and eventually returned to you. With transfers by giro, by contrast, you simply order your banker to pay the appropriate amount directly into your creditor's account. As with a cheque, you fill out a special form of instructions to your banker, normally in multiple copies to be used to notify the relevant parties that the transfer has been effected. However, unlike payment by cheque, the transfer is direct and simple. The circuitous routing of what one critic called the "peregrinating cheque" is avoided. As a result, the supporters argue, "There is no doubt that the giro method of payment is simpler and more straightforward, and therefore cheaper to operate, than the cheque method."[7]

A giro system is attractive for its simplicity. But such simplicity is most obvious only when both payer and payee have accounts with the same bank, even though in different cities. As a result most giro systems are operated by the national post office, which has a conveniently available nation-wide network of branch offices, including offices in the smallest of settlements. Indeed, a private giro system would seem impractical in a banking system as fragmented as that in the United States, but perhaps not inconceivable in Canada's concentrated system. (There are examples of giros operated by private banks through cooperative central arrangements and in competition with the national post offices.) Because of its association with the post office, some bankers have argued that the full costs of the giro cannot be ascertained, and they imply that the full costs may not be covered by the small charges levied and the implicit interest income derived from the balances deposited in giro accounts. Thus, they argue, the apparent low cost of the giro transfer system is spurious: it is a product of an implicit government subsidy.

In any case, the giro system seems to be used mainly by individuals making payments to each other and to business firms. It is less used for commercial payments among firms. Such systems have developed in the context of banking systems which did not provide low-cost chequing facilities for individuals desiring to make small and irregular out-of-town payments. In this sense the giro may be a substitute for such cash-transfer arrangements as postal money orders.

Is there a case for the establishment of a giro system in Canada, perhaps as a part of the post office? To our knowledge this matter has not been carefully examined, but since the banking system in Canada provides chequing facilities catering to the needs of "people requiring a standard, limited banking service, provided at the lowest possible cost, known in advance"[8] (both through personal chequing accounts and through the limited chequing privileges attached to some personal savings accounts), the case for such a departure in Canada would presumably be weak. It is unlikely that the savings resulting from the establishment of a giro in Canada would be great enough to merit public investment in the creation of the institutions (and in public education in the use of such institutions).

Computer Technology and the "Chequeless Society". A second proposal, of more revolutionary consequences, involves a major extension of the application of computer technology (and the omnibus credit card) to the payments process. In one version, it is suggested that a modern form of the telephone, connected to a central computer, coupled with a plastic identification card, could be used to effect payments.

> The plastic card contains pre-punched data whereby the contact through the telephone network can be automatically effected between a caller and a computer. The basic concept envisages indentification by the computer of the accounts of debtor and creditor through the medium of the pre-punched card and the instant transfer of funds between the two in accordance with the figures indicated by means of the keyboard. It is, therefore, possible to imagine the device being used in retail establishments or even in the customer's home for the settlement of accounts, without the need for cheques to be written or envelopes addressed. Transactions could be carried out at any time of the day or night.[9]

Clearly such a system possesses many technical and legal problems, including the problem of security. In the absence of a written document the bank (or the depositor) runs severe risks of the sort which are familiar to all users of credit cards, particularly as a result of loss or theft of the identification card. This is clearly a system of the future, not of the present, although it is not science fiction.

Neutrality of the Payments System

The neutrality of the Canadian payments system is now simply a question of the access of the near banks to the nationwide network of clearinghouses. As we noted earlier, near banks do not have access to the clearinghouses on the same basis as the banks. Many of the near banks contend that control of the clearinghouses by the chartered banks gives the banks a competitive advantage. They have argued that the chartered banks artificially raise the costs of clearing the cheques of near banks, and this artificial cost discourages the near banks from seeking additional chequing account business. The banks assert that there is no discrimination, and indeed that the near banks probably do not bear the full cost of clearing. Data are not available to definitely prove or disprove either contention. Therefore, perhaps in the spirit of eliminating any opportunity for discrimination, the Royal Commission on Banking and Finance recommended that:

> The clauses of the Canadian Bankers' Association Act which give the Association the right of operating the clearing system should be repealed, and an association of all clearing institutions formed to manage the system and allocate costs equitably among all members in relation to the work done by each.[10]

The Commission also recommended that all near banks belonging to the clearing system be required to hold reserve deposits with the Bank of Canada, and that the Bank of Canada assume the same role as the Federal Reserve System in the United States in collecting out-of-town cheques for those banks or near banks who desire to use this service. None of these proposed reforms was introduced in the 1967 revision of the Bank Acts.

As we noted above, prior to June 1970, Canadian banks assessed exchange charges on out-of-town cheques. This non-par clearing also affected the neutrality of the payments system, particularly since exchange charges were not uniformly applied. Many customers, particularly large accounts, paid no exchange charges. Indeed, large firms, with offices in several sections of the country, probably avoided most of these charges in any case by sending the cheques to the appropriate regional offices for collection (this is the equivalent of the problem of circuitous routing of cheques in the United States). Other customers, particularly small accounts, paid the full charges. The existence of the exchange charges probably also induced more use of alternative methods of payment (such as postal money orders) than would otherwise have occurred.

Non-par clearing thus created the possibility of widespread discrimination, although perhaps of relatively small magnitude. It is relevant to note, however, that the Royal Commission on Banking and Finance recommended:

> that there be a statutory prohibition on charges for the negotiation of out-of-town checks, the actual handling of which does not involve any significant extra cost to the institutions concerned.[11]

This reform was not included in the revision of *The Bank Act* of 1967, but in June of 1970 the banks voluntarily adopted it.

4/MONEY AND THE FLOW OF PAYMENTS

In our later analysis the concept of the demand for money will play a central role. Monetary policy — one of the central concerns of this book — involves manipulation of the supply of money.

What is the nature of the demand for money? What factors govern the quantity of money demanded at any point in time? We are not yet ready to examine these questions in any detail. However, our discussion of money as a medium of payment does suggest one factor of consequence. Surely, if money is a medium of payment, then quantity of money de manded must be related in some way to the value of payments to be made. This is correct, but the exact nature of the relationship is neither simple nor obvious.

The complication which arises in specifying the relationship between the value of transactions and the demand for money is that these are variables in different dimensions. The value of payments is a *flow variable*. It is something which occurs *over a period of time*: a day, a week, a month, or a year. By contrast, money is a *stock variable*. It is something which can be measured at a *point in time*: at a particular minute on a particular day. Thus, we cannot talk about the stock of money in the year 1971 in the same sense as we talk about the gross national expenditure in 1971. The stock of money must be measured at some particular point in time, such as the end of the business day, June 12, 1971. For purposes of analysis, of course, we might want to measure the *average* stock of money in existence during the year 1971. In principle, we should be measuring the average stock in existence at each successive instant during that year. In fact we would probably only measure the stock once a week or once a month, and average these observations to obtain the annual average.

It is true that the flow of payments involves money. Payments are effected by money changing hands. However, over any given period of time — such as a year — the same piece of money can change hands many times. Thus, the total flow of payments during the year can be many times the average stock of money in existence during the year. If money changes hands rapidly — if it has a high *turnover rate* or *velocity of circulation* — a very small average stock of money can support a very large flow of payments. If velocity is high, each piece of money is held for a short time between payments. A small stock of money is required to support a given flow of payments. If velocity is low, each piece of money is held for a long time between payments. A larger stock of money is required to support a given flow of payments. Clearly, we cannot derive the demand for money from a knowledge of the flow of payments without knowing something about the determinants of the velocity of circulation. That is a very complex topic which we are not yet ready to explore.

An analogy is sometimes helpful in thinking about these concepts. Such an analogy might be a fountain which continuously recirculates the same water supply by means of a mechanical pump. We might insert a meter into the pipe of the fountain and measure the total flow of water past that point in an hour. That would be analogous to the flow of payments in the economy at any given point in time. The total flow of water past our meter is effected by the continuous recirculation of the same water supply, and the magnitude of that flow depends directly on the speed at which we run the pump — i.e., the velocity or rate of turnover of the water supply. We cannot say how much water we require in the reservoir for any given flow of water per hour unless we know how fast the pump runs.

FOOTNOTES

[1] P. Einzig, *Primitive Money* (London: Eyre & Spottiswoode, 1948), p. 25.
[2] Why has gold been so widely selected as the commodity to be used as money? While there are clearly many cultural factors to be taken into account, early monetary economists argued that gold was *technically superior* to most commodities for this purpose. Gold is widely prized for decorative and other industrial purposes. Since it is also limited in supply it has "instrinsic" value, i.e., it would have value as a commodity even if it were not used as money. The supply is physically limited, apart from occasional major gold discoveries, and it tends to maintain its value over time. It has a relatively high value in relation to its weight, and in this sense is relatively portable. It is virtually indestructible. It is homogeneous and readily divisible. Finally, it is quite easily recognizable. A classic exposition of the "technical" requirements for a monetary commodity is provided by W. S. Jones, *Money and the Mechanism of Exchange* (New York, 1902), pp. 29-39. How does paper money compare with gold in terms of these technical desiderata? (Remember that, while paper money is far from "indestructible", a worn-out note is easily and relatively cheaply replaced).
[3] When the Bank of Canada was established in 1934 (it opened for business in 1935) Canada was *nominally* on the gold standard. However, the provision that Dominion Notes (the currency which Bank of Canada notes replaced) be convertible into gold on demand had been suspended in fact in 1929 and in law in 1931. Indeed, the gold standard was in suspension from 1914 except for the years 1926-1929. The Bank of Canada Act continued the nominal requirement for convertiblity of legal tender into gold, and added the obligation that the Bank of Canada should hold reserves of gold, silver or foreign exchange in the amount of 25% of its deposit and note liabilities. That requirement was also suspended in 1940. The revised *Bank of Canada Act,* passed in 1967, removed these provisions.
[4] It is interesting to note that on January 1, 1970, some $32 million, or just under 1% of the value of Bank of Canada notes outstanding, were in denominations of $1,000. What is the explanation for this? Surely notes of this size are not widely used in normal retail transactions.
[5] There are ten major clearing centers in Canada, normally called cash clearing centers. These are Ottawa, the eight cities in which the Bank of Canada has an agency and Quebec City. It is the clearings at these centers which are reported daily to the Bank of Canada and which are then settled on the books of the Bank of Canada.
    At all other clearing centers the net clearing balances are not settled by "cash" transfers. Rather, the banks which must make payments do so by drawing a draft, (i.e., an order to pay) on their main office in the nearest cash clearing center. The bank receiving payment will forward this draft to its main office in the nearest cash clearing center. The bank receiving payment will forward this draft to its main office in the cash clearing center for collection. Thus, the

draft, and hence the clearing balance of the outlying center, will appear (probably the next day) in the clearings of the cash clearing center, and will ultimately be settled on the books of the Bank of Canada.

In relatively small communities with more than one bank office, the volume of interbank clearings may not be great enough to justify the establishment of a clearinghouse. In such centers cheques are normally presented directly to the banks on which they are drawn, normally once each day. The net balance due will then be settled by draft in the same way as for outlying clearinghouses.

[6] Congress of the United States, House of Representatives, Committee on Banking and Currency (88th Congress, 2nd Session) *A Report On The Correspondent Banking System* (Washington, 1964).

[7] Sir Oscar Hobson, "Towards A Banking Democracy," in *The Banker*, Vol. 108 (Nov. 1958) pp. 710-715.

[8] Committee on the Working of the Monetary System, *Report* (London: H.M.S.O., 1959), pp. 329-332; p. 330.

[9] F. W. Gibson, "The Cashless Revolution" in *Westminster Bank Review*, (Feb. 1968), pp. 20-30.

[10] Canada, Royal Commission on Banking and Finance, *Report*, (Ottawa: Queen's Printer, 1964), p. 393.

[11] *Ibid.*, p. 394.

3

Financial Instruments and Financial Markets

In our economy the collection of financial surpluses and their allocation among alternate uses is primarily a market process. Individuals exchange their savings for financial instruments, claims on borrowers which entitle leaders to (certain or uncertain) returns in the future. The interaction of supply (from borrowers) and demand (on the part of lenders) in the market for financial instruments determines their market prices and in the process regulates the size, composition and direction of financial . flows in the economy. In this chapter we will discuss the characteristics of the most important types of financial instruments and some of the basic institutions of financial markets. In subsequent chapters we will develop a theoretical analysis of how these markets work.

1/THE CHARACTERISTICS OF FINANCIAL INSTRUMENTS

Definition

A financial instrument originates in an act of borrowing and lending — a transfer of purchasing power from a surplus spending unit to a deficit spending unit. It is what the borrower gives to the lender as evidence of the debt. In a more general way, we can define a financial instrument as *a claim to a future stream of payments*. It is a *contract* between a creditor (who will receive the payments) and a debtor (who will make the payments), one which in general can be bought and sold in the market at a market-established price. Thus, the initial creditor need not remain a creditor. He can sell the claim to someone else. A major part of our problem is to explain the price at which such transactions will occur.

Our definition of a financial instrument is perfectly general. Individual instruments will differ in a number of ways. First, we have not specified the *number* of payments to be received. It can range between a single payment and an infinite number of payments. Second, we have not specified the *timing* of the payments, only that they be made in the future, or at some unspecified time in the future. Third, we have not specified the *magnitude* of the payments. They may be large or small, of equal or of different size, and indeed they may vary in size from time to time. Finally, we have not specified that the payments will *necessarily* be made. A financial instrument is a *claim* to such payments: that claim may in fact be honoured in whole, in part, or not at all. At the moment we cannot know what will happen since the claim is for future payments.

Bonds as Financial Instruments

The most common of all financial instruments is what we shall call a *bond*. It has the amount of each payment and the number of payments (the length of the payments stream) specified in the contract. It is a *fixed income security*.

We are using the term "bond" in a very broad, generic sense to refer to all fixed income securities, regardless of the term to maturity, the number and type of payments, or the various provisions for the security of the bondholder (which will be set in a "Deed of Trust" accompanying the bond). In fact there are many types of bonds, and without attempting to provide a complete catalogue it may be useful to note the characteristics of some of the major varieties.

Term to Maturity. A major consideration in classifying bonds is the term to maturity, i.e., the time which must elapse before the final payment is due. At one extreme is a peculiar class of bonds issued by some governments, variously called *consols* or *perpetuities*. The contract calls for annual payments to the owner in perpetuity. By contrast, most bonds have a definite term to maturity. Those with a maturity date of ten years or over are normally classed as *long-term* bonds, those with maturities in the range three to ten years might be called *intermediate-term* bonds, and those with a maturity less than three years, *short-term* bonds. The shortest term bonds are those payable on demand, i.e., at any time specified by the holder.

Why is this classification by maturity important for our analysis? One of the characteristics of financial instruments which will assume importance in our analysis is the relative stability of market price in the face of changing interest rates. In general, stability of market price depends on the term to maturity. Those bonds with a short term to maturity tend to have a more stable price than those with a long term to maturity. This is a result of some importance which we will establish in Chapter 5.

Security of the Bondholder. Another major consideration in classifying bonds is the provision for the security of the bondholder. Some bonds are secured by a formal pledge of certain physical assets of the debtor. These are *mortgage* bonds, and in modified form are well known in real estate transactions. By contrast, some bonds are simply a charge against the general assets and earning power of the debtor, and are not secured by a pledge of any specific assets. These bonds are commonly called *debentures*, although if they are for a very short term they are more likely to be referred to as *promissory notes*, or *notes* for short. Some bonds also have a provision for a sinking fund, and hence are called *sinking fund bonds*. This form of bond requires that the debtor set aside a certain sum of money each year (frequently through the purchase of part of the outstanding issue of bonds) to provide for eventual retirement of the issue. This is supposed to provide additional security to the bondholder. Municipal governments generally issue *serial bonds* instead of sinking fund bonds to achieve the same purpose. A serial bond is in fact a package of bonds, each with a different maturity such that a portion of the total issue comes due for retirement each year during the term of the issue.

This brief survey hardly does justice to the variety of possible types of provisions for the security of bondholders, and hence to the possible types of bonds. However, they are only relevant in the present context because they have some bearing on the *risk* attached to the bond, and that is a factor of some interest for our analysis.

Credit Risk. Our definition of a bond stresses that it is a claim to a series of payments of fixed magnitude to be made in the *future*. However, the future can never be known in advance. There will always be some *uncertainty* about whether the payments will ever be made. Circumstances may change, such that even the most carefully formulated plans and expectations do not materialize, the debtor may be unwilling or unable to meet his obligation. In some cases this may only create costs of collection which cannot be fully recovered. In other cases, it may involve partial or total default on the obligation, with partial or complete loss to the creditor. In this event, the provisions for the security of the bondholder referred to in the previous section may take on more than academic significance.

We refer to this risk that the contractual payments may not be forthcoming as planned as the *credit risk*. In a sense it is a one-sided risk. The actual payments may be less than those called for in the contract, but they will never be more.

For reasons which we will explore more fully in Chapter 5, credit risk enters into the determination of the market price of bonds. In brief, other things being equal, investors will normally prefer less risky securities to more risky securities. As a result, if the promised stream of payments is the same for two securities, investors will offer a higher price for the less risky one. But if risk is to enter the investment decision, investors must be able to assess differences in credit risk. This calls for specialized skills in financial analysis. As a result, an industry has developed as an adjunct of financial markets providing information and professional advice to investors.

Nature of the Payment Stream. Another characteristic with respect to which bonds may differ is the nature of the stream of payments involved. In general, a bond will call for equal semi-annual payments (the interest or coupon payments) and a larger lump-sum payment on the maturity date (variously called the *face* value, the *par* value or the *redemption* value of the bond). Bonds are normally issued in denominations of $1,000 (although there are many exceptions to this). That is to say, the *redemption value* is $1,000. This should not be confused with the *market price* of the bond. A bond which has a redemption value of $1,000 may trade in the market at a price either greater or less than $1,000. If its price is less than its face value the bond is said to be trading at a *discount,* and if its price is greater than its par value the bond is said to be trading at a *premium.* Bonds are frequently issued at a discount or a premium. That is, the original issuer of a bond with a face value of $1,000 does not necessarily receive $1,000. He may receive less or more.

The annual interest payments (normally two coupons) can be expressed as a percent of the par value of the bond. Thus a $1,000 bond, bearing semiannual coupons for $25 each, would normally be referred to as a five percent bond. That is, the annual interest payment of $50 is 5% of the face value of the bond. This is a purely *nominal rate of interest.* Just as the market price of the bond may depart significantly from its par value, so the true rate of interest (what we shall call the yield) may depart significantly from this nominal rate. Indeed, as we just noted, at the time the bond is first issued, the issuer may receive less than the face value of the bond (he may sell it at a discount). As a result, he in fact pays a higher rate of interest on the money which he has actually obtained than that indicated by the nominal rate. The only significance of the nominal rate is to fix the size of the semi-annual coupon payments.

Not all the bonds will be in this coupon form, however. A particularly important variant is what we shall call a *bill.* This is a security calling for a single payment on a fixed date in the future. There are no periodic interest payments, only the final payment, the redemption value of the bill. Such bonds are normally very short-term, and perhaps the most important is the 91-day treasury bill issued by the Federal Government. It plays a particularly important role in the financial system and we will have occasion to refer to it frequently.

Bills always trade at a discount. The effective interest rate on a bill (the yield) depends on the relationship between its market price and its redemption value.

Marketability. Finally, it is necessary to mention another salient characteristic which may or may not be possessed by bonds (and other financial instruments): *marketability.* This refers to the ability of the holder to sell the security to someone else on short notice at a reasonably predictable price. Some instruments are not marketable because they are not transferable. That is, the sale of the security to a third party is prohibited. For example, Canada Savings Bonds contain the condition: "This bond is not assignable nor transferable." Other instruments are not marketable simply by virtue of the fact that an active market does not exist.

Such a statement must seem puzzling to a student of economics. A market exists whenever transactions occur. Thus, the very fact that the present purchaser of the security has purchased it must indicate that a market exists. Moreover, it is in general possible to find a buyer for most securities at some price.

In this connection it is useful to make a distinction between the primary and secondary markets for securities. By the *primary market* we mean transactions involving the issuance of new securities. By the *secondary market* we mean transactions in outstanding securities. Thus, the supply of securities in the primary market comes from individuals, firms and government agencies raising money for diverse purposes. The supply of securities in the secondary market comes from assetholders selling securities out of their portfolios.

While every credit transaction can thus be construed as a transaction in the primary market, the range of securities continuously traded in significant volume in the secondary market is relatively limited. These tend to be securities of well-known creditors whose credit worthiness can be relatively easily assessed and of which a relatively large volume is outstanding. Only these securities can be said to be highly marketable. True, most other transferable securities can be sold at some price: but perhaps only after considerable searching for a buyer, some delay, perhaps substantial cost, and possibly only then at a low price. The secondary market for such instruments is irregular and unorganized.

A marketable security is a security for which there is a developed secondary market in which there is a relatively large volume of continuous trading of the security.

Common Stock as a Financial Instrument

While the type of financial instrument which will occupy most of our attention in this book is the bond, there are other financial instruments in which the amount of each payment is not specified in the contract between creditor and debtor. The prototype of such securities is the common stock of corporations. Whereas a bond entitles its owner to a series of fixed payments a share of common stock entitles its owner to a *pro rata* share of such dividends as may be declared from time to time by the directors of the corporation. Dividends are normally thought of as a share of profits, although they are not rigidly tied to profits. The directors of a corporation might decide to retain some or all of the profits to finance the growth of the corporation, and on occasion they may decide to pay dividends even though the corporation is not making profits or perhaps is suffering losses. However, in general dividend payments will tend to reflect the profits of the corporation.

Also unlike most bonds, common stock does not have a definite maturity date. There is no fixed lump-sum redemption value, although the stockholders do not own residual rights to the assets of the corporation (i.e., after all other claims are allowed for).

The important point for our analysis is that just as the profits of a corporation may vary from time to time, so the dividend payments to the stockholder may vary over a wide range. Accordingly, we refer to such a financial instrument as a *variable income security*.

Stockholders as Creditors. Since our definition of financial instruments involved the concepts of debtor and creditor it may seem like we are stretching a point to include common stock. The owners of the common stock of a corporation are in law the owners of the corporation, not its creditors. Moreover, since they have a claim to a *pro rata* share of the profits (or better the declared dividends) of the corporation, their "instrument" has many of the characteristics of titles to physical capital rather than what we might normally think of as a financial instrument. These points are valid and important. However, we should distinguish between the corporation and its stockholders or owners; and it is *convenient* to treat the stockholders simply as creditors of the corporation with a particular type of claim on that corporation, a variable income claim. We should remember that the corporation is in itself a "legal person" with certain rights and obligations. The stockholders are not responsible for the actions and debts of the corporation, except to the extent that they may lose their investments in the corporation should it be unable to meet its obligations. Indeed, it is this fact of the "limited liability" of the stockholders — the fact of their divorcement from the obligations of the corporation — which makes the corporation such an effective form of business organization for ventures involving risk.

As a subsidiary point, it might be noted that while all stockholders have the right to vote at stockholders' meetings (which generally must be held at least once a year), in a typical corporation most do not participate actively in the management of that corporation. They treat their stock as an investment in someone else's venture; and they hold it in anticipation of a series of dividend payments whose magnitude is beyond their direct control. Even if a stockholder is in the management of the corporation, we should nonetheless regard his stock simply as a claim on a separate entity, the corporation. It is true that the fact of his ability to influence or control corporation policy may add an important dimension, a valuable characteristic, to that particular financial instrument; nonetheless, it is a financial instrument which provides a claim to a (probably variable) future stream of payments.

Other Variable Income Instruments. The common stock is the best known type of variable income security. However there are several other types of instruments which have variable payments streams. Basically they combine some of the features of common stock with some of the features of bonds. There are many subtle variations on the central principles, and we can only briefly mention some of the main types.

Perhaps the best known of such instruments is *preferred stock.* Unlike a bond, preferred stock does not have a fixed maturity, although it may be redeemable in the sense that the corporation has the option of retiring it on specified terms. The owner of preferred stock has a *prior claim* to dividends, up to a specified maximum rate, before any dividends can be paid on common stock. Moreover, some preferred stocks are participating. That is, they have the prior claim to dividends, but once dividends are paid on common stock at a certain specified rate the owners of the preferred stock share in any additional dividends declared. Thus, the specified rate is in fact a minimum rate, not a maximum.

There are also two classes of bonds which have variable payments streams, *income bonds* and *participating bonds.* These are bonds in the sense that they have a fixed redemption date and a fixed redemption value. However, in each case the annual interest payment is contingent on the earnings of the corporation, with participating bonds having the additional feature of a guaranteed minimum annual payment.

The endless varieties of financial instruments, with subtle differences in the characteristics, are evidence of the ingenuity of the participants in the financial system in designing instruments to suit the specific preferences of both debtors and creditors (including taking advantage of many complex provisions of tax laws).

Money as a Financial Instrument

In the previous chapter we offered a general definition of money as "anything which is normally accepted when a transfer of purchasing power takes place." Our concern was with the payments system, and our interest in money was as a *medium of exchange.* However, the very fact that money will normally be accepted in exchange for goods and services means that it is an asset. It is something which can be held as a *store of wealth.* In Canada today, money is simply one type of financial instrument which has the peculiar property of being acceptable at face value in exchange for goods, services and other financial instruments.

To some students this may seem a paradox. Financial instruments are claims for future payment. Future payments will be made in money. How then can money be both the means of payment and a claim for payment? Are we simply talking in riddles?

Perhaps no problem arises in connection with *bank money.* Chequable bank deposits can be regarded as claims for payment in legal tender money — claims which may be affected at the option of the depositor in whole or in part at any time in the future. We can take this as a limiting case in our definition of a financial instrument. It can be a claim for a *single payment* (the shortest possible stream of payments), payable *on demand* of the creditor (the shortest possible term to maturity).

This still leaves the problem of legal-tender money, however. As we noted in the previous chapter, legal tender in Canada in practice means notes issued by the Bank of Canada for use as currency, and these have the formal status as liabilities of the Bank of Canada. They are payable "on demand", although as we have seen, this inscription on Bank of Canada notes is quite meaningless. In what sense, then, can we say that legal tender money is a claim for payment?

Unit of Account. In order to answer this question we require another concept, that of the *unit of account.* This is the abstract unit by which we measure, record, and compare market values, the unit in which we keep our personal and business accounts. In Canada, the unit of account is the dollar (which is subdivided into 100 cents).

It is sometimes said that one of the functions of money is to serve as a unit of account. However, such a statement confuses two concepts. *Money* is an object, a financial instrument or (in some times and places) a commodity. It is something which changes hands in the process of exchange. The *unit of account* is an arbitrary unit in which we measure market value, *including the value of money*. It should be thought of in the same vein as one thinks of the ounce as an arbitrary unit in which we measure weight and the degree as the arbitrary unit in which we measure temperature. It is true that money is normally issued in denominations corresponding to the unit of account. That is not necessary, however. For example, in England values are frequently measured in guineas, a unit of account for which there is no monetary counterpart.

Money as A Generalized Fixed-Price Claim. In what sense, then is money (particularly legal-tender money) a claim for future payment? We should not regard it as a claim against any specific debtor (even though the government issues it). Rather, it is a claim for payment in that it is universally acceptable in exchange for goods, services or financial instruments of a given value, with the value measured in terms of the unit of account. A $10 Bank of Canada note can always be exchanged for goods, services or financial instruments whose market value equals $10. The Bank of Canada note — legal-tender money — is a general claim against society which can be effected at any time at the option of the holder.

Fixed Price vs. Fixed Purchasing Power. It is important to remember that to say that the price of money is fixed in terms of the unit of account is not to say that the purchasing power of money is always constant. A given quantity of money may not always command a fixed quantity of goods and services, only a fixed market value of goods and services. The prices of goods and services measured in terms of the unit of account may rise over time, and money, which always commands a *fixed value* of goods and services, will buy a *smaller quantity* of those goods and services. The purchasing power of money will have fallen. This process is called inflation, and one of the major tasks of monetary theory is to explain its causes, consequences and cures.

Summary: the Concept of Liquidity. In summary, we can say that money is a peculiar type of financial instrument. Regardless of the form in which it appears, money should be regarded as a claim against society as a whole rather than against any single debtor. *It is a financial instrument whose price, measured in terms of the unit of account, is fixed.* This is a vital property not possessed by most other financial instruments (or commodities).

The holder of shares of corporate stock or of government bonds faces the risk that their market values will fall. By contrast, the holder of money faces no such risk.

We call this property of money *liquidity*. It is possessed by other assets in varying degrees. That is, their market prices, measured in terms of the unit of account, are more or less stable. *Money, since its price is fixed, is the most liquid of financial instruments.*

2/THE INSTITUTIONS OF FINANCIAL MARKETS

To an economist the concept of a market does not necessarily imply a fixed location, any particular set of institutional arrangements or pattern of organization of exchange. A market exists whenever buyers and sellers agree to exchange, regardless of whether they are located in the same physical place and regardless of how their mutual interests are brought together. The tangible evidence of a market is not a structure of buildings or a particular set of institutional arrangements; it is simply a series of exchanges. In this sense, then, an economist would consider the financial market to be conterminous with the entire financial system. The financial system is basically a set of markets for particular types of financial instruments.

However, when we use the term financial market we have a narrower concept in mind. We can divide all financial transactions into two types, loan transactions and investment transactions. In the former category we place all transactions involving face to face negotiations between borrowers and lenders. The promissory notes involved are not normally designed to be re-sold, and hence they tend to remain lodged in the lender's portfolio (although this is not necessary, of course). In the second category we place all transactions in "public issues", financial instruments designed to be sold on an impersonal basis to any and all buyers. Inevitably, the distinction between the two categories is fuzzy at the margin. It is not clear whether certain transactions (e.g., negotiated private placements of long-term marketable bonds with a single institutional lender) should be considered a loans or investment type transaction. There is, however, a difference of substance. When we speak of financial markets in the narrow sense, we make reference to the second type of transaction – impersonal transactions in marketable financial instruments.

For most purposes of economic analysis, complete details on the institutional arrangements of markets are not necessary. Indeed, such details frequently get in the way of clear analysis. The institutions tend to adapt themselves to the particular market situation, and although they may have some impact on the efficiency and neutrality of the exchange process, they are seldom crucial to the outcome. This is equally true of the financial system. While it is important to know that certain types of markets exist, and to understand the institutions of those markets in broad outline, it is seldom important that all of the details of those arrangements be understood. All that is required here is a brief overview of the major institutions involved in exchanging financial instruments.

Brokers, Dealers and Underwriters

The central institutions of financial markets are a group of business firms called investment houses. They function as intermediaries in the marketing process, as brokers, as dealers or as underwriters.

A broker is a pure intermediary in market transactions. He is not a party to any transaction himself. Rather, he acts as an *agent* for his clients, be they buyers or sellers. He uses his information on the market — the basic ingredient in his activities — and his contacts to bring buyers and sellers together, at mutually acceptable prices, and provides the technical facilities necessary for the execution of the transactions. For his services, the broker charges his clients a fee or *commission* which is normally related to the value of the transaction.

A *dealer* is also an intermediary in the exchange process. However, in contrast to the broker, the dealer actually becomes a party to market transactions. In the jargon of the trade, he "makes markets". He holds an inventory of securities, buys in the market to add to that inventory and sells out of his inventory to other buyers, perhaps at a different time or place. He hopes to make a profit on a spread between buying and selling prices.

While techniques of underwriting vary depending on the circumstances, an *underwriter* is basically a dealer who handles new issues of securities. He buys them, and then sells them into the market hoping to make a profit on the spread between the selling and the buying price. Again, information and market contacts are the essential ingredients in the underwriter's activities.

Earlier in this chapter we distinguished between primary and secondary markets for securities. We can identify underwriting with the primary market and the main operations of brokers and dealers with secondary markets. This is an oversimplification, in part, because not all new issues of securities go through a formal process of underwriting. Thus, one vitally important group of bonds, those of the Government of Canada, are sold in the first instance to a large list of "primary distributors" including the chartered banks and the Montreal City and District Savings Bank as well as over 250 selected investment houses. If there is an underwriter, it is the Bank of Canada, but that hardly seems the appropriate designation of the Bank's activities. Similarly, a significant portion of corporate, provincial and municipal bonds are "direct placements" with large institutional lenders. The issuers negotiate directly with the lenders, generally with the assistance and advice of an investment house, but without benefit of an underwriting arrangement. This is an extension of the brokerage function to the new issue market.

The identification of underwriters with primary markets, and brokers and dealers with secondary markets is also an oversimplification, because it is difficult to separate the three activities. Investment houses in Canada, with some exception, do not narrowly specialize in one or the other line of activity. Thus, in the words of the Royal Commission on Banking and Finance:

> One of the distinguishing features of the Canadian industry is its relative lack of specialization. The largest and most profitable firms are fully integrated; they underwrite and distribute new issues, position and trade debt and other securities, sell wholesale and retail, operate in the money market, have membership in one or more stock exchanges, manage portfolios and in general perform the whole range of functions common to the industry.[1]

Moreover, the Commission notes, the "largest and most profitable" fully integrated firms dominate all aspects of the financial industry.

Patterns of Organization in Financial Markets

A study for the Royal Commission on Banking and Finance done in the early 1960's reveals that there are almost 400 firms acting as brokers, dealers and underwriters in Canada. Not all of these firms are independent. Many are specialized affiliates of other firms. Moreover, there is a marked degree of concentration in the business. A handful of integrated firms, with nation-wide branch organizations, account for the vast majority of business done in all aspects of the industry. Nonetheless, taking the industry as a whole, we are talking about a comparatively large number of firms who trade among themselves (wholesale transactions) and with the general public (retail transactions). How are their activities organized so as to produce an effective national market in securities?

Over-the-counter Markets vs. Organized Exchanges. Dealings with the general public are through a series of offices and branch offices throughout the country. Through salesmen or "customer's men" in these offices an investment house takes orders for purchases or sales, whether as a dealer selling or buying for its own account or as a broker taking orders for transactions to be effected in the market. In this respect, the securities industry is organized much like any other retail sales industry.

Perhaps the best known — and certainly the most spectacular — institutional arrangement for dealings among investment houses is the organized stock exchange. In Canada, there are six such exchanges in operation, two in Montreal (in the same building and with the same staff) and one each in Toronto, Winnipeg, Calgary and Vancouver. However, The Toronto Stock Exchange alone accounts for over 70% of the value trading in all stock exchanges, and the Montreal and Toronto Exchanges together account for over 95%. The smaller western exchanges provide an organized market for stocks of local enterprises, particularly mining and oil companies.

A stock exchange is a corporation, incorporated under provincial legislation. It provides a place where representatives of investment houses, admitted to membership in the exchange, can meet to buy and sell securities, on their own behalf or as agents for clients, and under rules established and enforced by the exchange. For the market to work effectively, of course, the traders on the floor must have almost instantaneous contact with their brokerage offices, and through these offices (and their branches throughout the country) indirectly with the firm's customers. Not all investment houses are members of organized exchanges (although many non-member brokers have access to the facilities of the stock exchanges through members, with whom they split the commissions). Thus, of an estimated 400 firms in the security business, perhaps 170 belong to one or more organized exchanges in Canada. Each exchange establishes its own rules governing membership, and in general each has established a fixed upper limit to the number of "seats" available. These seats can be bought and sold, but only with the approval of the exchange (and some members may own more than one "seat").

Just as not all investment houses are members of organized exchanges, so not all securities are traded on these exchanges. There is a second type of marketing arrangement connecting investment houses, the so-called over-the-counter market. In Canada, all bonds and many stocks are traded on the over-the-counter market. In some cases stocks are not "listed" on one of the stock exchanges because the corporation cannot meet the requirements of the exchange for listing; in other cases it is a matter of deliberate choice on the part of the management of the corporation not to seek listing. However, in the case of bonds, the stock exchanges have deliberately excluded bonds from trading on the floor of the exchange. The over-the-counter market is a telephone market. Deals are sought and consummated by telephone and telegraph, with the formal exchange of papers occurring subsequently. Much of the trading on the over-the-counter market involves dealers trading for their own account rather than as brokers.

A National and an International Market. The investment houses, many of them with nation-wide networks of branch offices, linked together through the stock markets and the over-the-counter markets in stocks and bonds, provide the institutional arrangements for a truly nation-wide market in all types of securities. Changes in demand or supply in any one section of the country will be felt almost immediately in all others. In part, this transmission of market changes will result from formal arbitrage operations. *Arbitrage* involves the simultaneous purchase and sale of a security in two different markets. Thus, if a particular stock listed on both the Toronto and Montreal markets should fall in price in Montreal at an instant, an alert investment house (probably with seats on both exchanges) could buy shares in Montreal and sell them in Toronto virtually simultaneously, making a profit in the transaction and tending to eliminate the price differential between the two markets.

Arbitrage of this sort appears to account for a small but significant portion of the activity in the organized stock exchanges. However, equally important in transmitting the changes in supply or demand among market areas are the activities of brokers and dealers on the over-the-counter market. In virtually constant communication with each other, traders at the leading investment houses seek out the best prices for their customers who wish to buy or sell, and are constantly alert for profitable buying and selling opportunities for the firm's own portfolio. The result is a fluid and continuous coast-to-coast market.

But the market connections established through the network of investment houses and formal stock exchanges is not confined to the boundaries of the nation. There are equally important international connections as well, and particularly strong connections with the financial markets of the United States. Thus, some Canadian stocks are traded on stock exchanges in the United States, and United States stocks in Canada. Leading Canadian investment houses have branch offices in the United States (and several other countries), and some investment houses operating in Canada are branch offices of United States firms. Canadian security dealers and brokers are in virtually continuous telephone and telegraphic contact with their counterparts in New York and elsewhere. These connections permit international arbitrage in both Canadian and foreign securities, and facilitate Canadian transactions in foreign securities and foreign transactions in Canadian securities. *The institutions of the financial markets are international as well as national in scope, and as a result market transactions flow easily across the country and across national boundaries.* This, as will become evident, is a fact of profound significance for Canadian monetary policy.

The Secondary Bond Market

As we will discover in a later section of this book, a major portion of the day-by-day operations of the Bank of Canada, including the implementation of monetary policy, involves purchases and sales of bonds in the open market. These are operations in the *secondary* bond market, and the nature and scope of that market can affect the magnitude, timing and nature of the operations which the central bank can effectively carry out. Hence, since it has particular significance for our later analysis, before we leave our brief description of financial markets we should examine the dimensions of the secondary bond market.

Table 3-1
The Primary and Secondary Bond Markets, 1961

Security	Sales	
	Primary Market	Secondary Market
	(Millions of Dollars)	
Government of Canada Bonds		
Treasury Bills	6,240	6,142
Short-term Bonds	1,325	4,618
Long-term Bonds	875	1,962
Provincial Government Bonds	952	1,289
Municipal Government Bonds	462	368
Corporate Bonds	666	1,400
	10,520	
less adjustment for Bank of Canada roll-over of portfolio*	1,015	
	9,505	15,780

* Securities taken by the Bank of Canada in exchange for maturing issues.
SOURCE: Investment Dealers Association of Canada, *Brief* to Royal Commission on Banking and Finance, 1962.

No statistics on the secondary bond market are collected and published as a matter of course. However, a study was conducted by the Investment Dealers Association of Canada at the request of the Royal Commission on Banking and Finance with reference to the year 1961. The results of that study are noted in Table 3-1. Unfortunately, these data are long out of date, but they are the only ones publicly available. It is reasonable to assume, however, that the picture which they give of the secondary bond market is still roughly accurate.

The Canadian secondary bond market is not highly developed. The bulk of secondary trading is in Government of Canada bonds, particularly short-term bonds (3 years and under to maturity). Thus, some 85% of all reported sales in 1961 were of Government of Canada bonds, and 68% of Government of Canada bonds with 3 years or less to maturity. One suspects that reported sales of longer-term bonds were also relatively heavily concentrated near the shorter end of the maturity range.

The market in short-term government securities is part of what has come to be called the *money market,* an open market in the short-term securities of selected "blue chip" borrowers. The money market has taken on an institutional identity of its own and has developed a peculiar significance within the financial system.

3/THE MONEY MARKET

The money market is effectively organized by a small number of money market dealers (or "jobbers" as they are sometimes called). These are investment houses which "make markets" in money market instruments. That is, they hold inventories of short-term securities, and stand ready to buy and sell short-term securities to be taken into and out of their inventories hoping to make a profit on the spread between buying and selling prices. The money market dealers tend to be the larger, better-known bond dealers, with nation wide networks of branches and international connections. They have lines of credit with the major Chartered Banks, and with the Bank of Canada.

Money Market Instruments

The money market is an active open market in *selected* short-term financial instruments.

Treasury Bills. Perhaps most important are the short-term obligations of the Government of Canada, including treasury bills. In one sense there has been a money market in Canada for a long time. That is, there is a long history of some trading in short-term securities. However, as we will see later, a primary function of the modern money market is to serve as a place in which financial intermediaries (and increasingly non-financial corporations) can make adjustments to their liquidity positions. This calls for not occasional, ad hoc trades, but continuous trading in a broad active market, and such a market requires a continuous supply of suitable money market instruments. The origins of the money market in this sense are generally identified with the first offering of treasury bills by competitive tender in 1934, although it is probably more accurate to date the market from 1953 or 1954.

The introduction of regular competitive tenders for treasury bills provided part of the requirements for an active money market. It guaranteed the market a regular supply of suitable instruments. From 1937 through 1952 an auction of treasury bills was held fortnightly, and in early 1953 the frequency of the auctions was increased to weekly.

The introduction of the treasury bill itself could not guarantee an active money market, however. Until the mid-1950's the money market remained primarily a market in short-term government securities, particularly treasury bills, and it was essentially a triangular market. Treasury bills were traded among the Government of Canada (as issuer), the Bank of Canada, and the chartered banks. Throughout the years 1946-1952 the chartered banks and the Bank of Canada between them tended to hold in excess of 85% of the total amount of treasury bills outstanding, and as late as December 1951 they held almost 95% of the $450 million in outstanding treasury bills.

In 1953 and 1954 a number of institutional changes in money market arrangements were promoted by the Bank of Canada which facilitated the development of a more active and broader money market.

Some of these changes related to the availability of short-term government securities. Thus, beginning in January 1952, treasury bills were auctioned weekly instead of fortnightly, and the total amount outstanding was sharply increased. In 1952 there was a fortnightly auction of $75 million of three-month treasury bills, with a total of $450 million outstanding at any one time. In 1953 the amount outstanding was increased to $650 million, and by late 1956 this had risen to $1,600 million. By early 1970 the Government of Canada was holding a weekly auction of $175 million of 3-month and 6-month treasury bills, with a total of $2,895 million of such bills outstanding at the end of the year. The increase in the amount of treasury bills outstanding was accompanied in late 1955 by an arrangement between the chartered banks and the Bank of Canada under which the banks agreed to invest a portion of their funds in treasury bills. The banks agreed to invest, at a minimum 7% of their Canadian dollar deposits in cash, day-by-day loans to security dealers, or treasury bills over and above the deposits which they had to maintain as cash reserves. This substantially increased the demand for treasury bills, as is evident on Chart 3-1. The 1967 revision of *The Bank Act* included a compulsory secondary reserve requirement.

Day-to-Day Loans. Some of the changes in money market arrangements related to the position of government security dealers in the market, and were designed to encourage these dealers to cultivate the market by holding inventories and actively trading money market instruments. Thus, certain bank charges arising out of inter-dealer transactions in securities were reduced and eventually eliminated in order to encourage active

Figure 3-1
The Development of the Canadian Money Market, 1946-1970

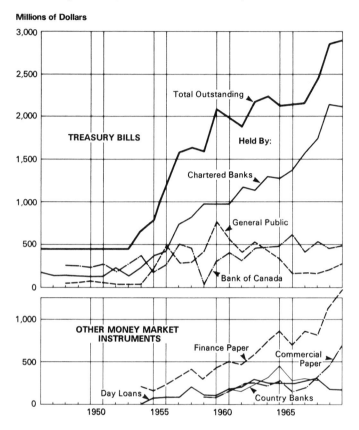

Millions of Dollars

trading. The chartered banks were also encouraged to make low cost "day-to-day" loans to the dealers to permit them to carry inventories of government securities, and the Bank of Canada offered lines of credit to a selected list of such dealers. Day-to-day loans (or *day loans* for short) are demand loans to money market dealers, secured by short-term Government securities. Such loans can be called by either party before noon for payment the same day. The rate of interest is determined by competitive forces in the market, but is normally substantially below the rate of interest on other money market instruments.

Bank of Canada Advances. Day loans from the chartered banks quickly became a primary source of finance for the money market dealers. As the market developed, other private sources of funds emerged as well. We will turn to these shortly. However, the lines of credit with the Bank of Canada were little used. This was largely by design. The Bank of Canada sees its role as a supplier of funds to money market dealers as that of a "lender of last resort" — a residual source of the finance should other sources dry up unexpectedly. The purpose is to relieve temporary pressures on the market and hence prevent short-term instability in the market resulting from the forced liquidation of money market dealer inventories. In accordance with this role, the interest rate on advances from the Bank of Canada to the money market dealers is set at 1/4 of 1% above the average yield on 3-month treasury bills. Other sources of finance are normally cheaper.

Advances from the Bank of Canada are in the form of "purchase and resale agreements", or "buy-backs". The securities are formally sold to the Bank of Canada, but the sale is accompanied by an agreement to repurchase the security on a specified date at a specified price. The difference between the price at which the dealer initially sells the security and that at which he agrees to repurchase it is calculated to yield the Bank of Canada the appropriate interest rate. This type of arrangement has broader applications in the money market as well.

Finance Paper and Commercial Paper. The institutional changes of 1953 and 1954 did not produce the money market. They could only facilitate its development. The really active force was a general rise in the demand for funds, accompanied by a general rise in interest rates. This development brought many new participants into the market, both to invest temporarily idle funds for short periods of time, and to borrow funds on short-term instruments. The former development produced what has come to be called "country banking" in short-term instruments. The range of instruments actively traded on the market expanded rapidly.

Among the earliest participants in the market were a group of sales finance companies who issued short-term notes, commonly called "finance paper". In the later 1950's, an increasing number of non-financial corporations began raising funds through money market issues, so-called "commercial paper". These firms include several retail stores, grain merchants, oil companies, and other industrial firms. In general, these firms found they could raise funds somewhat cheaper in the money market than through bank loans, although they generally have a line of credit with chartered banks as insurance.

In addition to finance paper, commercial paper and short-term Government of Canada securities, there are a number of other instruments traded in the money market. Some of the major municipal and provincial governments raise money through issues of treasury bills. Some banks and trust companies also use the facilities of the money market to attract funds into term deposits. There is also trading in foreign securities from time to time, and foreign participation in the Canadian money market.

"Country Banks." Finally, a development in the money market which has attracted some attention from time to time is the emergence of the *country bank.*

The role of the money market dealer in making markets in money market instruments is crucial to the efficient functioning of the money market. By standing ready to buy or sell securities the dealers provide continuity and hence a margin of stability to the market, reducing the risks of illiquidity for all participants in the market. However, to perform this role the dealer must be able to finance the acquisition and holding of inventories of securities. The dealer's own capital is one source of such finance, but in general, it only accounts for a small portion of the total funds used by money market dealers. As we have already seen, the chartered banks provide an important source of funds for money market operations through day loans. The banks also provide funds on conventional call-loans to investment dealers, some of whom will also be money market dealers. The Bank of Canada stands ready as a lender of last resort, but not as a continuing normal source of funds. The rest of the funds with which the dealers operate come from country banks: non-bank private lenders, mainly private corporations.

The typical country bank will be a corporation which has a large sum of money available for a short period of time, and which wishes to invest those funds in safe interest-bearing instruments. The investment dealer may bid for those funds on a competitive basis with banks and other possible short-term borrowers. These loans would be in the form of purchase and resale agreements, with the terms of the resale agreement tailored to the specific needs of the lender of the funds.

The Role of Money Market in the Financial System

The basic function of all financial markets is to mobilize the financial surpluses of the nation and to allocate these among competing deficit spending units. The money market, however, has another important role to play in the financial system. It provides a place where spending units and financial intermediaries can adjust their liquidity positions, and where the central bank can adjust the liquidity position of the entire economy. The vital quality of the money market is its breadth, activity and stability which can absorb substantial short-term shocks without excessive gyrations in market prices. Thus, corporations, banks or other financial intermediaries with temporarily surplus cash can put it to work, at a competitive rate of interest, in the money market, and be reasonably secure in the knowledge that the funds can be recalled on very short notice if needed. Likewise, the corporations, banks or other financial intermediaries which are short of cash can obtain it on short notice and for short periods of time, if that is desirable, by borrowing in the money market, or selling in the market any money market instruments that they may have been holding. The money market thus makes it possible for all types of firms and financial intermediaries to manage their financial affairs more efficiently, and particularly to economize on their holdings of money. It also provides a convenient point for the central bank to intrude into the operations of the financial system. The central bank can sell Treasury Bills and other short-term government securities in the money market in order to absorb what it might consider to be excess cash in the financial system. Likewise, it can purchase such money market instruments in exchange for cash if it feels that there is not sufficient cash in the system. We will have many occasions, as we progress through this book, to refer to the money market and its importance for financial intermediaries and the operation of monetary policy.

FOOTNOTES

[1] Royal Commission on Banking and Finance, *Report*, p. 302.

4

Elementary Theory of
Financial Markets, Part 1:
The Demand for Wealth

In Chapter 3 we described the major instruments exchanged in financial markets, and discussed the more important institutions of these markets in Canada. It is now time to turn to the more difficult task of exploring the process by which prices are formed in such markets. That is the purpose of this and the following two chapters.

When asked, "What determines prices in a financial market?" the average economics student will instinctively respond, "Supply and demand." This is true in a general sense, since all prices are determined by supply and demand, but unless we can put some content into the concepts of supply and demand, such an answer will not take us very far down the road to understanding the behaviour of financial markets.

1/THE DEMAND FOR FINANCIAL INSTRUMENTS

The Basic Decisions

The demand side of the market for financial instruments includes, at various times, virtually every spending unit in the economy — households, financial intermediaries, business firms, non-profit institutions and government agencies. Any spending unit with a need or desire to accumulate wealth will probably enter this market from time to time.

The role of financial intermediaries in financial markets raises special issues which are best considered separately. We will discuss them in Chapter 7. At the outset we also prefer to leave aside discussion of the demands of business firms, non-profit institutions and government agencies. With a few exceptions, particularly relating to the demand for money, they are peripheral to the main demand forces in financial markets. Thus, in this and the next chapter we will be focusing attention almost exclusively on household demands for financial instruments.

We will cast our analysis of household demands for financial instruments in terms of two basic decisions which every household must make:

(1) a decision on the *size* of total wealth holdings; and
(2) a decision on the *composition* of wealth holdings.
Wealth is the central concept in the analysis. Indeed, we will argue that financial instruments take on significance to households simply as forms in which wealth may be accumulated.

The first decision is the subject of this chapter, the second decision that of the next.

2/WEALTH AND SAVING

If wealth is to be the central concept in the analysis of demands for financial assets then the first task must be to define the concept of wealth and to explore the process by which wealth is accumulated. Our objective is the development of a theory of wealth accumulation.

The Concept of Wealth

As a start, we might define the household's wealth as *the value of the household's net equity in the things which the household owns.* While complex, this definition is designed to emphasize three essential elements. First, the concept of wealth relates to things which have value in the economic sense, i.e., *market value.* Second, it implies *ownership* — the right of the household to exclude others from the enjoyment of these valuable things. Finally, the definition recognizes that the household may formally "own" valuable things of greater aggregate value than the total wealth of the household. The difference is the aggregate value of the debts or obligations of the household. Thus, to cite the most familiar example, a family may "own" its house, and at the same time have an outstanding debt or mortgage against it, equal to a substantial portion of the market value of the house. The contribution of the house to the family's wealth is the difference between the value of the house and the value of the mortgage — the family's *equity* in the house.

The Accounting Framework

Three basic accounting relationships provide a simple framework for our analysis of the demand for wealth. Each of these can be expressed in the form of an equation, but an equation which is an *identity.* The two sides of the equation are equal by definition. One can take the left-hand side of each equation as a formal definition of the variable on the right-hand side. Unlike equations which embody *functional relationships*, identities do not tell us anything substantive about the demand for wealth. They do not purport to describe the behaviour of participants in the financial system. Rather, they specify *constraints* on behaviour. They tell us that certain combinations of events or activities are logically impossible. For example, the first identity tells us that it is impossible for a household's assets to increase while both its liabilities and its net worth are falling.

The Balance Sheet Identity. *Assets* are values which the household owns. *Liabilities* are the values which it owes. The difference between assets and liabilities is the equity in the value of things owed – the household's net worth or *wealth*. This fundamental relationship can be expressed in the balance sheet identity:

$$\text{ASSETS} \quad - \quad \text{LIABILITIES} \quad = \quad \text{WEALTH} \qquad (4.1)$$

Wealth need not always be positive. The assets of the household could exceed or fall short of liabilities, and accordingly wealth could be positive or negative. If wealth is positive, we can refer to the household as a *net creditor*, and if it is negative we can refer to it as a *net debtor*.[1]

The Saving Identity. The second basic identity is a definition of net saving. For every household, and indeed for the nation as a whole, it is true by definition that:

$$\text{INCOME} \quad - \quad \text{CONSUMPTION} \quad = \quad \text{SAVING} \qquad (4.2)$$

This identity is simply a statement of the fact that consumption and savings are alternative uses of the same scarce resources, the household's (or the nation's) income. In order to save, the household must choose to forego current consumption, and in this very basic sense current consumption foregone is the cost of saving. The decisions on consumption and on saving are two sides of the same coin. If you explain one, you explain the other.

There is nothing in the saving identity which· says that saving must be positive. Saving can be negative as long as current consumption exceeds current income (negative saving is sometimes called dissaving). Thus, saving is an economic variable which must be assigned an algebraic sign as well as a magnitude.

The Accumulation Identity. Assets, liabilities and wealth are *stock variables*. They are values measured at a point in time. Income, consumption and saving are *flow variables*. They are values measured over a period of time. The third identity – the accumulation identity – establishes a logical link between the stocks and the flows. It simply states that during any given period of time:[2]

$$\text{SAVING} \quad = \quad \Delta \text{ WEALTH} \qquad (4.3)$$

where Δ wealth means the *net change* in wealth.

The logic of this equation should be self-evident. If it is not, consider briefly what is involved in the act of saving. If the saving of a given household is positive during some month, the household receives more income than it spends on consumption during that month. What can the household do with the balance of its income? There are three possibilities. It might use this portion to acquire real or financial assets. This is a non-consumption use of the household's income, which results in an increase in its net asset holdings and hence its wealth. Alternatively, the household might use this portion of its income to pay off debts. Again, this is a non-consumption use of its income which, by reducing liabilities, increases the household's wealth. If it neither purchases assets nor pays off liabilities then the household must simply accumulate money in the amount of the excess of its income over its consumption. But money is also an asset. Its accumulation implies an equal increase of the household's wealth. *Positive saving implies a corresponding increase in wealth.*

The same points can be made regarding negative saving. If consumption is to exceed income, the household must somehow finance its deficit budget. It must either borrow, and thereby increase its liabilities and hence reduce its wealth, or it must draw down its assets, whether money or other assets, with the same effect on its wealth. *Negative saving implies a corresponding reduction in wealth.*

3/THE ECONOMIC THEORY OF THE SAVING DECISION

On any particular date which we can choose arbitrarily as the starting point for our analysis, each household in the population will have a measurable stock of wealth (positive or negative), and will expect a certain flow of income during the following time period, say one year. The household may plan to increase, decrease or make no change in its wealth holdings over that year. For our analysis, this is the fundamental decision to be made by each household — a decision about the size of its wealth holdings.

Equation 4.3 tells us that saving is the method by which any household adjusts the size of its wealth. This suggests that we should call this fundamental decision the *saving decision*. (It is important to remember that saving may be either positive or negative; wealth may be increased or decreased).

Specific Motives for Saving

If we asked people why they save part of their income we would probably be given a great variety of specific motives. It is quite likely that we would discover many instances in which saving was alleged to be quite *fortuitous* — an unplanned, inadvertent and perhaps random event. Aside from such short-term aberrations, however, we would probably discover that most households had in mind a fairly deliberate plan for saving. In some cases it might involve a general *income objective*, like the provision of a pension during years of retirement from active participation in the labour force or otherwise to increase the household's income in later years. In other instances we might be told about some specific *target* which the household has in mind, such as the purchase of a new house, a new automobile or some other major durable good, or even an intangible item such as a prolonged vacation, perhaps involving a trip to "the old country", or a university education or an inheritance for the household's children. In other instances we might discover that saving was simply an attempt to provide for general or specific *contingencies* which might occur in the future. Thus, a household might buy life or disability insurance on the main income earner, or it might build up a bank account "against a rainy day", or take advantage of unexpected future opportunities.

The variety of possible motives for saving is virtually endless, and no single theory can encompass all of them in detail. The problem is to distill from the endless complexities of reality a few generalizations which capture the "essence" of the behaviour of saving. In recent years, this has been the subject of much theoretical and empirical research. Without attempting a detailed review of the resulting literature, it is pertinent to note some of the highlights.

Income and the Saving Decision

The Keynesian Hypothesis. The theory of saving developed in most principles of economics textbooks is that embodied in the Keynesian consumption function. Its originator, J. M. Keynes, asserted that "the amount of aggregate consumption mainly depends on the amount of aggregate income," and this relationship exists because there is a:

> fundamental psychological law, upon which we are entitled to depend with great confidence, both *a priori* from our knowledge of human nature and from the detailed facts of experience . . . that men are disposed, as a rule and on the average, to increase their consumption as their income increases, but not by as much as the increase in their income.[3]

As equation 4.2 demonstrates, consumption and saving are complements. They are alternative possible uses of income, and if you explain one you necessarily explain the other. Thus, Keynes' consumption function can be readily translated into a saving function which says that "the amount of aggregate saving mainly depends on the amount of aggregate income," and "men are disposed, as a rule and on the average, to increase their saving as their income increases, but not by as much as the increase in their income." In most elementary economic theory it is assumed that the relationship between aggregate income and saving can be described by a straight line, such as that depicted in Figure 4.1. At low levels of income, saving is negative. At higher levels of income it is positive, and is an increasing function of income. The portion of income saved (the average propensity to consume) thus depends on the level of income, but the increase in saving is always a constant proportion (the marginal propensity to consume) of any increase in income.

Figure 4-1
Aggregate Saving Function: Keynesian Hypothesis

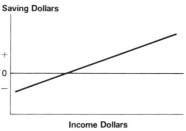

This assumed relationship between income and saving seems plausible enough. Since the accumulation of wealth is but one among the many competing demands on the limited income of each household, it would be surprising if the level of saving in the household was not affected by the household's income. Households with relatively high incomes are able to buy more of everything, including wealth, than are households with relatively small incomes. Moreover, at a low level of income, present consumption needs are likely in general to seem relatively more urgent than future requirements. We would therefore expect low-income households to save a smaller portion of their income than high-income families.

As it has been used in economic theory, the Keynesian hypothesis is primarily a relationship between *aggregate* income and *aggregate* saving. It is clear, however, from his "fundamental psychological law" that Keynes thought of his relationship applying at the *microeconomic* level as well — as explaining differences in individual household's saving. The validity of the hypothesis has been tested at both levels in a large number of studies. The aggregative studies have examined the relationship between income and saving for the nation as a whole over varying time periods extending well over half a century in length. The microeconomic studies, by contrast, examine the saving behaviour of a cross-section of households during a given period of time, normally one year.

At first glance, both the micro and macro studies appear to confirm the Keynesian hypothesis, at least in a general way. While the relationship may not be strictly linear, there is a clear, unmistakable positive relationship between saving and income, both in the aggregate and on the average for a cross-section of the population. That latter is illustrated in Table 4-1. However, in spite of this evidence, many economists have lingering doubts about the adequacy of the hypothesis.

These doubts are based in part on theoretical reasoning, involving the relationship between saving and wealth accumulation which we have already established. A low-income household which is dissaving must be simultaneously reducing its wealth, either by disposing of assets or increasing liabilities. The assumption that saving depends solely on income (if it is to conform to the facts of Table 4-1) implies a further assumption that households with chronically low incomes have unlimited means to finance consumption in excess of income. They must have unlimited assets which can be sold, or they must be able to increase their debts without limit. In general, this assumption is implausible.

Households with incomes above the zero saving level must be accumulating wealth. This includes the bulk of the households in the population. The hypothesis that saving depends only on the level of income implies the further hypothesis that households whose income remains continuously in this range have insatiable demand for wealth. While it does not do as much violence to our pre-conceptions about the world as does the first assumption (unlimited credit or assets for sale), this is also implausible. Households presumably demand wealth for any of the variety of purposes which we have noted earlier. None of these suggests an insatiable demand for wealth at moderate to high income levels regardless of all other considerations.

Empirical research appears to confirm these theoretical doubts. A careful sifting of the evidence shows that the Keynesian hypothesis does not

Table 4-1

Income and Saving of Families in Canadian Urban Areas, 1964

	All Classes	Under 2,500	2,500- 2,999	3,000- 3,499	3,500- 3,999	4,000- 4,499
Average Net Income	6,415	1,910	2,674	3,192	3,599	4,061
Consumption	6,046	2,345	3,167	3,455	3,800	4,220
Saving	+569	−366	−397	−201	−89	−28
Saving Ratio	+8.9	−19.2	−14.2	−6.3	−2.5	−.7

4,500- 4,999	5,000- 5,499	5,500- 5,999	6,000- 6,999	7,000- 7,999	8,000- 9,000	Over 10,000
4,466	4,933	5,385	5,968	6,801	8,072	12,090
4,540	5,035	5,464	5,744	6,716	7,380	10,002
+73	+26	+57	+466	+286	+951	+2,488
+1.6	+.5	+1.1	+7.5	+4.2	+11.8	+20.6

SOURCE: DBS 62-527 Urban Family Expenditure, 1964 (Ottawa: 1968), p. 37.

adequately explain all of the significant variations in saving behaviour among households, or all of the significant fluctuations in national saving behaviour. The Keynesian hypothesis appears to identify one important consideration in household saving, but as a total theory of saving it is at best only a first approximation.

The Permanent Income Hypothesis. One of the interesting regularities discovered in cross-sectional studies is that the saving behaviour of households which have recently experienced a significant *change* in income is different from the behaviour of households with the same present income level but which have not experienced a change in income. Households which have experienced a decline in income tend to save less than comparable households with a steady income, and households which have experienced a rise in income tend to save more than comparable households with a stable income. One possible explanation for this phenomenon is to be found in the so-called permanent income hypothesis.

According to this hypothesis, a household's consumption does not depend directly upon the household's current income. Rather, if we ignore a random or "transitory" component in consumption expenditures, it depends upon the household's "permanent income". The concept of permanent income is somewhat complex, and a formal definition is beyond our present exposition. However, we can roughly interpret it as that level of income which the household has come to expect as its normal income. The actual income may fall short of or exceed permanent income as a result of random "transitory" factors.

Illness or unexpected unemployment might reduce income below permanent income. Similarly, an unexpected gift or a sudden rise in the market price of a product produced and sold by members of the household would raise current income above permanent income. Thus both income and consumption have a permanent component (planned or expected) and a transitory component (a product of unexpected chance variations).

The permanent income hypothesis is normally presented as a theory explaining the behaviour of consumption expenditures. However, equation 4.2 permits us to reinterpret it as a theory of the behaviour of saving. According to this hypothesis, both income and saving have permanent and transitory components. Permanent (or planned) saving depends directly on permanent income, but actual saving may fluctuate about permanent saving as a result of chance factors. In most formal presentations of the permanent income hypothesis it is assumed that permanent saving is a constant proportion of permanent income — that the permanent marginal propensity to save is a constant.[4] The relationship observed in Table 4-1 is explained in terms of the transitory components of income and saving.

The permanent income hypothesis, if correct, provides a fundamentally different interpretation of the relationship between income and saving than does the Keynesian hypothesis. Moreover, the difference is a matter of considerable consequence for economic policy, as we will see in later sections of the book. Tests of the hypothesis have thus had a relatively high priority in empirical economics in recent years. Unfortunately, none of the variables involved — permanent income, permanent consumption, or permanent saving (or, for that matter, the corresponding transitory components) — can be observed directly. They are theoretical constructs. As a result, all of the tests have had to be indirect. Perhaps for this reason we must regard the formal statistical tests as inconclusive. Much of the evidence is favourable to the hypothesis, but the evidence is far from decisive.

The Life Cycle Hypothesis. In the simple form in which we have presented it, the permanent income hypothesis does not provide us with many insights into the saving decision. It only tells us that in part the saving decision is deliberate and in part a product of chance variations in income. It does not tell us what considerations govern the level of planned saving. (By definition, we cannot have a theory to explain the "random" component.) This is not a fault of the theory, but of our exposition, since we have not explored the theoretical foundations of the hypothesis.

The theory of household behaviour underlying the permanent income hypothesis is in all essentials the same as that underlying another contemporary theory of saving behaviour, the so-called *life cycle hypothesis,* which starts with the familiar assumptions that households seek to maximize utility, and that they derive utility only from the consumption of goods and services (and perhaps from leaving bequests to the next generation). However, households have a normal life span well beyond one year. Hence, the household will presumably seek to maximize the utility which it derives from consumption over its entire life span. This calls for a lifetime plan for consumption expenditures in the light of expected lifetime income.

A basic fact of life which the household must recognize is that the most desirable lifetime pattern of consumption will probably not conform exactly to the lifetime pattern of income which the household expects to receive. A typical life cycle is illustrated in Figure 4-2. In early years, as the household is formed, acquires the necessary durable goods and raises and educates children, it is quite probable that income will not exceed planned consumption by a substantial margin, and in many cases may fall substantially short of planned consumption.[5] In the middle years of the life span, by contrast, planned consumption will normally fall substantially short of earned income, as the children grow up and leave home. In later years, income from employment will probably drop substantially, particularly following retirement. Planned consumption will then greatly exceed income from employment.

Under these circumstances, the maximization of utility from consumption requires a redistribution of purchasing power between years of "surplus" income and years of "deficient" income. In addition, the household may wish to accumulate a reserve for contingencies, such as illness or unemployment, which might have a short-term impact on either income or consumption expenditures. The method of achieving both of these objectives is through saving. In years of surplus income the household can accumulate wealth (positive saving); in years of deficient income it can reduce its wealth, either through a reduction in asset holdings or an increase in liabilities (negative saving).

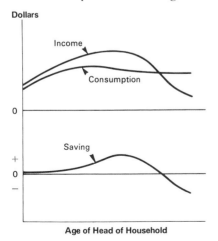

Figure 4-2
The Life Cycle: Income,
Consumption and Saving

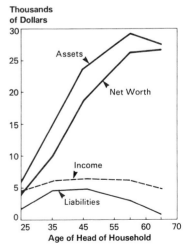

Figure 4-3
The Life Cycle: Income
and Wealth of Families
in Seven Canadian Cities, 1962

Some aspects of the life cycle in income and wealth for Canadian households are illustrated in Figure 4-3.

Expected Yield and the Saving Decision

The central variable in the Keynesian, permanent income and life cycle hypotheses is income. While the relationship between income and saving will depend in part on transitory factors and in part on the household's stage in the life cycle, it is conceded in general that the higher the level of income the higher will be the level of saving. There is also a second variable affecting the saving decision which has received much attention in the literature; this is the *expected yield on assets*.

Expected yield is the interest rate implicit in the relationship between the stream of future payments and the market price of the asset which provides those payments. A more precise formulation of the concept is developed in the Appendix to Chapter 5. However, in a very crude sense it is the ratio of the expected future payments to the current cost of the asset.

That expected yield should be a primary determinant of the demand for wealth should not be surprising. As we have already noted, the accumulation of wealth implies the sacrifice of current consumption in order to accumulate the means for larger future consumption. Depending on preferences between future and present consumption, saving — and hence, the net demand for wealth — should be more or less sensitive to changes in the yield on assets.

While saving should be sensitive to yields on assets, the direction of the effect is not always clear. From one perspective, the effect of higher yields is to provide a larger stream of future benefits from any given present sacrifice (e.g., a larger pension, or a larger estate for one's heirs). Since larger benefits are to be preferred to smaller, higher yields should stimulate saving. From a different perspective, however, the higher the yield the smaller the current sacrifice which is necessary to achieve any given future objective (e.g., a new house, or a round-the-world tour). A higher yield could conceivably reduce the incentive to save on the part of "target savers".

There is also another aspect to any increase in expected yields on assets. Higher yields also imply higher costs of borrowing funds (an interest cost to the borrower is an expected yield to the lender). The higher cost of credit should deter households from borrowing, and hence increase saving.

In summary, higher expected yields mean more favourable "terms of trade" between future and present. This should induce saving and hence increase the demand for additions to wealth. However, households with fixed targets for wealth accumulation can now achieve those targets with less saving. While the effect of higher yields could thus be perverse, most economists assume that higher yields lead to marginally higher saving rates (empirical evidence is somewhat equivocal).

Socio-Economic Factors in the Saving Decision

Current income, permanent income, stage in the life cycle, and expected yield are all "objective" factors affecting the saving decision. They
are factors in the outside world to which the household reacts. We should
not ignore the "subjective" or personal elements in the decision as well.
The tastes or preferences of households as between future and present
consumption and with respect to the provision of an estate for future gen-
erations may differ markedly. In technical terms, they may have very
different "time preferences". Some differences in time preference may be
related to other social or economic characteristics. Thus, survey researchers have discovered many interesting differences in saving behaviour as
between urban and rural families, home-owners and tenants, and persons
with different occupations, levels of education or racial backgrounds.

The Economic Theory of the Saving Decision: A Summary

The theory of demand developed in elementary economic theory has
its foundations in the concept of utility. People demand goods and services
because the consumption of these goods and services yields utility directly
to the consumer. In general, however, financial instruments are not in
this category. They do not yield utility directly in the same sense that
the consumption of a cup of coffee or a candy bar yields utility. The
demand for financial instruments is a demand for something to be held —
an asset — not a demand for something to be consumed. If households
seek to maximize the utility derived from the use of their limited incomes,
why then should they allocate part of their limited incomes to the
accumulation of non-utility-yielding financial instruments? Is their behaviour inconsistent with the general assumption of utility maximization?
Are asset-accumulating households acting irrationally.

In general, the answer to this last question is no. It may be quite
rational for a household which is seeking to maximize utility to devote
part of its limited income to the accumulation of financial instruments,
even though these instruments are not objects of consumption and hence
do not yield utility directly in the same sense as do consumer goods.
The rational head of the household must take a lifetime perspective on
utility maximization. He must plan his household's expenditures with
an eye to the future as well as the present. It may seem rational to
him to deliberately reduce the consumption of the household below its
potential levels at present in order to permit higher levels of consumption
in the future. Such a redistribution of income and consumption from
the present to the future requires an accumulation of wealth, and one
of the basic forms in which wealth may be accumulated is in the form
of financial instruments. *The demand for financial instruments has at its
roots a desire to accumulate wealth, and the desire to accumulate wealth
is in turn based on the desire to redistribute income and consumption
over time.*

FOOTNOTES

[1] This accounting definition of wealth is deceptively simple. We are in fact glossing over many of the complexities in the measurement of wealth, particularly in the measurement of the value of assets. In particular, we have ignored intangible assets, like the earning power of the members of the household — what some economists call human wealth. The measurement of the value of human assets is complicated by the fact that markets for such assets do not exist and as a result it is impossible to quote market values. Markets exist for the services of human beings, of course, but since the abolition of slavery there are no markets in which the *asset* which yields the services can be traded. This does not mean that the measurement of the value of the human asset is impossible. In the appendix to the next chapter we develop the concept of present value. The measurement of the value of a human resource — like the measurement of the value of any resource — is a problem in the calculation of present value.

If the value of human assets is included in the household's balance sheet, it is less likely that wealth could ever be negative.

[2] The validity of this identity depends on the appropriate definitions of income and consumption in equation 4.2, and hence the definition of saving. The problems arise because of three elements in the household's financial accounts: gifts, taxes, and changes in the market values of assets (capital gains or losses). We must make adjustments for each of these items. Capital gains and losses and gifts received must be counted as income (capital losses reduce income, of course). Gifts made by the household might be considered as a consumption use of income, but it is probably better to group gifts together with taxes paid as a deduction from income to obtain the household's disposable income.

[3] J. M. Keynes, *The General Theory of Employment, Interest and Money*, (New York; Harcourt, Brace & Co., 1936), p. 96.

[4] This is not a fully accurate statement of the position of the permanent income theorists. They argue that the ratio of permanent consumption to permanent income is independent of the level of permanent income. It does depend on a variety of other factors, however, including the level of interest rates and the household's "tastes and preferences for consumption versus additions to wealth". In the latter category, such objective factors as the size and age composition of the family and the variability of the household's income are suggested as important considerations. However, with all of these factors given, then the ratio of permanent saving to permanent income will be the same at all levels of permanent income. Cf., M. Friedman, *A Theory of the Consumption Function*, (Princeton: Princeton University Press, 1957), p. 26.

[5] It should be noted that the statistical relationship between age and savings depends on the definition of saving. This is particularly true in the early stages of the life cycle when the household is typically making heavy expenditures on durable consumer goods, including the purchase of a house. If all consumer durables are considered to be assets and hence included in the measurement of net worth, then only the "consumption" (i.e., depreciation) of these assets will be included in consumption expenditures. Saving is less likely to be negative under these circumstances than if these goods are not included in the measurement of net worth. Most statistical studies omit most of these consumer durables, largely because of the lack of reliable data. About the only durable good commonly included is the owner's equity in his house. This is the definition of assets used in measuring net worth as plotted in Figure 4-3, i.e., the household's equity in its house plus the value of its financial assets.

5

Elementary Theory of
Financial Markets, Part 2:
The Portfolio Balance Decision

The demand for wealth — the saving decision — is fundamental to household demands for financial assets. However, it is simply a decision about the *size* of total asset holdings, and must be accompanied by another decision about the *composition* of the collection of assets to be held.

It is convenient to term this collection of assets, an *asset portfolio* — or *portfolio*, for short. In selecting his portfolio the assetholder must be concerned with the balance between real assets and financial assets, and, of primary concern to us at the moment, within the category of financial assets he must be concerned with the balance between the different types of financial instruments discussed in Chapter 3. He must make choices among the great variety of financial instruments available in the market. *The portfolio balance decision thus translates a general demand for assets into specific demands for specific assets.*

For the sake of convenience we shall focus on choices among financial assets only. As we will see eventually, the same principles apply to the choice between real and financial assets.

In the first section of Chapter 3 we outlined the diversity of financial instruments in use in Canada today. This survey, although far from exhaustive, provided too great a range of characteristics to be maniuplated in a general theoretical analysis. For this we need a small set of concepts which capture the essential characteristics of the diverse financial instruments. While we will have occasion to discuss a few others, three concepts are basic: *expected yield, credit risk,* and *liquidity.*[1]

1/EXPECTED YIELD AND THE CHOICE AMONG FINANCIAL INSTRUMENTS

The central theoretical issue in any discussion of the portfolio balance decision is why any one financial instrument should be chosen over any other as the form in which the household accumulates wealth. One important factor in this choice should be quite obvious. Other things being equal, a rational assetholder will always prefer an asset with a high expected yield to one with a low expected yield.

The Concept of Expected Yield and Its Relationship to Market Price

We have already encountered the concept of expected yield in our discussion of the saving decision. You will remember that it is the interest rate which is implicit in the relationship between the market price of the financial instrument and the expected stream of future payments associated with that instrument. We noted that the effect of expected yield on the total demand for wealth was ambiguous. A higher expected yield might lead to greater or less saving. However, no such ambiguity exists in the effect of expected yield on the demand for particular assets. Since all assets are substitutes for each other as forms in which wealth may be accumulated, other things being equal, the demand for any particular instrument will be greater the higher the expected yield.

Normally, discussions of the demand side of a market focus on market price, and yet so far in our exposition we have scarcely mentioned market price. Rather, we have implicitly developed an argument that expected yield plays the central role in financial markets that price plays in other markets (although we have found a positive relationship between demand and yield, rather than the normal negative relationship between demand and price).

This difference from the standard discussion of demand is more apparent than real, however. The fact is that *for any financial instrument, market price and expected yield are inversely related.*

The validity of this statement should be obvious since, with the stream of future payments *fixed by contract*, the yield on the bond can only rise if the market price falls. This is implicit in the definition of expected yield. For example, in 1958 the Government of Canada issued a series of 25-year bonds maturing in 1983. The coupon rate was fixed at $4\frac{1}{2}\%$, such that the total annual interest payment on a $1,000 (par value) bond is $45. These securities are traded freely at prices determined in the open market. In early 1965, the market price of a $1,000 bond was approximately $940. At this price the yield is 5% per annum. Subsequently, bond prices fell. By late 1966, the price of a "$4\frac{1}{2}$ of 1983" was $860, implying a yield of 5.8%; and by early 1970 the price was $690, implying a yield of 8.4%. As bond prices fell, the yield increased.

It follows, then, that the statement that the demand for a financial instrument is directly related to its expected yield is the same as the statement that the demand for the instrument is inversely related to its market price.

The whole subject of market prices and yields on assets is so important, not only for our analysis, but also in any decisions relating to fixed assets, that we have taken pains to develop and explore the concepts more carefully and systematically in the appendix to this chapter.

2/RISK AND THE CHOICE AMONG FINANCIAL INSTRUMENTS

If expected yield were the only consideration in portfolio choices, then the rational assetholder, faced with the alternatives of one security yielding 5% and one yielding 10%, would always choose the latter. In the market, attempts of individuals to sell the 5% securities to purchase the 10% securities should drive the price of the former down (and the yield up) and the price of the latter up (and the yield down). The end result should be a rough equalization of yields on the two securities. In fact we observe in the market that the yields on different securities differ markedly and consistently. Why is this? The answer is that there are other factors which affect choices among assets, including credit risk, liquidity, the possibility of capital gains or capital losses, the risk of inflation, and differential taxation. We shall examine each of these factors in turn.

The first factor we want to consider is the possibility of the actual yield on the security being considerably different from the expected yield. We call this possibility credit risk. We shall see that credit risks associated with different securities differ markedly, and that differences in yield in the market place are, in part, a reflection of these differences in credit risk.

The Concept of Credit Risk

A financial instrument is a claim to a stream of future payments. Since those payments are to occur in the future, there will always be some uncertainty about whether the payments will in fact be made and, particularly in the case of variable-income securities, about the size of such payments. Correspondingly, there must be some uncertainty about the actual yield on any given financial instrument, since this yield depends on the size of the payments actually made in the future. It is because of this uncertainty that credit risk exists.

We can formalize the concept of credit risk by assuming that for any given financial instrument there is a range of possible yields at the present market price. If large future payments are made the yield will be high; if small future payments are made, the yield will be low. Indeed, if the future payments are very small, or, in the extreme, non-existent, the yield will be negative. It must be stressed that we refer to the actual yield on the investment — what actually materializes.

The individual contemplating the purchase of this security cannot know what the outcome will be. However, if he is to make a rational decision, he must somehow assess the likelihood of alternative possible outcomes, and select *the outcome which seems most likely*. It is this value to which we refer when we use the expression *expected yield*. Note that the expected yield is not the only outcome regarded as possible nor is it necessarily the outcome which will materialize.

For purposes of theoretical discussions we can formalize these elements of the portfolio-selection process by assuming that the assetholder has in mind a subjective probability distribution of possible yields on the asset, such as that drawn in Figure 5-1.

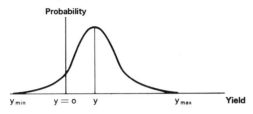

Figure 5-1
Probability Distribution of Possible Yields

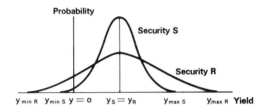

Figure 5-2
Two Probability Distributions: Same Expected Yield, Different Risks

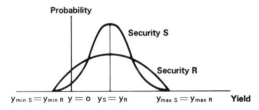

Figure 5-3
Two Probability Distributions: Same Range, Different Risks

The area under the bell-shaped curve is equal to 1, indicating that in the judgement of the assetholder (but not necessarily in fact) one of the possible alternative yields listed along the base of the curve must occur. That is, he feels that there is a probability of 1 (perfect certainty) that the actual yield will be among those listed on the base. The probability that any particular one of these yields will materialize is significantly less than 1. The yield ($\bar{y}$) which he feels has the greatest probability of occurance – the most likely outcome – is under the highest point of the probability distribution. In his judgement every other possible outcome has a lesser probability of occurance.

What we mean by credit risk is the *dispersion of possible yields around the expected yield*. Consider Figure 5-2, which shows two probability distributions of the type plotted in Figure 5-1. Each of these distributions represents the assetholder's subjective judgements about the possible yields on two different securities. Each security has the same expected yield. However, they differ markedly in terms of the associated degree of credit risk. In the case of security S (for "safe") the alternative possible yields are clustered closely about the expected yield. In the case of security R (for "risky") the alternative possible yields are more dispersed. The assetholder has less confidence that the actual yield will be the expected yield in the latter case. He subjectively assigns a lower probability to the expected outcome, and is willing to admit the possibility of a wider range of alternative outcomes.

Standard Deviation as a Measure of Risk. It is convenient for theoretical analysis to have a simple measure of risk in this probability sense. A number of possible measures are available. Perhaps the most simple measure would be the *range* of possible outcomes, i.e., the difference between the highest (y_{max}) and the lowest (y_{min}) yields which the assetholder would admit as possible outcomes. Formally, the range is

$$\text{RANGE} = y_{max} - y_{min}$$

As a measure of risk, the range is seriously defective because it takes into account only one of the two dimensions of risk. While it allows for the fact that the outcome may be different from the expected yield, it ignores the possibility that the assetholder implicitly assigns different probabilities to the alternative possible outcomes. Two securities might have the same range of possible yields, and yet one appears less risky than the other, because the assetholder assigns a lower probability to the extreme values, and hence has greater confidence in the accuracy of his estimate of the expected yield. This possibility is sketched in Figure 5-3.

What we need as a measure of risk, then, is a number which takes account of both dimensions, i.e., of the range of possible outcome and of the probability of each outcome. This measure is provided by a statistic called *the standard deviation,* commonly represented by the Greek letter sigma (σ), a complicated measure both in its computation and meaning. For now, all we need know is that it is a measure of the dispersion of the probability distribution about the expected yield. The more dispersed the distribution, (i.e., the larger the standard deviation), the greater the probability that the actual yield will be different from the expected yield, and hence the greater the credit risk associated with that security.

Credit Risk and the Choice Among Financial Instruments

We are now in a position to provide a major element in our formal theoretical answer to the question of why yields on two different securities of the same general term to maturity can be continuously and consistently different in the market place. While there are some factors on the supply side to be considered, the major consideration on the demand side is assetholders' reactions to credit risk.

Suppose an assetholder were faced with the two securities represented by the probability distributions in Figure 5-2. Both securities have the same expected yield $(\overline{y}_S = \overline{y}_R)$. However, the distributions of possible alternative yields about the expected yield are notably different. Would the assetholder nevertheless be indifferent as to which security he took into his portfolio?

The answer is surely not. He cannot ignore the fact that security R is more risky. While the expected yields are the same on the two securities, he is *less confident* that this yield will materialize in the case of Security *R* than in the case of Security *S*. Is this not a factor which he should take into account in choosing between the two assets? That is, should he not react to the credit risk on each of the two securities quite independently of the yield on each?

In deciding how he should react we must remember that the risk we are talking about has two sides. On the one hand, in the assetholder's judgement, there is a much greater probability that the yield on Security *R* will be less than the expected yield than is true in the case of the yield on Security *S*. On the other hand, there is also a greater probability that the yield on Security *R* will *exceed* the expected yield than is true in the case of the yield on Security *S*. *If the assetholder chooses the "safe" security he is also giving up the greater "risk" of a higher return.* Which will he choose?

Risk Aversion. In general, it is assumed that most assetholders are *risk averters*; that is, faced with the alternatives illustrated in Figure 5-2, the typical assetholder will always choose the less risky asset *(S)*. A risk averter places a higher subjective value (or utility) on the avoidance of extremely small yields (including negative yields) than he does on the possibility of unusually large gains. *A risk averter would demand a larger expected yield on the more risky security before he would choose it over a less risky security.*

Not everyone is a risk averter. Some assetholders, although they appear to be in the minority, are better described as risk seekers, in the sense that they value the chance of larger returns more than the risk of smaller returns. Such individuals, faced with securities *R* and *S* under the circumstances of Figure 5-2 would choose security *R*.

Summary: Risk and Expected Yield in the Choice Among Financial Instruments

Perhaps it would be helpful to summarize the argument to this point. We started with the general proposition that expected yield is the primary determinant of the demand for financial assets. However, we noted that since a financial instrument is a claim to payments to be made in the future, and since the future is unknown, the assetholder cannot be perfectly certain about the yield on financial assets. He must form an opinion about the range of possible outcomes and, in a general way, the likelihood of the alternative possibilities. In other words, he must form an opinion about the degree of risk attached to each security. For theoretical analysis we formalized this judgement into probability distributions of alternative yields on securities, with credit risk represented by the standard deviation of the distribution. The demand for any financial asset, then, depends not only on the expected yield but also on the degree of credit risk. *All financial instruments are substitutes for each other as forms in which wealth may be accumulated. However, securities with different degrees of credit risk attached are not perfect substitutes.* The greater the difference in credit risk, the more imperfect the substitute relationship.

We assume that most assetholders are risk averters, i.e., other things being equal, they prefer a less risky security. If a risk averter is to purchase a more risky security he will require a higher expected yield than that obtained on a less risky security. If most assetholders are of this frame of mind the structure of yields in financial markets will reflect it. In general, yields on more risky securities *will* be higher than yields on less risky securities — which is what we observe, as noted above. Credit risk is a major factor affecting relative yields on financial instruments.

The Determination of Credit Risk

Our exposition of the concept of credit risk and its role in the demand for financial assets has been abstract and theoretical. While such formal constructs are indispensable for theoretical analysis, we cannot realistically assume that each individual assetholder constructs a probability distribution of possible yields for each asset that he might consider taking into his portfolio, and calculates both the expected yield and the standard deviation. And yet, each rational assetholder must form some impression not only of the expected yield but also of the degree of credit risk.

In truth, little is known about how this is done. Sometimes people rely on hunches, or moon phases, or "inside information" or just some "feeling" about each asset. For concerned wealth owners, however, there are a group of professional investment counsellors, whose advice is frequently sought, and presumably used. These counsellors employ any of a variety of techniques of "security analysis" and frequently provide ratings of securities.

Past performance generally weighs heavily in such analysis, although the past is frequently a very poor guide to future prospects and history must be tempered with a careful assessment of the implications of current and pending developments. In the market, and particularly in the market for bonds, certain more or less standard rules of thumb have emerged, and

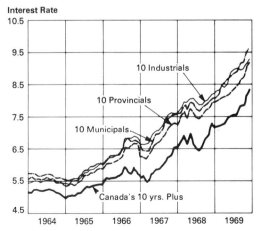

Figure 5-4

SOURCE: McLeod, Young, Wier

these are reflected in relatively standard differentials between yields on bonds of different types of borrowers. In Figure 5-4 we have plotted indices of yields on long-term bonds of several classes of borrowers over a number of years. Note that, in general, yields on Government of Canada bonds are less than those on bonds of all other borrowers. They are widely regarded as virtually riskless bonds. Yields on bonds of other borrowers range upward from those of the federal government. Of course, within each of the categories presented on this chart there will be a considerable range between individual borrowers of different "credit ratings", and the yields on many bonds will exceed those shown on the chart.

3/LIQUIDITY AND THE CHOICE AMONG FINANCIAL INSTRUMENTS

Our analysis of credit risk has taken us a long way in explaining how there can be different expected yields on different instruments in the market at the same time. However, differences of credit risk cannot fully explain the differences in yields which can be observed. There are other factors which must be taken into account, one of which is the *relative liquidity* of different instruments.

The "Normal" Yield Curve for Government Bonds

As evidence for the proposition that credit risk alone is not sufficient to explain observable and persistent differences in expected yields on financial instruments we need only consider yields on different financial instruments issued by the same debtor and for which credit risk is not a significant consideration. The one debtor which meets this requirement is the Government of Canada. Bonds issued by the Government of Canada can be regarded as riskless securities in that there is almost no chance that the contractual payments will not be made. Not only are the bonds backed by the general taxing powers of the Government, but also the contract calls for payment in Canadian legal tender and the Government of Canada has the ultimate power to manufacture legal tender. If all else fails, the Government can "print" the money to meet its legal obligations. Thus, if credit risk were the only consideration, yields on all government bonds should be approximately the same.

This is seldom the case. A fairly "normal" situation is depicted in Figure 5-5. On this chart we have plotted the yields on almost all Government of Canada bonds outstanding on June 30, 1964, with the bonds arranged in ascending order of term to maturity. The yields plotted on this chart were calculated on the basis of prices quoted in the market on that day, and on the assumption that the promised future payments (interest and redemption value) would in fact be made. A line — commonly called a *yield curve* — has been drawn indicating the general relationship between yield and term to maturity on that date. Not all yields lie exactly on the yield curve, but the curve is broadly representative.

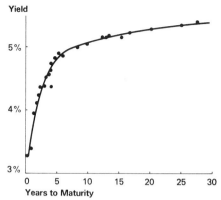

Figure 5-5
Yield Curve: Government of Canada Direct Securities, June 30, 1964

This is a fairly normal yield curve. The striking thing about it is that yields on very short-term bonds are very much lower than yields on longer-term issues. The curve initially rises very sharply to the right. Thus the yield on the shortest-term security plotted, a 91-day treasury bill, was approximately 3.25% per annum. The yield on a one-year bond was 30% greater (almost 4.2% per annum), and on a five-year bond 50% greater (4.9% per annum). By contrast, beyond ten years to maturity the yield curve is relatively flat. Thus a bond with ten years to maturity had a yield of 5.2% per annum, whereas the yield on one with over twenty-five years to maturity was only slightly greater at 5.3% per annum. Indeed, the yield on one bond with over thirty years to maturity (not shown on the chart) was only 5.1% per annum on that date.

One common theory offered to explain the relatively low yields on short-term bonds as compared to yields on long-term bonds is that asset-holders demand a premium for tying up their money for a longer period of time. While it is probably true that a premium yield would be demanded if the assetholder actually had his funds tied up for a longer period of time — i.e., if he could not get his money out until the bond matured — this argument overlooks an essential feature of these bonds. They are *marketable*. A secondary market exists, such that the holder of the bonds can sell them at the established market price at any time he chooses. As long as he has this option, his money is not "tied up". What, then, is the explanation for the "normal" shape of the yield curve?

The Demand for Liquidity and the "Normal" Yield Curve

One hypothesis, broadly consistent with the facts, is that shorter-term bonds have a greater degree of liquidity and this property of the short-term bonds is prized by assetholders to the extent that they are willing to sacrifice yield in order to obtain liquidity. That is, faced with two bonds with the same expected yield and the same credit risk the typical assetholder would normally prefer the one with the higher degree of liquidity. As a result, the typical assetholder would pay a premium price for the more liquid security, and hence (since price and yield move inversely) receive a lower yield.

The Determinants of Liquidity. We offered a general definition of the concept of liquidity in Chapter 3. In brief, *a liquid asset is one whose market price is relatively stable.* Thus money, a financial instrument whose market price is fixed in terms of the unit of account, is the most liquid of assets. If short-term government bonds are to be considered liquid assets their prices must be relatively stable, although not necessarily fixed. In seeking the factors which govern the relative liquidity of instruments we must uncover those factors which tend to produce variations in the market prices of financial instruments.

Three general factors affect the market price of a financial instrument: the size of the expected future payments, the risk associated with those payments, and the expected yield on alternative assets. A change in any one can be expected to produce a change in market price.

Clearly, a variable income security could not be a liquid asset. If the size of future payments is subject to change, then the market price of the instrument can be expected to change also, and perhaps over a very wide range. Thus, common stock in corporations cannot qualify as a liquid asset.

Similarly, a fixed income security such as a corporate bond, subject to substantial credit risk, cannot be a liquid asset. If there is substantial risk of default on the promised payments, substantial price changes cannot be ruled out. While more liquid than explicitly variable income securities, such bonds could still not be considered highly liquid.

These two points help us to narrow down the range of instruments which can be considered liquid. To be highly liquid a financial instrument must be a low risk claim to fixed future payments. This still does not narrow the field sufficiently. There is a third factor which might produce fluctuations in the market price of even riskless claims to fixed future payments. That factor is a change in the general level of yields on financial instruments, or, in other words, in the general level of interest rates. *The assertion that short-term government bonds* (riskless, fixed income securities) *are among the most liquid of assets is an assertion that their prices are not significantly affected as their yields rise or fall in sympathy with the general level of interest rates.* This is a property of short-term bonds not possessed by long-term bonds.

Price Stability and Term to Maturity. The basic mathematics of the relationship between yield term to maturity and market price are explored briefly in the Appendix to this chapter. The analysis in the Appendix shows that *as a general proposition* the market price and the yield on a bond will vary inversely, and that the decline in market price for any given increase in yield will be greater the longer the term to maturity. That this general relationship is not just a theoretical construct, but also exists in fact, is illustrated in Figure 5-6.

Figure 5-6
Prices and Yields: Short-term and Long-term Government Bonds

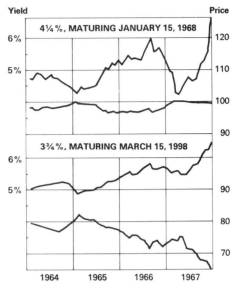

Shown in this Figure are the actual yields and market prices for two Government bonds during the period 1964-1967. The security on the upper panel was a bond which matured on January 15, 1968. At the beginning of the period it had a term to maturity of 4 years. By the end of the period it was on the verge of maturity. It was clearly a short-term bond, particularly in the latter part of the period. By contrast, the security on the bottom panel was a long-term bond throughout. Maturing in 1998, it had a term to maturity of 34 years at the outset and 30 years at the end of the period.

The contrast between the behaviour of yields and prices on the two bonds is striking. Although the yield on the short-term bond actually moved over a much wider range than did the yield on the long-term bond, the market price of the short-term bond showed much greater stability than did the price of the long-term bond. Indeed, as the short-term bond approached maturity in the latter half of 1967, the sharp rise in yields was barely reflected in the market price of the bond. By contrast, a parallel, but smaller, rise in the yield on the long-term bond involved a sharp drop in its market price. From the end of April to the end of December 1967, the market price of a $1,000 (par value) bond dropped over 13%, from $750 to $650.

Since we have defined liquidity in terms of stability of market price, it is clear that we must consider the short-term bond of the upper panel to be a much more liquid security than the long-term bond of the lower panel. Why should this be a significant consideration in the minds of asset-holders? In particular, why should the typical assetholder be willing to pay a premium price (that is, accept a lower yield) for the stability of the market price of the short-term bond?

The Demand for Liquidity

The particular motives of individual assetholders will be varied, of course, depending on individual situations. However, two major types of demand for liquid assets can be identified, one related to specific expenditure plans in the near future, and one related to uncertainty.

Specific Expenditure Plans. Part of the demand for liquidity is to create a bridge between the receipt of income and planned expenditures in the near future. An individual householder might hold a personal savings deposit with a chartered bank into which he deposits his monthly paycheck, in anticipation of paying assorted bills over the forthcoming month. Similarly, corporations will accumulate liquid assets of various types in anticipation of future payrolls and other current expenditures.

The significant thing about this type of demand for liquid assets is that it represents a matching of assets and liabilities in terms of term to maturity. It follows that an assetholder who has only very definite long-term liabilities may well have little demand for liquid assets. Indeed, he might prefer long-term, relatively illiquid assets to short-term, relatively liquid assets.

Uncertainty. The second major element in the general demand for liquid assets rest in our assumption that most assetholders are risk averters and in the fact that the future is replete with uncertainty. An assetholder cannot always anticipate when he will sell his assets. As time passes he may encounter *unexpected* expenses, calls for payment of debts, interruptions to his employment and income, or perhaps unusual opportunities to purchase major real or financial assets, or simply a change in his desires to purchase goods and services now as opposed to the future. Each of these contingencies involves unanticipated payments, calling for a sale of assets. If forced to sell when asset prices are low, he will incur substantial losses. However, if he holds short-term liquid assets he can make the unanticipated payments without incurring these losses.

To illustrate this point, refer again to Figure 5-6. Consider the position of an individual who purchased a $1,000 (par value) long-term bond at the end of 1966 for the then existing market price of $730. *If held to maturity*, the bond would have yielded 5.6% per annum. However, suppose the pressure of unanticipated expenditures forced him to sell the bond at the end of 1967. He in fact held the bond for one year, received interest payments from the Government in the amount of $37.50, and then sold it into the market for $650, or $80 less than he paid for it. Instead of the expected yield of 5.6% per annum, his actual yield was negative, −5.8%.

Suppose that instead, he held the short-term bond. He would have purchased it at the end of 1966 for $990, received interest payments from the government in the amount of $42.50, and sold it at the end of the year for $998, for an actual return on his investment of 5.1%. Although the expected yield (if held to maturity) of the long-term bond was greater than that on the short-term bond when purchased at the end of 1966, the actual yield on the long-term bond would have proven to be much less if the holder were forced to sell at the end of 1967.

In this sense, then, the demand for liquid assets is a reaction to a type of risk, that of having to make unexpected future payments. If we may be allowed a play on words, *the demand for liquid assets exists because as time passes every assetholder must expect to have unexpected expenditures.* As we will see, this is of vital concern to certain types of financial institutions, such as banks.

The Demand for Money and Other Liquid Assets. In the last section of Chapter 2 we raised the question of what determines the quantity of money demanded at any point in time. The answer we gave was that, since money is essentially a medium of exchange, the quantity of money demanded will depend in some way on the value of payments to be made. As we shall see in Chapter 19, the relationship between the flow of transactions and the demand for money is not that simple, but nonetheless, in a monetary economy, the workings of the exchange mechanism will create a *transactions demand for money.*

The analysis of this section suggests that there may be another source of demand for money as well. Money, after all, is the most liquid of assets. If there is a demand for liquid asset as a hedge against uncertainty, there should be a demand for money as a liquid asset. That is, in addition to the transactions demand for money, there must be an *asset demand for money.*

We have shown, however, that while money is the most liquid of assets, it is not the only highly liquid asset. There are other financial instruments which can be held as close (if imperfect) substitutes for money. Short-term federal government bonds, and notably treasury bills, are in this category, as are similar issues by some provincial governments. Note should also be taken of savings bonds issued by the federal government and some provincial governments (including "parity" bonds issued by certain Crown Corporations in British Columbia). While these are nominally long-term bonds, the issuing government has agreed to repurchase the bonds at a fixed price at any time at the option of the holder. They are in effect demand notes, and as such are highly liquid. In our survey of the money market we also noted the existence of many private short-term issues. Clearly, from the point of view of banks, day-to-day loans are highly liquid assets. Similarly, finance paper and commercial paper traded in the market, or the special arrangement with government security dealers that we referred to as the "country bank" serve the same purpose for corporations and other assetholders. It should also be noted that a line of credit with a bank, under which the corporation is entitled to loans up to a certain negotiated maximum, is also a liquid asset of considerable importance. As we discuss the various types of financial intermediaries in subsequent chapters we will discover that they also issue highly liquid financial instruments which can be held as substitutes for money. Indeed, we have already referred to such financial instruments as "near monies".

In satisfying their demands for liquidity, then, assetholders can choose from a wide range of instruments, including money. The choice actually made should depend, among other things, on relative yields on the various liquid assets. Thus, the demand for money as an asset should be sensitive to interest rates on other short-term financial instruments. The higher the level of short-term interest rates, the smaller the quantity of money demanded as an asset.

4/SPECULATION AND THE CHOICE AMONG FINANCIAL INSTRUMENTS

We now have three characteristics of financial instruments which enter into the demand for those instruments, i.e., expected yield, credit risk and liquidity. In general, we have concluded that, other things being equal, assetholders desire to avoid risk and prefer liquidity. As a result, expected yields on risky assets should normally be higher than expected yields on riskless assets, and expected yields on liquid assets should be lower than expected yields on illiquid assets.

A careful examination of Figure 5-6 should raise at least two sets of significant questions in your mind.

First, we have asserted that most assetholders are willing to sacrifice yield for liquidity, a set of preferences which implies that short-term bond yields should be lower than long-term bond yields. However, it is evident from Figure 5-6 that the yield on the short-term bond depicted in the upper panel was actually *higher* than the yield on the long-term bond on at least two occasions, i.e., in the late summer and fall of 1966, and in late 1967. Is this simply a peculiar aberration of the two bonds in question? Or is this a common phenomenon in financial markets? If it is common, how can we reconcile it with our earlier assertions about the general superiority of liquid financial instruments?

Second, in discussing the implications of changes in the market price of long-term bonds we laid great stress on the risk which this implied for the assetholder. However, does it not also create opportunities? Why could not a sharp operator in the market anticipate movements of bond prices, and profit by purchasing when bond prices are low and selling when bond prices are high? For example, could not an individual have purchased a $1,000 (par value) long-term bond for under $780 in late September 1964, and sold it for just over $810 at the end of January 1965? In doing so, he would have made a *capital gain* of $30 or almost 4% on his initial investment in 4 months (which is equivalent to an interest rate of approximately 12% per annum). This capital gain is in addition to any interest payments which the holder received from the government in this period of time. Moreover, in doing this the shrewd investor avoids holding the long-term bonds during periods of declining market prices, as for example the period January 1965 to August 1966. He would sell his long-term bonds when their price was at a peak (e.g., January 1965), thus making capital gains, and by switching his funds to short-term bonds whose market price is stable, avoid incurring *capital losses* during the period of declining market prices for long-term bonds. When long-term bonds are at their trough, this investor would then switch his funds out of short-term bonds and back into long-term bonds.

The issues raised by these two sets of questions are interrelated. Let us briefly consider the empirical question first, i.e., are long-term bond yields always higher than short-term bond yields?

An "Abnormal" Yield Curve

The answer is no. As evidence, we have plotted yield curves for three different dates on Figure 5-7. The top two panels of this figure relate to the dates cited above. In each case, the yields on very short-term securities are below the yields on long-term bonds. However, in each case the yield curve has a pronounced "hump". As a result, the yields on relatively short-term bonds were higher than the yields on long-term bonds. In the first instance the hump occurs in the range of three- to five-year bonds, and in the second case in the range five- to eight-year bonds.

It is unusual for the very shortest-term bonds to have a higher yield than long-term bonds. However, it is not unknown. The third panel in Figure 5-7 illustrates one instance in relatively recent history — mid-August 1959, when the yield curve had a reverse slope throughout.

The shape of the yield curve thus changes from time to time. Indeed, there is a fairly regular cyclical pattern to these changes. When the general level of interest rates is relatively low, the yield curve tends to have the shape of that in Figure 5-5. As interest rates rise, however, short-term interest rates tend to rise more rapidly than long-term interest rates. Remember that we said earlier that short-term yields move over a wider range than long-term rates, although the market prices of short-term bonds tend to vary over a narrower range. As a result, the yield curve becomes flatter. In periods of relatively high interest rates, the yield curve tends to develop a "hump", and in extreme circumstances it may develop the consistent downward slope of the third panel of Figure 5-7.

Speculative Demands for Bonds

We cannot develop a complete analysis of changes in the shape of the yield curve until we have considered the supply side of financial markets. However, a major part of the explanation for these gyrations rests in what we might call the *Speculative Demand* for financial assets.

Speculation and the Shape of the Yield Curve. Speculators can be expected to shift between long-term bonds and either short-term bonds or money in *anticipation* of changes in the market prices of long-term bonds. They seek to capture anticipated capital gains by purchasing long-term bonds (and selling short-term bonds, including money) when they expect interest rates to fall (and hence long-term bond prices to rise significantly).

Figure 5-7
Three Abnormal Yield Curves: Canadian Government Bonds

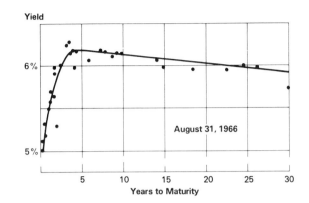

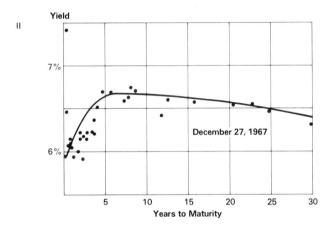

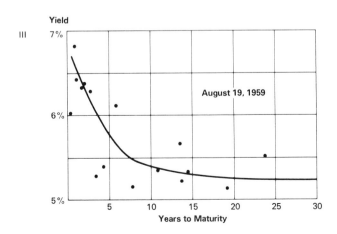

Similarly, they seek to avoid anticipated capital losses by selling long-term bonds (and purchasing short-term bonds), when they expect interest rates to rise (and hence long-term bond prices to fall).

Clearly, such activities will create pressures in financial markets tending to produce the characteristic changes in the shape of the yield curve. Thus, when interest rates are low and expected to rise, speculators will tend to sell long-term bonds and purchase short-term bonds or hold money. Their activities should therefore tend to further depress long-term bond prices, and raise short-term bond prices; or, what is the same thing, raise long-term bond yields relative to short-term bond yields. The activities of the speculator, therefore, will tend to accentuate the normal slope of the yield curve under these circumstances.

By contrast, when interest rates are high and are expected to fall, speculators will tend to purchase long-term bonds and sell short-term bonds or reduce their holdings of money (or perhaps borrow on short-term notes). Their activities in the market, therefore, should tend to support the price of long-term bonds and depress the price of short-term bonds; or, what is the same thing, to raise short-term bond yields relative to long-term bond yields. Depending on the intensity of the speculative pressures, this could produce the characteristic flattening of the yield curve, or the occasional reversing of the slope.

Successful speculators must be well-informed (or lucky). They must also be prepared to take risks. Moreover, it should be noted that speculation tends to add supply and demand pressures in the market which push prices in the direction which the speculators anticipated. Thus, speculation tends to eliminate the basis for speculation, and hence accelerate the transition to the new level and structure of interest rates. Therefore, the successful speculator must act early — he must outguess the market, and respond quickly to the signs of change.

Expected Yield for Short Holding Periods. Thus, a reasonably complete analysis of financial markets must take speculation into account.

It should be apparent, however, that to do so does not really call for a major departure in our analysis. What is involved is simply an application of the concept of expected yield. When we first developed the concept of expected yield we assumed that the security would be held to maturity. We defined expected yield as the interest rate implicit in the relationship between present market price of the security and all expected future payments to the holder of that security. In the interest of precision, perhaps we should call that concept *expected yield to maturity*. The present discussion of speculative capital gains and losses involves explicit recognition of the fact that the expected yield for shorter "holding periods" may be quite different. Thus, an assetholder seeking to maximize the return on his portfolio of assets may find it appropriate not to hold all assets until maturity. Periodic rearrangements of the balance of assets in his portfolio — involving active trading *in anticipation* of changes in market prices (it does little good to act after the fact) — may be highly profitable.

Speculation in Other Financial Markets

Our discussion of speculation as a factor in the choice among financial assets has focused on the government bond market. This is far too narrow a perspective. Speculative transactions are not confined to portfolio adjustments between long-term and short-term government bonds in anticipation of changes in the general level of interest rates. Clearly, whatever forces affect the market for government bonds must also affect the market for private bonds. This is evident from Figure 5-4. In the market for corporate stock, speculation as we have defined it (i.e., purchases in anticipation of short-term capital gains, or sales to avoid short-term capital losses) takes on a different character and assumes much greater importance. Rather than speculation on relatively regular and somewhat constrained movements in the general level of bond yields, speculation in the stock market involves anticipations of possibly spectacular changes in corporate fortunes. There are almost no limits to the possible changes in the market values of a share of stock, at least in the upward direction.

Speculation in Stock Markets. You will remember from our discussion in Chapter 3, a share of common stock is a claim to a *pro-rata* share of the profits of the corporation (or at least to that portion of the profits paid out as dividends). Just as the profits of the corporation can vary over a wide range, with abrupt changes in both magnitude and direction, so too can the market price of a share of stock of the corporation experience very sharp and very large changes. This is clearly fertile ground for the speculator, acting on hunch, rumour, or inside information.

These speculative activities are seen in their most dramatic form in the market for shares of stock in small companies engaged in exploration and development of oil and mining properties. The discovery of a rich body of ore, or of a potential oil well, will mean large long-run profit prospects for the company, and hence a rise in the market value of its outstanding shares of stock. The mere hint of such a discovery will attract speculative buying which will send the share prices shooting upward. A demonstration that the hints are false will "prick the bubble", producing an equally precipitous decline.

By way of example, one might cite the widely publicized Windfall affair of 1964. Under the influence of rumours that it had found a rich body of copper and zinc ore on its property (which was bordering on a proven rich find of such ore), the stock Windfall Oils and Mines Limited jumped from $0.56 per share on Friday, July 3, to $1.95 per share at the close of the market on Monday, July 6. This represented a gain of 250% over the weekend. In the face of persistent, but unsubstantiated (and also undenied) rumours, the market price per share rose intermittently to a peak of $5.60 on July 20, a gain of 900% in 17 days. This increase occurred in spite of the fact that the promoters of the mine sold a substantial amount of new stock in the market in this period. Had they not done so the rise could have been even sharper. The price then fluctuated between $3.00 and $4.50, closing at $4.15 on July 30th. It was then announced that the rumours were false: no commercial grade ore had been found. The price dropped to $0.80 when the market opened the next day, and by mid-August had returned to the level before the speculative surge. In subsequent years the price continued to sag, and in 1967 reached a low of $.15 per share. Fortunes were made and lost in the space of a month.

The Windfall case was unusual, although not unique. It would be wrong to assume that similar events are an everyday occurence in stock markets. Indeed, they are quite uncommon in markets other than markets for mining or exploratory oil company stock. Nonetheless, this case illustrates the potential force of speculative pressures in stock markets, and illustrates some of the extreme risks of investments in certain types of common stocks.

5/INFLATION AND THE EXPECTED YIELD ON FINANCIAL INSTRUMENTS

Inflation is a rise in the general level of prices of consumable goods and services where prices are measured in terms of the unit of account. Since the price of money is fixed in terms of the unit of account, inflation can also be defined as *a decline in the purchasing power of money.* A unit of money will buy a smaller quantity of goods and services. Indeed, *inflation involves a decline in the real value of anything whose nominal value (in terms of the unit of account) is fixed.*

Inflation and the "Real" Yield on Bonds

It should be evident from this statement that money is not the only financial instrument whose real value is affected by inflation. While there are few other financial instruments whose market prices are fixed, it must be remembered that bonds are claims to future payments which are fixed in terms of the unit of account. In a period of inflation, *the real value of these payments* will steadily decline. Thus the bondholder suffers a continuous erosion of his wealth.

Recognition of the possibility of inflation does not necessarily call for a radical revision of our analytical framework. It is significant because it is presumably the real rate of return on assets which is of concern to assetholders, both in their saving decisions and their portfolio balance decisions. But this means that the *expected rate of inflation must be allowed for in calculating the expected yields on financial assets,* and, by implication, *alternative possible rates of inflation must enter into the evaluation of the risks involved in holding bonds or money.* What we have done, then, in introducing the possibility of inflation, is to add another set of general considerations which must enter into the rational assetholder's calculations of expected yields and risks. Thus, to take a simple example, if an assetholder expects inflation at an annual rate of 1% per annum, then he must regard a bond with a nominal yield of 5% as having an expected *real* yield of 4% per annum. If he also considers, say, a

10% rate of inflation as a "possibility", then he must allow for this in evaluating the risks involved in holding bonds or money. Indeed, given the possibility of inflation, even government bonds and money cease to be riskless assets. *In making their portfolio, assetholders should be responsive to both the expected rate of inflation and the risk of inflation.*

Inflation and the "Real" Yield on Corporate Stock

Corporate stock differs in one vital respect from bonds, and this is significant in assessing the impact of inflation. Common stock is not a claim to a stream of fixed future payments, but rather to a share of profits which can be expected to rise in sympathy with any general rise in the price level. That is not to say that profits are tied directly to the price level. Many diverse factors affect profits for individual firms and in the aggregate. As a result, the profits of any individual company can move quite independently of the price level, depending on circumstances peculiar to that company and its industry, and profit levels in all or most industries can show wide short-term variation which have little or no apparent connection with movements in the general price level. These are all risks which the stockholder assumes. Nonetheless, the important point is that as the general price level is rising, the prices of things which business firms sell are rising as well as the prices of things which they buy. For a broad cross-section of firms (in the long run) this should mean that their profits have a built-in adjustment to changes in the price level.

There are many qualifications to this conclusion, and many interesting and unsettled empirical questions can be raised about the relationship between prices, costs, and profits. However, the important point for our analysis is that, unlike the bondholder who has a claim on fixed payments of declining real value, the stockholder has a claim on a variable payment, the real value of which is not necessarily eroded through inflation (and indeed may be enchanced through inflation).

The Redistributive Effects of Inflation: Adjustment of Prices and Yields. Does this analysis mean that the bondholder invariably loses real wealth through inflation while the stockholder invariably gains? In order to answer this question, let us briefly consider the adjustments which might occur in the face of a newly expected inflation.

Given the pre-existing market prices of stock and bonds, the initial effect of a new but widely held belief in the likelihood of inflation should be an attempt of holders of bonds (whose expected *real* yield is now lower in proportion to the expected annual rate of inflation) and money (whose expected real yield is now *negative* in proportion to the expected annual rate of inflation) to attempt to shift from these assets to common stocks. This shift in demand patterns should produce downward pressure on the price of bonds and upward pressure on the price of stocks. The existing holders of bonds will suffer capital losses and the existing holders of common stock will experience capital gains. Thus, because the expected rate of inflation had not entered into the valuation of these securities previously, that expectation will now produce a redistribution of wealth from bondholders to stockholders.

It should be noted, however, that the expectation of inflation, by lowering bond prices, will simultaneously increase bond yields. Therefore, someone who purchases a bond at its new market price will not necessarily lose as a result of inflation. The higher yield implied by the lower market price will tend to compensate him for the continual erosion of purchasing power as a result of inflation. Indeed, if inflation actually proceeded at the expected rate, and if expected yield were the only factor affecting demands for assets (i. e., ignoring credit risk and liquidity), the yield on the bond might adjust upward so as to fully compensate the holder for the rate of inflation. Thus, if the pre-existing equilibrium yield on bonds was 5% per annum, the expectation of inflation at an annual rate of 1% per annum might result in a decline in bond prices until the new nominal yield was 6% per annum. This would just compensate for the expected (and actual) 1% rate of inflation, and will re-establish the pre-existing real yield on bonds of 5% per annum. In this sense the purchaser of bonds at the market price will not suffer from inflation. (By the same token, the holder of bonds cannot improve his situation by selling those bonds in the market — he has already incurred his capital loss, and now the bonds which he is holding are as good an investment as ever at their new, lower market price).

This analysis of the impact of inflation on financial markets is far too simplistic to be useful beyond our very limited purposes. It implicitly assumes that the returns to the holder of common stock are adjusted upward in proportion to the expected rate of inflation, so that the inflation establishes the pre-existing real rate of return. It is far from obvious that this exact re-adjustment will occur. Moreover, the analysis ignores the fact that risk is also a factor in portfolio selection. Inflation, like other factors affecting the yield on securities, is a factor which cannot be foreseen with certainty. Thus, the *risk of inflation* may well affect the choices between money, bonds and stock. In particular, an increase in the *risk of inflation*, quite independently of an increase in the *expected rate of* inflation, should reduce demands for bonds and money, and increase demands for common stocks. This should have repercussions on the market prices of these instruments *in addition to* any effects produced by a change in the expected rate of inflation.

Conclusion: Inflation and the Choice Among Financial Instruments

Inflation reduces the real value of fixed payments. It thus reduces the real value of money, and of bonds. The expectation of inflation, therefore, should induce a shift in demand from money and bonds to common stocks, producing a decline in the price of bonds and an increase in the price of stock (the price of money is fixed).

Thus, inflation which has not been accurately anticipated will involve a redistribution of wealth among moneyholders, bondholders and stockholders. As a result, the possibility of inflation is a risk which must be taken into account in portfolio choices. Both the expected rate of inflation and the risk of inflation should affect the demands for financial instruments.

6/TAXATION AND THE EXPECTED YIELD ON FINANCIAL INSTRUMENTS

There is one other important factor affecting the choice among financial instruments which requires at least passing comment. That is the effect of a taxation system which involves differential tax rates on income obtained in different forms. Some of the differential effects of the tax system, such as the depletion allowances for mining and petroleum firms, affect the relative earning capacity of firms in different industries. They thus affect the choice among financial instruments *indirectly* by affecting the relative profit rates in different industries, and hence the expected yields on their securities (and particularly their common stocks). Other provisions of the tax system — like the special tax treatment of capital gains — have a *direct* impact on portfolio choices.

Traditionally, in Canada, capital gains were exempt from taxation, but under a 1971 tax bill capital gains on financial assets will be subject to taxation at half the normal progressive income tax rates. Although the effect is not as strong as earlier, the taxation system increases the expected yield (after tax) on securities which have the possibility of capital gains relative to all other securities (at least for individuals with high incomes and correspondingly high marginal tax rates). Of course, speculation on capital gains carries with it the *risk* of capital loss. However, because of differential taxation, the possibilities for capital gains must be given particular consideration in the portfolio choices of relatively wealthy people.

As in the case of anticipated inflation, the attempts of assetholders to adjust their portfolios to take advantage of differential tax rates should have the effect of adjusting the relative prices of securities to compensate for the tax differentials. Thus, the prices of securities which seem to promise capital gains should rise relative to the prices of other securities. However, only if everyone were in the same tax situation and had the same expectations for capital gains would the market price adjustment be complete.

7/THE SELECTION OF A PORTFOLIO

This chapter has introduced a large number of concepts. The problem now is to draw them together to see what they tell us about the nature of demands for financial instruments.

The Concept of a Portfolio

A basic concept, introduced early in the analysis, is that of a portfolio of assets. An assetholder's portfolio is simply the collection of assets which he chooses to hold.

We have already drawn certain strong conclusions about normal (i.e., risk averse) assetholders' preferences. We cast our analysis in terms of such abstract concepts as expected yield, credit risk, and liquidity, which we considered to be attributes of individual financial instruments. To complete our analysis we must consider the problem of choice among assets in the context of the selection of a complete portfolio. To that end, we must develop concepts of expected yield, risk and liquidity as attributes of portfolios.

Expected Yield of a Portfolio

Since he is only one among a great many participants in the market, each assetholder must take the expected yields on individual financial instruments as given. He cannot control them. He can only choose to hold or not hold the instrument. However, within limits set by the expected yields on instruments available in the market, each assetholder can control the expected yield on his portfolio through a careful selection of the instruments to be included in the portfolio.

Expected Yield on a Portfolio. The expected yield on a portfolio is simply the weighted average of the expected yields on the individual assets included in the portfolio — with the expected yield of each asset weighted by the proportion of the portfolio represented by that instrument.[2] Any assetholder can increase the expected yield on his portfolio by increasing the proportion of his portfolio invested in relatively high-yielding assets, and he can reduce the yield on his portfolio by increasing the proportion invested in relatively low-yielding assets.

Yield Preference. We have assumed that each assetholder has a strong preference for yield. The reason for this lies in our discussion of the saving decision (Chapter 4). Each household is presumably striving to maximize utility from its lifetime consumption potential. To accumulate wealth for the support of future consumption it must forego current consumption. The higher the expected yield on a portfolio the greater the future consumption which any given current wealth accumulation can be expected to support, i.e., the greater the lifetime consumption, and hence total utility, available to the household. A utility-maximizing household must therefore be attracted by higher yields. It must have a preference for yield. Faced with a choice between two financial instruments, other things being equal, it would choose the one with the highest yield.

What Does the Assetholder Maximize? But what is the import of the "other things being equal" assumption? What other things? Can we not assume that each assetholder simply maximizes expected yield without any qualifications?

We know know that the answer to this last question is no. If expected yield were the only consideration in the portfolio balance decision, assetholders would always choose instruments with high yields over those with low yields. Faced with assets with different expected yields, each asset-holder would include only one asset in his portfolio — the one which appeared to promise the highest expected yield. It does not take a sophisticated statistical survey to show that few assetholders have portfolios consisting of only one asset.

There is another interesting implication of assetholders maximizing expected yield. If all assetholders had roughly the same expectations with respect to each asset, equilibrium in the market would require identical expected yields on all assets. As assetholders attempt to purchase those instruments promising high expected yields, they create excess demand in the market which tends to drive up the price of those instruments. At the same time, they will be selling those instruments promising low expected yields, tending to drive down the price of those instruments. Remember, the market price and the expected yield on any instrument vary inversely. When the price of high-yielding instruments increases, the yield correspondingly drops, and vice versa for the low-yielding instruments. The end result should be a rough equalization of expected yields on all securities. At that time, if yield were the only consideration, assetholders would be indifferent between financial instruments. The instruments would be perfect substitutes for each other as forms in which wealth can be accumulated.

In general, we cannot observe either an equalization of expected yields or single-asset portfolios. Assetholders must react to other attributes of financial instruments besides expected yield. One of these attributes is credit risk. The assetholder must be concerned not only with the expected yield on his portfolio, but also with the risk on his portfolio.

Risk

We developed the concept of credit risk as an attribute of individual financial instruments. Like expected yield, the riskiness of an instrument is something over which an assetholder has no control. However, within limits, he can control the degree of risk on his portfolio through a careful selection of assets to be included in it. What is the relationship between the degree of credit risk on individual assets and the degree of risk on the portfolio?

The Riskiness of a Portfolio. By the risk on a portfolio we mean the standard deviation of the expected yield on the portfolio. The concept is parallel to that developed for the credit risk on individual assets, and indeed the risk on the portfolio depends on the risk on the individual assets included in that portfolio. However, unlike the relationship between the expected yields on the portfolio and the assets which comprise it, in all but the simplest case, the risk on a portfolio is not a simple weighted average of the risks on the individual assets. The relationship is much more complex. Nonetheless, we can assume that in most cases an asset-holder will increase the riskiness of his portfolio if he increases the proportion of relatively risky securities contained in that portfolio.[3]

Interdependence of Risk and Expected Yield

An assetholder can vary the degree of risk and the expected yield through a careful selection of the assets to be included in his portfolio. However, he cannot choose the degree of risk and the expected yield independently of each other. Since risk and expected yield are both attributes of individual financial instruments, when the assetholder selects a particular group of assets to be included in his portfolio he not only obtains the expected yield provided by that combination of assets, he simultaneously obtains the degree of risk provided by those same assets. To obtain a different degree of risk on his portfolio he must select a different combination of assets, and that means he will obtain a different expected yield on his portfolio.

In general, higher degrees of risk are associated with higher expected yields. Thus, to obtain a higher expected yield on his portfolio, the assetholder must include a higher proportion of relatively risky assets, and that generally means a higher degree of risk in the portfolio as well.

Risk Aversion. We have assumed that assetholders in general are risk averters. Risk is something which they prefer to avoid, and they have to be bribed to take on higher degrees of risk through the expectation of a higher yield. In general, a risk averter will not select the portfolio of assets with the highest expected yield. That would provide too high a degree of risk. Similarly, in general a risk averter will not select the portfolio with the lowest degree of risk. That would provide too low an expected yield. Because there is a subjective "trade-off" between risk and expected yield in his system of preferences, he will normally select a portfolio consisting of more than one asset, and one which is somewhere between the two extremes of maximizing expected yield and minimizing risk.

The Equilibrium Portfolio: Risk and Expected Yield. We have demonstrated the nature of the choice between risk and yield in a particularly simple case in Figure 5-8.

For the purposes of this diagram we have assumed that there are only two assets. One, a government bond, is regarded as perfectly safe (zero risk). The other, a corporate bond, has a higher yield, but it also has a relatively high degree of risk. If these are the only instruments available, what combination of the two will the assetholder choose?

In this figure, the expected yield on the portfolio (y_p) is measured along the vertical axis. It is the weighted average of the expected yields on the safe (y_s) and the risky (y_r) securities, with the weights being the proportions (a_s, a_r) in which the two assets are included in the portfolio That is,

$$a_s + a_r = 1 \qquad (5.1)$$

and,

$$y_p = a_s y_s + a_r y_r \qquad (5.2)$$

The risk on the portfolio (σ_p) is measured along the base axis. It depends upon the risks on the individual securities in the portfolio and the proportions in which these two securities are included in the portfolio.

Figure 5-8

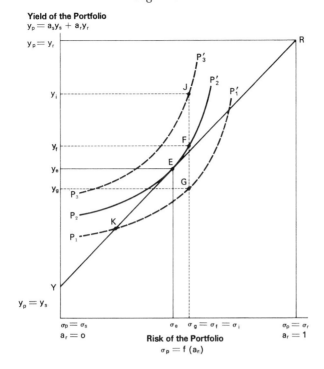

Yield of the Portfolio
$y_p = a_s y_s + a_r y_r$

In this particular case, the function linking the risks on the individual securities and the risk on the portfolio is simple. Since the risk on the government bond is zero $(\sigma_s = 0)$, given the risk on the corporate bond, the risk on the portfolio depends simply on the proportion of the portfolio devoted to the relatively risky security. That is,

$$\sigma_p = a_r \, \sigma_r \qquad\qquad (5.3)$$

This is a very special case. In general, the relationship is not that simple.

The line YR describes the combinations of expected yield and risk available to the assetholder by varying the proportions in which he divides his portfolio between the government bond and the corporate bond. At point Y the entire portfolio is invested in the government bond. The risk is minimized $(\sigma_p = 0)$, and the expected yield on the portfolio is minimized $(y_p = y_s)$. As we move out along the line YR, the proportion of the relatively risky security in the portfolio increases, and as a result, so do the expected yield and the risk on the portfolio. In the extreme, at point R, the entire portfolio consists of the relatively risky and high yielding corporate bond. At that point, both risk $(\sigma_p = \sigma_r)$ and expected yield $(y_p = y_r)$ are maximized.

Each point along the line YR, then, represents a different possible portfolio with different degrees of risk and different expected yields. Which of the alternatives available to him will the assetholder choose?

The general answer is that he will select that portfolio — that combination of risk and expected yield — which will provide him with the highest possible level of utility. We can identify that portfolio in a theoretical sense through an application of indifference curve analysis.[4]

The curves labelled PP' in Figure 5-8 are indifference curves which describe the assetholders' preferences as between expected yield and risk. They incorporate our assumption of risk aversion. Any one curve, say P_2P_2' identifies alternative combinations of expected yield and risk which the assetholder finds equally acceptable. He is indifferent between portfolios lying along this curve. Thus, he would find nothing to choose between the two portfolios represented by points E and F. While portfolio F involves a higher degree of risk, the assetholder would feel that he was fully compensated for assuming that higher degree of risk by the higher expected yield also associated with portfolio F.

While the assetholder would thus be indifferent between portfolios E or F, he would prefer either of these to the portfolio represented by the point G. This portfolio has the same degree of risk as portfolio F, but it also has a lower expected yield. There is a whole set of portfolios which the assetholder would regard as equivalent to portfolio G, including portfolio H. They all lie along the indifference curve P_1P_1', which then describes portfolios which are inferior to those lying along P_2P_2'.

Similarly, the assetholder would prefer the portfolio represented by joint J to either E or F. Portfolio J has the same risk as portfolio F, but a higher expected yield. There is a whole set of portfolios which the assetholder would regard as equivalent to portfolio J, all lying along the higher indifference curve P_3P_3'.

If the assetholder is to maximize utility, he must select that portfolio available on the market (and hence lying along the line YR) which he prefers most. Thus, between portfolios E and H, both of which are available to him, he would always choose E. By an extension of the same logic, between profolios E and K, both of which are available, he would always choose E. (Why?) By contrast, he would much prefer portfolio J to any of these, including E. However, portfolio J is not available in the market. That combination of risk and expected yield cannot be obtained, given the risk and expected yield on the two securities from which he must construct his portfolio.

Portfolio E, then, is the portfolio which would be selected. It is the *equilibrium portfolio*. It does not provide the maximum expected yield. Portfolio R would do that. It does not provide the minimum risk. Portfolio Y would do that. However, it is on the highest indifference curve between risk and expected yield which can be achieved by the assetholder, given the risk and expected yield on the financial instruments available in the market.

Conclusions: The Significance of Risk. The existence of risk and risk aversion means that financial instruments are not all perfect substitutes in the minds of assetholders. An increase in the yield on one security will lead to some substitution of the higher yielding security for the lower yielding security (it will induce assetholders to take on more risk), but it will not lead to total replacement of the low-yielding security asset portfolios.

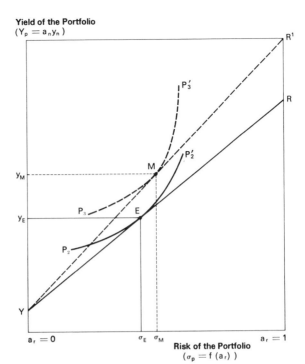

Figure 5-9

Yield of the Portfolio
$(Y_p = a_n y_n)$

R^1

P_3'

R

P_2'

M

y_M

P_3 E

y_E

P_2

Y

$a_r = 0$ σ_E σ_M $a_r = 1$

Risk of the Portfolio
$(\sigma_p = f(a_r))$

Figure 5-9 duplicates the essential feature of Figure 5-8, but allows for an increase in the yield on the corporate bond with no change in the yield on the government bond or in the risk on the corporate bond. The portfolio opportunity line thus becomes steeper. For any given degree of risk, the assetholder can now obtain a higher expected yield. The new equilibrium portfolio is now represented by point M on a higher indifference curve. The assetholder has assumed more risk and obtains a higher yield. As an exercise, the student should demonstrate what happens when:

   a. the expected yield on the "safe" security is lowered;

   b. the riskiness of the "risky" security increases;

   c. the expected yields on both securities increase proportionately (Remember: risk might be an "inferior good").

If we know the size of the assetholder's portfolio at that point in time, we can derive his demand for each type of security. Given the riskiness of each security, the demand for the risky security will be an increasing function of the differential between the expected yield on the risky and the "safe" securities. The opposite is true of the safe security. At wider and wider differentials the demand function probably becomes increasingly inelastic.

The market demand curve is the sum of individual assetholder's demand functions. The demand for risky securities, therefore, is presumably a function of the wealth of assetholders (and hence the size of portfolios) and the differential in yield between risky and safe securities.

Liquidity

The third basic attribute of financial instruments for which a risk-averting assetholder is presumed to have a preference is liquidity. We presume that, other things being equal, an assetholder prefers more liquid assets to illiquid assets.

The Liquidity of a Portfolio. Like expected yield and risk, liquidity is a property of individual financial assets. It becomes a property of a portfolio through the inclusion of highly liquid assets in the portfolio. Therefore, by the liquidity of the portfolio we mean simply the proportion of highly liquid assets in the portfolio, i.e., the ratio of liquid assets (L) to total assets (A).

The decision on the degree of liquidity is inseparable from the decision on the expected yield and the risk on the portfolio. However, as we did in the case of risk, we can analyze the choice between liquidity and yield, holding other considerations constant. Such an analysis is presented in Figure 5-10.

The vertical axis on this chart measures the yield on the portfolio. We assume that the portfolio consists only of a liquid asset (L) like money, which bears no interest, and an illiquid asset (N) like corporate stock, which has a positive expected yield (y_n). The expected yield on the portfolio depends simply on the proportion of the portfolio devoted to the illiquid asset $(1-l)$. That is:

$$y_p = (1-l) \ y_n$$

On the base axis we measure the liquidity of the portfolio; i.e., the proportion of the portfolio devoted to liquid assets (l). At point Y the entire portfolio is invested in liquid assets, and the expected yield on the portfolio is zero. At point Y_2 the entire portfolio is invested in illiquid assets, and the expected yield on the portfolio is y_{n2}, the expected yield on the illiquid asset. The line Y_2Y therefore traces the opportunities possible in the market. It shows the yield on alternative possible portfolios incorporating varying proportions of liquid and illiquid assets.

The lines labelled LP are indifference curves with respect to liquidity and expected yield. The determination of the equilibrium portfolio involves the same logic as that developed in the discussion of risk. The object is to achieve the highest possible indifference curve. If the expected yield on the illiquid asset is y_{n2} then equilibrium will be achieved at point B on curve LP_2.

We can trace what happens when the expected yield on the illiquid asset increases or decreases. If the expected yield rises to y_{n3}, the new equilibrium portfolio will be at C, with a smaller portion devoted to liquid assets. Similarly, if the expected yield on the illiquid asset is reduced to y_{n1} the new equilibrium will be at D, with a larger portion of the portfolio devoted to liquid assets. (As an exercise, the student should work out what would happen if the liquid asset had a positive expected yield.)

In other words, as the expected yield on illiquid assets changes, there is a general substitution between liquid and illiquid assets in assetholders'

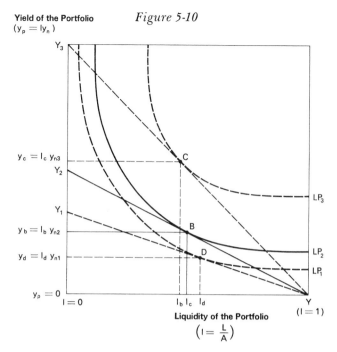

Yield of the Portfolio
$(y_p = Iy_n)$

Figure 5-10

Liquidity of the Portfolio
$(I = 1)$

$$\left(I = \frac{L}{A}\right)$$

portfolios. Given the size of the total portfolio, then, we can trace the assetholders' demand curve for liquid assets. It would show an increase in the quantity demanded as the yield on illiquid assets falls. Liquid and illiquid assets are imperfect substitutes for each other.

Other Dimensions of Portfolio Selection

This analysis of the selection of a portfolio has focused on two margins of choice, the expected yield-risk margin, and the expected yield-liquidity margin. Even if we limit ourselves to the three variables, expected yield, risk and liquidity, we must remember that there is a third margin of choice, risk versus liquidity. We have not explored that margin because it does not make an important contribution to our analysis. However, the student should remember that the degree of riskiness chosen may well affect the position of the LP curves, and hence may affect the choice of a degree of liquidity (the direction of the effect is not known).[5]

A second limitation of our analysis rests in the fact that we have only dealt with two-asset portfolios (including different assets when we discussed risk than when we discussed liquidity). This is necessary if we are to use geometrical constructions. The mathematics of multiple-asset portfolios becomes rather complex.

It should also be noted that we have implicitly assumed that the size of the portfolio does not affect preferences as between risk, liquidity and yield. It is not obvious that this is a valid assumption; however, we do not know how the functions shift with increasing portfolio size.

In the same connection, we have assumed that the rate of return on assets does not depend on the size of the portfolio. For reasons which we will discuss in Chapter 8, this is not necessarily the case, particularly since there are "transactions costs" involved in purchases and sales of assets (and hence in all rearrangements of portfolios) which depend largely on the number rather than the value of transactions. To rearrange a large portfolio, where the value of each purchase or sale of a security is relatively large, will involve smaller transactions costs per dollar invested. For this reason, the return to the portfolio may be greater than for a small portfolio.

Finally, we have used the concept of expected yield in this discussion as yield to maturity and we have ignored the effects of inflation. The earlier discussions of speculation and inflation should not be forgotten. There may be circumstances under which the yield for shorter holding periods is relevant, and all yields should be adjusted to a "real" basis (including the yield on money). Incorporating this in our analysis of the selection of a portfolio would make the whole matter impossibly complex.

8/THE DEMAND FOR FINANCIAL INSTRUMENTS IN A GENERAL EQUILIBRIUM CONTEXT

Developing the demand for financial instruments in the context of the selection of a portfolio makes it clear that all financial instruments are substitutes, although imperfect substitutes. This means that a rise in the expected yield on a short-term government bond does not confine repercussions to the government bond market. It will produce general substitution effects, altering the demand for other short-term securities, but also reaching out in much diminished magnitude as far as the market for speculative corporate stocks. As a result of substitutions in portfolios, yields on all financial instruments should tend to increase. Furthermore (and this will be of vital importance when we come to study monetary theory), substitutions may not be limited to financial assets. We earlier excluded consideration of choice between financial and real (or capital) assets. This was done primarily for convenience. But the reader should be aware that the change in the expected yield of one particular asset (be it real or financial) will in turn affect the demands for it and all other assets. Thus if we can change the yields on financial assets relative to the yields on real assets we can expect thereby to affect the demand for real assets.

FOOTNOTES

[1] In the first two sections of this chapter we have taken liberties with certain concepts which have more rigorous formulations in economic theory:

a. It will appear that we are defining the expected yield as the *mode* of the distribution of possible yields, when it is more common to define it as the mean or mathematical expectation of the distribution. When we come to a more rigorous definition (Appendix, Chapter 8) we will adopt the standard convention. However, in introducing the subject, theoretical precision is less important than conveying a general feeling for the concept.

b. Note also, that the probability distributions which we use in the next few pages are all symmetrical (a circumstance which, incidentally, makes the distinction between mean and mode unimportant in fact, if not in principle). Clearly, if we had in mind only bonds, the probability distributions could not be symmetrical. For simplicity, we are implicitly considering a wider range of securities.

c. We are ignoring the fact that different securities have different terms to maturity. This is not a factor in our analysis at this stage, but we will turn to it later.

d. In our discussion of expected yield and credit risk we are implicitly assuming that the assetholder plans to hold each security till maturity. We will turn later to the question of the significance of possible transactions in the open market, including the significance of changes in market price.

[2] If the portfolio consisted of three assets, with expected yields of 0, .05 and .10, then the expected yield on the portfolio would depend on the proportion of each in the portfolio. If the proportions were 10%, 30% and 60% respectively, then the expected yield on the portfolio would be

$$\bar{y}_p = \frac{.1 \times 0 + .3 \times .05 + .6 \times .1}{.1 + .3 + .6}$$

$$= \frac{.015 + .06}{1}$$

$$= .075$$

If, by contrast, the proportions were 60%, 30% and 10%, respectively, the expected yield on the portfolio would be

$$\bar{y}_p = \frac{.6 \times 0 + .3 \times .05 + .1 \times .1}{1}$$

$$= \frac{.015 + .01}{1}$$

$$= .025$$

[3] In fact, the relationship between the riskiness of the portfolio and the proportions of "risky" and "safe" assets in the portfolio is much more complicated than this. Full analysis of the topic — particularly if we admit the existence of a large number of different assets — requires relatively advanced mathematics. In a more advanced treatment of the subject it would be demonstrated that, *up to a point*, increasing the proportion of risky assets in the portfolio can reduce the riskiness of the portfolio as a whole. In other words, given the range of securities available in the market, there exists a combination of securities which is a *minimum risk portfolio*. In general, (although there are exceptions) that portfolio is a *diversified* portfolio. It does not consist of only the safest asset. Indeed, a portfolio consisting of several relatively risky securities *can* be less risky than a portfolio consisting of one relatively safe security. The main exception is when there is some security which is absolutely safe, i.e., there is no risk in holding it. Such a security might be money (although you should remember our discussion of the significance of inflation: If there is a risk of inflation, there is a risk of loss of real purchasing power – a risk of a negative yield – in holding money; perhaps in a more general framework, money is not a riskless security). If there is such a security, then a portfolio consisting only of it would be riskless, and hence, by definition, would be the minimum-risk portfolio.

These issues involve the *theory of portfolio diversification* which is introduced in Chapter 8 and considered somewhat more systematically but still on an elementary level in the Appendix to that chapter. In all of this discussion we are using the standard deviation of the yield on each asset and on the portfolio as the measure of risk.

[4] Students not familiar with such analysis should consult a good textbook on the principles of economics.

[5] In a more advanced analysis, liquidity preference would be developed as a special case of "risk aversion".

APPENDIX

CAPITAL VALUE AND YIELD: BASIC CONCEPTS OF FINANCIAL MARKETS

This Appendix provides a more complete and systematic discussion of the relationship between prices and yields on financial instruments. We also require the concept of capital value (or present value). It is easiest to explore these concepts initially with respect to bonds. We will then turn to variable income securities.

Capital Value and Yield on a Bill

Consider first the simple type of bond which we previously called a bill. This is a financial instrument which calls for a single lump-sum payment at the end of a fixed period of time, which we will assume is one year. For simplicity we assume that the bill has no credit risk. There is no question but that the payment will be made.[1]

Capital Value of a Bill. The basic question facing the potential purchaser of a bill is how much he should offer to pay for the bill (we assume that if he purchases it he will hold it until maturity). As with most questions in economics, the answer can only be given in terms of the alternatives open to him. Suppose he has the alternative of depositing the funds in the bank for one year (another riskless financial instrument) at a fixed rate of interest. If he chooses this alternative, by the end of the year he will have accumulated an amount equal to the amount deposited plus one year's interest on that sum. Then, since they are both riskless instruments, we can say that he should pay no more for the bill than the sum of money which he would have to deposit in the bank at the going rate of interest in order to accumulate, by the end of the year, an amount equal to the redemption value of the bill. That sum — the amount which he would have to deposit with the bank at the going interest rate — is the capital value of the bill.

We can define the capital value of the bill more precisely with the assistance of some basic financial mathematics. Suppose the going interest rates in riskless one year financial instruments is $100r\%$ per annum.[2] Then, V lent now, at this interest rate, will accumulate to;

$$\begin{aligned} A_1 &= V + Vr \\ &= V(1+r) \end{aligned} \qquad (5A.1)$$

by the end of the year. In other words, in order to accumulate the sum A_1 by the end of the year we would have to invest V at the going interest rate of $100r\%$ per annum. If A_1 is the redemption value of the bill, then V must be its present value. In general:

$$V = A_1 \left(\frac{1}{1+r} \right) \qquad (5A.2)$$

Thus, if the bill called for a single payment of $1,000 at the end of one year, and if the going rate of interest on riskless one year loans were 4%

per annum, the present value of the bill would be:

$$V = 1000 \ \left(\frac{1}{1 + .04}\right)$$
$$= 962$$

Yield on a Bill. Faced with the alternatives of a riskless bill and a riskless one-year bank deposit, an investor who has no other reason for preferring one instrument over the other should pay no more than $962 for the bill. If the market price of the bill (P) happened to be $962 a purchaser of the bill who held it to maturity and received the redemption payment of $1,000 would effectively earn 4% per annum on his investment. The yield on the bill would be 4% per annum. If the market price exceeded $962 the yield would be less than 4% per annum. If the price were less than $962, the yield would exceed 4% per annum.

In interpreting these statements it must be remembered that we calculated the capital value of the bill using the rate of interest on a closely competitive financial instrument. Thus, what we mean by *the yield on the bill is the interest rate which is implicit in the relationship between the market price of the bill and its redemption value. It is the interest rate at which the present value of the bill would be equal to its market price.* Given that we know the market price (P) and the redemption value (A_1) we can find the yield by substituting these values in equation 5A.2 and solving for the interest rate. For a one year bill, the yield (y) will be:

$$y = \frac{A_1}{P} - 1 \tag{5A.3}$$

If the market price of the $1,000 bill were $966 the yield would be $3\frac{1}{2}\%$ per annum. If the market price were $957 the yield would be $4\frac{1}{2}\%$ per annum. Note that *for a given future payment, market price and yield vary inversely.*

Effect of Term to Maturity. We have assumed that the bill has a one-year term to maturity. This is clearly a special case, one which we have assumed for convenience.

Suppose, instead, the bill had a two-year term to maturity. To find the present value we can ask what sum ($V) we would have to invest in order to accumulate A_2 by the end of the second year, when the interest rate is 100r% per annum.

From equation 5A.1 we know that $V will accumulate to $A_1 = V (1 + r)$ by the end of the first year. If this sum is then invested for a second year at the same interest rate, by the end of the second year we will have accumulated:

$$A_2 = A_1 + A_1 r$$
$$= V (1 + r) + V (1 + r) r$$
$$= V (1 + r) (1 + r)$$
$$= V (1 + r)^2 \tag{5A.4}$$

Or, dividing through by $(1 + r)^2$

$$V = \frac{A_2}{(1+r)^2} \tag{5A.5}$$

It can be shown that in general the present value of a single payment of $\$A_n$ to be made at the end of n years, where the prevailing interest rate for loans of that duration is $100r\%$ per annum is:

$$V = \frac{A_n}{(1+r)^n} \qquad (5A.6)$$

The present value of a given payment thus varies inversely with the term to maturity. It also varies inversely with the interest rate, and there is a strong interaction between term to maturity and the interest rate. This is illustrated in the following table.

Table 5A-1
Present Value of a $1,000 Bill*

Term to Maturity (Years)	Interest Rate (Yield) (Percent per Annum and Dollars)				
	3%	4%	5%	6%	7%
¼	993	990	988	985	983
½	985	980	976	971	966
1	971	962	952	943	935
2	943	925	907	890	873
5	863	822	784	747	713
10	744	676	614	558	508
20	554	456	377	312	258
50	228	141	87	54	34
∞	0	0	0	0	0

* Rounded to the nearest dollar. The present values for maturities of ¼ year assume compounding four times yer year; for ½ year, compounding twice per year; and for all other maturities compounding once per year.

Capital Value and Yield on a Bond

Capital Value of a Bond. The bill is a particularly simple type of bond which involves but a single future payment. In general a bond will involve a series of semi-annual payments (the coupon payments) and a final lump-sum payment (the par value or redemption value). If we assume for simplicity that the coupon payments are made once per year (rather than the usual twice per year) then what the purchaser is purchasing is a stream of payments of the order:

$$C_1 + C_2 + C_3 + \ldots\ldots\ldots + C_n + A_n$$

where $C_1 \ldots C_n$ are the annual coupons and A_n is the final payment, made at the end of the nth year. What is the present value of such a stream of payments?

To eliminate a difficult complication we will again assume that we are talking about a bond on which there is no credit risk, e.g., a federal government bond. If we then assume that the interest rate is the same for riskless loans of all maturities, the present value of the stream of payments associated with the bond is simply the sum of the present values of each of its component parts. That is, the present value of the stream of payments is:

$$V = \frac{C_1}{(1+r)} + \frac{C_2}{(1+r)^2} + \frac{C_3}{(1+r)^3} + \ldots + \frac{C_n}{(1+r)^n} + \frac{A_n}{(1+r)^n}$$

This equation can be simplified to:

$$V = \frac{A_n}{(1+r)^n} + C \left[\frac{1}{r} - \frac{1}{r(1+r)^n} \right] \tag{5A.7}$$

where $C_1 = C_2 = C_3 = \ldots = C_n$.

In the case of a consol, a bond with a fixed annual payment in perpetuity and hence no redemption value, the formula can be further simplified to:[3]

$$V = \frac{C}{r} \tag{5A.8}$$

The capital value of a bond thus depends in a rather complex fashion on the size of the annual coupon payments, $(C_1, C_2 \ldots C_n)$, the redemption value (A_n), the term to maturity, (n) and the going level of interest rates (r). The capital value varies directly with the size of the coupon and redemption value, and what is important for our analysis, *inversely with the market interest rate.*

Yield on a Bond. The concept of the yield on a bond is analagous to the yield on a bill in that it is the interest rate which is implicit in the relationship between the market price of a bond and the stream of coupon payments and the redemption value. *The yield on a bond is the interest rate at which the present value of a bond would be equal to its market price.* If the price of the bond is greater than present value calculated at the going market interest rate, then the yield is less than the interest rate. If the price is less than the capital value then the yield is greater than the market interest rate.

We were able to offer a simple formula for the calculation of the yield on a one-year bill. No such simple formula can be derived for the more general case of the yield on a bond. However, comprehensive tables of bond prices and yields are published. For a bond with a given coupon and term to maturity, it is possible to read the yield off the table if you are given the price (or the price if you are given the yield).

In table 5A-2 we have presented a small sample of prices and yields on a bond with annual interest coupons totalling $50 and a redemption value of $1,000. From this table we can see, for example, that a five-year bond selling for $957 will yield 6% per annum if held to maturity. Similarly, if it is to yield 6% per annum a twenty-five-year bond must sell for $871 and a consol for $833.

The market price of a bond, then, can be regarded as the present value of the stream of coupon payments and the final redemption payment when the present value is calculated at a particular rate of interest, i.e.,

Table 5A-2
Price and Yield* on a 5% Bond

(Years) Term to Maturity	Yield (Percent and Dollars)				
	3	4	5	6	7
1	1,020	1,010	1,000	990	981
2	1,038	1,019	1,000	981	963
3	1,057	1,028	1,000	973	947
5	1,092	1,045	1,000	957	917
10	1,172	1,082	1,000	926	858
15	1,240	1,112	1,000	902	816
20	1,299	1,137	1,000	884	786
25	1,350	1,157	1,000	871	765
	1,667	1,250	1,000	833	714

* Assuming Twice Annual Compounding. Prices have been rounded to the nearest dollar.

the rate of interest which is the yield on the bond. This is a true interest rate. It is the rate which a purchaser will earn on his investment if he buys the security at the market price. It is also the rate which a new borrower would have to pay if he borrowed money by issuing a comparable security. Thus, when we are considering the determination of the market price of a bond we are simultaneously considering the determination of an interest rate. As the price falls, the interest rate rises. They are linked mathematically.

It was demonstrated in Chapter 5 that interest rates on all types of securities are related to each other. While they are not rigidly tied to each other, they do not move independently of each other either. A general rise in interest rates will be reflected in the yields on all securities.

The Yield on Variable Income Securities

In principle the same concepts can be applied to variable income securities (or real assets, for that matter). That is, it should be possible to calculate the yield on such a security on the basis of the existing market price. However, a complication arises since, unlike a bond, a fixed stream of future payments is not specified in the contract of a variable income security. Both the size and length of the stream of payments depend on future developments which can never be perfectly foreseen. As a result, we can only calculate the present value of a share of common stock, for example on the basis of some *expected* stream of dividend payments which by its very nature must be conjectural. Individuals may disagree sharply on the most probable stream of future dividends, and individual opinions may be revised drastically from time to time as new information is forthcoming.

Risk on Fixed Income Securities. In our discussion of the yield on fixed income securities we ignored the risk that the "fixed" interest and redemption payments will not be made. However, such risk exists with respect to most bonds. In this respect a "high risk" bond has some of the characteristics of a variable income security. The actual payments may be less than those specified in the contract, or they may be delayed beyond the time specified in the contract (of course, they cannot be more than specified in the contract). This is something which should be taken into account in calculating yield.

Theoretical versus Expected Yield. We can refer to the yields calculated from information in the contract between borrower and lender as the *theoretical yield.* It is calculated on the presumption that the payments specified in the contract will all be made in full and on time. In the case of variable income securities no theoretical yield can be calculated, and in the case of high-risk bonds the theoretical yield may not be the most likely yield. We thus need the concept of *expected yield* to refer to the most probable yield, based on the assetholder's expectations of the size and timing of future payments. In the case of a perfectly safe bond, expected yield and theoretical yield will be the same.

By analogy with a consol, another security with no fixed maturity, the theoretical yield on common stock is sometimes measured by the ratio of current dividends to market price. This, however, could only be a valid calculation of the theoretical yield if the current dividend payments were expected to continue unchanged in perpetuity. Unlike the consol, for which the annual interest payment is fixed in perpetuity, in general there is no reason to expect the current dividend on common stock to continue indefinitely. As a result, the calculated dividend price ratio is not directly analogous to the yield on a consol, and indeed its meaning is not obvious.

Inflation and Taxes. We would remind you of two points made in the text of the chapter. First, if the general level of commodity prices is expected to change, then it is important that "real" yields rather than "nominal" yields be calculated. The nominal yields calculated as discussed above should be adjusted for the expected rate of inflation. Second, it will generally be the after-tax yield which is relevant for investor decisions. Given the nature of our taxation system, the adjustment for expected taxes may affect not only the general level of yields but also the relationship between yields on different types of securities.

Summary: Capital Value, Market Price and Expected Yield

The concepts of capital value and expected yield are basic to all economic analysis involving intertemporal decisions, i.e., decisions involving events which occur in more than one time period. These concepts are basic to the analysis of the determination of the market price of financial instruments because financial instruments are claims to payments to be made in future time periods. We will encounter the concepts again in discussing capital expenditure decisions of business firms since these are also decisions involving current expenditures (on plant and equipment) for the purpose of making profits in future time periods. The student is advised to review and master the concepts.

The main purpose of this Appendix has been to provide a more systematic definition of the concept of the expected yield on financial instruments, and a more careful development of the relationship between expected yield and the market price of the instrument. The important points to keep in mind are:

(1) If the stream of future payments is given, then the determination of the market price involves simultaneously the determination of the yield. Market price and yield are linked mathematically.

(2) Yield and market price vary inversely for any given stream of future payments.

(3) If the expected size of the future payments changes (as in a variable income security) then the price *or* the expected yield on that security must change in the same direction. Larger expected dividend payments on common stock in a corporation must mean either a higher price for the shares of stock, or a higher expected yield on the stock (or both).

(4) If the streams of payments on two financial instruments are different, then their market prices must be different if they are to give the same yield. Thus, if a 5%, twenty-year bond ($50 annual coupon) and a 3%, twenty-year bond ($30 annual coupon) are both to yield 4%, the price of the 5% bond must be $1,137 and the price of the 3% bond $863.

This last point is important. It is the price of financial instruments which is determined in the market place. However, since the characteristics of financial instruments are so diverse, market price does not provide a useful basis for comparison of financial instruments. Expected yield is the most useful common denominator for purposes of comparison and decision-making.

APPENDIX
FOOTNOTES

[1] This assumption is important. Toward the end of this appendix we will distinguish between the expected yield and the theoretical yield on financial instruments. The theoretical yield is calculated from information in the contract between the borrower and the lender. It presumes that all contractual payments will be made in full and on time. The expected yield allows for the possibility of partial or total default, or delays in payment. If there is complete certainty that payments will be made there is no need to distinguish between these two concepts, and we can refer to either simply as the yield.

[2] It may seem strange to quote interest rates at $100r\%$ per annum. The interest rate "4% per annum" can be written in ratio form as ".04". If we want r to represent this ratio i.e., $r = .04$, then we must refer to the rate of interest at $100r\%$ per annum (i.e., $r = .04$).

[3] A Consol calls for annual payments through all future time, i.e., $n = \infty$. But, as n approaches ∞, $\dfrac{1}{(1+r)^n}$ approaches O. Hence the terms $\dfrac{A_n}{(1+r)^n}$ and $\dfrac{C}{r(1+r)^n}$ both approach O, and the capital value of the bond approaches $\dfrac{C}{r}$.

6

Elementary Theory of
Financial Markets, Part 3:

Supply and Market Equilibrium

To this point we have discussed the theory of financial markets from the viewpoint of assetholders, the demand side of the market. We now turn our attention to the supply side, and to the nature of equilibrium in financial markets.

1/STOCKS AND FLOWS: TWO CONCEPTS OF SUPPLY

The supply of financial instruments has its origins in acts of borrowing and lending — in the demands of deficit spending units for funds to finance their deficits. However, in discussing the supply side of the market, it is important to make a sharp distinction between two different concepts of supply. One is the *stock* of financial instruments outstanding at a particular *point in time*, and the other the *flow* of new borrowing over a particular *period of time*.

At any point in time there will be an outstanding stock of financial instruments already in the hands of assetholders. Both the size and the composition of this stock is a reflection of past history. It reflects previous borrowings by households, governments and corporation. In our analysis of the financial system, this stock is something which must be taken as given — a predetermined variable.

The stock concept of supply is basic. However, we must recognize that over a period of time the outstanding stock is subject to change. Attempts of spending units to raise funds to finance deficits create a steady flow of new financial instruments onto the market which augment the basic stock. At the same time, partial or complete repayment of outstanding debts by some spending units work to reduce the outstanding stock. The difference between these two magnitudes — the flow of new borrowing and the flow of repayments — is the second concept of supply. It is supply as a *net flow*: *an addition to or subtraction from the basic stock over a period of time.*

Like the demand for financial instruments, the supply of financial instruments involves two fundamental decisions — a decision on the amount to be borrowed (the *borrowing decision*) and a decision on the types of financial instruments to be issued (the *liability balance decision*). A complete analysis of the supply of financial instruments must simultaneously explain both decisions.

2/THE BORROWING DECISION

One major conclusion which will follow from our analysis of the borrowing decisions of households, governments and corporations will be that, with certain important exceptions (including the borrowings of financial intermediaries, which fall into a class by themselves, and must be treated separately), the primary purpose of borrowing is to finance the purchase or construction of durable real assets. In the government sector these assets may consist of highways, schools or sewage disposal plants; in the corporate sector, factory buildings, machinery or equipment; and in the household sector, automobiles, household durables, or houses. The objects may be widely different, but they all have an extended life, and have value to their purchasers because they are expected to provide services either to be consumed directly or sold during future time periods. While the specific motivations of the individual sectors may differ widely, this aspect of the borrowing decision which all sectors have in common provides a convenient peg on which to hang our theoretical analysis.

The Consumer Sector

Since we have already made an extensive examination of the asset demands of households, it is convenient to begin our analysis with this sector. A simple adaptation of the balance sheet and accumulation identities of Chapter 4 provide a useful framework for the consideration of household borrowing decisions.

The Basic Identities Again. Consider first the balance sheet identity, which we previously wrote as:

$$\text{WEALTH} \quad = \quad \text{ASSETS} \quad - \quad \text{LIABILITIES} \qquad (4.1)$$

By splitting assets into the two categories, financial assets and real assets, and rearranging the terms, we can rewrite this equation as:

$$\text{LIABILITIES} \quad = \quad \frac{\text{REAL}}{\text{ASSETS}} \; + \; \frac{\text{FINANCIAL}}{\text{ASSETS}} \; - \; \text{WEALTH} \qquad (6.1)$$

Or, expressing the same relationships in terms of flows over time,

$$\triangle \, \text{LIABILITIES} = \triangle \, \frac{\text{REAL}}{\text{ASSETS}} \; + \; \triangle \, \frac{\text{FINANCIAL}}{\text{ASSETS}} \; - \; \text{SAVING} \qquad (6.2)$$

(Remember, the symbol $\triangle$ means "the change in", and from equation 4.3, saving $= \triangle$ wealth).

Equations 6.1 and 6.2 simply state that the decision of a household to go into debt involves a desire to hold assets, real or financial, in excess of the household's wealth. We have assumed that each household is striving to maximize the utility which it expects to derive from its lifetime income. Within the framework of the life cycle hypothesis, what reasons can we discover for household borrowing?

Categories of Borrowing. The first category might be called *transitory borrowing.* A chance illness to the head of the household, which both interrupts the flow of income and creates medical bills, might be the occasion of borrowing, particularly in the case of households which do not have many marketable assets. In terms of the concepts which we developed earlier, this is a case in which income is temporarily depressed below its "permanent" level, and consumption is raised above its "permanent" level. Borrowing is a response to transitory or random factors — an alternative to making more fundamental adjustments to the households "permanent" consumption plans.

In the second category we have borrowing which is part of a deliberate *plan to redistribute consumption over time* — a regular part of the life cycle of the household. A young family with good income prospects, might borrow in order to support a level of present consumption in excess of its present income, planning to repay the accumulated debt out of its expected higher future income. This might well be the case of a married student, paying his way through university with the assistance of loans.

While it is difficult to marshall statistical evidence to support the proposition, it is clear that these two purposes (transistory borrowing and redistributing income over time), account for a relatively small part of the total indebtedness of a typical household. The third category is of much greater importance. That is, *borrowing to finance the acquisition of specific assets.*

The typical household will presumably borrow to accumulate assets when the expected yield on those assets exceeds the expected interest cost on the debt. True, the desire for liquidity may be sufficiently strong that the household may borrow simply to create or maintain its stock of relatively liquid assets, even at some net interest cost to the household. However, the major rationale for borrowing will be the excess of expected yield on assets over the interest cost on liabilities.

In some cases these assets will be financial assets. Many households, particularly relatively high income households, borrow funds to purchase corporate stock upon which they expect to receive a relatively high return. Some of these funds will be borrowed from financial institutions, and some will be borrowed directly from stock brokerage firms. At the end of 1969, customer indebtedness to stock brokers amounted to some $392 million. Individuals also had debts of $573 million to Chartered Banks secured by marketable securities, but a large portion of these loans had probably been used for purposes other than the purchase of securities. In any case, borrowing for the acquisition of financial assets accounts for a small portion of the total indebtedness of the typical household.

Table 6-1
The Life Cycle in Household Debt, Assets and Net Worth

Age: Head of Household	Total Debt	Mortgage Debt	Installment Debt	Other Debt	Total Assets	Net Worth
			(Dollars)			
29 and under	1,950	1,300	390	260	5,977	4,027
30–39	4,660	4,070	330	270	14,728	10,066
40–49	4,860	4,350	270	240	23,726	18,867
50–64	3,050	2,580	240	230	29,317	26,271
65 and over	860	730	50	80	27,598	26,742
All households	3,590	3,080	270	230	20,421	16,830
(percent of total debt)	(100.0)	(86.0)	(7.5)	(6.4)		

Households in Seven Canadian Cities, 1962
Average Per Household

SOURCE: Royal Commission on Banking and Finance, *Appendix Volume* (Ottawa: Queen's Printer, 1964) .

If we take mortgage debt and installment debt outstanding as a measure of household borrowing to acquire real assets, it is apparent from Table 6-1 that household borrowing to finance the acquisition of real assets is the dominant factor in household indebtedness. Well over 90% of the debts of urban households included in the Royal Commission on Banking and Finance survey for 1962 were in these two categories. It is also interesting to note that the indebtedness of these households traces out a distinctive life-cycle pattern, as described in Chapter 4. In the early years, the accumulation of household assets is accompanied by increasing indebtedness. In later years, indebtedness falls off sharply.

The Expected Yield on Real Assets. A rational householder will only borrow to finance the purchase of real assets — a house or household durable goods such as furniture or appliances — if the expected yield on these assets is greater than the interest cost incurred by borrowing. It makes little sense to acquire an illiquid real asset expected to yield 2% per annum, if to do so you have to borrow and pay an interest rate of 12% per annum. Are householders rational in their borrowing decisions?

This is a difficult question to answer empirically since the yield on most household real assets is not monetary. Rather it is in the form of a stream of services consumed directly by the household. There is a market for many of these services (automobile rentals, coin laundries, movie theatres and frozen food lockers are some familiar examples) , and two Canadian economists have taken advantage of this fact to estimate the actual rate of return on selected consumer durables using the prices of equivalent services in the market place. They concluded that the implicit financial yield on the consumer durables owned by the typical household was very high indeed — frequently in excess of 25% per annum.[1] This calculation ignores such intangible values as the convenience, independence or security associated with owning rather than renting the object in question. Taking all things into consideration, the Royal Commission on Banking and Finance concluded:

> Our studies indicate that by and large Canadians manage their finances with greater wisdom than appears to be popularly believed . . . . Most households . . . . have made sensible use of installment and other credit to acquire physical assets that yield them high returns, not only in financial terms but in terms of convenience and ease of household living.[2]

This statement sounds faintly like a comfortable platitude, and certainly, the Royal Commissioners notwithstanding, if one allows for such intangible elements in the returns on consumer durables as "convenience and ease of household living", the true yield on such assets is impossible to measure. However, the point of relevance for us is that if households make some rough "calculation" of this sort, given the implicit yield on real assets, households should be less willing to borrow at higher interest rates. That is, *the supply of financial instruments from households should be an increasing function of the yield on consumer durable goods, and a decreasing function of the level of interest rates in financial markets* (i.e., of the yield on financial instruments).

Since the yield on consumer durables cannot be measured, this is a very difficult proposition to test. Numerous attempts have been made to identify the sensitivity of consumer borrowing to changes in the level of intterest rates. The results of such tests are at best inconclusive. However, most economists feel that such a relationship does exist, although it may be relatively weak.

The Corporate Sector

Most business firms are engaged in the production of goods and services for sale in the market place with a primary objective of making profit. The exceptions to the profit-seeking characterization of businesses are sufficiently unimportant that we can ignore them. Why should a profit-seeking business borrow funds?

Financing Real Capital Formation. As in the case of households, the primary, but not exclusive, purpose of borrowing by business firms is to finance the purchase or construction of real assets, capital goods to be used in the process of production (including inventories of raw materials, goods in process of production and finished goods awaiting sale) . The issuance of financial instruments, whether stocks or bonds, is not the only method of financing capital formation. A firm could also draw down holdings of financial assets accumulated in the past, or it could finance it out of "business saving". By business saving we mean that portion of the gross revenue of the firm which is not used to pay out-of-pocket costs such as wages, costs of raw materials purchased, interest on debts, etc., or is not paid out to the stockholders in the form of dividends. It is, in other words, the firm's capital consumption allowances plus its retained profits.

Millions of Dollars

Total Business Fixed Capital Formation

Gross Business Saving

Figure 6-1

Net New Issues of Corporate Securities

In Figure 6-1 we have presented some data to show the relationship between business borrowing and business capital expenditures. It should be noted that business saving in fact provides by far the largest portion of the funds required by businesses. However, the point of importance to us is the relatively close correspondence between business capital expenditures and the issuance of new corporate securities.

Interest Rates and the Yield on Capital Goods. Just as households cannot ignore the time dimension in planning consumption so as to maximize utility, business firms cannot take a static approach to the maximization of profits. The management must not only plan production with the production facilities presently at its disposal, it must also plan the expansion of those production facilities, at a rate and in directions which will maximize profits which the firm expects to receive in the future. This means that the management of the profit-maximizing firm must be continually alert for opportunities for capital expansion in which the expected yield will exceed the interest cost of the funds required to finance the expansion. Thus, the willingness of corporations to borrow, and hence the supply of financial instruments from corporations, should be directly dependent on the expected yield on real capital, and inversely dependent on the level of interest rates in the market. The higher the expected yield on real assets, the greater the volume of borrowing to be expected; the higher the level of interest rates (or expected yields on financial instruments), the smaller the volume of borrowing.

The Government Sector

The borrowing decisions in the government sector have some points of similarity with those in the household and corporate sectors, and some notable differences, particularly at the federal government level.

Provincial and Municipal Borrowing. Consider borrowing by the junior governments in Canada. The stock of outstanding provincial and municipal bonds for the period 1939-1968 is shown in Figure 6-2, and the relationship between junior government borrowing and capital expenditures in Figure 6-3. It is apparent from the latter chart that borrowing by provincial and municipal governments is closely related to provincial and municipal capital expenditures. The market rise in the outstanding debt of these governments in the 1950's and 1960's reflects a corresponding sharp rise in expenditures for social capital — highways, bridges, hospitals, schools, and so on. The trend in these figures is quite startling.

Expected Yield and Interest Rates. It is possible to think of social capital providing a yield to society. The rational government official, then, will only borrow to finance a capital project when the yield on the real assets exceeds the interest cost of the funds required to finance the expenditure. As in the case of real assets in the consumer sector, however, the returns on social capital are mainly non-monetary. Although there are some exceptions, the returns take the form of a stream of services, consumed collectively by the members of the society, with no (or perhaps a nominal) charge. The calculation of the yield on these assets requires the imputation of value to these services.

In principle, the supply of financial instruments from junior governments should be responsive to the level of interest rates. Like borrowing in the consumer and corporate sectors, borrowing by junior governments is

Figure 6-2
The Stock of Government Bonds, 1939-1968

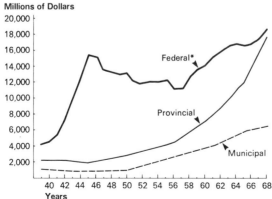

* Federal bonds outstanding net of bonds held by the Bank of Canada and federal government accounts.

Figure 6-3
Net Government Borrowing and Government Capital Expenditures, 1948-1969

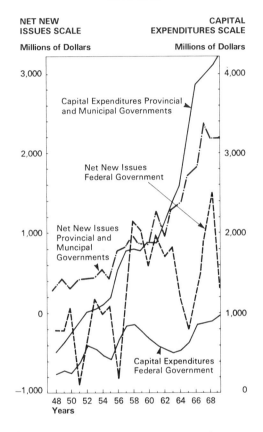

mainly to provide durable real assets which can be expected to provide a yield to the members of the society. The borrowing decision should involve a comparison of yield and interest cost: the higher the interest rate, the fewer the projects which will provide a yield in excess of interest cost, and the smaller the amount of borrowing.

The Federal Government. Borrowing by the federal government has a radically different character. Like all other sectors, the federal government borrows when its revenues fall short of its expenditures. However, as should be evident in Figure 6-3, there is no clearly definable relationship between federal capital expenditures and federal borrowing (indeed if there is such a relationship, it is inverse).

A glance at Figure 6-2 reveals that the net borrowing which accounts for most of the existing stock of federal government bonds occurred in two periods, 1940-1945 and 1958-1963. The former was the period of World War II, and the latter a period of relative stagnation in the Canadian economy. Indeed, if we omit exceptional events such as major wars, the bulk of the borrowing by the federal government is related to the general state of the national economy. When unemployment is high, the government tends to run a deficit in its budget and hence must borrow. In periods of high levels of economic activity, the opposite is true. For reasons which were explored in your principles of economics course, this is not only an automatic response to fluctuations in economic activity, it is a desirable response. The federal borrowing decision should be related to economic conditions in Canada, not to capital expenditures by the Federal government.

The Borrowing Decision: Summary

In all but the federal government sector, the borrowing decision is primarily related to the decision to acquire real assets. Thus, the supply of financial instruments from the consumer, corporate and junior government sectors is closely related to capital expenditures by these sectors (including the purchase of household durables as capital expenditures).

The capital expenditure decision can be considered as a process of comparing the yield on real assets with the interest cost of borrowed fund — i.e., with the expected yield on financial instruments. The higher the level of interest rates for any given level of expected yields on real assets, the less likely that any particular capital project will be undertaken. As a result, the supply of financial instruments from these sectors should be an inverse function of the level of interest rates.

The federal government is an exception to all of these generalizations. Peacetime borrowing by the federal government is more closely related to the level of economic activity than to the level of federal government capital expenditures.

3/THE LIABILITY BALANCE DECISION

Having decided to borrow, the household, corporation or government agency must choose the type of financial instrument to be issued. For the most part this is a question of whether to issue a long-term or a short-term bond, but in the case of a corporation there is also the question of whether to issue bonds or stocks.

This subject is far too complex for us to explore here. However, it should be clear that there is a parallel set of considerations to those which we discussed in connection with the portfolio balance decision on the demand side of the market.

Relative Yields. One consideration, clearly, must be the relative yields on financial instruments in the market. Other things being equal, the borrower will want to pay as low an effective interest rate as possible. As a result, he will be inclined to issue those financial instruments with the lowest effective yield.

Liquidity. Relative interest costs are not the only considerations. Liquidity may also be important. However, from the point of view of the borrower, rather than being a desirable property of a financial instrument, liquidity will normally be an undesirable property. You will recall that liquid instruments are short-term intsruments. A debtor with a major portion of his debt in liquid form, faces the risk of having to redeem these securities on short notice. If his assets will only yield returns over a long period of time, this can cause severe financial difficulties.

There are exceptions, of course. Some of the assets financed through borrowing may yield their returns over a short period of time. This would be true of inventories, for example. Thus, a firm with a fluctuating level of inventories might find that short-term liabilities are the most appropriate types.

Speculation. There are other exceptions to the general undesirability of liquidity as well. In particular, when interest rates are relatively high, borrowers may wish to speculate on a fall in interest rates in the future. Rather than contract for a long-term debt at relatively high interest rates, they may borrow on short term, planning to refinance the debt with long-term bonds when interest rates fall.

Borrower's Risk. Borrowers also assume a risk, of course, in committing themselves to fixed future payments. The assets, which they count on to provide the income to meet these payments, may not return the expected yield. This will affect the choice between stocks and bonds as financial instruments to be issued. If it is financed through common stock, inadequate returns on the asset will not force the firm into bankruptcy court (although if the venture is successful beyond expectations, the additional returns must be shared with the new stockholders).

Borrower's risk may also affect the borrowing decision. Any risk-averting borrower will demand an expected return substantially in excess of the interest rate on borrowed funds to compensate for borrower's risk before he will undertake the venture.

Inflation and Taxation. Expectations of inflation and taxation will also affect the choice between types of instruments to be issued. The effects are the opposite of those discussed previously in connection with the demand for such instruments. For example, expectations of continued rapid inflation would induce borrowers to borrow on as long-term a basis as possible, since future fixed-sum payments would be paid off in "cheap" inflated dollars.

A Note on the Federal Government

As in the case of the borrowing decision, the federal government should be (but is not always) an exception to all that we have said about the liability balance decision. The considerations governing the structure of the federal debt should be related to the general state of economic conditions rather than the range of considerations entering into the liability balance decisions of other spending units. This is a topic which we will consider in Chapters 20 and 23.

The Liability Balance Decision: Conclusions

Just as the assetholder must choose among alternative assets to be held, so the debtor must choose among alternative types of instruments to be issued. In general, the considerations entering into the debtor's choices are the same as those entering into the assetholder's choices, but they work in the opposite direction. Thus, debtors tend to prefer low-yielding instruments (to them, the yield is a cost) and to avoid liquidity. Risk aversion would probably lead them to issue variable income rather than fixed income securities. The important point to note, however, is that just as all financial instruments are substitutes for each other in asset portfolios, so they are substitutes for each other as methods of borrowing funds. A change in the yield on one financial instrument will not only set in train adjustments in the composition of asset portfolios, it will also lead to changes in methods used by borrowers to finance their current deficits.

4/MARKET EQUILIBRIUM

Until now, our discussion of the market for financial instruments has been primarily an analysis of the determinants of the behaviour of the individual participants in the market — the households, business firms and government agencies which are the ultimate lenders and borrowers. We examined how each participant might make decisions about the size and composition of his asset or liability portfolio by taking into account his reactions to liquidity and risk, and by taking the prices — or better, the expected yields — on the instruments as given. However, we cannot take prices and yields as given. They are determined in the market place through the interaction of the demand and supply forces which result from the portfolio selection decision of all of the individual borrowers and lenders. It is one aspect of the process by which the market allocates credit among all alternative possible uses.

Equilibrium Price

Equilibrium price is a familiar concept in economics: it is a price which, under existing conditions of demand and supply, has no tendency to change. Prices tend to rise under the pressure of excess demand, and to fall under the pressure of excess supply. An equilibrium price, therefore, is a price at which there is neither excess demand nor excess supply: a price at which market demand and supply are in balance. In the context of financial markets, this means a set of expected yields on financial instruments such that there is neither an excess demand for nor an excess supply of any category of financial instrument.

In a more advanced textbook the concept of equilibrium in financial markets would be the subject of very careful and extensive analysis. It is a difficult concept, because it involves two dimensions — stocks and flows. As we have seen, we can talk about supply both as a *stock* at a *point in time* (the stock of financial instruments outstanding) and as a *flow* over a *period of time* (the flow of net borrowing). Likewise we can talk of the demand for financial instruments as a stock (the desired stock at a *point in time*) and a *flow* (the flow of net saving over *a period of time*). A thorough analysis of financial equilibrium, which is beyond the scope of the present discussion, would have to explore both dimensions and to examine the interrelationships between them. For now, certain elementary points should be kept in mind.

Stock Equilibrium. If we could stop the clock and look at financial markets at a point in time, we would be faced with a situation in which the quantities of financial instruments outstanding are given. Given time, new securities can be issued, and existing securities retired. However, at any instant, the quantities are fixed by the cumulative effects of past history. In the immediate past, transactions in the market established a set of prices (and hence expected yields) for those securities. For this set of prices to be an equilibrium set in a stock sense, assetholders must have no incentive to alter the composition of their portfolios. *They must be content to hold the existing quantities of securities at the prevailing market prices for those securities.* This is the condition for stock equilibrium.

Suppose this is not the case and that there is a group of assetholders who feel that the market price for some of the securities which they are holding is too high (i.e., the expected yield is too low) relative to those on other assets (e.g. other securities, money, or physical assets). If we could somehow permit trading of securities without allowing time to pass (i.e., without changing the outstanding stocks of securities and other factors affecting demand and supply conditions), these assetholders would offer to sell what they consider to be the overpriced securities, and would submit bids for the underpriced securities. Since the quantities of these securities cannot change, the only effects of these transactions can be to rearrange portfolios (if the securities exist, some assetholder must have them in his portfolio) and to change prices. The price of the overvalued securities will be bid down, and the price of the underpriced security bid up, the adjustments presumably continuing until stock equilibrium is established.

In one case, which will assume major importance in our later analysis, it may be that assetholders in general have more money in their portfolios than is consistent with portfolio balance at existing prices and expected yields on securities. They will attempt to dispose of money in exchange for securities. This attempt at shifting portfolios will lead to a bidding up of the prices of all securities, (a lowering of interest rates). Neither the stock of money nor the stock of securities can change (remember we assumed them to be fixed in number) yet the level (and perhaps the structure) of interest rates will change.

It is this change in interest rates which allows the public to achieve portfolio balance with the given stock of money. The opposite adjustment would occur if there were an excess demand for money.

Flow Equilibrium. This analysis of the adjustment of prices and expected yields in the face of stock disequilibrium is highly artificial because it implies the passing of time without any changes in the external environment. However, time does pass, and as it does, the basic determinants of portfolio balance decisions change. The outlook for particular industries and hence the expected returns on outstanding securities and the expected yield on new physical capital formation, changes. Physical capital can be created or depleted. Income is generated, and consumption and saving occur. Government policy can be implemented or changed. Commodity price levels may rise or fall, perhaps accompanied by changes in employment levels. Expectations with respect to any of a great variety of relevant developments — including future security prices — may change slightly or drastically.

All of these considerations come to bear on two vital flows. First, as time passes borrowers can issue new securities and debtors can retire outstanding issues. Both the size and the structure of the stock of financial instruments available to be held will probably change. Second, the flow of saving during the period increases the size of assetholdings, thus increasing the demand for financial instruments. Dissaving has the opposite effect, or course. *Over that period of time, the prices* (and hence expected yields) *on financial instruments must adjust so that the increasing demands for financial instruments resulting from the flow of saving is just offset by the increasing stock of financial instruments resulting from borrowing to finance capital and other expenditures* (Remember: both the saving decision and the borrowing decision should be sensitive to the level of interest rates, although perhaps in varying degrees). This, then, is the condition for flow equilibrium.

It should be evident from what has been said that what we mean by "flow" equilibrium is in fact "stock" equilibrium at successive points in time, with the basic determinants of equilibrium changing from instant to instant.

Market Equilibrium and Resource Allocation

Most microeconomic theory focuses attention on the determination of relative prices in equilibrium. However, the underlying concern is always the allocation of scarce resources among alternative possible uses. Whether in the markets for bread and bicycles, or the markets for financial instruments, the process of price determination takes on importance because it is at the core of the process by which production and employment decisions are made in a market economy.

What is being allocated in the market for financial instruments is credit. Thus, the price of financial instruments not only determines the yield to assetholders, it also determines the cost of funds to borrowers. The yield to assetholders should affect savings decisions, thus affecting the share of income devoted to consumption and the share available to finance capital formation. The interest cost to borrowers should affect their willingness to engage in deficit spending, whether for consumption or capital formation. *Thus, the determination of equilibrium prices in financial markets should influence choices between present and future consumption, as well as the pace and industrial composition of capital formation.*

Market Equilibrium and Government Policy

There is also another aspect of equilibrium in financial markets which must be noted. We have seen that all financial instruments are more or less close substitutes, both as assets which might be held by assetholders and as liabilities which might be issued by debtors. This means that the markets for the various types of financial instruments cannot be considered separately. They are tightly interconnected, such that a disturbance to equilibrium in one market will also involve disturbances in others. But, as we have just noted, the prices of financial instruments also enter into decisions on consumption and public and private capital formation. This opens up the possibility that the government can engage in operations in the financial markets — altering the size of the outstanding stock of certain financial instruments, (e.g. government debt, money) — for the purpose of altering the level of expenditures on consumer goods and capital goods. It creates the possibility of a monetary policy to regulate the level of aggregrate demand for goods and services.

This is the topic of the second half of the book.

5/A QUANTITATIVE PERSPECTIVE ON CANADIAN FINANCIAL MARKETS

The past three chapters have been concerned primarily with theoretical abstractions. Perhaps it would be useful at this point to anchor the discussion in the real world by providing a brief overview of the flow of funds through the Canadian financial system.

The Financial Flow Accounts

In 1969, as part of a program to develop a comprehensive system of national accounts, the Dominion Bureau of Statistics began publishing a new set of data, the *financial flow accounts*.[3] When fully developed these data will be uniquely valuable for the analysis of financial activity in Canada. Unfortunately, the accounts are still incomplete (estimates of the stock of financial assets held are not available for some major sectors) and the known errors in the preliminary estimates are rather large. However, in what follows we use these preliminary estimates to describe some of the more important characteristics of the flow of funds through the Canadian financial system in 1969.

Sources and Uses of Saving

The financial flow accounts are, in the first instance, a statement of the sources and uses of saving in Canada. They show the gross and net saving generated in each of several "sectors" of the economy, and the corresponding gross real capital formation in each sector. The difference between saving and capital formation for any sector is its net lending or net borrowing: in our terminology, its financial surplus or financial deficit.

Table 6-2
Saving and Capital Formation in Canada, 1969
(millions of dollars)

	HOUSEHOLD SECTOR	BUSINESS SECTOR			GOVERNMENT SECTOR*		REST OF WORLD	TOTAL	DISCREPANCY	TOTAL
		Unincorp. Business	Corporate Business	Financial Intermed.	Federal	Prov. & Municipal		Sector Estimates		National Accounts
Capital Consumption Allowance		2,674	4,709	241				7,624	1,261	8,885
Net Saving	3,787		936	322	1,770	2,927	967	10,709	238	10,947
Residual error of estimate									−899	−899
GROSS DOMESTIC SAVING	3,787	2,674	5,645	563	1,770	2,927	967	18,333	600	18,933
GROSS REAL CAPITAL FORMATION	207	4,854	9,210	275	478	2,332	173	17,529	1,404	18,933
NET SURPLUS (+) OR NET DEFICIT (−)	+3,580	−2,180	−3,565	+288	+1,292	+595	+794	+804	−804	0

* Division of Social Security Funds between Federal and Provincial/Municipal Sectors estimated by authors.

SOURCE: *Canadian Statistical Review*, Vol. 45 (July 1970).

Sectors. In the financial flow accounts, a sector is defined as a grouping of economic units which share "certain common traits". They are, in fact, the familiar groupings of spending units — households; unincorporated businesses (which include households in their capacity as owner-occupiers of houses); public and private corporations; federal, provincial and municipal governments; financial institutions; and the rest-of-the-world. Data are provided for thirteen major sectors, and twice as many sub-sectors, although in constructing Table 6-2 we have consolidated these into seven sectors.

Surplus Sectors. As is evident in Table 6-2, the major source of financial surpluses in the Canadian economy in 1969 was the saving of *households.* This has been consistently the case in recent years (Table 6-3). It should be remembered, in this connection, that in the definition of sector, the activity of owning houses is included in the business sector.[4] That is, in the national accounts tradition, a household which owns a house is *in that respect* classified as an unincorporated business, even if it occupies the house itself. An owner-occupier is in the business of renting a house to himself; appropriate estimates of the implicit rental income and rental expense are included in the national income and expenditure accounts, and any new investment in housing is recorded as capital expenditure by unincorporated businesses. Thus, the apparent financial surpluses of the household sector do not take into account household investment in houses.

Table 6-3
Financial Surpluses in the Household Sector, 1962-1969

	Surplus (Millions of Dollars)
1962	2,467
1963	2,679
1964	1,977
1965	2,978
1966	4,211
1967	4,183
1968	3,278
1969	3,580

SOURCES: Dominion Bureau of Statistics, *Financial Flow Accounts, 1962-1967: A Preliminary Report* (Ottawa, 1969); *Canadian Statistical Review,* Vol. 45 (July 1970).

In 1969 the *government sectors* were also a net source of financial surpluses, although, as Table 6-4 shows, 1969 was not fully typical of recent experience. In general, municipal governments tend to be a net deficit sector, and the provincial governments a net surplus sector. The implementation of the Canada Pension Plan and the Quebec Pension Plan in 1966 significantly increased the share of the nation's savings which are directed through the government sectors.

Table 6-4
Financial Surpluses and Deficits in the Government Sector, 1962-1969

		Surplus or Deficit (−) (Millions of Dollars)			
	Federal	Provincial	Municipal	Municipal & Provincial	Total
1962	−572	95	−414	−319	−891
1963	−332	32	−451	−419	−751
1964	331	154	−477	−323	8
1965	608	284	−590	−306	302
1966	687	306	−701	−395	292
1967	403	75	−442	−367	36
1968	561	n.a.	n.a.	179	740
1969	1,289	n.a.	n.a.	596	1,885

SOURCES: Dominion Bureau of Statistics, *Financial Flow Accounts, 1962-1967: A Preliminary Report* (Ottawa, 1969); *Canadian Statistical Review*, Vol. 45 (July 1970).

Table 6-5
Financial Surpluses in the Rest-of-the-World Sector, 1962-1969

	Surplus (Millions of Dollars)
1962	874
1963	541
1964	424
1965	1,130
1966	1,137
1967	425
1968	109
1969	794

SOURCES: Dominion Bureau of Statistics, *Financial Flow Accounts, 1962-1967: A Preliminary Report* (Ottawa, 1969); *Canadian Statistical Review*, Vol. 45 (July 1970).

Finally, the importance of the *rest-of-the-world* as a net source of funds for investment in Canada should be noted. While the magnitude of the net surplus has varied from time to time (Table 6-5), the rest-of-the-world sector has been a net provider of funds consistently in recent years. Moreover as we shall see more clearly in the following chapter and in our discussion of monetary policy later in the book, the magnitude of the rest-of-the-world sector's contribution to gross domestic saving significantly understates the impact of world financial markets on the Canadian financial system. This will become an important theme in our later analysis.

Deficit Sectors. During 1969 the financial surpluses of the nation were absorbed, on balance, in what we have called the business sector. As we noted above, in some earlier years the *government sector,* and particularly the municipal government sector, was also in deficit. However, the persistent, large excesses of real capital formation over gross saving in recent years have been in publicly and privately owned firms producing goods and services for sale (Table 6-6).

A significant part of the *business sector's* deficit is always accounted for by unincorporated businesses, particularly residential housing. We have grouped public corporations (like the Canadian National Railways or Quebec Hydro) together with private corporations in the corporate sector. This group of firms consistently accounts for the largest part of the business deficit. For the purposes of Table 6-6 we have also assigned financial intermediaries to the business sector (although we will consider them separately in later discussion). Unlike other business firms, financial intermediaries have consistently had a financial surplus in recent years. However, as in the case of the rest-of-the-world sector, the net surplus or deficit is not a reliable index of the importance of financial intermediaries in the financial system. What it shows is simply the difference between gross saving (capital consumption allowances and undistributed profits) and real capital formation by financial intermediaries. The fact that the financial intermediaries have been a small surplus sector simply means that they have been more than able to finance their own capital expansion out of their own gross savings.

Balancing the Table. There are two accounting rules which must be applied to the financial flow accounts. The accounts must *balance,* and they must *reconcile* with the national income accounts. The balancing requirement is that the sum of gross domestic saving for all sectors must equal the sum of gross real capital formation for all sectors, such that the aggregate financial deficit or surplus for all sectors combined is zero. The reconciliation requirement is that aggregates such as gross domestic saving or gross real capital formation must equal their counterparts from the *national income and expenditure accounts.*

A glance at Table 6-2 demonstrates that these accounting rules do not hold. In some accounts the discrepancies are very large.

There are two types of errors which have to be allowed for in balancing the financial flow accounts and reconciling them with the national income accounts. The first is the residual error in the national income accounts themselves, an error which arises because of discrepancies between two different measures of national income. This error ($-899 million in 1969) is recorded in the last column of Table 6-2 as an adjustment to the sum of capital consumption allowances and net saving (which have been estimated separately) to obtain gross domestic saving (= gross real capital formation, estimated separately). The second is the set of errors which arise in the financial flow accounts themselves, giving rise to discrepancies between the sum of estimates for the sectors and the corresponding amounts shown in the national income accounts. These statistical discrepancies are recorded in the second-to-last column, "Discrepancy".

Table 6-6
Financial Surpluses and Deficits in the Business Sectors, 1962-1969

| | Surplus or Deficit (−) (Millions of Dollars) | | | |
	Unincorporated Businesses	Public & Private Corporations	Financial Intermediaries	Total
1962	− 698	−1,360	134	−1,924
1963	− 715	−1,381	100	−1,996
1964	− 810	−1,803	156	−2,457
1965	−1,424	−3,103	245	−4,282
1966	−1,271	−5,003	153	−6,121
1967	−1,320	−3,707	254	−4,773
1968	−1,198	−3,333	487	−4,044
1969	−2,180	−3,565	290	−5,455

SOURCES: Dominion Bureau of Statistics, *Financial Flow Accounts, 1962-1967: A Prelimi-nary Report* (Ottawa, 1969) ; *Canadian Statistical Review*, Vol. 45 (July 1970).

Financial Transactions Among Sectors

The financial flow accounts are more than a statement of the sources and uses of saving, by sector. They are also a fairly detailed statement of the types of financial assets and liabilities acquired by each sector during the period in question. Thus, the financial flow data provide insights into the asset and liability preferences of members of the various sectors, and permit some analysis of the financial transactions among sectors. Table 6-7 is a condensation of the financial transactions data for 1969.

Reading the Table. While it may appear somewhat formidable, Table 6-7 is actually quite simple.

The *rows* of the table relate to *financial instruments*, the names of which are listed at the left of the table. Each row shows the *net change during the year* 1969 in the value of a particular financial instrument held by (an asset = A) or issued by (a liability = L) each of the six sectors. For example, the first row tells us, among other things, that households increased their holdings of money market instruments (treasury bills, commercial paper and finance paper) to the extent of $203 million over the year, and corporations increased the value of their short-term marketable debt outstanding by $302 million. Similarly, the second to last row in the body of the table tells us, among other things, that households reduced their holdings of foreign securities by $262 million, and the rest-of-the-world reduced their total liabilities to Canadians in this form by $154 million.

It is important to remember that the assets of one sector are the liabilities of some other sector or sectors. This fact imposes an accounting rule on the table. Thus, if we add, along a row, the change in the holdings of a particular financial asset by all sectors, the total should equal the change in the total value of all sectors' liabilities in that form. Taking the

Table 6-7

Financial Transactions Among Sectors, 1969 (millions of dollars)

Net Change Of:	Household Sector			Business Sector					
				Unincorporated Business			Corporations		
	A	L	S or D	A	L	S or D	A	L	S or D
Fixed Income Securities									
Short-term Marketable Instruments	203						1	302	
Canadian Bonds:									
Government	− 9						31	443	
Corporate	22						− 57	780	
Canadian Loans:									
Consumer Credit		1,259		8			102		
Other Loans		− 266			803		522	1,856	
Mortgages					2,226		10	188	
Claims on Financial Intermediaries									
Currency and Deposits	1,696						− 324		
Life Insurance and Pensions	1,539								
Variable Income Securities									
Canadian Stocks	− 591						209	1,266	
Equity in Associated Enterprises	− 655				− 555		591	749	
Foreign Currency Investments									
Currency and Deposits	1,615						382		
Other Foreign Investments	− 262						180		
Other Financial Assets/Liabilities				186			690	− 35	
NET CHANGE	3,558	993	2,565	194	2,374	−2,180	2,337	5,549	−3,212
Discrepancy			1,015						− 353
NET SURPLUS OR DEFICIT (Table 6-2)			3,580			−2,180			−3,565

A = **F**inancial Assets; L = Liabilities; S or D = Net Financial Surplus or Deficit = A − L
SOURCES: As for Table 6-2.

(continued . . .)

Table 6-7 (. . . concluded)

Financial Transactions Among Sectors, 1969 (millions of dollars)

Net Change Of:	Government Sector			Rest-of-the-World			Financial Intermediaries			Total		
	A	L	S or D	A	L	S or D	A	L	S or D	A	L	S or D
Fixed Income Securities												
Short-term Marketable Instruments	14	70		248			304	398		770	770	0
Canadian Bonds:												
Government	1,455	1,990		1,042			37	123		2,556	2,556	0
Corporate	218			446			286	135		915	915	0
Canadian Loans:												
Consumer Credit	285						1,149			1,259	1,259	0
Other Loans	223	74		42	76		2,044	350		2,893	2,893	0
Mortgages							2,185	4		2,418	2,418	0
Claims on Financial Intermediaries												
Currency and Deposits	1,028	345		61			169	2,285		2,630	2,630	0
Life Insurance and Pensions		− 3						1,542		1,539	1,539	0
Variable Income Securities												
Canadian Stocks	29			257			636	393		540	1,659	−1,119
Equity in Associated Enterprises	1,538	29		694	255		200	871		2,368	1,249	1,119
Foreign Currency Investments												
Currency and Deposits	− 212				1,923		138			1,923	1,923	0
Other Foreign Investments	− 31				− 154		− 41			− 154	− 154	0
Other Financial Assets/ Liabilities	− 351	− 122		− 191	− 223		− 312	402		22	22	0
NET CHANGE	4,196	2,383	1,813	2,599	1,877	722	6,795	6,503	292	19,679	19,679	0
Discrepancy			72			72			− 2			− 804
NET SURPLUS OR DEFICIT (Table 6-2)			1,885			794			290			804

A = Financial Assets; L = Liabilities; S or D = Net Financial Surplus or Deficit = A − L

SOURCES: As for Table 6-2.

first row again, the increase in the total value of money market instruments held by households, corporations, government, the rest-of-the-world, and financial intermediaries was $704 million. This was the same as the increase of the money market instrument liabilities of corporations, governments and financial intermediaries during the year. Therefore, as the last column shows, the excess of the increase of assets over the increase of liabilities in that form was zero.

If you examine the table, you will see that there are two exceptions to this accounting rule, the row "Canadian Stocks" and the row "Claims on Affiliated Enterprises". The discrepancies arise in this case because of difficulties in collecting data to separate stock holdings from other types of financial advances by corporations to affiliated corporations. If the two rows are added together, however, the accounting rule holds.

The *columns* of Table 6-7 relate to *sectors*. Each sector has three columns: one (A) in which the *net change* in the sector's holdings of each type of financial asset is recorded; one (L) in which the *net change* in each of the sector's liabilities is recorded; and one $(S$ or $D)$ which shows the surplus or deficit for the sector as measured by the difference between the recorded net change in its total financial assets and the recorded net change in its liabilities. In principle, the surplus or deficit measured in this way should be the same as the financial surplus or deficit reported for that sector in Table 6-2. In practice, since different sources of information are involved, the two totals are seldom the same. The discrepancies for 1969 are shown at the foot of the table.

With this interpretation of the table in mind, we can consider what it tells us about the pattern of financial activity in Canada in 1969.

Household Sector. Consider first the household sector. The household sector had a net financial *surplus* in 1969, i.e., its financial assets increased by more than its liabilities. As we saw earlier, this was quite typical. In some other respects, however, the pattern of the households' financial behaviour in 1969 was not typical of earlier years. In particular, households appear to have made unusual reductions in their holdings of Canadian stocks and foreign investments, to have acquired unusually small amounts of Canadian bonds, and to have made unusually large increases in their holdings of foreign currency and foreign deposits.[5] In most years for which data are available, households devoted part of their resources to the acquisition of Canadian stocks and bonds and foreign securities, and investments in foreign currency and deposits were much less important.

Leaving these matters aside, the important point to note is the dominant role of financial intermediaries in the financial transactions of households. In 1969, as in most years, claims on financial intermediaries accounted for the largest part of the total increase in households' financial assets, and loans extended by financial intermediaries (particularly as "consumer credit") dominated the increase in their liabilities.

The Business Sector. As we noted earlier, the distinction between households and unincorporated businesses is somewhat artificial, particularly in respect to owner-occupied houses. It is therefore not surprising that as in the household sector, the striking characteristic of the financial transactions of *unincorporated business* is the dominant role played by financial intermediaries. This is true both with respect to the provision of mortgage credit for the construction of houses, and with respect to credit for other business activities. The offsetting entries in the category "Claims on Associated Enterprises" which appear in the accounts of both the household and the unincorporated business sectors reflect changes in householders' equity in unincorporated business, including primarily equity in the housing stock.

The situation is very different for businesses organized as *corporations*. The range of financing options is much wider, and the patterns of financial activity correspondingly much more complex. A range of financial instruments which can be sold in the open market assume much greater importance, as do financial transactions between parent companies and subsidiaries, and between governments and crown corporations. Transactions with financial intermediaries, particularly in the form of loans (recorded in the category "other loans"), are not negligible but they are far from dominant. However, another sector does assume major importance: the rest-of-the-world. Although the net inflow of funds from the rest-of-the-world was relatively small in 1969, it absorbed a major share of certain types of financial instruments issued by corporations, particularly long-term bonds and short-term money market instruments. The importance of the direct investment of funds by foreign parent firms in Canadian subsidiaries is also apparent in the category "Claims on Associated Enterprises".

Government Sector. The pattern of governmental financial activity is as complex as that of corporations. Part of the complexity arises because governments simultaneously acquire large quantities of funds in the market by issuing a variety of financial instruments, but particularly longer-term bonds, and advance funds both to other levels of government and to business enterprises (particularly government-owned corporations). Like corporations, governments have important transactions with financial intermediaries, but financial intermediaries are far from dominant in their activities. Also like corporations, governments have important transactions with the rest-of-the-world.

The Rest-of-the-World and Financial Intermediaries. This brief survey of the characteristics of financial flows in Canada suggests that our discussion of the theory of financial markets is seriously deficient in two respects. We have not explored the nature and significance of the international connection of our financial markets or of financial intermediaries. Given their quantitative importance in financial flows, we must correct this deficiency, a task undertaken in the next five chapters.

FOOTNOTES

[1] J. V. Poapst, and W. R. Walters, "Rates of Return on Consumer Durables," in *Journal of Finance*, Vol. XIX, No. 4 (Dec. 1964), pp. 673-677.
[2] Royal Commission on Banking and Finance, *Report*, p. 31.

[3] Dominion Bureau of Statistics, *Financial Flow Accounts, 1962-67: A Preliminary Report* (Ottawa: Queen's Printer, 1969).

[4] The rationale for this treatment of owner-occupancy of houses is discussed in Dominion Bureau of Statistics, *National Accounts, Income and Expenditure, 1926-1956* (Ottawa: Queen's Printer, 1958), p. 106.

[5] As the Dominion Bureau of Statistics acknowledges, the estimates for the household sector in the *Financial Flow Accounts,* are not very satisfactory. Indeed, since the sector's accounts are estimated as a residual from all of the other estimates, they reflect the net effects of all the errors in all the other accounts. Perhaps we should not place too much emphasis on the erratic behaviour of such difficult-to-estimate items as household holdings of stocks, bonds, foreign investments and equity in unincorporated businesses.

7

Elementary Theory of Financial Markets, Part 4:

International Aspects of Market Equilibrium

Our discussion of the flow of funds at the end of the previous chapter demonstrated the importance of international financial transactions. These transactions are facilitated by the fact noted in Chapter 3, that many of the institutions of the Canadian financial system are international in scope. An important question remaining to be answered is: What difference does the international connection make in the determination of equilibrium in Canadian financial markets?

1/WIDENING THE FIELD OF CHOICE

One obvious implication of this international connection is that it broadens the range of alternatives open to both assetholders and borrowers in Canada and in other countries. Canadian assetholders have the option of holding claims on non-residents as well as on residents of Canada. Thus they can purchase stocks and bonds of American corporations and governments (or similar securities issued in other countries) almost as easily as they can purchase the stocks and bonds of Canadian corporations and governments. Similarly, Canadian borrowers have the option of borrowing in financial markets throughout the world, as well as in the Canadian markets. (Or, putting the same proposition the other way around, non-residents have the option of holding claims on Canadian debtors as well as claims on debtors resident in their own countries.)

2/INTERNATIONAL YIELD DIFFERENTIALS AND MARKET EQUILIBRIUM

The widening of the field of choice for Canadian assetholders and debtors is important in itself. It should permit a much closer matching of asset holdings with asset preferences than would be possible with a narrower range of choice. However, the international connections of the Canadian financial system also impose a powerful constraint on the equilibrium level of security yields in Canada.

This conclusion follows from our earlier conclusion that expected yield is a major consideration in the selection of assets to be included in a portfolio, and the parallel conclusion on the liability side that the interest cost is an important consideration in the borrowing decisions. Given relatively easy access to foreign financial markets, it follows that both Canadian assetholders and Canadian borrowers should turn to these markets when there is a significant yield advantage to be gained in doing so. Indeed, if expected yield were the only consideration in portfolio management, Canadian assetholders would switch from Canadian to foreign securities whenever the expected yield on foreign securities exceeded that obtainable on comparable Canadian securities. Similarly, Canadian borrowers would borrow in foreign markets if the interest cost of doing so were less than the interest cost involved in borrowing in the Canadian market. Presumably foreign assetholders and borrowers would behave in a like fashion. Thus, higher yields in Canada would lead foreign assetholders to purchase Canadian securities (the counterpart of Canadians borrowing abroad), and lower yields in Canada would induce foreign borrowers to raise funds in the Canadian market (the counterpart of Canadians purchasing new foreign securities).

But that is not the end of the matter. Behaviour of this sort on the part of Canadian and foreign borrowers and assetholders will tend to equalize the yields on comparable securities in world markets. Thus, if Canadian security yields are relatively high, the combination of foreigners purchasing Canadian securities, and Canadians borrowing in foreign capital markets should depress yields in Canada while simultaneously increasing yields in

Figure 7-1
Quarterly Yields on U.S. and Canadian Long-term Federal Government
Securities

foreign capital markets. In this manner Canadian yields and foreign yields tend to be drawn together. In fact, it is not too much of a simplification to say that Canadian yields will be drawn to world, and particularly United States levels. We must remember that Canada is a small country in a large world, and our financial system has very close connections with that of the United States, a country whose economy is more than ten times as large as that of Canada. Under these circumstances, Canadian demands for foreign securities and Canadian borrowing in foreign markets are unlikely to have a major impact on foreign security yields. However, foreign demands for Canadian securities will have a major impact in this country.

What will be the relationship between equilibrium yields on Canadian securities and yields on securities in the United States? If Canadian and American securities were perfect substitutes for each other in the minds of both Canadian and American assetholders, and hence if relative yields were the only basis for choosing among these securities, the answer to this question would be quite straightforward. The process which we have just described would guarantee that yields on Canadian securities equalled yields on comparable American securities. Any departure of yields from equality would induce a shift of demands or supply between the markets, tending to re-establish equality.

Some Evidence: Long-Term Government Bond Yields

Is it the case that yields on comparable Canadian and United States securities tend to equal each other? The evidence provided by Figure 7-1 is interesting. It shows quite clearly that while yields on comparable securities in Canada and the United States tend to move up and down together, these yields are far from equal to each other. In the period in question, yields on long-term Canadian government bonds tended to remain roughly 25% higher than yields on comparable United States bonds. While the yields on these securities are obviously closely related to each other, apparently the equilibrium relationship is not one of equality. The differential is too persistent and too stable for this to be the case. How can we explain this?

3/THE FOREIGN EXCHANGE RISK

A major part of the answer lies in the existence of a type of risk which we have not yet discussed. This is a risk, peculiar to international transactions, which arises because two different currencies are involved, the currency of the lender and that of the borrower. The rate of exchange between the two currencies may change during the life of the financial instrument. We call this risk the *foreign exchange risk*.

The Foreign Exchange Rate

As far as residents of Canada are concerned, foreign monies are just so many other financial instruments, instruments which we can call *foreign exchange*. These monies are useful for making payments outside Canada.

As noted in Chapter 2, a foreign exchange market exists, in which the stock-in-trade is foreign monies. The prices established in those markets are called foreign exchange rates. Thus, *a foreign exchange rate means the Canadian dollar price of one unit of foreign money.* But this must mean that there are many foreign exchange rates, as many rates as there are foreign monies. This is true; however, in practice, the United States dollar plays the key role in the Canadian foreign exchange market. As a result, the expression *"the" foreign exchange rate has come to mean the Canadian dollar price of 1 United States dollar* and we will follow this practice.

It is important that you keep this convention in mind. There are few things in economics which generate as much confusion as foreign exchange and the foreign exchange rate, and very often this confusion has its roots in inconsistent usage of the expression "the foreign exchange rate".

The semantic problem arises because one can quote the foreign exchange rate either from the Canadian point of view (regarding it as a price in the domestic market) or from the foreign point of view (regarding it as a price in world markets). Thus, from the Canadian point of view the foreign exchange rate is the Canadian-dollar price of one United States dollar. From the American point of view, however, it is the United States-dollar price of the Canadian dollar. Mathematically, these magnitudes are reciprocals. That is, if the foreign exchange rate from the Canadian point of view is Can. $1.08, the price of the Canadian dollar from the American point of view is U.S. $.925. Many Canadians, nonetheless, cite the latter number as the foreign exchange rate. In order to minimize confusions, we will consistently call the former (Can. $1.08) the foreign exchange rate, and the latter (U.S. $.925) *the external value of the Canadian dollar.* When the foreign exchange rate rises (e.g., to Can. $1.09) the external value of the Canadian dollar falls (in this case to $\frac{1}{1.09} = $ U.S. $.917). Similarly, when the foreign exchange rate falls (e.g., to Can. $1.07), the external value of the Canadian dollar rises (in this case to $\frac{1}{1.07} = $ U.S. $.935).

We will not explore the organization and functioning of the foreign exchange market at this point, but merely note that an active market does exist, in which the forces of supply and demand are allowed to interact, to establish and to change the foreign exchange rate. By international agreement, fluctuations in the exchange rate are supposed to be confined to a band of 1% on either side of the official "par" rate of exchange. In Canada, the par rate on the United States dollar was approximately $1.08 from May 1962 through May 1970, so that the upper and lower limits to exchange rate fluctuations were approximately $1.09 and $1.07. However, at the end of May, 1970, the Canadian government withdrew the limits placed upon the movement of the exchange rate and allowed market forces wider scope in determining the exchange rate. This was presented as a transitional measure to facilitate the determination of a new par rate.

Even when an official par rate of exchange has been declared, international experience in recent years makes it obvious that the stated limits to exchange rate fluctuations should not be taken too seriously. Par rates of exchange are altered from time to time. For example, in 1967 the British devalued the pound by 14%, and in 1969 the French devalued the franc by 11% and the Germans appreciated the mark by 9%. One of the most dramatic events in international finance recently was a wholsale realignment of exchange rates in 1971. Lest it be thought that such major changes in exchange rates are something which happens only to foreign currencies, it is worth remembering that the Canadian dollar has not been immune to such developments. The events of 1970 are but the latest installment in a long history of devaluations and revaluations, stretching back long before World War II, and including a major devaluation in 1961-62.[1]

The Nature of the Risk

A Foreign exchange risk exists whenever an assetholder owns a financial instrument calling for fixed future payments in a foreign money, or whenever a debtor has an obligation to make fixed future payments in a foreign money. The risk is, of course, that on the payment date the foreign exchange rate will be such that the fixed sum of foreign money to be received or paid will amount to a different sum of domestic money than was initially expected. To the Canadian assetholder, the serious risk is that the foreign exchange rate will drop. The fixed sums of foreign money he will receive as interest and principal on his foreign assets will produce fewer Canadian dollars than expected, and the yield on the asset will correspondingly be less than expected. By contrast, to the Canadian borrower the serious risk is that the exchange rate will rise. If this happens, the fixed future payments of foreign money which he is obligated to make will cost him more Canadian dollars than expected, and the actual interest cost of the loan will be correspondingly greater than expected.

Major Adjustments vs. Minor Fluctuations

In part, the foreign exchange risk referred to is that of a major change in the par rate. Perhaps this can be effectively illustrated with reference to the British devaluation of November, 1967. Suppose a Canadian had purchased a "riskless" British Government bond for £100 in early October, 1967. At the time, the Canadian dollar price was approximately $300. Following the devaluation, if the British price of the bond remained at £100, the Canadian dollar equivalent would have been only $260. The wealth of the Canadian assetholder was reduced simply as a result of the change in the exchange rate.

Changes in official par rates are dramatic events which attract widespread attention. However, even if we leave these major adjustments aside, there remains a foreign exchange risk which also can have serious consequences, at least for short-term investments. This is the risk of small fluctuations of the exchange rate from day to day or week to week, around the official par rate of exchange but within the prescribed limits. As compared to a devaluation of 15% or so, fluctuations in the exchange rate of ½ or even 1% might seem like a pretty small issue to a potential purchaser of a foreign security. However, a drop in the exchange rate of as much as 1% can be catastrophic to the holder of 30-day or 90-day notes denominated in foreign currency.

We will not explore the mathematics of this proposition here, but perhaps an example will help clarify the point. For this purpose, consider the data set out as Example 7-1, in which we have assumed that on a particular day the yield on 90-day Canadian treasury bills was 4% per annum, whereas the yield on United States treasury bills was 5% per annum. Clearly, if yield were the only consideration, a Canadian assetholder would purchase a United States treasury bill in preference to a Canadian treasury bill. In doing so, he would obtain a yield which was a full 25% greater.

However, the example makes clear that this yield advantage in investing in the United States security would vanish if the exchange rate dropped by as much as one quarter of 1% in the 90-day period. A drop in the exchange rate of any more than 1.25% would produce an actual loss on the transaction (in the sense that the yield would be negative). Depending on the position of the exchange rate within the official limits on the day on which the investment is made, either of these changes is well within the realm of possibility. If we were talking about a 30-day security rather than a 90-day security the respective changes in the exchange rate would be even smaller. In our example, a drop of less than one-tenth of 1% would eliminate the yield advantage, and a drop of four-tenths of 1% would produce a negative yield. Thus, for short-term investments, the consequences of very small changes of exchange rates can be very great.

4/THE FOREIGN EXCHANGE RISK
AND MARKET EQUILIBRIUM

So much for the nature of the foreign exchange risk. The important question is: what are the implications of this risk for equilibrium in Canadian financial markets? In particular, why does this factor help explain the persistent and relatively stable divergence between yields on Canadian and United States securities shown in Figure 7-1?

Risk Aversion Once More

The answer can be found in the general assumption that assetholders are risk averters. That is, other things being equal, they will demand a higher yield before they will take the relatively more risky security into their portfolios.

It should be obvious that what we have said about the exchange risk facing Canadian assetholders who purchase foreign securities applies *pari passu* to foreign assetholders who purchase Canadian securities. Other things being equal, they will demand a relatively higher yield before they will choose a Canadian security over a comparable security denominated in their own currency.

Example 7-1
The Foreign Exchange Risk on Short-term Foreign Investments

(1)	UNITED STATES DOLLAR PRICE of U.S. Treasury Bill, yielding 5% per annum, par value U.S. $1,000 (Table 1, Appendix to Ch. 5)		= US$ 988
(2)	SPOT EXCHANGE RATE		= Can$ 1.08
(3)	CANADIAN DOLLAR PRICE of U.S. Treasury Bill (1) x (2)		= Can$ 1,067

Case 1
Spot Exchange Rate Constant at $1.08

(4)	RETURN at the end of 90 days (US$ 1,000 x $1.08)		= Can$ 1,080
(5)	GROSS GAIN (4) − (3)		= Can$ 13
	or: 1.25% for 90 days	= 5% per annum	
(6)	YIELD on Canadian Treasury Bills	= 4% per annum	
(7)	NET GAIN (5) − (6)	= 1% per annum	

Case 2
Spot Exchange Rate Falls by $\frac{1}{4}$% to $1.077

(8)	RETURN at the end of 90 days (US$ 1,000 x 1.077)		= Can$ 1,077
(9)	GROSS GAIN (8) − (3)		= Can$ 10
	or: 1.0% for 90 days	= 4% per annum	
(10)	YIELD on Canadian Treasury Bills	= 4% per annum	
(11)	NET GAIN (9) − (10)	= 0% per annum	

Case 3
Spot Exchange Rate Falls by $1\frac{1}{4}$% to $1.067

(12)	RETURN at the end of 90 days (US$ 1,000 x 1.067)		= Can$ 1,067
(13)	GROSS GAIN (12) − (3)		= Can$ 0
	or:	= 0% per annum	
(14)	YIELD on Canadian Treasury Bills	= 4% per annum	
(15)	NET LOSS (13) − (14)	= −4% per annum	

Some computations may not work out exactly because of rounding.

It is also important to note that during the period of time in Figure 7-1, Canada was a net capital importer. That is, foreign assetholders were continuously accumulating claims on Canadian governments, corporations and households much in excess of corresponding Canadian claims on non-residents. From 1950 through 1967 (later statistics are not yet available) Canada's net international indebtedness increased more than sixfold, from $4 billion to $25 billion. In this book, we cannot explore the underlying "real" economic forces inducing this heavy net international borrowing. However, it is useful to consider what was happening in financial markets to produce this result.

In terms of the analytical concepts developed earlier, at the prevailing level of yields on financial instruments the aggregate flow of funds demanded as a result of the borrowing decisions of Canadian spending units was continuously and significantly in excess of the supply of funds made available as a result of the simultaneous saving decisions of Canadian households. If an inflow of capital, in the form of foreign purchases of Canadian financial instruments, had not been possible, the excess demand for funds in Canadian capital markets would have forced Canadian security yields to higher levels. This would have resulted in a smaller accumulation of real assets in all sectors of the Canadian economy, i.e., by governments, consumers and particularly businesses. In other words, foreign assetholders were bribed to finance part of the capital formation which occurred in Canada during this period through the offer of an attractive yield on Canadian financial instruments. That yield had to be sufficiently in excess of yields in United States capital markets to compensate for all risks, including the foreign exchange risk.

5/THE AVOIDANCE OF RISK:
HEDGING AND FORWARD EXCHANGE CONTRACTS

It would be inappropriate to leave the discussion of foreign exchange risk without some consideration of techniques of avoiding this risk. The basic principle, called *hedging*, is quite straightforward. It simply involves the assumption of one risk to offset an equal and opposite risk.

In our discussion of the nature of the foreign exchange risk, we noted that the situations of an assetholder and a debtor were opposite. While the holder of a foreign currency asset *loses* if the exchange rate falls, the holder of a foreign currency liability *gains*. If the exchange rate rises the assetholder gains while the debtor loses. As a result, if someone holds simultaneously a foreign currency asset *and* a foreign currency liability of the same magnitude, he will have no foreign exchange risk. Whatever he loses on the asset as a result of a fall of the exchange rate he will automatically gain on the liability, and vice versa if the exchange rate rises. In other words, he has a *hedge* against exchange rate changes. *Foreign exchange rate risk exists only when one has an open position — when foreign exchange assets and liabilities are not equal.*

This principle is of vital importance to financial intermediaries, particularly chartered banks, which are heavily engaged in foreign exchange transactions but which do not wish to assume any significant foreign exchange risk. It also helps explain some borrowing in foreign financial markets. Thus, some business firms which have substantial continuing foreign exchange earnings as a result of their export business feel that this provides a natural hedge against foreign borrowing. However, the important application of the principle from our point of view involves the use of *forward exchange contracts* to eliminate the risk on short-term foreign currency investments.

Forward Exchange

In our discussion of the foreign exchange rate we did not recognize that at any time there may be several different prices in the foreign exchange market for the same foreign money, depending upon the *time of delivery*. The basic distinction of importance to us is the one between *spot exchange*, involving immediate delivery, and *forward exchange*, involving delivery on some specified future date.[2]

A forward exchange contract is an agreement calling for the purchase or sale of a specified amount of foreign money on a specified future date *at a price agreed upon at the time the contract is signed regardless of the actual spot exchange rate prevailing in the market on that future date*. A forward contract fixes the exchange rate for a particular transaction which will take place at a particular time in the future, and thus serves to *eliminate the foreign exchange risk for that transaction*.

We tend to think of the foreign exchange market in terms of transactions in spot exchange. However, an active market also exists in forward exchange contracts, although the market is largely confined to contracts of 180 days or less. Very long-term contracts are rare. Thus on any given day in the foreign exchange market there will be a structure of foreign rates, not just a single spot exchange rate. There will be a set of forward exchange rates, i.e., rates at which contracts can be negotiated for the purchase or sale of forward exchange 30 days, 60 days, 90 days, etc., in the future.

Forward exchange contracts are important to many firms engaged in foreign trade in goods and services where there is a delay between the time a contract is signed for the delivery of merchandise and the time at which payment is to be made. If payment is to be made in foreign currency, the profitability of the transaction may well depend on the level of the exchange rate. A rise in the exchange rate would increase the cost of goods and services to an importer, and a fall in the exchange rate would reduce the returns from sales of goods and services by exporters. Each can fix the foreign exchange rate for any given contract by means of a forward exchange contract — and since their interests are opposite (the importer wants to buy in the forward market, the exporter wants to sell) there is a basis for a market. The institutional arrangements are provided by the banking system. Banks will buy the forward exchange from the importer and sell it to the exporter. Of course the bank will sell at a slightly higher price than that at which it can buy forward exchange, the difference being its "fee" for the services rendered.

"Covered" Foreign Investments

Most transactions in forward exchange are related to attempts to avoid the foreign exchange risk on commercial transactions. However, forward exchange contracts also have obvious advantages for short-term international investors. They permit the purchaser of a foreign currency asset to fix the rate of exchange at which he will convert the proceeds of his investment back to his own currency, and thus eliminate the potential foreign exchange risk on his investment.

In Example 7-1 we assumed that the yield on 90-day Canadian treasury bills was 4% per annum while the yield on comparable United States securities was 5% per annum. As Example 7-1 made abundantly clear, any Canadian assetholder who was tempted by this yield differential into investing in the United States security would assume a serious foreign exchange risk. A very small change in the exchange rate could not only eliminate the underlying yield advantage to investing in the United States, but also turn a potential net gain into an actual loss. However, at the time he purchases the United States security the Canadian assetholder can avoid this risk by simultaneously entering into a forward exchange contract with his bank in which the bank agrees to purchase United States dollars in the amount of the redemption value of the United States treasury bills (i.e., U.S. $1,000 in the example) at an exchange rate agreed upon now.

Note carefully that two foreign exchange transactions are involved. The Canadian assetholder *simultaneously* purchases spot exchange and "sells" forward exchange. Such a pairing of spot and forward exchange transactions is commonly called a *swap*. When an assetholder makes a foreign investment in this way we say that the investment is *covered*. That is, the forward exchange contract serves to "cover" any potential foreign exchange risk.

A covered foreign investment, thus, will be riskless (assuming the foreign security is also riskless). The important question facing the Canadian assetholder is whether such an investment can also be *profitable*. Obviously, this depends not only on the level of yields in the two countries, but also on the relationship between the forward and the spot exchange rates.

The Yield on Covered Foreign Investments. Again, an example may be useful in order to develop this point. Example 7-2 incorporates the same assumptions about the spot exchange rate and relative yields on treasury bills as were used in Example 7-1. However, in the present case we assume that the funds invested in United States treasury bills are returned to Canada at the 90-day forward exchange rate prevailing in the market *now* rather than at the spot exchange rate which may prevail in the market at the end of 90 days. This makes the forward exchange rate a crucial factor in the investment decision.

Clearly, if the forward exchange rate is equal to the spot exchange rate (as in Case 1), there will be a strong advantage to the Canadian assetholder in investing in United States treasury bills rather than in Canadian treasury bills. Through the forward exchange market, the international investor can arrange to sell his United States dollars for the same price which he paid for them, and he will thus gain the full international differential in security yields, in this case 1% per annum. In the world of short-term investments, that is a very large differential — and, what is important, it is one which the purchaser of the United States treasury bill can obtain *with no additional risk*.

Example 7-2
The Forward Exchange Rate and the Net Yield on Covered Short-Term Foreign Investments

(1)	UNITED STATES DOLLAR PRICE of U.S. Treasury Bill, yielding 5% per annum, par value US$ 1,000 (Table 1, Appendix to Chapter 5)	= US$ 988
(2)	SPOT EXCHANGE RATE	= Can$ 1.08
(3)	CANADIAN DOLLAR PRICE of U.S. Treasury Bill (1) x (2)	= Can$ 1,067

Case 1
90-Day Forward Exchange Rate = $1.08

(4)	RETURN at the end of 90 days (US$ 1,000 x 1.08)		= Can$ 1,080
(5)	GROSS GAIN (4) − (3)		= Can$ 13
	or: 1.25% for 90 days	= 5% per annum	
(6)	YIELD on Canadian Treasury Bills	= 4% per annum	
(7)	NET GAIN (5) − (6)	= 1% per annum	

Case 2
90-Day Forward Exchange Rate = $1.077

(8)	RETURN at the end of 90 days (US$ 1,000 x 1.077)		= Can$ 1,077
(9)	GROSS GAIN (8) − (3)		= Can$ 10
	or: 1.0% for 90 days	= 4% per annum	
(10)	YIELD on Canadian Treasury Bills	= 4% per annum	
(11)	NET GAIN (9) − (10)	= 0% per annum	

Case 3
90-Day Forward Exchange Rate = $1.091

(12)	RETURN at the end of 90 days (US$ 1,000 x 1.091)		= Can$ 1,091
(13)	GROSS GAIN (12) − (3)		= Can$ 24
	or: 2.3% for 90 days	= 9% per annum	
(14)	YIELD on Canadian Treasury Bills	= 4% per annum	
(15)	NET GAIN (13) − (14)	= 5% per annum	

Some computations may not work out exactly because of rounding.

The difference that the level of the forward exchange rate can make is illustrated in Cases 2 and 3. The first of these cases demonstrates that if the forward exchange rate is as much as one quarter of 1% below the spot exchange rate, it eliminates any advantage to investing in the United States treasury bills in spite of the 1% yield differential. The reader should verify the fact that any lower forward exchange would make the purchase of United States treasury bills on a covered basis a losing proposition for Canadian assetholders. They would earn a higher net yield on Canadian treasury bills, in spite of the fact that the "raw" yield on treasury bills is lower in Canada. Case 2 thus illustrates the proposition that *if the forward exchange rate is lower than the spot exchange rate it will reduce the net yield on covered foreign investments.* In the case cited, the fact that the forward rate is approximately 1% above the spot rate more than doubles the net yield on investments in United States treasury bills. It should be apparent that this could make covered foreign investment profitable for Canadian assetholders even though foreign security yields were lower than those prevailing in Canada. To verify this fact, the student should recalculate Case 3 on the assumption that the yield on Canadian treasury bills is 5% per annum and the yield on United States treasury bills is 4% per annum. (Note: Table 1 of the appendix to Chapter 5 shows that the U.S. dollar price of a 90-day treasury bill yielding 4% per annum would be U.S. $990.)

Determination of the Forward Exchange Rate: The Interest Parity Theory. We have so far skirted around the question of how the forward exchange rate is set. Given the importance which this rate has assumed in our analysis, we must now face this issue head on.

We must remember that the forward exchange rate is simply a price. Agreed, it is a rather unusual price, since it is negotiated now for a transaction which will occur sometime in the future. Nonetheless, as a price it is set by the interaction of the forces of supply and demand in the market place. What can we say about supply and demand in the forward exchange market?

In fact, if you pause and think about it, we have already said quite a bit. At the very least we have identified two major classes of demand and supply, what we might call on the one hand *commercial demand and supply,* and on the other hand *assetholder demand and supply* (later we will have occasion to note the possibility of a speculative demand and supply as well). But we have also suggested the basic determinants of these demand and supply forces. We now need to draw these observations together.

Commercial demands for and supplies of forward exchange reflect attempts to hedge against normal foreign exchange risks on short-term commercial transactions. The commercial demand for forward exchange must therefore be related to the flow of Canadian imports since it results from attempts by importers to fix the foreign exchange rate on future payments for imports which they are presently contracting to purchase. Either because the level of the exchange rate will affect the demand for imports or because at relatively high forward exchange rates the importer may elect to "take the risk", we expect that this demand curve will slope downward to the right. That is, we expect that the higher the forward exchange rate, the smaller the quantity of forward exchange which will be demanded for commercial reasons.

Similarly, the commercial supply of forward exchange must be closely related to the flow of Canadian exports since it reflects the attempts of exporters to fix the exchange rate on payments which they expect to receive in the future for exports which they are presently contracting to sell. We would expect that this supply curve will rise to the right (like a normal supply curve). This in part reflects the fact that exports will be more profitable at higher exchange rates (and hence more will be offered for sale), and in part the fact that at relatively low forward exchange rates the exporter may be inclined to "take the risk" of not selling his foreign exchange earnings in the forward market.

We thus expect that commercial demand and supply in the forward exchange market can be described by curves of the "normal" shape, but asset-holder's demands and supplies are a different story. Return again to Example 7-2. It tells us that, given the difference in yields on short-term securities between Canada and the United States, and given the level of the spot exchange rate, there is a critical level of the forward exchange rate above which it is profitable for Canadian assetholders to rearrange their portfolios, selling their short-term Canadian securities, and replacing them with fully covered short-term United States securities. Moreover, since this can be done without altering the riskiness or the liquidity of their port-folios, assetholders should be prepared to move very substantial sums of money across the national border in response to such an incentive. All such transactions will create a supply of forward exchange since the Canadian assetholders will in each case be selling United States dollars in the forward market in the amount of the redemption value of their purchases of United States securities. At this point — determined by the level of the spot exchange rate and the difference between yields on short-term securities in the two markets — *the supply curve for forward exchange should become virtually perfectly elastic.* A small rise in the forward exchange rate above this point should induce large-scale readjustments in portfolios and hence large-scale supplies of forward exchange.

What is true of Canadian assetholders should be equally true in reverse for United States assetholders. A *rise* in the forward exchange rate for whatever cause should induce Canadians to make covered investments in the United States: a *fall* in the forward exchange rate should induce Americans to make covered investments in Canada.

To appreciate this point you must remember that the external value of the Canadian dollar and the foreign exchange rate move in opposite directions. As the spot exchange rate falls, the external value of the Canadian dollar rises. Similarly, if the forward exchange rate falls, the forward price of the Canadian dollar rises, and if the forward exchange rate is substantially below the spot exchange rate, the external value of the Canadian dollar is greater in the forward market than in the spot market. Thus, at low levels of the forward exchange rate, the American investor in Canada will gain any differential in interest rates plus the excess of the forward value of the Canadian dollar over its spot value. He will be that much more tempted to invest in Canada. He can do so with no risk, and with a higher yield than could be obtained in the United States on a corresponding short-term investment. As a result, if the forward exchange rate is driven down for any reason, there will come a critical point at which it becomes profitable for American assetholders to rearrange their portfolios, selling United States treasury bills and buying Canadian treasury bills on a fully covered basis. At this point — which again is determined by the level of

Figure 7-2
Demand and Supply for Forward Exchange
(Given the level of the spot exchange rate and short-term security
yields in Canada and the United States)

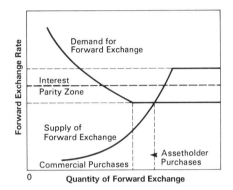

the spot exchange rate and the difference between yields on short-term
securities in the two financial markets — the demand curve for forward exchange should become virtually perfectly elastic. The supply of United
States dollars in the forward exchange market is the American demand for
forward Canadian dollars.

These points are illustrated on Figure 7-2. The demand for forward
exchange is depicted as having the shape normally associated with a demand
curve through most of its length. However, it is shown as becoming perfectly elastic at some point, and thus establishing a lower limit for the
forward exchange rate. Similarly, the supply of forward exchange is depicted
as having the shape normally associated with a supply curve through most
of its length, but becoming perfectly elastic at some point and thus establishing an upper limit for the forward exchange rate. It is perhaps paradoxical that while the bulk of the transactions in the market are "commercial" transactions, the forward exchange rate will in effect be set by the
possibly small flow of transactions on "assetholder" account. Regardless of
the balance of supply and demand pressures in the forward market resulting from normal commercial transactions, the reactions of Canadian and
American assetholders should hold the forward exchange rate within narrow
limits — limits which are set by the level of short-term security yields in the
two countries. The forward exchange rate is free to fluctuate, but only within these limits.

The range between the upper and the lower limits of the forward exchange rate might be called the *interest parity zone*. This range reflects the
fact that assetholders incur costs in adjusting their portfolios and in buying
or selling forward exchange. In part these are brokerage costs in the respective short-term money markets, and in part the "fee" which the bank charges
for its services in the form of a spread between the buying price and the
selling price for forward exchange (the bank sells forward exchange at a

higher price than it will buy it). In many expositions of the theory of forward exchange these transaction costs are neglected. As a result, the interest parity theory is presented as though it determined a precise forward exchange rate, rather than upper and lower limits to the rate. If we made this assumption, the interest parity rate would be the mid-point of the interval. It is marked with a dotted line on Figure 7-2.

Significance of the Forward Exchange Market for Equilibrium in Canadian Financial Markets. Having explored the mechanics of forward exchange and of covered foreign investment we must ask the significance of all of this for the things in which we are interested, and particularly for the determination of equilibrium in Canadian financial markets.

Before we introduced the topic of forward exchange contracts we had already established that there is an important international dimension to equilibrium in Canadian financial markets. As long as assetholders and borrowers are free to deal in either domestic or foreign financial markets, there should be a general tendency for yields on Canadian securities to be pulled toward yields in the relatively much larger foreign capital markets. Indeed, we have shown that in the Canadian case, there seems to be a relatively stable and persistent differential between security yields in Canada and those in the United States.

Now, however, our assertions about forward exchange seem to overthrow all of these propositions, at least for short-term securities. Forward exchange contracts serve to eliminate the foreign exchange risk. Thus, as far as a Canadian assetholder is concerned, a covered investment in a United States treasury bill should be in all relevant respects the same as an investment in a Canadian treasury bill. In neither case is there any foreign exchange risk. Moreover, they are of the same term of maturity, and thus have essentially the same degree of liquidity. They should be perfect substitutes for each other, and thus, forces in the market place should dictate that the yields on the instruments will be driven to equality with each other, in equilibrium. Note, however, that the United States yield relevant to this discussion is the United States treasury bill yield, *adjusted for the cost or gain on forward exchange contracts* (i.e., adjusted for the difference between the forward and the spot exchange rate). *It is this adjusted yield to which the Canadian treasury bill yield will be equated by market forces.* Except in the peculiar circumstance of the forward exchange rate and the spot exchange rate being equal, there is no reason why the "raw" yields on treasury bills in the two markets will be equal. Indeed, we can say that the forward exchange market drives a wedge between yields in the Canadian short-term security market and the United States short-term security market. In principle, this wedge should permit the "raw" yields to move independently of each other, with the forward exchange rate adjusting to keep the "adjusted" yields equal to each other. If we allow for transactions costs, of course, perfect equality cannot be expected. Rather, as Figure 7-2 shows, fluctuations in the adjusted yields should be confined to relatively narrow limits.

Some Evidence: Canada-United States Treasury Bill Yield Differentials. Do these theoretical conclusions bear any relationship to the facts? Some evidence is presented in Figure 7-3, in which we have plotted both the raw differential in yields on Canadian and United States treasury bills and that differential adjusted for the difference between the forward and the spot exchange rate.[3] On the bottom panel we have also plotted the differential between the spot and the forward exchange rates expressed in percent per annum.

Several conclusions seem to stand out from an examination of this chart.

(1) The "raw" differential between yields on Canadian and United States treasury bills has fluctuated over a relatively wide range in recent years.

It is instructive to compare the fluctuations in "raw" treasury bill yield differentials (Figure 7-3) with fluctuations in yield differentials on longer-term securities as presented in Figure 7-1. While there is a basic similarity in the pattern, the range of the short-term fluctuations is significantly widei

(2) Fluctuations in the differential between the spot exchange rate and the 90-day forward exchange rate almost parallel the fluctuations in the "raw" treasury bill yield differential.

Although it is quite clear that the correlation between these two series is less than perfect, a strong association is very evident. Remember that when the yield on Canadian treasury bills is substantially in excess of the yield on United States treasury bills, United States assetholders will attempt to buy Canadian securities. To cover the foreign exchange risk they will sell Canadian dollars in the forward market, or, what is the same thing, to buy United States dollars in the forward market. As a result, the forward exchange rate will be driven up relative to the spot rate, thus eliminating the advantage to Americans of investing in Canada on a covered (or riskless) basis.

(3) As a result, fluctuations in the covered yield differential were generally confined to a much narrower range than fluctuations in the "raw" differential.

This is what the interest arbitrage theory would predict.

(4) However, on several occasions fluctuations in the covered yield differential were outside the range which would seem reasonable under the interest arbitrage theory.

The winter of 1965-1966, the autumn of 1967 and mid-1959 are three obvious cases in point.

This evidence seems to suggest that the interest arbitrage theory of the forward exchange rate is substantially correct. However, it cannot explain all of the significant developments in the forward exchange market. Apparently Canadian assetholders are less sensitive to risk-free international yield differentials than this theory assumes. In drawing Figure 7-2 we assumed that both the demand and supply curves in the forward exchange market would become perfectly elastic at some point. Apparently this is not a valid assumption under all circumstances.

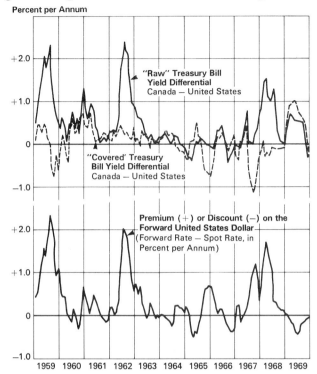

Figure 7-3
Foreign Exchange Rates and the Yield on Foreign Investments

6/OTHER FACTORS IN FOREIGN INVESTMENT: PORTFOLIO DIVERSIFICATION AND SPECULATION

Our analysis of international investment transactions suggests that Canadian assetholders will purchase foreign securities when the expected yield on those securities is sufficiently in excess of the expected yield on comparable Canadian securities to compensate for the additional (foreign exchange) risk of having foreign securities in the portfolio. In the special case of short-term securities, this risk can be avoided through a forward exchange contract, but for such "covered" investments to be worthwhile the forward exchange rate has to be outside a particular limit. However, these two propositions are insufficient to explain all international transactions in financial instruments. There are at least two other considerations which we have not yet taken into account: portfolio diversification and speculation on the forward exchange rate.

Portfolio Diversification

In our discussion of the economics of selecting a portfolio of assets in Chapter 5 we noted that in general a diversified portfolio is less risky than a portfolio containing a single asset, a point which will be considered further in Chapter 8. This same motive may lead many assetholders to include some foreign currency assets in their portfolios.

Speculation

It should also be obvious that speculation on changes in the exchange rate may provide a strong inducement to some assetholders to buy or sell foreign currency assets from time to time. Thus, anticipations of a rise in the exchange rate will induce purchases of foreign currency assets — including speculative purchases of forward exchange. Correspondingly, anticipations of a drop in the foreign exchange rate will induce sales of foreign currency assets — including speculative sales of forward exchange. As the Royal Commission on Banking and Finance showed in its *Report* (with reference to Canada in 1961-62) widespread anticipation of a major devaluation can bring forth very large speculative pressures.[4] However, there is also considerable scope for profitable speculation on changes in the exchange rate within the permissible limits around the official par rate of exchange.

Conclusion: International Capital Flows and Equilibrium in Canadian Financial Markets

We have now completed an exhausting but far from exhaustive discussion of some of the factors affecting international transactions in financial instruments. What is the upshot of this analysis?

You will recall that by "equilibrium in the financial markets" we mean a situation in which there is a set of yields on financial instruments at which there exists neither excess demand nor excess supply in the market. In our discussion of equilibrium we emphasized the importance of including both stock and flow concepts of supply and demand in the analysis. It should be apparent from what we have just said about international capital flows that there is another dimension to equilibrium as well. Full equilibrium calls for a set of yields on financial instruments for which there is neither excess demand nor excess supply in the market, taking into account demand and supply from *both* domestic and international sources.

That is not to say that equilibrium is incompatible with international capital flows. It is the demand and supply from domestic and international sources *combined* which is relevant, which means that, in equilibrium, yields on Canadian securities will be controlled to a substantial degree by yields on securities in world markets, particularly in the United States. An increase in the supply of financial instruments in Canada will tend to increase yields, but the amount of the increase which actually occurs will be limited by an inflow of funds from abroad. A widening of the international yield differential will attract foreign assetholders to Canadian securities (or will induce Canadian borrowers to approach foreign capital markets). We have shown that Canadian security yields will not be tied rigidly to foreign yields. Attitudes toward foreign exchange risk permits a range of variations about foreign yields. At the short-term end of the capital market an additional margin of flexibility is permitted by adjustments in the forward exchange rate. However, all things considered, the powerful impact of international capital markets on the Canadian market cannot be ignored.

FOOTNOTES

[1] The Canadian "devaluation" was much different than that which occurred in the case of the British pound. During the period from October 1, 1950 to May 2, 1962 there was no official par rate of exchange for the Canadian dollar. The Canadian dollar was allowed to "float": to find its own level in world markets depending on the pressures of supply and demand. For several years the Canadian dollar was very strong in world markets, and the foreign exchange rate was less than $1. Thus, in 1960 the price of the United States dollar in the Canadian foreign exchange rate averaged $.97. The "devaluation" of the Canadian dollar involved a sharp rise in the foreign exchange rate, from $.97 in 1960 to $1.05 in early 1962, capped off in May 2, 1962, by the declaration of an official par exchange rate of $1.08.

[2] Transactions in "spot" exchange involve the purchase or sale of claims to bank deposits in foreign financial centers. Thus, Canadian banks sell claims to their deposits with foreign correspondent banks, and they buy claims on foreign banks to be transferred to their accounts with these foreign correspondents. The instructions for such transfers are usually sent by telegraph (hence the expression "telegraphic transfer"), although the actual delivery of the funds in the foreign center normally will not occur until the next business day.

[3] Figure 7-3 reports international differentials in treasury bill yields. Of course there are other money market instruments (see Chapter 3). Of particular importance for international transactions are commercial paper and finance company paper. A major portion of international arbitrage transactions are in these instruments rather than treasury bills. While the behaviour of treasury bill yields will be substantially the same as the behaviour of commercial paper and finance paper yields, the correlation will not be perfect. As a result, the picture of international covered-yield differentials would look marginally different for commercial and finance company paper.

[4] Royal Commission on Banking and Finance, *Report*, pp. 297-299; pp. 486-488.

APPENDIX

SOME MATHEMATICS OF FORWARD EXCHANGE

In order to facilitate the exposition we have adopted the convention of identifying variables which are denominated in United States dollars or which refer specifically to the United States financial market with the subscript u. Variables which are denominated in Canadian dollars, or which relate to Canadian financial markets (with one exception) have no subscripts. In general we assume that the United States financial markets are the only ones relevant for Canadians.

In the Canadian market:

S = the spot exchange rate (the Canadian dollar price of one United States dollar for immediate delivery).

F = the 90-day forward exchange rate (the Canadian dollar price of one United States dollar for delivery in 90 days).

r = the yield on 90-day Canadian government treasury bills, in percent per annum.

In the United States Market:

r_u = the yield on 90-day United States government treasury bills, in percent per annum.

M_u = the market price of one United States treasury bill, priced to yield r_u percent per annum.

R_u = the redemption value of that treasury bill.

From the analysis in the Appendix to Chapter 5, we know that:

$$R_u = M_u \left(1 + \frac{r_u}{4}\right) \tag{7A.1}$$

It is important to note that the yield on the treasury bill, r_u, has been quoted in percent per annum. In equation (7A.1) this yield has been divided by four to make it percent per 90 days.

The Canadian Assetholder's Investment Decision

The Amount of the Investment. At the prevailing spot exchange rate, the Canadian dollar price of one United States treasury bill (M) will be:

$$M = SM_u \tag{7A.2}$$

This is the sum which we will assume may be invested.

The Canadian Dollar Return on the Investment. In order to avoid any foreign exchange risk, the Canadian purchaser of a United States treasury bill must simultaneously enter into a forward exchange contract to sell United States dollars in an amount equal to the redemption value of the bill. The bill will mature in 90 days. Under the terms of his forward contract, the Canadian assetholder will be required to sell his United States dollars for Canadian dollars at the agreed price (F) regardless of the spot exchange rate prevailing in the market at that time. Thus, the Canadian dollar return on the investment in United States treasury bills is:

$$FR_u = F \left[M_u \left(1 + \frac{r_u}{4}\right)\right] \tag{7A.3}$$

The Yield on a Covered Investment

Define a new variable, r_c, which is the yield in percent per annum to the Canadian assetholder on a covered investment in United States treasury bills. From (7A.2) and (7A.3) we know that:

$$SM_u \left(1 + \frac{r_c}{4}\right) = F \left[M_u \left(1 + \frac{r_u}{4}\right)\right]$$

$$S (4 + r_c) = F (4 + r_u)$$

$$r_c = \frac{F}{S} (4 + r_u) - 4$$

$$= \frac{4F}{S} - 4 + \frac{F}{S} r_u$$

$$= 4\left(\frac{F\text{-}S}{S}\right) + \frac{F}{S} r_u \qquad (7A.4)$$

The first term on the right hand side of this equation, $4\frac{(F-S)}{S}$, is the gain or loss on the foreign exchange "swap" on the purchase price of the United States treasury bill, expressed in percent per annum. If the forward exchange rate is less than the spot rate, this term will be negative. The cost of the swap will reduce the net yield on the covered investment.

The second term on the right hand side, $\frac{F}{S} r_u$, is the gain resulting from the yield on the treasury bill in the United States. Note that this yield is either augmented or reduced depending on whether the forward rate exceeds or falls short of the spot rate. In general, $\frac{F}{S}$ will be close to 1. Therefore, equation (7A.4) is commonly simplified to:

$$r_c \overset{\sim}{=} 4\frac{(F-S)}{S} + r_u \qquad (7A.5)$$

The Investment Decision. If the Canadian assetholder is to find covered investment in United States treasury bills a profitable transaction it must be true that: $\qquad r_c > r$

that is:

$$4\frac{(F\text{-}S)}{S} + \frac{F}{S} r_u > r \qquad (7A.6)$$

If the opposite is true, that is, if:

$$4\frac{(F\text{-}S)}{S} + \frac{F}{S} r_u < r \qquad (7A.7)$$

then United States investors will find it profitable to make covered investments in Canadian treasury bills. The yield on these investments will exceed the yield obtainable on United States treasury bills.

Market Equilibrium: The Interest Arbitrage Theory

The interest arbitrage theory assumes that assetholders in both countries will regard investments in domestic securities and fully covered investments in foreign securities as perfect substitutes for each other. As a result, the only condition compatable with equilibrium is:

$$r = r_c$$

$$= 4\frac{(F\text{-}S)}{S} + \frac{F}{S} r_u \qquad (7A.8)$$

If we take short-term security yields as given in the two markets, this becomes a theory of the determination of the forward exchange rate.

By manipulation of equation (7A.8) we obtain as the equilibrium forward exchange rate:

$$F = S \left(\frac{r + 4}{r_u + 4} \right) \tag{7A.9}$$

In other words, the equilibrium forward exchange rate depends on the level of the spot exchange rate and the relationship between short-term security yields in the two countries.

Some Qualifications

Term to Maturity. In all of these calculations we have assumed a 90-day term, with all security yields quoted in percent per annum. If we assumed a different term to maturity, the equations would be slightly different. Thus, for a thirty-day investment, equation (7A.9) would become:

$$F = S \left(\frac{r + 12}{r_u + 12} \right) \tag{7A.10}$$

The number 12 replaces the number 4 in the equation because we are now dealing with an investment for $1/12$ of a year rather than $\frac{1}{4}$ of a year. In general:

$$F = S \left(\frac{r + q}{r_u + q} \right) \tag{7A.11}$$

where $1/q$ is the fraction of one year for which the investment will be outstanding.

Transactions Costs. Like most expositions of the interest arbitrage theory, this discussion ignores transactions costs (i.e., brokerage fees for the several transactions in foreign exchange and in the security markets). If we allow for such costs, equations (7A-6) and (7A-7) do not hold precisely. The difference between yields must be great enough to cover transactions costs before the investment will occur.

Flexible Interest Rates. This statement of the interest arbitrage theory also assumes that yields on short-term securities are fixed, whereas the forward exchange rate is free to move. It is not clear that all of the adjustment will be taken up by movements in the forward exchange rate, however.

Suppose equation (7A-6) holds. That is, suppose there is some advantage to Canadian assetholders to make short-term covered investments in the United States. Their attempts to do so should simultaneously increase short-term security yields in Canada (as they sell, or refrain from buying, short-term securities), increase the spot exchange rate (as they attempt to purchase United States dollars), reduce short-term security yields in the United States (as they attempt to purchase United States securities), and reduce the forward exchange rate (as they arrange forward contracts to sell the United States dollars). Obviously, it is an oversimplification to assume that only the forward exchange rate adjusts.

8

Elementary Theory of

Financial Intermediation

In addition to the analysis of financial markets, the economics of the financial system is largely an analysis of the nature, operations and impact of a group of business firms which we call financial intermediaries. They loom so large in the financial system that their activities can have a decisive impact on the effectiveness of the system as a mechanism for the allocation of credit, and hence they can have a significant effect on both the composition and the level of economic activity. It is also important to note that government monetary policy is largely effected through financial intermediaries. Their economic importance is pervasive.

In Chapter 1 we made passing reference to financial intermediaries, their nature, function and importance. In this chapter we propose to examine them in greater detail, and in the process to develop an elementary theory of financial intermediation. In the following three chapters we will consider the specific characteristics of various types of financial intermediaries.

1/THE CONCEPT OF FINANCIAL INTERMEDIATION

A Conduit Between Ultimate Lenders and Ultimate Borrowers

In our earlier discussion of financial intermediaries we noted that financial intermediaries stand between the ultimate lenders (surplus spending units) and the ultimate borrowers (deficit spending units). They borrow from one group and lend to the other.

However, many economic units simultaneously borrow and lend: indeed, we might go so far as to say that at some time or other *most* (if not all) economic units do so. Thus, if we adopted a catholic definition of a financial intermediary we would have to include other economic units in addition to those firms, such as banks, trust companies and insurance companies, which we normally consider to be financial intermediaries. Many individuals or families are simultaneously creditors and debtors. They hold such things as bank deposits and saving bonds while at the same time they have outstanding consumer loans or mortgage debt. Similarly, many corporations extend trade credit and make long-term investments in other corporations while at the same time they have outstanding bank loans or long-term debt. Moreover, and especially in the postwar period, many corporations have become increasingly aware of the opportunity costs (in terms of income foregone) of holding large amounts of cash for lengthy periods. Therefore, they frequently invest their funds for short periods in various money market instruments. Indeed, corporations have become major suppliers of funds to the money market. Should we consider all such individuals and corporations to be financial intermediaries?

A More Specialized Concept

In one sense, all of these individuals and corporations are financial intermediaries. Perhaps we could call them *ad hoc* intermediaries. Their financial activities have an important place in the overall functioning of the financial system. Our concept of financial intermediation must be more specialized than this, however. We are concerned with a group of firms which make this type of financial activity their *primary business*. That is, their activities in simultaneously borrowing and lending are not an adjunct of some other activity, but rather are the essential reason for their existence. They are *continuously* engaged in the business of borrowing and lending (not just on an *ad hoc* basis), and in general (and with a few exceptions) they stand ready and willing to accept any and all funds placed with them at the posted interest rate.

Most financial intermediaries are private *profit-seeking firms*. There are exceptions. Two rapidly growing groups of intermediaries, *caisses populaires* and *credit unions*, are "cooperative banks". However, even these "cooperative banks" seek to make a return over and above costs, and in that sense they are profit-seeking institutions. Clearly, in order to earn profits *financial intermediaries must be able to borrow at a lower rate of interest than that at which they lend*. How can they do this? Why should any spending unit lend to a financial intermediary at a lower rate of interest than he could lend to the ultimate borrower (and to whom the intermediary will in fact lend the same money)?

Transmutation of Assets. The answer must be that depositors regard claims on financial intermediaries as in some sense superior to claims on ultimate borrowers. This means that if given the choice between a claim on an ultimate borrower and a claim on a financial intermediary *bearing the same effective yield*, these wealth-owners would always choose the claim on the intermediary, and would only choose the claim on the ultimate borrower if it bore a significantly higher effective yield.

It is for this reason that many economists argue that the essence of financial intermediation is the transmutation of assets. Transmutation means literally the transformation of something from one nature, substance or form into another. The financial intermediary accepts claims on ultimate borrowers which the ultimate lenders would not accept, and issues claims to be held by the ultimate lenders which have characteristics which the ultimate borrowers could not duplicate. The intermediary does not create real wealth, but *merely changes the form of the claims on real wealth held by the assetholders of the economy.* In this act of transmutation the financial intermediary creates an asset form with unique characteristics.

The unique properties of claims on financial instruments are varied. Thus, some intermediaries provide financial instruments which can be used as payments money, and which are in demand for that reason. Some intermediaries provide claims which are highly liquid, even though they are not money. Others provide claims in the form of insurance policies, where the claim is payable only in the event of a specified contingency (a fire, a death, or an accident, for example). Still others provide an instrument whose price behaves like a broad average of stock prices.

Underlying all of these specific characteristics, however, is *the central principle of portfolio diversification. A claim on a financial intermediary is in fact a claim on a diversified portfolio of assets and is but one claim in a diversified portfolio of liabilities.* It is the fact of diversification — primarily on the asset side but also on the liability side — which permits the intermediary to create financial instruments with all of these specific and valuable properties.

2/THE THEORY OF PORTFOLIO DIVERSIFICATION

The essential effect of portfolio diversification is that *it reduces risk.* Diversification of asset holdings reduces the risk of loss of the total value of asset holdings (and also the "risk" of unexpected gains in the total value of asset holdings). Diversification on the liability side reduces the risk of having to make payment simultaneously on all liabilities (and also the "risk" of unexpected increases in liabilities).

Diversification of Asset Holdings

A more precise statement of the theory of portfolio diversification is reserved for the Appendix to this chapter. That exposition is necessarily mathematical since the fundamental proposition is basically mathematical, being derived from a primary proposition of probability theory. However, on an intuitive level, this basic principle underlying diversification of asset holdings can be succinctly stated in the old adage "Don't put all of your eggs in one basket." In the present context, it might better be re-stated as "Don't put all of your wealth in one asset." In the case of the eggs in one basket, it only takes a single mis-step, a single fall, to break them all. In the case of investing all of your wealth in one asset, it only takes the failure of one debtor to mean your complete financial ruin.

In Chapter 5 we defined "risk" as the probability of significant variations in the actual yield on an asset around the expected or most likely yield. We might now extend these concepts and talk about the yield and the risk on a portfolio of assets. The yield on the portfolio will be the average yield on the assets which comprise the portfolio. The theory of portfolio diversification tells us, however, that the risk on the portfolio — the probability of significant variations in the actual yield about the expected or most likely yield on the portfolio — will be less than the average of the risks on the separate assets comprising the portfolio. Indeed, *the risk on the portfolio will vary inversely with the number of independent assets comprising the portfolio.* As the number of independent assets in the portfolio increases to a very large number (in the extreme, to infinity), the risk on the portfolio approaches zero. This is true even though each of the constituent assets of the portfolio has a significant risk attached to it.

This means that an assetholder faced with two assets equal in all relevant respects (i.e., same risk, same expected yield), should, if he has any aversion to risk at all, hold some of both assets rather than investing all of his funds in only one of them. By doing so he will have the same expected yield on his portfolio (the average of the two identical expected yields is the same as either of them) and at the same time have a lower degree of risk.

The principle of diversification also means, however, that it may be highly rational for an individual to hold some assets with a high risk and some assets with a low risk. Suppose, for example, an individual wealth-owner had only two alternatives to consider for investment, cash and shares of common stock in one particular corporation. He could choose to hold all his wealth in the form of cash. This alternative would offer some definite advantages. In addition to being perfectly liquid, the possibility of it becoming worthless (we ignore erosion of real purchasing power via price changes) is extremely remote under normal circumstances. There is a disadvantage associated with holding wealth in the form of currency, however. It earns no income, either in the form of interest or in the form of capital gains. Since our assetholder presumably desires to earn income as well as to avoid risk, a portfolio consisting of only cash is not optimal for him.

At the opposite extreme is a portfolio consisting of only shares of stock in the corporation. Unlike cash, common stock holds promise of a positive return either in the form of dividends or capital gains (or both). Stock, however, also has risk associated with it: the income of the corporation is far from certain, and fluctuations in the income of the corporation will be reflected in fluctuations in dividends paid and on the market value of the stock. In the extreme, the stock could become worthless (although, of course, it could increase in value, making the assetholder a very rich man indeed).

Should our wealth-owner, therefore, hold all his wealth in cash the possibility of loss is zero but so is the income, while on the other hand a portfolio consisting solely of stock will maximize his expected income but also maximize the risk of loss. If, as an alternative, the portfolio of the wealth-owner consisted of some of both types of asset then risk of loss would be reduced (should the corporation go bankrupt the loss would be only that portion of wealth held in stock) but so would the total expected income (less would be invested in stock thereby reducing expected income or capital gains).

In general (as was shown in Chapter 5) assets with high risks normally have high expected yields. As a result, diversification involving assets of high and low risk normally involves a reduction in the expected yield on the portfolio as a whole.

Independent and Dependent Assets

There is one vitally important qualification which must be made to these conclusions on portfolio diversification. In order to reduce risk, the assets in the portfolio must be at least partially *independent*. By independent assets we mean that the outcome of one asset is not directly associated with the outcome of any other in the portfolio.

Under what conditions might assets be dependently related? Suppose that between two assets, A and B, there existed a relationship such that if A (for example, an automobile company) failed, then B (a steel plant selling its entire output to A) would fail, we would say they were *dependently* related. Holding a portfolio of dependently related assets would not reduce risk.[1]

Remember, however, that while in a micro sense investments may be independent (e.g., a loan to a shoe store and a provincial bond) in a macro sense most assets are mutually dependent. If some calamity struck the entire economy, such as a major depression, most ventures would incur losses and many would collapse, with corresponding declines in the market values of most financial assets. Even in the ordinary course of business fluctuations, most industries tend to prosper or want together, and as a consequence their common stocks tend to rise and fall together. In this sense, then, there may be some limit to the reduction in risk that can be achieved through portfolio diversification.

Diversification of Liabilities

Since financial intermediaries borrow as well as lend, the risk of fluctuations in asset values are not the only serious risks that they face. They also face the possibility that their creditors may not extend their loans. That is, the holders of claims on financial intermediaries may all demand payment at the maturity of the loan. For easy reference we shall call this form of risk "banker's risk". For many financial intermediaries — for example, banks — this risk is particularly acute because a substantial portion of their liabilities are payable on demand. Under extreme circumstances, virtually the entire set of claims against the intermediary could be presented for payment in cash simultaneously, forcing total liquidation of the intermediary. This is a contingency which the management of the intermediary cannot ignore. The probability of a mass withdrawal of funds (a "'run" of the intermediary) may be extremely low, but certainly there is always a risk of significant withdrawals of funds in a short period of time.

In the earlier part of this century runs were rather common; in more recent times they have been rare but not unheard of. Indeed Canada's most recent experience with a run involved one of the savings banks in the city of Montreal and took place in the mid 1960's. A rumour spread through one district of the city that the bank had suffered some serious losses on its loans and would shortly be forced to close. Within 48 hours worried depositors withdrew more than ½ of the bank's deposits. The run was stopped only after the Minister of Finance announced in the House of Commons that the government had every faith in the management and would stand behind it to insure its continued operation.

It may well be that the run on the bank in Montreal will be the last one to occur in Canada. Recent legislation passed by the federal government requires banks and other federally chartered intermediaries that accept deposits to insure these liabilities up to the amount of $20,000 per individual account. Since this would cover, for example, all but a tiny share of total deposits in banks, most depositors need have no fear of suffering a loss should the banks fail. Yet, while runs may be a thing of the past, intermediaries cannot ignore the possibility of sizable fluctuations in the total level of their liabilities. As intermediaries gain experience with the changes in the levels of their liabilities, they are able to determine with some degree of certainty what a normal degree of variation will be. More important, they will be able to fix what portion of their total liabilities they can expect to have outstanding at all times. With the knowledge that, even though most or all of their liabilities are payable on demand, only a certain portion are likely to be cancelled at one time, they can in turn invest a portion of their total portfolio in the higher-yielding longer-term assets such as mortgages and government bonds. In effect, they can borrow short-term and lend long-term.

It is important to remember, however, that no intermediary will have complete certainty as to what proportion of its liabilities will be outstanding at any given time. The fact that these calculations are approximate and not exact creates a problem. Should the intermediary invest a large portion of its portfolio in long-term assets and then suffer a redemption of its liabilities larger than expected, it may be forced to sell these assets at a loss in an effort to raise cash. Similarly, excessive pessimism about the possible cancellation of liabilities may lead the intermediary to hold large amounts of short-term, low-yielding assets when it might well increase its return to the portfolio by holding more long-term assets.

The primary determinants of banker's risk are very complicated and are only now beginning to be explored fully. Recent empirical work, concerned with the nature of bank liabilities in particular, found that the level of banker's risk varied directly with the average liquidity of the deposits. Thus, the greater the percentage of total deposits not subject to chequing (i.e., payable on demand *de jure* or *de facto*) the larger was the portion of total deposits likely to remain with the firm at all times.

More importantly, given the risks of withdrawal by any one creditor of the intermediary, it is quite clear that the risk to the total portfolio is significantly reduced by diversification. Where there may be a significant risk that any one creditor will demand his money on any given day, the risk that all creditors will demand their funds at the same time is very small indeed.

But this proposition applies only if the creditors can be described as independent. Thus, if the depositors in a small bank in a small town are all employed in the same industry, the probability that they will all deposit and withdraw funds together may be very high indeed. They could not be described as independent. Similarly, if all creditors heard and believed the same rumour of impending failure of an intermediary, as in the Montreal case, the probability that they would all attempt to withdraw their funds again is very high indeed. They could not be described as independent.

As will become evident when we examine the various intermediaries in detail, the nation-wide branch bank networks in Canada, each with as many as 2 million or more separate depositors, have a high degree of independence with their liabilities. Furthermore, being highly concentrated, (only nine are chartered) there is a high probability that funds withdrawn from one insitution will be redeposited with it at the same or some other branch. Indeed, many people claim that the high degree of diversification both of liabilities and assets which results from nation-wide branching in large part accounts for Canada's freedom from bank failures for almost 50 years.

In summary the essential point is obvious. The asset portfolio of the intermediary must be managed with an eye to the risks involved on the liability side as well as the risks involved on particular assets. As we will see in our discussion of specific types of intermediaries in later chapters, the risks assumed on the liability side leave a decided imprint on the asset portfolio of the institution.

3/ECONOMIES OF SCALE IN PORTFOLIO MANAGEMENT

The reduction of risk on asset holdings through portfolio diversification is a general phenomenon. What a financial intermediary does for him in this way, any individual could, in principle, do for himself. Moreover, by lending directly to the ultimate borrowers the individual could avoid the costs of intermediation. (Remember: financial intermediaries are profit-seeking firms. In order to cover their operating costs and make a profit they must pay to their creditors a lower rate of interest than they earn on their diversified portfolios of assets.) While portfolio diversification is fundamental to financial intermediation, by itself it does not seem sufficient to explain the fact that intermediaries both exist and flourish.

Part of the explanation is that in the long run financial intermediaries are able to earn a substantially higher net return on their assets than could most individuals holding a similar range of financial assets. *The essential difference between individual portfolio diversification and a claim on a financial intermediary is that the latter is a proportionate claim on a much larger total portfolio.* The superior earnings position of the financial intermediary derives from economies of large-scale operations.

The concept of economies of scale should be a familiar one to all students of economics. Where economies of scale exist (and they are neither universal nor continuous through all scales of operations) a firm can achieve a lower level of costs per unit of output by increasing the scale of its operations, and making adjustments in techniques of production and organization appropriate to the larger scale.

All attempts to apply this concept to financial intermediaries have encountered the same problem: how do you identify and measure the output of financial intermediaries? The measurement of costs is relatively straightforward, but, as discussed in Chapter 1, the problem of measuring output in the sense of the value of the services performed by financial intermediaries has not been solved to the satisfaction of many economists. Without a fairly accurate measure of output how can we measure and discuss variations in costs per unit of output as the level of output changes?

Fortunately, in the present context we can beg the question. We are not immediately interested in costs in relation to the level of output of the intermediary (unless we take the size of the intermediary's portfolio of assets as an indicator of output, as many studies have done), but rather *in the impact of costs on the net return per dollar invested in diversified portfolios of different sizes.* It is in this unorthodox sense that we refer to economies of scale. The student should be aware that it is not exactly the same concept as that employed in the theory of the firm.

Why should there be economies of scale in portfolio management? We can divide the relevant considerations into three categories. In part, the economies arise because of indivisibilities in financial assets. Perhaps more obvious are economies which arise in connection with the decision-making processes relating to the management of the portfolio. To some extent economies also arise in connection with transactions in financial markets, and hence are dependent only indirectly on the size of the asset portfolio.

Indivisibility of Financial Assets

Not all financial assets are available in small denominations. For example, treasury bills only come in multiples of $1,000, or I.B.M. stock sells for more than $270 per share. These minimum unit sizes are beyond the financial capacity of many wealth-owners and, because of this, the range of alternative investment forms is limited. Could an individual with total assets of $5,000 invest in a diversified portfolio including several mortgages on residential property? Obviously not. However, a deposit in a Trust and Loan company effectively buys him a share of a portfolio including many such mortgages. The financial intermediary is able to hold a broader range of assets, including some higher-yielding assets, simply because of the larger total size of its portfolio.

Economies in Management

The management of an investment portfolio involves choices among alternatives. The essential inputs are prompt, accurate information on current and prospective developments in a broad range of economic activities, and technical expertise in interpreting the financial implications of these developments. Each potential investment (including those already in the portfolio) must be assessed in terms of probable return and risk, and its merits considered relative to all possible alternative uses of funds. A large investment portfolio will be able to support a group of individuals who will devote their full time to supervising the investment of funds. By working full time rather than part time on the problems of investment they frequently become specialists in particular industries, regions or groups of securities. They acquire an expertise and knowledge that frequently allows them to evaluate a particular investment opportunity quickly and shrewdly. It is almost impossible to imagine such expertise in a wide range of markets being possessed by any one individual.

It is true that such technical expertise is itself a marketable commodity. Individuals can hire the services of professional investment counsellors, and indeed many brokerage houses will offer advice of this sort as a part of their services to their customers. However, the fees of independent investment counsellors tend to bear more heavily on small portfolios than on large portfolios. Thus, suppose the fee of an independent counsellor is $100 per day or any fraction of a day. The larger the amount of wealth involved the lower will be the cost per each dollar of having this expert advice. For example, if the portfolio was worth $5,000 the cost per dollar of assets for the one day's advice would be 0.2¢ while if the portfolio was worth only $500 the cost would be 20¢ per dollar of assets. The larger portfolio is better able to combine expert, specialized advice with low cost per dollar of assets.

Economies in Market Transactions

The optimum portfolio for a wealth-owner or an intermediary will normally not be constant in size and composition over time. As wealth increases or the yields and risks associated with various investment alternatives change so will the composition or structure of the portfolio. But changes in the size and composition of the portfolio imply transactions in financial markets, and these transactions are far from costless. As we saw in Chapter 3 there are "transactions costs" in the form of fees and commissions of brokers and dealers as well as miscellaneous other costs involved in purchasing and selling securities in the market (and corresponding costs in making loans and handling deposit accounts). With few exceptions transactions costs are stated either as a flat sum per transaction or as a declining percentage of the value of the transaction. As a consequence, in most transactions, the larger the total amount involved the lower will be the transaction cost per dollar exchanged.

Clearly, if two equally diversified portfolios, one large and one small, were to involve the same number of market transactions in a given period of time, the burden of transactions costs would be heavier on the smaller portfolio than on the larger one. As a result, the net return on the smaller portfolio would be less than on the larger portfolio. The smaller one cannot get the benefits of the same degree of diversification, adapt to all market developments, and get the same return on the portfolio as can the larger.

Economies of Scale and the Role of Financial Intermediaries

If we regard the primary characteristic of the financial intermediary as the provision of a claim on a diversified portfolio of financial assets, this analysis suggests on *a priori* grounds one reason why such intermediaries should exist and flourish. Economies of scale in the management of investment portfolios, including economies in market transactions, permit the intermediary to obtain a higher net return on a diversified portfolio for any given degree of risk than could an investor with a relatively small sum to invest.

This also suggests that financial intermediaries should be relatively more important to investors with relatively small portfolios than to those with relatively large portfolios. There is some direct evidence that this is the case. Thus, a survey of consumers undertaken for the Royal Commission on Banking and Finance showed, among other things, an inverse correlation between total assets held and the percentage of earning assets held in the form of deposits with financial intermediaries.

4/OTHER ASPECTS OF THE MARKET POSITION OF FINANCIAL INTERMEDIARIES

Clearly, the analysis of portfolio diversification, including the analysis of economies of scale in portfolio management, is only a partial explanation of why financial intermediaries exist and flourish. We have neglected another minor element in the determination of the riskiness of claims on financial intermediaries. More important, we have not given due consideration to a point introduced earlier but not fully developed relating to the diversity of products offered by intermediaries.

The Capital Accounts and the Riskiness of Claims on Financial Intermediaries.

We should not forget that financial intermediaries are generally corporations, with stockholders who have subscribed capital to the corporation, and which have normally retained earnings over a period of time so as to accumulate surpluses and reserves. We can group all of these items together as the capital accounts of the intermediary. These accounts are in fact the excess of the value of the assets of the corporation over the value of the fixed dollar claims against that corporation. This excess of the value of assets over liabilities provides an additional margin of safety to the depositors since they have a prior claim to the earnings and assets of the corporation. That is, the claims of the depositors must be met before the claims of the stockholders can be considered. Some intermediaries will use their reserves to stabilize payments of interest to depositors in spite of fluctuations in earnings on the assets held by the intermediary.

Product Differentiation

We must re-emphasize, in explaining the growth of financial intermediaries, that they have succeeded in creating financial instruments with characteristics which could not be created by many ultimate borrowers. We need only think of the liquidity and convenience of demand deposits, or the special features of insurance or the diversified portfolio of stocks obtainable from a mutual fund to realise this.

As long as wealth-owners, or surplus spending units as we called them in Chapter 1, cannot obtain directly or by personal diversification a particular type of asset that they desire, there exists the possibility of an intermediary being created to provide the missing form. This is one of the primary reasons why we have such wide diversity in the types of intermediaries operating in Canada.

In a very general sense, these institutions are basically similar in that they all perform the function of financial intermediation. Thus the theoretical analysis of this chapter applies to all of them. However, in a more specific sense, each group plays a different role in the financial system. These differences are reflected in the types of liabilities which they issue as they collect funds, and in the types of assets which they acquire as they allocate those funds among the many investment alternatives. The main point of the next three chapters is to bring out the unique characteristics of each group of institutions, and hence to explore the role which each plays in the financial system. It should not be surprising, therefore, that our analysis focuses on the characteristic of the institutions' assets and liabilities.

FOOTNOTES

[1] There is one additional relationship which, for completeness, should be mentioned. Some assets might be inversely related: that is, if one is successful the other will fail by an equal amount. An example might involve two shipyards with only enough business to support one. Whichever yard gets to build the ship survives and flourishes. The other fails. Diversification with inversely dependent assets would reduce risk to zero and also reduce income to zero.

APPENDIX

PORTFOLIO DIVERSIFICATION AND RISK

The Concepts of Expected Yield and Risk

The concepts of expected yield and risk on an asset were introduced in Chapter 5. We noted that the yield on an asset is always uncertain. A number of alternative outcomes are possible, but some are less likely to occur than others. We represented this situation by a probability distribution of alternative possible yields, with the expected yield being the most likely of the alternative possible outcomes, and the risk being represented by the standard deviation of the probability distribution of these outcomes.

Expected Yield. What we mean by the expected yield is what the mathematicians refer to as the mathematical expectation of the probability distribution. It is simply the average of the alternative possible yields when each possible yield is weighted by the probability that it will occur. The formula for calculating the expected yield is:

$$\overline{y} = \sum_{i=1}^{\eta} p_i y_i \tag{8A.1}$$

where η represents the number of alternative possible yields in the probability distribution, y_i represents each of the alternative possible yields, and p_i represents the probability that that particular yield (the ith yield) will occur (remember that $\sum_{i=1}^{\eta} p_i = 1$).

Standard Deviation. The standard deviation, a complex measure of the distribution of the alternative possible yields around the expected yield, is a much more difficult concept. Its derivation and properties are explored in any basic textbook in statistics.[1]. In brief, it is the square root of the average of the squared deviations of the alternative possible yields from the expected yield. The mathematical formula is:

$$\sigma = \sqrt{\frac{\sum_{i=1}^{\eta}(y_i - \overline{y})^2}{\eta}} \tag{8A.2}$$

where the symbol σ (the Greek letter sigma) represents the standard deviation.

In the discussion of these problems another concept, the variance of the distribution, is sometimes used. The variance is simply the standard deviation squared. That is,

$$V = \sigma^2 = \frac{\sum_{i=1}^{\eta}(y_i - \overline{y})^2}{\eta} \tag{8A.3}$$

Expected Yield and Risk on a Portfolio

By a portfolio we mean a collection of assets. A portfolio is diversified if it includes more than one asset (providing the assets are independent to some degree).

Expected Yield of a Portfolio. The expected yield of a portfolio is simply a weighted average of the expected yields of the individual assets which comprise the portfolio. Thus,

$$\overline{y}_P = \sum_{i=1}^{m} x_i \overline{y}_i \tag{8A.4}$$

where m represents the number of assets in the portfolio, y_p represents the expected yield on the portfolio, y_i represents the expected yield on each asset comprising the portfolio, and x_i the proportion of the portfolio represented by that asset $\sum x_i = 1$. Thus, for a portfolio consisting of two assets, A and B, the expected yield would be:[2]

$$\overline{y}_P = x_A \overline{y}_A + x_B \overline{y}_B \tag{8A.5}$$

Risk of a Portfolio. The risk of a portfolio is the standard deviation of a probability distribution of the alternative possible yields on that portfolio. The risk of the portfolio depends on the composition of the portfolio (the relative shares of each asset in the portfolio), the risk on each asset in the portfolio, and the relationship between the yields on the assets included in that portfolio. In the comparatively simple case of a two-asset portfolio, it can be shown that:

$$\sigma^2_P = x_A^2 \sigma_A^2 + x_B^2 \sigma_B^2 + 2 x_A x_B R \sigma_A \sigma_B \tag{8A.6}$$

where σ_p is the standard deviation of the portfolio (σ_p^2 is the variance of the portfolio) and R is the coefficient of correlation between the yields on the two assets.

The coefficient of correlation is a new concept which requires brief explanation. (For a full exposition of its derivation and properties the student is referred to any basic textbook in statistics.[3]) For our purposes, suffice it to say that it is a measure of the extent to which the yields on the two assets tend to move together. If $R = 1$, then every time the yield on asset A increased, the yield on asset B would also increase by a predictable amount. This is a case of perfect positive correlation. Similarly, if $R = -1$, then every time the yield on asset A increased, the yield on asset B would decrease by a predictable amount. In the terminology used in the chapter, the assets are inversely dependent. And there is perfect negative correlation between their yields. If $R = 0$, then the yields on the two assets move quite independently of each other. Knowing the yield on asset A does not permit you to say anything definite about the yield on asset B. Of course R can have any of these three polar values or some value in between. But let us examine the three polar cases in detail, leaving it to the reader to work out the conditions for other values.

(1) Independent Asset.

In the case of independent assets, $(R=0)$, the term $2\chi_A\chi_B R\sigma_A\sigma_B$ in equation 8A.6 drops out. In this case, the *variance* of the portfolio is a weighted average of the variances on the individual assets. That is,

$$\sigma^2_P = \chi_A^2\sigma_A^2 + \chi_B^2\sigma_B^2 \qquad (8A.7)$$

However, the risk on the portfolio, represented by the standard deviation, is:

$$\sigma_P = \sqrt{\chi_A^2\sigma_A^2 + \chi_B^2\sigma_B^2} < (\chi_A\sigma_A + \chi_B\sigma_B) \qquad (8A.8)$$

In other words, the risk on the portfolio is less than the weighted average of the risks on the two assets comprising the portfolio. (Remember: the expected yield on the portfolio is a weighted average of the expected yields on the individual assets in the portfolio. *Diversification among independent assets thus reduces the risk for any given level of expected yield.*)

(2) Perfect Positive Correlation.

If the yields on the individual assets are perfectly correlated, $(R=1)$, then the variance of the portfolio becomes:

$$\sigma^2_P = \chi_A^2\sigma_A^2 + \chi_B^2\sigma_B^2 + 2\chi_A\chi_B\sigma_A\sigma_B \qquad (8A.9)$$

This is a familiar quadratic equation.
If we take the square root of this equation to obtain the standard deviation of the distribution of possible yields on the portfolio, we find that:

$$\sigma_P = (\chi_A\sigma_A + \chi_B\sigma_B) \qquad (8A.10)$$

The risk on the portfolio is the weighted average of the risks on the individual assets. Since the expected yield on the portfolio is also the weighted average of the expected yields on the portfolio, diversification does not reduce risk for any given level of expected yield.

(3) Perfect Negative Correlation.

Finally in the case of perfect negative correlation, $(R=-1)$. Equation A8.6 becomes:

$$\sigma^2_P = \chi_A^2\sigma_A^2 + \chi_B^2\sigma_B^2 - 2\chi_A\chi_B\sigma_A\sigma_B \qquad (8A.11)$$

Again, this is a familiar quadratic equation, the square root of which is:

$$\sigma_P = (\chi_A\sigma_A - \chi_B\sigma_B) \qquad (8A.12)$$

The significant thing about this portfolio is that there is some combination of the two assets in the portfolio $\left(\dfrac{\chi_A}{\chi_B} = \dfrac{\sigma_B}{\sigma_A}\right)$ in which the risk on the portfolio is zero.

Conclusions

The important results are those represented by equations 8A.4 and 8A.6. They tell us that the expected yield on a portfolio is the weighted average of the expected yields on the assets comprising the portfolio. It can be shown, however, that portfolios are wholly or partially independent of each other in a statistical sense $(D < R < 1)$, then the risk on the portfolio will be less than the weighted average of the risks on the assets comprising that portfolio. The results of portfolio diversification have been explored for portfolios consisting of two assets — it can be shown that they apply to assets consisting of more than two assets. The analysis can also be extended to determine the composition of the portfolio which provides the minimum risk. In general (contrary to the example developed in Chapter 5), this is a portfolio which includes some of each asset, with the proportion of each asset inversely proportional to the variance of its yield.

An Example. A simple example, for the case of a two-asset portfolio, can be developed using the data presented in Table 8A-1. If we assume $R = 0$ and the portion of the portfolio held in asset $A = .8$ and the portion held in asset $B = .2$.

The expected value of the portfolio equals

$.8 \times .05 + .2 \times .05 = .05$

Similarly the *variance* for such a portfolio is equal to

$(.8)^2 (.041)^2 + (.2)^2 (.105)^2$

$= .00152 = \sigma_P^2.$

∴ The standard deviation of the portfolio equals .039. Thus the portfolio of 80% asset A and 20% asset B has the same expected yield as an entire portfolio of either A or B and yet has a lower standard deviation (risk) than either of these alternative portfolios. We therefore say that such a portfolio is a more *efficient* portfolio.

Table 8A-1

Asset	Outcome			
	Rate of Return	Estimated Probability	Expected Value	Standard Deviation
A	.10	.33		
	.05	.33	.05	.041
	.00	.33		
B	.0605	.99	.05	.105
	−1.00	.01		

APPENDIX/FOOTNOTES

[1] See for example: Taro Yamane, *Statistics, an Introductory Analysis*, 2nd. ed. (New York: Harper and Row, 1967), pp. 61-63.

[2] See for example: Harry Markowitz, *Portfolio Selection*, Monograph 16 for the Cowles Foundation for Economic Analysis at Yale University, (New York: John Wiley & Sons, 1959), pp. 72-101.

[3] Yamane, *op. cit.* pp. 440-443.

9

The Chartered Banks

The most familiar, most pervasive, and perhaps most important type of financial institution is the bank. It has been the subject of more theoretical speculations and empirical studies by economists than any other type of financial institution and its name is enshrined in innumerable university courses and textbooks on money and banking. In basic economics textbooks it is identified as having unique, almost quasi-magical powers, to "create money". Perhaps as a result, it has been the principal target of monetary reformers, crank and otherwise, and certainly the banking industry is regulated and supervised to a more intense degree than almost any other class of business.

1/THE CONCEPT OF A BANK

Several definitions of a bank are possible. Indeed, in the most general sense all financial institutions which accept relatively short-term deposits from the general public might be classified as banks. All such institutions have some degree of what we called in Chapter 8 "banker's risk". That is, they all face the possibility that a substantial portion of their liabilities may be presented for payment over a short period of time.

The "Commercial" Bank Concept. Economists customarily distinguish between *commercial* banks and *savings* banks, primarily because of differences in the nature of their deposit liabilities and corresponding differences in the characteristics of their assets. A "pure" commercial bank (if it ever existed) would have short-term, highly volatile deposit liabilities which would be used as money in the normal course of events. It would have a relatively high degree of banker's risk, and as a result it would hold mainly short-term assets, including large quantities of short-term "commercial loans" (i.e., loans to businesses for working capital purposes). By contrast, a pure savings bank would have longer-term, lower-volatility savings deposits, and a correspondingly lower degree of banker's risk. As a result, it would mainly hold longer-term assets such as bonds, equities and mortgages (and hence would be involved primarily in financing the formation of fixed capital, assets with a long working life calling for long-term financing). The unmodified term "bank" would normally be applied to commercial banks.

The "Money/Money Substitutes" Concept. Despite the merits of classifying pure types of banking institutions for theoretical analysis, it is impossible to apply this dichotomy in practice. The important existing banking institutions are hybrids. Thus, in our discussion of the payments system in Chapter 2 we saw that a number of intermediaries issue liabilities which are used as money in the economy. Moreover, many financial institutions issue liabilities which are a close substitute for money as liquid assets, which led the Royal Commission on Banking and Finance to include in the concept of a bank:

> all private financial institutions issuing banking claims: that is, claims which serve as means of payment or close substitutes for them . . . We would include among banking liabilities all term deposits, whatever their formal name, and other claims on institutions maturing, or redeemable at a fixed price, within 100 days of the time of original issue or of the time at which notice of withdrawal is given by the customer.[1]

As the Commission notes, this is a very broad definition, which straddles the "pure" types discussed above, and encompasses

> the present chartered and savings banks, many trust and loan companies, some other deposit-taking institutions and [some] sales finance companies . . . It would also include the caisses populaires and credit unions . . .[2]

Such a definition makes an important point about the essential similarity and close competitiveness of institutions which bear different names and are regulated under different legislation. However, it does tend to obscure very real and important differences among institutions which can be included within this omnibus definition of a bank. As a result, neither the "pure" concepts of economic theory nor this broad definition by the Royal Commission provides a very useful basis for organizing a discussion of Canadian financial intermediaries.

A "Legal Status" Concept. In the absence of any more fundamental principle, we must fall back on the essentially arbitrary categories established through the legislative treatment of financial institutions. In this sense *a bank is simply an institution considered as such in the laws of the land* – an institution issued a charter under the terms of the *Bank Act,* and hence listed in Schedule A of the *Bank Act.* There are only nine such institutions in Canada.[3]

2/THE CHARTERED BANKS IN THE FINANCIAL SYSTEM

The chartered banks' claim to primacy of treatment in any discussion of the Canadian financial system is almost unquestionable on several counts.

The Money Issuing Function

One of the primary reasons why economists take an intense interest in the activities of financial institutions is their underlying concern with the causes and implications of changes in the size of the money supply. While our discussion of the payments system in Chapter 2 showed that other private financial intermediaries also issue claims which are used as money, it also showed that the deposit liabilities of chartered banks are of overwhelming importance in this regard. If the money supply is the focal point for our interest in financial intermediaries, then we must be primarily interested in the chartered banks. Indeed, if, as the Royal Commission on Banking and Finance (among others) argued, " . . . issuing of claims which serve as a means of payment . . ."[4] is the central principle for identifying a bank, then the chartered banks must be taken as banks *par excellence*.

Nature of Asset Holdings

The money-issuing function of the chartered banks is of vital importance, and that alone would be sufficient to demand that we pay close attention to them. However, financial intermediaries are also a vital part of the mechanism whereby the savings of society are allocated among alternative possible uses. The selection of assets by these intermediaries can have significant microeconomic consequences. The size and composition of their asset holdings set the chartered banks apart from other financial intermediaries. The next largest concentration of assets is in the hands of life insurance companies, with $12 billion (divided among a larger number of companies).

Concentration in Lending Activities

Like other financial intermediaries, part of the chartered banks' portfolios consists of *cash* and *marketable securities* (6% and 24% respectively of Canadian dollar assets). While these assets have particular importance to the banks (and while the banks are major holders of certain types of securities), we are more interested at present in the other major portion of their assets, loans.[5] The chartered banks lending activities are highly concentrated in a few categories of loans, with the result that they tend to dominate (although they seldom fully control) certain types of lending.

This is particularly true and particularly important in the case of short-term commercial loans to business firms and to farmers to finance inventories of raw materials, goods in process of production and finished products waiting to be sold. At the beginning of 1970 almost $11 billion (or 40%) of their Canadian dollar assets were in the form of such commercial loans. In this sense the chartered banks are "commercial banks". Although there are, of course, other commercial lenders, they are nowhere near as important as the chartered banks. At the beginning of 1970 there was approximately $700 million of "commercial paper" outstanding in the money market and approximately $1.2 billion in commercial loans outstanding from Sales Finance Companies.

The chartered banks are not exclusively commercial lenders in this narrow sense, however. They are also the primary sources of short-term loans for *provincial and municipal governments and non-profit institutions,* although together such loans account for only $1.2 billion or less than 5%

of total Canadian dollar assets. The banks also play a vital role in financing the activities of *brokers and dealers* in the *financial markets*. At the beginning of 1970, of total reported liabilities of investment dealers of $1,250 million, almost $790 million or 63% represented debts to chartered banks. These are all short-term business loans in one form or another. We should not forget that chartered banks are also a major factor in the provision of *consumer credit*. Thus, of an estimated total of just over $10.8 billion in consumer credit outstanding at the beginning of 1970, personal loans from banks accounted for more than 38%, much of it in the form of longer-term installment credit to finance the purchase of automobiles and other consumer durable goods. At the beginning of 1970, the banks also held $1,310 million worth of *mortgages* on residential property. While this represents less than 5% of their total Canadian assets, it is a type of lending which can be expected to grow significantly in the future. The banks also engage in some longer-term lending to businesses. Thus, a significant and growing portion of chartered banks' business loans are "term" loans (i.e, over two years to maturity), generally to smaller businesses for capital expansion purposes. Moreover, some portion of chartered banks' holdings of securities, particularly municipal and corporate bonds (but also some provincial bonds) might also be regarded as longer-term loans to these debtors, in the sense that an active secondary market for these issues does not exist and the banks acquire them in large blocks through direct negotiation with the issuer.

International Intermediation

There is another important dimension to the chartered banks' activities which merits at least passing mention in any discussion of their role in the financial system. While we customarily think of them in terms of their impact on the economy of Canada, we must remember that these banks are not simply domestic financial intermediaries. Of their total assets 27% are foreign currency assets. As noted in our analysis of the payments system, the chartered banks provide the link between the Canadian payments system and payments systems in the rest of the world. They buy and sell foreign exchange, and through their trade association they jointly operate the Canadian foreign exchange market. Dealing in foreign exchange, however, accounts for a small portion of their total holdings of foreign currency assets. In addition to the essentially mechanical activity of providing international payments facilities the chartered banks are important *international financial intermediaries*. That is, not only do they borrow from one set of individuals to lend to another, within Canada, they engage in such activities in other national financial systems and across national boundaries.

What is a Chartered Bank?

Chartered banks are not simply an example of a commercial bank. They are the department stores of the financial industry, not specialty shops. It is true that their lending activities are highly concentrated in short-term loans to business financial institutions, governments and consumers, and that in each area the chartered banks have a major and frequently a dominant share of the market. However, they also hold large portfolios of marketable securities, and they also engage in longer-term lending. We should make no mistake about it. From whatever vantage point you examine them, these are very complex institutions. Since we cannot hope to capture the full scope of their activities it is necessary to focus on a few essential features .

3/THE BALANCE SHEET OF THE CHARTERED BANKS

We have already encountered the concept of the balance sheet identity in Chapter 4. A balance sheet is simply an elaboration of that identity. It is a formal statement of the assets, liabilities and net worth of a firm, household or other institution, as of a particular date. In a balance sheet, the assets and liabilities will be shown in more or less detail depending on the purpose of the balance sheet, and will be organized into categories thought to reveal important characteristics of the business.

Table 9-1 presents a "consolidated" balance sheet for all of the chartered banks considered together as of January 1, 1970. Since it is in effect a balance sheet for the chartered banking industry, it conceals important differences among the several firms which comprise the industry. However, perhaps we can examine the structure of this balance sheet as though it were the balance sheet of a "typical" chartered bank.

The assets and liabilities in Table 9-1 are grouped into categories designed to highlight certain important features of the banking business. Perhaps the basic division to be emphasized is that between domestic intermediation on the one hand and international or foreign intermediation on the other. Within the domestic component of the balance sheet, note on the one hand the relative importance of deposits payable on demand among the liabilities and, on the other hand, the high degree of liquidity possessed by the asset portfolio. One of our major concerns will be to explore the relationship between these facts.

4/DOMESTIC INTERMEDIATION:
THE COLLECTION OF FUNDS

We have defined a financial intermediary as a firm whose primary business involves simultaneously borrowing from one set of spending units and lending to another, normally at a profit to the intermediary. In our discussion of financial intermediation in Chapter 7 we argued that this posed a paradox. To make a profit, the intermediary must lend at a higher interest rate than it borrows. Why, then, do not the ultimate lenders and borrowers by-pass the intermediary completely, with gains to both of them? Considering only the domestic aspects of the banks' operations initially, we must answer the questions: From whom do the banks borrow? Why are Canadian assetholders willing to hold claims on the chartered banks rather than potentially higher-yielding claims on ultimate borrowers? What are the characteristics of claims on chartered banks which make them attractive to these assetholders?

The Instruments of Intermediation: Deposits

Even if one includes the capital (or net worth) accounts as a domestic source of funds, about 90% of the funds which the banks have raised from domestic sources are in the form of deposits, of which almost ¾ are in fact, if not always in law, payable on demand. This suggests at least part of the answer to our question. To a large extent chartered banks raise funds by appealing to the assetholders' demands for liquidity, one of the three basic factors which we identified in Chapter 5 as entering into the portfolio balance decision.

The liquidity of most bank liabilities is a basic reality which pervades all aspects of the banking business. Every bank must so manage its affairs that it is able to meet all demands for the withdrawal of funds from demand deposits, and must always allow for the possibility of a very substantial withdrawal in a short period of time.

Liquidity is thus the key concept in exploring the place of banking liabilities in assetholders' portfolios. However, that is not the whole story. The chartered banks do not simply offer assetholders a single type of deposit with a single uniform characteristic – a high degree of liquidity. The chartered banks offer several types of deposits, each with particular and distinct characteristics designed to appeal to assetholders' multifarious asset preferences. While most chartered bank deposits are payable on demand, some can only be withdrawn at the end of a fixed term or after a specified period of notice. Some are transferable by cheque, others are not. Some pay no interest, others pay interest at substantially different annual rates. Why do banks offer so many different types of deposits?

Demand Deposits. As we saw in Chapter 2, demand deposits – or *current accounts* as they are sometimes called – must be considered to be money. They are almost perfect substitutes for currency in many uses, and indeed in some aspects of the payments process demand deposits must be regarded as superior to currency. Demand deposits are perfectly liquid, pay no interest, and are transferable by cheque. The regular current account is designed primarily for the use of business firms – or more generally for spending units which regularly make a large volume of payments. However, there is also a special form of demand deposit which is designed for the use of individuals, the so-called personal chequing account. Normally, banks levy a fee for each cheque written on a demand deposit, and in addition normally a monthly fee for servicing the account which will depend on the size of the balance maintained in the account. If the minimum balance is sufficiently large, the banks may waive service charges, and thus in a sense pay interest on the account.

It should be noted that not all demand deposits are held by individuals and business firms. The Government of Canada maintains very large balances with the chartered banks, as do provincial and municipal governments. There is also a significant amount of deposits by other banks. The

Table 9-1
Consolidated Balance Sheet of Canadian Chartered Banks, January 1, 1970

(Millions of Dollars)

I. DOMESTIC INTERMEDIATION

			DEPOSITS		
CASH			DEPOSITS		
Currency and Bank of Canada deposits	1,652		Demand deposits		
Deposits with other banks	147	1,799	General public	7,037	
			Provincial gov't	209	
			Gov't of Canada	1,308	
LIQUID ASSETS			Other banks	360	8,914
Treasury bills	2,087				
Short-term government bonds	1,327		Personal savings deposits	15,080	
Day, call and short loans	500	3,914	Other notice deposits	3,392	27,836
LOANS			OTHER LIABILITIES		
Mortgages	1,324		Bank of Canada advances		1
Other loans	17,600	18,924	Acceptances, letters of credit and guarantees (contingency)	1,263	
SECURITIES			All other liabilities	251	1,515
Long-term government bonds	1,654				
Other securities	1,450	3,104			
OTHER ASSETS					
Canadian dollar items in transit (float)	1,459				

(continued . . .)

Table 9-1 (concluded)

Assets			Liabilities		
Acceptances, guarantees, and letters of credit	1,263				
All other assets	638	3,360			
CANADIAN DOLLAR ASSETS			CANADIAN DOLLAR LIABILITIES		
FOREIGN CURRENCY CLAIMS on residents of Canada	31,101	1,060	FOREIGN CURRENCY DEPOSITS of Canadian residents	28,851	3,274
TOTAL: DOMESTIC ASSETS		32,161	TOTAL: DOMESTIC LIABILITIES		32,125

II. FOREIGN AND INTERNATIONAL INTERMEDIATION

Assets			Liabilities		
FOREIGN BRANCH ASSETS			FOREIGN BRANCH LIABILITIES		
FOREIGN CURRENCY CLAIMS on non-residents of Canada, at Canadian head offices	3,665	6,751	FOREIGN CURRENCY DEPOSITS of non-residents of Canada, at Canadian head offices	3,711	4,645
TOTAL: INTERNATIONAL ASSETS		10,416	TOTAL: INTERNATIONAL LIABILITIES		8,356

III. CAPITAL ACCOUNTS

Assets			Liabilities		
			RESERVES FOR LOSSES AND SHAREHOLDERS EQUITY		2,097
TOTAL: DOMESTIC AND INTERNATIONAL ASSETS		42,577*	TOTAL: DOMESTIC AND INTERNATIONAL LIABILITIES AND CAPITAL ACCOUNTS		42,578*

* Detail may not add to totals because of rounding.

SOURCES: Bank of Canada, *Statistical Summary*, and *Canada Gazette*.

latter are primarily deposits of foreign commercial banks who hold Canadian dollar balances so that they can effectively handle their customers' demands for Canadian dollars. These balances confirm the existence of a correspondent banking system (be it domestic or international) that we discussed in Chapter 2.

The Demand for Demand Deposits. In providing this type of deposit, then, the chartered banks are reacting to assetholders' demands for assets which can be stored cheaply and safely and which can be transferred from person to person, often over long distances, quickly and at low cost. They are satisfying the demand for an efficient medium of exchange.

If it is primarily a demand for a medium of exchange, the demand for this type of deposit should depend on the flow of transactions in the economy, and hence on the level of economic activity. Thus, as the value of the gross national product increases over time, the quantity of demand deposits demanded should similarly increase. If the rate of increase in the gross national product should falter, or indeed if the gross national product should fall, a corresponding change should occur in the demand for demand deposits.

Figure 9-1

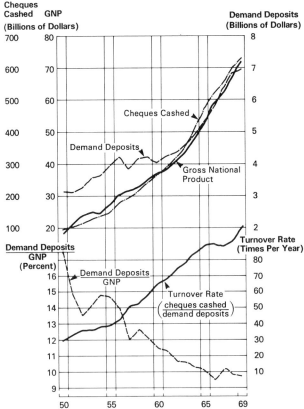

However, recent developments in economic theory suggest that the relationship between the level of economic activity and the quantity of the medium of exchange demanded should be neither rigid nor simple. The validity of this conclusion should be obvious from the information plotted in Figure 9-1. The upper panel of this chart shows the gross national product, the average stock of demand deposits, and the value of cheques cashed against demand deposits for the years 1950-1969. You should note the roughly parallel movements in the lines describing the behaviour of the gross national product (which can be taken as a measure of the level of economic activity) and the value of cheques cashed against demand deposits (which can be taken as a measure of the flow of expenditures effected using demand deposits). The behaviour of the stock of demand deposits over this period of time was also broadly similar. However, the relationship was much less close, and in particular there was a much smaller relative increase in the stock of demand deposits than in either of the other two series. As a result, the ratio of demand deposits to the gross national product declined substantially (but not continuously) over this period, and the rate of turnover (or velocity of circulation – see Chapter 2) increased approximately three-fold.

We will have occasion to explore the demand for money in greater detail in Chapter 19. At this point we can conclude that a basic determinant is the value of transactions to be effected, or the level of economic activity. However, over time, the spending units in the economy have found methods of economizing on their cash balances, so that the ratio of demand deposits to gross national product has been almost cut in half in a little over 15 years.

Personal Savings Deposits. Table 9-1 shows that the largest single source of funds for the chartered banks is personal savings deposits. In fact, this is not a homogeneous category of deposits. There are several kinds of personal savings deposits, with subtly different characteristics. However, all are designed as a safe, relatively liquid asset to be held in small or large amount by individual assetholders.

At the beginning of 1970 approximately 29% of all personal savings deposits were in a form which had a *fixed term* to maturity. This includes funds invested in savings certificates issued by some of the banks which have similar characteristics to Canada Savings Bonds. They are cashable at any time at a specified price, but offer a significantly higher yield if held to maturity.

Most of the funds in personal savings deposits are not in fixed term accounts, however. Over 75% of the funds are in what, for want of a better name, we might call *no-fixed-term* accounts. Such accounts are available in two forms, one subject to transfer by cheque and the other not directly transferable by cheque. Although the bank can legally require notice before any withdrawals, funds in these accounts are in fact withdrawable on demand.

Unlike the holder of a demand deposit, the holder of a chequable personal savings deposit receives interest on the funds left in the bank. However, he also generally pays a higher service charge per cheque written and very active use of the account is discouraged. The holder of a non-chequable personal savings deposit receives a still higher rate of interest on the funds left with the bank.

The Demand for Personal Savings Deposits. Citing research findings of the Royal Commission on Banking and Finance, one Canadian economist has noted that personal savings deposits tend to be the major financial asset held by a certain group of assetholders — a group which

> [has] unique preference patterns . . . [These individuals] prefer liquidity and safety over the rate of return to a much greater extent than do average investors . . . [They are likely to be] . . . unskilled portfolio holders with little wealth and low and irregular incomes saddled with the responsibilities of a large family . . . [For them] . . . it is rational behaviour . . . to be more concerned with the liquidity and safety of their total portfolio than with small marginal changes in its value and to place most of their earning assets with depository institutions.[6]

Certainly, the personal savings account in chartered banks must be one of the most widely held of financial assets. Thus, on April 30, 1969 there were some 15 million accounts on the books of the banking system, a figure which might be compared with the population of Canada which was estimated at 21 million at that time (of course, many individuals hold more than one account, and some accounts are held by clubs and similar organizations). Moreover, while the average balance in a personal savings account has been increasing over the years, it remains relatively small. On April 30, 1969 it was approximately $960. (as compared to $675 12 years earlier). It is also worth noting that half of these accounts had a balance of less than $100, and 79% had a balance of less than $1,000.

Although this type of account thus appears to have a particular appeal to the relatively small assetholder, we must not overlook the fact that there are some very large personal savings deposits as well. Thus, on April 30, 1969 there were some 225 thousand accounts with a balance of $10,000 or more, including approximately 2,700 accounts with a balance of $100,000 or more. While accounts in excess of $10,000 account for only 1.5% of the number of personal savings accounts, their relatively large size means that they provide a much higher proportion of the funds which banks raise through personal savings accounts.

The demand for personal savings deposits is thus primarily but not exclusively a demand on the part of assetholders with relatively small portfolios for a safe, highly liquid asset, bearing a modest but virtually guaranteed rate of return. We must not forget that in some part it is also a demand for a medium of exchange, a demand for a chequing account suitable for handling a relatively small number of monthly payments. As we have already noted, in January 1970 over 38% of the funds in personal savings deposits were in chequable accounts. However, this percentage has been falling rapidly (it was over 70% two years earlier), as individual assetholders are induced by higher interest rates to hold the non-chequable accounts and by lower service charges to hold personal chequing accounts.

People presumably hold chequable personal savings accounts partly as a medium of exchange, but the overall significance of such accounts in the

Table 9-2
Distribution of Personal Savings Deposits, 1967-70

Type of Deposit	1967 September	1968 December	1970 January
Fixed term	1,040	2,539	3,594
No Fixed Term:			
Non-Chequable	2,285	4,340	5,663
Chequable	8,148	6,583	5,634
	11,474	13,462	14,891
		Percent	
Fixed Term	9	19	24
No Fixed Term:			
Non-Chequable	20	32	38
Chequable	71	49	38
	100	100	100

payments process should not be exaggerated. There are no separate statistics for turnover rates on chequable and non-chequable savings accounts. However, in 1969 the rate of turnover of all personal savings accounts was 1.91 times per year. Since approximately 42% of all personal savings deposits were in chequable form during 1969, this implies a turnover rate for the "active" accounts of less than 4.5 times per year. By contrast, the turnover rate of demand deposits was 103.4 times per year.

Not only are chequable savings accounts much less active than demand deposits, cheques drawn on personal savings accounts are relatively unimportant in the total flow of payments through the economy. Such cheques accounted for less than 5% of all cheques cashed by chartered banks in 1969. A measure of the money supply held for transactions purposes which excluded personal savings accounts would not be grossly misleading. The primary economic significance of personal savings accounts, whether chequable or not, is as a safe, highly liquid asset bearing a moderate yield which is particularly attractive to individual assetholders with relatively little wealth.

Other Notice Deposits. The primary difference between fixed-term personal savings deposits and other notice deposits is a matter of size. Both represent funds deposited with the banks for fixed periods of time at predetermined rates of interest. However, deposit receipts, the major form of other notice deposits, are normally sold in denominations of $100,000 or more. Whereas personal savings accounts are directed at individual assetholders, other notice deposits are designed as temporary repositories of the excess cash balances of corporations, governments and other organizations.

The relatively high interest rate which banks pay for corporate notice deposits reflects the intense competition for these funds, both domestically (from other financial institutions and from the money market) and internationally. Indeed, for very large blocks of funds the rates are negotiated individually for each customer. However, the fact that these rates are much higher than those paid on personal savings deposits, let alone demand deposits, does not necessarily mean that the corporate notice deposit business is less profitable. The fact that funds are attracted in large blocks, and that they are for a fixed term, means that the administrative costs associated with them are relatively low per dollar of deposit.

It is also worth noting that corporate notice deposits carry with them a relatively high degree of banker's risk, even though each deposit is for a fixed term and hence is relatively illiquid. Since each deposit is relatively large, the bank cannot achieve the same degree of diversification of its liabilities with corporate notice deposits as it could, for example, with an equal value of personal savings deposits. As a result, corporate notice deposits tend to be more volatile in the *aggregate* than personal savings deposits.

Foreign Currency Deposits. It may be surprising to discover that not all deposits owned by Canadians in Canadian chartered banks are denominated in Canadian dollars. Indeed, in early 1970 Canadian residents held over $3 billion in deposits denominated in foreign currencies — over 10% of the domestic deposits of the chartered banks. These foreign currency deposits are almost exclusively in United States dollars.

The Demand for Foreign Currency Deposits. What accounts for the willingness of Canadian residents to hold United States dollar deposits with Canadian chartered banks?

Some part of the United States dollar deposits grow out of the normal international commercial activities of Canadian business firms. Just as business firms find it important to maintain working balances of Canadian dollars to facilitate their activities in Canadian markets, so firms which conduct a major portion of their transactions in international markets may find it very convenient to maintain working balances of United States dollars. Since these firms are resident in Canada, it is logical that they would prefer to hold some or all of these balances with their regular Canadian bankers. According to the Canadian Bankers' Association, the principal users of this facility have traditionally been:

> Canadian exporters, Canadian companies operating plants in the United States, and customers requiring a depository for investment capital awaiting exchange into Canadian dollars or repatriation to the United States.[7]

To this extent, the presence of United States dollar deposits does not raise any new issues in our analysis of the banking system. They are just another example of the role of bank money in the exchange process.

However, this explains only part of the holdings of foreign currency deposits in chartered banks by residents of Canada. To a very large extent foreign currency deposits are held by residents of Canada as a substitute for Canadian dollar time deposits, i.e., as a short-term liquid investment.

This fact again raises the issue which occupied so much of our attention in Chapter 7. Other things being equal, a Canadian assetholder is exposed to *foreign exchange risk* whenever he invests in a foreign currency asset, regardless of whether that asset is a claim on a non-resident or on a Canadian bank. It is the currency in which the claim is to be paid which creates the risk, not the country in which the debtor resides. You should also remember that this risk can be most devastating for relatively short-term securities, including short-term deposits.

Under these circumstances, why do Canadian assetholders purchase foreign currency term deposits with Canadian banks?

In some degree, Canadians invest in foreign currency deposits in spite of foreign exchange risk. Perhaps they are speculating on favourable movements in the exchange rate; perhaps they regard the risk as justifiable; perhaps they are diversifying their portfolios; perhaps because of offsetting risks elsewhere in their total financial situation (i.e., the presence of foreign currency liabilities) they have no net risk. However, to a major degree they avoid the foreign exchange risk through the now familiar device of the forward exchange contract. Thus, at the beginning of 1970, total resident-owned foreign currency deposits with Canadian banks amounted to just under $3.3 billion. Of these, some $1.6 billion were in the form of "swapped deposits," i.e., foreign currency deposits accompanied by a forward exchange contract under which the bank agrees to repurchase the United States dollars on maturity of the deposit at an agreed exchange rate. The yield to the depositor depends on the interest rate paid on the deposit and on the difference between the spot exchange rate (at which he purchases the United States dollars) and the forward exchange rate (at which he resells the United States dollars), as in the examples worked out in Chapter 7.

Why do Canadian investors invest in foreign currency deposits? Aside from the myriad of individual motives unique to the investor in question, the answer is simply that he can obtain a more attractive yield by so doing, often (through the "swapped" deposit) without any additional risk.

Trends in Domestic Deposit Liabilities

It should be evident by now that the various types of deposits issued by chartered banks are close but not perfect substitutes for each other. At one end of the spectrum are demand deposits which are highly liquid and non-interest bearing, and on the opposite end are long-term deposit certificates which are relatively illiquid and pay a premium interest rate.

If we examine behavior of bank deposits in the recent past (see Figure 9-2) we can see that the composition of deposit liabilities has been undergoing dramatic changes in recent years.[8] The relatively slow rate of growth of public demand deposits (4.8% per annum for 1950-69) stands in contrast to the somewhat more rapid rate of growth of personal savings deposits (7.0% per annum) and the very rapid rate of growth of other notice deposits (12.2%). The latter growth rate would be even higher if we focused exclusively on the period of the 1960's (21.8% per annum). We do not have data on resident-owned foreign currency deposits back to the early 1950's. However, in the 1960's the trend in such deposits was strikingly similar to that for other notice deposits (the growth rate was 19.0% per annum in the period 1960-1969).

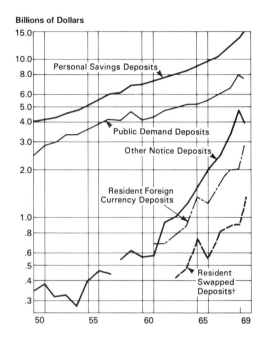

Figure 9-2
Trends in Chartered Bank Domestic Deposit Liabilities
(Semi-logarithmic Scale)

NOTE: Deposits as of December 31, except †, average of Wednesdays during December.

What accounts for these very different trends in the four main types of chartered banks' deposits? The answer lies in the banks' response to the competitive environment of the 1950's and 1960's.

Perhaps the crucial element in the new situation was the development of an active money market which was both domestic and international in scope. Corporate treasurers became increasingly aware of opportunities for investing excess cash balances in short-term assets such as treasury bills, finance company paper, and repurchase agreements with bond dealers. Holding large balances in demand accounts which paid no interest was, in terms of income foregone, an expensive proposition that offered few, if any, benefits.

The banks responded by offering interest rates on relatively large, term deposits — whether denominated in Canadian currency or "swapped" into United States dollars — which were competitive with rates offered on money market instruments. The result of this attempt to recapture short-term corporate funds has been very successful, if somewhat costly in terms of rates paid. For example, at the beginning of 1970 notice deposits amounted to more than $3.4 billion, and rates paid were 7% or more for money deposited for as little as 30 days.

A somewhat similar situation developed in the market for personal savings deposits. In this case, competition from the near banks made large inroads into the relative position of the chartered banks (See Table 9-3). Since the recent revision of the *Bank Act*, the banks have made strong efforts to recoup their position in this market.

Non-Deposit Sources of Funds

The balance sheet presented in Table 9-1 shows several other categories of domestic liabilities and the capital account as non-deposit sources of funds. Of these only the capital account has any major significance.

Acceptances, Guarantees and Letters of Credit. The account, *Acceptances, Guarantees and Letters of Credit* cannot really be described as a "source of funds" for bank operations. Unlike the other entries on the balance sheet, this represents a "contingent" liability. Although there are several different types of items recorded in this account, in general the bank has simply undertaken to guarantee certain liabilities of some of its customers (and hence there is an exactly offsetting asset account, *Customers' Liability under Acceptances, Guarantees and Letters of Credit*) in order to make those liabilities more acceptable in the market place. The bank could only be called upon to make payment in full out of its own resources if the customer failed to meet his obligation. In this sense it is a contingent liability. For this service, the bank charges a fee, and as a result it is useful to include such items in the balance sheet.

Other Liabilities. The other liabilities of the banks include such things as dividends payable but not yet collected by the shareholders, accrued tax liabilities, mortgages on bank property and other petty debts. This category also includes debentures which are long-term debts issued by the chartered banks. At the beginning of 1970 debentures issued totaled $40 million. The supposed advantage to the banks of raising funds via debentures is their relatively long term (usually 5 years or more) coupled with their exemption from any reserve requirements. To date only two banks have issued debentures and they were not very well-received in financial markets. This initial lackluster reception has apparently discouraged other banks from issuing similar instruments.

Another liability which is important, although its magnitude is generally very small (and most often zero) is *Advances from the Bank of Canada*. These are short-term loans made by the central bank to the chartered banks. When a bank for reasons of a sudden and adverse clearing against it or because of a sudden deposit withdrawal finds itself short of the legally required amounts of vault cash and/or deposits with the central bank it can borrow the needed funds for a short period of time from the central bank. This loan or *advance* gives the chartered bank time to liquidate some of its assets and then use the proceeds to repay the loan from the central bank. Later in this chapter, when we consider the position

Table 9-3

Personal Savings Held
with Various Financial Intermediaries

(Millions of Dollars)

TYPE	1945		1955		1965		1970	
	AMOUNT	% OF TOTAL	AMOUNT	% OF TOTAL	AMOUNT	% OF TOTAL	AMOUNT	% OF TOTAL
Chartered Bank Savings Deposits	2,635	78.7	5,633	73.0	9,725	54.9	15,030	55.3
Quebec Savings Bank Deposits	130	3.8	247	3.2	402	2.3	494	1.8
Credit Union and Caisse Populaire Shares & Deposits	135	4.0	598	7.7	2,275	12.8	3,778	13.9
Trust Company Deposits and Certificates	181	5.4	597	7.7	3,318	18.8	5,189	19.1
Mortgage Loan Deposits and Debentures	156	4.8	469	6.1	1,760	9.9	2,397	8.8
Government Savings Institutes	110	3.3	180	2.3	226	1.3	302	1.1
	3,347	100.0	7,734	100.0	17,706	100.0	27,190	100.0

SOURCES: Royal Commission on Banking and Finance, Report; Bank of Canada: Statistical Summary, June 1970, Supplement, 1969, 1970.

of the banks in the money market, and again in Chapter 17 when we discuss the functions of the central bank, we shall discuss various aspects of these advances in greater detail.

The Capital Account. What we are calling the capital account of the banks is simply the difference between the reported values of the banks' assets and liabilities. The sums recorded in this account derive from two sources, the capital subscribed by the original purchasers of shares of the banks' stock, and appropriations from the earnings of the banks over the years. They thus represent a source of operating funds for the banks, funds which can be ascribed directly or indirectly to the banks' shareholders.

In fact, the capital account has two separable components — *accumulated reserves for losses* and *shareholders' equity.* The distinction between these two components is important to the accountant concerned with measuring the profitability of the bank, or to the government concerned with assessing corporate income taxes (the banks are allowed to make limited additions to reserves for losses in most years without treating these funds as taxable profits). However, from our present point of view the distinction is not important.[9] They serve essentially the same function by providing a margin of safety for the bank's depositors and other creditors. This margin of safety is provided by the fact that the value of assets exceeds the value of creditors' claims by the magnitude of the capital accounts, and by the fact that the creditors' claims must be satisfied before any distribution of assets can be made to shareholders should the corporation be wound up. Thus, the capital accounts provide an estimate of the value of the residual claim of the shareholders to the assets of the bank: a claim which is legally "subordinated" to the claims of the bank's creditors, including depositors.

5/DOMESTIC INTERMEDIATION: THE ALLOCATION OF FUNDS

We have discovered that the liability side of the balance sheet of the chartered banks has a relatively unique structure, but that in recent years that structure has been undergoing rather dramatic changes. The same things can be said about the asset side of the balance sheet. There is a standard, historical mould, but the pattern of chartered bank involvement in the flow of credit to the economy has been changing significantly in recent years, and as a result the structure of the banks' asset holdings has been changing too.

If we want to analyze the banks' activities in the credit field, we must take account of four groups of factors: (1) the classic or historical pattern of chartered bank activities; (2) the incentives to change created by attempts to maximize profits in a changing economy; (3) the ever present necessity of coping with the high degree of banker's risk inherent in the structure of bank liabilities; and (4) a number of overriding legal constraints on what the banks are permitted to do.

The Allocation of Funds: Bank Loans

In a book which was for many years the standard exposition of Canadian chartered bank policies and practices, A. B. Jamieson asserted that:

> The chartered banks give two main functions: (1) to provide a safe depository for the funds of individuals and business concerns throughout Canada, and (2) within the limits of prudent banking to make these funds available to facilitate production and trade.[10]

Ten years later, in their brief to the Royal Commission on Banking and Finance, the Canadian Bankers' Association echoed agreement. Asserting that one of the primary functions of the chartered banks must be ". . . to make loans", they argued that

> the first priority in bank lending must still be given to short term business borrowing for working capital purposes.[11]

The management of all other aspects of the banks' asset portfolios, including the banks' investment activities, must normally be ". . . subsidiary to bank lending activities".

This is the traditional view of the role of the chartered banks in the flow of credit to the economy. Is it a valid description of the contemporary activities of the chartered banks?

We provided part of the answer to this question in the introduction to this chapter. The chartered banks remain today the primary source of short-term credit for businesses in Canada. But perhaps that should not be too surprising. The Canadian banking system developed over the years with the commercial lending function foremost in mind. As the Canadian Bankers' Association likes to emphasize, "there appears to be no other source similarly qualified to provide, administer and supervise this type of loan."[12] The business of making loans involves face-to-face negotiations between the lender and the borrower. The organization of the banking system facilitates this process. Thus, the banks have networks of branch offices, and in the case of the five largest banks these networks are nationwide in scope. In early 1969 the nine banks in operation had between them 5,959 offices in Canada, with the five largest banks accounting for almost 85% of them. These branch offices are in part deposit collection and administration points, but they are also loan offices, strategically located to service loan accounts. The business of making loans also involves a degree of skill in judging credit-worthiness. As the Canadian Bankers' Association again emphasizes:

> The training of branch managers is aimed at the development of officers who can seek out lending opportunities and make good loans. The manager's recognition and advancement depends to a significant degree on his abilities in making loans.[13]

Such, then, is the bankers' self-image. They consider themselves to be particularly well-adapted to make loans, especially commercial loans, and they consider commercial lending to have first priority in their credit activities. Are these assertions borne out by the facts?

Loans versus Securities. Consider first Figure 9-3. The upper panel shows trends in total Canadian dollar assets, loans and security holding since 1950 (unfortunately data are not available to permit inclusion of foreign currency claims on Canadian residents for all of this period). The lower panel shows the relative importance of loans and securities in the total Canadian dollar asset portfolio.

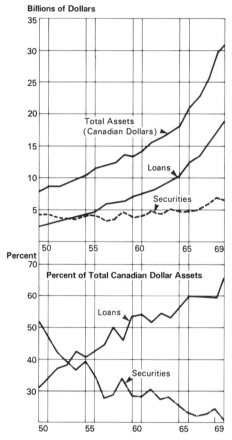

Figure 9-3

Figure 9-3 shows a very marked increase in the relative importance of loans among the total Canadian dollar asset holdings of the banks. From a minority position at the beginning of 1950 (31% of assets), loans have increased to a very dominant position in 1970 (62%). The importance of loans among the assets of the chartered banks is now greater than it has been at any time since the late 1920's.[14] There has been a corresponding decline in the relative importance of securities among the banks' assets, from 52% to 21%. Indeed, banks' holdings of securities were scarcely higher in 1970 than in 1950, although total Canadian dollar assets of the banks had almost quadrupled in the interval. What Jamieson said about the nature of the banking business in 1952, and what the Canadian Bankers' Association said in 1962 was even more true in 1970. The story of the growth of the chartered banks in the 1950's and 1960's has been a story of the growth of their lending business.

The Composition of the Loan Portfolio. The assertion that the main thrust in the banks credit activities takes the form of "making loans" is clearly correct. Security holdings are of much smaller relative importance. What about the additional assertion that bank loans are primarily "commercial" loans?

Table 9-4
The Chartered Banks' Canadian Dollar Loan Portfolio

	1950	1960	1970
Commercial Loans			
Farmers	243	420	1,135
Merchants	597	1,321	2,690
Other Industries	969	2,362	7,118
Total Commercial	1,809	4,103	10,943
Financial Loans	351	681	997
Commercial and Financial	2,160	4,784	11,940
Government and Institutional	186	538	1,222
Personal Loans			
Mortgages	—	971	1,324
Other Personal Loans	597	1,385	5,019
Total Personal	597	2,356	6,333
TOTAL CANADIAN DOLLAR LOANS	2,943	7,678	19,495
Percentage Distribution			
Commercial and Financial	74	62	61
Government and Institutional	6	7	6
Personal:			
Mortgages	0	12	7
Other Personal Loans	20	18	26
TOTAL	100	100	100

SOURCE: Bank of Canada *Statistical Summary,* June 1970.

Evidence on trends in the composition of the banks' loan portfolio is presented in Table 9-4. It is clear from these data that the "traditional" commercial lending business is still the dominant activity of the chartered banks, although it has been declining in relative importance. Perhaps the most notable change which is evident in Table 9-4 is the increased relative importance of personal loans. Almost one-third of the loan portfolio is in the form of mortgages and other loans to individuals and recent developments suggest that this component of the loan portfolio will increase in the future. Through the medium of the credit card and related arrangements the banks are pursuing the personal loan business with increasing vigour.

The Commercial Loan Theory of Banking and the Evolution of the Bank Act. We have seen that in contemporary practice, the chartered banks are primarily, but far from exclusively, providers of short-term credit to finance "production and trade". In an earlier day, banking theory made concentration on such loans a matter of high principle, and indeed it was argued that "any departure from this principle is bound to prove eventually disastrous."[15] The essential argument was that if the loans of chartered banks were used to finance the production and distribution of goods, the loans would be safe because they were "supported continually during their currency by the existence of the goods," and the loans would be "self-liquidating" because the goods when sold would provide the means to repay the loans.[16] This was an argument that the volume of bank credit would automatically be adjusted to the needs of trade, and therefore could be neither excessive nor deficient; and an argument that the banks would never have liquidity problems because of the revolving, short-term nature of their assets.

This is not the place to assess the merits of what has variously been called the "commercial loan" theory of banking or the "real bills" doctrine (commercial loans are "real bills" because they are backed by a corresponding value of real goods in the final stages of production). Suffice it to say that it was proven deficient both from the point of view of regulating the volume of credit and from the point of view of safeguarding the liquidity of banks. Indeed, institutional arrangements have been developed to supplant reliance on the commercial loan principle. As we will see, in contemporary banking practice, reliance is placed on the central bank to regulate the overall volume of credit, and on individual bank holdings of short-term financial instruments which can be sold in the money market and the reserve lending power of the central bank to safeguard the liquidity of the banking system.

Earlier versions of the *Bank Act* were firmly rooted in the commercial loan theory of banking. However, just as institutional arrangements for controlling the supply of credit and safeguarding the liquidity of the banking system have developed away from the real bills principle, so the lending powers conferred on the chartered banks in successive revisions of the Bank Act in recent years have embodied widening departures from the spirit of the commercial loan theory.

Early versions of the *Bank Act* contained a blanket prohibition against lending money

> upon the security, mortgage or hypothecation of any lands, tenements or immovable property, or of any ships or other vessels, or upon the security of any goods, wares or merchandise . . . except as authorized by this Act.

The crucial question, then, was what type of loans secured directly or indirectly by merchandise were explicitly authorized by the *Bank Act*.

The permissible scope of bank lending activities were spelled out in several sections of the *Bank Act*, including what have become the most famous sections of the *Act*, Sections 86 and 88. In general, these sections permitted the banks to make loans on the security of natural resources or manufactured goods in the process of distribution or production. Section 86 was primarily concerned with the distribution phase. It permitted loans secured by warehouse receipts or bills of lading for such products, i.e., on the security of evidence that such products had been placed in the custody of an independent warehouseman or a transportation company and could not be released without the bank's agreement. Section 88, by contrast, was of primary concern in the production phase. It permitted loans on the direct security of specified goods still in the hands of farmers, manufacturers and wholesalers.

In other words, Sections 86 and 88 of the *Bank Act* specifically permitted — perhaps we should say encouraged — the chartered banks to make the type of loan called for by the real bills doctrine: short-term, "self-liquidating" loans to facilitate production and distribution. By contrast, other sections of the *Act* specifically prohibited the chartered banks from making loans of a type which would violate the real bills doctrine: loans secured by long-lived capital equipment, buildings or land. It should be noted, however, that the banks were permitted wide latitude to hold stocks and bonds, to make loans on the security of stocks and bonds, or to make loans "without security".

The essential provisions of Sections 86 and 88, modified, sharpened, and broadened somewhat, remain in the *Bank Act* today (and with the same section numbers). However, the impact of the blanket prohibitions on other types of loans secured by real goods have been blunted or removed in special legislation and in successive revisions of the *Bank Act* since the late 1930's. In 1937 the banks were encouraged to make unsecured Home Improvement Loans, subject to a partial government guarantee. In the 1944 revision of the *Bank Act* the banks were permitted to make loans on the security of ships and ship equipment, fishing vessels and agricultural equipment, and under the *Farm Improvement Loans Act* of the same year they were permitted and, indeed, encouraged by a partial government guarantee to make longer-term loans for farm improvement on various types of security, including a mortgage on the farm. Similar provisions were made for longer-term loans to help establish veterans in a business or in a profession under the 1946 *Veterans' Business and Professional Loans Act*. (In 1960 the same type of guarantees were offered on longer-term capital loans to small businesses under the *Small Business Loans Act*).

These special provisions violated the spirit of the real bills doctrine, but in strictly limited amount and with most important cases, subject to governmental guarantee. The more significant changes were yet to come. One of these changes which had a profound effect on the character of the chartered banks' business, was a provision of the 1954 *Bank Act* which permitted the chartered banks to make loans to individuals who were neither farmers, manufacturers or wholesalers, on the security of chattel mortgage, that is:

upon the security . . . of household property, that is to say, motor vehicles and any personal or movable property for use in or about dwellings and lands and buildings appurtenant thereto . . .

The banks had long made personal loans, largely on the security of stocks and bonds or unsecured. This new provision opened the whole field of consumer installment credit in a fashion which was a complete violation of the real bills principle. At the time of the 1954 revision of the *Bank Act,* Parliament was not yet ready to extend similar blanket permission to enter the one major field of credit still closed to the banks, i.e., mortgage lending on the security of land and buildings. However, by the provisions of the *National Housing Act* of 1954 the banks were permitted to acquire mortgages which had been insured by the government of Canada. The final step was taken in the 1967 revision of the *Bank Act* when the prohibition against mortgage lending was removed, and the banks were given blanket permission to take as security for loans ". . . any real or personal, immovable or movable property," although a variable ceiling (initially 10% of Canadian dollar deposits) was placed on total holdings of non-insured mortgages.

Our earlier discussion of the banks' loan portfolios showed that commercial lending remains the core of their credit activities, and correspondingly Sections 86 and 88 retain a prominent and important place in the *Bank Act.* However, successive revisions of the *Bank Act* have relaxed the constraints imposed by the real bills doctrine, and the chartered banks have diversified their lending activities to a degree that they now deserve the sobriquet "the department stores of the financial system".

The Interest Rate Ceiling on Bank Loans. Another historical provision of the *Bank Act,* which was removed in the 1967 revision, has had an important impact on the banks' lending activities. That is the ceiling on the interest rate which the banks were permitted to charge on loans.

Prior to the 1967 revision of the *Bank Act* the banks were not permitted to charge interest on their loans at a rate in excess of 6% per annum. When interest rates were generally low this provision did not have a significant impact on bank operations. However, as interest rates increased in the 1950's and 1960's the banks argued that the interest rate ceiling hampered their efforts to develop new loan business.

The keystone of the structure of interest rates on bank loans is the prime rate or the rate charged on loans made to the very best customers. As the importance of the customer diminishes and the risk and cost of servicing the loan increases, the rate charged also increases. If the prime rate for some reason increases, so do the rates charged on most other loans made by the banks. But as the prime rate approached the old ceiling of 6% the banks argued that they were forced to deny credit to worthy customers because the permitted maximum of 6% did not adequately cover the cost of servicing and increased risk associated with these non-prime loans. By mid-1962 the chartered banks' prime rate was at the 6% ceiling, and from then until the removal of the ceiling in 1967 the prime rate remained at, or very little below, the ceiling. Clearly, this left little room within the law to differentiate among loan customers in terms of interest rates.

Part of the banks' reaction to this situation was to seek techniques to circumvent the restrictive impact of the ceiling. One method was to deduct the interest from the loan in advance — to discount the loan, in other words. On a loan repaid in installments, this would increase the interest rate substantially (perhaps to 9 through 12%) since interest was charged as though the entire loan was outstanding during the stipulated term. In fact, of course, the amount of the loan outstanding was continually diminishing as successive installments were paid. Increasing resort was also being made to the requirement of *compensating* balances. When a customer borrowed a large sum of money, the bank might require as a condition of the loan that the customer maintain at least a certain sum in an interest-free deposit account. Thus, if the customer borrowed $1 million for one year, at the ceiling rate of 6% and the bank required a compensating balance of $100,000 (so that the customer really only had use of $900,000, although he was paying interest on $1 million), the effective interest rate would have been increased to 6-2/3%. The larger the compensating balance, the higher the effective interest rate, of course. The most explicit avoidance of the 6% ceiling was in the field of consumer installment credit, in part through the device of collecting interest in advance, and in part through special service charges in addition to the regular interest rate.

In spite of these techniques to avoid the restrictive effects of the 6% interest rate ceiling, the Royal Commission on Banking and Finance found that the ceiling had had a significant effect on the development of bank lending. In particular, the Commission singled out term loans to business and mortgage lending as two serious cases in which the ceiling had inhibited lending because ". . . the banks have not always been able to charge rates commensurate with the risk of longer term lending."[17]

The case of mortgage loans is particularly instructive. Following the 1954 *Act* permitting the banks to acquire N.H.A.-insured mortgages, the banks' holdings of these mortgages increased rapidly to almost $1 billion in 1959. From that time on, interest rates, including mortgage rates, exceeded the ceiling, and bank mortgage lending ceased. In subsequent years, as mortgages were repaid, the banks' holdings fell steadily until late 1967, following the removal of the interest rate ceiling. Subsequently, the banks' holdings of mortgages (particularly uninsured, or "conventional" mortgages which carry a higher rate of interest than insured mortgages) have increased steadily. There also appears to have been an increase in term lending to business following the removal of the interest rate ceiling.[18] The removal of the interest rate ceiling has thus put the finishing touches on the banks, evolution away from the strict confines of the commercial loan principle of banking.

Safeguarding the Liquidity of the Banks

We must now turn our attention to an aspect of the banks' management of their asset portfolios that we have so far glossed over, their techniques of coping with the banker's risk which is inherent in the structure of their liabilities. How are the banks able to guarantee payment of such an overwhelming portion of their liabilities on demand?

Cash Reserves. A bank is required to be continuously willing and able to pay out cash when cash is demanded by its depositors. To a limited extent, normal cash drains will involve actual payments of currency over the counter in some or all of 5,960 bank offices across the country. To meet these potential over-the-counter cash drains each bank needs currency in the vaults of each of its offices across Canada. Primarily, however, cash drains will result from inter-bank settlements of net clearing balances. Since the clearing process is centralized, this implies that each bank needs funds at the Bank of Canada in Ottawa to meet potential clearing house drains (any reader who does not recall the nature of the cheque clearing process should review Section 2 of Chapter 2).

One obvious solution to the problem posed by possible cash drains would be for each bank to keep on hand at all times, both in its vaults and on deposit at the Bank of Canada, sufficient cash to meet all conceivable short-term demands for funds on the part of its depositors. As we have already pointed out, the bankers know that under normal circumstances it is highly unlikely that a large portion of deposits will be called for payment in a short period of time. As a result, the cash which they would have to hold to be "safe" would only be a fraction of their deposit liabilities — with the size of that fraction depending on the bankers' assessments of the probable volatility of their deposits and the degree of safety which they desire.

An examination of Table 9-1 reveals that the banks do in fact hold substantial amounts of cash, both in the form of currency in the vaults of their many banking offices and in the form of deposits with the Bank of Canada (and to a lesser extent with other banks). Is this, then, the bankers' primary method of hedging against banker's risk?

The Cash Reserve Requirement and Bank Liquidity. We have to be very cautious in placing such a construction on the relatively large holdings of cash by the chartered banks. The banks do not hold all of this cash voluntarily. Under the terms of the *Bank Act* they are *required* to hold cash, either in their vaults or in their deposits with the Bank of Canada, in the amount of 12% of all Canadian dollars demand deposits and 4% of all Canadian dollar savings and notice deposits. Given the composition of deposits at the beginning of 1970 this amounted to an average required reserve ratio of approximately 6.25% of total Canadian dollar deposits. Prior to June 1967, the required reserve ratio was 8% of all Canadian dollar deposits. There is no required cash reserve ratio against foreign currency deposits.[19]

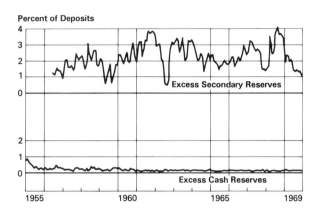

Figure 9-4
The Excess Reserves of the Chartered Banks, 1954-1969

One might argue that if the banks are required to hold this cash, then it cannot serve as a hedge against bankers' risk, because by definition the cash is not available to be paid out to depositors. Of course, this is not true of any excess reserves of cash, that is, holdings of currency and deposits at the Bank of Canada over and above those required by the *Bank Act*. Excess reserves are clearly available to be paid out to depositors. However, as the lower panel of Figure 9-4 demonstrates, excess cash reserves tend to be very small. In the past ten years they have rarely exceeded 0.1% of deposits in any month, and one has to go back 15 years to find a month in which they exceeded 0.4% of deposits. Surely excess reserves of that magnitude do not give the banks a significant margin of safety.

However, the apparent conclusion that the bulk of the banks' holdings of cash cannot be counted as a liquid asset must be modified somewhat because the legal cash reserve requirement is neither as simple nor as rigid as the above discussion implies. The actual cash reserve requirement, expressed as an equation, is as follows:

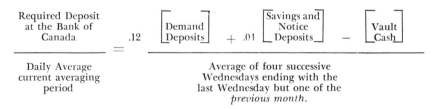

Take particular note of the time periods involved. Only the required deposit at the Bank of Canada refers to the present time period. All other elements in the equation relate to an earlier period.

From the point of view of the liquidity of the banks' cash holdings, there are two important elements of flexibility in the reserve requirement: (1) the fact that the reserve requirement need only be satisfied on a *daily average* over a set period of time; and (2) the fact that the vault cash (currency) which is to be counted in calculating the cash reserve was that held by the bank *last month.*

The significance of the first point should be obvious. Since the banks do not have to satisfy the reserve requirement every business day, they can draw their reserve deposits below the required level on some days as long as they exceed the requirement on other days by an amount sufficient to provide a daily average which satisfies the requirement. This introduces an important element of flexibility, making the banks' reserve deposits at the Bank of Canada more liquid than might appear at first glance.

Clearly, in assessing the liquidity of these deposits, an important question is how far the banks are willing to draw down their deposits below the required level on any given day. Since daily statistics are not published, we do not know. However, it undoubtedly depends in part on the *length of the averaging period.* The longer the averaging period the easier it will be for a bank to make up reserve deficiencies and hence the less reluctant will it be to fall substantially below its requirement on any given day. In Canada the reserve averaging period has traditionally been one month. Effective January 1969 it was reduced to 15 days.

The significance of the second point — the fact that it is last month's vault cash which enters the calculation of reserve holdings — may not be as obvious. However, it means that there is no legal impediment to a bank paying out currency which it has in its vaults. The entire holdings of currency could, in principle, be paid out without affecting the bank's legal reserve position. It is true that it will affect the reserve deposit which the bank must hold at the Bank of Canada on a daily average the *next month.*[20] However, paying out currency cannot create a reserve deficiency *this month.*[21] For this reason, cash in the vaults of bank offices across the country can be regarded as a perfectly liquid asset, at least for meeting over-the-counter drains.

The Demand for Excess Cash Reserves. We can conclude that bank holdings of cash provide only a *partial* hedge against banker's risk. Vault cash is available to satisfy over-the-counter demands for currency, and adverse clearing balances can be satisfied out of excess reserves or out of very temporary reductions in reserve deposits below the legal requirement. Clearly, the magnitude of the excess cash reserve is a crucial determinant of liquidity. However, we have seen that the banks in fact hold very small excess cash reserves. Given the banks' ever-present liquidity problem, is this not surprising? Should we not expect the banks to have a strong demand for liquidity, and hence to hold large sums of their most liquid asset, excess cash reserves?

The explanation for the low level of excess reserves among Canadian chartered banks is simple. The banks require sufficient stocks of liquid assets to meet possible clearinghouse drains. However, these liquid assets need not be excess cash reserves. They can be *any short-term asset which is virtually risk free and which can be converted into cash on very short notice.* While excess cash reserves do have the desirable property of immediate availability, they have the undesirable property of being sterile. By law the Bank of Canada cannot pay interest on the chartered banks' reserve deposits. By contrast, other liquid assets which the banks might hold do bear interest. As a result, a profit-maximizing banker will attempt to keep his excess cash reserves to a minimum, holding instead short-term liquid securities, as long as he can be confident that the securities can be converted into cash, on very short notice, and at a relatively small cost. This requires an active, efficient short-term money market (the nature of which was discussed in Section 3 of Chapter 3.)

Refer again to Table 9-1 and note the very substantial bank holdings of short-term, liquid securities. Almost 13% of Canadian dollar assets were in the form of day, call or short-loans, treasury bills, and other short-term Government of Canada bonds on January 1, 1970. These short-term, liquid instruments are normally referred to as the banks' *secondary reserves.*

The Secondary Reserve Requirement. As in the case of cash reserves, not all of the banks' holdings of secondary reserves are voluntary. Under a 1956 agreement sponsored by the Bank of Canada the chartered banks were obliged to hold cash, treasury bills or day-to-day loans in the amount of 7% of their Canadian dollar deposit liabilities over and above the cash reserve required by the *Bank Act,* making a combined reserve requirement of cash and liquid assets of 15% of Canadian dollar deposits.[22] In the 1967 revision of the *Bank of Canada Act* the Bank of Canada was given the statutory authority to formally establish such a secondary reserve requirement, and to change it from time to time subject to a maximum rate of 12%. The required ratio was initially established in March 1968 at 6% and almost immediately raised to 7%. In October, 1969, it was raised to 8%, and effective July 1, 1970 to 9%. With the cash reserve ratio in the neighbourhood of 6%, this makes the combined cash and liquid asset reserve requirement slightly more than 15% of Canadian dollar deposits. The combined ratio will change from time to time as the changing composition of bank deposits changes the cash ratio, or if the Bank of Canada elects to alter the liquid asset ratio.

Applying the same argument that we developed in the case of the cash reserve requirement, the existence of the secondary reserve requirement means that the banks' holdings of treasury bills and day-to-day loans are not fully liquid. To the extent that the banks' are obliged to hold these securities, they cannot be sold into the market to satisfy cash drains except on a very temporary basis. However, reference to the upper panel of Figure 9-4 shows that typically the banks have held excess reserves of treasury bills and day-to-day loans. The magnitude of these excess reserves has been quite variable, but has rarely been as much as 4% of Canadian dollar deposits. The *average* excess secondary reserve in recent years has been approximately 2% of deposits. Like the very small average excess cash reserve, this excess secondary reserve does not provide a very large margin of safety for the banks. Surely this is not the full extent of their hedge against their banker's risk.

Other Liquid Assets. The assets which may be held to satisfy the statutory secondary reserve requirement are very precisely defined. They are cash, treasury bills and day-to-day loans to investment dealers who have lines of credit with the Bank of Canada. No other assets can be included. However, there are other equally, or almost equally liquid assets which form part of the total hedge against banker's risk. In this latter category we would have to include all short-term government securities, call and short loans to other investment dealers, and some foreign currency assets — with longer-term government bonds and other marketable securities standing in a second rank of defense.

The Bank of Canada and Bank Liquidity. The analysis to this point shows that the banks' primary hedge against banker's risk consists of substantial holdings of liquid assets. This requires an active, stable money market which the banks can rely on to guarantee the liquidity of their secondary reserves. We have ignored the role of the Bank of Canada in safeguarding the liquidity of the banking system.

In fact the Bank of Canada enters the picture in two ways. In the first instance, the Bank of Canada will make short-term advances to the chartered banks. Such advances are for a minimum of seven days, and are made at an interest rate, called *the bank rate,* which is usually slightly higher than the treasury bill rate. If a second advance is granted during any averaging period it may be at a higher rate. This accentuates the idea that borrowing from the central bank should only be a last resort. In general the banks prefer not to borrow from the Bank of Canada, and as a result the average amount of such advances outstanding is very small.

The second contribution of the Bank of Canada to the overall problem of maintaining bank liquidity is to effectively underwrite the stability of the money market. It will be recalled that the Bank of Canada will also make advances to a selected list of government security dealers — the same dealers to whom the chartered banks may make call loans which can be counted as part of their secondary reserve requirement. This facility is used more actively than is the provision for direct advances to the chartered banks. Advances to the security dealers will be made at what we might call the *dealer rate.* It is the lesser of the bank rate or the treasury bill rate plus $1/4$ of 1%.

In addition to providing these lender-of-last-resort facilities, the Bank of Canada keeps a close eye on the money market with a view to maintaining "orderly" conditions. If necessary, the Bank will intervene in the market, buying or selling short-term government securities if it detects developments which might disrupt the functioning of the market.

The purpose of the reserve lending power and timely interventions of the Bank of Canada is to provide a broad, stable market which the banking system can rely upon for reserve adjustments. Thus banks with sizable cash drains have several options open to them. (1) They can temporarily draw down their cash reserves in the expectation of a reversal of the drain in the near future. (2) They can call day loans, i.e., assets which they have accumulated, confident that the security dealers will always be able to pay on demand. (3) They can sell into the money market any of a variety of short-term securities. Which technique they choose presumably depends on which one costs them least (i.e., in selling securities, which security produces the least income for them). Similarly, banks with cash inflows have several adjustment techniques, and they will choose among the alternatives on the basis of maximizing their returns. In general, we can expect most banks to be in the money market daily adjusting their cash holdings.

The Banks' Demands for Liquid Assets: Cyclical Aspects

Our discussion of the banks' demands for liquid assets has so far focused exclusively on the banker's problem of providing a hedge against banker's risk. This is not the only function which such liquid assets perform. Equally important is the role liquid assets play in helping to maximize bank income over time.

From our discussion of bank loans you will recall that the banks regard making loans as their first priority, with their investment activities "subsidiary" to their lending activities. The demand for loans — and particularly the prospects for making loans of suitable quality — varies with the level of economic activity. This is quite evident in Figure 9-3. The periods of strong increase in bank loans were 1956, 1959 and 1963-1969, all periods of expanding economic activity. The periods in between were years of comparative economic slack. The banks use their liquid asset portfolios to transfer lending capacity between these periods. That is, in periods of relatively slack demand for loans the banks will accumulate liquid assets. In periods of comparatively strong demand for loans they will dispose of the liquid assets to obtain funds to make loans. As is evident in Figure 9-5,

Figure 9-5
Chartered Banks' Secondary Reserves, 1955-1969

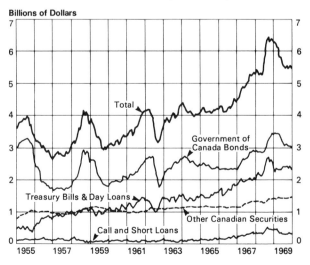

Government of Canada bonds are used primarily for carrying out such cyclical adjustments in the banks' asset portfolios.

The pattern of cyclical adjustments in the liquid asset portfolio is more clearly pronounced in the years 1954-1963 than subsequently (the pronounced dip in liquid assets in 1962 reflected special problems which arose at a time when Canada had a severe international balance of payments crisis). Indeed, in 1966-68, holdings of both loans and liquid assets increased. This, however, is not an exception to the general cyclical behaviour. What was different about the period 1966-68 was that total bank assets increased more rapidly than the demand for loans. In earlier periods of strong loan demand, total bank assets were not allowed to increase substantially (this is a matter within the discretion of the Bank of Canada, as we shall see later). It is this failure of total bank assets to increase sufficiently to accommodate what the bankers regarded as legitimate loan demands which produced the characteristic cyclical behaviour of bank liquid asset holdings.

Other Assets

We have not specifically discussed several categories of assets which appear on the domestic portion of the banks' balance sheet (Table 9-1). The account, *Items in Transit*, or bank *float* as it is sometimes called, includes such things as cheques which have been deposited with a bank but not yet collected from the bank on which they were drawn. The account, *Acceptances, Guarantees* and *Letters of Credit* is simply the asset counterpart of the contingent liability account of the same name which we discussed earlier. It appears as an asset because this is the liability of the banks' customers under the letters of credit or guarantees issued by the banks. *All Other Assets* is a grab bag of miscellaneous assets, including the banks' premises.

That leaves *foreign currency loans* to Canadian residents. Aside from drawing attention to the fact that the banks make such loans in sizable magnitude, little need be added to our earlier discussions of the foreign currency business of the banks in Canada. Just as corporations find it desirable to maintain United States dollar bank accounts, so many find it desirable to have their loans denominated in United States dollars.

6/INTERNATIONAL INTERMEDIATION

Aside from their size and nation-wide structure, perhaps the most distinctive feature of the chartered banks is the role which they play in international finance. There are, in fact, three aspects to the banks involvement in international finance.

As we have already seen, the banks provide part of the apparatus of the *international payments system*, i.e., the foreign exchange market and an international network of correspondent banks. Secondly, in areas such as the Caribbean, they provide *commercial banking services*. In many of the newly independent nations of the West Indies, Canadian banks are, in fact, the most important financial intermediaries. This commercial banking activity in the Caribbean, Latin America and parts of the western United States is primarily concerned with "retail" or consumer and small and intermediate business accounts. The major source of foreign business, however, and the one that truly involves the banks as intermediaries in international financial markets can be termed *"international wholesale" banking*. By this is meant the transacting of business in large multiples of funds (frequently $1 million or more) involving corporations, governments and other banking or financial firms. This market is truly international in scope. Funds borrowed in one country are lent in others. With very rare exceptions the typical consumer is excluded from this highly competitive global market.

We have already considered the international payments system extensively in Chapter 2. Our remarks in this section can be confined to the second and third aspects of the international business.

Foreign Commercial Banking Operations. The foreign branch business of the banks has a long history. The Maritime-based Bank of Nova Scotia was the first to venture abroad in 1889 and was subsequently followed by the Royal and Bank of Commerce. The main stimulant to this type of expansion was the obvious dependence of Canada on international trade and the particular role this trade played in the Caribbean and Latin America. On the west coast the first Bank of British Columbia (later absorbed by the Commerce) developed a branch network in Oregon and California.

The growth of deposits in these foreign branches has been uneven. Political events (such as the Cuban Revolution) resulted in some offices being closed. In some of the newer nations of the West Indies, there are strong government efforts to set up indigenous banks to compete with the foreign Canadian operations. More recently the Canadian operations in the western United States have been expanded by mergers with smaller banking firms. It can be expected that as trade increases in importance, especially with South America, the banks will continue to expand their overseas branch networks.

International "Wholesale" Banking. Almost all Canadian chartered banks maintain *agencies* in New York and other financial centers such as London and Paris. These offices function as branches, with the one notable exception that those in New York cannot directly accept deposits, but rather act as agents for the head office. For example, if an American corporation with a temporary excess of cash was encouraged to deposit some funds with a Canadian bank, these funds, although solicited by the agency, would be recorded as being carried in United States funds on the books of the head office in Canada. Since the chartered banks are forbidden by American law to directly solicit deposits to be held at their agencies they are effectively excluded from the local "retail" market. Given the nature of the wholesale market that they operate in, most of their deposits are closely akin to deposit receipts or certificates, i.e., they are left with the bank for stated periods of time at negotiated rates of interest.

Almost from their very beginning the Canadian chartered banks have held sizable amounts of their assets in forms denominated in foreign currencies. In part this was to be expected, given the importance of trade to the economy. Banks held balances with American and British banks as well as currency of the two nations to be able to meet the demands of their customers.

A sizable portion of foreign currency assets represents the counterpart of the liabilities obtained in their foreign branch networks. The Canadian banks that act as domestic banks in Trinidad, for example, not only collect deposits but make loans to consumers and businesses in their host country.

Yet the holdings of foreign assets throughout the history of banking in Canada have been the result of more than foreign exchange transactions and overseas branching operations. Of key importance has been the continuing substantial investment by Canadian banks in the New York money market. Prior to the establishment of a central bank and the consequent development of a truly effective domestic money market, the banks held a substantial portion of their liquid assets in New York. The most common form was short-term loans to stockbrokers and security dealers and United States treasury bills. When a bank in Canada was faced with a liquidity problem these assets could be quickly sold and converted into gold for return to Canada.

Even with the growth of the domestic money market the Canadian banks have not abandoned their investments in New York. It is here that the banks invest a large portion of the proceeds of their swap deposits and a portion of the deposits obtained through their agencies. Indeed the Canadian banks play a dominant role in financing Wall Street. At various times in the past few years, loans from Canadian banks have been equal to as much as 50% of the total financing received by New York brokers and dealers.

In the past decade and a half there has developed a new international financial market that deals in the lending and borrowing of large sums of United States dollar balances. While it is called the *Euro-dollar Market,* it is not strictly a European market. It accounts for a major part of the rapid expansion of foreign currency business done by the Canadian banks. A large part of the funds obtained by the banks' agencies in New York are invested in this market, as are some of the foreign currency deposits of Canadian residents.

The typical lender of dollar balances to the Canadian banks are major corporations. The banks in turn lend these funds to European or Asian banks, corporations, and occasionally governments. For the borrower, the market offers several attractions. It may be that domestic sources of credit are either unable or unwilling to extend credit to the borrower. Frequently, interest rates are lower in the Euro-dollar Market than in domestic markets. In some cases foreign currency, and especially United States dollars, cannot otherwise be obtained because of quotas or exchange controls.

For the lender of funds in the market (the Canadian banks among others), the attractions are also tempting. While competition among banks for Euro-dollar deposits frequently reduces the margin between the interest rate received and the interest paid to a fraction of 1%, on a large volume of transactions the revenue can be substantial. Moreover, the large size of each transaction, and the international reputations of most borrowers, make both the costs of intermediation and the credit risks extremely low per dollar of deposits. In addition, the banks may attract other business in this way. For example, they may gain the Canadian business of international corporations.

Why is it that corporations with excess funds do not participate directly in the market rather than using banks? The answer for the most part was given in Chapter 8 where we discussed intermediation. The banks, with their wide network of international correspondents are able to obtain a more precise picture of demand conditions in the market. But more important, even though these corporations may have several millions to invest, it is unlikely that they could obtain the degree of diversification and consequent reduction in risk that they enjoy when they put their funds with a bank. In essence, Canadian banks operating in the Euro-dollar market perform the same service for giant corporations that they do in the domestic market for individual savers, i.e., provide a means for asset diversification. It would be the rare though not inconceivable corporation that would find it worthwhile to participate directly in such a large financial market.

7/CONCLUSIONS: THE CHARTERED BANKS AS FINANCIAL INTERMEDIARIES

In their domestic operations, the chartered banks provide one classic stereotype of a financial intermediary. The banks collect funds by appealing to assetholders' demands for highly liquid assets, including assets which can be used as a medium of exchange. The banks have become increasingly successful in developing different types of deposits to appeal to many different specific asset preferences. On the other side of their operations, the use of the funds collected, the banks have primarily been short-term commercial lenders. This pattern of activities is also changing, as the banks extend more term loans, consumer loans and acquire more residential mortgages.

The banks also hold very sizable portfolios of marketable securities some long term but most short term. As we have seen, the main purpose of these securities is to provide a hedge against banker's risk, and to transfer lending power over time. As a result, bank holdings of securities fluctuate fairly widely, from day to day, week to week, month to month and year to year.

We also must not forget that the chartered banks are not simply domestic intermediaries. They have vast international operations, as commercial banks in several countries and as true international intermediaries. The banks also carry on a significant foreign currency business with residents of Canada.

FOOTNOTES

[1] Royal Commission on Banking and Finance, *Report*, p. 378.

[2] *Ibid.*, p. 363.

[3] At the end of 1967 there were only eight chartered banks. A new bank, The Bank of British Columbia, began operations during 1968. In 1969 one of the Quebec savings banks took out a charter as a chartered bank, but in mid-1970 it amalgamated with one of the established chartered banks.

[4] The Royal Commission added "or as close substitutes for such money claims." *Report*, p. 377.

[5] In Chapter 3, we distinguished between loan transactions and investment transactions as follows:

> In the former category we place all transactions involving face to face negotiations between borrowers and lenders . . . In the second category we place all transactions in "public issues", financial instruments designed to be sold on an impersonal basis to any and all buyers.

[6] V. Salyzyn, "The Behaviour of Personal Savings Depositors: A Rejoinder," in *Canadian Journal of Economics*, Vol. 1 (Feb. 1968), p. 111. (Reprinted by permission of the Canadian Journal of Economics.)

[7] Canadian Bankers' Association, *Submission to the Royal Commission on Banking and Finance*, July 1962, p. 101.

[8] The vertical axis on Figure 9-2 is a logarithmic scale. As a result, equal changes on any of the lines on the chart represent equal percentage rates of change, not equal absolute dollar changes.

[9] Prior to the revision of the Bank Act in 1967, the banks' reserves against losses were secret. In Table 9-1 the assets of the banks are reported at their true value, and the reserve for losses appears as a specific entry on the liability side of the balance sheet. In order to keep the reserves secret, the earlier practice had been to deliberately understate the value of assets. We can illustrate this with respect to December 31, 1966, a date for which we have the data based on the earlier system of hidden reserves, and the new system of reported reserves. The relevant information is as follows.

Hidden Inner Reserves of the Chartered Banks,
December 31, 1966

Assets whose Value was understated	True Value	Reported Value	Hidden Reserve
Call and Short Loans	291	285	6
Other Canadian Loans	12,118	11,849	269
Canadian Securities (other than Gov't. of Canada)	1,167	1,149	18
Foreign Currency Assets	5,643	5,562	81
Other Assets	479	478	1
Total of Above	19,698	19,322	377
TOTAL ASSETS	28,150	27,773	377

The net effect in terms of the margin of safety provided to depositors over and above that accounted for by shareholders' equity was the same whether the reserve was hidden or reported. However, when the magnitude of the reserve was hidden, the size of the margin of safety was never known by the public. Furthermore, since appropriations to hidden reserves (or, in some years, deductions from them) were also secret, the general public could never know the true profits of the banks in any given year. The reported profits would understate true profits by the amount of transfers to hidden reserves (or would overstate true profits by the amount of transfers out of hidden reserves). As a result, hidden reserves were the subject of much controversy. Of course, the Minister of Finance, with his interest in the taxation of the banks, exerted certain controls over the maximum amount of such hidden transfers. The whole topic of "inner reserves" is discussed thoroughly in the *Report* of the Royal Commission on Banking and Finance, pp. 144-5, and 386-9.

[10] A. B. Jamieson, *Chartered Banking in Canada* (Toronto: The Ryerson Press, 1953), p. 205.

[11] Canadian Bankers' Association, *Submission to the Royal Commission on Banking and Finance* (1962), p. 13.

[12] *Ibid.*, p. 13.

[13] *Ibid.*, p. 43.

[14] In the later 1920's loans accounted for between 55 and 60% of the banks' Canadian assets. During the depression of the 1930's this proportion fell to the neighbourhood of 30%, as bank loans to businesses and financial institutions fell off sharply. During World War II total bank assets increased sharply, from approximately $3.3 billion in 1939 to $7.2 billion in 1946. However, a large part of the increase in assets took the form of purchases of Government of Canada securities, issued to finance the war effort. As a result, the share of loans in the total portfolio continued to fall. In 1946 loans accounted for only 20% of Canadian dollar assets, whereas securities accounted for 58%, and well over 90% of those securities were Government of Canada bonds. In part, the long run trend so evident in Figure 9-3 is a prolonged adjustment to the very abnormal situation produced by the depression and the war.

[15] E. L. S. Patterson, *Canadian Banking*, rev. ed. (Toronto: The Ryerson Press, 1941), p. 193.

[16] *Ibid.*

[17] Royal Commission on Banking and Finance, *Report*, p. 124.

[18] *Bank of Canada Annual Report 1967*, p. 52.

[19] With respect to foreign currency deposits the Bank Act only requires that "the banks shall maintain adequate and appropriate assets against liabilities payable in foreign currencies." (Section 72 (7)).

[20] You should note that there are two effects on next month's reserves. The fact that cash holdings this month are lower increases the amount which must be held on deposit with the Bank of Canada next month. However, the reduction in cash holdings also reduces deposits this month, and that reduces the level of reserves which must be held next month. If all of the cash drain were a result of a reduction in demand deposits, every dollar of cash lost this month would increase the required reserve deposit next month by $.88 ($1—.12 x $1) .

[21] It should be noted that if the banks attempt to replenish the currency withdrawn by depositors by withdrawing currency from the Bank of Canada to be placed in branch vaults, that action will tend to create a reserve deficiency. However, it is the banks' attempt to keep their vault cash constant in the face of cash withdrawals by depositors, not the cash drain itself, which creates the dollar for dollar reduction in reserves with the Bank of Canada.

[22] The 1956 agreement served two purposes. It helped create a captive market for treasury bills and day-to-day loans to government security dealers, thus facilitating the rapid development of the money market. In addition, it served to impound large quantities of liquidity which the banks might attempt to use to increase bank loans at times when the Bank of Canada is attempting to restrict cash. It is presumably for the latter reason that the Bank of Canada reported in its 1967 Annual Report that "the present circumstances have not been regarded as appropriate ones in which to do away with the secondary reserve requirement." Bank of Canada, *Annual Report*, 1967, p. 49. We will have occasion to explore some of the economics of adjustments in the banks' asset portfolios later in the book.

10

The Near Banks as
Financial Intermediaries

In the previous chapter we considered a group of financial intermediaries which, by any definition, must be classified as banks. There are
only nine chartered banks, but in their hands we find the largest and
most diversified portfolio of assets held by any group of financial intermediaries in Canada. However, as we saw in Chapter 9, the relative position
of the chartered banks *vis-à-vis* other financial intermediaries has been
declining in recent years. Particularly important in contributing to the
erosion of the relative position of the chartered banks, has been intense
competition from a large number of generally smaller intermediaries which,
though in many ways different from each other, can be readily grouped
together in the general category of "near banks".

1/THE CONCEPT OF A NEAR BANK

Our definition of a near bank is quite simple. *It is a financial intermediary which raises a major portion of its operating funds by issuing
liabilities which are close, if not perfect, substitutes for the major liability
of the chartered banks, personal savings deposits.* In this sense, the bulk
of near bank liabilities are close substitutes for money as liquid assets, and
hence near banks belong in the category of financial intermediaries which
the Royal Commission on Banking and Finance argued ought to be
grouped together with the chartered banks for regulatory purposes.

The primary difference between the banks and the near banks lies in
their respective involvements in the payments system. Demand deposits
issued by the chartered banks are the primary medium of exchange in the
economy. Chequable savings deposits, whether issued by the banks or the
near banks, are much less important for this purpose. As a result, although
they issue liabilities which are the equivalent of chequable savings deposits
in chartered banks, the involvement of the near banks in the payments
system is comparatively minor. Indeed, although they compete strongly
with the chartered banks for deposit business, from a strictly institutional
point of view the near banks participate in the payments system through
the suffrage of the chartered banks (remember: the near banks cannot
belong to the Canadian Bankers Association, which operates the clearinghouses).

There are other differences between the banks and the near banks. The near banks do not have the massive involvement in international finance that is characteristic of the banks. The near banks are essentially domestic, personal savings banks. Given the dominant importance of personal savings deposits among their liabilities, in general, the average volatility of their liabilities is lower than that of the banks, and hence, the degree of banker's risk faced by these institutions is not as great as that facing the banks. Not surprisingly, as we shall see upon detailed examination, the structure of their asset portfolios is markedly different from those of the banks. It is also worth noting that for the most part, these institutions, unlike the banks, are under the jurisdiction of the provincial rather than the federal governments, though *de facto* the federal government is playing an increasingly important role in their inspection and supervision. The reader should bear in mind that while we emphasize these differences to permit us to obtain, for purposes of subsequent analysis, some sort of classification system, these firms all are engaged essentially in the same activity, financial intermediation. Their liabilities provide wealth-owners with asset forms that are preferable to the direct holding of claims on borrowers and at the same time provide borrowers with a lower cost source of finance than if they borrowed directly from wealth-owners. Thus the *essential differences between banks and near banks are in form and not in substance.*

2/THE QUEBEC SAVINGS BANKS

Of all of the near banks which we shall examine in this chapter, one category, the Quebec savings banks, constitutes an exception to the general rule of the primacy of provincial responsibility for the regulation and supervision of near banking operations. There is now only one firm in this category,[1] and it is regulated under the provisions of a federal law, the *Quebec Savings Bank Act,* which, like the *Bank Act,* is subject to revision every ten years. Its assets of slightly more than $590 million make it smaller than all but two of the chartered banks.

Regulation of the Quebec Savings Banks

Until recently, the Quebec savings banks have had a firmly established reputation for conservative management. Thus, as late as 1953, they had over 40% of their total assets invested in Government of Canada bonds and almost 70% of their assets in cash, and bonds of either the Government of Canada or one of the provinces. Indeed, it was not until 1959 that the latter ratio fell below 50%, nor until 1962 that it fell below 40%. These are relatively "safe" assets, and also relatively low-yielding.

This "conservatism" in the asset portfolio restricted the interest rate which the Quebec savings bank could offer on their personal savings deposits. In general, they offered the same interest rates as chartered banks. Perhaps for this reason, over the postwar period, when near banks in general were growing much more rapidly than the chartered banks, Quebec savings banks grew at roughly the same rate as chartered banks.

This "conservatism" cannot be laid entirely at the doorsteps of the management of the Quebec savings banks. In substantial part it was the product of the restrictive provisions of the law under which they operated. Unlike the *Bank Act,* which specifies the assets which the banks *may not* hold, the *Quebec Savings Bank Act* specifies which assets the savings banks *may* hold. All those not mentioned by name or class are excluded. This approach to regulation has impaired the flexibility of these institutions in branching into new lines of business and in adapting to changing market conditions.

Although the law has been progressively relaxed, the restrictions under which the Quebec savings banks have operated in recent years have been generally more severe than those affecting other near banks. Most important in this regard were restrictions on investment in mortgages. They were first permitted to invest a small portion of their assets in such securities in 1948, and subsequently the proportion of assets which might be held in this form has been progressively increased. It is also significant that until recently Quebec savings banks were not permitted to open branches outside the cities in which they had head offices. The severity of these restrictions undoubtedly explains why new institutions have not applied for charters under this *Act* (perhaps anticipating this result, the Act does not establish any procedures for granting new charters). The new near banks in the postwar period have all been in other categories. Indeed, the history of the Quebec savings banks may contain a significant moral. When the original legislation was passed, the government anticipated the rapid development of a nation-wide network of sound, federally supervised savings banks to parallel the chartered banks. However, the portfolio restrictions enacted to guarantee their soundness also stifled their growth in an environment in which their competitors were not similarly encumbered.

The Balance Sheet of the Quebec Savings Banks

The liability side of the balance sheet of the Quebec savings banks is notably simple. Some 91% of their funds are obtained from personal savings deposits. Like the corresponding deposit liabilities of chartered banks, savings banks legally can require notice of withdrawal of funds from these deposits. In practice, however, these deposits are payable on demand, and indeed are transferable by cheque.

The structure of the asset portfolio is in part a product of the regulations under which a savings bank operates. It is subject to a cash reserve requirement of 5% of deposits. This requirement may be satisfied either with cash held in the banks' vaults, deposits with the Bank of Canada, or deposits with a chartered bank. A Quebec savings bank is also subject to a secondary reserve requirement of 15% of deposits. This may be satisfied with cash, deposits with the Bank of Canada or chartered banks, or securities of the government of Canada or any province of Canada, provided that these securities are denominated in Canadian dollars.

The remainder of its asset portfolio consists of secured and unsecured loans (mainly to individuals) and mortgages. The ability to extend both

Table 10-1
Consolidated Balance Sheet of Quebec Savings Banks, December 31, 1969

ASSETS	Millions of Dollars	%	LIABILITIES	Millions of Dollars	%
Cash	26.8	5	Deposits		
Securities			Personal savings	499.9	91
Government of Canada	34.5	6	Government of Canada	17.9	3
Provincial governments	46.9	9			
Municipal governments	30.2	6	Advances from chartered		
Other	45.9	8	banks and Bank of Canada	—	—
Mortgages	269.2	50			
Loans			Capital accounts and others	29.5	6
Secured	16.0	3			
Unsecured	29.1	4			
Other	48.3	9			
	541.9			541.9	

SOURCE: Bank of Canada *Statistical Summary*, 1970.

mortgage and unsecured personal loans is one advantage which a savings bank has over most other near banks. A savings bank can now provide individual wealth-owners with virtually all of the services offered by the chartered banks except those involved in large-scale domestic and international payments. Indeed, until the recent revision of the *Bank Act*, the Quebec savings banks were the only banks or near banks which could extend both mortgage and personal loans (given the interest rate ceiling on chartered bank loans).

3/CO-OPERATIVE BANKS: THE CREDIT UNIONS AND CAISSES POPULAIRES

The Nature and Organization of Cooperative Banks

In organizational form, if not in substance, the next group of intermediaries which we want to consider are the very antithesis of the chartered banks. Whereas the chartered banks are privately owned, profit-seeking firms with centrally controlled, nation-wide branch operations, accepting deposits from and lending to the general public; the credit unions and *caisses populaires* are cooperative, non-profit seeking firms, with autonomous local, normally (but not exclusively) single-office operations, accepting deposits from, and lending money to members only. In the case of the chartered banks there is a clear distinction between borrowers and depositors on the one hand and the shareholders (or owners) on the other (although shareholders can be depositors and can borrow from the bank, of course). In the case of the cooperative banks both borrowers and depositors must be members, and as members, all have equal voting rights. In keeping with their local character, each credit union or *caisse populaire* is independent in its operating policies (although there are centralizing arrangements which we will examine shortly).

Local autonomy also brings with it diversity in character and organization, diversity which is accentuated by the tangled historical roots of the movement in Canada. Cooperative banking movements with somewhat different philosophies developed in Quebec at the turn of the century (the *Desjardins Caisses Populaires Movement*), in Ontario, and in the Maritimes in the 1930's (*the Antigonish Movement*). The latter movement subsequently spread to the prairie provinces as well. In the 1940's a major new thrust came from the United States when the *Credit Union National Association* (now called CUNA International) began organizing efforts in Canada. The indigeneous Canadian cooperative banking movements were predominantly rural, organized on community lines (including neighbourhood associations in cities) with membership open to all residents of the community, and stressed the savings aspect of the cooperative bank more than the lending aspect (much of the lending was for "productive" purposes, i.e., loans to small enterprises, farmers and fishermen). This was particularly true of the *caisses populaires* (which developed primarily, but not exclusively, in the Province of Quebec). As a result, cooperative banks in Quebec are normally organized on Parish lines, and the largest number are rural. However, in recent years the urban *caisses populaires* have been growing much more rapidly than their rural counterparts, both in number and in size, and the majority of *caisses populaires* assets are now in urban associations. However, the conservative nature of the lending policy and the emphasis on the stimulation of thrift among members has not disappeared from the movement. The CUNA-inspired credit unions, by contrast, tend to be organized on an industrial or occupational basis with membership open to all persons sharing the common industrial or occupational bond, and are much more deeply committed to a "liberal" policy of personal lending for a variety of purposes, including consumption. Such diversity makes it both difficult and potentially misleading to derive simple generalizations about the operations of cooperative banks in Canada.

The Growth of the Cooperative Bank Movement. Prior to the late 1930's, cooperative banking in Canada had a firm, broad base only in Quebec. Of the 277 local cooperative banks reported to be in existence in 1935, 239 were in the province of Quebec, and 47,000 of an estimated 52,000 members of cooperative banks in Canada belonged to Quebec local societies. The total assets of all co-operative banks was approximately $10.5 million, most of which was held by Quebec *caisses populaires*. Over the next three decades the growth of the movement was spectacular. Thus, by 1950, there were almost 3,000 local societies, with over one million members and total assets of $312 million. By 1968 there were more than 4,860 locals, with 4.6 million members and $3.7 billion in assets, representing increases over a 17-year period of 62% in the number of locals, 313% in the number of members, and 1,186% in the value of assets. Much of this growth has been outside Quebec, although in 1968 Quebec still accounted for over 35% of the locals and well over half of the members and of the assets of co-operative banks in Canada. It is also worth noting that there are substantially more *caisses populaires* than chartered bank offices in the province of Quebec, whereas in the rest of Canada there are four chartered bank offices for every three credit unions.

The growth of cooperative banks has been significant in shaping the development of financial intermediation in Canada in recent years. Moreover, while many of the individual operations are extremely small, their combined resources ($4 billion) are sufficiently large to make them an important factor in the functioning of the total financial system.

Centralizing Organizations. While local autonomy is a vigorously maintained basic principle of the cooperative bank movement, the local credit unions or *caisses* do not remain as islands unto themselves. There are several centralizing organizations. Thus, the *caisses populaires* in Quebec belong to one of two provincial *federations,* and credit unions inside and outside of Quebec belong to one of several *leagues.* While attempting to avoid interference with the autonomy of the local credit unions and *caisses,* the leagues and federations provide technical assistance to the locals, particularly in the organizational stages of new locals and in maintaining and supervising accurate bookkeeping and accounting.

The leagues and federations also provide educational services for local officers and members, and carry on lobbying and public relations activities for the cooperative banking movement. In Quebec the federations are also involved in the formal inspection and supervision of the activities of the local *caisses* to see that all legal conditions are satisfied and to ensure the soundness of the management practices in the interest of protecting depositors. In other provinces the formal supervisory function is performed by agencies of the provincial government.

Of more direct interest to us than the federations and leagues themselves are their financial arms, the *central credit societies* (or centrals, for short). Although the federations and leagues involve loose, joint affiliations of autonomous credit societies, the centrals take on some of the characteristics of central banks for groups of cooperative banks. They provide financial advice, do much of the systems' investing in stocks, bonds and other marketable securities, and act as lenders of last resort. They are credit unions for credit unions.

Most credit unions and *caisses populaires* hold deposits with a central credit society. In part, these deposits are surplus funds at the disposal of local societies. By lending such funds to individuals and to other credit unions with excess demands for funds, or by investing them in any of a variety of securities, the central provides a mechanism for the more effective utilization of the funds available within the cooperative banking system. But the role of the central credit societies goes well beyond arrangements for inter-credit union mobility of funds. By arrangements with the chartered banks, the centrals act as agents of the locals in the clearing and collection of cheques, and they hold and manage the liquid secondary reserves of the locals. Thus, the deposits with the central credit societies are in part clearing balances (out of which the central will pay cheques drawn on the local and to which it will credit the proceeds of cheques presented for collection on behalf of the local), and in part a pool of funds which can be drawn upon in time of need.

If the centrals are to serve effectively as a "mutual aid fund" for local credit unions, the centrals must pay careful attention to liquidity of their own asset portfolios. To this end the centrals hold substantial quantities of cash on deposit with chartered banks, and substantial portfolios of short-term securities. In addition, in 1953 a federal charter was obtained for what was planned as a nation-wide central credit society, the *Canadian Cooperative Credit Society*. It was planned that all provincial centrals would deposit funds with the national central, turning it into a central of centrals. The *Canadian Co-operative Credit Society* has not developed its full potential as a cooperative "central bank". Only four of the 20 central credit societies have joined the organization, and while the four are among the larger centrals (between them they account for over one-third of the total assets of central credit societies) they do not include the largest one, and they do not provide comprehensive geographical coverage.

The Balance Sheet of the Cooperative Banks

A consolidated balance sheet for credit unions and *caisses populaires* is presented in Table 10-2.

Sources of Funds. Consider first the liability side. The vast bulk of the cooperative banks' funds are derived from two sources, the capital subscribed as ownership shares by members, and fixed-interest deposits. The importance of funds subscribed by members in the form of shares is strikingly different from the situation in chartered banks. Thus, according to Table 10-2, shares accounted for more than 32% of total funds available to cooperative banks. The corresponding figure for chartered banks was only .9 of 1%.

Table 10-2

Consolidated Balance Sheet for Cooperative Banks:
Credit Unions and Caisses Populaires, January 1, 1970

ASSETS			LIABILITIES		
	Millions of Dollars	%		Millions of Dollars	%
Cash	431	11	Deposits:		
Loans	1,532	38	Term	424	
Mortgages	1,211	30	Demand	1,906	
Investments	728	18	Total	2,330	57
Other Assets	163	4	Shares	1,328	33
			Reserves and Surplus	255	6
			Other Liabilities	152	4
TOTAL	4,064	100	TOTAL	4,064	100

SOURCE: Dominion Bureau of Statistics, *Credit Unions, 1969* (Ottawa, 1971).

There are striking differences between the *caisses populaires* and the credit unions in this regard, as is suggested by Table 10-3. Deposits provide the vast bulk of funds for the cooperative banks in the province of Quebec, whereas, for cooperative banks outside Quebec, shares are very much important.

We should not make too much of the role of share capital in providing funds to cooperative banks, however. Like deposits, shares are in fact redeemable on demand (though technically subject to notice). However, they are not transferable by cheques, and as a result they are much less volatile than deposits. The average rate of turnover of shares ranges from once every 2.5 years for credit unions to once every 15 years for *caisse populaires*. From evidence cited by the Royal Commission on Banking and Finance it would appear that shares are held more as an intermediate or long-term asset rather than as a temporary abode of liquidity.

Deposits, by contrast, are more widely used for transactions purposes. In many instances they are transferable by cheque, and even when not legally subject to notice, they are *de facto* payable on demand. Since, with few exceptions, the bulk of deposits are held by individuals, the average deposit is relatively small (80% are for amounts of less than $1,000). Their annual rate of turnover varies from 2.5 to 40 times per year, the latter occurring in those unions where deposits are subject to chequing privileges.

Some credit unions (frequently the centrals) borrow funds from chartered banks and other lenders from time to time. These funds are included in the category of "other liabilities". Like other financial institutions, the cooperative banks have followed a practice of retaining part of their earnings to be accumulated as "surplus funds". This represents a share of the assets of the credit society which is not accounted for by deposits or other liabilities, and which have not been formally ascribed to shareholders.

Uses of Funds. The primary uses of the funds of cooperative banks are for loans to members, either in the form of mortgages or other loans. Some surplus funds are invested in securities, normally through the centrals, but most of the "investments" of the cooperative banks are short-term securities held (generally by the centrals) as secondary reserves. Cash, both in the form of till money and in the form of deposits with chartered banks, is held for the usual transactions reasons.

There are marked differences in the assets acquired by the *caisses populaires* and those acquired by the credit unions which are hidden in the consolidated balance sheet presented in Table 10-2. Some of these differences — reflecting different management philosophies — are brought out in Table 10-3.

In general, the management and investment policies of the *caisses* have been quite conservative when contrasted with those of the credit unions. Part of this may be a natural reflection of their differing clientele, since most of the *caisses populaires* are located in rural or relatively small settlements while a large bulk of the credit unions are located in the major urban manufacturing centres. It was the opinion of the Royal Commission that borrowing was regarded by *caisses populaires* members as a

Table 10-3
Differences between Credit Unions and Caisses Populaires
Percentage Distribution of Assets and Liabilities of Cooperative Banks
in Quebec and the Rest of Canada, January 1, 1970

	ASSETS			LIABILITIES	
	Quebec (Caisses Populaires) *	Rest of Canada (Credit Unions) *		Quebec (Caisses Populaires) *	Rest of Canada (Credit Unions) *
Cash	16	4	Deposits	81	29
Loans	24	53	Shares	12	57
Mortgages	33	26	Reserves and Surplus	6	7
Investments	22	13	Other Liabilities	1	7
Other Assets	4	4			
TOTAL	100	100	TOTAL	100	100

Composition of Investments		
Shares in Centrals	3	15
Term Deposits	5	47
Federal and Provincial Bonds	22	15
Municipal and Institutional Bonds	60	18
Other Securities	9	5
TOTAL	100	100

* The Quebec data include some credit unions operating in Quebec, and the rest of
Canada data include some *caisses populaires* operating outside Quebec.
SOURCE: Dominion Bureau of Statistics, *Credit Unions, 1969* (Ottawa, 1971).

necessary evil that was to be kept at a minimum. The main reason for
borrowing was for the purchase of land and housing and thus the holdings of mortgages are a significantly larger portion of total assets than is
true of credit unions.

Credit unions certainly do not regard borrowing as an evil. The union
is looked on by members as an accessible source of short-term consumer
finance and frequently as many as 50% of the membership will have loans
outstanding. The feature of accessibility appears to be one of the prime
attractions of the movement. Given the close association of members,
especially in the smaller industrial-based units, the management may have
a more personal knowledge of the individual's particular situation. Con-
sequently, a person not accommodated at a bank might obtain the needed
funds at the credit union and thereby avoid the higher rates usually charged
by the finance and consumer loan companies.

Finally, a significant aspect of the different characteristics of *caisses
populaires* and credit unions is revealed in the relative importance and
composition of their investments. *Caisses* hold a much higher proportion

of their assets in securities, the bulk of which are the bonds of local muni-
cipalities and religious and charitable institutions. By contrast, most of the
credit unions' investments are liquid reserves of term deposits, shares in
central credit unions and Government of Canada bonds.

In a word, the *caisses populaires* act like relatively conservative savings
banks, whereas the credit unions are more like mutual consumer loan
societies.

The Demand for Cooperative Bank Liabilities

It should be clear from what we have said that deposits and shares
in a credit union must be regarded as substitutes for personal savings
deposits in chartered banks. Why do some wealth-owners choose to hold
a portion of their assets in the form of claims on credit unions or *caisses
populaires*?

As with all aspects of the cooperative movement, ideology is probably
an important factor. The cooperative banks cannot be regarded simply as
another differentiated group of financial intermediaries. They represent a
movement with a particular philosophy which values voluntary co-operation
and mutual assistance in economic affairs. In the words of one spokesman:

> the whole idea of the Credit Union Movement is to ge tpeople to work to
> gether locally, to handle their own finances, to work (out) economic prob-
> lems which beset them as a particular group and to determine their own
> financial matters as much as possible to within the structure which has
> been created.[2]

Undoubtedly, many members hold funds in credit unions or *caisses populaires* simply because they subscribe to this philosophy (and many non-
members refuse to join because they object to this philosophy) .

Beyond this there are some important economic reasons. As we have
already pointed out, one is the possibility of relatively easy access to low-
cost credit associated with membership in the credit society. In other
instances there may be advantages associated with the location of the credit
society's offices. For example, in many industrial based credit unions, the
union office is located within the plant and it maintains hours which
coincide with work schedules. In some areas, particularly in rural Quebec,
the cooperative bank may be the only intermediary in the community.

It is doubtful that all of these considerations are sufficient to explain
the remarkable growth of cooperative banks in the postwar period. The
yields on shares and deposits in the cooperative banks relative to that on
personal savings deposits in the chartered banks must also be a vital factor.
Local autonomy complicates the picture. The cooperative banks do not all
pay the same interest and dividend rates. The dividend rate depends on
the "profitability" of the operations during the year. Not unexpectedly,
according to one careful study, relatively new institutions tend to have
lower dividend rates than do older, well-established institutions. Moreover,
there appear to be significant differences between dividend rates on cooperative bank shares in different provinces. Thus, for example, it was
reported in 1965 that the most common dividend rate in each province

ranged between 3% in New ·Brunswick and Saskatchewan and 5% in Ontario and Quebec. Similar diversity is to be noted in the rates paid on deposits. In spite of this wide diversity, it is nonetheless true that throughout the postwar period both the interest and dividend rates paid by the established cooperative banks have been somewhat above the rate paid on personal savings deposits by the chartered banks.

How can the cooperative banks simultaneously pay higher rates of interest and dividends on borrowed funds, and lend to members at lower rates of interest than competitive institutions? In many instances the office staff is minimal or entirely voluntary, so that administrative costs are low per dollar of assets. This is particularly important in small credit unions and *caisses populaires* where the diseconomies of small-scale operations would otherwise be a serious impediment to profitable operation. Secondly, since most loans are made to members who are known on a personal basis by the officers of the institution the rate of default is extremely low. It may also be of some importance that as cooperatives the credit unions and *caisses populaires* are not subject to corporate income taxes. Their entire "profit", aside from necessary additions to reserves, can be paid out as interest or dividends to members.

4/THE TRUST COMPANIES

Canadian trust companies are in a sense simultaneously two businesses within the same organization. On the one hand they act as trustees, managing or administering estates and other trust funds and on the other hand they are true financial intermediaries, collecting funds through deposits and investing those funds in the hopes of making a profit.

The Estate, Trust and Agency Business

Our primary concern will be with trust companies' activities as financial intermediaries, but we should briefly review the other side of their operations, referred to as the *Estate, Trust and Agency* business.

When a trust company is acting as a financial intermediary, it is a principal in the financial transaction. It collects money by issuing claims on itself, and it then purchases assets for its own account. Profits, if any, are a result of differences between the yield on the assets and the interest paid on liabilities. When the trust company is acting as a trustee, by contrast, it is not a principal in the transaction (although it may legally "own" the assets). Rather, it acts as an *agent,* administering trust funds for a set fee for services rendered. Under some arrangements the trust company has no discretion in the investments to be made. It merely acts as an agent for the owner of the funds, carrying out his explicit instructions (although perhaps offering him advice). This is the so-called agency business, and in 1961 (the only year for which data are available) it accounted for almost half of the funds under administration. Under other arrangements the trust company has a wide range of discretion with respect to the investments to be made: the company is a trustee in the true sense. However, even in the case of these trusts, the company's discretion may be limited by the agreement under which the trust was created, or by applicable provincial trusteeship laws. The range of activities incompassed by the ETA accounts is broad. For example, the companies act as administrators of estates and personal trust funds, they manage pension funds, and they administer funds set aside by corporations for the repayment of bonded debt.

Over the past 15 years the ETA business has increased rapidly. From $3.9 billion in 1952, the book value of assets under administration increased to $7.4 billion in 1960, and to $18.8 billion in 1969. These accounts represent a very sizable concentration of assets: in 1969 they were more than three times the value of assets held by trust companies as the result of their business as intermediaries. While the trust companies have complete discretion with respect to the employment of very few of these funds, the policies pursued by the trust companies in administering the ETA funds over which they do have control can have a profound effect on the flow of credit through financial markets. Therefore, to consider only their activities as financial intermediaries would be to vastly understate their importance in the financial system.

Use of Funds. Data covering the deployment of the funds entrusted to the administration of the trust companies are sketchy at best. The best available information relates to 1962, and is the product of a special survey of some of the major offices of three large trust companies undertaken for the Royal Commission on Banking and Finance. The results of that survey are reported in Table 10-4. If these companies are at all representative (and if the information is still accurate) it would appear that the ETA accounts are primarily a source of funds for investment in equities and longer-term bonds. Little more can be said.

Table 10-4
Distribution of Assets of E.T.A. Accounts: 3 Major Trust Companies, 1962

		Percent
Cash		3
Government of Canada Bonds		
Short-Term	2	
Long-Term	9	11
Provincial and Municipal Bonds		13
Other Bonds and Short-Term Paper		
Canadian	10	
Foreign	1	11
Mortgages		2
Equities		
Canadian	48	
Foreign	12	60
TOTAL		100

SOURCE: *Royal Commission on Banking and Finance, Appendix Volume* (Ottawa: Queen's Printer, 1964), pp. 233-246.

The Trust Companies as Financial Intermediaries

The trust companies' business as financial intermediaries has grown even more rapidly than their business as trustees. In 1952 the book value of assets held in ETA accounts was more than eight times the value of assets held on an intermediation basis. By 1969, that ratio had fallen to three times. As financial intermediaries, the trust companies are the single most important group of near banks and are strong competitors of the chartered banks in the market for personal savings deposits. They also offer the banks effective, though somewhat restricted, competition in some aspects of what has been called the "wholesale" deposit market (i.e., the market for relatively large blocks of funds on short-term deposit). Indeed, many observers believe that the rapid growth of the trust companies intermediary business in recent years has been largely at the expense of the chartered banks.

Not all trust companies operate an intermediary business. Those that do must operate under a charter issued by either the Federal Government or one of the provincial governments. However, all trust companies must register with the appropriate authorities in the provinces in which they do business, and must conform to the regulations of those provinces regardless of the province in which they are chartered. Most of the large trust companies have operations in Ontario, and hence must abide by Ontario regulations. As a result, there is less diversity in the applicable regulations than might otherwise be the case. These regulations restrict the types of assets in which trust companies can invest funds derived from deposits (so-called "guaranteed" funds). However, the range of permissible investments is wide enough to allow broad latitude to the trust companies in deciding on investment policies.

Sources of Funds. Like the chartered banks, the trust companies offer two kinds of deposits which are nominally subject to notice, but which are in fact payable on demand. One type is chequable whereas the other is not, and both are directed at personal savings, extremely active use of the chequing privilege being discouraged.

But the most important single source of funds for the trust companies comes from term deposits or guaranteed investment certificates. Usually sold in denominations of $1,000 or more the latter are funds left with companies for prescribed periods of time at predetermined interest rates. Generally, though not always, they are non-transferable. It is in this market that the companies have been successfully attracting corporate funds as well as individual savings. Trust companies have been willing to pay premium rates and have exhibited a continued willingness to "tailor" their certificates of deposits in terms of both size and maturity. As a consequence of this willingness to provide an asset form that closely matches the wealth-owner's preferences, the Royal Commission on Banking and Finance found that in 1961 more than 40% of the total amount of these longer-term funds were derived from corporate sources. The preponderant portion were in the 1- to 6-year maturity range when initially taken out.

Use of Funds. The trust companies, like other banks and near banks, must manage their asset portfolios with one eye on the ever-present banker's risk. This risk is clearly less for the trust companies than for the chartered banks since the former do not participate in the same central way in the payments system. Nonetheless, the trust companies must hold substantial quantities of liquid assets, including cash and short-term marketable securities. Unlike the chartered banks, the trust companies are not required by law to hold cash reserves in any specified ratio, nor to hold cash deposits with the Bank of Canada. As a result, their cash holdings can be kept to a working minimum (although, under Ontario law, they are required to hold "liquid assets" in the amount of 20% of deposit liabilities). As is shown on Table 10-5, their total Canadian cash holdings amounted to less than 2% of their total assets. (However, what is perhaps more relevant, they amounted to over 7% of the deposits payable on demand.)

Beyond their cash holdings, they do hold substantial quantities of short-term marketable securities and short-term deposits with chartered banks and other trust and loan companies. We have included among the liquid assets "secured loans". These are largely short-term loans to investment dealers to finance their inventories of securities. These loans reflect the trust companies' involvement in the money market as country banks (see Chapter 3). At the beginning of 1970 liquid assets amounted to over 20% of the total assets of the trust companies.

In this respect the trust companies are not significantly different from the other banking type institutions which we have examined. The strikingly different aspect of these companies is their very large holding of mortgages. At the beginning of 1970, over 57% of the total assets of the trust companies were in the form of mortgages. Indeed, one might well describe the trust companies as warehouses for mortgages.

One factor explaining the high degree of concentration of assets in mortgages is the relatively low degree of banker's risk facing the companies. More than one half of the total liabilities are for fixed terms and of the remainder the non-chequable deposits have relatively low annual rates of turnover (about two times per year). As a "savings bank', a trust company does not have to be overly concerned with holding a relatively high proportion of its assets in quite illiquid forms.

It is also relevant to note that the trust companies did not suffer from a prohibition against holding mortgages or a relatively low ceiling on the interest rates on loans such as that which effectively kept chartered banks out of the mortgage market in the early postwar years and in the early 1960's. At times when the demand for housing was increasing rapidly, a major potential competitor of the trust companies was effectively ruled out of the market. The trust companies' ability to step into this market undoubtedly goes a long way toward explaining their ability to compete successfully with the chartered banks for funds, and hence to grow so rapidly.

The trust companies also hold sizable portfolios of securities, particularly provincial, municipal and corporate bonds.

Summary. What then can we say about the trust companies as financial intermediaries? In a word, they are a classic example of a savings bank,

Table 10-5
The Trust Companies as Financial Intermediaries: Consolidated Balance Sheet, January 1, 1970

(Millions of Dollars)

Assets			Liabilities & Equity		
CASH			**PERSONAL SAVINGS DEPOSITS**		
Canadian dollars	97		Chequable	438	
Foreign currency	184	231	Non-chequable	901	1,339
OTHER LIQUID ASSETS			**TERM DEPOSITS**		
Treasury bills	11		Less than 1 year	1,058	
Government of Canada bonds	583		1–6 years	2,772	
Term deposits (Banks, trust companies)	105		Over 6 years	20	3,850
Other short-term paper	297		**OTHER LIABILITIES**		167
Secured loans	163	1,159	**SHAREHOLDERS' EQUITY**		415
MORTGAGE LOANS					
N.H.A. insured mortgages	594				
Conventional mortgages	2,670	3,264			
SECURITIES					
Provincial & municipal bonds	381				
Corporate bonds	329				
Corporate shares	107				
Foreign securities	63	880			
OTHER ASSETS		238			
TOTAL ASSETS		5,771			5,771

(Percentage Distribution)

Assets	%	Liabilities & Equity	%
Cash	4	Personal savings deposits	23
Other liquid assets	20	Term deposits	67
Mortgage loans	57	Other liabilities	3
Securities	15	Shareholders' equity	7
Other assets	4		
	100		100

offering the public a range of deposit forms, but heavily emphasizing term and savings deposits. This stress on notice deposits combined with their peripheral involvement in the payments system via chequable savings accounts results in a very low degree of banker's risk compared to the banks. As a result, they are free to invest a substantial portion of their funds in long term, illiquid assets. Indeed, the trust companies have been a primary source of mortgage funds in recent years.

5/THE MORTGAGE LOAN COMPANIES

In terms of their role as intermediaries the mortgage loan companies are practically indistinguishable from the trust companies. With the exception of the absence of estate and trust agency business, the differences in form and the markets in which they operate are minor. Mortgage loan companies tend to be more localized (frequently operating within one country or province) and they tend to rely more heavily upon the issue of debentures rather than deposits. Several companies do not accept any deposits and unlike trust companies have not participated to any great extent in financing security dealers and finance companies or in country banking.

The Balance Sheet of Mortgage Loan Companies

Following our discussions of the chartered banks and the trust companies, the balance sheet of the mortgage loan companies requires little explanation. A consolidated balance sheet for January 1, 1970 is presented in Table 10-6.

Sources of Funds. Like trust companies, the mortgage loan companies accept deposits which are to all intents virtually the same as personal savings deposits at chartered banks, except that they have normally paid a somewhat higher rate of interest. Some of these accounts are chequable, and some (paying a higher rate of interest) are non-chequable. Both types are in fact payable on demand, although notice can legally be required for withdrawals, and both types are held almost exclusively by individuals rather than by businesses. These deposits are in effect demand liabilities.

Like the trust companies, the mortgage loan companies raise most of their funds by issuing longer-term financial instruments, and particularly debentures with an original term to maturity in the range of 1 to 6 years.[3] The mortgage loan companies also borrow substantial sums of money from banks, trust companies and other institutional lenders.

Uses of Funds. Given the low volatility of most of their liabilities, the mortgage loan companies have found it unnecessary to hold a large share of their assets in highly liquid form. Their cash holdings at the beginning of 1970 amounted to just over 1% of their total assets (although they did represent over 7.7% of the deposits payable on demand). Holdings of other liquid assets are held down proportionately, amounting to less than 7% of total assets. The dominant investment is in mortgage loans, and particularly relatively higher-yielding conventional mortgages. Additional long-term assets are held in the form of government and corporate securities.

Table 10-6

Mortgage Loan Companies as Financial Intermediaries
Consolidated Balance Sheet, January 1, 1970

(Millions of Dollars)

CASH		34	PERSONAL SAVINGS DEPOSITS		
			Chequable	162	
OTHER LIQUID ASSETS			Non-chequable	279	441
Treasury bills	12				
Gov't of Canada bonds	123		DEBENTURES AND TERM DEPOSITS		
Term deposits and short-term paper	20		Original term		
Collateral loans	28	183	Less than 1 year	46	
			1–6 years	1,295	
MORTGAGE LOANS			Over 6 years	615	1,956
N.H.A. insured	210				
Conventional	2,298	2,508	OTHER LIABILITIES		468
SECURITIES					
Provincial and municipal bonds	60				
Corporate bonds	33				
Equities	73		SHAREHOLDERS' EQUITY		427
Foreign securities	8	174			
OTHER ASSETS		393			
		3,292			3,292

(Percentage Distribution)

Cash	1	Personal savings deposits	13
Other liquid assets	6	Debenture and term deposits	60
Mortgage loans	76	Other liabilities	12
Securities	5		
Other assets	12	Shareholders' equity	13
	100		100

6/GOVERNMENT SAVINGS DEPOSITORIES

In addition to all these various near bank competitors of the chartered banks there exists a group of institutions which compete for the same pool of savings, but which are generally not true intermediaries. Most of these government-owned institutions only perform *half* of the intermediation function: they collect funds by issuing savings deposits, but they do not lend funds to other spending units (unless one wishes to argue that they lend the funds to the government). The only exceptions are the Alberta Treasury branches which engage in some lending to the general public.

Government savings institutions are in a sense vestiges of the past when they were relatively important as storehouses of wealth (e.g., the government post office savings accounts in the late 19th and early 20th centuries) or when they were considered to be a source of funds for provincial treasuries (e.g., Ontario Savings offices and the Alberta Treasury branches). In recent times their growth rates have been extremely low and their combined assets of $330 million do not make them an important factor in the financial sector. In late 1969 the federal Postal Savings Bank stopped accepting deposits, and is now out of business.

In many ways, Canada Savings Bonds and similar securities issued by provincial governments, perform similar functions as deposits with government depository institutions. That is, they provide a safe, and by virtue of their instant convertibility to cash, perfectly liquid asset offering a relatively high rate of return. Data on total issues of savings bonds by provincial governments are not available. However, as is noted in Table 10-7, the total value of Canada Savings Bonds outstanding is 25 times as great as total deposits in government depositories. These bonds do provide strong competition for funds with private depositories.

Table 10-7
Deposits with Government Savings Institutions, February, 1971

(Millions of Dollars)

Post Office Savings Bank	4
Province of Ontario Savings Office	104
Alberta Treasury Branches	
Public Deposits	
Not bearing interest	43
Bearing interest	152
Provincial Government Deposits	27
TOTAL	330
Canada Savings Bonds	6,591

SOURCE: Bank of Canada *Statistical Summary*, February 1971.

7/THE BANKS AND THE NEAR BANKS

What we have chosen to call near banks are a diverse group of institutions, which range from cooperatives like the *caisses populaires,* which have virtually displaced chartered banks in many small communities, to government-operated depositories, which are not true financial intermediaries. The unifying feature of these institutions is that they all offer liabilities which are close substitutes for liabilities of chartered banks, primarily personal savings deposits but also longer-term deposits. Not only are their liabilities close substitutes, but most of these institutions (the exceptions are the government depositories) have competed aggressively and successfully with the chartered banks for funds. They have generally offered more attractive interest rates, and have frequently been willing to tailor their office locations, business hours and services to more effectively attract customers. The results of this competition were reported in Table 9-2. To provide a visual image they are summarized again in Figure 10-1.

Figure 10-1
Growth Rates: *Banks and Near Banks*

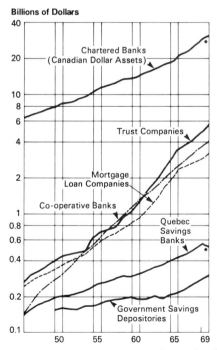

*Reflects, in part, the change in status of one Quebec saving bank to a chartered bank.

SOURCE: Bank of Canada, *Statistical Summary,* 1955-1970.

The striking feature of this chart is the very much more rapid rate of growth over the whole postwar period of trust companies, mortgage loan companies and cooperative banks than either chartered banks on the one hand or Quebec savings banks and government savings depositories on the other. Many factors undoubtedly contributed to these divergent growth rates. However, it is significant that the rapid growth institutions were those which offered premium interest rates on their deposits: premium rates made possible in part by their low operating costs (in the case of many small cooperative banks) and the relatively high-yielding assets which they were willing and able to acquire. The growth of trust and loan companies is a reflection of the demand for housing in Canada. In a positive way, the aggressive business policies, including the vigour and imaginativeness of their competitive efforts, were also vital to the growth of the rapid-growth institutions. But we must not forget that in a negative way, many governmental regulations contributed to the retardation of the growth of the slow-growth institutions. It is relevant that a significant change in relative growth rates appears to be emerging at the end of the time period, as the competitive policies of the chartered banks changed in response to a thorough revision of the *Bank Act*.

FOOTNOTES

[1] In 1969 the Quebec City Savings Bank changed its status from that of a Quebec savings bank to that of a chartered bank, with the name *The People's Bank*. This left only the Montreal City and District Savings Bank in the Quebec savings bank category. In early 1970 the People's Bank merged with La Banque Provinciale du Canada.

[2] Royal Commission on Banking and Finance, *Hearings* (Toronto: F. J. Nethercut and R. J. Young, 1962), p. 3066.

[3] The difference between the mortgage company's debentures and the trust company's guaranteed investment certificates is a distinction in law, not in economic signficance. Trust companies in general are not permitted to borrow. They may accept funds in "trust", with a specific earmarking of assets to which the "trust" funds are applied. Loan companies are permitted to borrow, and do so largely through the insurance of debentures. These are bonds (mainly short- to intermediate-term in this case) which are a general claim on the assets of the company but do not involve any specific assignment of assets.

11

Other Financial Intermediaries

In the previous two chapters we examined financial institutions whose liabilities are either money or near substitutes for money. To round out our discussion of Canadian financial intermediaries we must now turn our attention to a heterogeneous collection of intermediaries whose liabilities do not have this characteristic. That is not to say that these institutions have little economic significance, for a major portion of the savings of society are channeled through them. They now hold total assets in excess of $35 billion, with their relative importance in the financial system continuing to increase.

The range of activities of firms in this residual group is extensive. At one extreme we have the mutual fund, a type of intermediary which simply provides portfolio diversification and professional selection of securities for the assetholder. The liabilities of the mutual fund do not have the special property of liquidity like those of deposit-type institutions. At the other extreme are insurance companies, a set of institutions whose liabilities have very specialized characteristics, the special nature of which makes it easy to forget to include the companies in a list of intermediaries. One tends to forget that they borrow or lend, and to regard them simply as firms selling a service, insurance.

Between these two extremes are several other more or less specialized intermediaries, which seek out sources of funds to be borrowed on a wide variety of terms, lend for specialized purposes, and, by holding a diversified portfolio of securities, perform the essential function of risk spreading. These specialized intermediaries are so numerous and so varied that they almost defy systematic cataloguing, and the list is continually changing as firms are established to take advantage of new opportunities for profitable intermediation.

1/PURE INTERMEDIATION: THE MUTUAL FUND

The Nature of a Mutual Fund

The concept of a mutual fund is relatively simple. Individuals contribute funds to a central investment pool by purchasing shares or "units" in the fund. This pool is used to purchase a portfolio of securities. Part of the income earned on the portfolio is used to cover management expense, with the residual income either paid out to the members as dividends or added to the pool of funds available to purchase securities. Members' claims on the fund are proportionate to the *number* of units which they own Over time, the value of any given portfolio of securities will change as a result of changes in the market prices of the securities comprising the portfolio. As a result, the value of each unit will change. Furthermore an "open-ended" fund will sell additional units to old or new members thus acquiring additional funds for investment, and producing a further change in the total value of the portfolio. The cost of each new unit will depend on the value of the portfolio of securities at the time the new unit is issued. This may be higher or lower than the costs of the original units, and earlier subscribers will correspondingly earn capital gains or capital losses on their units. Open-ended funds will also cash in the units of their members for whatever is their unit value at that point in time (less certain charges), selling securities out of the portfolio for this purpose if necessary.

In principle any group of individuals could organize such a "fund" For example, you and nine other friends could decide to form a mutual fund. You might decide that the value of the initial units will be $10 Each purchases one unit, providing an investment fund of $100.

As the value of the assets purchased with the original subscribed capital rises or falls so does the value of the units. But since it is an open ended fund, the number of units is not limited to the original number and the value of a unit is not fixed at the original value. Thus, if after one month the value of the portfolio has increased so that the unit value is $12, (i.e., the total fund is now worth $120) additional units would cost $12 each. Similarly if, in the following month, because of an adverse turn in the market, the total portfolio falls in value so that the unit value is but $8, then additional units can be purchased at that price, and existing units can be cashed in for that price. Why? Because that is the value of the assets which must be sold out of the fund so that a unit can be cashed in.

Such a mutual fund is more likely to be called an "investment club" Unlike a true mutual fund it does not sell units to the general public but rather confines its membership to a specified group of individuals Such clubs are increasingly common, and the arrangements normally called for fixed monthly subscriptions by each member of the club. Given the small scale of the typical club's investment portfolio, the opportunities for portfolio diversification are limited, as are the possibilities for expert management (see the discussion of economies of scale in financial inter mediation in Chapter 8). People frequently join such clubs to learn about the stock market and to gain experience in making investment decision while pooling the limited time which each one can devote to research on securities. On a small scale, the basic principle is the same as that involved in a true mutual fund (although the operations of true mutual funds are supervised by government agencies).

The Asset Portfolios of Open-Ended Mutual Funds

A consolidated statement of the assets of Canadian mutual funds is shown in Table 11-1. The contrasts between the portfolio of this inter

Table 11-1
The Assets of Open-ended Mutual Funds, January 1, 1970

(Market Value)

LIQUID ASSETS	Millions of Dollars		%
Cash (Canadian and Foreign)	159		
Short-term Notes	134	293	9
FIXED INCOME SECURITIES			
Government of Canada Bonds	34		
Provincial and Municipal Bonds	32		
Corporate Bonds	77		
Mortgages	9		
Preferred Stock	134		
Foreign Bonds	56		
Other Securities	0	342	10
VARIABLE INCOME SECURITIES			
Canadian Common Stocks	1,311		
Foreign Stocks	1,230	2,541	78
OTHER ASSETS		90	3
		3,266	100

SOURCE: Bank of Canada, *Statistical Summary*, 1970.

mediary and those of most of the other financial intermediaries which we have examined so far are very pronounced.

Liquidity. You should note particularly the relatively small holdings of cash and other liquid assets which is characteristic of the mutual funds. Unlike intermediaries such as banks or trust companies, mutual funds do not face a high degree of banker's risk, and hence they do not have a strong liquidity preference; but, like banks, their liabilities are payable on demand (the units can be cashed in at any time). Unlike banks the dollar value of the claims is not fixed, but fluctuates in value with changes in the market value of the asset portfolio.

Concentration on Equities. An equally important point to note in Table 11-1 is the overwhelming importance of equities among the assets of mutual funds. At the beginning of 1970 Canadian and foreign common stocks accounted for over 80% of the market value of the assets of all mutual funds taken together. For many funds, this proportion would be very much higher.

Foreign Securities. It is also interesting to note the relatively high proportion of the assets of mutual funds which are foreign, primarily United States, equities. Most funds hold some foreign securities, and some hold them exclusively. This overall proportion of foreign securities has been increasing in recent years, from 20% in 1963 to 41% by 1970. As a result, the mutual funds have become a primary means by which Canadians make investments abroad.

The Demand for Mutual Fund Shares

Growth Rate. While not as spectacular as the growth of the inter-mediary business of trust and loan companies and the cooperative banks, the growth of mutual funds in recent years has been quite striking. In the period 1959-1970 the market value of the total assets of mutual funds increased almost 300%. A significant part of this growth can be attributed to capital gains on securities held in the mutual funds' portfolios as a result of rising prices for corporate stocks. However, well over half of the increase in total assets represented new funds subscribed by shareholders. In this period the number of active mutual funds almost doubled as well. What accounts for this strong demand for mutual fund shares?

Risk Spreading and the Demand for Mutual Fund Shares. In Chapter 5 we analyzed the demand for financial instruments in terms of a choice at the margin between expected yield, risk and liquidity, with inflation and taxation as important considerations entering into the calculation of the "real" yield on the instruments. Although shares of mutual funds are more liquid than many assets, it is clear that, unlike banks and trust companies, mutual funds do not appeal to assetholders' demands for liquidity. Rather, it is in the realm of risk and expected yield that we must find the answer to our question.

The essential characteristics of common stock as a financial instrument were discussed in Chapter 3. The point stressed was that these securities involved a residual claim to the potentially highly variable profits of a business enterprise. Considered individually, therefore, common stocks are relatively *risky assets.* Assetholders with a strong aversion to risk might be expected to eschew heavy investment in stocks unless their asset port-folios were large enough to permit substantial portfolio diversification and to generate sufficient income to permit the purchase of professional investment advice. A mutual fund, by pooling the funds of many small assetholders, can achieve the necessary scale of operations to afford professional selection of securities and to achieve substantial portfolio diversification.

You will recall from Chapter 8 that the expected yield on a diversified portfolio of securities is the weighted average of the yields on the individual securities included in the portfolio. In this sense, the mutual fund does not alter the yields available in the market place. What the fund does is to reduce the risk associated with any given level of expected yield. Thus, *the mutual fund effectively improves the trade-off between risk and expected yield available to assetholders,* particularly to those with relatively small asset portfolios.

Are Mutual Fund Shares Riskless? It is worth noting that although a mutual fund effectively reduces risk through portfolio diversification, even a mutual fund which invests in a broad range of corporate stocks cannot render negligible the total risk to its shareholders. As noted in Chapter 7 portfolio diversification is only effective in reducing risk if the yields on the assets included in the portfolio are *independent*. To some extent this is true of the yields on common stocks. Individual companies may prosper or fail regardless of the fates of other companies. However, because of broad cyclical movements in the economy as a whole, the profits of all companies have a tendency to rise and fall together. Thus, the yields on common stocks are not completely independent, but have some degree of positive correlation. The shares of even a widely diversified mutual fund cannot be riskless.

Specialization Among Mutual Funds. Note also that the degree of portfolio diversification varies widely among funds. Thus, there are funds which invest almost exclusively in companies with new mining properties, or in companies engaged in the production, transmission or distribution of oil, gas, or electricity, or in insurance companies, and there are even funds which invest exclusively in other mutual funds. Clearly, while all funds achieve some risk spreading through diversification among companies, the degree of risk spreading may vary between funds.

This fact reflects the different investment objectives of mutual funds. For example, many funds assert that they are "growth" oriented. That is to say, the investment policies of the fund are aimed at maximizing capital gains with little if any concern for income in the form of dividends. Other funds, however, stress a regular flow of income. Such funds usually consist primarily of bonds, and they appeal most to persons who are retired or are about to retire, and to whom a regular flow of income is important. Other funds aim at a "balance" between income and capital gains, and their portfolios contain both bonds and equities. Finally, there is a group of funds that are "fully managed". This means that the management of the fund is not restricted to any particular investment policy, but will adjust the composition of the portfolio from time to time, and perhaps quite radically, in response to anticipated developments in securities markets.

At the beginning of 1970 approximately 36% of total mutual funds assets were in stock funds with primary growth objectives, 32% were in fully managed funds, and 20% in "balanced funds". Bond funds are of negligible importance. These proportions represent a dramatic change in recent years. As recently as 1963 balanced funds accounted for 40%, fully managed funds 34% and stock funds only 19% of total assets. While all three major types of funds have grown rapidly, the growth of stock funds has been particularly spectacular.

What explains this fact, particularly since we have assumed that most investors are risk averters, and many of these stock funds are highly specialized, with consequent relatively high degrees of risks?

Inflation and Taxes. An important attribute of common stock (which we discussed at some length in Chapter 5), is that, unlike bonds and other fixed income securities, the *real value* of common stock is not necessarily eroded as a result of inflation, and may even be enhanced by it. Through portfolio diversification, mutual funds consisting almost exclusively of common stock reduce some of the risk attached to holdings of common stock, while at the same time they provide a *hedge against the risk of inflation*. This appears to be a significant consideration leading to investment in mutual fund shares.

In Chapter 5 we also noted that the taxation system may affect choices among financial instruments. The particularly important consideration in this regard is the fact that capital gains are not taxed as income in Canada. This makes specialized stock funds, with the possibilities of very substantial capital gains, highly attractive assets to many investors.

Mutual Funds: A Pure Intermediary

We can summarize the essential contribution of mutual funds to the structure of the financial system by saying that the mutual fund provides the individual assetholder with a better trade-off between risk and yield on corporate securities (and particularly common stock) then he could obtain in the market place. In part this is accomplished by taking advantage of economies of scale in portfolio management: through professional appraisal, selection and trading of securities. Indeed, the performance of the mutual fund depends directly on the abilities of the management firm. The integrity and abilities of management are another source of risk to the individual investor. However, the fundamental principle through which the mutual fund alters the risk-yield trade-off is portfolio diversification. Indeed, if we regard portfolio diversification as the *sine qua non* of financial intermediation, perhaps we could say that mutual funds are "pure intermediaries". They are an important and growing factor in financial markets, and have come to represent one of the more important forms in which wealth-owners hold wealth. After reviewing their operations through 1962 the Royal Commission on Banking and Finance concluded:

> On balance, they [the mutual funds] play a constructive role in mobilizing savings for equity purchases, particularly from smaller investors. They have also improved the workings of markets and can play a useful role in increasing Canadian ownership of domestic industry.[1]

2/PURE INTERMEDIATION: THE CLOSED-END INVESTMENT FUND

The mutual funds which we have been discussing are all open-ended funds, in that they involve unlimited provision for the issuance of new shares or units. In one sense they are a comparatively recent innovation in the Canadian financial system. The first funds were established in the early 1930's, but widespread recognition and rapid expansion did not occur until the mid-1950's and early 1960's. Indeed, by far the largest number of funds now in operation have charters that date no earlier than the mid-1950's.

However, the basic principle upon which the mutual funds operate – improving the trade-off between risk and yield for individual assetholder by spreading risks over a diversified portfolio of securities – is very simple and in this respect mutual funds were long anticipated by the operation of investment companies or closed-end investment funds.

Table 11-2
The Assets of Closed-end Investment Funds, January 1, 1970

	(Market Value)	
LIQUID ASSETS	Millions of Dollars	%
Cash (Canadian and Foreign)	9	
Short-term Notes	6	
Other Liquid Assets	5	20	2
FIXED INCOME SECURITIES		
Government of Canada Bonds	9	
Other Canadian Bonds	3	
Mortgages	13	
Foreign Bonds	2	
Preferred Shares	52	79	9
VARIABLE INCOME SECURITIES		
Canadian Common Shares	710	
Foreign Shares	35	745	88
OTHER ASSETS		7	
		851	100

Like a mutual fund, a closed-end investment fund is a pool of funds for investment in a diversified portfolio of securities. As is apparent from Table 11-2, by far the most important assets of these funds are common stocks of Canadian corporations. Thus, again like mutual funds, they perform the function of risk spreading for individual investors wanting to hold corporate shares. However, unlike mutual funds, at any point in time a closed-end fund has a fixed ceiling to the number of its shares outstanding. New issues of shares are possible, of course, in much the same way as new issues of any corporate shares are possible. However, the closed-end fund does not stand ready to cash in its shares for the prevailing pro rata value of its assets, nor does it stand ready to issue new shares on demand at that same price. Instead, the fixed number of shares outstanding are traded in the stock markets just like other equities. Moreover, closed-end funds generally issue both preferred and common shares, and some have a limited amount of bonded indebtedness outstanding as well.

Most funds have strict limits to the amount of their investment in any particular firm, particularly in voting shares. Such rules are in part designed to ensure diversification, but they also have the effect of ruling out the possibility of the fund exerting effective control over the operations of the enterprise. While some closed-end investment funds have a similar limitation, others take an active role in the management of enterprises in which they have a large financial interest. If an investment fund does take an active role in management of enterprises it is problematic whether we should continue to consider it to be a financial intermediary. There is a subtle, ill-defined line across which the fund becomes in effect a holding company, controlling and operating a diversified, conglomerate industrial empire.

3/CONSUMER LOAN AND SALES FINANCE COMPANIES: SPECIALIZED LENDING TO HIGH-RISK BORROWERS

In Chapter 9 when we discussed the portfolio changes that had occurred in the banking industry, we pointed out the very rapid growth of personal loans. From 1950 to 1970 they increased from slightly under $600 million to over $4.8 billion. A large portion of this growth was in loans secured by chattel mortgages, i.e., term loans for the purchase of consumer durables and, more recently, consumer services such as vacations. The banks, however, were not the sole lenders in this field. The Quebec savings banks, and more importantly the *caisses populaires* and credit unions were also important participants in this burgeoning market. Yet in spite of the large-scale participation by these intermediaries in the consumer loan market they still accounted for only 45% of the outstanding consumer debt in 1970. At that time more than 25% of the total amount of such debt outstanding was held by companies that specialize in lending in this market: sales finance and consumer loan companies.

Consumer Loan Companies

The consumer loan companies specialize in direct cash lending to individuals. There are a large number of firms in this business. Most of them are small local operations with one or two offices but several have large-scale, nation-wide chains of branches. At the end of 1967 there were 76 firms registered with the government of Canada under the *Small Loans Act* operating over 2,000 offices across Canada.[2] The five largest firms between them accounted for almost 60% of the offices and over 70% of the assets of registered companies.

Normally the loans are cash loans, and are for relatively small amounts. Over two-thirds of the total loan balances outstanding on the books of registered companies at the end of 1967 were in "small loan" accounts, i.e., the original loan was for $1,500 or less. The average size of small loans made during 1967 was $597, and over 45% of all small loans were for sums less than $500.

The vast bulk of the loan applicants are wage earners with monthly incomes of less than $600, and about 75% have previously borrowed from similar companies. Almost half of all applications for loans are refused because the applicant is considered to be an unworthy risk given past experience, because it is felt that he is currently over-extended in his debt commitments, or because security, if required, is not deemed to be adequate. In spite of this high refusal rate, almost a quarter of all loans balances outstanding at the end of 1967 were in "delinquent" accounts. Indeed, 11% of the balances were in accounts which were at that time delinquent over three months. Actual losses are very much less than this of course, partly because many delinquent accounts are subsequently repaid and partly because the loan company ultimately has resorted to security offered for the loan. (The most common security is a chattel mortgage. In the event of default, the loan company will take possession of the chattels.) Most loans are granted either for purposes of debt consolidation or for essential purchases such as food, housing and clothing. In recent years, however, the companies have begun lending to people for other reasons such as financing vacations or automobile purchases. However, the consumer loan companies are primarily engaged in cash lending to a relatively risky clientele, a clientele who, for the most part, turn to these companies because they are unable to find credit accommodation elsewhere.

Sales Finance Companies

Unlike consumer loan companies, sales finance companies have little if any direct contact with the public. Rather than actively solicit business from the public, as the loan companies do, almost all of their business in consumer lending originates with some other business firm. For example, an automobile dealer will sell a car to a customer with a time purchase plan. The customer signs a contract agreeing to pay a certain sum each week or month for a specified period of time. The dealer in turn takes this contract to a sales finance company which purchases or *discounts* the contract. The dealer by this method receives the proceeds (or more accurately the proceeds less the discount charged by the finance company for taking over the contract) of the sale at once rather than receiving the funds over an extended period of time.

While the financing of consumer purchases of durable goods is the most familiar aspect of the sales finance companies operations, a major part of their lending involves the financing of dealer inventories, particularly for automobile dealers (dealers in other durables are most commonly financed directly by manufacturers or by bank loans). In this respect the sales finance companies compete directly with the chartered banks. The rates charged on inventory loans to dealers usually are much lower than rates charged on the high-risk term contracts made with the public. In 1964 the Royal Commission reported that inventory loan rates were close to 6% while term contracts ranged from 12½% to 19%. Finance companies find that dealers whose inventories they finance bring most, if not all, of their term purchase contracts to them, so the tie-in becomes quite strong. Two of the largest firms in the business are in fact subsidiaries of automobile manufacturers and are considered to be an integral part of the total marketing approach of these companies.

Finally, sales finance companies have begun to diversify their lending activities even further. As the banks and near banks began to make inroads into the field of consumer finance the sales finance companies responded by reversing the process. They began lending on a term basis to companies that, because of the risk or term demanded for loans, were unable to find accommodation at chartered banks. While such term lending is still a relatively small portion of the total business done by such companies (perhaps as much as 16%) it appears to be a growing sector.

In summary, as in the case of consumer loan companies, a large part of the lending activity of the sales finance companies is concentrated in a relatively risky sector of the economy. Many of their indirect consumer

Table 11-3

Consumer Loan and Sales Finance Companies: Consolidated Balance Sheet, January 1, 1970

(Millions of Dollars)

LIQUID ASSETS				**SHORT-TERM LIABILITIES**		
Cash	127			Bank loans	403	
Short-term notes and bills	78			Notes–Canadian dollar	1,401	
Government of Canada bonds	28	233		Notes–Foreign currency	139	1,943
ACCOUNTS AND NOTES RECEIVABLE				**LONG-TERM LIABILITIES**		
Consumer loan companies				Bonds–Canadian dollar	1,077	
Cash loans	1,672			Bonds–Foreign currency	429	
Installment credit	110	1,782		Owing affiliated companies	856	2,362
Sales finance companies						
Consumer goods	1,279			**OTHER LIABILITIES**		764
Commercial and industrial goods	738					
Dealer inventories	560	2,577		**CAPITAL ACCOUNTS**		583
Other receivables		666	3,243			
OTHER ASSETS			394			
TOTAL ASSETS			5,652	**TOTAL LIABILITIES**		5,652

SOURCE: Bank of Canada *Statistical Summary*.

loans are to people who have been refused accommodation at some other financial intermediary. This high risk is in part evidenced in the relatively high rates they charge on loans. In addition, however, the sales finance companies are important in financing dealer inventories of certain durable consumer goods, and they compete with the chartered banks in this field.

Source and Use of Funds

As is evident in Table 11-3, over 85% of the assets of consumer loan and sales finance companies are in accounts and notes receivable. Less than 5% of their assets are in liquid forms, even when we define the category of liquid assets broadly enough to include all government of Canada bonds. The deliberate assumption of high-risk, relatively small personal and commercial loans is the hallmark of these institutions. How can they do this, and not only survive but actually thrive?

Part of the answer lies in the much-repeated statement — through portfolio diversification they spread the risk and hence somewhat reduce the significance of risk in their overall operations. Another part of the answer lies in the fact that most of their loans are secured either by merchandise which can be repossessed, or by other security. Indeed, when sales finance companies discount paper for dealers, part of the risk is frequently borne by the dealer. Another factor is their interest rates, which are commensurate with the risks assumed, and at times the level of these rates is the subject of public concern and opprobrium. Equally important, however, is the nature of their liabilities. Clearly, sales finance or consumer loan companies could not pursue their present patterns of activities if they faced the degree of banker's risk associated with the liabilities of banks or trust companies.

Because of consolidation, the data in Table 11-3 conceal major differences between consumer loan and sales finance companies. As we have seen, the consumer loan companies carry the riskier, least liquid assets. Correspondingly, their sources of finance tend to be relatively more secure, long-term arrangements. Thus, for the smaller, independent consumer loan company, the major sources of funds are capital subscribed by the shareholders (including retained earnings) and term loans from chartered banks. Larger independent firms also issue long-term debt and sometimes borrow on shorter-term on the open market. Many of the larger firms are owned either by American firms or by larger Canadian sales finance companies. In these cases, long-term loans from the parent firms provide the bulk of the operating funds.

The sales finance companies are larger, more diversified borrowers than are the consumer loan companies. A major portion of their funds is obtained on long- or medium-term bases, either through the issuance of longer-term bonds, or through retained earnings and capital subscribed by shareholders. This provides an element of stability to their financial position. However, in an industry which has substantial cyclical and seasonal swings in demand, reliable short-term accommodation is also essential. As in the case of the consumer loan companies, the traditional source of such funds has been bank loans, particularly for the smaller finance companies. However, on various occasions the finance companies found that excessive reliance on bank borrowing had some disadvantages. In periods of general credit restraint, which coincided with periods of relatively strong demand for finance company loans, the chartered banks reduced their lines of credit to the finance companies. These restrictions were particularly severe in 1956-57 and 1959-60. Although short-term borrowing outside the banking system had already developed as an important source of finance, these episodes induced the finance companies to actively cultivate such resources. As a result, finance companies played a major role in the development of the short-term money market in Canada (see Chapter 3). Finance paper became one of the major instruments traded in that market, and short-term borrowing in the money market by finance companies is now more than double their short-term borrowing from banks. At times in the recent past (before the failure of a large sales finance company) open-market borrowing has had even greater relative importance.

Conclusions

Although their operations are somewhat different, the consumer loan companies and sales finance companies are commonly grouped together: in both cases, loans are largely made directly or indirectly to persons, and their loans are relatively risky. Inevitably, their operations impinge on those of other financial intermediaries. They compete with various lending institutions in the consumer loan field, and they compete with the chartered banks in some aspects of the commercial loan field. However, they are primarily specialized intermediaries which have developed skills in intermediating a particular type of risk, associated with relatively small personal loans. They have sought out sources of finance to meet their needs, and in the process have played a major role in the development of the short-term money market in Canada.

4/SPECIALIZED INTERMEDIATION:
INSURANCE COMPANIES

The combined assets in Canada of the general insurance companies (i.e., those specializing in insurance against fire, theft, automobile accidents, disability, etc.,) and the life insurance companies totaled almost $17 billion at the beginning of 1970. This represented the largest pool of funds administered by any single group of financial intermediaries aside from the chartered banks. Clearly, the insurance companies represent a major concentration of financial resources. But is it legitimate to refer to them as financial intermediaries? Selling insurance seems to have little in common with commercial banking.

Insurance as an Asset

Before attempting to answer this question, we should first explore the nature of insurance as an asset.

"Pure" Insurance. In its "pure" form, insurance simply involves a pooling of risks. Life insurance is probably the most familiar type of insurance, hence an example involving life insurance may help make the point.

Imagine that you are one of a 100 people all of the same age and sex who decide to insure each others lives for the forthcoming year. The agreement is that if anyone of the group dies during the year his estate will be paid $1,000. By consulting an actuary — a person trained, among other things, to derive probabilities of people of specified characteristics dying over a specified time period on the basis of mortality tables (historical records of the incidence of death) — you discover that it is most probable that one of the 100 people will die during the course of the year. This means that each member of the group must expect to contribute $10 during the year. Of course, the incidence of death is uncertain. It may be greater or less than the most probable number, and the necessary individual contribution may be higher or lower than $10. However, actuarial estimates of the death rate are surprisingly accurate, at least for large groups. For a small group — and 100 is a small group — the risk to the insurers will be relatively great.

In order to avoid the risk that some member will not pay their share when called upon, you may agree to form a mutual insurance company, with each paying his contribution — his premium — in advance. In order to cover the expected payments from the fund during the year, each member's premium would have to be $10. The higher the probability of death within the specified time period, or the larger the payment to be made upon death, the higher the premium would have to be. The insurance company must also recognize that the death rate may be higher than predicted, and it must make financial provision for such a contingency — it must maintain "reserves". In order to accumulate funds for this purpose, and in order to cover the costs of administering the company (collecting the premiums, keeping the company's books, managing its funds, dealing with policyholder's claims, selling insurance, etc.), the premium will have to be substantially higher than $10 — perhaps $12 to $15.

A life insurance policy is an asset to each policyholder: a claim on the insurance company. But it is a very unusual asset. Unlike a bond, for example, the date of future payment is not fixed, and indeed the fact of payment is not certain. Payment will only be made if a specified event (in this case a death) occurs during a specified time period (the term of the policy, in this case the following year). If that event does not occur during that time period, and it may not, then no payment at all will be made and *the policyholder has no further legal claim on the insurance company.*

The Present Value and Expected Yield on "Pure" Insurance. If pure life insurance is an asset which can be purchased in varying quantities in the market place, then rational choice presumably calls for a comparison of the present value of the insurance with its market price, or alternately of the expected yield on insurance with the yields on other assets which might be purchased with the same funds.

Consider again the earlier example of an insurance policy calling for a payment of $1,000 should the insured die during the forthcoming year. Since the amount of the payment is uncertain — it may be either $1,000 or $0 — we can only calculate the present value of the asset on the basis of the expected value of the payment (i.e., taking account of the probability that a payment of $1,000 will be made). In the present case, given that there are two possibilities, a payment of $1,000 with a probability of .01, or a payment of $0, with a probability of 0.99, the present value of the insurance payment is:

$$\bar{v} = (0.01) \ (\$1,000) + (0.99) \ (0)$$
$$= \$10$$

In other words, the purchaser of this insurance policy must pay perhaps $15 for a claim to a possible future payment, when the present value of that claim is only $10! Clearly, *the expected yield on such an asset is negative.* The same basic principles can be applied to pure insurance policies written for contingencies other than death, and, while the calculations are more complicated for terms longer than one year, always with the same result. *If insurance companies are to cover all administrative and selling costs and to make a profit, the expected yield on pure term insurances must be negative.*

There is always a wide variety of assets available in the market place having expected yields which are greater than zero. Why, then would anyone purchase pure insurance as an asset?

The Demand for "Pure" Insurance. Our analysis of the problem of asset selection in Chapter 5 stressed that expected yield was not the sole criterion governing such choices. Rather, the problem is that of choice, at the margin, between expected yield, risk and liquidity. Purchasers of pure insurance are acquiring an asset designed as *a hedge against the risk of financial loss,* and they are doing it at some expected net cost in the sense that the expected yield on the asset is negative. In general, insurance is purchased to hedge against the risk of destruction or impairment of other assets, such as the risk that fire may destroy a house or factory, or that illness or death of the major bread-winner might impair the future income of the household. However, it may also be taken out as a hedge against a great variety of other financial contingencies, including very commonly the risk of legal liability for automobile accidents.

Insurance Policies as a Vehicle for Systematic Saving

Not all insurance policies sold by life insurance companies are of this "pure" or "term" variety. A "pure" insurance policy cannot be used as a vehicle for the accumulation of savings since at the end of the specified term, if the event against which insurance was taken out (death, fire, accident) has not occurred, the policyholder has no further claim on the company. However, life insurance companies also offer a variety of policies which permit the systematic accumulation of savings. The periodic "prem ums" paid to the insurance company include the cost of insurance *per se* (plus the administration costs, of course) plus an additional sum which constitutes a periodic payment into a cumulating fund. At the end of a fixed term, the policyholder has a claim to a specified lump sum payment from the company (whether he dies within the period or not), and during its life the policy has a cumulating cash value which the policyholder can claim (by surrendering his policy) or frequently borrow against. Such a policy involves the principle of co-insurance. In the early years of the policy the insurance is primarily provided by the insurance company, whereas in the later years of the policy the insurance element declines sharply, with protection provided primarily by the policyholder's own savings accumulated with the company.

It is difficult to calculate the rate of return on such savings-type life insurance policies. However, most calculations that have been made suggest that the rate of return is generally low relative to yields available on alternative assets.[3] Nonetheless, such insurance policies are very popular, with the result that life insurance provides a major vehicle for personal saving in Canada. Indeed, it has been estimated that approximately one-quarter of personal saving each year is accomplished through life insurance.[4] Why is this such an attractive vehicle for savings?

In part, the answer may be that the policyholders do not know the rate of return on their savings accumulated with life insurance companies. In part they may be attracted by the very fact that insurance is combined with saving. They may also be impressed with the apparent safety of their funds with insurance companies. Also, policyholders are clearly attracted by the systematic nature of the savings process.

Insurance Companies as Financial Intermediaries

At the end of 1967 there were 397 insurance companies registered with the federal government, of which 127 were incorporated in Canada. In addition, insurance was also written by 48 fraternal benefit societies, and a number of smaller provincially incorporated insurance companies. Considered as an industry, the insurance business is more international in scope than any of the other groups of financial intermediaries which we have examined. Thus, although Canadian fire and casualty insurance companies do relatively little business outside of Canada, well over one-quarter of the life insurance policies of Canadian life insurance are written outside Canada. For several of the larger life insurance companies foreign policies account for well in excess of 40% of their total life insurance business. At the same time, many foreign insurance companies are active in Canada. Thus, at the end of 1967 almost one-third of the life insurance policies and more than one-half of other insurance policies in effect in Canada had been written by foreign insurance companies. Foreign insurance companies doing business in Canada must register with the federal Superintendent of Insurance, and must maintain assets in Canada equal to their Canadian liabilities (calculated on an actuarial basis).[5] These funds are included in the asset data reported in Table 11-4.

As noted above, some insurance companies operating in Canada are incorporated and supervised exclusively by provincial governments, and some insurance is written by fraternal societies. However, over 90% of the life insurance and more than 85% of the fire and casualty insurance in effect has been written by federally registered and supervised companies.

Such, in crude outline, is the insurance industry. However, we have left hanging the question raised earlier: Can we legitimately consider insurance companies to be financial intermediaries?

Are Insurance Companies Financial Intermediaries? When we explored the concept of financial intermediation we saw that it has two important aspects. On the one hand a financial intermediary issues financial instruments, claims on itself, and uses the funds so collected to make loans and acquire a variety of financial assets. On the other hand, by holding a large, diversified portfolio of assets, a financial intermediary takes advantage of economies of scale and spreads risk, permitting it to offer a class of financial instruments with a better trade-off between risk, expected yield and/or liquidity than would otherwise be available in the market.

Many economists would argue that, given this concept of a financial intermediary, insurance companies can only be considered to be financial

Table 11-4

Assets of Insurance Companies in Canada, January 1, 1970

	Life Insurance Companies*		General Insurance Companies	
	Millions of Dollars	%	Millions of Dollars	%
LIQUID ASSETS				
Cash	53.6	.4	118.0	4.2
Short-term Notes and Deposits	†		132.2	4.8
FIXED INCOME SECURITIES				
Government of Canada Bonds	307.1	2.5	572.6	20.8
Other Bonds	3,706.3	30.4	997.1	36.2
VARIABLE INCOME SECURITIES				
Common and Preferred Shares	719.5	5.9	385.5	14.0
LOANS				
Mortgages	6,210.7	50.8	34.0	1.2
Policy Loans	568.7	4.6	—	—
OTHER ASSETS	656.8	5.4	519.1	18.8
TOTAL ASSETS IN CANADA	12,222.7	100.0	2,758.5	100.0

* For 16 companies holding approximately 86% of all life insurance company assets.
† Data not available separately.
SOURCES: Bank of Canada, *Statistical Summary*; Dominion Bureau of Statistics, *Business Financial Statistics*.

intermediaries to the extent that they issue life insurance policies with a savings feature attached. Financial intermediation involves the holding of a diversified portfolio of assets in order to spread risks. Pure insurance is different. It simply involves a pooling of risks. For pure insurance there need be no necessary accumulation of assets, and hence no lending activities. By this criterion, companies which do not issue savings-type life insurance policies (e.g., most general insurance companies) should not be classified as financial intermediaries.[6]

However, the business of an insurance company does not simply involve its acting as an agent to effect a pooling of risks among its policy-holders. The company stands as a true intermediary in the process. An insurance policy is a claim on the insurance company, just as a bank deposit is a claim on the bank. And just as the bank cannot know with certainty the portion of its deposits which will be called for payment in any given period of time, so an insurance company cannot know with certainty the claims for payment which will be made under outstanding policies during any period of time. Accordingly the insurance company, like the bank, must make provision for the possibility that its estimates are wrong. It must accumulate a pool of assets — contingency reserves — to guarantee its ability to make the contractual payments. And the composition of the portfolio of assets must be adapted to the degree of risk which the insurance company has assumed. While it is true that the major accumulation of funds administered by insurance companies is the savings of life insurance policyholders, there would seem to be little merit in the argument that general insurance companies (or life insurance companies with respect to their "term" insurance business) are not financial intermediaries. Moreover, as is apparent in Table 11-4, we are talking about a sizable concentration of financial assets.

The Deployment of Insurance Company Funds. The degree of risk assumed by general insurance companies is greater than that assumed by life insurance companies. The accidental destruction of real property like railroad rolling stock, a house, or an automobile is much less predictable than death or retirement. Since the requirements for funds to make payments on policies are correspondingly less predictable, the general insurance companies find that they must keep relatively more liquid asset portfolios than do the life insurance companies. This is illustrated in Table 11-4, which shows the assets held in Canada by both groups of companies. You should note the relatively small holdings by life insurance companies of both cash and Government of Canada bonds (unfortunately, information is not available on their holdings of other short-term liquid assets).

The other important difference in their asset portfolios is the life insurance companies' relatively heavy concentration on mortgages. As a long-term, relatively illiquid asset, mortgages are not particularly suitable assets for general insurance companies. Life insurance companies are a major factor in the mortgage market — indeed, they are the largest private institutional lenders in this market.

Competition Between Insurance Companies and
Other Financial Intermediaries

While insurance is clearly a rather unique type of financial instrument, we should not assume that insurance companies and other financial intermediaries do not compete for funds. While the competition may be more remote than that between banks and trust companies for term deposits, it *is* there, particularly in regards to life insurance with a savings feature.

During the past two decades there have been significant changes in the market for long-term consumer savings. Whereas life insurance was at one time virtually the only form of long-term contractual savings available there have developed in recent years a number of substitutes, the most important of which are the mutual funds and pension funds. The life insurance companies also faced renewed attacks from other longer-established forms of saving, such as time deposits with chartered banks and Canada Savings Bonds. Rates paid on these forms of saving rose steadily throughout the past two decades and the low rates paid on life insurance savings served to reduce the relative appeal of this form of saving. The life insurance companies responded to these competitive challenges in various ways. First, there has been a gradual increase in the rates paid on savings held by the Life companies. Second, they have increased their efforts to sell combined packages of group term, health, and disability insurance along with pension fund administration. By this scheme, an insurance company agrees to provide low-cost group term and other insurance and at the same time undertakes to administer the pension fund of the employer. Finally, the insurance companies have in recent years attempted to increase the attractiveness to individual savers of their own insurance policies by embellishing with additional services such as medical coverage, and occasionally disability insurance.

Most recently, however, the insurance companies have faced a new entrant into the market in the form of the government-administered Canada Pension Plan. While the plan is relatively new and therefore its impact upon the economy is not clear, its effect on savings flows could be important. One preliminary indication relates to the growth of life insurance assets. The plan was introduced in 1966 but its first full year of operation was 1967. Prior to 1967 the annual rate of increase in assets held by the companies had been close to 10%. In 1967, however, while the Canadian economy was enjoying continued economic expansion, life insurance assets increased by only 6.5%. In 1968 the growth in assets held by 16 companies with more than 85% of total assets in the industry fell to 5.8% and in 1969 the growth declined further to 4.2%. It may be therefore that the accumulation of long-term consumer savings is changing in favour of pension plans and, more importantly, pension plans administered by the public and not the private sector.

5/SPECIALIZED INTERMEDIATION: PENSION FUNDS

Like insurance companies, we must consider pension funds to be one group of financial intermediaries offering a highly specialized product — a pension. In our discussion of the demand for financial instruments in Chapter 4 we argued that the underlying demand for wealth reflected a desire to redistribute income and consumption over time. A pension plan does this explicitly. It collects a portion of each member's income during his working life and returns it (plus interest) in the form of an annual pension following retirement. Most pension plans involve an element of insurance as well. That is, members of the plan who live unusually long will continue to receive their pension in spite of the fact that their lifetime contributions by themselves would not have been adequate to purchase such a stream of retirement income. At the present time, in addition to the Canada Pension Plan operated by the government of Canada, there are more than 4,000 "trusteed" other pension plans with total assets of almost $9 billion dollars administered by trust companies and insurance companies.[7] Between 1952 and 1970 the increase in assets held by these funds was more than $7.5 billion so that they have become a major collector and investor of long-term consumer savings.

The Investment of Pension Funds

Since the managers of the funds can predict with great certainty both the inflow of funds and, more importantly, the outflow (they know when each member will retire and have some experience with early withdrawls due to death) the funds have little need for liquidity. As is evident in Table 11-5, their assets are primarily concentrated in the long-term forms with only minimal amounts in cash or other short-term assets. Perhaps

Table 11-5

Assets of Trusteed Pension Funds, January 1, 1970

	Millions of Dollars	Percentage Distribution
LIQUID ASSETS		
Cash	104	1.2
FIXED INCOME SECURITIES		
Government of Canada Bonds	491	5.6
Provincial and Municipal Bonds	3,242	36.1
Other Bonds	1,269	14.1
VARIABLE INCOME SECURITIES		
Canadian Stocks	1,445	16.1
Foreign Stocks	522	5.8
Investments in Pooled and Mutual Funds	725	8.1
LOANS		
Mortgages	775	8.6
OTHER ASSETS	371	4.4
	8,972	100

SOURCE: Bank of Canada *Statistical Summary*.

because of the fact that most pension plans promise a *fixed income* during retirement, the bulk of the assets are fixed income securities, and particularly provincial, municipal and corporate bonds. However, the portion of variable income securities is increasing, particularly as some pension plans have begun to offer variable income pensions designed partially to provide a hedge against the risk of inflation.

There is one further aspect of pension funds which merits passing mention. Table 11-5 shows a relatively heavy concentration of investments in provincial and municipal bonds. Closer examination of detailed data reveals that this concentration is particularly heavy among pension plans of provincial, municipal and educational institution employees. Thus provincial and educational employee funds respectively held 63% and 76% of their assets in the form of provincial bonds, and municipal employee funds held 43% in provincial bonds and 34% in municipal bonds. Federal government employee funds also show a relatively heavy concentration in Government of Canada bonds, although nowhere near the extremes of the provincial and municipal funds (17%). In short, apparently the administrators of many pension funds, and particularly those administered by provincial and municipal governments use the funds as a source of self-finance. The Royal Commission on Banking and Finance commented:

> Clearly pension fund investment decisions — particularly in plans at each level of government — are not made exclusively in terms of yields available on different assets. At the extreme, some funded plans administered by provincial governments held non-marketable long-term obligations of the government concerned — which is virtually equivalent to operating an unfunded plan. Given the size of the flows involved, this tendency to disregard market considerations on the part of many funds, particularly some of the large ones, can lower both the returns to the members on their pension savings and the efficiency of capital allocation in the market.[8]

Can such pension funds really be regarded as financial intermediaries?

6/OTHER SPECIALIZED INTERMEDIARIES

In addition to the various types of intermediaries that we have already discussed, there exist many other firms that in one form or another provide specialized intermediation. For example, there is one firm established by two chartered banks and a trust company that provides long-term loans to small- and intermediate-size businesses. Originally this firm was established as a method of avoiding some of the restrictions contained in the *Bank Act*. Now, even though the *Bank Act* has been revised so as to remove these artificial restraints the company continues to thrive and expand because it has proved to be such a profitable venture.

There are other firms, frequently referred to as development corporations, that both lend and participate directly via equity holdings and/or management in smaller- and intermediate-size firms. To a large extent they provide venture capital to firms that cannot raise funds via bank loan or are too small or closely held to warrant bond and/or equity issues.

Indeed, close scrutiny of the system would probably turn up a number of intermediaries which we do not even suspect exist. Unfortunately, data concerning the activities of all these "other" intermediaries are either non-existent or sketchy at best. Many of the private intermediaries by their very nature prefer to be anonymous and thus are not anxious to provide information concerning their activities. We suspect, however, that if the data were available most of these unclassified intermediaries would be shown quantitatively to play only a very minor role in the total financial sector. That is not to say that they are either unimportant or irrelevant.

7/GOVERNMENT LENDING INSTITUTIONS

There are a number of government-operated lending institutions which are important participants in the financial system, although, like the governmental savings institutions discussed in Chapter 9, they are not true financial intermediaries. Some provide insurance, such as the Export Credit Insurance Corporation which insures loans taken out by exporters and also provides finance for exports by direct loans. Other agencies insure farm crops, and provide loans to veterans, small business, and students. While these various insurance programs are important in some contexts the two institutions operated by the federal government that are of most direct and immediate importance to the financial sector are the Industrial Development Bank and the Central Mortgage and Housing Corporation.

The Industrial Development Bank is a wholly owned subsidiary of the Bank of Canada. Founded in 1944 by act of Parliament it was established to provide medium- and long-term financing for business firms unable to obtain financing on reasonable terms and conditions elsewhere. At first the Bank was restricted to lending to manufacturing enterprises but this constraint was removed in 1961 and now the institution lends to almost any business enterprise.

Loans are normally for relatively small amounts (the average is about $25,000) which highlights the fact that the primary customers of the bank are relatively small, high-risk business ventures. At the beginning of 1970, total loans outstanding amounted to slightly more than $437 million.

Originally the *Central Mortgage and Housing Corporation* was established to administer the National Housing Act. Since its creation in 1945, the Corporation has undergone several transformations so that at present it has four major fields of activity. First it insures mortgages under the NHA. By that we mean that it guarantees the loans made by private investors to individuals for the building of new homes or for the purchase and rehabilitation of existing residences. Second, the Corporation lends directly to individuals for housing construction, to nonprofit organizations for the construction of low-cost, low-income rental housing, to various organizations for the construction of student accommodation and to local governments for the construction of sewage treatment plants. Third, the Corporation tries to promote uniform building standards and codes throughout the nation. Finally, it is involved in providing short-term finance to mortgage lenders and is attempting to develop a secondary market for mortgages.

The insuring of mortgages by the Corporation helps to reduce the cost of mortgages to the borrower and provides a high-yield, low-risk, but still relatively illiquid, asset to the borrower. Normally, the difference in rates paid on an insured mortgage and a "conventional" or non-insured mortgage is between one half and one full percent. Furthermore, insured mortgages can be granted for up to 90% of the value of the house while conventional first mortgages are normally limited to 75% of the value of the purchase.

The program of direct lending has been instrumental in providing low-cost, low-income rental housing in major urban areas. The Corporation's lending for the construction of student accommodation has provided the bulk of the funds available in Canada for this purpose. At the beginning of 1970, the Corporation had loans outstanding of over $3 billion. In 1969 alone it lent more than $600 million and its total loans for the period 1954-1970 were in excess of $4 billion. Thus, in terms of its direct lending and insuring of mortgages, the Corporation plays a major role in the mortgage market.

Finally, the efforts of the Corporation to establish a secondary market in mortgages have had only limited success. Mortgages by their very nature are non-homogeneous even when sheltered under the protection of NHA insurance. Normal purchasers of mortgages frequently prefer to deal directly with the lender in an effort to tie in other business. Firms that might deal in the secondary market, therefore, are either already in the market or can find equally long-term substitutes which are more homogeneous and which have less risk associated with them. Furthermore, loans for low-income housing or dormitories for students are for abnormally long terms (30-40 years) and have artificially low rates of interest. In recent months, however, several private institutions have begun to sell packages or mortgages that are guaranteed by the selling institution and this may add further stimulus to the development of the secondary market.

8/COMPETITION AMONG TYPES OF INTERMEDIARIES

We have now completed our detailed survey of Canadian financial intermediaries. For purposes of description we have divided the intermediaries into groups or categories. While most of these groupings have roots in federal or provincial laws, we also discovered that each group had a rather distinctive pattern of assets and liabilities. On this basis we could say that each group represented firms engaged in a particular field of financial intermediation. However, it should also be obvious that from an economic point of view the various categories of financial intermediaries are largely — but not completely — arbitrary. The activities of firms in each group impinge directly on those of some, if not all, other groups.

Consider, for example, the chartered banks. While the banks are unique, in that part of their liabilities constitute a substantial portion of the money supply, they still face strong competition in other sectors. Thus the trust companies, the mortgage loan companies, and the *caisses populaires* and credit unions all compete with the banks for personal savings deposits. In assets, the banks face competition with the sales finance companies for consumer loans, with the trust companies, mortgage loan companies, credit unions, *caisses populaires* and insurance companies for mortgages.

While the banks are much less specialized in their intermediation than is the case with some other intermediaries, their example should make the major point. *The activities of intermediaries do not fit into tight, specialized compartments. The patterns of overlapping activities among groups of intermediaries are both complex and quantitatively important.* Moreover, as the discussion in the previous chapters suggests, *these patterns are not static: they are continually changing.*

These are points which should be kept in mind as we turn our attention to questions of public policy with respect to competition and soundness in the financial system.

FOOTNOTES

[1] Royal Commission on Banking and Finance, *Report*, p. 256.

[2] Under the Small Loans Act, anyone engaged in the business of "money-lending" (excluding chartered banks and licensed pawnbrokers) must obtain a license from the Minister of Finance and conform to the regulations of the Act if he makes loans of less than $1,500 and if he charges interest on those loans at the rate of 1% per month or greater. Firms which make personal loans of greater than $1,500 *exclusively*, or which invariably charge lower rates of interest, need not register. The main provisions of the Act call for regular inspections by the Superintendent of Insurance and place a ceiling on the rate of interest which may be charged. That ceiling varies with the size of the loan, and ranges from 24% per annum for loans of $300 or less to 15.2% per annum for loans of $1,500. Loans in excess of $5,000 made by registered companies are exempted from the interest ceiling.

[3] See, for example: Royal Commission on Banking and Finance, *Report*, p. 241.

[4] The Canadian Life Insurance Officers Association, *Submission to the Royal Commission on Banking and Finance* (Toronto, 1962) , pp. 34-37.

[5] That is, taking account of the probability of the insured event occurring. They do not have to maintain assets in an amount equal to the total value of insurance policies in effect. For example, at the end of 1967 foreign life insurance companies had $26.4 billion worth of life insurance policies in effect in Canada, but were required to hold only $3.1 billion of assets in trust in Canada under the law. Their actual Canadian assets were slightly higher.

[6] The Royal Commission on Banking and Finance was of this point of view. Thus, The purchaser of general insurance does not accumulate financial assets . . ., he simply buys a service; these companies are thus not financial intermediaries in the full sense. (Royal Commission on Banking and Finance, *Report*, p. 250.) The Bank of Canada is apparently also of this view. Statistics on general insurance companies are not reported in the Bank of Canada's *Statistical Summary* along with the statistics of other financial intermediaries. It is tempting to turn the issue on its head. Since an essential aspect of financial intermediation is the spreading of risks through portfolio diversification, and since insurance is simply a pooling of risks, is not financial intermediation then an aspect of insurance?

[7] In addition to the "trusteed" pension funds there are untold numbers of unfunded plans. A trusteed plan is a financial intermediary in the usual sense. The pension is a financial claim against the fund, and the fund accumulates a diversified portfolio of financial assets. By contrast, an unfunded plan could not be considered a financial intermediary. Such a plan does not have assets sufficient to match its liabilities. Typically, the pension is a claim against the future earnings of the corporation itself, rather than a claim against a diversified portfolio of assets.

[8] Royal Commission on Banking and Finance, *Report*, p. 260.

12

The Development of the
Canadian Financial System

Our major concern in this chapter is with the evolution of the industrial structure of financial intermediation in Canada. Together with the
following chapter on the financial system of the United States, this is an
essential prelude to the discussion of public policy toward the structure of
the financial system in Chapter 14.

1/DOMINANT THEMES

From a relatively uncomplicated beginning in the colonies of British
North America, the Canadian economy's growth and increasing complexity
called for the development of our present complex network of financial
institutions and markets. Economic growth created demands for an infinite
variety of specialized financial services and specialized forms for the accumulation of wealth. At the same time, changes in the structure and performance of the economy, including its proclivity to develop periodic
crises, posed frequent challenges and tests for financial institutions. The
system had to adapt continuously to the changing economic environment.

However, as we shall see more clearly in the next chapter, the product
of this historical process to date is a financial system which is vastly different from that of the United States, although the two systems developed
under similar economic conditions. It is clear that there is something else
which is important in explaining the development of the Canadian system.

The Content of Public Policy

In large part, the mould for the Canadian system was cast at the
outset. Unlike their counterparts in the United States, the authorities in
what was to become Canada adopted a system of commercial banking
involving a few very large-scale banking firms. These firms developed
substantial economic and political power, and *the vested interests of the
established banks emerged as a very powerful conservative force* in the
evolutionary process.

Beyond these first steps, *the content of public policy continued to be
the decisive factor shaping the development of the system.* Deliberation

urrounding successive revision of banking legislation became the arena
or struggles between opposing interests. In part, changes in public policy
elated directly to *the structure of the industry*, as, for example, govern-
nent measures affecting the ease of establishing new banks or the ease
.f merging existing firms into an even smaller number of larger firms.
)ther concerns of public policy related to the *development of effective
nstitutions for the regulation of the money supply in the public interest,*
nd the *continuing search for institutions and policies which would guar-
ntee the stability of banks* and other financial institutions (individually
nd in the aggregate), and which would protect unsuspecting creditors
rom severe financial loss.

As we shall see, the struggle began with the government casting envious
yes on the banks' rights to issue notes for circulation as currency. At
arious stages it focused on proposals to effectively lodge part of the public
lebt in the banking system, proposals for compulsory government inspec-
ion of financial institutions, and the establishment and control of the
•perations of a central bank. Most recently it has involved proposals to
xtend federal supervision to provincially supervised companies, and the
›rovision of compulsory deposit insurance. More often than not, the debates
nvolved an impassioned conflict between the public's concern for safety
nd the bankers' desires for freedom from cumbersome, perhaps costly,
estrictions.

The Impact of the United States

The development of Canadian public policy toward the financial
ystem was not simply a groping for solutions to internal Canadian finan-
ial problems. It was also heavily influenced from time to time by develop-
nents in the financial system and the financial policies of the United States.
\t times the Canadian reaction was one of imitation. Thus, the model
or the original Canadian bank charters was an early American bank
although the fundamental concepts had deeper British roots). At other
imes, the Canadian reaction was one of revulsion. On balance, the latter
eaction has dominated. As a result, the Canadian financial system, and
›articularly the banks, developed along radically different lines from the
\merican counterpart.

2/THE FIRST THREE DECADES OF THE NINETEENTH
CENTURY: THE ORIGINS OF CANADIAN BANKING

Banking, or at least efforts to establish banks, began almost simul-
aneously in the three colonies of Upper Canada, Lower Canada and
Nova Scotia. In these three areas, where the problems of economic survival
.nd growth were formidable, there were neither organized financial markets
.or formal financial intermediaries. While private financing could be
›btained, normally from merchants who acted as primitive private bankers,
he supply was irregular and interest rates were frequently very high.
:apital was scarce, risks were high and financial markets were extremely

imperfect. Moreover, there was no official provision of a stable, uniform currency which would expand with the growth of the colonies. In the absence of such a currency, the money supply consisted of a polyglot mixture of private script issued by merchants and frequently proving to be worthless, the remnants of some ad hoc government issues, some French coins left over from the old regime, and an infinite variety of foreign coins and notes (which circulated at varying rates of exchange). In the words of one student of Canadian banking history:

> During the second quarter of the nineteenth century the office of a Canadian currency broker was a veritable curiosity shop, exhibiting the remnants of several national currencies in the last stages of demoralization. There, from a currency point of view, the halt, the blind and the disowned of many mints foregathered in shabby company. Their thin, worn and battered faces mutely witnessed to a long and busy life with much travel and hard usage. Only the chronic scarcity of coinage in times of peace enabled this motley crew to occupy the market-place and brazen their way into fairly respectable company.[1]

In such an environment, banks were sometimes regarded as a panacea. To the merchant they held out the promise of a reliable source of commercial credit at reasonable rates. To individuals, they offered a convenient method for the safekeeping of wealth. To the economy as a whole, they promised an elastic supply of a uniform currency: bank notes.

Bank Notes as Currency. It may seem strange to think of privately owned banks as a source of currency. We are accustomed to thinking of governments as issuing currency while banks, to the extent that they issue money, have demand deposits transferable by cheque. Historically, however, the right of banks (and others) to issue notes was rooted in common law (it has been argued that governments in fact usurped a common law right of banks), and in any case, the use of cheques to effect transactions was little developed in the early nineteenth century. Bank notes, designed to circulate as currency, were the major liability of the early banks. Indeed, so important was the right to issue notes that it is doubtful whether without this power a bank could have survived and developed. In this regard the nature of commercial banking was very different in this period than it is today. By way of illustration, Table 12-1 traces the changes in the structure of the balance sheet of one bank, the Bank of Nova Scotia, from 1833 to the present. Note the dramatic decline in the importance of notes in circulation and the capital accounts (funds provided by the owners of the bank) and the equally drastic rise in the importance of deposits as a source of funds. Note also the change in the relative importance of gold and silver among the assets of the bank. By law, all bank notes were convertible into specie on demand, a fact which made it necessary for note-issuing banks to hold very substantial gold and silver reserves. In the early days these were foreign coins, some of which had formal status as legal tender.

Contrary Political Forces. While the obvious need for greater uniformity in the currency and for improved credit facilities seemed to argue strongly for the establishment of banks, this view was not unanimous. The

Table 12-1
The Bank of Nova Scotia, 1833-1970
Composition of Liability and Asset Portfolios

	1833	1863	1892	1931	1970
Liabilities		(Percent)			
Notes in Circulation	19.4	28.0	11.2	4.9	—
Deposits	22.0	34.6	61.6	78.9	92.0
Other Liabilities	—	4.7	1.3	1.9	3.4
Capital Accounts	58.6	32.7	26.0	14.2	4.6
TOTAL	100.0	100.0	100.0	100.0	100.0
Assets					
Gold and Silver	32.3	12.7	3.7	0.8	1.1
Coin and Legal Tender	2.0	—	4.8	8.6	3.1
Other Bank Notes	0.3	0.8	3.4	0.3	—
Foreign Currency	—	—	—	0.6	0.2
Correspondent Balances	0.2	—	3.0	5.8	14.8
Securities	65.3	85.4	16.7	24.1	12.1
Loans	—	—	66.6	53.5	61.5
Other Assets	—	1.2	1.7	6.2	7.2
TOTAL	100.0	100.0	100.0	100.0	100.0
	(thousands of dollars)		(millions of dollars)		
TOTAL ASSETS	85.9	1.7	10.0	262.5	

SOURCES: The Bank of Nova Scotia, 1832-1932 (Toronto: Bank of Nova Scotia, 1932); Canada Gazette (Ottawa: Queen's Printer, February, 1970).

ad experiences of the United States and their paper currencies coupled with comparable experiences in Canada with various private and public issues had soured many individuals on any form of paper money. Moreover, many believed banks would soon establish a stranglehold on the economy, the government, and eventually the farmer so as to preclude him from gaining a fair share of the growing prosperity of the region. The rivalry between the rising wealthy merchant class, with their limited political power, who favoured the establishment of banking, against the empowered agrarian aristocracy of the Family Compact and Chateau Clique who favoured banking only on their terms (i.e., that they own them) makes it easy to see why it was not until 1820 in Nova Scotia that the first bank was chartered. (The Bank of Montreal began business as a private firm in 1817 after repeated attempts to secure a charter had been bogged down in the political infighting of the day, but it did not obtain a charter until 1822.)

The First Bank Charters

The first bank charters set the pattern in which the Canadian banking system developed. It is striking that, even down to detailed wording, they were based upon the charter which Alexander Hamilton, the first Secretary of the Treasury of the United States, drew up for the first Bank of the United States. However, it is also important to note that Hamilton's charter was based on concepts of banking developed in Great Britain, and particularly in Scotland. Although this concept of banking was eventually discarded in the United States, the Imperial connection served to strengthen the concept in Canada.

Hamilton envisaged the first Bank of the United States as an embryonic central bank which would regulate and bring order to the American banking industry, and would provide a pattern for the orderly future development of that industry. At the time the First Bank of the United States was established (1792) the American banking system was a disparate collection of state-chartered and private banks, many of which followed questionable, often fraudulent, banking practices with the result that some banks failed, bank notes were frequently worthless, and many unsuspecting individuals lost heavily. Hamilton's charter gave the first Bank of the United States wide powers to open branches, to issue currency and to compete with, and hence discipline and supplant, shaky local banks. By wholesale adoption of this charter, the early Canadian banks obtained the same rights, and the Canadian banking system developed along Hamilton's lines.

Principles Established by the Early Bank Charters

Legislative Chartering. Like all limited liability companies at that time, banks were chartered by a special act of the relevant legislature (a few private banks emerged which had no charters — they were in effect partnerships with unlimited liability — and a few banks for a time held charters from the Imperial government). This principle of legislative chartering of banks was subsequently rejected in the United States in favour of chartering through executive action. In Canada, aside from a short period to be discussed subsequently, the principle of legislative chartering for fixed term subject to extension by subsequent legislation was retained.

"Commercial" Banking. In the early bank charters, the scope of the business of banks was defined through specific prohibitions against certain activities. The banks were implicitly permitted to do anything which was not specifically prohibited (this is in contrast to common practice in the United States in which the charter specifies what the bank may do, with all other activities implicitly prohibited). The effect of the prohibitions in the first charters was to establish Canadian chartered banks as "commercial" banks. They were prohibited from dealing in goods and services or real estate, and were prohibited from lending on the security of mortgages on real estate, i.e., their activities were effectively confined to short term commercial and personal lending, and international finance.

Bank Notes. The banks were permitted to issue bank notes designed to circulate as currency, with certain limitations on the total amount outstanding at any one time, and subject to the requirement that they be convertible into gold or silver on demand.

Branching. It is also significant that the first bank charters did not contain any prohibitions against the opening of branches. They thus permitted Canadian banks to develop networks of branch offices, including offices in colonies other than the one in which the bank was initially chartered. This laid the groundwork for the most striking difference between banking systems in Canada and the United States; the nation-wide branch banking system.

Protection of the Public. Perhaps reflecting the acrimonious debates surrounding the initial chartering of banks, the early charters also contained primitive arrangements for "the better security of the public", i.e., the depositors and note holders who were the creditors of the banks. Thus, a ceiling was established on total bank debts, the directors of each bank were made personally responsible for bank debts in excess of the legal limit, and the government was given the power to call for periodic reports from the banks on their paid-in capital, total debts, deposits, notes in circulation and cash on hand.

3/THE 1830'S TO CONFEDERATION: "POPULIST" PRESSURES ON THE BANKING SYSTEM

With the formation and early success of the first banking corporations several groups emerged who wanted to enter what appeared to be a profitable venture. But, as the clamor for new bank charters increased, the imperial authorities became concerned lest charters be granted to individuals more intent on quick speculative gains via extensive note issue than on long-term profits through "sound" banking practice. The British Government began to send to each of the various colonial legislatures long lists of suggestions on how existing and future charters might be improved, to minimize the risk of failure and hence of loss to depositors and note holders. In several cases, whether for political reasons (Family Compact versus outside applications) or financial reasons, the authorities in England disallowed charters which had been granted by local governments. The effect was to strengthen the concept of banking set out in the original charters.

In spite of this external intervention, both the number of banks and their total assets continued to grow. In 1830 there were six banks in Canada (with unknown total assets). Between 1830 and the end of 1867, 50 new banks were successfully established. Taking account of mergers, repealed charters and failures (17 banks failed between 1830 and 1867, or almost one out of every three banks in operation at some time during this period), only 35 banks, with total assets of $84 million, remained active at the end of 1867. Over the same period, the number of active banks in the United States increased by 1,579, from 329 to 1,908.

"Populism" and "Free Banking"

The growth of the banking system, and particularly the concentration of that growth in the hands of a few firms, did not meet with universal acclaim. An essentially agrarian "populist" reaction emerged, rooted in a fear of the "money trust" and drawing much of its inspiration from opinions which were widely held and politically very influential in the United States.

"Populism" in the United States. Hamilton's First Bank of the United States was extremely successful in disciplining the more adventurous local banks in the United States. However, its very success earned it lasting enemies. When its charter came up for renewal in 1811, it was allowed to lapse by a hostile Congress. The financial problems which the American government encountered by relying on the fragmented banking system for financing the War of 1812 led them to charter a second Bank of the United States in 1816. However, it met the fate of its predecessor this time at the hands of Andrew Jackson and his populist supporters.

The Banks of the United States served as a focal point for agrarian discontent. The populists were suspicious of the banks' dominant position in the financial system, and resented the conservative banking policies which the Banks attempted to enforce throughout the country. The populist believed that the Banks were in league with other money interests in the financial centers of Philadelphia, New York and Boston to exploit the rural areas. It was argued that conservative commercial banking principles discriminated against them — an allegation which had some substance, in that land or mortgages on land were not considered bankable assets on conservative commercial banking principles. Moreover, the instability o agricultural crops and markets made any loans to farmers a risky asset and called for premium interest rates (if indeed credit would be extended at all).

The populists favoured "free banking", that is, they wanted banking legislation making it easy to establish small banks under local control, using local funds, and, most importantly, making local loans (primarily to farmers). The free banking principle involved the granting of a bank charter by executive action to any group which met the minimum requirements set out in the legislation. In general these minimum requirements – and particularly the minimum amount of capital which had to be subscribed to the new bank — were kept low, for the express purpose of facilitating the entry of small banks. Restrictions were normally placed on the opening of branch offices to encourage retention of local control.

The free banking principle was rooted in a concern for ready access to credit rather than a concern for the protection of depositors and note holders. However, state free banking acts generally included provisions requiring specified collateral (typically government bonds) against bank notes outstanding. While not widely successful as a device for protecting the note holder, this did have the incidental effect of creating a captive market for government securities.

The Free Banking Movement in Canada. In Canada, populist fears of a bank conspiracy against the farmer and little merchant throughout the 1830's and 1840's brought about recurrent agitation, particularly in the legislature of Upper Canada, to permit free banking. The legislature eventually did pass a free banking statute and its provisions reflected the populists' philosophy. Bank charters could be issued by executive decision, capital requirements were low, and free banks were precluded from branching. Furthermore, the amount of notes which could be issued was limited to the amount of government debt held by the banks, and the banks were required to maintain redemption centers for their notes at various points throughout the colony. This final feature was included to prevent the notes of the bank being discounted in places distant from the bank's office. (Discounting was a common feature when information as to the soundness of the bank and its ability to redeem its notes in gold was lacking. To offset the possible risks of holding the notes, individuals and businesses would only accept them at less than their face value.)

To some extent, the free banking movement failed to obtain widespread acceptance in Canada because legislative charters could still be obtained. In those States where free banking was established the provision for legislative charters was simultaneously abolished, so that new banks had to conform to the free banking principle. In Upper Canada, however, the option of a legislative charter proved to have strong attractions, particularly in the right to open branch offices and more liberal provisions for note issue. Only six banks were established under the *Free Banking Act*, one of which had previously been operating under an Imperial charter. Two of these failed quickly, and the others soon converted to legislative charters.

While the principle of free banking was not established in Canada, populist suspicions of an eastern "money trust" which would discriminate against rural and western interests did not die. Indeed, it persists in some sectors of the country today.

The Banks and Governmental Finance

The controversies surrounding the banking system in this period brought to the fore another important issue: the financial relations between government and the banks.

The period was marked by several attempts on the part of the colonial governments to encroach on the traditional rights of the banks to issue bank notes. Some of the proposals simply involved requiring banks to hold government securities as collateral behind bank notes outstanding. Others, pushed more vigorously, involved the substitution of a government-issued paper money for bank notes. The motivations underlying these proposals were undoubtedly complex, but two themes stand out clearly from the debates: a desire to protect the public from the consequences of the competitive over-issuance of bank notes by the banks, and a desire to augment the financial resources of the government.

The attractiveness to the government of a governmental monopoly over the issuance of paper money should be obvious. It permitted the creation of *interest-free* public debt. Its unattractiveness to the banks is equally obvious. Interest-free government debt was being substituted for interest-free bank debt. Moreover, the sums involved were significant. In 1861, notes in circulation accounted for over 21% of the total funds (liabilities plus capital stock) of the banks in the Province of Canada, and they were substantially more important as a source of funds than interest free deposits.[2] It is not surprising that the banks opposed such scheme vigorously (and, during this period, quite successfully).

The regulatory significance of such schemes is not as obvious. The proposed governmental issue of paper money was to have a fixed gold reserve. It is true that the banks were required by their charters to convert their notes in gold and silver on demand, but they were not required to maintain any fixed minimum relationship between their notes and their holdings of gold and silver. The bankers argued that the absence of such restraints on the issuance of paper money was essential if the money supply was to have adequate "elasticity" to meet seasonal and secular demands for money. The government argued that elasticity created the danger of over-issue.

Formal proposals for a government monopoly in Canada over paper money were defeated in 1841 and 1860. In the midst of a minor financial crisis in 1865 a partial measure was enacted, permitting a limited issue of government paper money. In the following year the first issue occurred with the cooperation of the government's fiscal agent, the Bank of Montreal which restricted its bank notes outstanding. The new government notes were used to a limited extent as bank reserves, partially replacing specie for that purpose. While it was a limited measure, with limited effect, the *Bank Note Act* of 1866 was important in that it ended the chartered banks monopoly of note issue.

The Beginnings of Diversified Financial Intermediation

Although the chartered banks continued to totally dominate the financial system, the seeds of various other types of financial intermediation were planted in this period.

As we have seen, the chartered banks were conceived as "commercial banks". They were discouraged from making long-term loans, and were prohibited from lending on the security of real estate. This left major gaps in the financial system. In response, several financial intermediaries specializing in longer-term, particularly mortgage, financing made their appearance. A number of "building societies", precursors of the modern mortgage loan company, were established in Upper and Lower Canada as early as 1845, and two Quebec savings banks were established in 1846 and 1848. The early building societies were heavily involved in farm mortgages. Insurance companies also began to emerge as important financial intermediaries in this period. The first insurance written in Canada was by agencies of British companies (fire insurance in 1804 and life insurance in 1846), but by the end of the period a number of Canadian companies were well established.

4/CODIFICATION OF THE BASIC PRINCIPLES: CONFEDERATION TO 1891.

The first two decades following Confederation was a period of rapid growth in the banking system. From 1867 to 1890 total bank assets increased three-fold, from $84 million to $260 million. Initially, the growth in total assets was accompanied by an increase in the number of firms.

In the seven years 1868 - 1874 20 new banks were established, and after several failures and mergers the total number of active banks increased from 35 to the all-time peak of 51. In the following 17 years six more banks were established, but four mergers and 12 failures gradually reduced the number of active firms to 41 by the end of 1890. The number of bank offices rose from 123 in 1867, to 230 in 1874, and 426 in 1890. Chartered banks were not the only financial intermediaries to experience substantial growth during the period. Previously established savings banks, building societies and insurance companies continued to expand, and several new types of intermediaries were established. Consolidation in the banking system was accompanied by increased diversification in financial intermediation considered as a whole.

The Legal Framework

The British North America Act assigned responsibility for the regulation of currency and banking to the federal government. As a result, one of the first orders of business for the first Government of Canada was to formalize arrangements in these areas.

Monetary Legislation. The first problem to be tackled was the issuance of paper money. Following temporary legislation in 1868, resolutions were introduced into the Parliament by the Minister of Finance calling for a restructuring of Canadian banking and monetary legislation on the model of the *National Bank Act* of the United States (1864). The resolutions incorporated both the principle of linking paper money to government financing, and populist concepts of the appropriate banking structure. The banks were to be deprived of the right to issue bank notes on the security of their general credit and restricted to issuing government printed notes on the security of an equal value of government bonds deposited with the Minister of Finance (such notes would be legal tender, would be convertible into gold on demand, and would be backed in addition by fixed gold reserves held by the banks). The plan also called for the creation of small local banks, with small capital requirements, so as to achieve greater "diffusion of banking interests in different localities".[3] This re-emergence of populist concepts was again decisively rejected in a one-day debate in the House of Commons.

The monetary legislation which was passed, the *Dominion Notes Act* of 1870, was a compromise. The concepts of a government monopoly over paper money, and of government bond-secured bank notes were rejected.

The right of the banks to issue bank notes on their own security was confirmed, but restricted to notes with a denomination of $4 or greater. Thus the government established a monopoly over small-denomination ($1 and $2) notes. As a further measure to increase governmental participation in the profits from note issuance, the banks were required to hold at least half of their cash reserves in Dominion notes. The Dominion notes themselves had fractional gold reserves behind them, and in this sense the Act officially established the gold standard in Canada. Aside from periodic increases in the ceiling on the amount of Dominion notes which could be outstanding and changes in the gold backing for these notes, no major changes in the principles underlying the issuance of currency occurred until Canada abandoned the gold standard (1914). Dominion notes gradually increased in importance, but not until 1908 did the total value of Dominion notes outstanding exceed the total value of bank notes in circulation, and even then almost 85% of the outstanding Dominion notes were lodged in bank vaults. At no time, until they were superseded by Bank of Canada notes, did Dominion notes account for a major fraction of currency in circulation.

The First Bank Act. If the monetary legislation of 1868-1870 represented a compromise with the concepts of American populism, no such compromise was evident in the *Bank Act* of 1871. Although provisions for the security of depositors and note holders were extended, the Act codified the principles which had been set out in the first charters and firmly established through practice.

The rejection of populist ideology is most clearly marked in the provisions for establishing new banks. The Act continued the principle of legislative chartering of banks, with each charter subject to renewal every ten years. The Act also provided specific authorization for the banks to open branches "at any place or places in the Dominion", and established a substantial financial hurdle for new banks in the form of a minimum capital requirement. A new bank was required to have $500,000 of capital subscribed and $100,000 actually paid-in within two years, with the balance of the requirement callable as necessary. In the United States at that time a National Bank, i.e., one chartered by the federal government, could be established in a small town with capital of $50,000 and charters could be obtained from most states for banks with even less capital. Clearly, the framers of the first *Bank Act* intended to have no truck with American-style "free banking".

With respect to the business of the banks, no significant innovations were introduced. The "commercial" character of the banks' business was reinforced. Provisions were introduced permitting "commercial" lending, provisions which evolved into the familiar Section 88, and the established prohibitions against mortgage lending and dealing in real estate were continued. The provisions of the *Dominion Notes Act* of 1870 with respect to bank notes and bank reserves were also incorporated in the *Bank Act,* and extended somewhat. For the greater security of the public, shareholders of banks were subjected to double liability, and the banks were required to submit more detailed periodic reports to the government.

Unsettled Issues: Inspection, Reserve Requirements, and a Central Bank. In the two subsequent revisions, 1880 and 1890, only minor changes were made in the *Bank Act*. A redemption fund was established to guarantee the redemption of the notes of failed banks, the share of Dominion notes in bank reserves was increased, bank notes were confined to denominations in multiples of $5, and the scope of commercial loans (Section 88) was expanded. As a harbinger of future developments, the minimum capital requirement for new banks was altered so that $250,000 had to be paid in before the bank could commence business, and the bank had only one year from the time it obtained its charter to raise this capital.

The central concern underlying most of these adjustments to the *Bank Act* was the security of bank creditors. Between 1871 and 1890 thirteen banks failed, including four in 1878 and five in 1887. The failure of a few others was averted through amalgamation with other sound institutions. In general it was the smaller banks which failed, and frequently they were relatively new institutions. The measures which were taken, then, were designed to protect the note holders (the "unsuspecting creditors") of failed banks, who accepted the notes in good faith as currency, and to make it more difficult for small, new banks to be established.

Even more radical solutions to the problem of bank instability were proposed. The concept of a government monopoly over the currency supply, through the creation of a government bank of issue — a prototype central bank — was in the air, but gained little support. Direct attempts to impose governmental inspection on the banks and to require fixed-percentage cash reserve requirements were advanced by the government, but successfully warded off by the political pressures mounted by the banks. Indeed, in the case of the fixed-reserve requirement, the bankers were permitted to argue their case before the cabinet — a highly irregular procedure. These reforms remained "unfinished business" for some time to come.

Profile of the Financial System in 1890

The development of other financial institutions continued apace with the refinement of the chartered banking system. New intermediaries continued to be established. Indeed, the government itself established two savings banks, the Post Office Savings Bank and the Dominion Government Savings Bank. Of more lasting importance was the fact that the first trust company made its appearance in Ontario in 1882. In addition to these new types of institutions, insurance companies and mortgage loan companies continued to grow, both in total assets and in numbers. As a result, by 1890 non-bank financial intermediaries — and particularly intermediaries specializing in long-term mortgage financing — were emerging as significant factors in the financial system.

Table 12-2 presents a profile of financial intermediation in Canada in 1890 on the basis of the limited statistical information available.

Table 12-2
The Canadian Financial System, 1890

I. THE MONEY SUPPLY

	Millions of Dollars	Percent
Dominion Notes (held outside banks)	5.9*	6.2
Bank Notes	35.0	37.0
Public Demand Deposits with Chartered Banks	53.7	56.8
TOTAL	94.6	100.0

* The banks held $9.7 million of Dominion Notes

II. THE ASSETS OF FINANCIAL INTERMEDIARIES

The Chartered Banks	260	54
Quebec Savings Banks*	11*	2
Government Savings Banks*	43*	9
Mortgage Loan Companies (Building Societies)	123*	26
Trust Companies	n.a.	—
Life Insurance Companies	43	9
General Insurance Companies	n.a.	—
TOTAL	480	100

* Deposits
SOURCES: Urquhart and Buckley, *Historical Statistics of Canada; Statistical Year-Book of Canada*, 1891 (Department of Agriculture).

5/CONSOLIDATION AND GROWTH: 1890-1914

In the 25 years between 1890 and the outbreak of World War I both the Canadian economy and the banking industry experienced a fundamental change in structure and size. In the economy, agriculture declined in relative importance, the industrial base emerged as an increasingly important factor, and international trade expanded rapidly. Partly in response to these changes in the structure of the economy, and partly as a result of increased sophistication in management, the banking system underwent a fundamental structural change as well. Growth and consolidation were the orders of the day. Thus in less than 25 years, bank assets increased from $260 million to more than $1.55 billion and the number of branches rose from 426 to over 3,000. Yet, in spite of this growth the number of banks declined from 41 in 1890 to 22 in 1914.

The Merger Movement

Various factors contributed to the consolidation of the banking system in this period.

Legislation. Changes in the *Bank Act* were conducive to consolidation. We have already mentioned the change in the capital requirements enacted with the revision of 1890. This increase in minimum capitalization tended to restrain entry. Thus, in the 24-year period 1890-1913, only 11 new banks were established as compared to 28 in the previous 24 years, although the rate of growth of bank offices and bank assets in the second period was almost double that in the first.

While entry was restrained, mergers were facilitated. In 1900 the *Bank Act* was changed to permit a bank to purchase the assets of any other bank. Prior to this change, all mergers required a special Act of Parliament. Following this simplification of merger procedures, 17 mergers were consummated before the end of 1914. In the previous 33 years there had only been six mergers.

Economic Factors in Mergers. The legislative changes of 1900 facilitated mergers. However, the incentive for these amalgamations had to rest elsewhere. The owners of one bank had to have an incentive to sell, and the owners of another to buy. That is, the assets of the absorbed bank had to be worth more to the buyer than to the seller. What might cause such a divergence in valuations? Little substantive research has been done on bank mergers in this period, so we do not know the answer to this question. However, some hypotheses have been advanced.

Impending insolvency is frequently suggested as the common reason for selling a bank. Relatively *high costs* appear also to have plagued some banks, whether through *inefficiency* in management or through the inability of very small banks to exploit *economies of scale*. It is also important to note that small localized banks could not achieve the degree of *diversification in asset holdings* common to very large institutions.

For some purchasing institutions, merger may have provided a relatively cheap method of *penetrating markets* where they previously had little or no representation. For example, certain regions of the Maritimes were regarded as areas suitable for expansion, not so much because the demand for loans would be heavy but rather because the supply of deposits would be in excess of local needs. Here then was a ready source of finance for the expanding markets in the west.

For the bank desiring to enter a new market the choice was either to buy an existing bank or start from scratch. In general, the first alternative was preferred since it provided the purchaser with the office and personnel along with established accounts and loans. The purchase also served to eliminate a potential competitor.

Even in the absence of significant penetration of new market areas, the existence of *economies of scale* would create an incentive to merge. The merged banks would have lower costs than either of the original firms. In some cases a drive to be the largest bank seems to have been operative, and the simple desire to reduce the degree of competition in the market place may have been a powerful consideration.

Bank Failures

Limitations on entry and bank mergers were only two of the three elements in the consolidation process. The third was the failure of banks. In this period 11 banks disappeared through failure (and two others had their charters suspended).

Bank failures more often than not were the result of poor management. Excessively risky loans were made which subsequently proved to be worthless and this meant the financial position of the bank was impaired. The inability of some smaller banks to achieve a high degree of diversification in asset holdings also left them in an exposed position. In several cases, however, the failure was the direct result of the fraudulent practices of the general manager or directors who had used the funds of the bank for private investment schemes or similar dubious ventures. As a result the bank would find it had few tangible assets and therefore would be forced to end business.

In two cases, the manner in which the failures were handled was rather unusual. Normally, because of the double liability provision, a failure implied the loss to the shareholders of their equity plus that sum again. Not infrequently these amounts plus what could be recovered from the sale of the bank's assets were not sufficient to cover the bank's liabilities and as a result depositors also suffered losses. The failure of a large bank could affect the entire banking community. To avoid such repercussions, the Bank of Montreal agreed to take over the failing Ontario bank in 1906. The other remaining banks agreed to participate in losses suffered by the Bank of Montreal as a result. Because of this action the loss to the depositors was zero and the financial disaster that would have followed had the bank failed was avoided. In 1908, when the Sovereign bank failed, 12 chartered banks divided the existing branch network of the Sovereign bank among them and agreed to share losses in proportion to the value of the deposits that each had assumed.

These arrangements amounted to a primitive ad hoc deposit insurance scheme. It could not be relied upon in all cases, however, and indeed not even in all large-scale failures (as the spectacular failure of the Home Bank in 1923 was to demonstrate).

In summary, the structure of the chartered banking industry underwent a major transformation between 1890 and 1913. This transformation was facilitated by legislation permitting mergers and restricting entry, and was partly effected through mergers and partly through bank failures. At the end of 1914 there were only 22 banks remaining in active operation in Canada.

Profile of the Financial System: 1914

The growth of non-bank financial intermediaries continued during this period, but not at as rapid a rate as the growth of the chartered banks. Thus, as Table 12-3 shows, the chartered banks actually increased their share of the total assets of Canadian financial intermediaries. This increase

Table 12-3
The Canadian Financial System, 1914

I. THE MONEY SUPPLY

	Millions of Dollars	Percent
Subsidiary Coin	19.7	4.0
Dominion Notes (outside banks) *	19.2*	3.9
Public Demand Deposits with Chartered Banks	350.0	70.7
Bank Notes	106.0	21.4
TOTAL	494.9	100.0

* The Banks held $143 million of Dominion Notes.

II. THE ASSETS OF FINANCIAL INTERMEDIARIES

The Chartered Banks	1,556	60
Quebec Savings Banks	42	2
Government Savings Banks	56	2
Caisses Populaires	2	—
Mortgage Loan Companies	479*	19
Trust Companies†	19†	1
Life Insurance Companies	370	14
General Insurance Companies	48	2
TOTAL	2,572	100

* 1913.

†Federal Trust Companies only. Provincial companies probably had assets several times as great as federal companies. E. T. & A. account of federal companies as $30 million in 1914.

SOURCES: Urquhart and Buckley, *Historical Statistics of Canada; The Canada Year Book; Statistical Year Book of Quebec.*

---

in asset holdings was financed by a sharp increase in total deposits in banks, and particularly interest-bearing savings and notice deposits. Both notes in circulation and capital accounts declined in significance as a source of funds. Thus, the banks began to compete effectively for funds with the non-bank financial intermediaries on their own grounds.

An important new type of near bank was introduced in this period when the first *caisse populaire* was organized in Levis, Quebec, in 1900. By 1915 there were 91 societies with 23,614 members and total assets in excess of $2 million.

6/WAR FINANCE: 1914-1920

The Bank Act of 1913

In 1913 parliament undertook the revision of the *Bank Act* that had been delayed for three years. The changes that were enacted did not constitute a major overhaul of the legislation, but nevertheless, some of these alterations were important.

The battle over outside inspection which had occupied so much of the debate from 1880 onwards was partially resolved by the institution of a shareholders' audit. Each year the shareholders were to elect a firm to carry out a complete audit of the bank and the results were to be distributed to the shareholders and the Minister of Finance. The aim, of course, was to reduce the possibility of fraud which had been found to be the cause of several recent spectacular failures.

The demands from the west for increased credit facilities had been partially solved by the enactment in 1908 of a temporary provision whereby the banks during certain portions of the year, could issue notes in excess of the legal limit (provided that such excess issue was backed by gold or Dominion notes of a like amount). In 1913 this temporary provision was made permanent, and as an additional measure banks were authorized to make loans secured by threshed grain grown upon the borrower's land.

Finally, because of growing agitation on the part of many who believed that mergers were threatening the country with a money trust and a consequent diminution of competition, all subsequent mergers required the approval of the Minister of Finance.

The Finance Act

Less than a year after the revision of the *Bank Act* Canada was at war. The rules so carefully reviewed and redrawn just 12 months earlier now appeared inadequate.

The first problem was one of liquidity for the nation and the banks. At the outbreak of the conflict, European banks had experienced heavy withdrawals of deposits in the form of gold. In the unsettled environment of mid-1914, many thought the Canadian monetary system equally vulnerable. In principle, Canadian money was convertible into gold on demand, but gold held by the government and the banks was only a fraction of their combined monetary liabilities outstanding. Under normal circumstances the banks could also draw on their assets held in New York (primarily call loans in the securities markets), and transfer the proceeds in the form of gold to Canada. However, if the demand had been large and continuing, these foreign assets would also have been quickly exhausted.

Runs on some banks did develop, as depositors and note holders demanded payment in gold. To avoid the massive drain of gold, including a possible flow of capital out of the country, and to preserve the stability of the banking system, the government made two important changes in the rules governing the Canadian monetary system.

Termination of the Gold Standard. On August 3, 1914, the government, by Order-in-Council (subsequently ratified through legislation), suspended the gold standard. That is, it "temporarily" revoked the requirement that Dominion notes and bank notes be convertible into a fixed amount of gold on demand. This meant that, as far as the internal affairs of Canada were concerned, gold was legally just another commodity, although one of peculiar international significance. Gold's role as the "standard" money into which all other monies were legally convertible was assumed by Dominion notes (although bank notes themselves were made a quasi-legal tender since the banks were empowered to meet all depositors demands for payment with their own bank notes. The depositor was permitted to exchange one bank liability for another, but could demand neither gold nor Dominion notes). Aside from a brief period in the late 1920's Canada never returned to the formal gold standard. The 1914 suspension was in effect the termination of the gold standard.

A Lender of Last Resort. The second major change involved in the enactment of the *Finance Act,* provided for the first time in Canada an official "discount window" through which the banks could obtain additional cash reserves virtually on demand. Under the *Dominion Notes Act* the issuance of new Dominion notes was strictly limited. Under the *Finance Act,* these controls were virtually removed. The Minister of Finance was authorized to advance Dominion notes to the banks upon the pledge of securities approved by the Treasury Board including the banks' own promissory notes. This meant that the Minister of Finance was acting as lender of last resort where the banks could always find accommodation in times of need. As Easterbrook and Aitken comment " . . . The Act in effect gave control of the ultimate source of credit, the cash reserves of the banks, into the hand of an agency of the government and in so doing may have helped to prepare the way for a central bank".[4]

One of the common criticisms of the operation of the *Finance Act* was that the Minister of Finance never chose to use the power given him to control bank reserves. Rather, he left the initiative completely in the hands of the banking system itself.

Table 12-4
The Canadian Money Supply, 1913-1920

	1913	1920	Increase
	(Millions of Dollars)		
Subsidiary Coinage	19	30	11
Dominion Notes			
Total Outstanding	131	312	181
Held by Banks	111	279	168
Held by Others	20	32	12
Bank Notes Outstanding	109	229	120
Total Currency in Circulation	148	292	144
Bank Demand Deposit Liabilities	381	657	276
TOTAL MONEY SUPPLY	529	949	420

SOURCE: Urquhart and Buckley, *Historical Statistics of Canada.*

These provisions permitted a major wartime expansion of the mone⋅
supply, as is indicated in Table 12-4. It is striking that almost all of the
expansion of money in the hands of the public was bank money — ban⋅
deposits and bank notes. Most of the increased supply of Dominion note
remained lodged in the banks' vaults, out of public view and perhap
symbolic of the dominant role of the chartered banks in the monetar⋅
system.

As dramatic as the monetary expansion was, the lasting significance o⋅
the *Finance Act* of 1914 remained elsewhere. It set the nation's monetar⋅
system on a course which culminated in the establishment of a true centra⋅
bank.

Profile of the Financial System: 1920

As is evident in Table 12-5, one of the effects of war finance was to
temporarily increase the relative importance of the chartered banks in the
financial system (a phenomenon which was repeated during World Wa⋅
II). Indeed, this marked a watershed in the dominance of the chartered
banks over the financial system. From this date on their relative position
vis-à-vis other financial intermediaries declined. While the banks continued

Table 12-5
The Canadian Financial System, 1920

I. THE MONEY SUPPLY

	Millions of Dollars	Percen⋅
Subsidiary Coin	30	3.⋅
Dominion Notes (Outside Banks)	32	3.4
Bank Notes	229	24.⋅
Public Demand Deposits with Chartered Banks	657	69.⋅
TOTAL	949	100.⋅

II. ASSETS OF FINANCIAL INTERMEDIARIES

The Chartered Banks	3,057	75
Quebec Savings Banks	63	1
Government Savings Banks	43	1
Caisses Populaires	6	—
Mortgage Loan Companies	189*	5
Trust Companies	83†	2
Life Insurance Companies	590	14
General Insurance Companies	125	3
TOTAL	4,066	100

* 1922.   † Excluding E. T. & A. accounts of $722 million.
SOURCES: Urquhart and Buckley, *Historical Statistics of Canada; Canada Year Book*
   Statistical Yearbook of Quebec.

Figure 12-1
Chartered Banks: Major Liabilities, 1867-1940

o grow in size (and diminish in number by mergers and failures), both new and existing non-bank intermediaries enjoyed even faster rates of expansion.

Neufeld has argued that the relative decline of the banks was an inevitable result of their failure to innovate.[5] The banks did not develop new types of financial instruments which would be attractive forms in which the nation could accumulate its savings. In Canada, as elsewhere, as the wealth of the community increased, money declined in relative importance as a form in which claims to wealth were held. This affected the banks, particularly since they were the major issuers of money, and the retardation of their growth was particularly noticeable in their monetary liabilities — demand deposits and notes in circulation — as is evident in Figure 12-1. If the banks were to continue to outstrip the rising demand for money (which depended roughly on the rate of growth of aggregate output) they had to attract a substantial portion of the savings of the nation to their savings and notice deposits. In the competition for these savings the banks lost ground both to near banks, offering comparable instruments at somewhat higher yields, and to other intermediaries, particularly life insurance companies, offering very different types of instruments. They also began to face greater competition from the attractions of direct investment in stocks and bonds.

Development of the Capital Market. The war period did not produce any fundamental changes in the structure of financial intermediation, but

DEVELOPMENT OF THE CANADIAN FINANCIAL SYSTEM   267

merely postponed the gradual erosion of the position of the chartered banks. However, the war did have a major direct impact on the development of the capital market and its institutions in Canada.

Such markets predated the war, of course. Stock exchanges had been organized in Montreal and Toronto long before Confederation. Thus, the Montreal Stock Exchange traces itself back to an informal arrangement of 1832, and the Toronto Stock Exchange to 1852. Several exchanges were incorporated formally in the years following Confederation and a number of bond underwriting and distributing houses were established. However, it is unquestionably true that these were satellite organizations. As far as the financing of Canadian development was concerned, the relevant capital market was not in Canada but rather in London, England, and to a lesser extent in New York. Thus, for example, it is estimated that between 1904 and 1914 some $2,186 million worth of Canadian government and corporate bonds were issued of which almost 70% were sold in the United Kingdom and an additional 9% in the United States. Between 1900 and 1914 total foreign investments in Canada are estimated to have increased from $1,232 million to $3,837 million, with over 70% of the latter owned in the United Kingdom and 23% in the United States. Although estimates of capital formation in Canada at this time are at best rough, the increase in foreign capital invested in Canada in this period appears to have accounted for over 40% of total capital formation![6]

One of the direct effects of the war was to drastically curtail Canada's access to the London capital market at a time when financing requirements — particularly of the federal government — were increasing markedly. New York replaced London as the dominant external source of capital funds. At the same time, Canadian capital market institutions became firmly established. Thus, in the years 1915-1920, new Canadian bond issues amounted to $3,428, more than double the previous six-year period, of which 67% were sold in Canada with most of the balance sold in the United States. The Bond Dealers' Association of Canada was established in 1916 with 32 members. By 1921 it had expanded to 103 members.[7]

Although foreign capital markets continued to loom large in Canadian financial affairs, and although an important volume of activity already existed in Canadian markets, we can roughly date the emergence of a viable Canadian capital market from this period.

7/THE FINANCE ACT AND
THE CENTRAL BANK ISSUE: 1920-1935

The two decades between the wars marked the final act in the long struggle between the banks and the government to determine who would be dominant in controlling the money supply. In many ways it marked the transition of the government's role from that of an almost passive participant to a potentially strong though immature manager of the financial system. This was a period of great stress upon the financial system, containing one of the most impressive waves of expansion experienced in the 20th century as well as the worst depression. When the system was found weak

n several spots the government stepped in and finally assumed a role which
n many ways it had sought to avoid, and did so in the face of strong oppo-
ition from a large portion of the body politic.

Government Inspection of the Chartered Banks

The government first began to take over its new role as a result of
Canada's last and most spectacular bank failure. In the spring of 1923 the
Iome bank failed. This institution had gained its charter in 1905, although
rior to that time it had been a savings institution without the power of
ote issue. Just before its collapse its position had been considered quite
ound and with assets in excess of $27 million, while small by average
ndustry size, it was an important financial institution. Following a change
n management, substantial losses were uncovered along with evidence of
nisconduct on the part of several officers of the firm.

A Royal Commission was appointed to examine the reasons for the
ailure and as a result of that report, together with increased demands from
he public for greater safety, an Act was passed providing for annual gov-
rnment inspection of all banks. A special branch of the Department of
'inance was established under the directorship of an Inspector General of
Banks, empowered to carry out the inspections and to report irregularities
o the Minister.

The question of external inspection, as we have seen, dated back to the
880's. From the very beginning the banks had fought successfully to avoid
vhat they considered would be an unwarranted invasion of their privacy
nd a costly and time-consuming nuisance. Only under great pressure had
hey accepted the external audit in 1913. When that compromise had
roven deficient their ability to resist government inspection was gone and
hey begrudgingly accepted the inevitable.

The Central Bank Controversy

The other major change in the system that occurred during the inter-
var years was the establishment of a central bank in Canada.

At the turn of the century, neither Canada nor the United States had
central bank. G. E. Foster, the Canadian Minister of Finance, had urged
he creation of such an institution as early as 1890, but he was over-ruled
y his colleagues in the government. In the United States, Congress ap-
ointed a National Monetary Commission in 1908 to study the structure
nd performance of the American financial system. The Commission recom-
nended the establishment of a central bank, and, although it did not con-
orm fully to the Commission's proposal, the Federal Reserve System was
stablished in 1913.

The report of this Commission had some impact in Canada. As early
s 1913, in the hearings on the revision of the *Bank Act,* various witnesses
vere questioned on the recommendations made by the National Monetary
Commission. Most believed that such a system was either not needed or not
easible in the Canadian setting and so there was little interest on the part
f the Committee in establishing such an institution in Canada.

However, as we have seen, a major step was taken at the outset of World War I when, under the *Finance Act* of 1914, the gold standard was abandoned and rediscounting facilities established at the Ministry of Finance. For some time, the rediscounting facilities were the focus of the debate over the establishment of a central bank. In 1918, for example, the president of the Canadian Bankers Association urged the abolition of these facilities in favour of a central bank of discount. He argued that the *Finance Act*, while helpful, meant that the government in the future would play a direct and increasingly important role in the banking industry. He believed the risk of political interference should be avoided at all costs. The Association, with the approval of the Minister of Finance, went so far as to set up a committee to study the subject. But the strong opposition of some member banks, combined with the obvious lack of interest on the part of the government, caused the question to be quietly dropped. Instead the *Finance Act* of 1923 was enacted, making the rediscount facilities a permanent fixture.

With this action, the focus of the debate shifted to the second major question: the adequacy of the *Finance Act* as a substitute for a true central bank.

Deficiencies of the Finance Act

Lender of Last Resort. **One** of the traditional functions of a central bank is to act as a "banker's bank" — a lender of last resort for the financial system. In this function it can be said that the *Finance Act* did for the Canadian financial system what the Federal Reserve System did for the United States financial system, and did it more simply. In place of the network of twelve Federal Reserve Banks and their branches was the already existing administrative machinery of the Treasury Board and the Department of Finance. The fact that the system worked, and apparently without political intervention, was one of the strong arguments advanced by the bankers in opposition to a central bank. In short, they argued that with the *Finance Act,* a central bank was not necessary.

Monetary Management. **Such** a conclusion, however, implies a very narrow concept of the role of the central bank in the financial system. While we have not yet explored this aspect of central banking, the management of the money supply is an essential function of a modern central bank, and in this respect the *Finance Act* cannot be considered to have been a substitute.

The *Finance Act,* it will be recalled, was adopted simultaneously with the termination of the gold standard in 1914. The gold standard arrangement as it had existed prior to 1914 had left little scope for governmental management of the money supply. While gold directly constituted a very small fraction of circulating money, the portion of the money supply which the government directly issued (and hence, in principle could control) was directly linked to the gold holdings of the government. Thus, as Figure 12-2 illustrates, there was a close (but far from rigid) relationship between official gold reserves and Dominion notes outstanding.

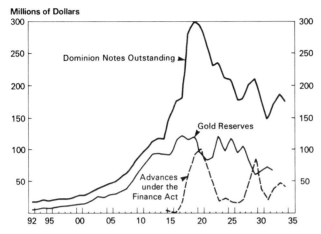

Figure 12-2

The *Finance Act* provided a method for changing the supply of Dominion notes outstanding which was unrelated to gold reserves. Indeed, as Figure 12-2 illustrates clearly, major changes in the supply of Dominion notes outstanding after 1914 were dominated by advances under the *Finance Act* rather than changes in gold reserves. Indeed, large changes in the supply of Dominion notes occurred during World War I and again in the late 1920's in spite of opposite changes in gold reserves.

However, the significant thing is that the *Finance Act* mechanism for changing the money supply was not designed (and was certainly not used) to give the government the *initiative* in controlling the money supply. The *government was a passive participant. The initiative for bringing the mechanism into play rested solely with the chartered banks.* They had to want advances under the *Finance Act* for monetary expansion to occur, and could choose to repay advances at any time, thus effecting monetary contraction. The government could alter the interest rate charged on such advances (the discount rate), but there is no evidence that they even considered using this power to systematically encourage or discourage borrowing in the interests of steady monetary expansion. Indeed, it was forcefully argued that the *Finance Act* contained no authority to use the discount rate in this way.

The Finance Act and the Gold Standard. The gold standard was re-established in Canada on July 1, 1926, when convertibility of Dominion notes into gold was resumed. Gold was money internationally. It could be used to make international payments. Thus, when, in 1928-29, a deficit emerged in the Canadian balance of international payments (in the sense that exports and net sales of securities were not sufficient to pay for imports) gold was drained out of the Canadian financial system. However, contrary to the gold standard principle, the money supply was not allowed to contract. Indeed, the very economic expansion which produced the balance of payments deficit also produced increased demands for money and credit which were accommodated by advances under the *Finance Act*. The combined expansion of the money supply and precipitous decline in gold reserves (Figure 12-2) led to a second suspension of gold convertibility and the final termination of the gold standard in Canada.

The *Finance Act* was adopted in 1914 because of an unwillingness to accept the discipline of the gold standard at a time when the gold standard dictated severe monetary contraction. The experience of 1927-1929 demonstrated that the *Finance Act* and the gold standard were incompatible. Again the gold standard was abandoned in favour of the *Finance Act* when the gold standard dictated monetary contraction. It is paradoxical that the *Finance Act* proved incapable of coping with, and indeed contributed to an even more severe monetary contraction in the following year. The great depression provided the definitive demonstration that the *Finance Act* did not provide a true central bank.

The Great Depression. The great depression was world-wide in scope. The Canadian economy, exposed as it was to developments in world markets, was severely hit. Thus, the value of exports of goods and services was cut in half between 1929 and 1932, net sales of new Canadian securities in world capital markets stopped ('indeed, retirements slightly exceeded new issues by 1932), and what had been a substantial inflow of capital for direct investment in Canada turned into a large net outflow. Inside Canada economic activity ground to a standstill. By 1933 capital expenditures by business were only 20% of what they had been in 1929, and the gross national product 58% of its 1929 market value. Of course, a substantial part of the drop in each case was accounted for by the precipitous decline in the price level. However, the *real* gross national product (adjusted for changes in prices) fell by almost 30% in four years, and by 1933 official estimates show 20% of the labour force unemployed (and these are widely regarded as conservative estimates).

Monetary contraction paralleled and reinforced the decline in output. Thus from 1929 to 1933, chartered bank deposits and currency in circulation fell by 12.5% (Figure 12-3). Even more dramatic declines occurred in total bank assets (20%) and bank loans in Canada (36%).

The Macmillan Commission and the Central Bank. As the economic situation grew worse and the banks continued their contraction, criticisms of the financial system intensified. The government finally yielded to the pressure for some type of reform by appointing a Royal Commission chaired by Lord Macmillan to study the desirability of establishing a central bank in Canada. Its major recommendation was that a central bank be established, which, to minimize possible political interference, would be privately owned, with its liabilities limited to four times its holdings of gold. It was to be given a monopoly over the issuance of currency (i.e. replacing both Dominion notes and bank notes with Bank of Canada notes). The recommendation was followed and the Bank of Canada began operations in March, 1935.

The steps toward the final achievement of government control of the stock of money had been slow and hard-won, beginning with the *Bank Note Act* of 1866, to the *Bank Act* of 1871, the *Finance Act* of 1914 and then the Royal Commission. It is not surprising therefore that when the

Figure 12-3
The Money Supply and Aggregate Output, 1900-1934
(semi-logarithmic scale)

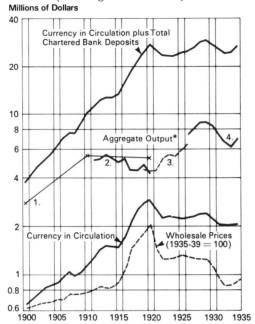

*There is no continuous series for aggregate output back to 1900. The four series used are those of (1) Firestone, (2) Deutsch, (3) Jones, (4) D.B.S. Cf. M. C. Urquhart and K. A. Buckley, *Historical Statistics of Canada* (Toronto: Macmillan, 1965), pp. 112-138. The early estimates have been deflated by the wholesale price index.

Bank began operations its first steps were hesitant and its immediate impact was largely psychological.

Assessing the Finance Act. The *Finance Act* had been widely regarded as a failure. Indeed, some would go so far as to argue that it was a disaster. It is clear that it was an important step in the direction of establishing a central bank (since it broke the shackles of the gold standard), but it is also likely that it delayed the coming of a true central bank.

It is interesting to speculate whether our monetary experience in the 1920's and 1930's would have been different had a central bank been established earlier. For this purpose it is instructive to contrast the Canadian record with that in the United States.

Critics of the Finance Act argued that the Act was inflationary because it left control of the money supply at the mercy of competitive pressures in the banking system, with no discipline either from the government or from the gold standard. However, it is apparent that in spite of a more rapid rate of increase in output, the money supply expanded less rapidly in Canada than it did in the United States during the 1920's (i.e., 1922-1929). As measured by wholesale price indexes, price levels behaved similarly in the two countries, and indeed remained on balance roughly stable, as did the foreign exchange rate which was free during part of this period. The *Finance Act* did not have inflationary consequences for Canada during most of the 1920's, but for the very end of the 1920's, the critics of the *Finance Act* have an important point. Whereas the Federal Reserve System took steps to retard monetary expansion in 1928, no significant retardation of the expansion is evident in Canada. However, in the subsequent contraction, monetary contraction in Canada was less severe than in the United States where bank deposits and currency in circulation dropped by almost 25% from 1929 to 1933.

What can we make of these observations? Not much, perhaps, given the fact that financial institutions in the United States are notably different than in Canada (see Chapter 13). Moreover, the behaviour of the Federal Reserve System would not necessarily have been duplicated by a Canadian central bank. However, there are obvious grounds for doubting that a central bank would have performed notably better than the *Finance Act* during the 1920's. Although a central bank would have established the *potential* for governmental management of the money supply, the U.S. experience suggests that that potential might not have been used effectively.

Table 12-6
The Canadian Financial System, 1934

I. THE MONEY SUPPLY

	Millions of Dollars	Percent
Subsidiary Coin	27	4
Dominion Notes (Outside Banks)	34	4
Bank Notes	123	16
Public Demand Deposits with Chartered Banks	575	76
TOTAL	759	100

II. ASSETS OF FINANCIAL INTERMEDIARIES

	Millions of Dollars	Percent
The Chartered Banks	2,919	49
Quebec Savings Banks	75	1
Government Savings Banks	45	1
Credit Unions and *Caisses Populaires*	9*	—
Mortgage Loan Companies	207	3
Trust Companies	228†	4
Life Insurance Companies	2,340	39
General Insurance Companies	171	3
Small Loan Companies	2	—
Sales Finance Companies	n.a.	—
Mutual Funds and Investment Companies	n.a.	—
TOTAL	5,996	100

* Loans   † Excludes E. T. and A. accounts of $2,436 million.
SOURCES: Urquhart and Buckley, *Historical Statistics of Canada; Canada Year Book; Statistical Yearbook of Quebec.*

Profile of the Financial System in 1934

The interwar period saw a further proliferation of type
intermediaries, including the establishment and rapid growth
finance companies, and the continued rapid growth of life ii
trust companies (particularly their non-intermediary or E. T
count business). The relative position of the chartered banl.. ....ued
to decline.

8/REFINEMENT OF CENTRAL BANKING
INSTITUTIONS: 1935-1970

The Bank of Canada

When the Bank of Canada opened its doors in March 1935 it was a
privately owned bank with approximately 12,000 individual shareholders.
Following the election of 1936, the government assumed majority ownership
of the bank (through the expedient of issuing new shares), and appointed
a majority of the Board of Directors. Complete nationalization was achieved
in 1938 when the Government purchased all privately held shares. The
Bank of Canada is now a crown corporation, with the Minister of Finance,
on behalf of the Government of Canada, the sole shareholder. All profits
from the Bank's operations accrue to the Government.

The Bank's management is nominally in the hands of a government-
appointed Board of Directors, including 12 directors "from diversified occupations" appointed for three-year terms, a Governor and a Deputy Governor, appointed for seven-year terms. The Deputy Minister of Finance
also sits on the Board as an *ex officio* member. An Executive Committee
comprised of the Governor, the Deputy Governor, one Director and the
Deputy Minister of Finance (without vote) meets weekly, with the full
Board meeting a few times a year to review developments and ratify the
decisions of the Executive Committee. Although the Minister of Finance is
kept fully informed, in practice, the continuing operations of the Bank are
in the hands of the Governor and his professional staff.

Monopoly of Currency. Under the original Bank of Canada Act,
the chartered banks were required to gradually reduce their notes outstanding over a ten-year period to approximately one-quarter of their 1934
value. In 1944, however, the banks' right to issue notes was revoked, and
by 1950 chartered bank notes were formally retired from circulation. The
Bank of Canada was given a monopoly over paper money. Thus, the banks
finally lost a right which they had fought a long hard battle to maintain.
However, as Figure 12-1 confirms, by the early 1930's the relative importance
of banks' notes in circulation as a source of funds for the banks had declined very substantially.

Fiscal Agent of the Government. The Bank of Canada also assumed
a role which had historically been the prerogative of the Bank of Montreal,

that of fiscal agent for the Government of Canada. In this capacity the bank manages the Government's cash position, operates its chequing account, makes arrangements for the issuance and retirement of government debt, and handles the Government's foreign exchange transactions. In these respects the Bank's role is that of banker, not policy maker.

Cash Reserves of the Banks. When the Bank of Canada was established, the chartered banks were compelled to sell their gold held in Canada to the Bank of Canada, and were required to hold cash reserves in the amount of 5% of their Canadian deposits in the form of either Bank of Canada notes or deposits at the Bank of Canada. A long battle against required reserves had been lost, although the reserve requirement as established was less onerous than most banks had been accustomed to maintaining. These requirements were eventually increased and made more effective.

It is also interesting to note that a vestige of the gold standard was maintained. The Bank of Canada was required to hold gold reserves in the amount of 25% of its note and deposit liabilities, but the requirement was immediately suspended and was eventually removed from the Act.

Lender of Last Resort. The Bank of Canada replaced the Department of Finance as lender of last resort for the chartered banking system. Unlike experience under the *Finance Act,* this facility was in fact little used until the late 1950's when monetary policy became effectively more restrictive the money market was more highly developed, and the nature of the discounting arrangements altered substantially. The Bank of Canada was also empowered to make advances to the Government of Canada and to the provincial governments, although the Bank has declined to become involved in provincial government finances.

Monetary Manager. The primary function of the Bank of Canada is to formulate and execute monetary policy, i.e., to manage the supply of money and credit and hence influence the level of interest rates in Canada. We will analyze this aspect of the Bank of Canada's operations in considerable detail in Chapter 17. The important point is that the combination of a fixed cash reserve requirement, which eventually became an effective constraint on the banks, and the ability of the Bank of Canada to buy and sell securities in the open market in order to regulate the quantity of reserves available *made it possible for the Bank of Canada to take the initiative in changing the Canadian money supply.* This represented the major change from the arrangements under the *Finance Act.*

The Development of the Central Banking Apparatus

We do not intend to examine the history of monetary policy under the Bank of Canada in this chapter. However, in order to bring to a close the analysis of the evolution of the financial system it is useful to point out a few milestones in the development of the central banking apparatus from 1935 on.

Institutional Gaps. With the passage of the central banking legislation, management of the money supply became a direct responsibility of a
government agency. But the simple conferring of power did not imply that
the Bank of Canada was immediately capable of taking a confident, independent stance and able to impose its will upon the system. Central banking skills had to be learned, and since, at its inception, the Bank was largely
staffed by former chartered bankers, commercial banking attitudes had to
be forgotten. The Bank of Canada's task was further complicated because
certain crucial institutions, like a short-term money market, did not really
exist in Canada. Partly as a result of this the chartered banks were reluctant
to operate with cash reserves close to the legal requirements, and developed
the habit of keeping large excess reserves. Thus, whereas the banks were required to hold reserves equal to 5% of their Canadian deposit liabilities, in
the early years of the Bank of Canada they actually held more than twice
that amount. This provided a cushion which partially insulated the banks
from the Bank of Canada's monetary policies, and complicated the problem
of monetary management.

In any case, the Bank of Canada soon became totally immersed in the
problems of war finance and postwar re-adjustment, during which time the
concept of a central bank pursuing an active, periodically restrictive and
independent monetary policy was deliberately suppressed. Indeed, almost
from its inception until the early 1950's, the Bank of Canada was pre-occupied with problems of government finance and the stability of the government bond market at low levels of bond yields. As long as it was committed
to operations to peg the price of government bonds it could not simultaneously restrict the money supply since such restriction would have
implied higher bond yields. As a result, the problem of adapting the structure of the financial system to better facilitate active, independent central
banking operations was postponed until the revision of the *Bank Act* in
1954.

Bank Act of 1954. A few changes were made in the chartered banks
lending authority in 1944 (e.g., for intermediate term credit to farmers and
fishermen) and 1954 (e.g., loans on insured mortgages and chattel mortgages), most of which were discussed in Chapter 9. However, the main
change of concern to us is the revision in the cash reserve requirement. In
place of a daily requirement of 5% of Canadian deposits the banks were
now required to maintain a monthly average reserve equal to 8% of
deposits (see Chapter 9). In addition, the Bank of Canada was given the
authority to increase this requirement by no more than 1% per month to
a maximum of 12%.

The banks responded by bringing their actual cash reserves into line
with required reserve, reducing their average cash reserve from 10.24% in
1953 to 8.29% in 1956 (again, see Chapter 9). This meant that the banks
no longer had a cushion of "excess reserves." The availability of cash was
a highly effective constraint, and given the Bank of Canada's ability to control the supply of cash, this gave it effective control over the supply of
money and credit.

The Money Market. The second major change involved the develop
ment of a broad, active short-term money market. The Bank of Canada'
actions in effecting this institutional development were discussed in Chapter
3. This was important in making it feasible for the banks to operate with
very small excess reserves, and it provided a solid market in which the
Bank of Canada could buy and sell securities to affect the availability o
cash to the banking system.

These two measures completed the development of the central banking
apparatus as we have it today. The only other important consideration
was the status of the Bank of Canada within the government heirarchy, and
particularly the status of the Governor of the Bank of Canada.

Status of the Bank of Canada. As we have noted, from 1938 the Bank
of Canada has been wholly owned by the Government of Canada, the Di
rectors and Governor of the Bank are appointed by the Government, and
the Deputy Minister of Finance is an *ex officio* member of both the Board
of Directors and the Executive Committee. However, until the revision of
the *Bank Acts* in 1967 there was no clear, legal definition of the degree of
independence possessed by the Bank of Canada in formulating monetary
policy. Can the Governor and his Board of Directors make major policy
decisions independently or are they directly responsible to the Government
of the day, such that the Bank is simply responsible for implementing the
Government's monetary policy?

The tradition of an independent central bank which can, among other
things, impose a measure of monetary discipline on the government of the
day is of long standing. It was again endorsed to a limited degree by the
1964 Report of the Royal Commission on Banking and Finance on grounds
of:

> the historical tendency of governments of all forms to develop the habit
> of inflating the currency. Since the process of inflation is understood by
> relatively few people and since it has few organized opponents in our society,
> a special responsibility is imposed on the central bank to see that the ob-
> jective of price level stability is not forgotten by government merely because
> other goals have more political popularity in the short run.[8]

Governments can be trusted with taxation, conscription, and capital pun-
ishment, but not with management of the money supply.

As we saw, the Macmillan Commission proposal dealt with this problem by creating a privately owned central bank. By definition it was "independent". While the degree of autonomy of the nationalized institution
was not defined, it was generally understood that the Governor was responsible to the Minister of Finance in the sense that the Bank could not
legitimately pursue a line of policy which was contrary to that of the government. At the same time, the first Governor of the Bank made it abundantly clear that since the *Bank of Canada Act* gave the Bank responsibility
for monetary policy he would not implement a policy with which he was
in fundamental disagreement. He reserved the ultimate right to resign in
protest.

In fact, conflict between the Bank and the government on matters of policy never became an issue until the late 1950's and early 1960's. At that time the "sound" money policies of the second Governor of the Bank, Mr. James Coyne, came into sharp conflict with the expansionary policies of the government. Moreover, the Governor effectively challenged the implicit supremacy of the government in determining the course of monetary policy, and went so far as to publicly criticize government fiscal policy. The conflict was resolved in mid-1961 when the House of Commons passed a bill declaring the office of Governor of the Bank of Canada vacant. While the Senate refused to accede to the bill, the Governor resigned immediately after the Senate vote. On taking office, the third Governor of the Bank of Canada, Mr. Louis Rasminsky, formally accepted the principle of joint responsibility, with the government having the ultimate right "to direct the Bank as to the policy which the Bank is to carry out".[9] This principle was formally incorporated in the Bank of Canada Act in the revision of 1967.

Profile of the Financial System in 1967

Table 12-7 provides a profile of the Canadian financial system in the late 1960's. As is evident, the Canadian financial system is now infinitely more complex than in 1920, let alone in 1866 or 1830.

Table 12-7
The Canadian Financial System, 1967

I. THE MONEY SUPPLY

	Millions of Dollars	Percent
Subsidiary Coin	328	2
Bank of Canada Notes	2,408	14
Public Demand Deposits at Chartered Banks	6,330	36
Other Chequable Deposits	8,314	48
TOTAL	17,380	100.0

II. ASSETS OF FINANCIAL INTERMEDIARIES

Chartered Banks	31,649	48
Life Insurance Companies	12,912	20
General Insurance Companies	2,307	4
Mortgage Loan Companies	2,751	4
Trust Companies	4,311	7
Quebec Savings Banks	506	1
Credit Unions and *Caisses Populaires*	3,367	5
Government Savings Banks	254	—
Consumer Loan and Sales Finance Companies	4,500	7
Mutual Funds and Investment Companies	2,762	4
TOTAL	65,319	100

FOOTNOTES

[1] Adam Shortt, "The Early History of Canadian Banking," in *Journal of the Canadian Bankers' Association*, Vol. V., pp. 13-14.

[2] R. M. Breckenridge, *The History of Banking in Canada*, (Washington: Government Printing Office, 1910, for the National Monetary Commission), p. 85.

[3] *Ibid.*, p. 95.

[4] W. T. Easterbrook and H. G. J. Aitken, *Canadian Economic History*, (Toronto: Macmillan, 1958) p. 468.

[5] E. Neufeld, "The Relative Growth of Commercial Banks," in *Essays in Money and Banking in Honour of R. S. Sayers*, edited by C. R. Whittlesey and J. S. G. Wilson (Oxford: Clarendon Press, 1968), pp. 130-150.

[6] J. Viner, *Canada's Balance of International Indebtedness, 1900-1913* (Cambridge, Mass.: Harvard University Press, 1924).

[7] *Submission of the Investment Dealers Association of Canada to the Royal Commission on Banking and Finance*, p. 2.

[8] Royal Commission on Banking and Finance, *Report*, p. 541.

[9] "Statement of the Governor of the Bank of Canada issued August 1, 1961," Bank of Canada, *Evidence of the Governor before the Royal Commission on Banking and Finance*, (Ottawa: 1964), pp. 131-132.

13

The Banking System of the United States:

Structure and Public Policy

Given the important role which the United States plays in Canadian economic activity, and given the large-scale, and virtually unrestricted flow of financial transactions in both directions across the international border, we cannot hope to understand Canadian banking developments, problems and policies without reference to events in the United States. Every student of the economics of the Canadian financial system should have a basic understanding of the American banking system as well. Unfortunately, the structure of the American banking system and the nature of American governmental institutions are so radically different from our own that many Canadians find them perplexing.

The purpose of this chapter is to help bridge that particular gap in understanding by providing a brief analysis of banking institutions and policies in the United States, highlighting the most striking differences from Canadian institutions and policies. The point is not to discover which system is "best", but rather to suggest evidence from a radically different experience which may assist us in evaluating the policy alternatives open to us in Canada. Some relevant material has already been discussed in earlier chapters, particularly the American payments system in Chapter 2 and some aspects of American financial history in Chapter 12.

1/COMMERCIAL BANKING

The American counterparts of Canadian chartered banks are called, simply, commercial banks. In some ways they are very different from Canadian banks, but they perform essentially the same functions in the financial system.

The Balance Sheet of Commercial Banks

One method of highlighting the similarities and differences between American and Canadian banks is by comparing their balance sheets.

Table 13-1
Comparative Balance Sheets of Commercial Banks
The United States and Canada, January 1, 1970

(Billions of Dollars)

	UNITED STATES		CANADA	
	(US $)	(%)	(C $)	(%)
ASSETS				
CASH ASSETS				
Currency and coin	7.4	1.4	0.6	1.9
Deposits with central banks	21.5	4.0	1.1	3.6
Deposits with other banks	20.8	3.9	—	—
ITEMS IN PROCESS OF COLLECTION	40.6	7.6	1.5	4.9
MONEY MARKET LOANS				
Federal funds sold	9.9	1.8	—	—
Day-to-day loans	—	—	0.2	0.6
Broker and dealer loans	5.7	1.1	0.3	1.0
SECURITIES				
Federal government bonds	55.0	10.3	5.1	16.5
Other government bonds	59.4	11.1	0.7	2.3
Other securities	12.2	2.3	0.7	2.3
MORTGAGES	70.7	13.2	1.3	4.2
LOANS				
Commerce, industry, agriculture	119.7	22.3	10.8	34.9
Personal	67.3	12.6	5.0	16.2
Financial institutions	17.6	3.3	0.5	1.6
Other	7.4	1.4	1.2	3.9
OTHER ASSETS	20.0	3.7	1.9	6.1
TOTAL ASSETS (gross)	535.6	100.0	30.9	100.0
LIABILITIES				
DEPOSITS				
Public: Demand	209.9	39.2	7.2	23.3
Personal savings	95.1	17.8	15.0	48.5
Other time	101.6	19.0	3.4	11.0
Government	5.3	1.0	1.3	4.2
Other banks	28.0	5.2	0.4	1.3
TOTAL DEPOSITS	439.9	82.1	27.3	88.1
OTHER LIABILITIES	49.3	9.2	1.5	4.9
CAPITAL ACCOUNTS	46.4	8.7	2.1	6.8
TOTAL LIABILITIES	535.6	100.0	30.9	100.0

SOURCES: Federal Deposit Insurance Corporation, *Annual Report,* 1969. Bank of Canada *Statistical Summary, Supplement,* 1969.

Relevant asset and liability data are presented in Table 13-1.[1] It is apparent from these data that the nature of financial intermediation by the two sets of banks is broadly comparable, but that there are some interesting differences. First consider the asset side of the balance sheet.

Loan and Security Holdings. In discussing the business of Canadian chartered banks in Chapter 9, we noted that according to the bankers' self-image, the main focus of their attention is loans, and particularly short-term business loans. Although personal loans have been increasing in importance, business loans remain the core of the Canadian banks' asset portfolios. Security holdings perform the secondary functions of safeguarding liquidity, transferring lending capacity over time, and permitting broader portfolio diversification.

Table 13-1 suggests similar preoccupations among American commercial bankers. Although loans account for a significantly smaller proportion of total assets than in Canada (particularly if mortgages are considered separately from the loan portfolio), they are clearly the dominant earning asset. The bulk of the loan portfolio consists of business loans, but personal loans are also of major importance (they account for a smaller portion of total assets than in Canada, but a larger proportion of total loans apart from mortgages).

The composition of the security holdings of American commercial banks is notably different from that of Canadian banks. Whereas the American banks have very large holdings of state and local government bonds, the Canadian banks' holdings are overwhelmingly federal government securities. However, we should remember that the Canadian banks' choice of securities is affected by the secondary reserve requirement. Treasury bills held to satisfy this requirement amounted to over 25% of all federal securities held at the end of 1968. There is no general requirement of this sort in the United States, but many state chartered banks are permitted to satisfy part of their legal reserve requirement with holdings of federal or state bonds. In considering the American banks' large holdings of state and local government securities it is also relevant to note that interest on these securities is tax exempt, and, in a sense which is not true in Canada, American banks are locally oriented institutions. We will return to this point later.

Table 13-1 gives a picture of American banking at one point in time. An analysis of changes in the composition of commercial banks' asset portfolios over time would reveal a pattern of interaction between loans and security holdings similar to that observed in the case of Canadian banks. Security holdings increase in importance in periods of weak demand for loans, and decline in importance in periods of strong demand for loans. Thus, as in Canada, one of the important functions of banks' portfolios of securities is to transfer lending capacity between time periods. However, for some banks, security investments are a primary use of funds. Thus, at the end of 1968, there were some 300 banks in the United States whose holdings of federal government securities exceeded half of their total assets. These were primarily small, rural banks, with few lending opportunities.

Mortgages. The relatively smaller holdings of business and personal loans on the part of American commercial banks is largely offset by much greater relative holdings of mortgages. As we saw in Chapters 9 and 12, traditional banking theory in Canada held that mortgages were not appropriate assets for commercial banks. This principle was incorporated in the *Bank Act,* and it was not until 1954 that Canadian banks were permitted to hold mortgages which had been insured by the federal government (although, as we saw earlier, the ceiling on interest rates which banks could charge on loans deterred the banks from acquiring insured mortgages after 1959), and it was not until 1967 that they were permitted to hold uninsured mortgages.

American banks have not been subject to such a blanket proscription of mortgage loans. Historically it is true that the proposition that mortgages were not appropriate assets for commercial banks had considerable support in the United States. Indeed, in the *National Bank Act* of 1864, national banks were prohibited from holding mortgages. However, this provision did not affect the asset holdings of state chartered banks, a fact which helped these institutions to survive and prosper in the face of competition from the national banks which were supposed to replace them, and in spite of punitive measures taken against them by the federal government. Morever, when the Federal Reserve System was established in 1913, the prohibition on national bank mortgage investments was relaxed, and permissible mortgage holdings were tied to the stockholders equity or the savings and time deposits of the bank.[2] It is widely argued that the importance of loans directly or indirectly linked to real estate among the assets of commercial banks, and particularly of small, rural, state-chartered banks, was one of the factors contributing to the high rate of bank failures in the United States, and general instability of the system in the 1920's and 1930's.

Interbank Deposits and Loans. One of the singular characteristics of the American banking system, discussed in Chapter 2, is the existence of correspondent relationships among banks. This is reflected in the consolidated balance sheet in the importance of *Deposits With Other Banks* (a small part of *Loans to Financial Institutions* is also loans to correspondent banks). In Canada, inter-bank deposits are very small, and are mainly related to international correspondent relations. In the United States they are large and vital to the operation of the domestic banking system.

In some states, banks are permitted to count deposits with other banks as part of their cash reserves. However, most interbank deposits reflect services rendered by big city banks to their country correspondents. Thus, 70% of all interbank deposits are with the 100 largest banks, and 40% are with banks in New York and Chicago.

Cash Reserves. Like Canadian banks, American banks must satisfy minimum legal cash reserve requirements. However, in contrast to the relatively simple set of reserve requirements in Canada, the American system of reserve requirements is very complex, reflecting both the fragmentation of the banking system and the structure of regulatory authority (both of which are discussed later). A bank's cash reserve requirement depends on the *regulatory status* of the bank, its *location*, its *size*, and the *composition of its deposits*.

Banks which are members of the Federal Reserve System (member banks) must satisfy the requirements set down by the Board of Governors of the Federal Reserve System. As can be seen in Table 13-2, these requirements are higher for the 178 banks in major cities which are classified as "Reserve City Banks", than for the remaining 5,700 member banks which are classified as "Country Banks". At both classes of banks, they are higher for demand deposits than for time and savings deposits, and are higher for deposits in excess of $5 million than for deposits of less than $5 million.

Table 13-2
Member Bank Minimum Cash Reserve Requirements, January 1, 1970

	Reserve City Banks	Country Banks
NET DEMAND DEPOSITS*		
Under $5 million	17	12½
Over $5 million	17½	13
SAVINGS DEPOSITS	3	3
TIME DEPOSITS		
Under $5 million	3	3 .
Over $5 million	6	6

* Gross demand deposits less cash items in process of collection and less demand balances due from domestic banks.
SOURCE: Federal Reserve *Bulletin*, June 1970.

State chartered banks which have not joined the Federal Reserve System (non-member banks) must satisfy the reserve requirements established by the state authorities. These differ markedly from state to state, but are generally less onerous than the federal requirements. As Table 13-3 shows, while on average the actual cash reserves of non-member banks are not significantly different from those of member banks (when expressed as a percentage of total deposits), they are held in very different forms. The federal reserve requirement can only be satisfied by deposits with a Federal Reserve Bank or currency held in the bank's vault. State requirements can generally be satisfied by cash in the vault, deposits with other commercial banks (non-members do not have the option of maintaining reserve deposits with the Federal Reserve System), or in some cases state or federal securities. The monetary liabilities of the federal government — what we will later call "high-powered money" — are a small part of the total cash reserves of non-member banks. Correspondent balances are much more important.

The Banks and the Money Market. In our discussion of the Canadian banking system we emphasized the importance of the money market as the

Table 13-3
Cash Reserves of Member Banks and Non-member Banks
December 31, 1968

	Member Banks	Non-Member Banks	All Banks
	(Billions of Dollars)		
Deposits with Federal Reserve Banks	21.2	—	21.2
Vault Cash	5.6	1.6	7.2
TOTAL FEDERAL MONETARY LIABILITIES	26.9	1.6	28.4
Balances with Domestic Banks	11.3	7.6	18.9
TOTAL CASH	38.1	9.2	47.3
TOTAL DEPOSITS	355.4	78.9	434.3
	(Percent of Total Deposits)		
Deposits with Federal Reserve Banks	6.0	—	4.9
Vault Cash	1.6	2.0	1.7
TOTAL FEDERAL MONETARY LIABILITIES	7.6	2.0	6.6
Balances with Domestic Banks	3.2	9.7	4.4
TOTAL CASH	10.8	11.6	10.9

SOURCE: Federal Reserve *Bulletin*, July 1969.

place where banks make day-by-day adjustments in their cash reserve positions (see Chapters 9 and 3). These adjustments can be made by buying or selling short-term securities in the market, or by varying the amount of credit extended to dealers in government securities, particularly credit in the form of day-to-day loans.

The money market performs the same function in the American banking system, but on a much larger scale and with somewhat different institutional arrangements. As in Canada, the basic money market instruments are short-term government securities, particularly treasury bills, and selected short-term commercial and finance paper. The banks can make adjustments to their cash positions daily, by purchasing or selling short-term financial instruments, either out-right or on purchase-and-resale agreements, by varying the credit which they extend to security houses, or by borrowing from the central bank.

However, the American money market has an important adjunct not found in Canada, a market in bank reserves *per se*, called the *federal funds market*. Federal funds are deposits with Federal Reserve Banks. They are funds which member banks can use to satisfy their legal reserve requirements. Through the agency of a federal funds broker, banks with temporarily excess reserves can lend them to banks with deficient reserves, normally for an overnight period. The interest rate on such loans is set competitively, and is highly sensitive to shifts in demand and supply pressures.

Transactions in the federal funds market are for relatively large sums of money, such that only the larger banks can effectively participate in the market. As a result, while the American banking system as a whole normally has a significant volume of "excess reserves", i.e., cash reserves over and above those required to satisfy the minimum legal requirement, these excess reserves tend to be held mainly by smaller, country banks. The federal funds market provides an efficient mechanism by which the large city banks can keep their actual cash holdings very close to the legal requirement.

The amount of federal funds indebtedness outstanding varies widely from time to time. The amount outstanding at the end of 1969 is shown on Table 13-1 as an asset item "'Federal Funds Sold". Since these are inter-bank transactions there is a corresponding liability, included in this table in the account "other liabilities".

In recent years the banks have developed two other techniques for adjusting their cash positions, particularly when they are short of reserves. The first involves variations in their own negotiable certificates of deposit outstanding. Certificates of deposit are short-term money market instruments, issued in denominations of $100,000 or more. Unlike regular time deposits, they can be traded in a secondary market. They have become a major liability of American banks. Thus, at the end of 1968 negotiable certificates of deposit amounted to over 20% of the time and savings deposit liabilities of large commercial banks. The fact that they are traded in a competitive market makes it possible for a bank to take the initiative in changing the volume of its certificates outstanding, at least within limits, and hence to use these certificates to adjust its cash reserve position. By issuing certificates at competitive rates a bank can attract reserves from other banks, and by retiring maturing issues can reduce excess reserves.

The second new technique of cash adjustment involves borrowings in the Euro-dollar market.[3] You will remember that the Euro-dollar market is an international market in United States dollars (Chapter 8). By borrowing in that market, typically through the agency of its own foreign branches, a large American bank can bolster its own cash reserve position. In mid-1969 Euro-dollar borrowings reached such proportions that the Federal Reserve System imposed a special 10% reserve requirement against this type of indebtedness.[4]

Deposit Liabilities. There are also interesting differences in the composition of the deposit liabilities of Canadian and American banks, and particularly in the relationship between demand, personal savings and time deposits as sources of funds. Canadian banks appear much more like personal savings banks than do banks in the United States, which are relatively more dependent on demand deposits and time deposits as sources of funds.

In this connection, it should be noted that a much sharper distinction is drawn between savings and demand deposits in the United States. We have seen that in Canada, some savings deposits are chequable (almost 38% at the beginning of 1970). In the United States, personal savings accounts are not chequable, and can only be withdrawn on presentation of the passbook.

The Industrial Structure

The most striking contrasts between the banking systems of Canada and the United States relate not to the nature of their assets and liabilities, but to the number and size of commercial banks: to the structure of the commercial banking industry. We should perhaps expect that a nation which has ten times our population and almost thirteen times our gross national product will also have many more banks. However, the actual difference in the number of firms in the commercial banking business is far greater than can be explained by these scale factors alone. Whereas Canada had nine commercial banks at the end of 1969, the United States had almost 13,700.

Banking Firms versus Banking Offices. While the United States has many more *banking firms* than we might expect on the basis of the relative sizes of the two economies, it has relatively fewer banking *offices*. In the United States there are some 33,800 commercial bank offices, approximately one for every 6,000 people. In Canada there are 5,900 offices, one for every 3,600 people. A few banks in the United States have very extensive networks of branch offices. For example, in the State of California, the Bank of America alone operates 980 offices, more than all but the largest three Canadian banks (see Chapter 14), and four other banks each operate more than 200 branch offices. However, over 70% of American commercial banks are *unit banks*, operating only one office, and of the 19,000 branch offices throughout the country, 70% are in the *same county* as the head office of the bank, and 85% in that county or *contiguous counties*. State-wide networks of branches are relatively rare, and nation-wide networks unknown. On the average, the 3,700 branch banking firms operate only six offices. Among Canadian banks, by contrast, the average number of offices is 590, and the five largest banks each have more than 700 offices spread across Canada.

Size Distribution of Banks. One direct consequence of the prevalence of unit banking in the United States is a proliferation of commercial banks with very small financial resources, as is evident in Table 13-4. Thus, at the end of 1968 over 85% of all American commercial banks had total deposits of less than $25 million — less than those of Canada's newest and smallest bank, which had then been in business less than six months. These very small banks typically have only one office, and solicit deposits and make loans in a very limited local market, usually a small town and its immediate hinterland. A high proportion of their loans are for agricultural purposes, and they are little involved in commercial and industrial finance. They do not participate actively in the national money market, have almost no dealing in foreign exchange, and rely heavily on their big city correspondents (Chapter 2), for assistance and advice, and for the provision of specialized banking services for their customers.

Not all American banks are small local institutions. There are many medium-sized institutions which carry on a normal range of commercial

Table 13-4

Number of Commercial Banks and Total Deposits, by Size of Bank
The United States, December 31, 1968

Size of Bank: Deposits	Number of Banks*		Total Deposits	
	Number	Cumulative Percentage	Amount	Cumulative Percentage
(Millions of Dollars)			(Billions of Dollars)	
less than 1	371	2.7	0.2	—
1–2	1,257	11.9	1.9	0.5
2–5	3,669	38.6	12.5	3.3
5–10	3,430	63.7	24.7	9.0
10–25	2,967	85.4	45.7	19.5
25–50	1,030	93.0	35.3	28.3
50–100	476	96.5	32.8	35.0
100–500	390	99.2	82.5	53.8
500 or more	108	100.0	201.8	100.0
	13,698		437.5	

* Includes 50 non-deposit trust companies.
SOURCE: Federal Deposit Insurance Corporation, *Annual Report*, 1968.

banking activities in cities throughout the nation. In addition, the large metropolitan areas contain some of the world's major banks, including the largest bank in the world, the California-based Bank of America. The four next largest are all American banks.

This means that there is an extreme range between large and small banks in the United States. While there are over 300 banks with total assets of less than $1 million, there are three banks with total assets in excess of *$20 billion*, and 13 banks with assets of *$5 billion or more*. In contrast to the tiny local banks, the giant institutions carry on banking activities which are national and international in scope. Most of them have representatives (but not branches) in major cities throughout the country in order to service their large industrial customers, and like the major Canadian banks, they generally have branches or agencies in the world's financial centers. Some of the major American banks also operate networks of branch offices carrying out a normal commercial banking business in other countries, particularly in South and Central America.

In terms of the magnitude of the financial resources at their disposal, the very large banks dominate the American banking system. As we saw in Table 13-4, the 108 banks with total deposits of $500 million or more (less than 0.8% of all banks) held almost half of all deposits with commercial banks in 1968. One study revealed that in 1964 the largest bank alone held over 4% of deposits, and the ten largest over 20%.[5]

Group and Chain Banking. The figure of 13,700 incorporated banks somewhat exaggerates the number of *independent* banking firms in the United States. Many banks belong to either banking groups or banking chains.

A banking group exists when two or more banks are controlled by a holding company.[6] At the beginning of 1970 there were 197 independent holding company groups owning 723 banks in 32 states and the District of Columbia. Most of these groups are relatively small, including a few small unit banks in a single state. However, in 1968 there were six with aggregate deposits in excess of $3 billion, and the largest had deposits of $8.3 billion, making it, in effect, one of the six or seven largest banks in the nation.[7]

Group banks account for only 10% of the offices and 14% of the deposits in commercial banks in the United States. On a nation-wide scale they do not have a significant effect on the banking structure. However in some states their impact is substantial. For example, the State of Minnesota has strict limitations on branch banking, and as a result there are 723 unit banks in the state. However, 117 of these, holding 60% of all deposits in the state, belong to five holding company groups. Similarly in Nevada, a state permitting state-wide branch banking, one group, controlling two of the states' nine commercial banks, holds 60% of all deposit in the state. Other states present much less extreme pictures.

Although inter-state branch banking is prohibited in the United States, four holding company groups operate banks in more than one state. For example, the largest holding company, based in California, owns 23 bank with 587 offices in 11 western states.[8]

Chain banking differs from group banking only in that no holding company is involved. Rather, control of two or more banks is in the hand of an individual or a partnership. Unlike banking groups, chains do not have to register with the federal banking authorities, and hence there are no data on them. One study, which covered only banks which were member of the Federal Reserve System, identified 431 chains involving 1,169 bank in 1962.[9] Most chains involved only two banks, but some involved more and one involved 21 banks. Chain banks are mainly located in small town in states which prohibit branch banking.

Even taking chain and group banking organizations into account, there are 11,000-12,000 *independent* banking firms in the United States. Does this mean that the American banking industry approximates the economists idealized concept of a "purely competitive" industry?

Banking Markets and Banking Competition. It would be a mistake to think that all 12,000 independent banking firms compete in the same market. Banks are multi-product firms. They provide a variety of service for, accept deposits from, and extend credit to, customers who differ greatly in their access to alternative sources, partly because of the cost and inconvenience involved in dealing with relatively remote banks (another case of the importance of transactions costs), and partly because of the importance of information on credit worthiness in the functioning of loan markets.[10] Thus, it is generally argued that the market for services provided to households (chequing accounts, personal savings accounts, safety deposit boxes, mortgage credit, consumer credit, etc.) is largely local in scope. In the case of business firms: small, local firms in the distributive trades are primarily dependent on local banks; larger firms with more established regional reputations may have ready access, with little or no additional costs or inconvenience, to banks over a much wider area; and very large firms, with established nation-wide reputations, have access to the large banks in all parts of the country. Many of the very large firms have regular dealings with several banks, sometimes because of a provision in American banking laws which limits the amount of credit which can be extended to any single borrower to 10% of the bank's capital.

It is important to keep this hierarchy of markets in mind in interpreting the structure of the American banking system. While the national banking market may be highly competitive in many respects, local banking markets are much more concentrated and apparently less competitive, particularly outside the larger urban areas, and in spite of the fragmentation of the banking system into small unit banks. Thus, a study for 1959 revealed that 55% of all unit banks were in towns with only one banking office, and 92% were in communities with no more than two banking offices.[11] Including both branch banking and unit banking states, there were over 10,000 communities in the United States which had only one banking office, and 15,400 which had no more than two offices. They were almost exclusively communities with less than 25,000 inhabitants, but among them they accounted for two-thirds of the banking offices in the United States. For these communities, the fragmentation of the banking system does not mean the absence of monopoly in local banking markets.[12]

The same study also revealed a high degree of concentration of bank deposits in larger urban areas. Indeed, in all but the largest metropolitan areas in unit banking states, the degree of concentration in deposit holdings is approximately the same as it is in Canada on a nation-wide basis (see Chapter 14).

It has been argued that modern developments in transportation and communication reduces the significance of local banking monopolies defined in this geographic sense. Customers can now deal with banks in a broader area with little additional cost or inconvenience. However, several studies have produced evidence showing that concentration in this sense has a decided impact on interest rates charged and paid by banks. In general, interest rates on loans and service charges on accounts tend to be higher, and interest rates paid on deposits to be lower, the higher the degree of concentration in the banking market.[13] The most competitive rates are those set in the national market for big business accounts.

Evolution of the Banking Structure

We have described the structure of the banking system of the United States as it was on December 31, 1968. The structure is not static, but is undergoing rather fundamental changes. It is perhaps useful, therefore, to briefly consider the structure of the system in historical perspective.

Figures 13-1 and 13-2 trace the numbers of banks and banking offices in the United States at five-year intervals since 1900. These charts show a history of amazing gyrations.

Figure 13-1
Number of Commercial Banks in the United States, 1900-1968

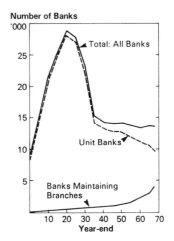

SOURCES: U.S. Bureau of Census, *Historical Statistics of the United States, Colonial Time to 1957* (Washington: 1960), *Federal Reserve Bulletin.*

Figure 13-2
Number of Banking Offices in the United States, 1900-1968

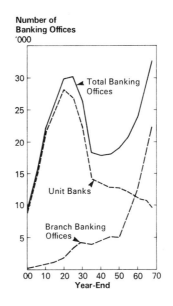

SOURCES: U.S. Bureau of Census, *Historical Statistics of the United States, Colonial Times to 1957* (Washington: 1960); *Federal Reserve Bulletin.*

1900-1929: Expansion and Retrenchment. During the first two decades of this century, there was a strong, virtually uncontrolled upsurge in the number of banks, almost all of which were unit banks, and many of which were heavily involved in agricultural development. From 8,700 in 1900, the number of banks increased more than three-fold to 29,000 in 1921.

The decade of the 1920's, by contrast, was a period of retrenchment in numbers of banks and offices. The forces of expansion (opening of new banks and branches) were gradually overwhelmed by the forces of contraction (mergers, voluntary liquidations and failures). Many of the new banks proved to be unsound, and a relatively large number of bank failures had become almost commonplace in the American banking system. Thus, an average of 85 banks closed each year from 1900 through 1919 because of financial difficulties. This figure rose ominously to 505 in the troubled year of 1921, and in spite of general prosperity continued to rise to 775 in 1924 and to a temporary peak of 976 in 1926. In effect, the banking system was painfully purging itself of the chartering excesses of the pre-World War I era. To Canadian observers, accustomed to only occasional failures, the apparent instability of the American system was astounding (and, many said, instructive).

The Banking Crisis of 1933. The onset of the depression of the 1930's was accompanied by a violent contraction of the banking system. Between 1928 and the end of 1933, the number of commercial banks dropped from 25,000 to under 14,000. Over 4,000 banks failed in 1933 alone, and some 9,100 failed in the four years 1929-1933. Total collapse of the system was only narrowly averted through emergency measures, including a bank "holiday" in 1933, following which only demonstrably sound banks were allowed to open for business. This cathartic experience engendered a continuing fear that a banking system based on virtually free entry, open competition and limited controls over asset holdings was inherently unstable. As we shall see, this argument still has a profound effect on the content of public policy with respect to the structure of the banking system.

In response to the banking crisis of 1933 the Federal Government extended its authority over the banking system. Bank failures dropped immediately to their pre-1920 level, and from 1942 on became comparatively rare. There followed a prolonged period of stability. Indeed, by 1950 there were roughly the same number of commercial banks and only 11% more banking offices than there had been in 1933.

Expansion through Branch Banking. The 1950's saw a new type of upsurge in the banking system. The number of *banks* continued to decline, but the number of *banking offices* increased rapidly. While unit banks remain more numerous than banks operating branches, there are now many more branch bank offices than there are unit banks — and the trend is continuing.

As can be seen in Figure 13-3, aside from a temporary aberration in the years 1963-65, there has been a steady decline in the population of commercial banks since 1950, at an average rate of about 50 banks per year. This has been the net result of the chartering of about 100 banks and the disappearance through mergers of about 150 banks annually. Bank failures have played a negligible role.

This pattern of development has been a direct product of governmental regulation of the banking industry. Indeed, it seems clear that the structure of the American banking system has been kept in a chronic condition o disequilibrium by state and federal banking authorities. Two types o powerful market forces have been partially restrained by these authorities

Both the overall growth of the economy and of population and change in the geographic structure of the population (both inter-state movement and movements to the suburbs) resulted in rapid growth of the deman for new banking facilities. As we have seen, the primary accommodation to these demands has been a rapid expansion of branch banking office (although such an adjustment is not possible in states which prohibit o severely restrict branch banking). It can be argued, however, that th growth of banking facilities has not been rapid enough to remove th tension between demand and supply in the market.

It is interesting, in this regard, to consider the bulge in new bank opening in the years 1963-65, which we noted earlier (Figure 13-3). Th new banks chartered in this period were predominantly national banks in contrast to preceding experience.[14] This can be directly attributed t the appointment of a new Comptroller of the Currency, James Saxon, th federal officer responsible for the chartering and supervision of nationa

Figure 13-3
Components of the Changing Structure of the Banking System of the U.S.
New Banks, Bank Mergers and Banks Closed, 1950-1968

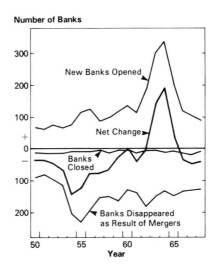

SOURCES: U.S. Bureau of Census, *Historical Statistics of the United States, Colonial Time to 1957* (Washington: 1960) ; *Federal Reserve Bulletin.*

anks. Among other things, Mr. Saxon drastically altered existing policies governing the granting of national bank charters in the interests of stimulating competition, thus contradicting a basic tenet of post-depression banking policy.[15] The new policy was short-lived. At the end of Mr. Saxon's short term of office, the old pattern of change in the population of commercial banks re-asserted itself. However, the bulge in new bank charters in 1963-1965 seemed to indicate that there was a substantial number of potential bankers, who thought they saw profitable opportunities for new banks (which may in part have been a product of restrictions on the expansion of branch banking), but who were kept out of the market by federal regulations. One statistical study estimated that the cumulative effect of restrictions on entry between 1936 and 1962 was to reduce the total number of banks in the industry by 1,500.[16]

The second important force was internal to the banks. Economies of scale in banking created strong pressures to increase the size of banking firms. In some instances, this was accomplished through branch banking, and in some cases through bank mergers. However, both state laws limiting branch banking and federal policies with respect to bank mergers have restricted the pace of these adjustments.

In short, it might be argued that while it started with a very different structure, the American banking system has been making small, tentative steps in the direction of a structure like that of the Canadian banking system. That is, the branch banking form of organization has been growing at the expense of unit banking. However, the extent of this movement has been restricted by both federal and state policies, and the present structure of the system still stands in stark contrast to the structure of the Canadian system. In the meantime, the United States has attempted to achieve through governmental regulation the type of stability in their banking system which Canada obtained from nation-wide branch banking and virtual cartelization of the industry (this issue is discussed further in Chapter 14).

As we saw in Chapter 12, and again in this chapter, the nature of public policy has a profound effect on the development of the banking system. We will return to this theme in Chapter 14. However, since we are presently comparing American and Canadian institutions, it is perhaps appropriate to devote a few pages to an examination of the rationale for American banking policies.

2/GOVERNMENT REGULATION OF BANKING: THE BASIC PRINCIPLES OF PUBLIC POLICY

To a Canadian observer, the arrangements for the chartering, regulation and supervision of banks in the United States are of bewildering complexity. This is not a product of a conscious design. Rather, it reflects a long and contentious history of interaction between state and federal governments, and among agencies within the federal government. The unique product has been labelled the "dual banking system".

The Dual Banking System

The Constitutional Issue. The issues between the federal and state authorities have their roots in the interpretation of the Constitution of the United States. Like Canada, the United States has a federal form of government, with governmental responsibilities constitutionally divided between the federal and the state authorities. The constitution explicitly assigns to the federal government the power to "coin money and regulate its value", but, in contrast to the British North America Act, it makes no mention of the regulation of banking. Since powers not specifically granted to the federal government were reserved to the states, the states claimed the right to incorporate and regulate banks.

First and Second Bank of the United States. The right of the individual states to charter and regulate banks thus has a firm constitutional basis. However, the federal government also claimed this right. In 1971 the federal government chartered the First Bank of the United States, and following its demise, chartered the Second Bank of the United States in 1816. These banks carried on a commercial banking business through branches in various parts of the country (providing the model for the Canadian banking system — Chapter 12), but they were also incipient central banks, striving to bring order and stability to a banking system populated by state-chartered institutions, many of which were small, unreliable, "wildcat" banks. In the face of strong political pressures, the charters of the federal banks were revoked, although their constitutionality was affirmed by the Supreme Court. This not only delayed the establishment of a true central bank, but also meant that the principle of nation-wide branch banking under the supervision of the federal government was never established in the United States.

The National Bank Act. The *National Bank Act* of 1863 created a permanent federal presence in the field of commercial banking. This act provided for the chartering of a new class of commercial banks, to be called national banks. In general, the federal requirements for a bank charter were more restrictive than state requirements. Cash reserves and minimum capital requirements were higher, there were stricter controls over loans and investments (e.g., mortgage loans were prohibited initially) and there were superior provisions for the security of banknote holders. Significantly, however, the legislation left the status of branch banking ambiguous, neither granting nor explicitly denying the right to operate branches. However, the lack of explicit authority to open branches was interpreted as denying permission. It was not until 1927 that national banks were permitted to open branches, and then only in the city in which their head office was located. In 1933 this restriction was removed. National banks were permitted to open branches providing they abided by whatever restrictions the state in question had imposed on branch banking by its state banks. In this way the principle of state precedence in the matter of branch banking was accepted, and *nation-wide* branch banking by national banks effectively prohibited (except through inter-state group banks).

It was hoped that the stricter controls over national banks would give them an appearance of greater security and stability which would provide a competitive advantage over state banks, such that state-chartered institutions would be driven from the industry. However, the demise of state banks did not materialize, in spite of a discriminatory tax imposed on bank notes issued by state banks. As a result, the United States ended up with a "dual banking system" — a system under which there are two parallel sets of laws, regulations and regulatory authorities governing banks and banking. Indeed, since each state has its own laws and regulations, there are in effect 51 banking systems.

It could be argued that the existence of 51 chartering authorities does not necessarily imply the high degree of fragmentation of the banking system which we observe in the United States. Indeed, if all 51 governments had similar banking statutes, put no limits on branch banking, and allowed full rights to banks chartered in other states on a reciprocal basis, the structure of the American system might be only marginally different from our own. However, the fact is that the states did not develop a uniform approach to banking regulation and do not grant reciprocal rights to banks chartered in other states.

Principles of Public Policy

It is difficult to account for the extreme diversity of banking policies among states and between the state and federal governments without a searching examination of American banking and political history. However, there are at least four themes which stand out in the historical record: "populism", the search for stability through a central bank, the avoidance of "overbanking", and the preservation of competition. Their interaction has produced an amazing tangle of regulatory authorities with differing, and often conflicting, objectives.

"Populism" and the Banking Structure

Fragmentation of the banking system occurred as a matter of deliberate design in many states, particularly in the mid-west and south. During the formative period in banking legislation, what we earlier called "populism" was the dominant political force in these areas (as, in some respects, it still is). Basic to this doctrine was the belief that local affairs (very broadly defined) should be locally controlled. This manifests itself partly in pressure for the decentralization of political authority (local authority versus the state, states rights versus the federal government), and partly in a fear of centralization of economic power through ubiquitous industrial and financial "trusts".

Unit Banking. Banking was obviously of critical importance from the populist point of view, and decentralization of banking could be best achieved through unit banking. Branch banking was prohibited or severely restricted in most states in this area, and the "populist" forces fought bitterly against the First and Second Banks of the United States, and against

all subsequent moves to create uniformity and to expand federal authority
Even the central bank, when it was eventually established in 1913, was de
centralized. It was a system of 12 regional central banks, owned by the
commercial banks themselves, and with only limited centralized co-ordina
tion.

Although state banking laws have been changing, and many exception
to once rigid legal restrictions have been allowed, there are still 15 state
in the south and midwest which are generally considered "unit banking"
states. In another 19 states, predominantly in the same area but including
some of the major eastern states (i.e., Massachusetts, New Jersey and New
York), branch banking is severely restricted, in some cases to the count
in which the head office is located and in other cases to that and contiguou
counties. Only 19 states, and the District of Columbia, permit unlimited
state-wide branch banking. These states are predominantly in the east and
the far west. Inter-state branch banking is prohibited, except, as we hav
seen, through the device of group banks. As we noted earlier, nationa
banks are required to abide by the relevant state banking regulations with
respect to branch banking.

Free Banking. In addition to restrictions on branch banking, populis
banking policy involved "free banking" (Chapter 12). Pioneered in New
York in 1838, the free banking principle for the granting of bank charter
soon spread to all states, and was incorporated into the *National Ban
Act* of 1863. This principle required the banking authority to grant
charter to any individual or group which satisfied certain minimur
requirements set down in the statute. It allowed no administrative discre
tion. The purpose was to prevent the granting of monopolistic privilege
by opening the industry to all who thought they could make a profit. The
effect was a rapid proliferation of small banks.

The Search For Stability: The Central Bank

If populist banking policies meant free entry to the banking industry
and banks which were small, locally owned, and sensitive to local cred
requirements, it all too often also meant banks which had weak manage
ment and insufficiently diversified portfolios, and which were peculiarl
vulnerable to bankruptcy. As we have already seen, the American bank
ing system had a history of devastating instability. The search for method
to eliminate this instability provided a second theme in American publ
policy, and, since it was inevitably centralizing in its effects, this searc
came into sharp conflict with the populist principle.

There were several early attempts to bring discipline and stability
the banking system, some by state governments and some by the federa
government. We have already seen that the First and Second Banks
the United States and the *National Bank Act* were both unsuccessful a
tempts on a national level. The same might be said of the eventual establis
ment of a central bank in 1913.

The Federal Reserve System: A Compromise With Populism. I
principle, a central bank should be able to underwrite the stability of the

banking system. While it may not be able to prevent the failure of selected individual banks which have been the victims of fraud, bad management, or an unfortunate combination of circumstances, by standing as a lender of last resort it should be able to prevent the failure of some banks from bringing down other banks in their train. However, the Federal Reserve System proved incapable of saving the system in the 1929-1933 debacle. Part of the problem was the nature of the central bank. While the National Monetary Commission had recommended the establishment of a strong central bank with broad powers, what was enacted was a compromise with populism.

The pre-eminence of states' rights meant that membership in the Federal Reserve System could only be made compulsory for national banks. Membership was voluntary for state banks. On the eve of the crisis in 1929, two-thirds of the commercial banks in the United States (holding however, only one-third of bank assets) were not members of the Federal Reserve System. Even in 1968 over 56% of all commercial banks were non-members, although they held only 17% of all assets. This voluntarism was a serious limitation to the extension of federal control over the banking system. It meant not only that most banks did not have access to the central bank as a lender of last resort, but also that the Federal Reserve System could not impose strict standards on its members without inducing many of them to forsake membership (including, perhaps a national bank charter) for non-membership.

In its internal organization, the Federal Reserve System was decentralized. It was not to be a monolithic national central bank, but a federation of 12 regional reserve banks. Moreover, the individual Federal Reserve Banks were not to be owned by the federal government, but by the member banks, with elaborate controls to ensure that the boards of directors could not be dominated by the larger banks in the district. The national body that was also created, the Federal Reserve Board, with members appointed by the President of the United States, had very little power.

The Federal Reserve Banks were to hold the cash reserves of member banks, and, within limits, they could issue notes to be used as currency. However, their main activity was to make advances to member banks, as necessary. A crucial restriction was that all such advances had to take the form of "rediscounts" of "eligible paper" — short-term promissory notes which the member banks had taken in security for normal commercial loans to farmers, merchants or industrial firms. That is, the Federal Reserve Banks were not given full discretion in managing the supply of money and credit, but had their actions tied to the real bills principle (see Chapter 9 and Chapter 17). The extension of credit by the Federal Reserve Banks was to be dictated by the "need of trade", as interpreted by member banks. The Federal Reserve System was not designed as a vehicle for a vigorous, centralized national monetary policy.

Reform of 1933-34: Moves to Centralization. The crisis of 1933 produced a fundamental change in the Federal Reserve System. The appearance of decentralized service organization for member banks was maintained, but the substance of it was revoked. Two interrelated centralizing institutions were created. First, the weak Federal Reserve Board was transformed into a strong Board of Governors of the Federal Reserve System, with statutory independence from political pressures (each governor is appointed by the President of the United States for a 14-year term, with only one governor retiring every other year). Second, an *ad hoc* coordinating committee for transactions in government securities which had emerged in the 1920's was given legislative status as the Open Market Committee. It is a 12-man body, including the seven Governors and five representatives of the 12 Federal Reserve Banks. The Open Market Committee has sole authority over Federal Reserve transactions in U.S. government securities.

On the operational side, the link to the real bills doctrine was discarded, and along with it the notion that the Federal Reserve System should play a passive role in the financial system. In spite of the relaxation of the rules governing advances, quantitatively, discounts and advances declined to insignificance. Transactions in government securities became the primary vehicle for the extension of credit to the banking system. This placed the initiative for credit policy in the hands of the centralized Open Market Committee, not the individual Federal Reserve Banks or the discounting member banks. Moreover, the Board of Governors was given the power to vary the cash reserve requirements of member banks, a powerful, if blunt, instrument of monetary control. (These matters are discussed further in Chapter 18.)

The transformation of the Federal Reserve System into a centralized agency for monetary policy was not the only significant change in government policy toward the banking structure in the period 1933-35. Perhaps equally important was the creation of the Federal Deposit Insurance Corporation.

The Avoidance of "Overbanking": Restrictions on Entry and on Competition

While not the primary purpose of the plan, as it turned out, the establishment of the Federal Deposit Insurance Corporation made it possible for the Federal Government to exert considerable control over the subsequent evolution of the structure of the banking system.

The Federal Deposit Insurance Corporation. The F.D.I.C. provide insurance to bank depositors, guaranteeing the safety of their deposits in insured banks.[17] Membership in this plan was made compulsory for all members of the Federal Reserve System, but was also made available to non-member banks who could qualify under the F.D.I.C.'s strict standard. The plan proved to be immensely popular. By the end of the first year of operation, 85% of all non-member banks had been admitted to the insurance plan, and as of December 31, 1968, 98% of all commercial bank (accounting for over 99% of commercial bank assets) were insured by the F.D.I.C.

New Banking Policies. With federal deposit insurance virtually *sine qua non* of banking, the federal government was placed in a strong position to impose new policies on the whole banking system. A new pattern of banking policies emerged, emphasizing the soundness of assets and management policies, limitations on "destructive competition", and the avoidance of "overbanking".

In order to improve the quality of assets and management policies, federal supervision was extended to all state banks which joined the F.D.I.C. This involved new, conservative criteria for the valuation of bank assets, and regular inspection by federal officials. Federal bank examiners not only assess and report on the quality of the bank's assets, but also on the quality of the bank's management.

Both competition for deposits among established banks and the entry of new banks were restricted. Thus, the payment of interest on demand deposits was prohibited, and the Federal Reserve System and the F.D.I.C. were required to set ceilings on interest rates which could be paid on savings and time deposits. It was argued that free competition via interest rates had contributed to the instability of the banking system. Badly managed and irresponsible banks were said to have paid excessive interest, forcing otherwise sound institutions into financial difficulties. Initially, the ceiling was accepted with enthusiasm by many bankers, but in recent years it has become an object of controversy. In the face of rising interest rates, the ceiling established under the Federal Reserve's "Regulation Q" has limited the banks' flexibility in meeting competition from near-banks, foreign banks, and the money market, and as a result there has been considerable agitation to eliminate or modify it.[18]

Entry was regulated on all sides. A new bank not only had to obtain a charter from the state or national authorities, but also a certificate of insurance from the F.D.I.C.[19] Both the Comptroller of the Currency, in issuing new bank charters, and the F.D.I.C., in issuing new insurance certificates, were required to consider such things as the bank's "future earnings prospects", "the general character of its management", and "the convenience and needs of the community to be served". A bank similarly had to obtain approval for an increase in its capital or for the opening of new branches, with the same criteria to be applied by the regulatory authorities.

We saw earlier how the new policies affected the development of the banking structure. Bank failures became relatively rare, and losses to depositors even rarer, the number of banks in the system declined steadily, and, until the early 1950's, the number of bank offices increased slowly. Branch banking became the dominant form for the expansion of banking facilities.

The Preservation of Competition as a Policy Objective

The reforms of the 1930's were designed to rationalize and stabilize the banking system, in part by restricting competitive forces. More recently, renewed emphasis has been placed on the preservation of competition in banking markets, particularly where competition is threatened by a proliferation of bank holding companies or by bank mergers. Thus, under the *Bank Holding Company Act* of 1956, bank holding companies are required to register with the Board of Governors of the Federal Reserve System, and the Board's approval is required for all acquisitions of banks by holding companies. In addition to various factors relating to the management and financial condition of the banks and the "needs and convenience" of the community, the Board is required to consider the impact on competition in assessing such applications. Similarly, under the *Bank Merger Act* of 1960, all bank mergers involving banks under federal jurisdiction require prior approval of the regulating authorities, and again the impact on competition is one of the factors which must be considered in assessing merger applications. Indeed, the Attorney General of the United States is required to submit a brief to the bank regulatory authorities offering his assessment of the competitive impact of the merger. Moreover, recent Supreme Court decisions have held that banks are subject to the anti-trust laws, which in effect made the impact on competition the primary consideration in considering applications for mergers. The effect has been to retard bank mergers, and hence to reinforce the traditional fragmentation of the banking system.

Public Policy and the Banking Structure

The banking system of the United States has developed under the often conflicting pressures of public policies administered by state governments and several agencies of the federal government. Indeed, the very complexities of the banking structure which are so perplexing to Canadian observers are themselves a direct product of complex and conflicting public policies. The role of "the authorities" is ubiquitous. Thus:

> Private entrepreneurs are not permitted to enter the banking industry without the consent of the public authorities. Where they are allowed to enter, they may branch or merge only with the approval of the public authorities. While private entrepreneurs are left the choice whether to seek entry or to seek expansion of their banking operations, the ultimate decisions on bank entry and bank expansion through branching or merger is assigned to the public authorities.[20]

This represents a degree of governmental control over the banking system which is unknown in Canada.

But even the structure of the regulatory authorities is complex and tangled. Each successive reform involved the super-imposition of a new institution on the existing structure. Thus the national banking system under the Comptroller of the Currency was super-imposed on the pre-existing state banking systems. The reforms of 1913 and 1933-35 added two new agencies, the Federal Reserve and the F.D.I.C., without altering the earlier ones. And the new emphasis on competition has, in effect, also brought the Attorney General's office into the picture. All of these agencies have some regulatory authority, and their jurisdictions overlap.

To minimize inter-agency conflicts, primary responsibility for the various banking policies has been divided up among the agencies, but not along functional lines. Thus, the Federal Reserve administers interest-rate ceilings for member banks, and the F.D.I.C. for insured non-member banks. Clearly, there is a very real danger that the same policy will be administered according to different standards by the three agencies, leading to discrimination among competitive institutions.

3/NEAR BANKS

The United States has a rich variety of specialized financial intermediaries in addition to commercial banks. Many of these — insurance companies, pension funds, mutual funds, finance companies — are the direct counterparts of institutions found in Canada and discussed in earlier chapters. Although there are differences in detail, the operations of these intermediaries are sufficiently similar in both countries that we need not discuss them further. Indeed, many insurance and finance companies have operations on both sides of the border.

Moreover, as is apparent in Table 13-5, while near banks have a slightly greater relative importance in the United States, and life insurance companies in Canada, the structure of the financial system is almost identical in the two countries, except within the near bank sector. In the case of

Table 13-5

Comparison of the Structure of the Financial Systems
of Canada and the United States
Total Assets of Major Financial Intermediaries, January, 1969

	United States		Canada	
(Billions of Dollars)	Dollars	Percent	Dollars	Percent
Commercial Banks	509.5	41.5	28.5*	38.5
Near Banks	238.2	19.5	12.1	16.3
Savings and Loan Ass'ns.	(152.8)	(12.5)		
Mutual Savings Banks	(71.2)	(5.8)		
Credit Unions	(14.2)	(1.2)	(3.4)	(4.6)
Trust & Loan Companies			(7.9)	(10.7)
Quebec Savings Banks			(0.6)	(0.8)
Gov't Savings Banks			(0.3)	(0.4)
Other Financial Institutions				
Life Insurance Companies	182.6‡	14.9	13.7	18.5
Other Insurance Companies	48.4‡	3.9	2.5	3.4
Pension Funds	144.1	11.8	9.0	12.1
Mutual Funds	52.7	4.3	3.4†	4.6
Finance Companies	49.9‡	4.0	4.9	6.6
TOTAL	1,225.4§	100.0§	74.1§	100.0§

*Canadian dollar assets only. †Includes closed-end investment companies.
‡Financial assets only.
§Detail may not add to totals because of rounding.
SOURCES: Bank of Canada, *Statistical Summary, Supplement 1969; Statistical Abstract of the United States,* 1969; Federal Reserve *Bulletin,* June 1970.

near banks, the United States has institutions which have no exact counterpart in Canada, and vice versa. Given the importance attributed to near banks in recent discussions of the effectiveness of monetary policy and the extent to which we rely on empirical research on this problem which has been done in the American context (these issues are discussed in Chapter 23), these institutions merit brief discussion.

Types of Near Banks

Savings and Loan Associations. The most important type of near bank in the United States is the savings and loan association. The consolidated balance sheet for all savings and loan associations is summarized in Table 13-6.

Savings and loan associations play the same role in the financial system of the United States as do trust and mortgage loan companies in Canada. They intermediate between individual savers and the mortgage market. Their major liabilities are savings deposits, highly liquid, relatively safe financial instruments which are attractive substitutes for money in the portfolios of individual assetholders. The major use of funds is to extend mortgage loans. Indeed, savings and loan association asset holdings show a singular concentration in mortgages. They hold a much higher

Table 13-6

*Savings and Loan Associations and Mutual Savings Banks
Assets and Liabilities, January 1, 1969*

(Billions of Dollars)	Savings and Loan Associations		Mutual Savings Banks	
	Dollars	Percent	Dollars	Percent
ASSETS				
Cash	3.0	2.0	1.0	1.4
Mortgages	130.8	85.5	53.3	74.9
U.S. Gov't Securities	9.5	6.2	3.8	5.3
Other Assets	9.5	6.2	13.1	18.4
Other Securities			(10.4)	(14.6)
Other Loans			(1.4)	(2.0)
Other Assets			(1.3)	(1.8)
TOTAL ASSETS AND LIABILITIES	152.8	100.0	71.2	100.0
LIABILITIES				
Deposits (including shares)	131.6	86.2	64.5	90.6
Other Liabilities	10.9	7.1	1.4	2.0
Reserve Accounts	10.3	6.7	5.2	7.3

SOURCE: Federal Reserve *Bulletin*. June 1970.

proportion of their assets in this form than either Canadian trust companies (55%) or mortgage loan companies (75%).

Dualism is also present in the savings and loan association system. Like commercial banks, savings and loan associations may be incorporated by either the federal government or state governments. All federal associations must be "mutual", i.e., owned by their depositors, like a cooperative bank or a mutual insurance company. The "deposits" in a mutual association are actually "shares" on which dividends are paid. Some states permit "stock" associations to be incorporated as well. A stock association is like a regular commercial corporation. It has a separate set of stockholders who own the business and share in its profits. (At the end of 1967 less than 13% of the 6,000 savings and loan associations in the United States were stock associations.)

Mutual Savings Banks. Next in importance to savings and loan associations are mutual savings banks. The consolidated balance sheet of mutual savings banks is also summarized in Table 13-6.

As their name implies, these banks are also mutual associations, owned by their depositors. They operate under charters issued by 17 states, primarily in the north-east (and particularly in New York, Massachusetts and Pennsylvania). Thus, like Quebec savings banks, they are a regional rather than a nation-wide institution. At the end of 1968 there were approximately 500 mutual savings banks in operation in the United States.

As can be seen in Table 13-6, the primary business of the mutual savings banks is also intermediation between households and the mortgage market. Their main source of funds are savings deposits, and their main use of funds mortgage loans. Thus, both in their organization and in the nature of their financial intermediation they are much like savings and loan associations. However, they operate under charters which permit them to follow a much more flexible investment policy than savings and loan associations.

Credit Unions. American credit unions are essentially the same as Canadian credit unions (as distinguished from *caisses populaires*). This should not be surprising since, as we saw in Chapter 10, the Canadian credit union movement drew a major stimulus from the American movement in the early 1940's. Credit unions are local mutual associations, normally organized on industrial or occupational lines. They accumulate funds in savings "shares" or deposits, and make personal loans to members for a variety of purposes. They have federal or state charters, and the federal institutions are supervised and inspected by the Bureau of Federal Credit Unions.

Credit unions are relatively less important in the financial system of the United States than they are in Canada (but remember, the Canadian figures include *caisses populaires*). However, they have experienced an exceptionally high rate of growth in the postwar period, increasing from less than 1.5% of near banks assets in 1945 to 6% in 1968. They can no longer be ignored as a factor in the financial system.

Characteristics of Near Banks

The major types of near banks in the United States have several characteristics which distinguish them from Canadian institutions.

Non-chequable Savings Deposits. In Canada, both banks and near banks offer savings deposits which are transferable by cheque. In the United States this is not permitted. Both savings deposits at commercial banks and savings deposit or shares in the near banks are "passbook" accounts. Although notice of withdrawal can be required by the bank, funds can normally be withdrawn on demand with presentation of the passbook. However, funds cannot be transferred to a third party by cheque.

Trusteeship Function. In Canada, chartered banks have not been permitted to assume trusteeship functions. A separate group of institutions, trust companies, exist for this purpose, and they have developed into the country's largest, and most important near banks. Given the close connection between commercial banking activities and the trusteeship business, the chartered banks developed working arrangements with trust companies, and indeed some chartered banks have close ownership affiliations with trust companies. In the United States, by contrast, the trusteeship function can be freely assumed by commercial banks. As a result, there are few trust companies which are not commercial banks, and those that do exist are not deposit-accepting institutions. The peculiar Canadian near bank, the non-bank trust company, does not exist in the United States.

Dualism and Fragmentation. The system of dual control which we discussed earlier in connection with commercial banks, is also characteristic of the near banking system. A division of authority between federal and provincial governments is also present in Canada, but here it has not prevented the development of nation-wide networks of branch offices by major trust and loan companies. Savings and loan associations and mutual savings banks are permitted to operate branches in most states, but large nation-wide firms cannot exist. There are some inter-state holding companies which control several stock savings and loan associations, but legislation in 1959 prohibited the formation of additional holding companies or the acquisition of new associations by existing holding companies.

Deposit Insurance. In 1967 Canada established a system of deposit insurance for banks and certain near banks (Chapter 14). In the United States a system of federal insurance for mutual savings banks and saving and loan associations is of longer standing, dating from the banking reform of the early 1930's.

Mutual savings banks are eligible for insurance by the Federal Deposit Insurance Corporation, the agency which insures deposits in commercial banks. Two-thirds of the mutual savings banks, holding over 85% of all deposits in mutual savings banks, are so insured. In addition, the State of Massachusetts operates its own deposit insurance plan for mutual savings banks.

Savings and Loan Associations can obtain similar insurance from another federal agency, the Federal Savings and Loan Insurance Corporation. All federal associations must take out this insurance, but it is optional for state-chartered associations. Almost three-quarters of all associations are so insured. In addition, three states, Massachusetts, Maryland and Ohio, have their own deposit insurance plans. Credit Unions do not have Federal deposit insurance.

Lender-of-Last-Resort Facilities. As in Canada, near banks do not have direct access to central bank credit in the United States.[21] However, unlike Canada, the United States has developed a special lender of last resort for savings and loan associations and mutual savings banks — the Federal Home Loan Bank System.

The Federal Home Loan Bank System was established in 1932 to provide lender-of-last-resort facilities to institutions involved in residential mortgage lending. In structure it is similar to the Federal Reserve System. Thus, there are 12 regional Federal Home Loan Banks, under the supervision of the Federal Home Loan Bank Board. Like the Federal Reserve Banks, the Home Loan Banks make short-term emergency loans to members faced with unexpected withdrawals of deposits (called withdrawal advances), but unlike Federal Reserve Banks they also make longer-term loans to members as a more or less permanent addition to the borrowing association's resources (called expansion advances). The Banks finance their advances with deposits by member associations, including interest-bearing time deposits, and with funds raised on the open market. The System also has a $1 billion line of credit with the Federal Treasury which could be drawn upon in an emergency.[22]

The presence of a lender of last resort of this type undoubtedly helps explain why savings and loan associations hold such a large portion of their assets in otherwise illiquid mortgages in spite of the fact that their deposit liabilities are effectively payable on demand. The banker's risk is, in effect, shifted to the Federal Home Loan Banks. However, the Federal Home Loan Banks also serve another purpose. They mobilize funds, largely in the open market but partly from members in areas where there are surplus savings, for investment in areas of the country where the supply of mortgage money is relatively least adequate and mortgage rates relatively the highest. To a limited extent, they thus substitute for nation-wide branch organizations and help surmount the imperfections of the national capital market. In recent years, advances from Federal Home Loan Banks have amounted to less than 4% of the assets of savings and loan association, but their importance is increasing.

To a limited extent, the Federal Home Loan Bank System can also operate like a central bank, deliberately manipulating the volume of funds available to member institutions. On occasion, by restricting the availability of "expansion advances" to members the System has helped reinforce the policies of the Federal Reserve System.[23]

Membership in the Federal Home Loan Bank System is compulsory for all federal savings and loan associations, and is optional for mutual savings banks and state savings and loan associations. Most savings and loan associations are members, but few mutual savings banks have joined.

Competition Between Banks and Near Banks

We saw in Chapter 10 that throughout most of the postwar period, near banks grew more rapidly than chartered banks. As is apparent in Figure 13-4, this was also true in the United States, although, except in the case of credit unions, the difference in relative growth rates was not as pronounced as in Canada (compare Figure 13-4 with Figure 10-1).

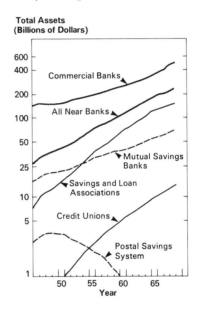

Figure 13-4
The Growth of Banks and Near Banks, 1946-1968
(semi-logarithmic scale)

As in Canada, the growth of near banks in the United States was partly fostered by controls over the banks. In particular, the rate of interest which commercial banks could pay on time and savings deposits was limited by Regulation Q (in Canada, you will recall, the comparable control was a ceiling on the rate of interest which banks could charge on loans). Until 1966 there was no such control on near banks (except those mutual savings banks which were insured by the Federal Deposit Insurance Corporation). In that year insured Savings and Loan Associations and mutual savings banks were brought under a comparable ceiling administered by the Federal Home Loan Bank Board.[24] At the same time, however, commercial banks were not prohibited from acquiring mortgages. As we mentioned earlier, this may partly account for the difference in the relative performance of banks in Canada and the United States.

4/CONCLUSIONS

We have only been able to scratch the surface in our analysis of the complex American financial system. However, perhaps we have succeeded n conveying an understanding of the basic elements of the system.

In comparing the banking system of the United States to that of Canada, one point which should stand out is the high degree of fragmenation of the former system. This has meant a much greater dependence on pen markets for such things as the inter-regional movement of funds than s true in Canada. Transfers of funds which are carried out within branch anking organizations in Canada must be effected through inter-bank transctions in the United States. It has also meant a much greater reliance on governmental regulation of financial institutions and financial markets than s typical in Canada. Stability in the banking system has been sought hrough a combination of careful supervision, restrictions on entry and estraints on competition. In Canada, stability has been achieved through he predominance of very large firms in the industry, a high degree of conentration in asset holdings, and inter-bank agreements to restrict competition. Are these the only routes to financial stability? Must competition in he setting of interest rates be stifled either by government regulation or by private agreement? Or are there alternative methods of ensuring that we have a stable, efficient banking system?

FOOTNOTES

[1] The data on the assets and liabilities of the Canadian chartered banks in Table 13-1 differ from those presented in Table 9-1. The latter was a complete balance sheet, including assets and liabilities denominated in foreign currency as well as Canadian dollars. In order to maintain comparability with the American data, Table 13-1 includes only assets and liabilities denominated in Canadian dollars (plus the net foreign asset position). This is the concept of the balance sheet of the banking system which is commonly cited in discussions of Canadian banking.

[2] Banks are permitted to hold uninsured mortgages to the extent of their stockholder's equity or 70% of their combined time and savings deposits, whichever is greater. There is no limit on holdings of federally insured mortgages.

[3] The American banks' involvement in the Euro-dollar market as a technique for domestic cash adjustments is discussed briefly in "Euro-dollars: A Changing Market," in *Federal Reserve Bulletin*, Vol. 55 (Oct. 1969), pp. 765-784.

[4] Widespread resort to the Euro-dollar market at this time is usually attributed to the fact that Federal Reserve regulations prevented the banks from offering high enough interest rates on certificates of deposit to make them competitive in the money market. "Euro-dollars: A Changing Market," pp. 756-757; "Reserves Against Certain Foreign Deposits," in *Federal Reserve Bulletin*, Vol. 55 (Aug. 1969), pp. 656-657.

[5] J. M. Guttentag and E. S. Herman, "Banking Structure and Performance," in *The Bulletin*, New York University, Graduate School of Business Administration, Institute of Finance, No. 41/43, (Feb. 1967), p. 43.

[6] Under federal law, a bank holding company is one which owns, directly or indirectly, 25% or more of the voting stock of two or more banks, or which is able to control in any manner the election of a majority of the directors of two or more banks.

[7] *Federal Reserve Bulletin*, Vol. 55 (Aug. 1969), p. A96. At that date there were 80 registered holding companies, but because of inter-corporate links only 71

separate holding company groups.

[8] Board of Governors of the Federal Reserve System, *Subsidiary Banks of Bank Holding Companies,* December 31, 1968 (mimeographed, n.p.).

[9] J. C. Darnell, "Chain Banking," in *National Banking Review,* Vol. 3 (Mar. 1966), pp. 307-331.

[10] The classic discussion of these issues is D. Alhadeff, *Monopoly and Competition in Banking* (Berkley, California: University of California Press, 1954). See also C. H. Kreps, Jr., "Characteristics of Local Banking Competition," in D. Carson, ed., *Banking and Monetary Studies* (Homewood, Illinois: R. Irwin, 1963), pp. 319-332; Guttentag and Herman, *op. cit.,* pp. 34-38.

[11] Guttentag and Herman, *op. cit.,* pp. 47-50. Similar data are reported in C. H. Kreps, Jr., *op. cit.,* and "Changes in Banking Structure, 1953-62," in *Federal Reserve Bulletin,* Vol. 49 (Sept. 1963), pp. 1191-1198.

[12] The presence of group and chain banking also increases the degree of concentration in local banking markets. We noted some aspects of this in our discussion of group banks. There is little comparable information for chain banks, but the study referred to earlier found that in 1962 over half of all chains had their affiliated banks in one county, suggesting that chains did increase concentration in certain local markets in a significant degree. Darnell, "Chain Banking."

[13] The relevant evidence is surveyed by Guttentag and Herman, *op. cit.,* pp. 80-103.

[14] In the years 1947 through 1962 some 351 national and 1,225 state banks were chartered, an average of 22 national and 76 state banks per year. In every year new state charters were several times as numerous as new national charters. In the years 1963 through 1965 some 457 national and 382 state charters were issued, an average of 152 new national and 127 new state banks per year. The preceding relationship between new national and state charters was reversed. From 1966 on, the old pattern re-emerged, as new national charters fell to 25, 14 and 16 in 1966, 1967 and 1968 respectively. Cf., Comptroller of the Currency, *Annual Report,* 1964; *Federal Reserve Bulletin,* various issues.

[15] The whole issue is discussed in the Comptrollers' *Annual Report,* 1964.

[16] S. Peltzman, "Bank Entry Regulation: Its Impact and Purpose", *National Banking Review,* Volume 2 (Dec. 1965), reprinted in *Studies in Banking Competition and the Banking Structure* (Washington: The Administrator of National Banks, 1966), pp. 285-299.

[17] The insurance policy is actually taken out by the bank on behalf of its customers, and the bank pays a premium based on its total deposits. Each account is only insured up to $10,000, but since the F.D.I.C. can generally arrange to have a failing bank merged into a sound bank (making an appropriate financial adjustment to compensate for the short-fall of assets in the failing bank), losses to depositors have been small.

[18] Regulation Q applies to member banks, but the F.D.I.C. adopts the same ceilings for non-member insured banks. In 1966 a similar ceiling was imposed on rates paid by savings institutions, administered by the Federal Home Loan Bank Board. We will discuss this institution later.

[19] Unless, of course, it chooses to operate without F.D.I.C. insurance. It has been reported, however, that many state banking authorities refuse to issue a charter unless the F.D.I.C. will issue a certificate of insurance (see Comptroller of the Currency, *Annual Report,* 1964, p. 242).

[20] A. Brimmer, "Market Structure, Public Convenience and the Regulation of Bank Mergers," in *The Banking Law Journal,* Volume 86 (Sept. 1964), pp. 773-793.

[21] Mutual Savings Banks are eligible for membership in the Federal Reserve System, but none have chosen to join. However, mutual savings banks in New York have organized their own "central bank", the Savings Bank Trust Company, which is a member of the Federal Reserve System.

[22] The Federal Home Loan Bank Board is also responsible for the Federal Savings and Loan Insurance Corporation which also has a $750 million line of credit with the Treasury. Under recent legislation, the Federal Reserve System was given the authority to purchase bonds of agencies like the Federal Home Loan Bank Board, and has used this power to a limited extent. This also provides a residual source

of liquidity for the system.

[23] For a discussion of such a case, see Federal Home Loan Bank Board, *34th Annual Report, 1966* (Washington: 1967) , pp. 45-56.

[24] The Board attempted to implement such controls a year earlier without legislative authority, by the expedient of denying advances to associations which violated Board-established interest rate ceilings. This experiment was not successful. The 1966 legislation was justified on the now familiar grounds that while a limited amount of competition in the financial system is desirable, "it could be carried beyond reasonable limits". *Ibid.*

14

The Social Interest in the
Structure of the Financial System:

Issues in Microeconomic Policy

Our discussion of the microeconomics of the Canadian financial system so far has been in *positive* terms. We have described some important features of the structure and history of the system, and have developed an elementary analysis of the function of financial markets and financial intermediaries. However, in spite of our avowed concern with public policy, and with the exception of some matters relating to the payments mechanism, we have so far avoided the discussion of *normative* issues. The purpose of this chapter is to explore some of these issues. It is concerned with the objectives and content of public policy with respect to the structure and functioning of the financial system.

1/THE CONSTITUTIONAL PROBLEM

Canada is a federal state, with a constitutional division of powers and responsibilities between federal and provincial governments. The *British North America Act* assigned to the federal government exclusive responsibility for public policy relating to many aspects of the financial system, including interest rates, bills of exchange and promissory notes, currency and coinage, the incorporation of banks, savings banks and "banking" in general.

If we accept a comprehensive definition of the concept of "banking" this would seem to give the federal government broad powers over most financial intermediaries. However, neither the constitution nor the court has provided a definition of "banking", and the effective working definition is very narrow. It is limited to those institutions specifically enumerated in the *Bank Act* or the *Quebec Savings Bank Act,* and only those institutions are permitted to use the words "bank", "banker" or "banking" to describe their business.

The *B.N.A. Act* assigned to the provinces exclusive jurisdiction over "property and civil rights" and the incorporation of companies "with provincial objects". This has meant that the responsibility for regulating many kets in securities is provincial, and the provincial governments have the right to charter and supervise all types of financial institutions except "banks"'. Even the requirement that provincial companies must have "provincial objects" has proven to be of little significance. Simply by registering in other provinces as extra-provincial companies, many provincially incorporated financial institutions are able to carry on a nation-wide business.

Because we have 11 centers of policy making with overlapping jurisdictions, it is not surprising that the Royal Commission on Banking and Finance found "a mixed and sometimes confused pattern of regulation".[1] The constitutional division of powers places a major obstacle in the way of a unified national policy. To obtain such a policy would require federal-provincial and interprovincial cooperation, or definitive legal interpretations (e.g., of the scope of "banking") permitting the assertion of federal supremacy in the regulation of financial affairs. Substantial progress has in fact been made through provincial government cooperation to develop uniform regulations for security trading. Furthermore, there is considerable similarity among provincial laws governing provincially incorporated financial institutions. (Provincial arrangements for continuing inspection and supervision in both fields, however, differ significantly.)

The Royal Commission, in an effort to achieve a uniform policy, urged the more radical approach of unilateral federal assertion of jurisdiction over all private financial institutions enaged in the "business of banking", broadly defined to include the issuing of all

> . . . claims which may be transferred immediately or on short notice by cheques or on customers orders . . ., other demand liabilities . . .,[and] term deposits, whatever their formal name, and other claims . . . maturing or redeemable at a fixed price within 100 days of the time of original issue or of the time at which notice of withdrawal is given by the customer. . . [2]

Such a definition would include all provincially incorporated near banks. Furthermore, since the Commission recommended that all other institutions should be "prohibited unequivocally from operating as banks",[3] the result would have been a substantial reduction in provincial responsibility for and power over financial institutions.

While Parliament adopted many of the recommendations of the Royal Commission in the recent revision of the *Bank Act*, it did not act on this central proposal for a truly comprehensive banking law. There were some suggestions by the government of the time that further legislation along this line could follow, although many authorities doubted that it would be constitutional, or if constitutional that it would be politic in view of contemporary federal-provincial relations. In any case, as we will see, the implementation of federal deposit insurance has indirectly achieved part of the Royal Commission's objective.

2/COMPETITION AS AN OBJECTIVE OF PUBLIC POLICY

While the federal government thus does not have power to regulate all financial institutions or all financial markets, it directly controls certain vitally important institutions. Federal policy, particularly with respect to the chartered banks, can have wide repercussions on the whole financial system.

For example, in 1967 several laws were passed by the government of Canada which together were the most important expression of public policy towards the financial system in recent years.[4] These legislative changes had the greatest impact on the operations of the chartered banks. However, they also had important direct and indirect effects on a much broader range of institutions.

The government made it abundantly clear in introducing the *Bank Acts* of 1967 that *the primary objective of the changes was to increase the degree of effective competition in the financial system.* The government was concerned not just with competition among the several chartered banks, but also with competition between banks and near banks.

Competition as a Policy Objective

It is true that economists commonly advocate a high degree of competition as an objective of public policy towards most industries in the economy, but should we treat the financial system in the same manner in which we treat other industries? Is not the financial system different in an important sense which makes competition an *inappropriate* objective of public policy with respect to it?

Competition and Economic Efficiency. At the root of public policy designed to stimulate competition is a concern for *economic efficiency* — a concern that society obtain the maximum possible benefit from the limited real productive resources at its disposal. Economic efficiency has two basic dimensions. The first is that excessive resources not be absorbed in the production of any product. That is, each good or service which is produced must be produced at the *least attainable cost.* If the quantity of output of every product were predetermined, that would be all that there was to economic efficiency. However, all resources have alternative possible uses. The range of products produced and the quantity of each product produced can be altered. Therefore, the second condition for economic efficiency is that all resources must be allocated to their most valuable uses. That is, *optimum quantity* of each good or service must be produced. One of the important conclusions of elementary economic theory is that, if we accept relative valuations of goods and services implicit in consumer demand curves, then, with certain exceptions, *highly competitive markets provide the most reliable mechanism for achieving economic efficiency in both senses.*

Competition and Efficiency in the Financial System. As was argued in Chapter 1, the financial system can be considered an industry — a collection of firms producing financial services. The production of these services absorbs part of the scarce resources of the economy. As in any other industry, then, it is important that the appropriate quantity of financial services be provided, and that they be provided at least attainable cost.

However, to rest the case for a high degree of competition in the financial system on such an analogy with other industries is to miss an important dimension of the matter. The significance of the financial system cannot be assessed simply in terms of the resources absorbed in producing financial services — in terms of value added in banking and finance. The financial system is, above all else, a mechanism for allocating credit to alternative possible uses, and a mechanism for providing assetholders with convenient forms in which they may accumulate wealth. The allocation of credit affects the structure of economic activity: it determines among other things what lines of activity will expand and what new ventures will get off the ground. The range of financial instruments available, and the yield on each instrument, affects the welfare of all assetholders. The fundamental case for a policy of stimulating competition in the financial system must rest on the importance of competition in *ensuring that credit is allocated to its most valuable uses* (i.e., to the uses promising the highest rates of return) *at the minimum attainable cost*, and in *ensuring that a broad range of financial instruments is made available to assetholders on the best possible terms* (i.e., offering the most favourable combinations of risk, liquidity and expected yield) .

Concentration and Competition in the Canadian Financial System

There is, then, theoretical justification for a policy encouraging competition. However, the Banking Acts of 1967 were not based simply on theoretical speculations about the benefits which might be derived from a high degree of competition in the financial system. They were also based on evidence produced by the Royal Commission on Banking and Finance that in important respects the financial system was not as competitive as it could be.

Competition Among Whom? From our earlier discussion of financial markets it should be obvious that in one sense there are always a very large number of participants in the financial system, both as lenders and as borrowers. Virtually every household, business-firm, non-profit institution and government agency in Canada, plus many foreigners, are involved in one side of the market or the other. Since a very large number of participants on both sides of a free market virtually guarantees a high degree of competition, does it not follow that the financial system is highly competitive?

Not necessarily. *What we have to be concerned with is not the number of ultimate participants in financial markets — households, business firms, etc. — but the number of firms and the state of competition among firms which bring the ultimate borrowers and lenders together.* We must be concerned with competition among firms acting as brokers and dealers in financial markets on the one hand, and firms acting as financial intermediaries on the other. Although there are many households and firms on each side of the market, the market cannot be highly competitive unless the intermediaries in the marketing process are also competitive. What are the facts?

Findings of the Royal Commission on Banking and Finance. The Royal Commission's studies, as set out in their *Report,* provide the only comprehensive analysis of concentration and competition in the Canadian financial system. Their survey revealed that a high degree of concentration of business in the hands of a few large firms was typical of many segments of the Canadian financial system. While a high degree of concentration is inimical to active price competition, it does not necessarily imply a lack of such competition. However, the Commission did discover some evidence of *a serious lack of active price competition* in some aspects of the system.

Concentration and Competition in Financial Markets. Consider first competition among brokers and dealers in Canadian stock and bond markets. The Commission found a large number of firms (over 400) engaged in such activities. However, it also found that there was a relatively high degree of concentration of business in the hands of a few large firms, and that the competitive situation was very different in major segments of securitites markets. In the short-term money market the "professionalism" of the market's participants ("mainly corporate treasurers and others skilled in the financial business") has forced a high degree of competition involving "vigorous innovation and price cutting".[5] While similar tendencies were noted in the longer-term bond market, the Commission was concerned with the high degree of concentration in the underwriting of new security issues. Thus, they found that in 1960 six firms accounted for the underwriting of 90% of all public utility issues, 60% of all industrial bond issues, 65% of all stock issues and "also dominated" new issues of provincial and municipal bonds.[6] The Commission noted that the cost of underwriting in Canada was generally higher than in the United States, and suggested that this was partly due to

> the comparative lack of competitive bidding for new issues (except for municipals . . .) and the general failure of the industry to engage seriously in competition for underwritings.[7]

The degree of concentration in secondary trading in securities — particularly stocks — is significantly less than in the underwriting of new issues. However, it should be noted that the commissions which brokers charge for their services are not established by the forces of competition. Rather, standard commissions are established by agreement, with the incorporated stock exchanges, of which the major brokerage firms are members, providing the vehicle for such agreements. In general, the schedule of commissions in Canada are somewhat higher than in the United States.

Note that the stock exchanges are not simply places where stock trading takes place. These corporations have important regulatory functions as well. They establish rules of conduct for member firms, and supervise the activities of these firms to ensure that the rules are abided by. This contains obvious dangers to the public — dangers of conflicts of interest, dangers that the institution will act like "a private club to be conducted in accordance with the interests of its members [rather than as a] public in situation [which] exists apart from its members".[8] Similar regulatory functions are performed by trade associations in other branches of the securities industry, including most importantly the Investment Dealers Association of Canada. Indeed, one of the notable features of the securities industry in

Canada is the extent to which formal supervision and regulation is left to trade associations as opposed to governmental agencies, although all provinces have regulatory agencies, and generally the cooperation between the government and the relevant associations is close. The Royal Commission urged that the staffs of provincial securities commissions be improved both in size and quality so as to assume more of the regulatory functions.

What can we conclude about competition among firms offering brokerage and dealership services in securities markets? According to the Royal Commission studies, it is a mixed picture. In some segments of the industry there is a high degree of competition. In others, the competitive situation is less intense. Apparently the economists' ideal of prices set in an intensely competitive environment is not met uniformly in securities markets.

Concentration in Commercial Banking. The previous chapter reviewed some of the major differences between the structure of the financial systems in the United States and Canada. One of the striking conclusions to be drawn from such a comparison is the relatively higher degree of concentration in the commercial banking system in Canada.

In Canada there are at present only nine chartered banks.[9] As can be seen in Table 14-1, only five of these can be said to be nation-wide "retail" banking firms, with significant branch banking operations in most, if not all provinces. These five banks between them hold over 93% of total assets of chartered banks (the three largest account for two-thirds of total assets). Two smaller banks are primarily regional in their operations, with most of their offices concentrated in the Province of Quebec and contiguous areas (generally in French-speaking communities). The largest of these two banks has less than half the assets of the smallest of the big five. There are also two very small banks. One is new, and is presently regional in nature, confining its operations to British Columbia. The second is longer established, but has only nine offices in seven major cities across Canada and is relatively specialized in international finance (although it is actively expanding its Canadian business relative to its international business).

Concentration and Competition. Does it necessarily follow that because there is a high degree of concentration in an industry that active competition cannot exist?

The Canadian commercial banking industry obviously falls in the analytical category of "oligopoly" — an industry in which there are a few dominant firms, each of which must be continuously conscious of the high degree of interdependence in their market positions. It is a market structure in which the competitive strategies of each firm must be dominated by a careful assessment of the probable reactions of the few other firms. A fully satisfactory theory of price and output determination in oligopoly has yet to be developed. However, you will recall from your principles of economics course that there are a few generalizations about competitive behaviour which apply to most oligopolies most of the time.

Perhaps the most significant generalization is that *oligopolists are normally reluctant to use price aggressively as a competitive weapon.* There is a general fear that price cutting will degenerate into mutually destructive

Table 14-1

Concentration in the Canadian Chartered Banking System, January 1, 1970

	Total Assets		Canadian Assets		Offices*					
	Millions of Dollars	Percent	Millions of Dollars	Percent	British† Columbia	Prairie‡ Provinces	Ontario	Quebec	Atlantic Provinces	Canada
Royal Bank of Canada	10,652	25.0	7,014	22.8	133	277	413	182	132	1,137
Canadian Imperial Bank of Commerce	9,470	22.2	7,244	23.6	209	328	642	183	67	1,429
Bank of Montreal	8,401	19.7	6,276	20.4	137	237	369	205	89	1,037
Bank of Nova Scotia	5,935	13.9	3,559	11.6	82	135	311	73	147	748
Toronto-Dominion Bank	5,165	12.1	3,779	12.3	82	149	411	75	11	728
Banque Canadienne Nationale	1,723	4.0	1,703	5.5	–	5	16	556	–	577
La Banque Provinciale du Canada	891	2.1	870	2.8	–	–	22	247	20	289
The Mercantile Bank of Canada	192	0.5	173	0.6	1	2	1	3	2	9
Bank of British Columbia	78	0.2	66	0.2	4	–	–	–	–	4
La Banque Populaire	71	0.2	70	0.2	–	–	–	–	–	–
	42,578	100.0	30,755	100.0	648	1,133	2,185	1,524	468	5,958

SOURCE: *Canada Gazette.*
* May 31, 1969.
† Includes Yukon.
‡ Includes Northwest Territories.

"price wars". As a result, there are strong pressures inherent in the market structure to induce firms to agree on prices. Carried to the extreme, such agreements transform the oligopoly into a *cartel* — a monopoly by agreement. Even in the absense of formal cartel arrangements, the market structure induces firms to be very cautious about price cutting, and perhaps to implicitly acknowledge one firm as the "price leader", effectively setting the price for the whole industry. Competitive energies are then directed to other "non-price" strategies. Rivalry for market shares takes the form of competitive variations in the nature and quality of the product, or in ancillary services rendered to customers. Many economists argue that, carried to the extreme and without the safeguard of price-cutting competition, such non-price competition can involve substantial economic waste in the sense that excessive resources are absorbed in the production of the output which is produced. Because the price is higher than necessary, an inappropriate amount of the product is produced.

Concentration, then, does not necessarily imply an absence of competition, but it is inimical to aggressive competition, and partciularly to the use of price as a competitive weapon. What direct evidence do we have on the competitive behaviour of Canadian commercial bankers?

Competition in Commercial Banking. The Royal Commission on Banking and Finance concluded that "banking is in many ways a highly competitive business",[10] but, with some exceptions, competition did not extend to interest rates paid on deposits or charged on loans. Rather, such rates tended to be established by interbank agreements. Thus,

> there is a strictly limited amount of price competition among banks in their lending business . . . Their rates are subject to agreed minimum levels. Price competition has been further restricted in periods of credit restraint by agreements among the banks to the effect that no banks will take over an account from another by offering a better rate or a larger line of credit.[11]

Similarly on the deposit side, the Commission found that "price competition among the chartered banks is severely limited" by interbank agreements.[12] Active price competition was discovered only in the market for very large-size term deposits (primarily deposits by corporations), including large-size foreign currency deposits. This is an aspect of the high degree of competition in the short-term money markets discussed earlier.

Interest rates paid on deposits and charged on loans are not the only significant "prices" charged by banks for their services. Other charges, such as service charges on deposit accounts, can be of equal importance to many customers. Historically, these charges have also been the subject of "discussions" and "understandings" between banks.[13]

The bankers appear to have regarded such discussions and understandings as a necessary method of avoiding a form of competition which they felt was likely to give rise to "unsound" banking practices. Thus, for example, in testimony before the Standing Committee of the House of Commons in 1954 the then president of the Canadian Bankers' Association concluded that:

> the competition between banks is keener today than I have ever seen it . . . Basically we compete on the question of service, reputation and general

ability to convince people that we are as good or better than our competitors
. . . *I hope that there is no price cutting competition . . . because I regard
that as being poor competition* [our italics].[14]

Similarly, in commenting on "price competition" in their brief to the
Royal Commission on Banking and Finance the Canadian Bankers' Associa
tion argued that "Among the chartered banks themselves . . . competition
must take a different form",[15] i.e., it must take the form of competition in
the quality of the services provided.

The Royal Commission concluded, however, that exclusive emphasis
on the quality of service in the competitive process had led to "a waste
ful form of competition", particularly through excessive proliferation o
bank branches.[16] Increased price competition would lead to more concern
with efficiency, the more careful tailoring of the "quality" (and also the
price) of banking services to customers' demands and a reduction in the
proliferation of bank branches.

The historical record, then, is reasonably clear. The banks, by their
own admission, engaged in only limited competition by way of interest
rates, and limited their competitive actions to "non-price" competition
Some of the Royal Commission's recommendations and the revisions of the
Bank Acts which were derived from them were a reaction to this state o
affairs. What has happened since the revision of the *Bank Act*? Has the
historical pattern been broken?

While it is perhaps too early to give a conclusive answer to this
question, it is clear that significant changes are occurring in chartered bank
policies. There are signs of increased price competitiveness, particularly
in the market for savings deposits. We do not know if these changes in
policy will be permanent and there has not yet been a comprehensive assess
ment of their effects on the structure and behaviour of the financial system.

The Importance of Entry. Another of the significant generalizations
which can be drawn from investigations of oligopoly is that inter-firm agreements will be ineffective in maintaining high prices if entry into the
industry is relatively easy. Concern that high returns to the established
firms will attract new competitors places an upper limit on the price which
the oligopolists will collectively charge.

Table 14-2 provides a historical perspective on the existing structure o
the Canadian banking system, summarizing information discussed more
fully in Chapter 12. In the hundred years covered by the table, the structure
of the system changed significantly, evolving from a system comprised o
35 banks with an average of 3.5 offices per bank to one comprised of ten
banks with an average of 596 offices per bank. However, it is important
to note that the major transformation was basically completed by 1925.
Thus, in spite of the entry of 37 new banks between 1867 and 1925, the
total number of active banks declined from 35 to 11, partly as a result o
bank failures and partly as a result of bank mergers. Since 1925, the
process of consolidation through merger has continued, although on a much
diminished scale. However, it is significant that *since 1925 only four new
banks have been successfully established.* Of these two were organized by

large, well established foreign banks (one English and one Dutch), one was created out of another federally supervised financial institution (a Quebec savings bank), and one was inspired by a provincial government (although as a result of federal opposition it was ultimately organized by private interests).[17] Neither of the foreign-owned banks grew to be a significant factor in the domestic banking business. Neither established a nation-wide chain of branches to compete directly with the "big five" in offering a full range of banking facilities. Indeed, one of these banks — Barclay's Bank of Canada — was eventually absorbed by another of the larger Canadian banks, as was the bank created out of the Quebec savings bank. *In recent years, entry into the banking business in Canada has not been easy, and the entry of new banks has not provided a vital external source of competitive pressures.*

Table 14-2

The Changing Structure of the Banking System
New Banks, Mergers and Failures, 1867-1968

| Year End | Number of Active Banks | New Bank Charters | | Banks Closed | | No. of Bank Offices |
		Not Used	New Active Banks	Mergers	Failures	
1867	35					123*
1900	35	(20)	26	7	19	708
1925	11	(15)	11	26	9	3,840
1950	10	(1)	1	2	0	3,679
1960	9	—	1	2	0	5,051
1968	9	(1)	1	1	0	5,922†
Net Change						
1867–1925	−24	(35)	+37	−35	−28	
1925–1968	− 2	(2)	+ 3	− 5	0	

* 1868.
† May 1, 1968.
SOURCE: Buckley and Urquhart, *Historical Statistics of Canada.*

Barriers to Entry. There are several barriers to entry into the commercial banking industry in Canada. There is an *incorporation barrier*, for, unlike the incorporation of most companies, the incorporation of a chartered bank requires a special act of Parliament. Such a bill must be introduced as a private member's bill, and must be passed in the private member's hour. Under Parliamentary rules it is comparatively easy for a few members to hold up the procession of the bill. Once passed second reading, the bill must be referred to a standing committee, where the sponsors of the bill may be cross-examined and asked to "show their capacity, their financial position, and their intent . . . to demonstrate their capacity to carry on the banking business"[18] before the bill is reported to the House for third reading. Once the act of incorporation is passed and the charter granted, the sponsors of the new bank must still obtain a certificate from the government entitling them to commence business. Before issuing this certificate, the government must satisfy itself that all legal requirements have been met. The delays can be lengthy. Thus while the first version of the bill involved some very contentious issues relating to provincial government participation in a chartered bank, it is sobering to note that the total time elapsed between the receipt of the petition by the Senate of Canada (May 4, 1964) and the opening for business (July 17 1968) of Canada's newest bank, the Bank of British Columbia, was over four years.

In addition to these qualitative controls, the *Bank Act* also erects a *financial barrier* to entry in the form of a minimum capital requirement. Thus, a new bank must have at least $1 million of capital subscribed before it can be allowed to commence business (of which $500 thousand must be deposited with the Minister of Finance, to be held in trust, before a regular board of directors can be elected and application made for a certificate permitting the bank to commence business), and the bank must raise these funds within one year of its incorporation or else its charter lapses. The minimum capital requirement had been $500,000 prior to 1954. When it was raised to $1 million, one puzzled M.P. was inspired to ask "Should we make it more difficult to go into the banking business?"[19] By way of contrast, in the United States minimum capital requirements for national banks range between $50,000 and $200,000 depending on the size of the city in which it is located. State requirements are generally similar although in several states they are even lower.[20]

These legislative barriers to entry are undoubtedly significant in restricting entry. However, the more fundamental barriers are those inherent in the *market structure* and in the existence of substantial *economies of scale* in banking.

Various aspects of the market structure are relevant. On the lending side a new bank must attract customers from the existing banks if it is to establish itself as a commercial lender. But given their size, nation-wide branch organizations, intense involvement and long experience in the capital, money and foreign exchange markets, and world-wide banking connections, the established banks are able to offer business firms a wide range of services which a new bank will find it almost impossible to duplicate immediately. On the deposit (and personal lending) side, a new bank must somehow find a place for itself in a market already saturated with branches of established banks, and must somehow convince depositors that it is a sound institution (clearly, deposit insurance is a major benefit in this respect). Unlike the United States, there are no controls over the opening of new bank branches. As a result, the established banks can respond rapidly to every shift in the market for bank deposits, whether through population growth and redistribution or otherwise, with a corresponding adaptation of their branch organizations leaving no obvious gaps to be filled by new institutions.

Economies of Scale. Recent research suggests that banking is an activity which is subject to economies of scale. If so, new banks not only

have the immediate problem of breaking into the market, but, as long
as they remain small, will probably suffer from an inherent cost disadvantage.

Unfortunately, all of the research on bank cost functions has been
done in the United States. The relevant cost information for individual
banks is not available to permit a duplication of such studies for Canada,
and given the marked differences in the structure of the banking systems
of the two countries it is not clear that the American results can be
applied directly to the Canadian case. One problem involves the size of
banks studied. Most of the banks included in the American studies were
much smaller than the smallest Canadian bank. Moreover, the clearest
evidence of substantial economies of scale is for banks which by Canadian
standards are very small indeed. As a recent review of the literature noted,
"Regarding scale economies among large banks, the evidence is inconclusive,"[21] and most of the banks included in the "large" category are
still small by Canadian standards.

Moreover, one discovery of recent research is that the behaviour of
costs depends not simply on the size of the bank, but in the nature of
the business done (strong scale economies were discovered in managing
the securities portfolio and in "business development", less pronounced
economies were discovered in handling demand deposits, business loans and
administration, and no economies were found in handling time deposits),
and on whether the bank was a unit bank or had a system of branch offices
(on this the evidence is quite equivocal).[22] Unfortunately, given the vast
differences in size and organization, it is difficult to translate the findings
to interpret the Canadian situation. For example, we cannot answer the
question of whether, on balance, costs would be higher or lower if the
existing bank offices in Canada were organized into unit banks or smaller
chains of branch offices. However, it does seem clear that while in some
activities (e.g., the collection of time deposits and making installment
loans) a small new bank may not be at a serious cost disadvantage, in its
essential operations in the national money and capital markets (and
probably the foreign exchange market, a function not examined in the
American studies) it would have a significant disadvantage.

The existence and extent of economies of scale and economies of
branch banking are important issues in other ways as well. If such economies exist and are substantial, economic efficiency requires industrial
concentration. That is, it requires large-scale branch organizations which
can take advantage of scale economies. It is unfortunate that data do not
exist to permit an investigation of the problem in the Canadian context.

Concentration in Other Branches of Financial Intermediation. In
Chapters 10 and 11, for purposes of description, we grouped financial intermediaries into several categories based largely on legal distinctions but also
reflecting significant differences in the composition of asset and liability
portfolios. If we examine each of these categories separately, a relatively
high degree of concentration of assets in the hands of a few large firms
seems to be typical of most types of financial intermediation in Canada.
Thus, for example, the percentages of assets held by the five largest firms

in several of the major categories in 1966 were as follows:[23] trust companies, 53%; mortgage loan companies, 75%; life insurance companies, 48%; consumer loan companies, 68%; mutual funds, 69%. While they do not display the same intense degree of concentration as we noted in the case of commercial banking in Canada, each of these categories of financial institutions contains a few firms which, at least in terms of asset size, are dominant.

The lower degree of concentration in the various categories of non-bank financial intermediation in part reflects the fact that there are many more firms in these categories than in chartered banking. Thus, at the end of 1966 there were almost 4,800 cooperative banks, 135 life insurance companies, over 300 general insurance companies, over 100 trust and loan companies, over 80 consumer loan companies, and over 60 mutual funds. Unlike chartered banks, the large, financially dominant, non-bank financial intermediaries are surrounded by a sizable fringe of smaller firms. Many of the smaller firms carry on a highly specialized or localized business; however, many are in full and direct competition with the larger enterprises.

A Broader Concept of Competition. While concentration is inimical to active competition, to place exclusive emphasis on the apparently high degree of concentration in the asset holdings of non-bank financial intermediaries is to miss certain essential elements in their competitive situation.

The measures of concentration which we have used are based on legal definitions of industries which do not always make economic sense. The concept of an industry is one of the most widely used concepts in economics, but in a world in which the goods and services produced by different firms are seldom indentical but frequently similar, the concept of an industry is somewhat vague, and the groupings of firms used for statistical analysis are generally quite arbitrary. This is clearly true in the case of financial intermediaries. For example, considered as financial intermediaries (i.e., ignoring the E.T. and A. business) the operations of many of the trust and mortgage loan companies are virtually indistinguishable although they operate under different laws. They draw on the same sources of funds (term and savings deposits) and use those funds to acquire the same types of assets (primarily mortgages). Indeed, there are sharper differences in operations among firms within each of the categories "trust companies" and "loan companies" than between "typical" firms in each category. And what is true of trust and loan companies is true of many other categories of intermediaries. Thus trust and loan companies are faced with competition from cooperative banks, Quebec savings banks, chartered banks and governmental depositories in the market for funds, and in addition, from life insurance companies in the market for assets.

This suggests that in analyzing concentration and competition in financial intermediation we ought not to look at legal categories, but ought to examine separately each line of financial activity (e.g., savings deposits, demand deposits, commercial lending, mortgage lending, consumer lending, etc.). Moreover, various studies show that frequently it is a mistake to think of a single national market. Many borrowers, particularly individual and small firms, cannot compete for funds on a nation-wide basis, but are effectively confined to local lenders. A truly comprehensive analysis of concentration and competition ought to take this into account.

Such a study has not been undertaken for Canada. As a result there are few strong conclusions which can be drawn. However, it is clear that the activities of financial intermediaries overlap in a very complex pattern, that competition has impinged in varying degrees and at various points on the activities of chartered banks, and that this has been a primary factor eroding the banks' dominant position in the financial system in recent years. *Active competition among non-bank financial intermediaries and between these institutions and the chartered banks has been a major dynamic force in the Canadian financial system.*

It is important to note that, unlike chartered banking, entry into most categories of non-bank financial intermediation has been comparatively easy in recent years. This in part reflects the fact that most types of non-bank financial intermediaries can be chartered by provincial governments which are themselves in competition for new businesses. In each of the categories referred to above there has been a major expansion in numbers between 1950 and 1966: on the order of 50% in the case of cooperative banks, 100% in the case of trust and loan companies, and 90% in the case of life insurance companies. Although there continues to be a high degree of concentration of asset holdings among non-bank financial intermediaries, *the relatively easy entry of new firms has provided a vital source of competitive pressures.*

Conclusions: Competition and Public Policy

A concern for economic efficiency provides a powerful argument for a public policy directed toward the stimulation of competition, and particularly price competition, as long as increased competition does not preclude taking advantage of significant economies of scale. We have seen that there is evidence of significant restraints on competition in some parts of the financial system, and evidence of active competition in others. The *Bank Acts* of 1967 were partly directed at heightening competition in crucial areas where there were several obvious constraints, i.e., competition among chartered banks and between chartered banks and other financial intermediaries. What were the major provisions of the *Banks Acts* of 1967 which were directed to this objective?

3/A LEGISLATIVE STIMULUS TO COMPETITION: THE BANK ACTS OF 1967

In previous chapters, as we discussed the various types of financial intermediaries, we encountered most of the pro-competitive provisions of the *Bank Acts* of 1967 in an *ad hoc* fashion. It is useful now to bring all of these provisions together in summary form.

Anti-Combines Provisions

Some of the provisions of the new *Bank Acts* were designed to compensate for the fact that the *Combines Investigation Act* does not apply to financial institutions. While the Act prohibits inter-firm agreements or conspiracies in restraint of trade, it only applies to trade in "articles" and not to trade in "services". The relevant innovations in the new *Bank Acts* are as follows:

1. Prohibition of Interbank Agreements on Interest Rates and Charges
(Section 138)

All interbank agreements to fix interest rates or other charges on loans or deposits are prohibited for the first time. This strikes directly at the agreements which the Royal Commission found to be commonplace in banking, and which they considered to be a primary restraint on active price competition.

2. Prohibition of Interlocking Directorates
(Section 18)

Certain interlocking directorates are prohibited. Thus, effective January 1, 1970, a person cannot be a director of a chartered bank if he is simultaneously the director of another chartered bank, a Quebec savings bank, or a trust or mortgage loan company which accepts deposits from the public, and effective July 1, 1971 the directors of any one bank cannot constitute more than one-fifth of the directors of any corporation incorporated in Canada.

3. Restrictions on Dominant Share Holdings
(Sections 53, 54, 76)

The *Bank Act* introduces two new rules — what we might call the *Ten Percent Rules*. Any chartered bank is prohibited from directly or indirectly owning more than 10% of the voting shares in any relatively large Canadian corporation or more than 50% of the shares of a smaller corporation, with certain specified exceptions (essentially corporations providing ancillary services directly to the bank). Similar in effect is a provision designed to limit control over chartered banks by individuals or closely associated groups of individuals. Thus, the transfer of shares to any individual is prohibited if the transfer would increase his holdings to more than 10% of the outstanding shares of stock. The transfer of *any* share to the federal government, or any provincial or foreign government is also prohibited.

Through the Ten Percent Rules the government is seeking to maintain a clear separation between the banks and their customers. The bank may not control important customers; and important customers may not control the banks.[24]

Relaxation of Legislature Constraints on Banking

The second major group of pro-competitive innovations involved a general relaxation of the legislative restrictions on the business of chartered banks. These changes were designed to modify or eliminate discriminatory constraints on the ability of the chartered banks to meet competition from other financial institutions, particularly in attracting savings deposits and in extending mortgage credit. The intent again is to increase the degree of competition, although some economists are concerned that the effect may well be to increase chartered bank domination over the financial system to the general detriment of effective competition.

4. Broadening of the Lending Authority of Chartered Banks

The chartered banks were permitted for the first time to make "conventional" mortgage loans (i.e., mortgage loans which had not been guaranteed by an agency of the federal government). An upper limit on mortgage holdings was established, with a provision for this limit to be gradually increased to 10% of each bank's total Canadian dollar deposits and debentures.

5. Broadening of the Borrowing Authority of Chartered Banks

The banks were given the authority to issue debentures as well as to accept deposits. Debentures are marketable securities, representing a general claim on the assets of the bank which is subordinated to that of depositors. Under the *Act*, bank debentures must have a minimum term to maturity of five years, and unlike regular term deposits the banks are specifically prohibited from cashing the debentures before the expiration of the minimum five-year term.

6. Removal of the Interest Rate Ceiling on Bank Loans

The 6% ceiling on the interest rate which could be charged by chartered banks and Quebec savings banks was initially raised to 7¼% per annum, and under a complicated provision was removed entirely, effective January 1, 1968.

7. Reduction in the Level and Changes in the Form of the Cash Reserve Requirement

In place of the former 8% cash reserves behind all Canadian dollar deposits, banks are now required to hold 4% cash reserves against deposits "payable after notice" and 12% against deposits "payable on demand". By early 1970, given the composition of deposits, this had the effect of lowering the average required cash reserve ratio from 8% of Canadian dollar deposits to 6.2%. The right of the Bank of Canada to vary this reserve ratio was rescinded. However, a secondary reserve ratio was enacted, which can be varied by the Bank of Canada. The banks are presently required to hold an additional 9% of their Canadian dollar deposits in cash, day-to-day loans, or treasury bills. This ratio could be raised to a maximum of 12%. As before, the banks have no required reserve against foreign currency deposits. They are only enjoined to hold "adequate and appropriate assets" against such liabilities.

The lagged form of the cash reserve ratio (discussed in Chapter 8) was retained and extended to the secondary reserve ratio, but the Bank of Canada was given the authority to reduce the averaging period from one month to one-half month. The Bank of Canada did reduce the averaging period effective January 1969.

The reduction in the level of the cash reserve requirement, like the removal of the interest rate ceiling and the broadening of lending authority, should permit the banks to increase the average earnings on their assets, thus removing the basis for the common argument that the banks cannot pay competitive interest rates on savings deposits. The new form of the cash reserve requirement is also significant from this point of view. It provides a relative reduction in costs for that part of the deposit business in which the chartered banks compete most directly with the near banks.

Improving the Competitive Position of New Banks and Near Banks

The primary effect of the provisions reviewed so far is to improve the competitive position of the chartered banks *vis-à-vis* the near banks, and they do nothing to stimulate competition from newly established financial institutions. The *Bank Acts* made one important step in that direction through the provision of deposit insurance.

8. Deposit Insurance

The *Canadian Deposit Insurance Act* (1967) enacted by the government of Canada and the parallel (but not exactly similar) *Quebec Deposit Insurance Act* (1967), enacted by the Province of Quebec in response to the federal legislation, represent a significant new departure in public policy in Canada. For the first time, Canadian governments guarantee the safety of deposits with certain financial intermediaries.[25]

The federal act created the Canada Deposit Insurance Corporation and required all federally incorporated financial intermediaries which accept deposits from the general public in Canada — the chartered banks, Quebec savings banks, and federal trust and loan companies — to take out deposit insurance with the Corporation. Provincially incorporated trust and mortgage loan companies are permitted to join the insurance plan if they meet certain minimum qualifications, obtain permission from their provincial government, and agree to conduct their business in accordance with the provisions of the Federal *Trust Companies Act* or *Loan Companies Act* whichever is relevant. In fact, most provinces have passed legislation requiring provincially chartered trust and loan companies to join C.D.I.C., and the Corporation now insures deposits in trust and loan companies chartered by all provinces except Quebec.

While formally the Corporation will only guarantee a single deposit up to a maximum of $20,000, in fact the broad powers of the Corporation are designed to provide protection to all depositors. Thus, the Corporation is required to inspect each member institution at least once each year, to ensure that it is in sound financial condition and that it is conducting its operations in accordance with "sound" business and financial practices. In the event of temporary financial difficulties, the Corporation is empowered to purchase assets from any member institution, to make loans to a member or guarantee loans made by others, or to deposit funds with a member, if such actions seem appropriate to maintain the liquidity of the institution and hence to guarantee the safety of public deposits in it. In the event of insolvency of a member, the Corporation will make payment to each depositor in cash or will provide him with a deposit in another sound institution, in the amount of his deposit up to the legal maximum of $20,000.

The Corporation's funds are derived from two sources. At the outset the federal government subscribed $10 million capital funds. Beyond this, each member institution must pay an annual insurance premium equal to $500 or 1/13 of 1% insured deposits, which ever is greater. All premiums are credited to a Deposit Insurance Fund. If at any time, in the judgement of the Corporation, this Fund becomes adequate, the Corporation can reduce the annual premium. If necessary, the Corporation also has the power to borrow up to $500 million from the federal treasury.

The *Quebec Deposit Insurance Plan* has wider coverage than the federal plan. While the maximum insurance per deposit is the same, deposits in a broader class of financial institutions are covered, including most importantly the *caisses populaires* and credit unions. Indeed *every* deposit-accepting institution in the province of Quebec (aside from the federally chartered banks) is required to register with the Quebec Deposit Insurance Board, which has broad powers to supervise each institution's operations (including the power to cancel its registration). Since only registered institutions are allowed to accept deposits, the power to cancel a firm's registration gives the Board a powerful basis for regulating the provincial financial system.

Arrangements have been made to avoid duplication in insurance coverage and to coordinate the activities of the Canada Deposit Insurance Corporation and the Quebec Deposit Insurance Board. Trust and loan companies incorporated outside Quebec are to insure their Quebec deposits with the Q.D.I.B., and trust and loan companies incorporated in Quebec can choose to insure their deposits outside Quebec with the C.D.I.C. Where it is relevant, provision is made for the joint inspection of trust and loan companies. Also, under a revision of the Canada Deposit Insurance Act, the C.D.I.C. is empowered to lend money to the Q.D.I.C. if necessary,

Increasing competition was only a subsidiary theme in the decision to institute deposit insurance. Nevertheless, the existence of deposit insurance should have a significant impact on the competitive environment. By removing part of the risk to depositors — both through the formal guarantee of part of each intermediary's deposits and through the requirement of more consistent and rigorous inspection procedures — it should improve the

competitive position of new banks and less well-established loan and trus
companies (and, in Quebec, the *caisses populaires*). The established char
tered banks argued strongly that they did not require deposit insurance –
that their record for depositor safety spoke for itself. It was also arguec
that if the established institutions were required to join the insurance plan
since their deposits involved a lesser risk, the insurance principle shoulc
dictate that they pay lower premiums. The fact that they were nonetheles
required to pay the same premiums as new or more risky institution
suggests that the insurance premium is in part a "competition tax", th
proceeds of which are implicitly used to promote the competitive positio
of less well-established institutions.

Restraints on Competition: Soundness and Canadianization

While increasing the degree of competition in the financial systen
was the primary objective of the new *Bank Acts,* the revisions did no
pursue this objective single-mindedly nor to what might be regarded a
its logical extreme. The new *Bank Acts* both retained established provision
which restrict the nature and degree of competition, and introduced som
new constraints on competitive processes. Some of these restrictive provision
are designed to ensure the soundness of financial institutions, and some t
encourage Canadianization of the financial system.

"Soundness" as a Policy Objective. The bankruptcy of financial insti
tutions, whether through embezzlement, fraudulent mismanagement, ba
judgement in asset selection, or external events over which the managemen
could have no control (e.g., a depression or financial crisis), has alway
been a matter of serious concern to governments. As we saw in Chapte
12 and 13, "soundness" was long a dominant pre-occupation of bankin
policy in the United States and the continuing search for more and bette
safeguards against the insolvency of financial institutions has been a
important theme in the history of banking legislation in Canada. In par
this reflects concern for *the fate of unsuspecting depositors,* frequently th
financially unsophisticated; however, even very sophisticated investors ar
unlikely to have adequate information to permit them to identify unsound
ness in a bank or a trust company. In part, it has been motivated b
concern for the *stability of the financial system as a whole,* and with tha
the stability of the economy. World history is replete with examples of on
institution's failure initiating a chain reaction which brings down othe
sound institutions. In the extreme, the very financial stability of the natio
can be impaired. In part, also, this search may have been motivated b
concern for the *efficiency of the financial system.* As we have seen, b
spreading risks and taking advantage of economies of scale, financial inte
mediaries can reduce the costs involved in moving funds from certain saver
to investors, thus improving the efficiency of the financial system. Howeve
if there is a high degree of risk of loss through the failure of financial inte
mediaries, the costs of intermediation will increase and the developmen
of financial intermediaries will be stunted.

Constraints in the Interest of Soundness. Several types of measures have traditionally been used by governments in their attempts to ensure the financial integrity of financial institutions. Perhaps most common is legal specification of types of assets which may or may not be held by these institutions. Such controls might be designed to relate the structure of the institution's asset portfolio to the nature of its liabilities. While they serve a different purpose now, cash reserve requirements for commercial banks had their origins in this type of consideration. Similarly, as we noted in Chapter 9, the impact of the commercial loan theory in shaping early versions of the *Bank Act* provides a prime example. Alternatively, the purpose might be to prohibit the institution from holding excessive amounts of highly speculative assets, as in the case of restriction on the holding of common stock by insurance companies.

Legal controls over asset holdings serve little purpose if they are not vigorously enforced. It is a short jump in principle (although a major jump in history) to the requirement of formal external audits of the books and formal governmental inspection. As we saw in Chapter 13, government inspection of banks in Canada was only implemented following revelations that the last bank failure, that of the Home Bank in 1923, involved blatant violations of the *Bank Act*. Inspection is accompanied by the enforcement of conservative accounting procedures to avoid overstating the size or profitability of the institution.

There are other common devices, involving restrictions on the institutions' freedom of action, but perhaps the most significant from our present point of view is control over entry into the industry and official toleration (if not official encouragement) of restraints on price competition.

Restrictions on Entry. Some governments have a formal policy of restricting entry into the financial industry. As we saw in Chapter 12, the authorities in the United States responsible for extending deposit insurance coverage to banks — and hence effectively regulating entry into commercial banking — are required by law to have regard to a new banks' "future earnings prospects", "the general character of its management", and "the convenience and needs of the community to be served". The effect of these provisions has been to deliberately restrict entry to commercial banking.

In Canada, a similar deliberate policy has not been formulated. However, as we have seen, the *Bank Act* imposes significant qualitative and financial hurdles in the way of new entry to commercial banking. In the interests of increasing competition, many people have advocated a streamlining of the procedures for granting a bank charter. It is interesting to note that the first version of the new *Bank Act* Bill (C-102), introduced in May 1965, contained a radically different procedure for chartering banks. A new bank was to be incorporated through the issuance of letters patent by the Governor General in Council. These letters patent had to be laid before Parliament within 15 days, with Parliament then having the opportunity to annul them. The legislation required a decision within 40 days if Parliament was in session (or, if not in session within 40 days of the opening of the next session). In introducing the bill, the Finance Minister

(Mr. Gordon) emphasized that this was a major pro-competitive change and that it was designed "to make it easier for applicants to get a bank charter when they can meet all the specific requirements of the *Act*". In withdrawing the streamlined provision in favour of the pre-existing arrangements in 1967, the new Finance Minister (Mr. Sharp) expressed concern that " . . . if the bill had been approved in its original form there would have been some reason for regret", in that unsound institutions might have been speedily incorporated. The chartering of provincial institutions is much easier, and many critics contrast unfavourably the failure rate of such institutions (there have been several major failures in recent years) with the failure rate of chartered banks (there have been no failures since 1923), and urge more control over entry, and more careful inspection. It will be interesting to see if the Canadian Deposit Insurance Corporation begins to play a major role in restricting entry in many fields of financial intermediation through the selective refusal of deposit insurance.

Restraints on Price Competition. In the United States there has also been a deliberate policy of restricting the use of interest rates by banks as a competitive weapon in attempting to attract deposits. Thus, banks which are members of the Federal Reserve System or are insured by the Federal Deposit Insurance System have a legal ceiling on interest rates which they may pay on savings deposits (a ceiling which may be changed from time to time by the Federal Reserve Board under its regulation Q), and they are prohibited from paying any interest on demand deposits. These regulations originated in the crisis atmosphere of the mid-1930's when it was felt strongly that aggressive competition among banks was impairing the financial integrity of some institutions and hence contributing to the instability of the financial system (Chapter 13).

Canada has not had a similar policy of imposing a ceiling on interest rates which banks may pay on deposits (the controversial interest rate ceiling in Canada was on loans, not deposits. The effect on the banks' ability to compete for funds was similar although more indirect). However, a similar effect was achieved through approval of increasing concentration in banking through mergers (all mergers of chartered banks must have government approval) and through implicit toleration of interbank agreements on interest rates and other charges (no move was made to bring the banks within the purview of the *Combines Investigation Act*, until the 1967 revision of the *Bank Act* provided a substitute arrangement). Indeed the record of stability of the Canadian banking system during the 1930's which stands in stark contrast to the experience in the United States, is frequently pointed to with pride as evidence in favour of a highly concentrated banking system with minimal unsound competition through interest rates.

Constraints in the Interest of Canadianization. The new *Bank Acts*, in company with other federal legislation relating to most financial institutions under federal jurisdiction, introduced new measures designed to promote Canadian ownership and control of financial institutions.

The central measure, affecting the chartered banks, Quebec savings banks, and federally incorporated trust, loan and life insurance companies is what we can call the *Twenty-five Percent Rule*. This is a prohibition against the transfer of shares to non-residents if the transfer would increase non-resident holdings to more than 25% of the outstanding shares (remember, under the Ten Percent Rule there is an upper limit of 10% of outstanding shares beyond which no more shares may be transferred to any one individual, whether resident or non-resident). The *Bank Acts* also require that three-quarters of the directors of a chartered bank or Quebec savings bank must be citizens of Canada ordinarily resident in Canada.

The provisions relating to trust, loan and insurance companies were designed to prevent institutions presently controlled by Canadians from falling under foreign control. The provisions were not retroactive. Institutions controlled by non-residents at the time the law was introduced in Parliament were specifically exempted from these regulations. This principle was not carried forward in the *Bank Acts*. Rather another new rule relating to existing non-resident stockholdings was introduced, the *Twenty Times Authorized Capital Rule*. This rule is retroactive. Any chartered bank which was controlled by non-residents at the time the new *Bank Act* was introduced into Parliament is required to restrict its total size (liabilities plus capital accounts) to twenty times its authorized capital unless non-resident share holdings fall below 25% of outstanding shares. This provision, which comes into effect on January 1, 1973, only applies to one bank, the Mercantile Bank, since this was the only institution with substantial non-resident ownership (it was wholly owned by the First National City Bank of New York).

It is true that the measures taken to restrict foreign ownership and control of financial institutions can be considered but one aspect of a broader policy of ensuring "that no one or related group of shareholders is to dominate any of our banks, whether he is a Canadian or a foreigner".[26] However, it is also clear that *this policy conflicts with a policy of increasing the degree of competition*. We have already seen that entry of new banks is a vital source of competitive pressures, and that barriers to entry are substantial. Prohibition of foreign-owned banks may effectively close off one important potential source of new entrants. (Remember: two of the four banks successfully established in Canada between 1925 and 1970 were foreign owned.) In any case, the restrictions imposed on the one existing foreign-controlled bank had the immediate effect of restricting the growth and hence the competitive potential of a vigorous new entrant to the banking business.

In fact, of course, the Mercantile Bank was not a new firm, nor had it been previously Canadian controlled. It was established in 1953 as a wholly owned subsidiary of a Dutch bank. In 1963 it was purchased from its Dutch owners by the first National City Bank of New York. The takeover could be regarded simply as a change of foreign owners. However, the takeover also effected a significant transformation in the bank. During the years 1953-1963 the Mercantile Bank was not a vital factor in the Canadian banking system. It had only three offices in Canada (in Montreal, Toronto

Table 14-3
The Mercantile Bank, 1955-1968, Selected Assets and Liabilities

| | Total Assets | Foreign Currency Deposits | Canadian Currency Deposits | | | Current Loans in Canad |
			Personal Savings	Notice	Demand	
		(Millions	of Dollars)			
December 1955	11.5	1.0	0.6	2.7	1.7	4.4
December 1960	82.2	60.0	1.6	4.5	7.8	16.5
June 1963	83.9	64.3	1.4	3.2	5.7	17.6
December 1964	138.0	92.9	1.4	13.5	13.4	21.1
December 1965	208.9	142.6	1.9	26.7	12.4	58.4
December 1966	234.0	132.9	3.0	38.8	23.8	74.0
December 1967	198.0	94.2	5.1	45.7	25.7	89.5
December 1968	190.5	76.5	8.6	46.0	28.5	121.7
December 1969	191.5	84.3	10.1	30.9	28.2	148.2

SOURCE: *The Canada Gazette.*

and Vancouver), and as Table 14-3 shows clearly, its Canadian currenc business was both very small and stagnant. Indeed, from December 196 to December 1963 its Canadian currency deposits actually *fell* (total Cana dian dollar deposits in Canadian banks increased by 25% over this period) The transformation which occurred following the takeover is evident i Table 14-3. Not only did total assets take a major jump, but the Canadia portion of the business began to accelerate. In this period the bank opene new offices in four other Canadian cities.

That the new provisions were an effective constraint on the bank i also evident from Table 14-3. At the time the *Bank Act* was passed, th Mercantile Bank's ratio of total liabilities to authorized capital was 22. just in excess of the limit (in the case of other banks the ratios range between 28.1 and 70.7, with the big five all having ratios in excess of 50) Given authorized capital of $10 million (which can only be increase by cabinet approval) the bank is effectively frozen at its present size unle the required change in ownership occurs.

Conclusions: The Content of Contemporary Public Policy

The **main thrust of** contemporary Canadian public policy with respe to the structure of the financial system is to increase the degree of compet tion. However, this policy is not carried to its logical extreme. Certai restraints on competition are preserved, and particularly restraints on entr into banking (indeed, there are strong pressures to tighten up conditior of entry into other lines of financial intermediation). This reflects a naggin concern that wide-open competition may be inconsistent with the soun ness of financial institutions, and the belief that soundness must be pre-eminent objective of public policy. Additional constraints on the con petitive process have also been introduced in the interests of promotin Canadian ownership and control of financial institutions.

4/THE POLICY DILEMMA: ARE COMPETITION AND FINANCIAL STABILITY INCONSISTENT OBJECTIVES?

It should be obvious from this discussion that those charged with the ormation and administration of public policy are faced with a fundamental sue. Both a high degree of competition and financial stability are objecves in which the general public has a very vital interest. Are they inconstent objectives? Is it necessary to constrain competition in the general terests of financial stability?

In considering this matter, a distinction should be drawn between e stability of the financial system and the solvency of individual financial stitutions. While financial instability involves the failure of financial stitutions, the failure of selected institutions need not imply general nancial instability. The problem is to prevent the failure of one institution om setting off a chain reaction. For this purpose, the government has o primary instruments: the central bank as lender of last resort and eposit insurance.

The Central Bank and Financial Stability. As we have seen, the Bank f Canada has essentially unlimited powers to issue legal tender. The ntral bank, therefore, is in a key position to facilitate financial stability. y acquiring assets from, or extending loans to otherwise sound institutions, can provide those institutions with as much liquidity as necessary to meet panic-induced "run".

In fact, the Bank of Canada will extend loans directly only to chartered anks and to those government security dealers which have established lines credit with the Bank of Canada. However, in the event of pressure on ny large financial institution, the Bank of Canada can support the market r securities which the institutions might be forced to sell, and can make nds readily available to chartered banks which may wish to extend mporary credits to the institution. The Bank of Canada demonstrated e importance of its indirect intervention in 1965 when the failure of a ajor sales finance company, the Atlantic Acceptance Corporation, threated to set off a chain reaction affecting both other finance Companies and me trust companies.

Nonetheless, the effectiveness of the Bank of Canada in this regard ould be increased if all institutions with highly liquid liabilities (e.g., all ar banks) maintained reserve deposits with the Bank of Canada and nce had direct access to Bank of Canada advances.

Deposit Insurance and Financial Stability. The central bank works hind the scenes, providing liquidity as necessary. Deposit insurance has more direct psychological effect. By guaranteeing the safety of deposits, has the effect of heading off runs before they start.

It should also be noted that the Canadian Deposit Insurance Corporaon and the Quebec Deposit Insurance Board also provide lender of last sort facilities to member institutions who may not have access to the ank of Canada. If it were not for the fact that, outside Quebec, coperative banks are excluded from the plan this would close one institional gap in the Canadian financial system.

Should Banks Be Allowed to Go Bankrupt? Given that institutions for underwriting the stability of the financial system exist, the question is whether the government must create an environment in which it is virtually impossible for *any* financial institution to go bankrupt.

The possibility of bankruptcy performs an important economic function. It forces the owners and managers of a business to accept ultimate financial responsibility for their actions (although, given limited liability provisions, their responsibility is limited to the value of their investment). Such responsibility is presumably an incentive to efficiency, responsiveness to market developments, and competitive innovation.

Strong arguments can be made that banks and other financial institutions ought not to be an exception to the general rule that bad management produces either bankruptcy or takeover by other interests. It is clear however, that this view is not widely accepted, and is not consistently adhered to in the recent revision of the *Bank Act*.

FOOTNOTES

[1] Royal Commission on Banking and Finance, *Report,* p. 362.

[2] *Ibid.,* p. 378.

[3] *Ibid.,* p. 364.

[4] While several pieces of legislation are involved, including revisions to the *Bank Act,* the *Quebec Savings Bank Act,* and the *Bank of Canada Act,* and the passage of a new law, the *Canada Deposits Insurance Act,* we can refer to them collectively as the *Bank Acts of 1967.*

[5] Royal Commission on Banking and Finance, *Report,* pp. 301-302.

[6] *Ibid.,* p. 303.

[7] *Ibid.,* p. 312.

[8] Ontario, *Report of the Royal Commission to Investigate Trading in the Shares of Windfall Oils and Mines Limited,* (Toronto, 1965), p. 105.

[9] We have excluded *La Banque Populaire* from all of these discussions. As we have already noted, *La Banque Populaire* was created out of one of the Quebec savings banks in early 1969. However, in mid-1970 it was merged with *La Banque Provinciale du Canada.*

[10] Royal Commission on Banking and Finance, *Report,* p. 369.

[11] *Ibid.,* p. 127.

[12] *Ibid.,* p. 369-370.

[13] Canada, House of Commons, Standing Committee on Banking and Commerce, *Proceedings, Decennial Revision of the Bank Act* (Twenty Second Parliament, First Session, 1954), p. 253.

[14] *Ibid.,* p. 234.

[15] The Canadian Bankers' Association, *Submission to the Royal Commission on Banking and Finance* (July 1962), p. 157.

[16] Royal Commission on Banking and Finance, *Report,* pp. 120-121.

[17] Barclay's Bank of Canada was established in 1929 by the English bank of the same name. It was purchased by the Imperial Bank of Canada in 1953. The Mercantile Bank of Canada was established by the National Handelsbank of Holland in 1953. The original bill to establish the Bank of British Columbia (introduced in the Senate in 1964) was sponsored by the government of the province, which had commited itself to purchasing 25% of the initial issue of shares. As a result of federal government opposition, the bill was withdrawn and a new one introduced in 1966 omitting provincial government participation, but with the same group of provisional directors. The initial success of the bank in raising capital funds and attracting deposits was undoubtedly in part a result of its provincial identification. Two other bills to incorporate new banks were

introduced into Parliament in 1964. In one case — the proposed Laurentide Bank — the bill was withdrawn when the parent finance company experienced financial difficulties. The other, the Bank of Western Canada, was passed, but following a disagreement among its sponsors and financial problems encountered by its parent finance company, it was decided to wind up the bank before it ever opened for business.

[18] Canada, House of Commons, Standing Committee on Finance, Trade and Economic Affairs, *Proceedings, Decennial Revision of the Bank Acts,* (February 7, 1967), p. 1739.

[19] Canada, House of Commons, Standing Committee on Banking and Commerce, *Proceedings, Decennial Revision of the Bank Act,* May 13, 1954.

[20] These are minimum requirements. The authorities can require more capital for a new bank, and in practice many state and federal authorities appear to do so. Thus, in a study of banking in Illinois, it was reported: "The statutory minima bear no relationship to recent practice. Both the State authorities and the F.D.I.C. regard the statutory capital requirements as far too low." I. Schweiger and J. S. McGee, "Chicago Banking," in *The Journal of Business,* Vol. 34, (July 1961), p. 297.

[21] J. M. Guttentag and E. S. Herman, "Banking Structure and Performance," in *The Bulletin,* New York University, Graduate School of Business Administration, Institute of Finance No. 41/43 (Feb. 1967), p. 118.

[22] *Ibid.,* pp. 114-123; 181-196; F. W. Bell and N. B. Murphy, *Costs in Commercial Banking: A Quantitative Analysis of Bank Behaviour and its Relation to Bank Regulation,* Federal Reserve Bank of Boston, Research Report No. 41 (1968).

[23] Some of these figures are estimates only. One of the side effects of the decentralization of responsibility for the chartering and supervision of financial institutions is that in many categories accurate, comprehensive information on individual firms —including in some cases simply a list of firms — is not available. This makes it difficult to make precise statements about concentration in each category. The numbers cited here and later in each category have been culled from a variety of official and private publications. Cooperative banks have been omitted from the discussion of concentration since the normal concept does not seem to apply to these essentially localized institutions. In the case of mutual funds, all funds which are operated by the same management firm have been grouped together as a single fund.

[24] It is not clear that the concept of maintaining the independence of banks from domination by single groups of economic interests is fully consistent with the basic policy of stimulating competition. The provision virtually prohibits the "takeover" of an existing bank except through amalgamation with an existing bank. A "take-over" can be an effective device for installing a new, more effective management team in a firm which is not achieving its full market potential, i.e., to improve efficiency, the fundamental purpose of a policy of stimulating competition. It is not obvious, therefore, that the 10% rule is perfectly consistent with the rest of the pro-competitive policy.

[25] Following the introduction of the Canada Deposit Insurance Act in Parliament in January 1967, and in the face of a run on a trust company, the government of Ontario introduced and quickly passed an almost identical bill in the Ontario Legislative Assembly. Thus, the government of Ontario has the honour of establishing the first deposit insurance scheme in Canada. Shortly after the federal act was passed, the Ontario Act was revised to require trust and loan companies incorporated or registered in Ontario to insure deposits with the Canada Deposit Insurance Corporation.

[26] Canada, House of Commons, *Decennial Revision of the Bank Acts,* Proceedings of the Standing Committee on Finance, Trade and Economic Affairs (27th Parliament, First Session, 1966-67), Vol. 2, p. 1655.

15

Transition to Macroeconomics

The preceding sections of the book were concerned with the micro economics of the financial system. We now turn to macroeconomic problems

Macroeconomics versus Microeconomics

Microeconomics is concerned with the *composition* of economic activ ity. Applied to the financial system, it is an analysis of the behaviour o individual decision-making units (households, firms and governments ir their roles as assetholders and debtors) and of the process by which thei interaction in the market place determines a set of prices for financia instruments and the allocation of credit among alternative uses. By con trast, macroeconomics is concerned with issues relating to the *stability* o economic activity. The basic units of analysis are broad aggregates like "the money supply", "consumption", or "investment", and the analysis focuse on such variables as the general level of prices or the general level of em ployment. Monetary theory, as a branch of macroeconomics, is concernec primarily with the implications of the size of the stock of money for eco nomic stability.

The Historical Roots of Monetary Theory

Monetary theory has had a long and contentious history including many diversions into the search for monetary panaceas for deep-seated socia ills, and for a monetary constitution appropriate to fundamental reform o the social structure. However, modern monetary theory can be regarded as having two primary roots in the history of economic analysis. The first, anc in a sense the most fundamental, is *the classical quantity theory of money* This theoretical analysis is familiar to students of introductory economic as a proposition that in a static, fully employed economy there is a direc and proportional relationship between the stock of money and the genera level of prices. In some ways it is unfortunate that the hypothesized relation ship between money and prices has become the centre of attention in dis cussions of classical monetary theory. What is of greater significance in the present context is one of the "building blocks" of the classical analysis. Tha is the assumption that in general there is a *stable demand for money func tion*. As we will see, this is one of the two central propositions of monetary theory. Indeed, most of the heated debates in theoretical and empirica monetary economics in recent years have related to the nature of this func ion, its stability, the relevant variables in it, and the relative size of the various parameters.

The second major root of modern monetary theory is John Maynard Keynes' *General Theory of Employment, Interest and Money*. Published in 1936, in the midst of the most devastating depressions the industrialized world had ever experienced, this book was an attempt to develop a consistent theoretical explanation of why the self-regulating mechanisms of a market economy are in general insufficient to guarantee continuous full employment of the nation's productive resources. As a theory of how an economy could be in stable equilibrium at less than full employment, *The General Theory* has been subjected to increasingly effective theoretical criticisms in the three decades since its publication. Nonetheless, it has had a profound and lasting impact on economics. While it would be stretching a point to say that it created modern macroeconomics, it did produce a reorientation of theoretical macroeconomics away from preoccupation with the general level of prices and the general "business cycle" in favour of the determination of an equilibrium level of employment. The central analytical concept became the level of aggregate demand, and with it came a whole new set of theoretical concepts with which to explore macroeconomic problems. As one of the most effective critics of Keynesian theory noted recently:

> In one sense, we are all Keynesians now; in another sense no one is a Keynesian any longer. We all use the Keynesian apparatus; none of us any longer accepts the initial Keynesian conclusions.[1]

The impact of Keynesianism on monetary economics is difficult to summarize. In part it was theoretical. Keynes took over the Classicists' concept of the demand for money, explored and extended it, and drew conclusions which had profound new implications for the effectiveness of monetary policy in regulating the level of aggregate demand. In major part, however, the impact was empirical. The controversies over the theoretical implications of Keynes' assumptions about the demand for money produced a spate of increasingly refined attempts to quantify the demand for money function. Similarly, Keynesian pessimism over the general effectiveness of monetary policy in influencing aggregate demand has produced many penetrating empirical studies of the impact of monetary variables on economic activity. Macroeconomic model building and testing have become major preoccupations of monetary economists.

The Two Basic Propositions of Monetary Theory

We make no attempt in this book to explore all of the subtleties of post-Keynesian macroeconomic models. We want to focus on the impact of monetary variables on the level of aggregate demand and hence on certain crucial macroeconomic variables like the general level of prices and the general level of employment. However, one of the things which has been learned from the endless controversies over the Keynesian treatment of monetary factors is that they cannot be considered in isolation. We cannot avoid exploring general macroeconomic models. It is a question of emphasis. Since our primary concern is with monetary phenomena, we will concentrate mainly on the monetary sectors of such models.

Our development of monetary theory in the next few chapters is organized around two basic propositions.

(1) The institutional arrangements are such that the government (the "monetary authorities") has the potential to control the supply of money.

(2) There is a measurable, and normally relatively stable, demand for money function.

Monetary theory, in this sense, is simply an application of elementary demand and supply analysis to money. Monetary policy involves the deliberate creation of either an excess demand for money or an excess supply of money. As we will see, the controversial issues in monetary economics at present are how the economic system purges itself of such disequilibria in the financial system. How and to what degree does an excess supply of money decrease the aggregate demand for real goods and services?

The Microeconomic Foundations of Monetary Theory

Microeconomics and macroeconomics appear to be very different. They are concerned with different ranges of problems, and as a result they employ different types of analytical concepts to explore different kinds of economic relationships. However, they must not be thought of as unrelated fields of study. In spite of their notable differences, *they involve the study of the same behaviour from different vantage points.*

On a very general level the relationships between the two are quite obvious. The behaviour studied in macroeconomics is simply an aggregation of the corresponding aspects of the behaviour of decision-making units studied in microeconomics. While the points of emphasis may differ, macroeconomic theory should have its foundations in microeconomic theory.

The link between macroeconomic theory and microeconomic theory is one of the most difficult and least explored branches of economic theory. Economic theorists have had little success in deriving macroeconomic propositions from the common assumption of microeconomic theory that the decision-making units maximize something (be it utility or profits). As a result, most macroeconomic relationships must be regarded simply as "plausible" generalizations, perhaps with recognized empirical justification rather than propositions derived in a consistent fashion from familiar propositions of microeconomic theory.

It follows that any observations which we make on the microeconomic foundations of monetary theory must be of the most general sort. With that caveat, it is useful to draw together a few basic microeconomic propositions which we have already examined and which can be regarded as providing the foundations for the two basic propositions of monetary theory.

Consider first the question of the *demand for money*. We have already established that money is a financial instrument with certain peculiar characteristics. It is technically designed to be an efficient medium of exchange and as a result, considered as an asset to be held in a portfolio, it has a very igh degree of liquidity. Liquidity is a characteristic of assets which is ighly prized by many assetholders. Indeed, we have demonstrated that under normal circumstances many assetholders are willing to pay a premium (in the form of potential interest income foregone) in order to hold assets which are highly liquid. That is, we have demonstrated that in a micro-conomic context, many individual assetholders will have a demand for liquid assets.

Money is not the only liquid asset. However, the macroeconomic theory of the demand for money — one of the two basic propositions of monetary theory — rests loosely on the microeconomic foundations which we have established in our discussion of the portfolio balance decision. That is, it rests on the assumption that individual assetholders will choose to hold part of their wealth in the form of money, in part because of the technical qualities of money as a medium of exchange, and in part because money is the most liquid of assets. Since money is not the only liquid asset, however, our microeconomic theorizing suggests that the aggregate demand for money should depend in part on the yield and availability of other highly liquid assets — close substitutes for money. Some of the major recent controversies in monetary theory have focused on the nature, extent and strength of such substitution effects in the demand for money. Our microeconomic theory cannot provide answers to these questions, although it does suggest that, large or small, such effects should exist.

On the *supply side*, the relevant microeconomic propositions relate to the behaviour of financial intermediaries. It was established in Chapter 2 that the money supply consists mainly of the liabilities of private, profit-seeking financial intermediaries, particularly the chartered banks. Such institutions extend credit out of borrowed funds. But, *whenever they borrow money they create money*. This seeming paradox arises because, as evidence of the debt created through the act of borrowing, the bank issues a financial instrument which is used as money. The process of money creation, then, is but an aspect of the process of financial intermediation which we explored in several of the preceding chapters.

We will be primarily concerned with the ability of the monetary authorities to control the supply of money. Clearly, this is a matter of their ability to control the willingness or ability of the money-creating private financial intermediaries to borrow and lend. As we explore this question it will turn out that the central proposition in the analysis is one which we have already examined. That is the proposition that profit-maximizing bankers are generally unwilling to hold "excess" cash reserves, and are not permitted to hold "deficient'" cash reserves. As a result, by the manipulation of the quantity of cash in bank vaults, the monetary authorities have substantial leverage over the banking system.

In summary, as we turn our attention to the macroeconomic issues relating to the functioning of the financial system, you would be well advised to review quickly some of the basic elements of our microeconomic analysis of individual demands for wealth and of the behaviour of financial intermediaries. They are the microeconomic foundations of monetary theory.

FOOTNOTES

[1] Milton Friedman, *Dollars and Deficits: Inflation, Monetary Policy and the Balance of Payments* (Englewood Cliffs: Prentice-Hall, 1968), p. 15.

16

The Control of the Money
Supply: Part 1

The Banks and Near Banks

Our first task in exploring the macroeconomics of the financial system
is to examine the mechanism by which the supply of money is expanded
and contracted. As a preliminary step we should remind ourselves of the
nature and composition of the Canadian money supply.

1/THE MONEY SUPPLY

You will remember that our major conclusions in Chapter 2 about
the Canadian money supply were that (1) the appropriate scope of the
money concept is ambiguous, but (2) if we adopt a medium of payments
concept of money, the money supply consists of currency in circulation and
chequable deposits with financial intermediaries. Government-issued currency is legal tender, but chequable deposits in financial institutions are
more important as a medium of exchange. They constitute the largest part
of the total supply of payments money outstanding, and they account
for an even larger share of the total flow of transactions in any given period
of time. Moreover, among the various types of chequable deposits available, demand deposits with chartered banks, while accounting for less than
half of the total outstanding, are used with such intensity as to be overwhelmingly important as a medium of payments. In recent years, for
example, the rate of turnover of demand deposits with chartered banks
has been in the neighbourhood of 2 times per year. Total cheques cashed
against demand deposits in 1969 amounted to $700 billion, compared to
$35 billion against personal savings deposits, in spite of the fact that the
average balance in demand deposits during the year amounted to only
$6.5 billion as compared to $14.6 billion in personal savings accounts (of
which $5.6 billion was in chequable accounts) .

2/THE PROCESS OF DEPOSIT CREATION

Clearly, our first task in the analysis of the supply of money must be
to explain what controls the supply of demand deposits.

The Principle of Deposit Expansion

To set the basic mechanism controlling the supply of deposits in clear relief, let us assume that we have a financial system with only one chartered bank, that this bank issues only demand deposits, and that these demand deposits are the only type of money in circulation.

The basic principle by which this bank can expand the money supply follows directly from the concept of money and the nature of financial intermediation. You will recall from Chapter 8 that a financial intermediary finances its portfolio of earning assets by issuing liabilities, claims upon itself, which have particular valued characteristics (like liquidity, relatively low risk, etc.). Normally, in order to acquire more earning assets a financial intermediary must first *sell* its own liabilities. It must exchange its liabilities for money, offering them at a sufficiently attractive yield that assetholders will be willing to take them into their portfolios. However, the liabilities of our financial intermediary, a bank, have the peculiar characteristic that *they are money*. Thus, when the bank wants to acquire earning assets it does not have to sell its liabilities for money first. Since its liabilities are money, it can exchange them directly for earning assets, adding to the stock of money outstanding in the process. In other words, by the very process of financial intermediation, this bank creates money. This is the basic principle of deposit expansion. *Deposit expansion occurs whenever banks make a net addition to their earning assets (loans or securities) which is not financed by capital subscribed by the banks' owners (or by non-deposit liabilities).*

Credit Creation. It is important to keep in mind that both sides of the balance sheet are involved in this process. *When a bank creates deposits it simultaneously creates credit.* Indeed, the creation of deposits is not the primary objective. Rather, it is to add to the portfolio of earning assets and thereby to increase the profits of the bank (it follows that credit creation will only occur when a bank finds profitable loans or securities to add to its portfolio). The creation of deposits occurs as a by-product. It is the method by which the banks finance the net addition to the stock of credit extended directly or indirectly to businessmen, consumers and governments.

Money Creation and Wealth. Note that the money created in this way will be an asset to whoever receives it, but in the aggregate *it does not increase the wealth of the community directly*. In the books of the bank there has been an equal increase in assets and liabilities. The bank's net worth has not increased. Similarly, in the books of the community at large there has been an equal increase in assets (money) and liabilities (debt to the bank). The public's net worth has not increased. In the technical jargon of the economist, money created in this way has come to be called "inside money". It is money offset by an equal value of private debt.

An Example. To make these points quite clear and explicit consider Example 16-1.

Example 16-1
Deposit Expansion by a Monopoly Bank
(Thousands of Dollars)

. *Initial Balance Sheet*: Monopoly Bank

Assets		Liabilities	
Loans	5,000	Demand Deposits	9,000
Securities	5,000	Capital Accounts	1,000
	10,000		10,000

. *Transaction:* The bank makes a loan to a businessman.

Bank				Businessman			
Loans	+10	Deposits	+10	Deposits	+10	Loans	+10

. *Closing Balance Sheet*: Monopoly Bank.

Loans	5,010	Demand Deposits	9,010
Securities	5,000	Capital Accounts	1,000
	10,010		10,010

Net Change:

	Money Supply	+10
	Credit	+10

The structure of the initial balance sheet of the bank is quite simple. We have assumed that the assets consist of equal proportions of loans and securities, and that the sources of funds are either demand deposits or capital subscribed by shareholders. You should note that this bank has no cash reserves among its assets. By assumption there is no other type of money besides its demand deposits. There is nothing to hold as cash reserves, nor is there need for such reserves.

The bank makes a loan for $10,000 to a businessman, crediting the businessman's demand deposit with that sum of money. To this point, the transaction is simply an exchange of assets and liabilities. The bank gains a claim on the businessman; the businessman gains a claim on the bank. Neither the net worth of the bank nor the businessman have changed; the assets and liabilities of both have increased by like amount. However, the businessman now has in his possession money which previously did not exist. The businessman is free to spend the funds he has borrowed to meet his payroll, purchase raw materials, pay for capital equipment, etc. As he makes those payments, the money created by his act of borrowing from the bank enters into general circulation. The money supply has expanded by $10,000. When the loan is repaid, a corresponding contraction of the money supply will occur, unless the bank replaces the loan with another of equal value.[1]

It should be obvious that the bank does not have to wait for someone to approach it for a loan in order to expand the money supply. If the bank enters the open market and purchases government bonds (or any securities), making payment by crediting the sellers' demand deposit, the same effect will occur. The money supply will expand by an equal amount. Indeed, whenever the bank purchases any asset this will happen (or even whenever the bank pays for goods or services rendered to it).

3/CONSTRAINTS ON DEPOSIT CREATION

The context in which we have developed the basic principle of deposit creation is highly artificial. Given our unrealistic assumptions, there is no effective constraint on the ability of the bank to create money other than its ability to find acceptable assets to purchase. By relaxing these assumptions we can identify the constraints which actually exist.

Cash Reserves and "Excess Reserves"

Banker's Risk. We have so far assumed that there is only one type of money: demand deposits. Relaxation of this assumption reveals an important constraint on the banks, imposed by what we earlier called "banker's risk".

It does not matter what we assume to be the other money, providing only that it is not issued by the bank itself. If we take an historical perspective we might assume that it is gold or silver coin. However, in the contemporary world it is more likely to be inconvertible paper money, issued by a central bank or other governmental agency, and endowed with legal tender status. The important point is that *the bank is required to convert its deposit liabilities into legal tender, at par, and on demand.* Therefore the bank's portfolio must be managed with one eye on its ability to meet possible demands for payment in legal tender.

The Demand for Cash Reserves. This means that the banks will have a demand for legal tender to be held as cash reserves, and this demand will depend, among other things, on the size and potential instability of its deposit liabilities. The smaller the bank's cash reserves relative to its deposits the greater the risk that it will not be able to meet all depositors demands for cash. However, it is highly unlikely that all, or even a large portion, of total deposit liabilities will be presented for payment in a short period of time. As a result, the bank does not have to hold cash equal in value to its deposit liabilities, or even nearly equal in value. The bank must hold cash reserves, but these can be a fraction of total deposit liabilities.

The banker's problem in managing his cash reserve position is simply another example of the problem of portfolio selection which we examined in some detail in a different context in Chapter 5. The banker is deciding on the composition of his portfolio as between earning assets (loans and securities) and non-earning, but highly liquid, assets (cash). The larger the proportion of reserves, the higher the degree of safety. But the larger the proportion of reserves, the smaller the interest income. As in the case of any portfolio manager, the banker must balance these considerations at the margin.

It is commonly assumed that banks will hold cash reserves in a *fixed percentage of* deposit liabilities. However, if we view the decision as a problem of portfolio balance, it would be surprising if the banker chose

Figure 16-1
Bank Cash Reserve Ratios, 1892-1934*

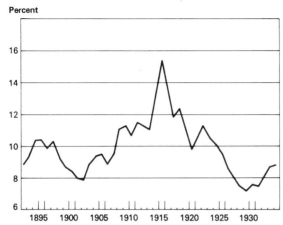

Percent

SOURCE: *Canada Year Book,* 1927-28; *Canada Year Book,* 1934-35.
Ratio of cash on hand to net liabilities.

he same proportion of cash reserves under all circumstances. A drop in the
isk of cash withdrawals (as he perceives that risk) or a rise in interest
ates (and hence in the opportunity cost of holding reserves) should induce
iim to reduce the cash reserve ratio. A decline in interest rates or a rise
n the risk of withdrawals should have the opposite effect. In any case,
iistorical experience before the implementation of required cash reserve
atios, shows that the banks' cash ratio was far from constant. By way of
an example, Figure 16-1 shows the average annual ratio of cash reserves
o the liabilities of Canadian chartered banks for the years 1892-1934. The
ange of fluctuations is wide. From 1902-1915 the average ratio was almost
doubled, while from 1915-1929 it was more than cut in half again. Moreover, an aggregate ratio, such as that plotted on this chart, effectively con-
eals the behaviour of many individual banks which had widely different
eserve policies, and the fact that annual averages are plotted conceals
horter-term fluctuations in the aggregate ratio.

Legal Reserve Requirements. As we saw in Chapter 12, the system
n which the banks themselves decided on the appropriate level of their
ash reserves eventually gave way to a system in which the government
pecified *minimum* acceptable ratios of cash reserves to deposits. At times
'e.g., 1935-1954) the legal requirement was not an effective constraint on
he banks. They chose to hold cash reserves substantially in excess of those
equired by law. At other times (e.g., 1954 to date) the cash reserve require-
nent was effective. The minimum cash reserve ratio specified by law was
it least equal to, and apparently substantially greater than, that which
he banks would have chosen to hold voluntarily. As a result, the cash
eserve requirement introduced an important rigidity into the manage-
nent of the banks' asset portfolios, and the cash reserve ratio became very

stable. In fact, it is appropriate in the modern world to assume a fixed cash reserve ratio.

By making the assumption of a fixed cash reserve ratio plausible, the fact of an effective legal cash reserve ratio thus simplifies the analysis of the banks' demands for cash reserves. It is important to remember, however, that while this assumption is in accord with recent experience, it is neither necessary nor representative of a longer run of historical experience.

Excess Reserves and Deposit Expansion. We have already established that, in our simple case, deposit expansion occurs when the bank makes loans or buys securities. However, the bank's willingness to do this will be governed by its cash reserve position. We established in Chapter 9 that a profit-maximizing banker will want to keep his non-earning cash assets to the minimum dictated by prudent banking practice. When the required cash reserve ratio is higher than that which the bank would hold voluntarily, the profit motive dictates that the bank keep its non-earning assets close to the minimum permitted by law. We can define *excess cash reserves* as the difference between the cash reserves actually held by the bank ("actual" reserves) and those which the bank is required to hold by law ("required" reserves). Then, the profit motive dictates that when the bank has excess cash reserves it will acquire more earning assets. Deposits will expand. Conversely, if the bank has deficient cash reserves, it will dispose of earning assets. Deposits will contract.

This is a very important point. It is the second principle of deposit expansion: *Deposit expansion will only occur when banks have excess cash reserves, and it will continue until the excess reserves are exhausted.* A reserve deficiency (negative excess reserves) will correspondingly produce a contraction of deposits which will continue until the reserve deficiency is eliminated.

An Example. This principle can best be explored by way of an example. For the purposes of Example 16-2 we have modified the initial balance sheet of the "Monopoly Bank" to allow for a 12% cash reserve requirement (the same as that currently applicable to Canadian demand deposits at chartered banks). At the outset the bank has no excess reserves. It is required to hold cash in the amount of 12% of deposits, and it chooses not to hold more.

In the next chapter we will explore the various ways in which the cash reserves of the banks may increase or decrease. In order to minimize the complications, we can assume that the government prints $10,000 of new currency, which it deposits in the bank, and then spends. Total deposits and cash reserves increase in the same amount, but the *required* cash reserve increases by only 12% of that sum, i.e., by $1,200. The bank has excess reserves of $8,800.

Given this excess cash reserve, on which it earns no interest income, the bank's asset portfolio is not in equilibrium. In order to achieve portfolio balance, the profit motive dictates the acquisition of more earning assets. In the example, we assume that the bank extends more loans

Example 16-2
Deposit Creation by a Monopoly Bank with a Twelve Percent Reserve Ratio
(Thousands of Dollars)

A. Initial Balance Sheet

Assets		Liabilities	
Cash Reserves	1,080	Demand Deposits	9,000
Loans	5,000	Capital Accounts	1,000
Securities	3,820		
	10,000		10,000

B. Deposit Expansion

STAGE I: (a) The government deposits $10 thousand of newly printed currency, and (b) then makes equivalent payments by cheque to the general public.

	Bank		Government		Public	
(a) Cash +10	Deposits Gov't +10		Deposits +10	Currency +10		
(b)	Deposits Gov't −10 Public +10		Deposits −10		Deposits +10	
NET: Cash +10	Deposits +10				Deposits +10	

Bank Reserve Position (end of Stage I)

Total Deposits	9,010.00
Required Reserves	1,081.20
Actual Reserves	1,090.00
EXCESS RESERVES	8.80

The Money Supply (net change)

	Demand Deposits
Stage I	+10
CUMULATIVE (to the end of Stage I)	+10

STAGE II: The Bank makes loans in the amount of its excess cash reserves crediting $8.8 thousand to the deposits of businessmen.

	Bank		Public	
Loans +8.8	Deposits Public +8.8		Deposits +8.8	Loans +8.8

Bank Reserve Position (end of Stage II)

Total Deposits	9,018.80
Required Reserves	1,082.26
Actual Reserves	1,090.00
EXCESS RESERVES	7.74

The Money Supply (net change)

	Demand Deposits
Stage I	10
Stage II	8.8
CUMULATIVE (to the end of Stage II)	18.8

STAGE III: The bank makes loans in the amount of its excess cash reserves, crediting $7.74 thousand to the deposits of businessmen.

Bank			Public	
Loans +7.74	Deposits Public +7.74		Deposits +7.74	Loans +7.7

Bank Reserve Position (end of stage 3)		The Money Supply (net change)	
			Demand Deposit
Total Deposits	9,026.54		
Required Reserve	1,083.18	Stage I	10.00
Actual Reserves	1,090.00	Stage II	8.80
EXCESS RESERVE	6.81	Stage III	7.74
		CUMULATIVE (to the end of Stage III)	26.57

C. Final Balance Sheet

Assets		Liabilities	
Cash Reserves	1,090.00	Demand Deposits	9,083.3.
Loans	5,073.33	Capital Accounts	1,000.0
Securities	3,820.00		
	10,083.33		10,083.3.

Bank Reserve Position		The Money Supply (net change)	
Total Deposits	9,083.35		
Required Reserves	1,090.00		*Demand Deposit*
Actual Reserves	1,090.00	Stage I	10.00
EXCESS RESERVES	0	Stage II	8.80
		Stage III	7.74
MULTIPLIER		Stage IV	6.81
		...	...
Deposit Multiplier $= \dfrac{\Delta D}{\Delta R} = \dfrac{1}{r} = 8.33$		Stage n	0
		CUMULATIVE (to end of process)	83.33

although it might well acquire additional securities, particularly short-term liquid securities. In either case, the proceeds are credited to someone' demand deposit, providing a net addition to the money supply.

This is far from the end of the story, however. The extension o $8,800 of loans will not re-establish portfolio balance, as is evident from the fact that excess reserves of $7,740 remain at the end of Stage II i the example. Given the fractional reserve requirement, the increase i deposits has impounded as required reserves only a fraction of the exces reserve. Thus, when deposits increase by $8,800, required reserves increas by only $1,060, leaving excess reserves of $7,740. Again, the profit motiv dictates the extension of loans in the amount of the excess reserves, an an additional $7,740 is credited to the public's deposits with the bank.

This process will go on until all excess reserves have been purge from the system. As is shown on the final balance sheet, that will b when total deposits have increased by $83,330, or 8.33 times the initial deposit of currency.

Algebraic Representation: A Simple Deposit Expansion Multiplier.
Using very elementary mathematics, it is possible to derive a general expression for the deposit expansion multiplier implied by our very simple assumptions. Let R represent cash reserves, D deposits, and r the reserve ratio (which has a value greater than zero but less than one).

For equilibrium in the bank's portfolio, there must be no excess reserves. Actual reserves must equal what the bank feels it is required to hold (to satisfy legal requirements plus any extra which it requires for safety). That is, in equilibrium:

$$R = rD \tag{16.1}$$

or

$$D = R\left(\frac{1}{r}\right) \tag{16.2}$$

It follows that if equilibrium is to be maintained in the face of an increase in cash reserves:

$$\Delta D = \Delta R\left(\frac{1}{r}\right) \tag{16.3}$$

That is, given an increase in reserves, to maintain equilibrium in the bank's portfolio, deposits must expand by the factor, $\left(\frac{1}{r}\right)$. We call this the deposit expansion multiplier. Given a reserve ratio of .12, the multiplier is 8.33. The higher the ratio the smaller the multiplier. Thus, if the ratio were .2, the multiplier would be 5. By contrast, if the ratio were .04, the multiplier would be 25.

The Constraints on Deposit Creation.
The multiplier formulation provides a simple, explicit statement of the basic constraints on deposit creation in the banking system. These are (1) the quantity of cash reserves, and (2) the effective reserve ratio.

Although the multiplier formulation suggests that the process of deposit creation is simple and mechanical, it is neither. Both the quantity of cash reserves in the banking system, and the effective reserve ratio are affected by a complex of portfolio balance decisions made by the general public and other financial institutions, as well as by the banks. Thus, the quantity of cash reserves is affected by decisions of the public about the form in which they will hold their cash balances — demand deposits or currency. The effective reserve ratio is affected by decisions of the public as to whether to hold time deposits or demand deposits, and whether to hold time deposits in banks or near banks. It is also affected by decisions made by near banks as to the level of their cash reserves, and the form in which they will be held — cash in the vault or demand deposits with chartered banks. And of course, the portfolio balance decisions of the public are conditioned by the incentives by banks and near banks in the form of interest payments on time deposits and other considerations. In the next several sections we explore some of these complications of the basic analysis.

Cash Drain

Our development of the deposit expansion multiplier ignores the effects of the public's demand for currency as opposed to demand deposits as a medium of exchange. However, in discussing the composition of the money supply in Chapter 2 we noted that currency was more efficient than demand deposits for certain types of transactions. As a result, as the money supply expands, the amount of currency in circulation is likely to rise as well.

This increase in currency in circulation is significant because every dollar of currency in circulation is a potential dollar of bank cash reserves which, if it were lodged in the bank's vaults, would serve to support several dollars worth of bank deposits (depending on the reserve ratio). In this sense, currency in circulation and bank cash reserves are both what some economists call *high-powered money*. Given the total supply of high powered money, an increase of currency in circulation will reduce bank reserves and will reduce the total money supply by a multiple of the cash drain. Correspondingly, a reverse drain from currency in circulation into bank reserves will expand the total money supply by a multiple of the increase in bank reserves.

In the example explored in the previous section we assumed an increase in bank reserves resulting from an increase in the total amount of high-powered money in existence. Clearly, if a drain of currency into circulation accompanies the expansion of the money supply, the total expansion will be less than that shown in Example 16-2. In order to see this, consider the following example.

An Example. In order to demonstrate the effects of the cash drain in Example 16-3 we have assumed a currency-deposit ratio of .5. That is, we assume that in equilibrium, currency is 50% of deposits. Otherwise the figures used in this example are the same as those from Example 16-2. As can be seen by comparing these examples, *the effect of cash drain is to reduce the monetary expansion produced by the introduction of a given amount of new high-powered money into the financial system.*

Example 16-3
Deposit Creation with Cash Drain
Monopoly Bank with a 12% Cash Reserve Ratio
(Thousands of Dollars)

A. Initial Balance Sheet

Assets		Liabilities	
Cash Reserves	1,080	Demand Deposits	9,000
Loans	5,000	Capital Accounts	1,000
Securities	3,820		
	10,000		10,000

B. Deposit Creation

STAGE I: (a) The Government deposits $10 thousand of newly printed currency & (b) makes equivalent payments by cheque to the general public. The public's demand for currency can be described by the equation $C = 0.5\ D$. (c) The public divides its increased money holdings between currency and deposits on this basis, taking $3.33 thousand in currency and holding $6.67 thousand in deposits.

(a)

Bank		Government		Public	
Cash +10	Deposits Gov't +10	Deposits +10	High-powered money +10		

(b)

	Deposits Gov't −10 Public +10	Deposits −10		Deposits +10	

(c)

Cash −3.33	Deposits Public −3.33			Cash +3.33 Deposits −3.33	

NET CHANGE:

Cash +6.67	Deposits +6.67		High-powered money +10	Cash +3.33 Deposits +6.67	

Bank Reserve Position
(end of Stage I)

The Money Supply
(net change)

			Deposits	Currency	Total
Total Deposits	9,006.67				
Required Reserves	1,080.80	Stage I	+6.67	+3.33	+10.00
Actual Reserves	1,086.67				
EXCESS RESERVES	5.87				

STAGE II: The bank makes loans in the amount of its excess reserves from Stage I (5.87 thousand). The public takes the proceeds partly in currency ($1.96 thousand) and partly in deposits ($3.91 thousand), according to the demand for currency function.

Bank		Public	
Cash −1.96 Loans +5.87	Deposits Public +3.91	Cash +1.96 Deposits +3.91	Loans +5.87
NET: Assets +3.91	Deposits +3.91	Money +5.87	Loans +5.87

Bank Reserve Position
(end of Stage II)

The Money Supply
(net change)

			Deposits	Currency	Total
Total Deposits	9,010.58				
Required Reserves	1,081.27	Stage I	+6.67	+3.33	+10.00
Actual Reserves	1,084.75	Stage II	+3.91	+1.96	+ 5.87
EXCESS RESERVES	3.48	CUMULATIVE (to end of Stage II)	+10.58	+5.29	+15.87

STAGE III: The bank makes loans in the amount of its excess reserves from Stage II ($3.48 thousand). The public takes the proceeds partly in currency ($1.16 thousand) and partly in deposits ($2.32 thousand), according to the demand for currency function.

Bank

| Cash −1.16 | Deposits |
| Loans +3.48 | +2.32 |

| NET: | Deposits |
| Assets +2.32 | +2.32 |

Public

Cash +1.16	Loans +3.48
Deposits	
+2.32	

| Money +3.48 | Loans +3.48 |

Bank Reserve Position
(end of Stage III)

Total Deposits	9,012.90
Required Reserves	1,081.55
Actual Reserves	1,083.59
EXCESS RESERVES	2.04

The Money Supply
(net change)

	Deposits	Currency	Total
Stage I	+6.67	+3.33	+10.00
Stage II	+3.91	+1.96	+ 5.87
Stage III	+2.32	+1.16	+ 3.48
CUMULATIVE (to end of Stage III)	+12.90	+6.41	+19.35

C. Final Balance Sheet

Assets		Liabilities	
Cash Reserves	1,081.94	Demand Deposits	9,016.13
Loans	5,014.19	Capital Accounts	1,000.00
Securities	3,820.00		
Total	10,016.13		10,016.13

Bank Reserve Position
(end of process)

Total Deposits	9,016.13
Required Reserves	1,081.94
Actual Reserves	1,081.94
EXCESS RESERVES	0

The Money Supply
(net change)

	Deposits	Currency	Total
Stage I	+6.67	+3.33	+10.00
Stage II	+3.91	+1.96	+ 5.87
Stage III	+2.32	+1.16	+ 3.48
Stage IV	+1.36	+0.68	+ 2.04
...		...	
CUMULATIVE	+16.13	+8.06	+24.19

NOTE:

High-powered Money Outsanding	+10.00
Currency in Circulation	+ 8.06
Bank Cash Reserves	+ 1.94

MULTIPLIERS

$$\text{Money Supply Multiplier} = \frac{\Delta M}{\Delta H} = \frac{24.19}{10.00} = 2.42$$

$$\text{Deposit Multiplier} = \frac{\Delta D}{\Delta H} = \frac{16.13}{10.00} = 1.61$$

As a result of cash drain, some bank reserves are drawn out of the banks and into circulation as currency while deposit expansion proceeds. In the example, the money supply multiplier is reduced from 8.33 to 2.42

(the deposit expansion multiplier is reduced from 8.33 to 1.61). The larger the cash drain, the smaller the multiplier and the smaller the share of the banking system in the total monetary expansion. Thus, if the cash drain coefficient were .80, the money supply multiplier would be 1.96, and the deposit multiplier 1.09. By contrast, if the cash drain coefficient were .20, the money supply multiplier would be 3.75 and the deposit multiplier 3.12.

Other Banks: Clearinghouse Drain

An additional source of artificiality in our analysis of the deposit expansion process is the assumption that there is only one bank with a monopoly of the demand deposit business, when in fact, in Canada, there have never been fewer than eight banks, and at times there were more than 35. In the United States, there are more than 13,000. Does this make a difference to the deposit expansion process? *The presence of more than one bank alters the details of the deposit expansion process but not the basic principles.*

The complication which arises from the existence of other banks is that any bank engaging in monetary expansion will likely experience a *clearinghouse drain.* That is, as cheques are written against its deposits, and payments are made, *some or all of the funds will be deposited in other banks in the system.* Thus, a bank which makes loans in the amount of its excess reserves, creating an equal amount of new deposits, is exposed to the risk that the entire sum will be withdrawn and deposited in other banks. This forces the first bank to pay over an equal value of reserves. Its excess reserves disappear. The important point, however, is that unlike a cash drain, the clearinghouse drain does not eliminate excess reserves from the banking system. *It merely transfers them to other banks.* These banks, impelled by the same profit motive, will make loans or purchase securities, initiating the second round of deposit expansion. They will also likely experience a clearinghouse drain, moving the reserves and the base of deposit expansion throughout the banking system. Eventually most banks will probably have had some share of the increased deposits. The process of expansion will stop when all excess reserves have been purged from the system. Unless the risk of clearinghouse drain induces banks to hold larger cash reserves than would a monopoly bank, the total expansion of deposits will be the same with many banks as with one bank.

Will the reserve ratio be higher in a banking system with several banks? On *a priori* grounds one would think so, although the development of an efficient, active short-term money market has reduced the need to hold cash reserves by making it possible to make reserve adjustments in the money market. Secondary reserves may substitute for cash reserves as a hedge against clearinghouse drains. In any case, it is clear that in Canada in recent years, the required cash reserve ratio has been at least as high as, and probably considerably higher than, that which the banks would hold voluntarily. Thus, as we saw in Chapter 9, Canadian banks normally hold virtually no excess cash reserves. We can assume, therefore, that the existence of several banks does not increase the effective cash reserve ratio.

Example 16-4

Deposit Creation with More than One Bank
(Thousands of Dollars)

STAGE I: As in Example 16-2. (It is assumed that the deposits are initially held at Bank A.)

Bank A

| Cash | +10 | Deposits | +10 |

Bank B

| Cash | 0 | Deposits | 0 |

Bank C

| Cash | 0 | Deposits | 0 |

Public

| Deposits | +10 | | 0 |

Bank Reserve Position
(cumulative change to the end of Stage I)

		Cash Reserves		
	Deposits	Actual	Required	Excess
Bank A	+10	+10	+1.2	+8.8
Bank B	0	0	0	0
Bank C	0	0	0	0
System	+10	+10	+1.2	+8.8

The Money Supply
(cumulative change to the end of Stage I)

	Deposits
Stage I	+10
Total	+10

STAGE II: (a) Bank A makes loans in the amount of its excess reserves, crediting $8.8 thousand to demand deposits. (b) These deposits are withdrawn almost immediately and deposited in accounts with Bank B.

(a)

Bank A

| Loans | +8.8 | Deposits | +8.8 |

Bank B

Bank C

Public

| Deposits | +8.8 | Loans | +8.8 |

(b)

Bank A

| Cash | −8.8 | Deposits | −8.8 |

Bank B

| Cash | +8.8 | Deposits | +8.8 |

Bank C

Public

| Deposits | +8.8 |

NET CHANGE:

Bank A

| Assets | 0 | Deposits | 0 |

Bank B

| Cash | +8.8 | Deposits | +8.8 |

Bank C

Public

| Deposits | +8.8 | Loans | +8.8 |

Bank Reserve Positions
(cumulative change to the end of Stage II)

	Deposits	Cash Reserves		
		Actual	Required	Excess
Bank A	+10	+ 1.2	+1.2	0
Bank C	+ 8.8	+ 8.8	+1.06	+7.74
Bank B	0	0	0	0
System	+18.8	+10.	+2.26	+7.74

The Money Supply
(cumulative change to the end of Stage II)

	Deposits
Stage I	+10
Stage II	+ 8.8
Total	+18.8

STAGE III: (a) **Bank B makes loans in the amount of its excess reserves, crediting $7.74 thousand to demand deposits. (b) These deposits are almost immediately withdrawn and deposited in accounts with Bank C.**

(a)

Bank A		Bank B		Bank C		Public	
		Loans +7.74	Deposits +7.74			Deposits +7.74	Loans +7.74

(b)

Bank A		Bank B		Bank C		Public	
		Cash −7.74	Deposits −7.74	Cash +7.74	Deposits +7.74		

NET CHANGE:

Bank A		Bank B		Bank C		Public	
		Assets 0	Deposits 0	Cash +7.74	Deposits +7.74	Deposits +7.74	Loans +7.74

Bank Reserve Positions
(cumlative change to the end of Stage III)

	Deposits	Cash Reserves		
		Actual	Required	Excess
Bank A	+10	+1	+1	0
Bank B	+ 8.8	+1.06	+1.06	0
Bank C	+ 7.74	+7.74	+ .93	+6.81
System	+26.54	+10	+2.99	+6.81

The Money Supply
(cumulative change to the end of Stage III)

	Deposits
Stage I	+10
Stage II	+8.8
Stage III	+7.74
Total	+26.54

STAGE n: This process continues until excess reserves are exhausted.

Bank Reserve Positions
(cumulative change to the end of Stage n)

| | Deposits | Cash Reserves | | Excess |
		Actual	Required	
Bank A	+10	1.2	1	0
Bank B	+8.2	1.06	1.06	0
Bank C	+7.74	.93	.93	0
Bank D	+6.81	.82	.82	0
Bank E	+5.99	.72	.72	0
. . .		. . .		
Bank n	0	0	0	0
System	+83.33	+10	+10	0

The Money Supply
(cumulative change to the end of Stage n)

	Deposits
Stage 1	+10
Stage II	+9
Stage III	+8.1
Stage IV	+7.29
Stage V	+6.56
. . .	. . .
Stage n	+0
Total	+83.33

MULTIPLIERS

$$\text{Deposit Expansion Multiplier} = \frac{\Delta D}{\Delta R} = \frac{83.33}{10} = 8.33$$

An Example. Deposit expansion with more than one bank (but ignoring the cash drain) is illustrated in Example 16-4. We have assumed a very simple pattern of clearinghouse drain. The initial deposit stays with the bank in each case, but any deposits created by the bank are withdrawn almost immediately and deposited in some other bank. We do not know what a "realistic" pattern of drains would be (in Canada, with so few banks, it is generally assumed that each bank would retain its proportionate share of any deposits created). However, regardless of the pattern, the basic point is the same. *Even if the deposit-creating bank loses all of its excess reserves at each stage in the expansion process, those excess reserves immediately reappear in some other bank. For the system as a whole the total expansion of deposits through all stages is not affected by the presence of several banks.* Each bank presumably shares proportionately in the total expansion.

Savings and Time Deposits

To this point in our analysis we have assumed, unrealistically, that the banks issue only chequable deposits. The banks issue non-chequable savings and time deposits. On our narrow definition of the money supply these deposits are not money since they are not in a form which can be used as a medium of exchange. However, they are very liquid, and indeed a large portion of them are payable on demand. While they are not money, they are a very close substitute for money as a liquid reserve against contingencies. How do they affect the process of deposit creation?

This question is actually two-fold: (1) How does the presence of time deposits affect the creation of *monetary deposits,* and (2) how does the presence of time deposits affect the creation of *total deposits?* Throughout we take the level of cash reserves in the banking system as given, and to minimize complexities we ignore cash drain. However, we must allow for the possibility of different cash reserve requirements for time and demand deposits.

Time Deposits and Money Creation. Any bank depositor is free to choose whether he will hold his funds in a demand deposit on which no interest is paid[2] but which is designed to be used as a medium of payment, or in a time deposit bearing a positive rate of interest but not designed to be used as a medium of payment. Although we have little empirical evidence on factors governing this choice, theoretical reasoning suggests that it will depend, among other things, on the level of interest rates paid on time deposits. In any case, we are interested at the moment in the effect of a transfer of funds from demand deposits to time deposits on the total supply of money and credit.

The immediate impact is obvious. If holders of demand deposits convert them into time deposits there is an immediate reduction in the stock of demand deposits outstanding. The money supply is reduced. But how permanent is this reduction? Can the banks then make additional loans, creating new demand deposits to replace those which have been converted into time deposits?

The answer to this follows directly from our earlier analysis of the process of deposit creation. *Additional deposits can only be created if the transfer to time deposits produces excess reserves in the banking system.* If time deposits are subject to the same reserve requirements as demand deposits, no excess reserves will be created by the transfer. The restriction of the money supply will be "permanent" (i.e., will last as long as the funds are kept in time deposits, or until more cash reserves are available), but the total deposits in and total credit extended by the banking system will be unchanged. However, if the time deposits are subject to a lower reserve requirement, the transfer will produce excess reserves. Additional deposits can be created. As long as the reserve requirement for time deposits is greater than zero, however, the demand deposits lost in the transfer cannot be fully replaced (some "permanent" reduction in the money supply will result). Nonetheless, total bank deposits will have increased, and with it total bank earning assets. If the reserve ratio behind time deposits is zero, no monetary restriction will occur, and total bank deposits will be greater by an amount equal to the amount of deposits transferred to time deposits.

An Example. These points are illustrated in Example 16-5, which considers three possible cases: where the reserve ratios for demand and time deposits are the same; where the reserve ratio for time deposits is less than that for demand deposits; and where the reserve ratio for time deposits is zero. The effects of a transfer of $10,000 from demand to time deposits is traced through for each case. When the reserve ratios are assumed to be the same (Case 1) total deposits are unchanged but demand deposits (the money supply) fall by the amount of the transfer. When the reserve ratios are assumed to be 4% and 12% (Case 2), the bank is able to create deposits to replace two-thirds of the demand deposits which were transferred to time deposits. Total deposits expand by $6,670, and the net reduction in demand deposits is only $3,330 (half of the transfer). When it is assumed that no reserves are held against time deposits (Case 3), the bank is able to create deposits to replace all of the demand deposits transferred to time deposits. As a result, total deposits expand by the full $10,000.

Example 16-5

Time Deposits and Deposit Expansion
(thousands of dollars)

Case 1

Reserve Ratios:	Demand Deposits	0.12
	Time Deposits	0.12

$10 thousand is transferred from demand deposits to time deposits.

Bank			Public		
Deposits			Deposits		
Demand	−10		Demand	−10	
Time	+10		Time	+10	

	Bank Deposits				Bank Reserve Position		
	Demand	*Time*	*Total*		(net change)		
					Demand	Time	Total
Net change	−10	+10	0	Deposits	−10	+10	0
				Reserves			
				Actual			0
				Required	−1.2	+1.2	0
				EXCESS			0

Case 2

Reserve Ratios: Demand Deposits   0.12
                 Time Deposits   0.04

STAGE I: $10 thousand is transferred from demand deposits to time deposits.

Bank			Public		
	Deposits			Deposits	
	Demand	−10		Demand	−10
	Time	+10		Time	+10

	Bank Deposits				Bank Reserve Position		
	(net change)				(cumulative change to end of Stage I)		
	Demand	Time	Total		Demand	Time	Total
Stage I	−10.0	+10.0	0	Deposits	−10	+10	0
				Reserves			
				Actual	—	—	0
				Required	−1.2	+0.4	−0.8
				EXCESS	—	—	+0.8

STAGE II: The Bank makes loans in the amount of its excess reserves from Stage I. $0.8 thousand are credited to *demand deposits* of the general public.

Bank				Public			
Loans	+0.8	Deposits		Deposits			
		Demand	+0.8	Demand	+0.8	Loans	+0.8

	Bank Deposits				Bank Reserve Position		
	(net change)				(cumulative change to the end of Stage II)		
	Demand	Time	Total		Demand	Time	Total
Stage I	−10.0	+10.0	0	Deposits	−9.2	+10.0	+0.8
Stage II	+0.8	0	+0.8	Reserves			
CUMULATIVE	−9.2	+10.0	+0.8	Actual	—	—	0
(to end of				Required	−1.10	+0.4	−0.70
Stage II)				EXCESS	—	—	+0.70

STAGE III: The bank makes loans in the amount of its excess reserves from Stage II. $0.7 thousand are credited to *demand deposits* of the general public.

Bank				Public			
Loans	+0.70	Deposits		Deposits			
		Demand	+0.70	Demand	+0.70	Loans	+0.70

	Bank Deposits (net change)					Bank Reserve Position (cumulative change to the end of Stage III)		
	Demand (Money)	Time	Total			Demand	Time	Tota
Stage I	−10.0	+10.0	0		Deposits	− 8.50	+10.0	+1.5(
Stage II	+ 0.80	0	+0.80		Reserves			
Stage III	+ 0.70	0	+0.70		Actual	—	—	0
CUMULATIVE (To end of Stage II)	− 8.50	0	+1.50		Required	− 1.02	+ 0.40	−0.6:
								+0.6:

STAGE n: The process continues until excess reserves are exhausted.

	Bank Deposits (net change)					Bank Reserve Position (cumulative change to end of n stages)		
	Demand (Money)	Time	Total			Demand	Time	Tota
Stage I	−10.0	+10.0	0		Deposits	− 3.33	+10.0	+6.6
Stage II	+ 0.80	0	+0.80		Reserves			
Stage III	+ 0.70	0	+0.70		Actual	—	—	0
Stage IV	+ 0.62	0	+0.62		Required	− 0.40	+ 0.40	0
. . .		. . .						
Stage n	0	0	0		EXCESS	—	—	0
CUMULATIVE	− 3.33	+10.0	+6.67					

Case 3

Reserve Ratios: Demand Deposits   0.12
                              Time Deposits   0

STAGE I: $10 thousand is transferred from demand deposits to time deposits.

Bank				Public		
Deposits				Deposits		
Demand	−10			Demand	−10	
Time	+10			Time	+10	

	Bank Deposits (net change)				Bank Reserve Position (cumulative change to the end of Stage I)		
	Demand	Time	Total		Demand	Time	Tot.
Stage I	−10	+10	0	Deposits	−10	+10	0
				Reserves			
				Actual			0
				Required	− 1.2	0	−1.:
				EXCESS			+1.:

STAGE II: The bank loans in the amount of its excess reserves from Stage I. $1 thousand is credited to *demand deposits* of the general public.

Bank		Public	
Loans +1.2	Deposits Demand +1.2	Deposits Demand +1.2	Loans +1.2

Bank Deposits (net change)	Demand	Time	Total	Bank Reserve Position (cumulative change to the end of Stage II)	Demand	Time	Total
Stage I	−10.0	+10.0	0	Deposits	− 8.8	+10.0	+1.2
Stage II	+ 1.2	0	+1.2	Reserves			
CUMULATIVE	− 8.8	+10.0	+1.2	Actual			0
(To end of				Required	−1.056	0	−1.056
Stage II)				EXCESS			+1.056

STAGE n: The process continues until excess reserves are exhausted.

Bank Deposits (net change)	Demand	Time	Total	Bank Reserve Position (cumulative change to the end of n stages)	Demand	Time	Total
Stage I	−10.0	+10.0	0	Deposits	0.0	+10.0	+10.0
Stage II	+ 1.2	0	+1.2	Reserves			
Stage III	+ 1.056	0	+1.056	Actual	—	—	0
Stage IV	+ 0.929	0	+ .929	Required	0	0	0
. .			. . .	EXCESS	—	—	0
Stage n	0	0	0				
CUMULATIVE	0	+10.0	−10.0				

In summary, *as long as time deposits are subject to a lower reserve requirement than demand deposits, any transfer of funds to time deposits will lead to a net expansion of total deposits and total bank credit.* The effective cash reserve ratio is reduced by such a transfer.

The Limit to Deposit Creation with Time Deposits. This analysis makes it clear that any transfer of funds from demand deposits to time deposits will increase the total deposits and total earning assets of the chartered banks. Other things being equal, such transfers would appear to be profitable for the banks. If so, what limits such transfers? What restricts the expansion of credit through this mechanism?

We must remember that the banks cannot reclassify accounts at will. To increase their time deposits they must induce people to give up demand deposits in favour of time deposits. The prime incentive to do so is the rate of interest paid on time deposits.

This suggests the nature of the limiting mechanism. Additional time deposits can only be gained by offering higher interest rates on time deposits. This increases the opportunity cost (the interest foregone) of holding demand deposits, and induces depositors to economize on their demand deposit balances, transferring a portion to time deposits. However, this cannot be done without limit or without inconvenience and cost to the depositor. Demand deposits are mainly held by business firms to facilitate the transactions of the firms. They cannot be dispensed with readily. As a result, the banks will find that to attract more time deposit they will have to pay higher interest rates and hence incur higher costs.[3]

Banks are business firms, striving to maximize profits. As you will recall from your principles of economic course, if marginal revenue (the revenue derived from producing and selling an additional unit of output) exceed marginal cost (the cost of producing an additional unit of output) the firm can increase its profits by increasing output. If marginal revenue is less than marginal cost, the firm can increase its profits by reducing output. Only when marginal revenue equals marginal cost will profits be maximized.

This rule can be applied to banks. Our assertions about the cost to the bank of attracting more time deposits can be interpreted to mean time deposits are subject to rising marginal cost. The additional earning asset which can be acquired as a result of the increase in time deposits produce an increase in interest income (marginal revenue). It is only profitable then, for the bank to strive for higher levels of time deposits if the expected marginal revenue exceeds anticipated marginal cost. With rising marginal cost, and a given yield on new earning assets, this establishes a definite limit to the share of time deposits in the total deposits of the banking system.

In short, *the limit to credit creation through the time deposit mechanism lies in the increasing cost of attracting additional time deposits.* Attempts to expand time deposits beyond some point will simply not be profitable.

Time Deposits and the Money Multiplier. This analysis of the impact of time deposits on deposit creation assumed a single lump-sum transfer of funds from demand deposits to time deposits (perhaps in response to a change in interest rates; perhaps for a variety of other reasons). What if there is a systematic relationship between demand deposits and time deposits? For example, what if, other things being equal, some fraction of any increase of demand deposits is normally transferred to time deposits

It should be obvious from what has gone before that such a relationship between time deposits and demand deposits will alter the size of the deposit multiplier. As long as time deposits are subject to reserve requirements, any transfer of funds from demand deposits to time deposits will reduce the amount of demand deposits which can be created on the basis of a given increase in bank reserves. The money supply multiplier will be reduced. At the same time, if the reserve ratio applied to time deposits less than that applied to demand deposits, any such transfer will increase the total deposits of the banking system. What we might call the total deposit multiplier will be increased. The smaller the reserve ratio applied to time deposits the larger the money supply multiplier and the total deposit multiplier. At the extreme, if the reserve ratio for time deposits zero the money supply multiplier will be the same as if time deposits did not exist.

These points are explored in the Appendix to this chapter.

Secondary Reserve Requirements

Throughout this analysis of the deposit expansion mechanism we have implicitly assumed that all of the reserves held by the banks, either as a hedge against banker's risk or to conform to legal requirements, are in the form of high-powered money (either cash in the vault or deposits with the central bank). However, we know that in Canada the banks also have a secondary reserve requirement, which can be satisfied by holding treasury bills, day-to-day loans, or cash. Moreover, we saw in Chapter 9 that the chartered banks in fact hold very large reserves of call loans and short-term, marketable securities as their primary hedge against banker's risk. In contrast to cash reserves, the banks normally have substantial excess reserves of liquid assets, which, unlike cash, are earning assets. Thus, the secondary reserve requirement is less onerous for banks than a corresponding cash reserve requirement would be. Does it have the same effect in restricting the expansion of deposits?

In general, the answer to this question is no. *Unless the supply of eligible liquid assets is less than the amount which the banks require, the liquid asset ratio will not impose a constraint on the amount of deposits which the banks can create on the basis of a given amount of high-powered money.*

This is not to say that the secondary reserve requirement has no significance. It clearly affects the composition of any increase in the banks' asset portfolios, and in this sense affects the form of the credit which may be extended. Thus, it could prevent the banks from increasing their loans as rapidly as they might otherwise do, thus restricting the availability of credit to certain sectors of the economy. By preventing the banks from taking on a larger proportion of high yielding assets it may also affect bank earnings (and have a marginal effect on the incentive to more credit creation).

4/NEAR BANKS AND DEPOSIT CREATION

One of the more contentious issues in the theory of the supply of money is whether near banks can create deposits.

Many economists argue that only true commercial banks have deposit-creating powers. In this regard, commercial banks are said to be unique among financial intermediaries. Near banks can increase their deposit liabilities by attracting deposits from commercial banks. They cannot "create" deposits.

Other economists disagree, denying the validity of the sharp dichotomy between banks and near banks, and asserting that any differences are just a matter of degree, and that near banks participate actively along with banks in a complex process of deposit creation.

Near-Bank Liabilities and Bank Money. One factor in the debate is the monetary status of the liabilities of near banks. As we have seen, in the United States the liabilities of near banks are not transferable by cheque. By our definition they are not money. By contrast, in Canada most near banks have some deposits which are transferable by cheque. While their rate of turnover is not high as compared to demand deposit it chartered banks, they must be admitted as part of the money supply An obvious answer to the question of whether near banks can create money then, might be that those in Canada can, but those in the United State cannot.

This answer is too facile, however. It does not clarify the centra issues. To do so we will consider a simple example, and in order to explore the matter in its "pure" form we will assume that United States' institution prevail; that is, that near banks do not have chequable deposits.

An Example. In Example 16-6 we trace through the effects of transfer of $10,000 from a demand deposit with a chartered bank to a non chequable time deposit with a trust company. We are using the trus company in the example as a stereotype of a near-bank. Several specia assumptions are involved in the example, each of which is based on th characteristics of trust companies and their role in the financial systen which we identified in Chapter 10. Two assumptions are particularly im portant.

Example 16-6
Deposit Creation by Near Banks: Case 1
(Thousands of Dollars)

STAGE I: $10 thousand is transferred from DEMAND DEPOSITS with chartere banks to time deposits with a trust company. The trust company deposi the funds in its demand deposit with its banker.

Trust Co.		Bank		Public	
Reserves	Deposits +10	Deposits		Deposits	
Deposits		Public −10		Bank −10	
+10		Trust +10		Trust +10	

The Trust Company desires to maintain cash reserves in the form c correspondent balances with its banker in the amount of 4% of its depos liabilities.

	Public Deposits (net change)				Reserve Position (cumulative change to the end of Stage I)		
	Trust Co.	Bank	Total		Trust Co.	Bank	Tot.
Stage I	+10	−10	0	Total Deposits	+10	0	+10
				Reserves			
				Actual	+10	0	+10
				Desired	+ 0.4	0	+ 0.4
				EXCESS	+ 9.6	0	+ 9.6

STAGE II: The Trust Company makes mortgage loans in the amount of its exce reserves. The $9.6 thousand is deposited in *demand deposits* of the gener public, entering general circulation.

Trust Co.		Bank		Public	
Reserves Deposits 　　−9.6 Loans　+9.6		Deposits Trust　−9.6 Public +9.6	Deposits Bank　+9.6	Loans　+9.6	

Public Deposits (net change)				Reserve Position (cumulative change to the end of Stage II)			
	Trust Co.	Bank	Total		Trust Co.	Bank	Total
Stage I	+10	−10	0	Total Deposits	+10	0	+10
Stage II	0	+ 9.6	+9.6	Reserves			
				Actual	+ 0.4	0	+ 0.4
CUMULATIVE	+10	− 0.4	+9.6	Desired	+ 0.4	0	+ 0.4
				EXCESS	0	0	0

The first crucial assumption is that trust companies keep any addition to their cash reserves in the form of a deposit with chartered banks. This is quite realistic. Currency in their vaults — the only other method of holding cash reserves — is typically a very small portion of total cash holdings of trust companies. For the purposes of the example we have arbitrarily assumed a fixed reserve ratio of 4% for all trust company deposits, the same ratio as we employed earlier for time deposits with chartered banks. Recent experience suggests that this is somewhat high.

The second basic assumption derives from our desire to consider the extreme case posed by American institutional arrangements. We assume that since near bank liabilities are not money, when the trust company makes a mortgage loan, or otherwise invests its funds, the proceeds are all deposited in demand deposits with chartered banks, thus entering the general monetary circulation. There is no return flow into deposits with trust companies.

In Example 16-6, the *immediate impact* of the transfer of funds from banks to near banks is to increase the deposit liabilities of the near banks *without reducing the deposit liabilities of the banks*. It is true that the ownership of deposits in the banking system has changed significantly. Trust companies now own deposits which were previously owned by members of the general public, and by consequence *the publicly owned money supply has fallen*. However, since the banks have the same total deposits, their cash reserve position is not changed (they have neither excess reserves nor deficient reserves), and they have no incentive to contract credit and deposits.

At the same time, *the trust companies do have excess reserves.* Their portfolios are in disequilibrium. The profit motive will dictate that they acquire more earning assets, and in making new loans or acquiring securities, they will be adding to the total stock of credit available to the economy. In this sense, by attracting deposits from the banking system, the trust companies are expanding the total supply of credit.

What happens to deposits and the money supply? As the trust companies lend their excess reserves, they will lose those excess reserves in their entirety. Borrowers — probably housebuyers — want money which can be spent. They do not want non-monetary claims on near banks. As a result of the loan, then, the trust companies' reserve deposits with chartered banks will be transferred to housebuyers, and as the funds are spent they will enter the general monetary circulation. Thus, unlike the case of a normal cash drain (Example 16-3) there is no transfer of excess reserves among financial institutions. Because the excess reserves were in the form of deposits at a bank, they disappear once the loan is made. There is no secondary credit and deposit expansion.

The upshot is that *the interaction between the near banks and the banking system has in fact "created" both credit and deposits.* It is true that *there is a small reduction in the publicly-held money supply,* narrowly defined, accounted for by the cash reserve which the trust companies hold in deposits with their correspondent banks against their increased deposit liabilities. The smaller the trust companies' reserve ratio, the smaller this contraction will be. At the extreme, if the trust companies do not increase their reserves with the increase in its deposits (i.e., their marginal reserve ratio is zero), no contraction of the money supply will occur. In any case the overall effect is to increase the total of highly liquid deposits held by the general public.

Credit Creation and the Competition for Deposits. At first glance the mechanism involved in this process of credit creation may appear to be different from that which we explored before. The availability of excess reserves of "high-powered money" proved to be the driving force behind the creation of credit by the chartered banks. In the present case, the competition for deposits between near banks and the chartered banks appears to be at the heart of the process. In fact, however, the mechanism is exactly the same. *The transfer of deposits to near banks leads to the creation of credit because it creates excess reserves of high-powered money in the financial system.*

Excess reserves emerge because the near banks hold their cash reserve in deposits with chartered banks. This economizes on high-powered money since the only high-powered money involved in the reserves behind the deposits in near banks is that held by the chartered banks as reserves behind the reserve deposits of the near banks. Reserves of high-powered money are a fraction of a fraction of deposits in the near bank. Let us define the *equilibrium effective reserve ratio* as the ratio of high-powered money to total deposits (in banks and near banks) when no excess reserves remain in either banks or near banks (i.e., when the portfolios of both groups of institutions are in equilibrium). Then we can say that the transfer of deposits from banks to near banks creates credit because it reduces the equilibrium effective reserve ratio.

Moreover, as Example 16-7 makes clear, this expansion in deposits and credit will occur even if (as may be more likely) the funds which are attracted from the chartered banks come out of time deposits subject to the same nominal reserve requirement (in the example, 4%). The expansion occurs because the near bank holds its reserves in deposits with chartered bank, thus reducing the equilibrium effective reserve ratio.

Example 16-7

Deposit Creation by Near Banks: Case 2
(Thousands of Dollars)

STAGE I: $10 thousand is transferred from **TIME DEPOSITS** with chartered banks to time deposits with a trust company. The trust company deposits the funds in a demand deposit with its correspondent bank.

Trust Co.

Reserves +10	Deposits +10

Bank

	Deposits
	Time −10
	Demand +10

Public

Time	
Deposits	
Bank	−10
Trust Co.	+10

The trust company desires to maintain cash reserves in the form of correspondent balances with its banker, in the amount of 4% of its deposit liabilities. The Bank maintains a 4% reserve behind time deposits and 12% behind demand deposits.

Public Deposits
(net change)

	Time Deposits		Demand Deposits	Total
	Trust Co.	Bank		
Stage I	+10	−10	0	0

Reserve Position
(cumulative change to the end of Stage I)

	Trust Co.	Bank		Total
		Time	Demand	
Total Deposits	+10	−10	+10	+10
Reserves				
Actual	+10	0	0	+10
Desired	+0.4	−0.4	+1.2	+1.2
EXCESS	+9.6	−0.8		+8.8

STAGE II: The trust company makes mortgage loans in the amount of its excess reserves. $9.6 thousand is transferred from trust company demand deposits to public demand deposits in the banking system.

Trust Co.

Loans	+9.6
Reserve Deposit	−9.6

Bank

	Demand Deposits	
	Trust Co.	−9.6
	Public	+9.6

Public

Demand Deposit	+9.6	Loans +9.6

Public Deposits
(net change)

	Time Deposits		Demand Deposits	Total
	Trust Co.	Bank		
Stage I	+10	−10	0	0
Stage II	0	0	0	+ 9.6
CUMULATIVE	+10	−10	+ 9.6	+ 9.6

Reserve Position
(cumulative change to the end of Stage II)

	Trust Co.	Bank		
		Time	Demand	Total
Total Deposit	+10	−10	+10	+10
Reserves				
Actual	+ 0.4	0	0	+ 0.4
Desired	+ 0.4	− 0.4	+ 1.2	+ 1.2
EXCESS	0		− 0.8	

STAGE III: Simultaneously the banks reduce their portfolios of earning assets, refusing to renew loans in the amount of their reserve deficiency.

Trust Co.

Banks

Loans	−0.8	Demand Deposits
		Public −0.8

Public

Demand Deposits	−0.8	Loans −0.8

Public Deposits
(net change)

	Time Deposits		Demand Deposits	
	Trust Co.	Bank	Demand Deposits	Total
Stage I	+10	−10	0	0
Stage II	0	+ 9.6	+ 9.6	+ 9.6
Stage III	0	0	− 0.8	− 0.8
CUMULATIVE	+10	−10	+ 8.8	+ 8.8

Reserve Position
(cumulative change to the end of Stage III)

	Trust Co.	Bank		
		Time	Demand	Total
Total Deposits	+10	−10	+ 9.2	+ 9.2
Reserves				
Actual	+ 0.4	{ 0 }		+ 0.4
Desired	+ 0.4	− 0.4	+ 1.0	+ 0.6
EXCESS	0	{ −0.6 }		− 0.6

STAGE n: This process of bank deposit contraction continues until the reserve deficiency is eliminated.

Public Deposits
(net change)

	Time Deposits		Demand Deposits	
	Trust Co.	Bank	Demand Deposits	Total
Stage I	+10	−10	0	0
Stage II	0	0	+ 9.6	+ 9.6
Stage III	0	0	− 0.8	− 0.8
Stage IV	0	0	− 0.6	− 0.6
. . .				
Stage n	0		0	
CUMULATIVE	+10	−10	+ 2.93	+ 2.93

Reserve Position
(cumulative change to the end of Stage n)

	Trust Co.	Bank		
		Time	Demand	Total
Total Deposits	+10	−10	+ 3.33	+ 3.33
Reserves				
Actual	+ 0.4	{ 0 }		+ 0.4
Desired	+ 0.4	− 0.4	+ 0.4	+ 0.4
EXCESS	0	{ 0 }		0

In order to consolidate your understanding of this point, it might be useful for you to do the following two exercises. First, trace through what would happen if near banks held their cash reserves in the form of currency in their vaults. Second, trace through what would happen if the chartered banks held most of their cash reserves in the form of correspondent balances with each other. In assessing the relevance of the latter, remember that while correspondent balances are mainly connected with international banking operations in Canada, in the United States they are an important part of domestic banking. Indeed, in some states, state banks can count correspondent balances as part of their required cash reserves.

Limits on Near-Bank Credit Creation. This analysis demonstrates that any transfer of funds from banks to near banks will lead to an expansion of the supply of credit and the stock of liquid assets in the economy. We have seen that the amount of credit which can be created from any given transfer is strictly limited by the reserve ratios of the banks and near banks. However, we have not established that there is any limit to the amount of funds which will be transferred. Will such transfers go on indefinitely? What limits the ability of the near banks to attract deposits and expand credit?

The answer is exactly the same as that which we developed in the case of time deposits at chartered banks. It is a matter of profitability.

If the near bank is to gain more deposits it must persuade depositors to shift their accounts. To do this, it must offer terms which are sufficiently attractive to depositors to induce them to alter their banking habits. This may involve many factors in addition to interest rates paid on deposits including such conditions as the location of branches, the hours of business at branch offices, service charges on accounts, advertising, gifts for opening new accounts, etc. To all of this, the banks can be expected to respond in some degree. As a result, the near banks can only obtain more deposits by being successful in a process of competitive bidding, and in doing so they will encounter rising costs. In brief, *near bank deposits are subject to rising marginal costs.*

Given the yield which can be expected on new assets acquired by the near bank — marginal revenue — there is some point beyond which the competition for deposits is no longer profitable. Thus, competition for more deposits will only appear profitable if expected marginal revenue exceeds marginal cost. When marginal revenue equals marginal cost equilibrium will have been established, including an equilibrium distribution of deposits between banks and near banks.

This, then, establishes the limit to credit creation by near banks. It is inherent in the profit motive.

5/SUMMARY

In this chapter we have explored the mechanics of the creation of deposits and credit in the private sector of the financial system. What have we established?

First, we have shown that *the creation of deposits and the creation of credit are intimately connected.* One is the obverse of the other. Thus deposit expansion occurs as financial institutions make net additions to their total assets, i.e., as they increase the volume of credit extended to the economy.

Second, we have demonstrated that, given the rules under which financial institutions must operate (e.g., legal reserve requirements), and management policies of financial institutions, *the quantity of "high-powered money" available in the financial system is the basic determinant of the stock of deposits and credit.* Any increase in the quantity of high-powered money will lead to a multiple increase in deposits and credit.

Third, underlying all of this, and providing *the driving force, is the striving of financial intermediaries to maximize profits,* subject to the constraints imposed on them by the monetary authorities (i.e., reserve requirements) and subject to the willingness of the public to hold various types of claims on financial intermediaries. The profit motive induces the chartered banks to pare their excess cash reserves to the minimum consistent with legal requirements and prudent banking practices. This behaviour is basic to the multiple expansion of deposits. The profit motive also determines the extent to which banks and near banks will compete for time deposits. When time deposits are subjected to lower effective reserve requirements — and particularly when near banks hold their reserves as deposits with banks — any increase in time deposits in banks or near banks will expand the supply of credit and deposits.

Under any given set of circumstances — given the quantity of high-powered money, individual preferences as between time and demand deposits, and the general level of interest rates and demands for credit — there will be a determinate level of credit and deposits at which the portfolios of all financial institutions will be in equilibrium. Change any of these determinants and the equilibrium quantities will change.

The Supply of High-Powered Money. All of our analysis in this chapter has taken the supply of high-powered money as given. We have not explored the determinants of the quantity of high-powered money, although clearly this is a crucial consideration in determining the total supply of deposits and credit. That is the subject of the next two chapters. As we will see, even our implicit assumption in this chapter that the quantity of high-powered money is beyond influence by private financial institutions is not quite correct.

APPENDIX

MONEY SUPPLY MULTIPLIERS

It is customary to develop the analysis of the creation of money by means of money supply multipliers of varying degrees of complexity. The purpose of this appendix is to review some basic multiplier models.

1/THE RELEVANCE OF MULTIPLIER MODELS

It is possible to develop a great variety of multiplier models, each one more complex than the other. The important question is: Do they have any relevance? Or are they just toys, designed to show off (very elementary) algebraic virtuosity?

Complex multipliers make an important point, although there is a major danger in using this approach to the analysis of the determination of the money supply.

The danger of the multiplier approach to the analysis of the supply of money and credit is that it seems to suggest that the expansion (or contraction) of the supplies of money and credit is a simple *mechanical* process. A complex multiplier, constructed from several ratios, regulates the relationship between changes in the quantity of high-powered money and changes in the supply of money and credit in the economy, just as the gears in an automobile regulate the relationship between the speed of the engine and the speed of the wheels. This mechanical analogy is unfortunate. It assumes constant things which are demonstrably not constant.

Each of the ratios involved in the more complex forms of the multipliers is in fact an assumption about the behaviour of participants in the financial system. Thus, the reserve ratios are presumed to represent decisions made by banks with respect to the level of their cash reserves, and the cash drain coefficient and the time deposit coefficient represent decisions made by members of the public as to the form in which they are going to hold liquid assets (currency, time deposits or demand deposits). The complex multipliers make a very important point by emphasizing that the demands for currency and time deposits are relevant to the deposit expansion process. However, it is unreasonable to assume that these instruments are always held in portfolios in fixed proportions to each other, regardless of the level of interest rates and regardless of the level of income. Recent research suggests that portfolio balance decisions are much more complicated than that.

As a result, *we can only take the multiplier model as a first approximation to a much more complicated model of portfolio selection, incorporating a great variety of other factors explaining the critical ratios.*

2/THE BASIC MULTIPLIER

In the text we developed the formula for the basic deposit expansion multiplier, assuming only one type of deposit (demand deposits) and ignoring cash drain.

$$D = R \left(\frac{1}{r} \right) \tag{16.2}$$

We developed this multiplier from the basic equilibrium condition that there should be no excess reserves in the banking system. It is sometimes developed in a different way, as the sum of a geometrical progression.

Deposit Expansion as a Geometrical Progression

STAGE 1   Currency is deposited in the banking system. Cash reserves (R) and deposits (D) increase by the same amount.

$$\triangle D_1 = \triangle R \qquad (16A.1)$$

Excess Reserves:
Required reserves (R_r) increase by a fraction (r) of the increase in deposits.

$$\triangle R_r = r \triangle D_1$$
$$= r \triangle R \qquad (16A.2)$$

Leaving excess reserves (R_e):

$$R_e (1) = \triangle R - r \triangle R \qquad (16A.3)$$

STAGE 2   Loans are made, and deposits created, in the amount of excess reserves from Stage 1.

$$\triangle D_2 = \triangle R - r \triangle R$$
$$= \triangle R (1 - r) \qquad (16A.3)$$

Cumulative Expansion:
At the end of Stage 2, total deposits have increased:

$$\triangle D_1 + \triangle D_2 = \triangle R + \triangle R (1 - r) \qquad (16A.4)$$

Excess Reserves:
At the end of Stage 2, excess reserves remain in the amount of:

$$R_e (3) = R_e (2) - r \ [R_e (1)]$$
$$= \triangle R (1 - r) - r \ [\triangle R (1 - r)^2]$$
$$= \triangle R (1 - r)^2 \qquad (16A.5)$$

STAGE 3   Loans are made, and deposits created, in the amount of the excess reserves from Stage 2.

$$\triangle D_3 = \triangle R (1 - r)^2 \qquad (16A.6)$$

Cumulative Expansion:

$$\triangle D_1 + \triangle D_2 + \triangle D_3 = \triangle R + \triangle R (1 - r) + \triangle R (1 - r)^2 \qquad (16A.7)$$

Excess Reserves:

$$R_e (3) = R_e (2) - r \ [R_e (2)]$$
$$= \triangle R (1 - r)^2 - r \ [\triangle R (1 - r)^2]$$
$$= \triangle R (1 - r)^2 \ (1 - r)$$
$$= \triangle R (1 - r)^3 \qquad (16A.8)$$

STAGE n

Cumulative Expansion:
If we allow this process to continue for n periods, the cumulative expansion of deposits appears as the sum of a geometric progression, with

first term R and common ratio $(1-r)$. It is shown in elementary algebra that the sum of such a geometric series is:

$$\triangle D = \frac{\triangle R \quad [1 - (1-r)^n]}{1 - (1-r)} \tag{16A.9}$$

Excess reserves will remain until n approaches infinity, and hence $(1-r)^n$ approaches zero. The expression for the cumulative expansion of deposits then becomes:

$$\triangle D = \triangle R \left[\frac{1}{1 - (1-r)} \right]$$
$$= \triangle R \left(\frac{1}{r} \right) \tag{16A.10}$$

The deposit expansion multiplier is $\left(\dfrac{1}{r} \right)$.

3/THE MULTIPLIER WITH CASH DRAIN

The basic multiplier focuses attention on the cash of the banking system, on the assumption that these reserves are not drained out of the banks in the process of deposit expansion. However, bank reserves and currency in circulation are interchangeable. As the money supply expands, some bank reserves are likely to be drawn into circulation. The second deposit expansion multiplier takes such a cash drain into account.

While there are both long-term trends and short-term fluctuations in the relationship between currency and demand deposits, as a first approximation we can assume that there will normally be a fixed ratio (c) between currency (C) and demand deposits (D). That is, in equilibrium we assume.

$$C = cD \tag{16A.11}$$

From our definition of high-powered money (H), we know that:

$$H = C + R$$
$$= cD + R \tag{16A.12}$$

Or,

$$R = H - cD \tag{16A.13}$$

But we also know that:

$$D = R \left(\frac{1}{r} \right) \tag{16.2}$$

Therefore,

$$D = (H - cD)\frac{1}{r} \tag{16A.14}$$

Reorganizing, we get

$$D = H\left(\frac{1}{r + c}\right) \qquad (16A.15)$$

In other words, in order to maintain equilibrium in the face of an increase in high-powered money (which may be used either for bank reserves or currency for circulation) total deposits must increase by a factor of $\left(\frac{1}{r+c}\right)$. This is a modified *deposit expansion multiplier*, allowing for an increase in currency in circulation as the money supply expands. Gixen the same reserve ratio, this multiplier is smaller than the basic multiplier.

It should be noted, however, that the total expansion of the *money supply* is somewhat *greater* than the expansion of deposits. The money supply (M) is composed of both deposits and currency in circulation. That is,

$$M = C + D \qquad (16A.16)$$

On the assumption of proportionality between currency in circulation and demand deposits,

$$\begin{aligned} M &= cD + D \\ &= D\,(1 + c) \end{aligned} \qquad (16A.17)$$

Substituting 16A.15 in 16A.17:

$$\begin{aligned} M &= \left(\frac{H}{r + c}\right)\,(1 + c) \\ &= H\left[\frac{1 + c}{r + c}\right] \end{aligned} \qquad (16A.18)$$

The expression in square brackets is the equilibrium *money supply expansion multiplier*, allowing for cash drain.

4/THE MULTIPLIER WITH TIME DEPOSITS

As we noted in the text, if a portion of any increase in demand deposits is automatically drawn into time deposits with a lower cash reserve ratio it becomes necessary to distinguish between the money supply multiplier and the total deposit multiplier, and the relationship between demand deposits and time deposits has a complicated effect on the size of these multipliers. For the purposes of the following analysis we are ignoring the complications introduced by cash drain, and are assuming a simple proportional relationhip between time deposits (T) and demand deposits (D). That is:

$$T = tD \qquad (16A.19)$$

Let the reserve ratio applicable to time deposits be r_t and that applicable to demand deposits be r_d, where:

$$0 < r_t < r_d < 1 \tag{16A.20}$$

In equilibrium, total reserves (R) will be divided between demand deposits and time deposits such that no excess reserves remain. That is,

$$R = r_d D + r_t T \tag{16A.21}$$

Substituting

$$
\begin{aligned}
R &= r_d D + r_t \,(tD) \\
&= D \; [r_d + r_t t]
\end{aligned}
\tag{16A.22}
$$

or:

$$D = R\left[\frac{1}{r_d + r_t t}\right] \tag{16A.23}$$

The expression in square brackets is the *demand deposit multiplier,* allowing for time deposits. As long as $t > 0$, or $r_t > 0$, then:

$$\frac{1}{r_d} \; > \; \frac{1}{r_d + r_t t} \tag{16A.24}$$

That is, if positive cash reserves are maintained behind time deposits, the drain of funds into time deposits will reduce the demand deposit multiplier.

The total deposit multiplier will be greater than this. Total deposits are the sum of demand deposits and time deposits.

From 16A.23 and 16A.19:

$$
\begin{aligned}
D + T &= R\left[\frac{1}{r_d + r_t t}\right] + tR\left[\frac{1}{r_d + r_t t}\right] \\
&= R\left[\frac{1 + t}{r_d + r_t t}\right]
\end{aligned}
\tag{16A.25}
$$

The expression in square brackets is the *total deposit expansion multiplier,* allowing for time deposit drain. It can be shown quite easily that this will be greater than the basic multiplier, if $r_d > r_t$.

5/THE MULTIPLIER WITH TIME DEPOSITS AND CASH DRAIN

Combining the analysis of Section 3 with that of Section 4 we can derive an even more complicated set of multipliers, allowing for all three effects: the applicable reserve ratios; the cash drain; and the time deposit drain.

From 16A.12 and 16A.21:

$$H = cD + r_d D + r_t T \tag{16A.26}$$

Substituting 16A.11 and 16A.19 in 16A.26:

$$H = cD + r_dD + r_ttD$$
$$= D(c + r_d + r_tt)$$

or:

$$D = H \left[\frac{1}{c + r_d + r_tt} \right] \tag{16A.27}$$

The expression in square brackets is the *demand deposit multiplier,* allowing for both cash drain and the time deposit drain.

Substituting 16A.11 and 16A.27 in 16A.16:

$$M = C + D$$
$$= cD + D$$
$$= H \left[\frac{1 + c}{c + r_d + r_tt} \right] \tag{16A.28}$$

The expression in square brackets is the *money supply multiplier,* allowing for cash drain and time deposit drain.

We can also derive a total deposit multiplier by a similar process. The result is:

$$D + T = H \left[\frac{1 + t}{c + r_d + r_tt} \right] \tag{16A.29}$$

For additional models see: J. Galbraith, " A Table of Banking System Multipliers", *Canadian Journal of Economics,* Vol. 1, No. 4, pp. 763-771.

APPENDIX
FOOTNOTES

[1] It is logical to ask: but what about the interest on the loan? Since the businessman must repay more than he has borrowed, will not the net effect of the extension and repayment of the loan be to reduce the money supply?

To the extent that the bank makes a profit on the loan and does not distribute that profit as dividends to its shareholders, any payment received by the bank tends to reduce the money supply. The bank debits the relevant demand deposit. However, any payment by the bank tends to expand the money supply. The bank credits the relevant demand deposit. Thus, the receipt of interest will tend to reduce the money supply. However, the payment of wages, salaries and other expenses, and the payment of dividends out of profits, will offset this. Thus, the net reduction in the money supply amounts to the value of retained earnings. The bank's total assets remain the same; its liabilities contract and its capital account expands by the amount of the retained profit.

[2] We are ignoring the presence of chequable deposits on which interest is paid (at a lower rate than on non-chequable deposits) .

[3] The banker may feel that he is attempting to attract funds which would otherwise be invested in other financial instruments, such as stocks or bonds (we will consider the special case of deposits in other financial intermediaries in the next section) . However, if someone is to sell stocks or bonds to place the funds in a time deposit, he must find someone with money (demand deposits or currency or another time deposit) to sell it to. If there is to be a net addition to time deposits, the funds must come out of demand deposits (or currency in circulation) directly or indirectly.

17

The Control of the Money Supply: Part 2

The Bank of Canada (Major Instruments)

In the previous chapter we analyzed the process by which money and credit are created and destroyed in the private sector of the financial system. We discovered several aspects of the behaviour of banks, near banks and the general public which affect the supply of money, but underlying all of this as the basic determinant is the supply of *high-powered money*.

1/THE CONCEPT OF HIGH-POWERED MONEY: THE MONETARY BASE

We introduced the concept of high-powered money in the previous chapter, defining it as the sum of currency in circulation and bank cash reserves. This is sometimes called the *monetary base* (for obvious reasons).

The concept of the monetary base implies an equivalence between currency in circulation and bank reserves. We have already seen that they are not equivalent in terms of their impact on the total supply of money. The *composition* of the monetary base is an important variable from this point of view, and one which *cannot* be controlled by the monetary authorities. However, currency in circulation and bank reserves are equivalent in another sense. They are directly convertible into each other. A dollar of currency when deposited in a bank becomes a dollar of bank reserves. And vice versa, a dollar taken out of the bank in the form of currency reduced bank reserves by a dollar.

The important point to note is that with the exception of subsidiary coinage, (which we can ignore) *the monetary base is comprised of liabilities of the Bank of Canada.* Currency takes the form of notes of the Bank of Canada and bank reserves are either Bank of Canada notes or deposits with the Bank of Canada.

2/THE BANK OF CANADA

We have already encountered the Bank of Canada at several points in our analysis of the financial system. It is Canada's *central bank,* the organiz ition and functions of which were outlined in Chapter 12. In brief, we can describe it as the bank for the financial system. It holds the bulk of the chartered banks' cash reserves; handles the settlement of inter-bank clearing balances; makes advances to the chartered banks and approved security dealers; manages the nation's central reserve of foreign exchange; and issues notes to be used as currency. In addition, the Bank of Canada acts as the fiscal agent of the Government of Canada (manages the government's cash balances, handles government security transactions, etc.) and acts as the Canadian correspondent of foreign central banks. However, the aspect of the Bank of Canada which is of immediate concern to us is its function as manager of the money supply. When we ask what controls the size of monetary base, one possible answer is the Bank of Canada. To see how, we must first analyse the Bank of Canada's balance sheet.

Table 17-1
The Bank of Canada, Balance Sheet, January 1, 1970

	Millions of Dollars	Percent
ASSETS		
Government of Canada securities*	4,018	82
Advances to banks and security dealers (including banker's acceptances and purchase and resale agreements on government securities.)	43	1
Foreign currency assets	161	3
Items in process of collection	177	4
All other assets	489	10
TOTAL ASSETS	4,889	100
LIABILITIES		
Bank of Canada notes outstanding		
In circulation	2,903	59
Held by chartered banks	544	11
Deposits		
Chartered banks	1,109	23
Government of Canada	81	2
Other	42	1
Items in process of settlement	155	3
All other liabilities (including the capital accounts)	55	1
TOTAL LIABILITIES	4,889	100

* Securities held under repurchase agreements have been deducted from reported holdings of government securities.
SOURCE: Bank of Canada *Statistical Summary*, 1970.

The Balance Sheet of the Bank of Canada

Assets. As compared to most of the other financial intermediaries which we have examined, the composition of the asset portfolio of the Bank of Canada is exceptionally simple. Indeed, from this vantage point the Bank appears to be nothing other than a warehouse for government securities. At the beginning of 1970, fully 84% of the Bank of Canada's assets were government bonds, and these holdings accounted for about 17% of the total public debt of Canada outstanding at that time.[1] Interest on government securities is the major regular source of income for the Bank of Canada.

Another earning asset of the Bank of Canada is "Advances to Banks and Security Dealers". This account reflects the Bank of Canada's activities as lender of last resort for the financial system. You will recall from our earlier discussions that the Bank of Canada is empowered to make very short-term advances to the banks and to enter into purchase and resale agreements with approved government security dealers. While the latter are not in the form of advances, they have the same effect and purpose, and so we include them in the advances account.

The account "Foreign Currency Assets" includes the Bank of Canada's correspondent balances with other central banks and some foreign currency securities. At times, changes in holdings of foreign currency securities have been an important element in Canada's international monetary policy. We will return to this point later.

The remainder of the Bank of Canada's assets have been grouped together into two accounts. The title of the first of these, *Items in Process of Collection,* is amply descriptive. It includes cheques which have been received by the Bank of Canada, either for its own account (e.g., in payment for securities sold), or for the account of the Government of Canada. In later analysis it is set off against the corresponding liability account. The residual we will call Bank of Canada float.

The *Other Assets* of the Bank of Canada are principally accrued interest on its portfolio of securities and the value of the Bank's premises.

Liabilities. The liability side of the Bank of Canada's balance sheet is only slightly more complicated. The primary liability of the Bank is its notes, which we have seen are legal tender and comprise the bulk of the supply of currency in the country. Most of these notes are in active circulation, although a significant amount are lodged in bank vaults as cash reserves.

The other liability of major consequence is the deposits of the chartered banks. Along with Bank of Canada notes held in their vaults, these are the cash reserves of the banking system, held to satisfy legal requirements. Together, chartered bank deposits and Bank of Canada notes outstanding account for 94% of the total liabilities of the Bank of Canada.

The Bank of Canada also has other depositors. Principal among these is the Government of Canada itself. Indeed, the management of the government's cash balances raises some particular problems for the Bank of Canada which we will have occasion to examine in the next chapter. The other depositors are primarily government of Canada crown corporations and foreign central banks which have business in Canada, either on their own account or for the account of their governments.

The account *Items in Process of Settlement* includes outstanding cheques upon which the Bank of Canada will have to make payment when they are cleared through the banking system. The "Other Liabilities" account is principally the capital account. It measures the Government of Canada's net equity in the assets of the Bank of Canada.

Two Identities: The Monetary Base Equation and the Bank Reserve Equation

We are not interested in the formal structure of the Bank of Canada's balance sheet for its own sake. Rather, we are interested in what it can tell us about the mechanism by which the Bank of Canada can control the supply of money and credit.

As we have seen in earlier analysis a balance sheet can be interpreted as an equation. Like other equations, the balance sheet identity can be manipulated algebraically to derive other analytically useful equations.

The Monetary Base Equation. In Table 17-2 we transform the balance sheet identity into an equation explaining the monetary base in terms of other accounts in the balance sheet of the Bank of Canada. The resulting equation is as follows (the figures in brackets are millions of dollars and refer to January 1, 1970) :

$$
\begin{aligned}
\underset{(4,556)}{\underset{\text{BASE}}{\text{MONETARY}}} \;=\; & \underset{(1,109)}{\underset{\text{BY BANKS}}{\text{DEPOSITS}}} + \underset{(3,477)}{\underset{\text{OUTSTANDING}}{\text{NOTES}}} \\[2ex]
=\; & \underset{(4,018)}{\text{SECURITIES}} + \underset{(43)}{\text{ADVANCES}} + \underset{\substack{\text{ASSETS}\\(161)}}{\text{FOREIGN}} \\[2ex]
- & \underset{(81)}{\underset{\text{DEPOSITS}}{\text{GOVERNMENT}}} + \underset{(22)}{\text{FLOAT}} + \underset{\substack{\text{(NET)}\\(342)}}{\text{OTHER ASSETS}}
\end{aligned}
$$

(17.1)

In this equation, float is the difference between the asset *Items in Process of Collection* and the liability *Items in Process of Settlement*. The remaining assets and liabilities (*Other Assets, Other Liabilities and Other Deposits*) are included on a net basis. The point of the equation is the demonstration that *any change in the size of the monetary base must be reflected simultaneously in at least one other account in the balance sheet of the Bank of Canada.*[2] Or, turning the proposition around, *a change in the magnitude of any of the Bank of Canada's asset or liability accounts, unless offset by an equal and opposite change in some other account on the right-hand side of the equation, will produce an equal change in the monetary base.* Thus, an increase in any of the bank's assets — whether through the purchase of securities, the granting of an advance, or, indeed, the purchase of a new building — taken by itself, will involve an equal increase in the monetary base. Likewise, an increase in any of the bank's non-monetary liabilities — perhaps an increase in government deposits or in deposits of other central banks — taken alone, will involve an equal reduction in

Table 17-2
Derivation of the Monetary Base Equation

SYMBOLS

Government Securities	= S	Notes in circulation	= N_c
Advances	= A	Notes in banks	= N_b
Collection Items (asset)	= C_a	Bank deposits (at B of C)	= D_b
Foreign Assets	= E	Government Deposits	= D_g
Other Assets	= OA	Other deposits	= D_o
Float	= F	Settlement Items (liab.)	= C_1
Other Assets (net)	= OA_n	Other liabilities	= OL
Monetary Base	= B		

DERIVATION

The Bank of Canada balance sheet (Table 17-1) can be rewritten as an equation:

$$S + A + E + C_a + OA = N_c + N_b + D_b + D_g + D_o + C_1 + OL \tag{1}$$

By definition,

$$B = N_c + D_b + N_b \tag{2}$$

Substituting equation (2) in equation (1), and rearranging the terms:

$$B = S + A + E + C_a - C_1 + OA - OL - D_o - D_g \tag{3}$$

By definition:

$$F = C_a - C_1; \tag{4}$$

and

$$OA_n = OA - OL \tag{5}$$

Substituting (4) and (5) in (3), and rearranging the terms:

$$B = S + (E - D_g) + A + (F + OA_n) \tag{6}$$

THIS IS THE MONETARY BASE EQUATION.

---

the monetary base. These principles should be familiar. They are exactly the same as those which we encountered in Chapter 16 in the analysis of the expansion and contraction of the money supply by private financial institutions. The motives of the firms and the details and ultimate limits of the process may be very different. However, it is important to remember that *the principles by which the central bank can create high-powered money are exactly the same as the principles by which commercial banks can create payments money.* Thus, as when the commercial banks create money, *the effective decision taken by the central bank in order to increase the money supply is a decision to increase its asset holdings.*

The Bank Reserve Equation. The monetary base is comprised of currency in circulation and bank reserves. However, as we have seen, a reduction in bank reserves will have a much more powerful impact on the supply of money and credit than will an equal increase in the amount of currency in circulation. Thus, the transfer of currency from bank reserve to active circulation will actually lead to a contraction of the total money supply, other things being equal. For this reason, it is frequently more important to examine changes in bank reserves than in the monetary base *per se*.

By subtracting currency in circulation from each side, we can transform the monetary base equation into a bank reserve equation, as follows:

$$\underset{(1,653)}{\underset{\text{RESERVES}}{\text{BANK}}} = \underset{(4,556)}{\underset{\text{BASE}}{\text{MONETARY}}} - \underset{(2,903)}{\underset{\text{CIRCULATION}}{\text{CURRENCY IN}}}$$

$$= \underset{(4,018)}{\underset{\text{SECURITIES}}{}} + \underset{(43)}{\underset{\text{ADVANCES}}{}} + \underset{(161)}{\underset{\text{ASSETS}}{\text{FOREIGN}}} - \underset{(81)}{\underset{\text{DEPOSITS}}{\text{GOVERNMENT}}}$$

$$+ \underset{(22)}{\underset{\text{FLOAT}}{}} + \underset{(392)}{\underset{\text{(NET)}}{\text{OTHER ASSETS}}} - \underset{(2,903)}{\underset{\text{CIRCULATION}}{\text{CURRENCY IN}}}$$

$$(17.2)$$

The Instruments of Monetary Control. These equations can be used to make a point of very considerable importance for our analysis. The previous chapter demonstrated the vital importance of the monetary base, and particularly of bank reserves, for the determination of the supply of money and credit. Control of the monetary base is an essential function of the central bank. However, equations 17.1 and 17.2 demonstrate that *not all of the determinants of the monetary base or of bank reserves are under the direct control of the central bank*. They are not all instruments of monetary control.

Consider first the *monetary base equation* (17-1). As we will demonstrate more clearly in subsequent sections, normally the Bank of Canada can directly control only three of the terms in the equation: government securities, foreign assets and government deposits. The first of these is the major instrument for positive monetary control. The scope for large-scale manipulation of the second and third is strictly limited. They are at best auxiliary instruments.

First, Bank of Canada advances fall into a different category. The initiative for making and repaying such advances rests with the chartered banks and security dealers, not with the Bank of Canada. While the Bank of Canada can influence the level of advances outstanding, it has only *partial control,* and advances cannot be considered a positive instrument of monetary control.

Second, Bank of Canada float is a phenomenon of the postal service and of the clearing system. While the speed with which major cheques are cleared and collected can sometimes be influenced by the Bank of Canada, in general we must regard the behaviour of float as beyond central bank control. It is normally a very small element in the monetary base equation, yet in the very short run, it can have a significant impact on changes in the monetary base. Let us classify it as a *technical factor* in the equations.

We have grouped all other asset and liability accounts together to consider them on a net basis. Again, with this residual we have a factor in the determination of the monetary base over which the central bank has little, if any, direct control. Some of the components in this sum involve longer-term arrangements (e.g., interest accrued on investments, or the value of bank premises) and others involve decisions made by outside agencies (e.g., the deposits of foreign central banks and others). Like float, Other Assets (net) must be considered a *technical or external factor*. It cannot be considered an instrument of monetary control.

In order to summarize these propositions, we can rewrite the monetary base equation as follows:

$$
\begin{aligned}
\text{MONETARY} \\
\text{BASE}
\end{aligned}
=
\left[
\left(
\begin{array}{c}
\textit{primary} \\
\textit{instrument} \\
\text{SECURITIES}
\end{array}
\right)
+
\left(
\begin{array}{c}
\textit{auxiliary instruments} \\
\text{FOREIGN} \quad - \quad \text{GOVERNMENT} \\
\text{ASSETS} \qquad\quad \text{DEPOSITS}
\end{array}
\right)
\right]
$$

$$
\textit{Bank of Canada controlled}
$$

$$
+
\left[
\begin{array}{c}
\textit{banks and dealers} \\
\textit{controlled; B of C} \\
\textit{"influenced"} \\
\text{ADVANCES}
\end{array}
\right]
+
\left[
\begin{array}{c}
\textit{technical and} \\
\textit{external factors} \\
\text{FLOAT} \ + \ \text{OTHER ASSETS} \\
\text{(NET)}
\end{array}
\right]
$$

$$(17.3)$$

The Bank of Canada, then, does not control all of the determinants of the monetary base. Since the bank reserve equation derives from the monetary base equation, it follows that the Bank of Canada does not control all of the determinants of bank reserves. Indeed, as the bank reserve equation makes clear, the determination of bank reserves involves an additional factor beyond the direct control of the central bank – the amount of currency in circulation. It is determined solely by members of the general public when they decide whether to hold their money balances in the form of currency or in the form of bank deposits. The Bank of Canada and the chartered banks are passive agents in this process.

With this in mind, we can then re-write the bank reserve equation, identifying the loci of control as follows:

$$
\begin{aligned}
\text{BANK} \\
\text{RESERVES}
\end{aligned}
=
\left[
\left(
\begin{array}{c}
\textit{primary} \\
\textit{instrument} \\
\text{SECURITIES}
\end{array}
\right)
+
\left(
\begin{array}{c}
\textit{auxiliary instruments} \\
\text{FOREIGN} \ - \ \text{GOVERNMENT} \\
\text{ASSETS} \qquad \text{DEPOSITS}
\end{array}
\right)
\right]
$$

$$
\textit{Bank of Canada controlled}
$$

$$
+
\left[
\begin{array}{c}
\textit{banks and dealers} \\
\textit{controlled; B of C} \\
\textit{"influenced"} \\
\text{ADVANCES}
\end{array}
\right]
$$

$$
\textit{technical and external factors}
$$

$$
+
\left[
\begin{array}{c}
\text{FLOAT} \ + \ \text{OTHER ASSETS} \ - \ \text{CURRENCY IN} \\
\text{(NET)} \qquad\qquad \text{CIRCULATION}
\end{array}
\right]
$$

$$(17.4)$$

Given that so many important factors in these equations are beyond the control of the central bank, can we really say — as is commonly alleged, and as we suggested at the outset of this chapter — that the Bank of Canada determines the size of the monetary base, the level of bank reserves and hence the money supply?

Defensive versus Dynamic Operations. The answer must be a *qualified* yes.

It should be obvious that although some of the terms in the monetary base and bank reserve equations are beyond central bank control, this is not in itself sufficient to vitiate the proposition that the central bank can control the total amount of high-powered money outstanding and the size of bank reserves. *The central bank can still achieve such control if it can anticipate and offset the effects of changes in the exogenous factors.* Such operations have been called *defensive operations*—designed to defend a given monetary policy from extraneous influences — to distinguish them from the more familiar *dynamic operations* designed to change the money supply with a view to influencing the level of economic activity.[3] For example, the monetary effects of a reduction in float or in the deposits of other central banks could be offset by an equal increase in holdings of government securities. Or, the effects on bank reserves of a decline in currency in circulation could be offset by a corresponding increase in government deposits at the Bank of Canada. This suggests that in spite of its inability to control each and every item in the basic equations, the Bank of Canada can exert quite detailed control over the aggregrate levels of the monetary base and bank reserves.

This answer must be qualified under some circumstances. If the actions of the central bank indirectly induce a partially offsetting reaction in some other account, then the central bank's control is obviously weakened. Thus, for example, if the attempt to reduce the monetary base by sales of government securities produced an increase in central bank advances, the intentions of the central bank would be partially frustrated. This is a matter which requires further, more detailed investigation.

We can presume that under normal circumstances the Bank of Canada has sufficient power to control both the size of the monetary base and the level of bank reserves.

We now turn to a more detailed examination of the major tools of central bank control.

3/THE MECHANICS OF MONETARY CONTROL: OPEN MARKET OPERATIONS

From the point of view of the implementation of monetary policy, the most important factor in the monetary base equation is the Bank of Canada's holdings of government bonds. Not only is this the *largest* element in the equation but also *it plays the central role in the implementation of changes in the supply of* high-powered money.

Transactions in the Open Market: The Locus of Initiative

The Bank of Canada can obtain government securities either by purchasing new issues directly from the government, or by purchasing outstanding issues in the government securities market. Likewise, the bank can reduce its holdings either by not replacing maturing issues when they are redeemed by the government, or by selling bonds out of its portfolio to other participants in the government securities market. Transactions in the government securities market — commonly called *open market operations* — are particularly important in this respect because they permit the Bank of Canada to make frequent adjustments to the monetary base *on its own initiative.* As long as there is a broad, active market, with a large volume of transactions occurring every day, the Bank need only enter the market as a buyer or seller on the same basis as any other participant in order to effect the appropriate adjustments in the monetary base.

Given the importance of the government securities market in the analysis, it may be useful for you to review the discussion of the organization of Canadian financial markets presented in Chapter 3. You will recall that there is outstanding a very large stock of government bonds (almost $19 billion in private hands at the start of 1970), covering almost the entire range of possible maturities, and held by a wide variety of assetholders, both in Canada and abroad. These bonds are actively traded in the market — indeed, the secondary bond market is dominated by government bonds — through the intermediary of investment houses which act both as dealers and brokers. The largest volume of continuous trading is in the short-term maturities, including treasury bills. As with other participants in the market, when the Bank of Canada engages in open market operations, it submits bids and offers through the intermediary of the government security dealers.

An Example. The mechanics of the process by which the Bank of Canada can expand the monetary base by purchasing government bonds in the open market is illustrated in Example 17-1.

Example 17-1
Open Market Operations

The purchase of government bonds in the open market by the Bank of Canada

STAGE I: The Bank of Canada purchases from government security dealers government bonds worth $100 thousand. These bonds were previously held in the private sector of the economy, and offered for sale to any buyer in the market. The Bank of Canada pays for the bonds with cheques drawn on itself.

Bank of Canada		Security Dealers	
Gov't. bonds +100	Cheques outst. +100	B. of C. cheques +100	
		Gov't. bonds −100	

STAGE II: The government security dealers deposit the cheques in their accounts with chartered banks.

Security Dealers		Chartered Banks	
B. of C. cheques $\qquad$ −100 Bank deposits $\qquad$ +100		B. of C. cheques $\qquad$ +100	Deposits $\qquad$ +100

STAGE III: The outstanding Bank of Canada cheques are cleared and collected, and the $100 thousand is credited to chartered bank reserve deposits with the Bank of Canada.

Bank of Canada		Chartered Banks	
	Cheques outst. −100 Deposits of banks $\qquad$ +100	B. of C. cheques $\qquad$ −100 Cash reserves $\qquad$ +100	

NET CHANGE:

Bank of Canada		Security Dealers		Chartered Banks	
Gov't. bonds +100	Deposits of banks $\qquad$ +100	Gov't. bonds −100 Bank deposits $\qquad$ +100		Cash reserves $\qquad$ +100	Deposits $\qquad$ +100

NOTES:

1. There has been no change in the society's wealth. The private sector of the economy has taken non-interest-bearing claims on the government in exchange for interest-bearing claims.
2. The security dealers will use their new bank deposits to purchase other securities (or to pay off other debts). The new deposits will go into general circulation.
3. The deposit liabilities and the cash reserves of the chartered banks have increased by the same amount. The chartered banks will therefore have excess cash reserves, and will further expand the supply of money and credit.
4. The overall effects would have been the same if the Bank of Canada had purchased the bonds from members of the general public (other than the security dealers) or from the chartered banks.

The monetary repercussions of the transaction follow from the method by which the Bank of Canada makes payment for the securities purchased. The Bank of Canada does not hold chequable deposits with commercial banks. Unlike a private purchaser, it does not make payment by writing cheques, ordering a chartered bank to make payment to the seller of the bonds. Rather, it draws a cheque on itself, and when that cheque is presented for payment by the seller's bank, an equal sum is credited to the bank's cash reserve deposit with the Bank of Canada. High-powered money has been created in the transaction, and the monetary base has been expanded. As we saw in the previous chapter, this lays the basis for a further (multiple) expansion of the supply of money and credit by private financial institutions.

The effects of a sale of securities by the Bank of Canada is exactly the opposite. The purchaser of the securities makes payment to the Bank of Canada by a cheque drawn on a chartered bank, and, when the cheque is collected, the appropriate sum is deducted from the bank's reserve deposit with the Bank of Canada. The supply of high-powered money has been reduced by an equal amount, and the monetary base contracted. There follows, as outlined in Chapter 16, a further contraction of the supply of money and credit by private financial institutions.

Open Market Operations and Interest Rates. We emphasized that in open market operations the adjustment of the monetary base occurs at the initiative of the Bank of Canada, but we must qualify this proposition.

It is correct to say that in principle the initiative in open market operations always rests with the central bank. However, open market operations cannot be undertaken in any significant volume without affecting the market price and hence the yield on government bonds. The sale of bonds by the Bank of Canada will depress prices and hence raise yields. Conversely, the purchase of bonds by the Bank of Canada will raise prices and hence reduce yields. Subsequent portfolio adjustments by private asset-holders coupled with the effects of changes in the supply of money and credit from private financial intermediaries induced by the change in the monetary base, will generalize the change in government bond yields to a change in the general level of interest rates. *The Bank of Canada is free to take the initiative in open market operations only if it is free to ignore the repercussions on interest rates.*

There are two relevant aspects to this *caveat*. The first is that *the Bank of Canada's open market operations must not be guided by a profit motive.* The Bank cannot be deterred from selling government bonds by the knowledge that in doing so it will incur substantial financial losses. Profits have no place in the policy decisions of a central bank.

Secondly, the Bank of Canada can only have freedom to initiate open market operations *if the level of interest rates is not an independent objective of government policy.* Indeed, under the extreme circumstances in which the level of interest rates — or perhaps more precisely, the level of yields on government bonds — is pegged as a matter of government policy, the Bank of Canada may have to assume a completely passive attitude in open market operations. It will have to respond to every initiative emanating from the market, buying bonds whenever private selling pressures would otherwise depress prices and raise yields. The Central Bank's open market operations then become the vehicle for implementing a particular interest rate policy, and the size of the monetary base adjusts to whatever level is consistent with the chosen level of interest rates. The level of interest rates and the size of the monetary base cannot be chosen independently of each other.

This proposition assumes major importance when we consider the international constraints on monetary policy. Under certain circumstances the Bank of Canada may have little control over the monetary base, but rather may have to respond to the securities market in order to keep Canadian bond yields within a certain range of United States bond yields. This problem is discussed further in Chapter 21.

The proposition also has importance in explaining the behaviour of the monetary base and hence the supply of money and credit during and after World War II. At that time, both in Canada and the United States, the maintenance of fixed, low levels of yields on government bonds was a primary objective of financial policy.

4/THE MECHANICS OF MONETARY CONTROL: CENTRAL BANK ADVANCES

Central Bank advances are an enigma. Quantitatively, they appear to be of minor importance in contemporary monetary systems. Even at times of peak central bank lending, advances account for only a minor fraction of total bank reserves let alone of the monetary base. Yet such advances have been the subject of a vigorous controversy among monetary economists in recent years. Defenders of the existing mechanisms argue that they perform a *vital* auxiliary function in the process of monetary control. They ameliorate the difficult situations created for individual banks or financial houses from time to time, thus permitting a more vigorous pursuit of monetary controls. Some critics argue, by contrast, that the provision of central bank credit in this fashion weakens the central bank's control of the monetary base, and hence that central bank lending ought to be abolished, or at least the arrangements for it significantly transformed. At the opposite extreme is a group of critics who find fault with the relegation of advances to an auxiliary role in monetary control. They argue that the mechanism for such advances ought to be rehabilitated to its classical position as the basic instrument of monetary policy.

Given the relatively small sums of money involved, the vehemence of the controversy surrounding this aspect of central banking is perhaps surprising. Our task in this section involves not only the exploration of how the mechanism works in Canada today, but also an exploration of the issues underlying the controversy. For this purpose we must consider the role of central bank advances in classical theories of central banking, and briefly the operations of the "discount window" of the Federal Reserve Banks of the United States. But first we must review the relationship between central bank advances and the monetary base.

Advances and the Monetary Base

Forms of Advances. There are three basic types of central bank advances: rediscounts, loans secured by appropriate collateral, and purchase and resale agreements. In Canada today, only the last two are relevant.

The *rediscounting* of commercial paper is the classic form of central bank advance. It involves the purchase from a bank of the promissory notes of the bank's commercial customers. These notes have been endorsed by the bank so that they are simultaneously the liability of the bank and the commercial customer. The notes are purchased by the central bank at a posted rate of discount from their face value. Such advances are rediscounts because the central bank is discounting the notes of a third party — notes which the commercial bank itself has previously "discounted." In popular parlance, however, and particularly in the United States, all central bank advances (except, perhaps, purchase and resale agreements) have come to be called "discounts", the interest rate for all advances the "discount rate", and the mechanism for such advances the "discount window".

In contrast to rediscounts, *direct loans* by the central bank involve only the promissory note of the bank which is borrowing. However, the bank must normally pledge acceptable assets as security for the loan. The most common type of collateral is government bonds, although some central banks will accept other assets.

The *purchase and resale agreement* is the normal method by which a central bank makes advances to security dealers. The central bank purchases securities from the dealer, but at the time of the purchase the dealer signs an agreement to repurchase the securities from the central bank on a particular date and at a specified price. The difference between the buying and selling prices determines the rate of interest on such advances. Short-term government bonds are the most common type of security used in these arrangements, although some purchase and resale agreements are also made with banker's acceptances.

Monetary Effects. As the monetary base equation makes clear, the extension of central bank advances expands the monetary base, and the repayment of these advances contracts it. The process is illustrated in more detail in Example 17-2. Central bank advances appear to be no different from open market operations. The extension of advances has the same effects as the purchase of government bonds (or the acquisition of any asset), and the repayment of advances has the same effect as the sale of bonds.

Locus of Initiative. However, there are important qualitative differences. Unlike open market operations, central bank advances involve direct, face-to-face negotiations between borrower and lender. They are not impersonal transactions in the securities of a third party which are traded actively in the open market.

Example 17-2
Central Bank Advances

A purchase and resale agreement between the Bank of Canada
and government security dealers

STAGE I: A government security dealer enters into a purchase and resale agreement with the Bank of Canada. The Bank of Canada purchases $100 thousand worth of government bonds from the dealer, and the dealer simultaneously signs an agreement to repurchase the securities from the Bank of Canada in 5 days. The Bank of Canada pays for the securities with a cheque drawn on itself.

In the following accounts, in order to minimize complications, we treat this transaction as though it were a direct advance from the Bank of Canada to the dealer — which in effect it is.

Bank of Canada				Security Dealer			
Advances	+100	Cheques outst.	+100	B. of C. cheques	+100	Advances from B. of C.	+100

STAGE II: The dealer deposits the cheque with his bank

Security Dealer			Chartered Bank			
B. of C. cheques	−100		B. of C. cheques	+100	Deposits	+100
Bank deposits	+100					

STAGE III: The outstanding Bank of Canada cheque is cleared and collected, and the $100 is credited to chartered banks cash reserves.

Bank of Canada			Chartered Bank			
Cheques outst.	−100		B. of C. cheques	−100		
Deposit of bank	+100		Cash reserves	+100		

NET CHANGE:

Bank of Canada		Security Dealers		Chartered Banks	
Advances +100	Deposits of banks +100	Bank deposits +100	Advances from B. of C. +100	Cash Reserves +100	Deposits +100

NOTES:
1. There has been a direct increase in the money supply of $100 thousand. It is presently in the hands of the security dealers, but they will use it to pay off other (private) debts or to purchase securities. The money will go into general circulation.
2. The deposit liabilities and the cash reserves of the chartered banks have increased by the same amount. The banks now have excess cash reserves which provide the base for a further expansion of the supply of money and credit.
3. While the initial impact would have been different, the overall effect would have been the same if the Bank of Canada had made the advances directly to the chartered banks.

REPAYMENT:
When the advance is repaid (i.e., the securities repurchased) exactly the opposite set of transactions will occur. The dealer will pay by cheque, when the cheque is cleared and collected chartered bank reserves will be reduced, and credit contraction should ensue. You should note that, because of the interest charges involved, a larger sum will be repaid than was lent.

The locus of initiative for the two types of central bank operations is correspondingly different. Open market operations are normally entirely at the initiative of the central bank. Advances are at the initiative of the banks and security dealers. The central bank establishes the line of credit available to each borrower, sets the conditions for advances, and posts the interest rates at which advances will be made. While it can make the term for advances more or less favourable, for example by lowering or raising the relevant interest rates, the central bank must then sit back and await the decisions of possible borrowers. It can *offer incentives* but *cannot initiate* the advances which will change the quantity of high-powered money outstanding.

In the eyes of most contemporary economists, monetary policy is *quantitative*: it involves the direct manipulation of the *size* of the monetary base and hence the money supply. While central bank advances affect the size of the monetary base, since they cannot be sensitively adjusted at the initiative of the central bank, they are not widely considered an effective positive instrument of monetary control. Rather, they are assigned a minor supporting role in monetary control.

This was not always the case. In one theory of central banking — we can call it the classical theory — the roles of the discount mechanism and open market operations are reversed, with the former being dominant and the latter assuming the supporting role. We cannot fully understand current controversies surrounding central bank advances without briefly reviewing classical theory and particularly American experience, before turning to an examination of the contemporary Canadian situation.

The Role of Central Bank Advances: Classical Theory

The central bank of classical theory did not have the same modern quantitative preoccupation. It was not thought of primarily as an institution engaged in continuous, direct and detailed regulation of the size and growth of the money supply. Rather, emphasis was placed on its role as guardian for the financial system. It was to use its powers to prevent excessive monetary and credit expansion and hence to head off financial crises, to stabilize the banking system in times of crisis, and above all to protect the nation's gold reserves from international pressures. It was expected that central banking operations would have a strong international preoccupation.

In some respects, this describes a more passive institution than we have in mind today. However, it would be a mistake to think that classical theory did not call for active intervention on the part of the central bank to attempt to direct financial developments. It was the method of intervention which was markedly different. *The primary instrument of central bank intervention was the discount rate* — the interest rate applicable to central bank advances. Open market operations were considered to be a method which might be used from time to time to make an increase in the discount rate "effective".

Role of the Discount Rate. It was assumed that the banking system would normally be in debt to the central bank, and that each commercial bank would regularly use its line of credit with the central bank in the management of its liquid asset position. It would borrow to obtain more cash, and repay debt as it became more liquid. Central bank credit would be sufficiently important to the banking system that the banks would be highly sensitive to any change in the discount rate. A rise in the rate would lead to a reduction in commercial bank borrowing, and therefore total reserves. This in turn would cause a reduction in the total supply of money and credit, and hence a rise in market interest rates. A reduction in the rate would presumably have the opposite effect.

This meant that *the discount rate was the pivotal rate in the money market.* Indeed, because of the expectations which it would create, a change in the discount rate could be expected to have direct repercussions on all other interest rates even before true credit restraint set in.

Role of Open Market Operations. To the extent that open market operations had any function in this system of monetary control, it was in support of the discount mechanism. If banks were very liquid, the money market might not respond sensitively to a rise in the discount rate. In such circumstances, open market operations might be used to "force the market into the bank". That is, by selling securities the central bank could absorb cash forcing the banks to seek central bank advances, thus driving the market interest rates up with the discount rate.

Theory and Practice. These classical principles of central banking were largely developed in England, and reflected practices evolved by the Bank of England — in many ways the quintessential central bank. In the United States and Canada, however, central banking developed along somewhat different lines.

There are many similarities between the policies of the Federal Reserve system and those of the Bank of Canada, and yet there are sharp contrasts as well. The American mechanism is very active, has been subject to careful analysis by many economists, and has provoked a significant controversy. The Canadian mechanism is less active, little analyzed, and passes virtually unnoticed in the literature. Although the problem occasioning the debate does not have a direct counterpart in Canada, the principal issues in the controversy are in a sense universal. For this reason it is useful to examine the American case first.

The Role of Central Bank Advances: American Experience

History: Automatic Credit to Credit for Unusual Circumstances. The American central bank, the Federal Reserve System, was initially established on what might be construed as a version of classical principles. The original legislation (1913) contained no provisions for the Federal Reserve Banks to purchase government securities (although a provision was introduced during World War I, permitting the Federal Reserve Banks to hold limited quantities of government bonds). It was envisaged that the Federal Reserve Banks would extend credit only to member commercial banks, and only on the security of the promissory notes of the member bank's commercial customers. In this way the supply of Federal Reserve credit was supposed to adjust automatically to meet the legitimate demands of business and commerce — an interesting extension of the commercial loan theory of commercial banking to central banking. The commercial paper was to be "rediscounted" by the Federal Reserve Banks at a discount rate established from time to time by the Federal Reserve Banks "with a view to accommodating commerce and business". In the early 1920's over 70% of the member banks had occasion to borrow from the Federal Reserve System during each year, and discounts accounted for roughly the same proportion of total bank reserves.

The original charter thus seems to have implied a passive role for the Federal Reserve System in the financial system. The supply of Federal Reserve credit was to be regulated primarily by the supply of "eligible paper" rather than by the judgment of a centralized monetary authority. Indeed, although their actions were subject to review by the Federal Reserve Board, each of the twelve Federal Reserve Banks was free to establish its own discount rate, applicable for loans to member banks in its district. The institutions were hardly designed for the implementation of a vigorous national monetary policy.

In the 1920's, some experiments were conducted with the use of the discount rate as a regulating device, more or less in accordance with classical principles. Gradually, however, reliance came to be placed on open market operations, supervised by an *ad hoc* "open market committee" of the Federal Reserve Banks. With this change in emphasis, a new policy emerged with respect to the discount window. Continuous borrowing by member banks was discouraged, with the discount window to be used for "seasonal and temporary requirements of members", and particularly to meet "unusual circumstances", such as those caused by "adverse economic circumstances in their localities and among their customers".

The importance of the discount window as a source of bank reserves declined somewhat in the mid-1920's, but nonetheless extensive use of this facility continued until the early 1930's. Following the banking crisis, and major revisions in the legislation governing the operations of the Federal Reserve System, reliance on the discount window by member banks declined sharply.[4] The volume of discounts remained insignificant, until the early 1950's, by which time the new concept of the role of the discount window in policy formation was firmly established. The principles underlying access to the discount window have not changed significantly from those evolved in the 1920's and 1930's, yet a new controversy has welled up. What is the debate all about?

Cyclical Behaviour of Advances. The basic issues derive from the fact that Federal Reserve advances undergo systematic and relatively wide fluctuations. The behaviour of Federal Reserve advances in recent years is shown in Figure 17-1, including separate data on the two components, "discounts and advances" and "purchase and resale agreements". The cyclical behaviour of total advances is obvious, as is the fact that the fluctuations in the total are dominated by changes in advances to member banks, called in the statistics "discounts and advances". Advances to security dealers in the form of purchase and resale agreements are relatively much less important.

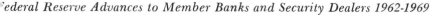

Figure 17-1

'ederal Reserve Advances to Member Banks and Security Dealers 1962-1969

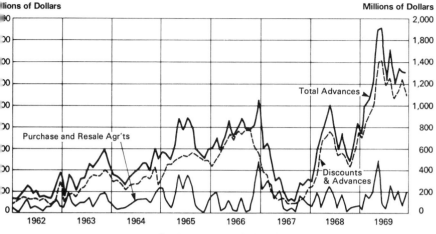

SOURCE: Federal Reserve Bulletin, 1963-1969

The important point is that the *fluctuations in advances are closely elated to changes in Federal Reserve monetary policies.* Periods of substantial increase in advances tend to be periods when the Federal Reserve is pursuing a restrictive monetary policy, using the instruments of monetary control to restrict the growth of the monetary base relative to rising demands for money and credit. Periods of major decline in advances tend to be periods when the Federal Reserve is pursuing an easier monetary policy, using the instruments of monetary control to actively expand the monetary base.

As we have seen, an increase in central bank advances adds to the monetary base, whereas a reduction in such advances decreases the monetary base. For this reason, then, *monetary policy and the discount window seem to work in opposition to each other.*

Determinants of Central Bank Advances. We cannot explain this cyclical pattern in central bank advances, nor fully understand the controversy surrounding it unless we know something about the determinants of central bank advances. Analysis of this matter has focused almost entirely on discounts and advances to member banks. We can only do likewise.

Why do member banks seek loans from their Federal Reserve Banks? What factors govern the magnitude of member banks borrowing?

To a banker, borrowing from the central bank is one technique of adjusting to a deficiency in his cash reserve position. Faced with legal minimum cash reserve ratios, prudent banking practice calls for immediate measures to correct any deficiency. In doing so, the banker is faced with several options. For example, he may call outstanding call-loans; sell short-term liquid assets in the money market; borrow reserves from other banks through the Federal Funds market, or, on occasion, through the Euro-dollar market; compete vigorously for large blocks of corporate cash balances through the issuance of negotiable certificates of deposit; or borrow from his Federal Reserve Bank. Various considerations will affect the choice, including the size of the bank (a small country bank is unlikely to enter either the certificate of deposit, the Euro-dollar, or the Federal funds markets), the size and expected duration of the reserve deficiency, and the size of the bank's liquid asset holdings. However, one of the basic considerations is the relative cost of the alternative adjustment techniques. In the case of borrowing, the obvious cost is the interest which must be paid. In the case of selling short-term liquid assets, it is the opportunity cost of interest foregone. Borrowing from the Federal Reserve System should then be affected by the relationship between the discount rate and other money market interest rates.

Several studies have demonstrated that the differential between the discount rate and money market rates is an important determinant of member bank borrowing from the Federal Reserve System,[5] but how does this help explain the cyclical behaviour of Federal Reserve advances, and the opposition of open market operations and discount window operations?

Determinants of the Cyclical Pattern of Advances. During a period of credit restraint, several forces will bear upon the commercial banking system simultaneously. In general, the demand for loans will be strong and expanding rapidly; although this may not be true of all banks. The central bank will resist the credit and monetary expansion implicit in the rising loan demand by restricting the monetary base. It should be noted that this need not imply a contraction of the monetary base. I may simply mean a lower rate of increase than that implicit in the expansion of economic activity. Our analysis in Chapter 16 demonstrated that restricted expansion of the monetary base means restricted expansion of total deposits in the banking system. As a result, collectively (there may be many individual exceptions) the banks will find increasing loan demand rapidly outrunning the increase in their resources.

The banks may respond to this situation in two ways. On the one hand they may compete vigorously with each other for the available supply of deposits, particularly in the market for negotiable certificates of deposit. On the other hand, they may rearrange their asset portfolios disposing of short-term liquid assets in the money market (and probably also some longer-term marketable bonds) in order to make room for additional loans. The liquidity of the banks' asset portfolios will be reduced bond prices will be depressed, and, correspondingly, market interest rate will be bid up.

The discount rate is changed only at discrete intervals, and then usually by relatively large amounts ($\frac{1}{4}$ or $\frac{1}{2}$ percentage point). When it takes such a jump, the discount rate cannot help but affect the level of other short-term interest rates. However, between jumps a significant gap frequently opens between the discount rate and the continually changing narket rates. Overall, the discount rate gives the appearance of a runner who makes occasional spurts to the fore, but who generally lags behind he pack. In a period of generally rising interest rates this creates an obvious inducement for banks to borrow from their Federal Reserve Banks, and for this reason alone, central bank advances can be expected to increase in periods of monetary restraint. In addition, the incidence of credit restraint among banks may be very uneven. Some banks may experience severe cash drains, and given their reduced holdings of liquid assets, may find they cannot cope with their cash deficiencies other than by borrowing from their Federal Reserve Bank or by making a fundamental retrenchment in their lending policies or in their investment portfolios. Given the relatively high cost implied in calling loans or disposing of longer-term bonds in a depressed bond market, they will be driven to borrowing from their Federal Reserve Banks. Such borrowing would occur even if the

Figure 17-2
The Discount Window and the Money Market: United States, 1962-1969

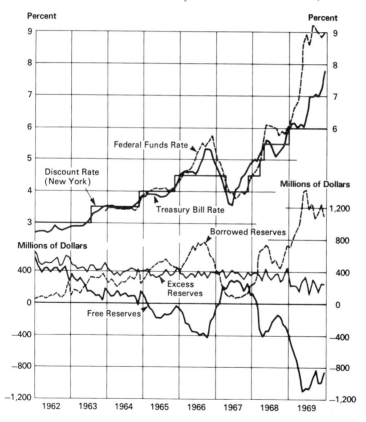

SOURCES: Federal Reserve Bulletins, 1963-1969.

discount rate were continuously kept equal to short-term money marke╵ rates such as the treasury bill rate.

In a period of monetary restraint, then, more banks will be borrowing larger sums for longer periods of time. Federal Reserve advances will in crease, providing additional high-powered money, and thus offsetting some of the restriction of the monetary base.

Some such relationship seems fairly obvious in Figure 17-2, particularly if you focus attention on the gap between the federal funds rate and the discount rate of the Federal Reserve Bank of New York (the federal funds rate is a crucial money rate, and the New York discount rate can be taken as representative of the rates of all 12 Federal Reserve Banks). As the whole level of interest rates increased from 1962 to 1968, the level of bor rowing from Federal Reserve Banks also increased. Particularly sharp in creases in Federal Reserve advances occurred in 1966 and 1968 when the federal funds rate rose considerably above the discount rate. When the pressure on the federal funds market relaxed, the level of borrowing also fell off sharply. Since these were periods of restrictive monetary policy, this seems to provide evidence in support of the critics of the discount mech anism.

The "Free Reserve" Doctrine. The implication that the operation of the discount window partially frustrate the operations of monetary policy are vehemently denied by the Federal Reserve System and by many mone tary economists.

One argument which is advanced is that the discount window is an essential *safety valve.* By providing them with a reliable emergency source of funds it cushions the impact of monetary restraint on individual bank which might otherwise be very adversely affected. It is argued that this permits the Federal Reserve System to ignore some of the harsher individual consequences of its monetary actions, and thus permits it to pursue a more vigorous policy than it would otherwise be able to do.

Moreover, it is asserted that the reserves which the banks have bor rowed from the Federal Reserve System are not really the same thing a the reserves which the banks own outright. This follows because banker are allegedly reluctant to be in debt to any other bank, including the centra bank. Tradition has it that such indebtedness is a sign of poor ban management.

Like many similar "traditions", the precise meaning of this one i difficult to define. Bankers certainly do borrow from the central bank an from other banks, when there is some advantage in doing so. However whatever the precise meaning of the bankers' "reluctance to borrow", th Federal Reserve Systems regulations governing the use of the discount win dow are calculated to reinforce it. The regulations emphasize that borrow ing is a "privilege" of membership in the Federal Reserve System, not "right". Members may borrow only on short term and for "appropriate purposes. Borrowing from the Federal Reserve is not to be a continuin source of funds to finance bank operations, and continuous or frequent bo rowing is a matter for official concern and scrutiny. (Notice how radical ifferent is this approach from the classical theory we discussed earlier.) Jnder these circumstances, it is argued, banks which are in debt to the Federal Reserve System will feel themselves under continuous pressure to restrict redit in order to repay their debt and to make a more fundamental adjustnent to their deposit situation. The object of policy will be achieved, albeit radually rather than abruptly. *Bank borrowing from the Federal Reserve ystem does not offset the restrictive effects of open market operations. It imply alters the way in which such effects are transmitted to the economy.*

Proponents of this view argue that the purpose of monetary policy is to ffect the cost and availability of credit, and particularly the availability f loans from commercial banks. The willingness of banks to extend new redit can be gauged by the level of "free reserves" in the banking system. This is a new concept for us, which strictly has relevance only in the American banking system but which has sometimes been used in discussing Canadian banking developments as well. A formal definition is:

$$\begin{array}{ccc} \text{FREE} & & \text{EXCESS} & & \text{BORROWED} \\ \text{RESERVES} & = & \text{RESERVES} & - & \text{RESERVES} \end{array}$$

Excess reserves are cash reserves over and above those required by law, nd borrowed reserves are outstanding advances from the Federal Reserve ystem.

The excess reserves of American commercial banks tend to be relatively table. Thus, major changes in free reserves result from changes in the evel of indebtedness to the Federal Reserve System. When banks have large ree reserves, they have excess cash and they are not heavily in debt to he Federal Reserve System. Because they are not worried about a shortage f cash, nor under pressure to repay outstanding advances, they are willing o extend more credit. By contrast, it is argued, when free reserves are small, nd particularly when they are negative (i.e., borrowings exceed cash eserves) the banks are under substantial pressure. They have pared down heir cash somewhat, and are heavily in debt. They must give top priority o repaying Federal Reserve advances and rebuilding their cash positions, nd hence are reluctant to extend more credit.

In this way, it is argued, the level of free reserves is a sensitive ndicator of the availability of credit from the banking system, and hence sensitive indicator of the degree of tightness of monetary policy. Refer gain to Figure 17-2. As it suggests, under relatively "easy" monetary conditions American banks will have some excess cash reserves — perhaps $400 million to $500 million, spread across all 6,000 member banks. At the same ime, member bank indebtedness to the Federal Reserve System would normally amount to about $100 million, leaving net free reserves of $300 million to $400 million. Under tight money conditions the banks will educe their excess cash reserves, but only slightly, and will borrow heavily rom the Federal Reserve Banks. Free Reserves will become negative. Thus, n early 1968, a period of relatively tight monetary conditions, the free eserves of member banks amounted to — $400 million. In the extreme ightness of mid-1969 they fell to less than — $1,000 million!

The Role of Central Bank Advances: Canadian Experience

One of the recurring themes in the development of the Canadian financial system (explored in Chapter 12) is the impact of American institutions, ideals, and developments. In some cases Canada adopted aspects of the American system, and in others reacted strongly against it. The result is a subtle mixture of similarities and differences. The same can be said of the discount mechanism.

Early History: The Finance Act. The classical theory of central banking never had serious application in Canada. Indeed, until 1935, when new principles had emerged in the United States, Canada did not even have a central bank. It is true, as we saw in Chapter 12, that the *Finance Act* provided a "discount window" for the chartered banks as early as 1914, and that this mechanism had extensive use during the 1920's. In a sense it was Canada's answer to the Federal Reserve System of the United States. However, it was an emergency measure which became institutionalized without any explicit underlying philosophy, and certainly with no conception of using it for monetary control. No serious consideration was given to using the Department of Finance as a classical central bank, manipulating the discount rate to exert rational control over the financial system.

The Bank of Canada, 1935-1955: An Inactive Discount Window. When the Bank of Canada was established, it took over the *Finance Act's* function as lender of last resort for the banking system. However, until the mid-1950's, its role in this capacity was almost hypothetical. Aside from a few wartime advances in support of bank financing of Victory Loan campaigns, the discount mechanism was rarely used by the banks, which had, in any case, substantial excess cash reserves throughout the period.

Likewise, the discount rate was not used as an instrument of policy prior to the mid-1950's. When the Bank of Canada opened for business, it simply carried on the $2\frac{1}{2}\%$ discount rate then in effect under the *Finance Act.* This rate was continued until February, 1944, when it was reduced to $1\frac{1}{2}\%$ because $2\frac{1}{2}\%$ was "out of line with the current market".[6] The Governor took pains to emphasize that this did not signal a change in credit policy. A second change of the rate occurred in October, 1950 when it was increased to 2%. Although it was announced that this was part of a new policy of higher interest rates, the change did not in fact foreshadow active use of the rate as an instrument of policy. No further change occurred until the rate was reduced to $1\frac{1}{2}\%$ in February 1955, following which the official conception of the role of the discount rate entered a new phase which we will discuss later.

Thus, during the first 20 years of the Bank of Canada the discount rate was changed only three times — in 1944, 1950 and 1955. This record could hardly be called aggressive use of the rate as an instrument of credit policy! (In order to maintain perspective on the discount rate, however, it should be noted that interest rates were effectively pegged at a low level hrough most of this period, with the result that there was virtually no active use of any of the formal instruments of quantitative monetary policy). In this context, the discount window had no clearly defined function in the financial system. It was an inactive and apparently re-lundant appendage to the central bank.

Reforms of 1953-54. On several previous occasions we have referred to the major changes which were introduced into the Canadian financial system in 1953 and 1954. Among other things chartered bank cash reserve requirements were altered and made more effective in the sense that the banks stopped holding large excess reserves, and the Bank of Canada took measures to develop an active, open short-term money market. The banks were encouraged to work close to their required holdings of cash reserves, and were provided with a short-term money market in which they could invest any temporary excess liquidity and in which they could obtain additional cash on short notice (by calling day loans or selling short-term securities) as necessary.

A revision of the provisions for central bank advances was an integral part of these reforms. By making advances available to approved govern-ment security dealers (in the form of purchase and resale agreements) the Bank of Canada made it clear that it was underwriting the stability of the market. Such a guarantee was important to the banks if they were going to depend on the market for day-to-day reserve adjustments. It should be noted also that in encouraging the banks to work closer to their minimum cash reserve requirements, and thus removing the cushion of excess cash reserves, the Bank of Canada almost guaranteed that the discount window would receive more use than it had in the previous 20 years.

The Role of the Discount Window. In breathing life into its redund-ant appendage, the Bank of Canada adopted the American concept of the function of central bank advances. Thus, in his 1956 Annual Report, the Governor of the Bank of Canada warned:

> The purpose of Bank of Canada advances to the chartered banks is not to provide loanable funds to the banking system but simply to enable an in-dividual bank to replenish its cash reserves or its total liquid assets at a time when these have been depleted by unexpected withdrawals.

And likewise, advances to dealers are not to be regarded as a continuing source of dealer finance. Rather, they are designed to

> provide an underlying assurance of liquidity to the money market and to encourage the use of the money market mechanism in the adjustment of cash reserves.[7]

However, the fact that the underlying policies with respect to advances are the same does not mean that central bank advances have the same importance in the two financial systems.

Continuity of Advances. The advances accounts in the balance sheet₁ of the Federal Reserve Banks are seldom empty. There are always some security dealers or member banks with outstanding indebtedness.

Table 17-3
Bank of Canada Advances and Chartered Bank Reserves, 1956-1968

	Number of Days Advances Outstanding		Daily Average Amount Outstanding	
	to Banks	to Security Dealers*	Banks	Security Dealers*
1945	74		0.6	
6	12		—	
7	6		0.1	
8	12		0.1	
9	14		0.1	
1950	6		—	
1	—		—	
2	—		—	
3	30	293	0.2	15.2
4	62	124	2.4	14.5
1955	98	48	4.2	1.9
6	105	62	7.6	2.0
7	59	103	3.5	6.5
8	40	50	1.4	2.6
9	53	64	2.1	3.0
1960	25	75	1.5	4.7
1	5	55	0.2	3.0
2	37	50	3.0	3.4
3	20	48	0.4	2.4
4	15	49	0.2	2.4
1965	48	42	1.8	2.8
6	5	48	0.1	3.7
7	24	72	1.1	7.6
8	14	35	0.2	4.3
9	35	93	1.2	9.4

* Purchase and resale agreements.
SOURCE: Bank of Canada, *Annual Reports,* 1945-1969.

As is evident from Table 17-3 this cannot be said of Canada. For ex ample, in 1968, a year of moderate borrowing, advances were outstanding to chartered banks on only 14 business days and to security dealers on only 35 days. On all other days there were no advances outstanding. Thus, while in the United States central bank advances continuously provide bank reserves, in Canada they do not.

Quantitative Importance. These facts seem to suggest that the dis count window is less important in Canada than in the United States. But continuity may not be the most relevant measure of the significance of central bank advances. We should also consider their quantitative import ance as a source of bank reserves.

As we saw earlier (Figure 17-2), Federal Reserve advances are quantitatively insignificant in periods of monetary ease. For example, in 1961 and 1962, discounts, advances, and purchase and resale agreements provided less than 0.5% of the reserves of member banks. However, in years of monetary restraint and relatively heavy borrowing from the Federal Reserve System, this proportion is in the range of 3% to 4% (in mid-1969 it exceeded 6%), a small but nonetheless significant figure (perhaps more significant than the proportion itself is the increase in a short period of time). In sharp contrast (again referring to Table 17-3), even during years of relatively heavy borrowing, such as 1960, 1967, or 1969, Bank of Canada advances in all forms accounted for only 0.5% to 0.7% of bank reserves. In years of light borrowing the proportion was less than 0.2%

It is also interesting to contrast the composition of central bank advances in the two countries. In the United States advances are predominantly direct loans to member banks. In Canada, purchase and resale agreements with security dealers are several times as large as advances to banks in almost every year. If the American discount window is predominantly a mechanism for reserve adjustments by banks, the Canadian counterpart is predominantly a device for underwriting the money market. It is very little used directly for bank reserve adjustments.

Overall, the discount mechanism is quantitatively less important in Canada than in the United States, and is designed for a somewhat different purpose. Given our interest in monetary control, however, the relevant question is whether the Canadian mechanism displays the same cyclical characteristics.

Cyclical Behaviour of Advances. Comparison of Bank of Canada advances with relevant Canadian money market rates in Figure 17-3 reveals no strong, systematic relationship of the type which we discovered in the United States.[8] Apparently, central bank advances do not provide a systematic offset to monetary policy in Canada. Why is the behaviour of central bank advances different in the two countries?

Part of the explanation lies in the differences in the structures of the two banking systems. In Canada, including the Quebec Savings Bank, there are only 9 banks which have lines of credit with the Bank of Canada. A substantial and sustained increase in the banking system's indebtedness to the central bank could only occur if some individual banks repeatedly borrowed increasing sums — something virtually prohibited by the Bank of Canada's regulations.[9]

The Federal Reserve System, as we have seen, has similar regulations restricting repeated and large-scale borrowing by individual banks, but there are over 6,000 banks with access to the Federal Reserve System's discount windows. The banking system can be continuously in debt to the Federal Reserve System without any individual banks being continuously in debt. A substantial increase in the banking system's indebtedness to the Federal Reserve System can occur simply by a larger proportion of the member banks borrowing, even though each bank borrows a limited sum for a relatively short period of time.

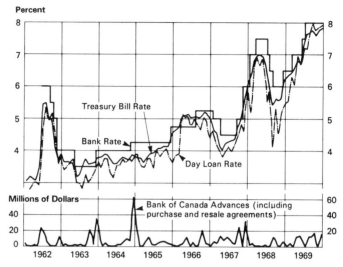

Figure 17-3
Bank of Canada Advances* and the Money Market; Canada, 1962-1969

*Averages for Wednesdays.

Beyond this, it should be noted that in the period of time covered by Figure 17-3, the entire period during which Canada had a discretionary Bank Rate, the Bank Rate remained consistently above the treasury bill and day-loan rates. Unlike the Federal Reserve System's discount rate, which frequently lagged behind relevant market rates in this period, at least at cyclical peaks, the Bank of Canada's Bank Rate was almost consistently a *penalty rate*. It was normally kept at a sufficiently high level to avoid creating an incentive to borrow, without at the same time imposing a serious burden on those dealers or banks who were forced by circumstances to borrow.

Bank Rate Policy. We saw that during the first 20 years of the Bank of Canada's existence, the discount window was virtually a redundant appendage to the central bank. When the mechanism was rehabilitated in 1955, the Governor of the Bank of Canada warned that the public would have to become accustomed to more flexible use of the bank rate in the future. Certainly the early record was not difficult to beat. From early August 1955, through mid-October 1956, the Bank Rate was increased on six separate occasions. In a little over a year there were twice as many changes as had occurred in the first 20 years of the Bank's history. On November 1, 1956, the Bank of Canada took the final step in the direction of flexibility and formally tied the Bank Rate to market interest rates. The Bank Rate was fixed at $1/4\%$ above the yield on 90-day treasury bills as established at the last weekly auction of treasury bills.

The Canadian experiment with floating discount rate was regarded with interest by economists. However, in late June, 1962, at the height of a foreign exchange crisis, the experiment was abruptly terminated and shortly thereafter the Governor of the Bank of Canada stated publicly, "I regard the argument about the relative merits of a fixed bank rate and a floating bank rate as over."[10] Actually, the Governor was not contrasting the floating rate with a "fixed" rate. Rather, he had in mind what we might call a "discretionary" Bank Rate — one which is posted, and in that sense fixed, but which is subject to change from time to time at the discretion of the Bank of Canada.

The Bank of Canada did not adopt a fully discretionary Bank Rate arrangement. It opted for a mixed system, with two rates. The Bank Rate, applicable to advances to banks, is discretionary. However, security dealers have the option of borrowing at the posted Bank Rate or a special Money Market Rate, whichever is lower. The Market Rate is a floating rate, pegged at $1/4\%$ above the rate on 90-day treasury bills as established at the preceding weekly auction.

What are the relative merits of discretionary and floating Bank Rate systems? Why did Canada adopt a floating rate, then abandon it in favour of a mixed system?

The Floating Bank Rate. There are two major advantages of a floating Bank Rate. First, it automatically guarantees that the Bank Rate will continuously be a penalty rate in the sense noted above. This does not mean that it will be higher than the rates earned by banks or security dealers on all of their short-term assets. Rather, it means that it will consistently be somewhat higher than the rates on certain key money market instruments commonly used for reserve adjustments (e.g., treasury bills and day loans). While movements in the Bank Rate may not be predictable from week to week, its relationship to certain other rates is consistent and predictable.

This could presumably be achieved through frequent changes in a discretionary Bank Rate. However, there is a potentially disturbing "mystique" about announced changes of the Bank Rate.

A change in a discretionary Bank Rate is a deliberate, calculated act of intervention on the part of the central bank, dramatized through a public announcement. Invariably this stimulates a spate of speculation in the financial papers. What does the rise in the Bank Rate "mean"? Does the central bank see storm clouds on the economic horizon? Or is it really an indication of continued economic expansion? Is the central bank simply adjusting to rising interest rates in the market? Or is it attempting to push the market to higher levels of interest rates? Is the country in for a period of tighter money and credit? The central bank normally finds it necessary to dispel uncertainty through a public statement of the purpose of the move (which sometimes provokes further speculation as the financial editors attempt to read between the lines to discover what the Bank "really" intends). By itself, the Bank Rate is an inefficient device for communicating complex information.

The two major advantages of allowing the Bank Rate to float are that it guarantees a suitable "penalty rate" at all times, and that changes in the rate will not provoke disturbing speculation about the economic prognosis and about the central bank's intentions.

The Discretionary Bank Rate as a Signal. Paradoxically, the latter "advantage" of the floating rate is also cited by its critics as a major disadvantage. That is, it is argued that if the Bank Rate is allowed to float, the central bank loses a valuable weapon from its limited armoury. It can no longer use changes in the Bank Rate as a dramatic signal of its intentions.

There is considerable confusion regarding what information can be communicated by changes in the Bank Rate. As we have already seen, as a technique of communicating the central bank's views on the state of the economy and on appropriate economic policy, the Bank Rate is at best inefficient and at worst confusing and perhaps perverse. As the Governor of the Bank of Canada has acknowledged,

> The easiest method of communicating ideas is that of using the English language. If the central bank has something . . . to say . . . the most natural thing for the central bank to do is to make a speech or to issue a statement.[11]

Some economists call this "open mouth operations".

What, then, can be efficiently signalled by way of a discretionary change in the Bank Rate?

The Bank Rate can be used to provide guidance to participants in the money market as to the level of short-term interest rates which the central bank thinks is appropriate under the circumstances. By eliminating uncertainty about the central bank's intentions in this regard, the Bank Rate provides a clear focus for participants in the market, without tying the market rigidly to any particular level or structure of rates.

Normally, the central bank adjusts the Bank Rate in response to changes emerging in the money market (perhaps under central bank pressure). However, the Bank Rate can also be used to lead the money market to new levels of rates — something which could be accomplished through open market operations, but which might be effected more simply and more directly through the device of an abrupt, dramatic change in the Bank Rate. Perhaps the clearest instance of this use of the rate was provided by the circumstances in which the floating rate was abandoned in June, 1962. At the height of the foreign exchange crisis, the Bank of Canada led the money market to much higher levels of interest rates by dramatically raising the Bank Rate to 6% and fixing it there. The results can be seen quite clearly in Figure 17-3.

Some economists have argued that the central bank can obtain the best of both worlds by allowing the Bank Rate to float with the money market, but with the margin between the Bank Rate and the key market rate subject to discretionary changes as a signal. The Bank of Canada has adopted a different compromise. A discretionary Bank Rate is maintained as a money market signal, but quantitatively the most important volume of borrowing is done at the floating Market Rate.

Central Bank Advances: Summary

Central Bank advances should not be thought of as a positive instrument for monetary control. They provide a safety valve for individual banks and security dealers faced with severe but temporary cash deficiencies. Under some circumstances, however, these advances can have a perverse effect on the total supply of bank reserves in terms of the objectives of monetary policy. While the free reserve doctrine holds that these fluctuations are simply part of the complex mechanism by which monetary policy is transmitted to the economy, many economists argue that they weaken the force of monetary policy and that for this reason the discount mechanism ought to be abolished. As long as the discount mechanism exists, however, a careful and flexible Bank Rate policy must be followed. This does not preclude the use of the Bank Rate as a money market signal, but it does suggest that the Rate should be a penalty rate.

FOOTNOTES

[1] Remember: The Bank of Canada is owned by the government of Canada. The $4.1 billion of government securities held by the Bank of Canada is *intra-governmental debt*. It is owed by one branch of the government to another. As a result, if we want to calculate the *net* public debt (claims on the government held outside the government) we should deduct the value of the securities held by the Bank of Canada (along with those held by other agencies).

By the same reasoning, the liabilities of the Bank of Canada to the general public (currency in circulation), the chartered banks and other depositors should be included in the public debt, and this is a somewhat larger figure (almost $4.8 billion at the beginning of 1970). However, there is one significant difference between the liabilities of the Bank of Canada and the rest of the public debt. The former do not bear interest. If we are concerned with the interest-bearing public debt, the Bank of Canada's holdings should be deducted. In this connection you may recall the historical controversy discussed in the section on "The Banks and Government Finance" in Chapter 12.

Finally, in this connection, it should be remembered also that all profits from the Bank of Canada's operations revert to the central treasury of the Government (prior to 1956 part of the profits were retained to build up a financial reserve). In effect, the payment of interest on the Bank of Canada's holdings of government bonds is simply a complicated method of meeting the expenses of the Bank of Canada out of the public treasury, although it gives the Bank the appearance of financial independence and profitability.

[2] This statement requires qualification. Remember that we are ignoring *coin* in circulation and in bank vaults, which is part of the monetary base but not a liability of the Bank of Canada. However, since this is a relatively small component of the monetary base ($481 million, or 10.5% on January 1, 1970), and, more importantly, since the volume of coin in circulation can be expected to adjust fairly systematically to the amount of other money in circulation, its existence as part of the monetary base does not impair Bank of Canada control over the monetary base.

[3] The terminology is that of Robert Roosa, who was for many years an important officer of the Federal Reserve Bank of New York. His pamphlet *Federal Reserve Operations in the Money and Government Securities Markets* (New York: Federal Reserve Bank of New York, 1956) is one of the best available discussions of the inner workings of a central bank. As Roosa makes clear, most of the day to day operations of such a bank are defensive in nature.

[4] Important among the changes were a broadening of the lending authority of the

Federal Reserve Banks (by eliminating the restrictive link to "eligible" commercial paper) ; the formalization of the institution of the open market committee; and the introduction of variable cash reserve requirements. A brief history of discount window policy in the United States is contained in Bernard Shull, *Reappraisal of the Federal Reserve Discount Mechanism: Report on Research Undertaken in Connection with a System Study*, (Washington D.C.: Board of Governors of the Federal Reserve System, 1968) .

⁵ Perhaps the best known study is A. J. Meigs, *Free Reserves and the Money Supply* (Chicago: University of Chicago Press, 1962) . Other studies are briefly reviewed in D. M. Jones, *A Review of Recent Academic Literature on the Discount Mechanism* (Washington: Board of Governors of the Federal Reserve System, 1968) , pp. 13-17.

⁶ Bank of Canada, *Annual Report*, 1943 (Ottawa, 1944) , p. 4.

⁷ Bank of Canada, *Annual Report* 1956, p. 13.

⁸ The data on Bank of Canada advances in Figure 17-3 are not fully comparable with the American data in Figure 17-2, and are not ideal for our purpose. Until recently the Bank of Canada has not published monthly averages of daily borrowings by banks and security dealers, but rather it published balances outstanding on each Wednesday. These figures capture all bank borrowing (which are for a minimum term of seven days) , but will not necessarily capture all dealer borrowing. Loans taken out between Thursday and Tuesday, and repaid in the same period, will be missed. The annual data in Table 17-3 are daily averages, as published annually in the Bank of Canada's *Annual Report*.

Furthermore, in interpreting Figure 17-3 it should be noted that three of the major fluctuations in advances recorded on the chart are a product of extraneous considerations and should be ignored, *viz.*, those at the end of 1963 and 1964 and in late 1967. In each case the Bank of Canada was experimenting with techniques for offsetting the impact of the seasonal drain of currency into circulation on bank reserves. In the terminology developed earlier, these represented *special defensive operations*. In December 1963 the Bank entered into $45 million worth of longer-term (one month) purchase and resale agreements with security dealers at a special low rate of interest. In December 1964 the same arrangements were made, but for $100 million, placed by competitive tender.

The 1963 and 1964 special repurchase agreements added to the monetary base at a time when the Christmas drain of currency into circulation would normally reduce bank reserves. The agreements thus obviated an equal value of open market operations. In January, when the agreements expired, a corresponding reduction in the monetary base would occur at the time when the currency drain normally reversed itself.

Cf., Bank of Canada, *Annual Report*, 1963, pp. 45 and 48; 1964, pp. 36-37.

⁹ In 1968 the Bank of Canada shortened the averaging period for cash reserve requirements from one month to one-half month. At the same time the Bank announced a new, less restrictive policy with respect to advances. Each bank and security dealer was given a larger basic line of credit, and the minimum period for advances to banks was reduced from seven days to two or three days. In addition, banks are now permitted to take out a one-day advance on the last day of any given averaging period if their cash reserves have been equal to or greater than the legal minimum up to that time. However, at the same time the Bank announced that the basic concept of the discount window remains the same. That is, the Bank

expects that each bank will be able in the ordinary course of events to adjust its cash position through the money market, that advances will be relatively infrequent, and that more than one advance to a bank in the same averaging period will be rare.

Bank of Canada, *Annual Report*, 1968, p. 41.

¹⁰ Bank of Canada, *Evidence of the Governor Before the Royal Commission on Banking and Finance* (Ottawa, 1964) , p. 55.

¹¹ Bank of Canada, *Annual Report*, 1956, p. 46.

18

The Control of the Money

Supply: Part 2 (Cont'd):

The Bank of Canada (Auxiliary Instruments)

While Bank Rate policy is an important dimension of central banking, in the modern context the primary instrument of monetary control is unquestionably open market operations. Appropriate Bank Rate policy reinforces open market operations — it does not supplant them. However, there are at least two other potential instruments of monetary control which can be used *instead* of open market operations under certain circumstances. These are government deposits and foreign currency assets. Since they have restricted usability we refer to them as auxiliary instruments.

1/GOVERNMENT DEPOSITS

Among its many functions, the Bank of Canada serves as the banker for the Government of Canada. However, while the Bank of Canada holds the government's chequing account, it normally holds only a small fraction of the total cash balances of the government. The bulk of the government's funds are in deposits with the nine chartered banks, divided among the banks on the basis of an agreed formula. At the outset of 1970 the Government of Canada had over $1,400 million in accounts with the chartered banks, Quebec savings banks and the Bank of Canada. Of that, the Bank of Canada held only $81 million, or just under 6%.

The Bank of Canada is the government's own bank and all profits from its operations revert to the government. Why, then, does the government rely so heavily on the chartered banks as depositories for its cash balances? Why does it not have the Bank of Canada do all of its banking business?

The Management of Government Cash

The division of the government's cash balances between the Bank of Canada and the chartered banks is a matter of deliberate policy. Indeed, the obvious policy of holding all of the government's cash with the Bank of Canada would create severe and unnecessary complications for the Bank of Canada in managing the monetary base. It would require frequent, massive "defensive" open market operations.

To understand this, you should keep in mind two basic points: government deposits are highly volatile; and changes in government deposits at the Bank of Canada have a direct impact on the monetary base.

Volatility of Government Deposits. The volatility of total government cash balances is obvious from Figure 18-1. In the period 1962-1969 government deposits with the chartered banks, and hence total government deposits, underwent very wide swings. A change of several hundred million dollars in the space of a month was not unusual. There is evidence of a strong seasonal movement in the balances, reflecting systematic differences in the timing of tax collections and government expenditures, but there are also other irregular influences, including the issuance and retirement of government bonds.

Figure 18-1
Government of Canada Deposits*, 1962-1970

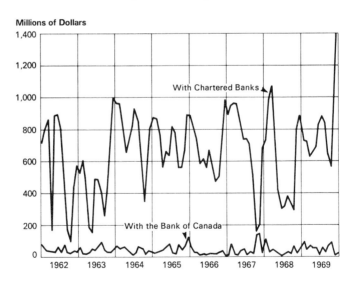

* Average of Wednesdays.
SOURCE: Bank of Canada, Statistical Summary, 1966 *Supplement,* 1969 *Supplement.*

Government Deposits and the Monetary Base. If the government held all of its cash balances at the Bank of Canada, the volatility of its deposits would be very troublesome, because any change in government deposits at the Bank of Canada has an equal and opposite effect on the monetary base. An increase in government deposits at the Bank of Canada tends to reduce the monetary base by an equal amount; a reduction in these deposits tends to increase the monetary base. These relationships are apparent in the monetary base equation, and are demonstrated in more detail in Example 18-1.

Example 18-1
Government Deposits

Case A

Tax collections – deposited at the Bank of Canada

STAGE I: Taxes are paid by members of the general public, with cheques drawn on accounts at chartered banks. The government deposits these cheques in i*s account with the Bank of Canada.

Bank of Canada		Public	
Cheques on banks +100	Deposits of gov't. +100		Tax liability −100
			Cheques outst. +100

STAGE II: When the outstanding cheques are cleared and collected, bank reserve deposits at the Bank of Canada are reduced by an equal amount.

Bank of Canada		Public		Chartered Banks	
Cheques on banks −100	Deposits of banks −100	Bank deposits −100	Cheques outst. −100	Reserve deposits −100	Deposits of public −100

NET CHANGE:

Bank of Canada		Public		Chartered Banks	
	Deposits of banks −100	Bank deposits −100	Tax liability −100	Reserve deposits −100	Deposits of public −100
	of gov't. +100				

NOTE:
The deposit liabilities and cash reserves of the chartered banks have been reduced by the same amount. The banks will now be deficient in their reserve positions, and multiple credit contraction will follow.

Case B

Tax collections – deposited at chartered banks

Taxes are paid by members of the general public, with cheques drawn on accounts at chartered banks. The government deposits these cheques in its accounts with chartered banks.

Bank of Canada		Public		Chartered Banks	
		Bank deposits −100	Tax liability −100		Deposits of public −100
					of gov't. +100

NOTE:

The total deposit liabilities and cash reserves of the chartered banks are unaffected by this transaction. No general credit contraction will occur. The publicly owned money supply has been reduced by the amount of the tax collection.

Government expenditures would have opposite effects. If they are made out of deposits with chartered banks only the ownership of the money supply is changed (as in Case B): if they are made out of deposits with the Bank of Canada, total chartered bank reserves and deposit liabilities will be increased by the same amount, leaving excess reserves and inducing further credit expansion.

Case C

Transfer of government deposits

Government deposits with chartered banks are withdrawn and redeposited with the Bank of Canada.

Bank of Canada		Chartered Banks	
	Deposits of banks −100 of gov't. +100	Reserve deposits −100	Deposits of gov't. −100

NOTE:

The deposit liabilities and cash reserves of the chartered banks are reduced by the same amount, leaving the banks with deficient reserves. Multiple credit contraction will follow.

A transfer of deposits from the Bank of Canada to the chartered banks would have the opposite effect, creating excess reserves and inducing general credit creation.

Clearly, if the government kept all of its cash balances at the Bank of Canada, the Bank would have to engage in massive open market operations to offset the monetary repercussions of government transactions, since monthly changes in government cash balances are frequently many times greater than the total of transactions in government securities which the Bank of Canada would enter into in a similar period for all other reasons. We are not talking about a minor complication.

The Two-Deposit Policy. These complications can be minimized (but not avoided entirely) by the simple expedient of a two-deposit policy. All government expenditures are made out of the account with the Bank of Canada. However, the bulk of the government's cash is kept in accounts with the chartered banks, and transferred to the Bank of Canada only as needed. As a result, government cash outlays tend to reduce government deposits at the chartered banks, transferring the ownership of bank deposits from the government to the general public, but without any repercussions on the monetary base. Government cash inflows are deposited with chartered banks, again transferring ownership of bank deposits without affecting the monetary base.

As a result, the major fluctuations in government cash balances are confined to accounts with chartered banks. Balances at the Bank of Canada are kept small and *relatively* stable (see Figure 18-1). The monetary complications of government transactions are thereby minimized.

Government Deposits as a Policy Instrument

There is thus good reason for the government to maintain bank accounts at both the Bank of Canada and the chartered banks. But the existence of the two sets of accounts also creates a potential auxiliary instrument of monetary control. The size of the monetary base can be adjused just as effectively by a transfer of funds between the government's accounts with the chartered banks and the Bank of Canada as it can by open market operations. Indeed, the deposit transfer is a simpler and more direct method of changing bank reserves.

With the concurrence of the treasury (on whose behalf they act) the Bank of Canada has considerable latitude in managing the government's cash balances. However, there is little evidence of vigorous, prolonged use of this instrument. The Bank seems to regard it as a temporary expedient only. When the government's balances at the Bank of Canada are already very low, there is no scope for substantial transfers of government funds from the Bank of Canada to the chartered banks as a method of increasing the monetary base. Transfers in the opposite direction are generally more feasible. However, a longer-term reduction in the level of deposits at chartered banks presupposes a substantial margin of cash in the hands of the government in excess of requirements. Such surpluses can be engineered through excess taxation or borrowing, of course, but if special arrangements of this sort are necessary, this technique of policy would normally have nothing to commend it over direct open market operations by the central bank. (Remember: government borrowing is in principle no different from the sale of government securities by the Bank of Canada out of its portfolio.)

The use of transfers of government deposits for the purpose of adjusting the monetary base have been reported by the Bank of Canada on a few occasions in recent years.[1] Frequently, such transfers have been associated with the use of a secondary auxiliary instrument, the Bank of Canada's foreign currency asset account.

2/FOREIGN CURRENCY ASSETS

One of the points made by the monetary base equation is that any purchase of assets by the central bank, regardless of what those assets are, will add to the monetary base unless offsetting measures are taken. The disposal of assets will have the opposite effect. If the asset has an active market, like government bonds, it is a potential instrument of monetary control. Among the assets of the Bank of Canada, other than government bonds, the only one which has an active, broad market is foreign exchange. Since whatever the Bank of Canada can achieve through operations in the government bond market it can also achieve through transactions in the foreign exchange market, the Bank's foreign currency assets must also be regarded as a potential instrument of monetary control.

The Foreign Exchange Account versus
the Bank of Canada's Foreign Currency Assets

It is important to distinguish between the Foreign Exchange Fund account and the Bank of Canada's own Foreign Currency Asset account.

In principle, if the foreign exchange rate was a perfectly flexible price, the Exchange Fund account would not have to exist. It is a product of the government's commitment to stabilize the foreign exchange rate. At times when the exchange rate has been allowed to "float", the government has used the account to minimize erratic fluctuations. At times when the exchange rate has been fixed, the government has used the account to keep the rate within 1% on either side of the official par rate. Under both regimes, the government purchased foreign exchange to be added to the account whenever pressures of private supply and demand tended to depress the rate to an unacceptable level, and sold foreign exchange out of the account whenever market pressures tended to drive the rate up to an unacceptable level.

The Exchange Fund account is managed by the Bank of Canada as the fiscal agent for the Minister of Finance. However, it is conceptually separate from the Bank of Canada's own Foreign Currency Asset account. While, as we shall see, it is sometimes used for other purposes, the latter is primarily the Bank of Canada's working balances in foreign exchange that are held to facilitate foreign payments either on behalf of the Bank's "clients" (primarily Government departments), or the Bank itself.

Foreign Exchange and the Monetary Base

When the Bank of Canada purchases foreign exchange for its own account, it makes payment with a cheque drawn on itself. When this cheque is deposited in the vendor's account with a chartered bank and is cleared and collected, bank reserves are augmented by an equal amount. Bank of Canada sales of foreign exchange in the open market have the opposite effect. Payment is received in the form of a cheque drawn on a chartered bank, and that amount will be deducted from the bank's reserve deposit at the Bank of Canada.

Such monetary repercussions do not necessarily follow if the foreign exchange transactions are for the Foreign Exchange Fund account. Indeed, *transactions of the Foreign Exchange Fund will only affect the monetary base if they result in a change in the size of government deposits with the Bank of Canada.* It is the change in government deposits which affects the monetary base. Changes in the Foreign Exchange Fund *per se* have no such monetary implications: the Foreign Exchange Fund does not appear in the monetary base equations.

To illustrate this point, consider Example 18-2. For the purposes of this example we have assumed that the Foreign Exchange Fund purchases $100,000 worth of foreign exchange in the open market. If we stop at the end of Stage II, this transaction would increase chartered bank cash reserves and deposit liabilities by $100,000 each, giving the banks excess cash reserves and hence the basis for further credit creation. However, in the normal course of events Stage III will follow. That is, the government will transfer funds from its balances with the chartered banks to its balances with the Bank of Canada to cover the foreign exchange purchase. This neutralizes the potential impact on the monetary base. The monetary base will only increase if government deposits at the Bank of Canada are allowed to run down as a result of the transaction.

Example 18-2
The Foreign Exchange Fund

STAGE I: The Foreign Exchange Fund purchases foreign exchange in order to support the foreign exchange rate. The foreign exchange is paid for by a cheque drawn on the government's account with the Bank of Canada. In the books of the government, this shows up as an advance from the government to the Foreign Exchange Fund.

Government		Public		Foreign Exchange Fund	
Advance to F.E. Fund +100	Cheques outst. +100	Cheques on B. of C. +100 Foreign exchange −100		Foreign Exchange +100	Advance from gov't. +100

STAGE II: The government cheques on the Bank of Canada are deposited in accounts with the chartered banks, cleared and eventually credited to the banks' reserve deposits with the Bank of Canada.

Bank of Canada		Government	
	Deposits of gov't. −100 of banks +100	Deposit at B. of C. −100	Cheques outst. −100

Public		Chartered Banks	
Cheques on B. of C. −100 Deposits at chartered banks +100		Reserve deposits +100	Deposits of public +100

STAGE III: As a matter of normal policy, funds are transferred from the government's accounts with the chartered banks to its accounts with the Bank of Canada to cover the outlay on foreign exchange.

Bank of Canada		Government		Chartered Banks	
	Deposits of gov't. +100 of banks −100	Deposits at B. of C. +100 at chart- ered banks −100		Reserve deposits −100	Deposits of gov't. −100

NET CHANGE:

Bank of Canada		Government	
	Advance to F.E. Fund +100 Deposit at chartered banks −100		

Foreign Exchange Fund	
Foreign exchange +100	Advance from gov't. +100

Public		Chartered Banks	
Foreign exchange −100 Deposit at chartered banks +100			Deposits of gov't. −100 of public +100

NOTE:

Total bank deposit liabilities and cash reserves are unchanged. Since no excess reserves (positive or negative) are created, no credit expansion or contraction occurs. All that has changed is the ownership of the money supply.

If this transaction leaves the government short of cash balances, it may have to borrow additional funds in the money or capital markets. This transaction will not affect the monetary base unless the Bank of Canada purchases some of the bonds. As an exercise, this should be traced through.

Foreign Exchange as a Policy Instrument

The Bank of Canada's power to trade in the foreign exchange market on its own account in order to alter the monetary base (the obvious way in which the Bank's foreign exchange assets could be used as a policy instrument) is in fact severely circumscribed under normal circumstances. In the first place, the Bank's holdings of foreign exchange are relatively small, no more than required for operational purposes. This means that the Bank cannot easily sell foreign exchange to contract the monetary base which, of course, does not prohibit foreign exchange purchases to increase the monetary base. However, except in unusual circumstances, the second alternative is effectively ruled out by the fact that the government has an independent policy on the level of the foreign exchange rate (this is the same point discussed earlier with respect to interest rate policy and open market operations). The Bank cannot buy and sell foreign exchange without influencing the foreign exchange rate, which would normally bring the Bank's operations into conflict with official exchange rate policy.

"Swaps" with the Exchange Fund. The Bank has developed a tech-nique of entering into a "swap" arrangement with the Foreign Exchange Fund in order to temporarily increase the level of government deposits at the chartered banks, and hence to temporarily increase the size of the monetary base. You will recall that a "swap" involves the pairing of a spot foreign exchange transaction with an opposite forward contract (Chapter 7). In this case, the Bank of Canada purchases foreign exchange from the Foreign Exchange Fund, simultaneously executing a contract to resell

the foreign exchange to the Fund on an agreed date in the future. The Bank credits the government's account with the appropriate sum, which is then transferred to the government's deposits with chartered banks. Bank reserves and the monetary base are increased by the amount of the purchase. The following net changes would be registered in the monetary base equation:

$$B = S + (E - D_g) + A + (F + OA)$$
$$\text{(net change)} \quad (+100) \quad (0) \quad (+100) \quad (0) \quad (0) \quad (0) \quad (0)$$

(18.1)

When the forward contract expires, the transaction will be reversed, producing a corresponding decline in the monetary base.

The Bank of Canada has used such transactions on a fairly large scale since late 1964 for temporary adjustments to the monetary base, for example, to compensate for seasonal drains of currency into circulation.[2] The resulting change in the behaviour of the Bank's foreign currency assets is quite noticeable in Figure 18-2. Prior to late 1964 the account was relatively stable, if we allow for the large jump in 1962 which was a result of measures taken during the foreign exchange crisis of that year.[3] From late 1964 on, the account shows much larger fluctuations, which are the mirror image of the Foreign Exchange Fund's forward contracts with the Bank of Canada (upper panel). However, if we allow for swaps with the Foreign Exchange Fund, and for another special crisis measure in early 1968, the Bank's foreign asset account continues to display considerable stability.

Figure 18-2
Foreign Exchange: The Bank of Canada and the Foreign Exchange Fund*

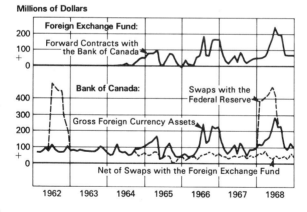

Month-end.
SOURCE: Bank of Canada, Statistical Summary.

Swaps with the Foreign Exchange Fund have become an important, basic instrument for defensive monetary operations. They are simply a rather complicated method of temporarily augmenting government deposits at the chartered banks. Direct Bank of Canada advances to the government would achieve exactly the same effect (although, perhaps, not without political repercussions).

On occasion, the Bank of Canada has also adjusted the timing of the transfer of its profits to the government as a technique of monetary control. When the Bank's profits are paid over to the government and deposited in the government's account with the chartered banks, bank reserves increase by a like amount. By choosing the time at which such transfers will be made, the Bank can harmonize this impact on bank reserves with other aspects of its monetary control policies.[4]

3/VARIABLE RESERVE REQUIREMENTS

With the exception of some aspects of Bank Rate policy, all of the techniques of monetary management which we have discussed so far involve the control of the size of the monetary base. In this task the central bank has a range of options open to it, particularly for shorter-term, temporary adjustments, but the main instrument of policy is undoubtedly open market operations in government securities. To a very large extent, this is what central banking is all about.

Although we have focussed on the control of the monetary base, it is important that we not lose perspective on the purpose of central bank operations. Control of the monetary base is merely a means to an end — a method of regulating the supplies of money and credit in the economy. But control of the monetary base is not the only possible technique by which the central bank can influence these variables. Two other types of measures have been used in certain situations: the variation of minimum legal reserve requirements and direct or selective credit controls (including what is usually referred to as "moral suasion").

Discretionary Cash Reserve Ratios

We demonstrated in Chapter 16 that the money supply can be related to the monetary base by a "multiplier", the value of which depends, among other things, on the cash reserve ratio maintained by the commercial banks. The higher the cash reserve ratio, the smaller the multiplier, and vice versa. Under normal circumstances, the banks will have little incentive to hold substantial excess cash reserves. This means that the size of the multiplier depends on the minimum cash reserve ratio required by law.

Provided that they have the authority to vary the required reserve ratio, this relationship gives the monetary authorities an additional instrument for monetary control. By lowering the required cash reserve ratio, the central bank can create excess cash reserves in every bank simultaneously, inducing monetary expansion throughout the banking system. Similarly, by raising the required cash reserve ratio, the central bank can create deficient reserves in every bank in the system, forcing monetary contraction. A variable cash reserve ratio, then, can be a powerful and pervasive instrument of policy, which is independent of central bank operations in the open market.

American and Canadian Experience. The Federal Reserve System was given the authority to vary the required cash reserve ratios of member banks within certain limits in 1935.[5] This power was used almost immediately, as the ratios were doubled in three stages in 1936 and 1937, raising them to their legal maximums. In subsequent years, the power has been used on several occasions (see Table 18-1), most recently to increase the ratios in January 1968 and again in April 1969.

Table 18-1
The Variable Cash Reserve Requirement: The United States, 1935-1969

Ratio in effect as of:*	Central Reserve City Banks	Demand Deposits Reserve City Banks	Country Banks	Savings and Time Deposits
Dec., 1935	13	10	7	3
May, 1937	26	20	14	6
April, 1938	22¾	17½	12	5
Nov., 1941	26	20	14	6
Oct., 1942	20	20	14	6
Sept., 1948	26	22	16	7½
Sept., 1949	22	18	12	5
Feb., 1951	24	20	14	6
Dec., 1960	16½	16½	12	5

	Demand Deposits Reserve City Banks		Country Banks		Time and Savings Deposits	Time Deposits	
	Deposits up to $5 mill.	Deposits over $5 mill.	Deposits up to $5 mill.	Deposits over $5 mill.	Savings Deposits	Deposits up to $5 mill.	Deposits over $5 mill.
Mar., 1967	16½	16½	12	12	3	3	6
Jan., 1968	16½	17	12	12½	3	3	6
April, 1969	17	17½	12½	13	3	3	6

* High or low point of reserve ratios, except for 1968-69.
SOURCE: Federal Reserve *Bulletin.*

The Board of Governors of the Federal Reserve System has made it clear that it does not regard the variable cash reserve ratio as a *normal* tool of monetary policy but rather as one to be used in exceptional circumstances. This is particularly true of increases in the ratio, which the Board regards as a drastic move not to be taken without careful study and long deliberation. Thus, following the increase in the rates to their legal ceilings during the Korean War, the Federal Reserve System did not use its power to raise the ratios again for 16 years, in spite of several periods of sharply restrictive monetary policy.

The Bank of Canada first gained the power to vary the required cash reserve ratios of the chartered banks, within the limits of 8% to 12%, in

1954. The maximum increase in any one month was limited to 1%, and a month's notice had to be given before any increase could be brought into effect. This power was withdrawn in the 1967 revision of the *Bank Acts*, *without ever being used*. In its place a variable secondary reserve requirement was introduced, which we will examine shortly.

The Equivalence of Open Market Operations and Variable Cash Reserve Ratios. The mechanical multiplier model of monetary expansion (see the Appendix to Chapter 16) suggests that open market operations and reserve ratio variations are equivalent methods of achieving a given objective, i.e., a particular change in the size of the money supply. That is, a desired increase in the money supply could be obtained either by holding the reserve ratio constant and increasing the monetary base, or by holding the monetary base constant and reducing the reserve ratio. The opposite would be true for a desired reduction in the money supply. For this reason, it is sometimes suggested that open market operations and cash reserve ratio variations are perfect substitutes as policy instruments, and that the central bank should be indifferent as to which it uses in any particular circumstance.

Our brief survey of the use of cash reserve ratio variations in Canada and the United States implies that the central banks in these two countries do not regard these techniques as perfect substitutes. They have revealed a strong preference for open market operations as the technique of policy under normal circumstances. Why?

There are important differences between open market operations and cash reserve ratio variations considered as policy instruments. Open market operations have much greater *flexibility*. They can be conducted in large or small amounts, and both the magnitude and the direction of the operations can be changed from day to day or week to week as necessary. This makes possible relatively delicate adjustments to the monetary base, and permits a gradual approach to monetary restriction or monetary ease. Mistakes can be quickly and easily corrected.

By contrast, changes in cash reserve ratios are only feasible at distinct intervals. That is, changes must be made to coincide with the start of a new averaging period, which in Canada is now 15 days. Frequent changes in the continuous use of a variable reserve ratio as an instrument of policy is only compatible with very short reserve averaging periods.

In this connection it should also be noted that the monetary repercussions of seemingly small changes in the required cash reserve ratio can in fact be quite large. The smallest increase in the cash reserve ratio in the United States in recent years has been 1/2%. A corresponding increase in the reserve ratio in Canada in 1968 would have added $117 million, or just under 8%, to the *required* reserves of the chartered banks. If the Bank of Canada did not make the additional reserves available (which would defeat the purpose of the operation, of course), this would have forced a contraction of the total deposits of the chartered banks of up to $1,700 million, or just over 7% — all in one jolt.[6] So powerful is the initial impact of a change in the reserve ratio that the central bank normally finds it has to offset it with large-scale open market operations.

It has been quite reasonably pointed out that the central bank is not constrained to reserve ratio changes in the traditional magnitudes of multiples of $1/2\%$. It could change the ratio by smaller fractional amounts, such as 0.1%. However, the possibility of frequent, though small, variations in the required reserve ratio introduced a new source of uncertainty for bankers, which cannot help but alter their management policies, and particularly to induce them to hold a larger share of their assets, on the average, in liquid form.

This reaction to *uncertainty* about the required cash reserve ratio is related to but conceptually different from the direct impact of higher reserve ratios on bank portfolio management policies. This points to what is perhaps the most significant difference between open market operations and cash reserve ratio variations. While both can be used to change the size of the bank's asset portfolios, changes in the reserve ratio also impose *a constraint on the composition of the bank's asset portfolios.* An increase in the reserve ratio reduces the share of earning assets in the bank's operations. (Consider, for example, the implications of raising the cash reserve ratio to 100%). It is not difficult to understand why commercial bankers are strongly opposed to increases in cash reserve ratios as a technique of monetary restraint (although they are generally quite happy to see cash reserve ratios reduced in periods of monetary ease). In general, variable cash reserve ratios have an unsettling effect on bank operations.

Finally, it is important to note that the cash reserve requirement cannot be changed without a public announcement, giving rise to speculation regarding the implications of the change. As in the case of discretionary changes in the discount rate, many economists argue that because their impact on economic activity is unreliable, such *announcement effects* should be avoided whenever possible.[7]

Use of Variable Cash Reserve Ratios. The general thrust of the points made in the previous section is critical of the use of variable cash reserve ratios as an instrument for monetary control. Not all economists agree that variable reserve ratios are of limited use in central banking.[8] Some would argue that the pervasive, dramatic and rapid impact of reserve ratio changes is a positive attribute. All banks are affected simultaneously and immediately, in contrast to open market operations, which have their immediate impact at the financial centers and then gradually filter out to the rest of the banking system. (Given the difference in the structure of the banking systems, this argument is much less persuasive in Canada than in the United States. Why?) It is argued that bankers will soon become accustomed to reserve ratio changes, that errors of magnitude can be adjusted through appropriate open market operations, and that unfortunate effects on individual banks can be taken care of through the discount window.

Without attempting to evaluate the relative merits of the pro and con arguments, it is instructive to briefly review the circumstances under which the Federal Reserve System in fact used its power to vary cash reserve ratios. The initial use of the variable cash reserve ratio prior to World War I was an attempt to impound the very sizable "excess reserves" which had suddenly been created in the banking system as a result of a flood of gold into the country from war-threatened Europe. The Federal Reserve System was concerned about the inflationary potential in the credit expansion which these excess reserves seemed to portend. The Federal Reserve action has been roundly criticized as overly drastic, and as responsible for the subsequent recession.

The actions taken in 1948 and 1951 were again attempts to impound what the Federal Reserve System regarded as excessive liquidity in the banking system under inflationary conditions. In this case, the liquidity took the form of large holdings of government bonds, the prices of which were virtually pegged by government policy. The pegging of bond prices immobilized the Federal Reserve System's primary instrument of policy, open market operations.

The final case was somewhat different. The 1968 and 1969 increases in the reserve ratios, both of which were relatively moderate and aimed primarily at the larger banks, had a primarily psychological purpose. Concerned that widespread expectations of inflation were weakening the impact of higher interest rates, the increases in reserve ratios were intended as dramatic evidence of "the system's determination to resist inflationary pressures".[9] In other words, the Federal Reserve System was deliberately capitalizing on the so-called announcement effects.

In summary, the Federal Reserve System has used what it regards as a drastic, blunt tool of policy primarily to impound large blocks of liquid assets in the banking system, and secondarily to capitalize on the announcement effects.

Variable Secondary Reserve Ratios. Many of the same things can be said about variable secondary reserve ratios. Their primary use is to impound excess liquidity in the banking system: to prevent the banks from selling off liquid assets in order to make more loans. However, in one important sense, they are much less drastic than variable cash reserve ratios. While an increase in the secondary reserve ratio may force the banks to hold a larger share of the eligible securities (directly or indirectly these are usually government bonds) than they would voluntarily choose to do, at least, unlike cash, these are interest-bearing assets. The income penalty is not as great as in the case of an increase in the required cash ratio.

It should be noted again that an increase in the secondary reserve ratio would normally have no implications for the money supply: that is unless the eligible securities are in very limited supply, or the government is pegging interest rates on government bonds. For this reason, those who argue that the only proper concern of the central bank is the size of the money supply also argue that secondary reserve requirements have no value as a tool of monetary policy. They are merely a device for creating a market for government bonds. Those who argue that the supply of bank credit is an important variable in its own right feel that a variable secondary reserve ratio may be a valuable instrument of policy if it can be used flexibly. It can be used to regulate the volume of bank loans extended with any given level of the money supply.

In early 1969 the Bank of Canada increased the required secondary reserve ratio from 7% to 8%, and, effective July 1, 1970 raised it again to 9%, as a measure of credit restraint.

4/DIRECT CREDIT CONTROLS

Another option which is sometimes open to central banks is the direct regulation of some of the activities of banks and other financial institutions. These regulations may have their roots in legislation which compels compliance and imposes formal legal penalties in proven cases of non-compliance, and they may be administered by an agency other than the central bank. Alternatively, the "controls" may be based on the moral authority of the central bank to command voluntary compliance. The latter type of control is commonly called "moral suasion". All direct controls tend to have a selective impact on financial activity, and hence are sometimes referred to as "selective controls".

The Purpose of Credit Controls

Direct controls restrain a specific type of financial activity which it is felt is producing undesirable pressures on the economy. Some examples may help clarify the point.

Consumer credit is a favourite target for direct controls, particularly in periods when strong consumer demand for durable goods is alleged to be producing inflationary pressures. Thus, during the Korean War, a sharp upsurge occurred in consumer purchases of all types of goods, perhaps because of memories of severe shortages during World War II. The government responded by imposing compulsory higher-than-normal down payments and shorter-than-normal repayment periods on installment credit extended by banks and other financial institutions and on residential mortgage credit.

Foreign exchange is perhaps an even more common target of direct controls. Indeed, in many countries there is virtually no legal free foreign exchange market. All transactions must be approved by the foreign exchange authority. In Canada, formal foreign exchange control of this type was imposed as a wartime measure in 1939, and finally abandoned in 1951, by which time the controls had effectively become non-operative. Foreign exchange controls are usually implemented when there is a strong excess demand for foreign exchange at the official exchange rate, and for some reason the government does not want to change the exchange rate. The controls are to conserve the limited supply of foreign exchange for "high priority" uses, to prevent speculation and a flight of capital from the country, and in general to prevent private demands for foreign exchange from imposing impossible pressures on the foreign exchange market. When the Canadian controls were in full effect, all foreign exchange in private hands had to be sold to the Foreign Exchange Control Board (through its agents, the chartered banks), and foreign exchange could only be purchased with a permit from the Board.

These are examples of formal direct controls, backed by legislation. More common, certainly in Canada, is the informal type of control which we call "moral suasion". It involves the use by the central bank of its "moral authority" to command "voluntary" compliance — although there may be subtle threats in the background.

Moral Suasion

Examples of moral suasion are abundant in Canadian central banking history. Indeed, in times such as the late 1950's, moral suasion appeared to be the primary operating technique of the Bank of Canada.

Thus, in 1947 and 1948, a period of heavy capital expenditures and rapid inflation, the Bank of Canada "suggested" that banks refrain from extending bank credit to finance capital expenditures.[10] The "suggestion" was withdrawn in 1949. Again in February 1951, during the Korean War inflation, the Bank of Canada supplemented the government's direct controls over consumer and mortgage credit with a "suggestion" to the banks that total bank credit for all purposes should not increase, and that particularly severe restrictions should be placed on term loans to finance capital expenditures, loans to finance stock market speculation, and installment credit.[11] These "suggestions", including the ceiling on total bank loans, were effective. In spite of boom conditions in the economy with associated strong demands for bank credit, and the absence of vigorous policies to control the monetary base, no increase in bank loans occurred for a full year, the duration of the "suggestion".

These early cases of moral suasion occurred at times when the Bank of Canada's other tools of policy were partially immobilized by other aspects of government policy, and particularly the policy of stabilizing government bond prices and yields. In 1955 a new period of active use of moral suasion started, with partially new objectives, which could not have the same rationale. By this time the immediate postwar shackles on quantitative monetary control had been completely removed, and restrictive monetary policy was pursued vigorously. Selective controls through moral suasion were used to supplement quantitative measures, not to substitute for them. The objective was to influence the *distribution* of the available funds — to " . . . make possible a wider access . . . to funds."[12]

The range of moral suasion was considerable. Thus, in late 1955 the Governor of the Bank of Canada "suggested" that the banks severely limit term loans to corporations. This was a return to the concern, so prominent in the use of moral suasion in 1947-48 and 1951, that bank credit was being used "inappropriately" to finance capital expenditures (shades of the commercial loan theory). Initially the banks were to confine their term lending to loans of less than $250,000, a limit which was raised to $1 million in early 1958, and later to $2 million before the "suggestion" was finally withdrawn. The ceilings appear to have been effective, although a more fundamental 1957 "suggestion" that the banks formally segregate their commercial banking operations from their savings banking operations was rejected by the banks after considerable controversy (this appears to be the only "suggestion" which received outright rejection by the chartered banks, although, as we will see, suggestions to other financial institutions were turned aside).

The Bank of Canada also attempted to impose direct controls over consumer credit when the government declined to implement legislation to that end. Thus, in 1956 the Governor held discussions with finance companies and major department stores with a view to restricting installment credit, but "It turned out that agreement of all concerned could not be reached."[13] However, a "suggestion" to the banks apparently was effective, such that the Governor could report in early 1957 that "the banks have not increased in 1956 their lines of credit to finance companies and retail stores providing installment finance facilities".[14] What could not be achieved directly was attempted indirectly, with some success.[15]

Perhaps the most enduring "suggestion" of the Bank of Canada was the 1955 proposal that the chartered banks maintain a 7% secondary reserve ratio in addition to their 8% cash reserve ratio. As we have seen, this became a permanent feature of chartered banking operations and was finally written into the law in 1967. It provided a guaranteed market for government bonds and helped stimulate the development of the money market, but the official rationalization of the policy was as a measure to restrict banks from selling government bonds to obtain resources to extend more loans to business.[16]

Moral suasion is usually used to restrain some type of financial activity. The Bank of Canada also attempted to put it to positive use to shape bank-ending policies. Thus, in 1956 the Bank urged the chartered banks to take care not to discriminate against small businesses. Indeed, the very nature of the term loan ceilings could be interpreted as a device to direct bank funds to smaller firms. In 1957 the Bank of Canada also became concerned about the apparent withdrawal of the chartered banks from the market for N.H.A.-insured mortgages. After discussions, the Governor reported that he had obtained agreement from the banks that they would "resume operations" in the N.H.A.-mortgage lending field "on much the same scale as in 1956". [17]

This is indeed a record of continued reliance on moral suasion. In his 1956 report the Governor of the Bank of Canada acknowledged that his "suggestions" to the banks had "gone about as far as this kind of voluntary informal action can go" without "some form of legally inforceable regulatory action."[18]

Since the 1955-58 episode, the major use of moral suasion has been in connection with foreign exchange transactions. Thus in the midst of the 1968 foreign exchange crisis, the Bank of Canada asked financial intermediaries, and particularly the banks, not to facilitate "swapped deposit" transactions (see Chapter 9), and not to extend credit to finance abnormal transfers of funds from Canadian subsidiaries to foreign parent firms. Both "suggestions" seem to have been effective in terms of their objectives

Effectiveness of Moral Suasion. In general, moral suasion is designed to override the profit motive. It is used to restrain financial institutions from activities which they would normally undertake, or to induce them to undertake activities which they would not do voluntarily. If the discrepancy between the dictates of the profit motive and the dictates of central bank "suggestions" is great, there is a strong incentive to evasion – an incentive which is accentuated if some firms suspect that others are evading or will evade the regulations. The central bank has the best chance of success if the financial institutions are vulnerable to central bank sanctions, if evasions can be detected easily, and if the financial institutions constitute a relatively small, closely knit and hence self-policing group. It should not be surprising that the Bank of Canada obtained agreement from the chartered banks for all but the most drastic suggestions for reorganizing their business (e.g. the separation of commercial and savings business) but could not obtain full cooperation from department stores and finance companies. The latter firms were not directly dependent on the central bank (although they proved to be indirectly vulnerable), and therefore were not obliged to provide a continuous flow of detailed statistical information on their operations. Furthermore, they were not as highly concentrated and centrally organized as the chartered banks.

It should also be noted that even though direct controls are successful in achieving their proximate objective, such as the control of term loans by chartered banks, they will not necessarily be effective in achieving their ultimate objective, the elimination of inflationary pressures on the economy. Selective controls attack the symptoms of the economic ailment, not the causes. If the problem is an excessive supply of money and credit, the suppression of its expression in certain forms (e.g., particular types of credit, or credit extended by particular types of firms) will result in its expression in other forms. Borrowers will seek out alternative sources of credit: lenders will find loopholes and disguised forms for extending the proscribed type of credit; pressures for the evasion of the regulations will build up, and "black markets" (and perhaps corruption) will be encouraged. There is evidence that selective controls can have the desired macroeconomic effects in the short run. In the face of sustained use, the market system is highly inventive, and the success of the controls is far less certain.

Selective Control and the Allocation of Credit

Perhaps the most serious aspect of moral suasion and other forms of selective controls is that if they are subject to comprehensive, sustained and effective use, they introduce a new dimension to central banking. The central bank is no longer simply an arbiter of macroeconomic balance in the economy; it becomes an important arbiter of the allocation of credit and hence of resources. The collective judgement of "the market" as reflected in the interaction of supply and demand and the behaviour of prices and profits is overruled by a centralized judgement as to the "national interest". If, as argued in Chapter 14, the competitive market is the most reliable mechanism for achieving an efficient allocation of resources in the economy effective and sustained moral suasion is likely to produce serious distortions in resource allocation (unless it somehow compensates for distortions resulting from a lack of effective competition). It is not surprising that vigorous advocates of the freely competitive market system denounce selective controls as harmful to the economy — and, indeed, argue that they do the least damage when they are evaded!

5/THE PROCESS OF MONETARY CONTROL

Together, Chapters 17 and 18 suggest a few important conclusions. We saw in Chapter 16 that the supply of money and credit can be expanded and contracted by actions of private financial institutions. The important regulators are the supply of high-powered money and the cash reserve ratio. Both of these variables can be subjected to central bank control (although the Bank of Canada no longer has the legislative authority to vary the cash reserve ratio). This provides the basis for central bank control of the supply of money and credit. The basic tool of central bank control is open market operations in government securities. However, the central bank in fact has a wide range of other techniques at its disposal, particularly for temporary adjustments to the monetary base. Variations of the cash reserve ratio as a technique of policy suffers from inflexibility, and, like selective credit controls, it interferes unnecessarily with the operations of the banks.

FOOTNOTES

[1] For example, see Bank of Canada, *Annual Report,* 1965, p. 41; 1966, pp. 42-44; 1967, p. 49; 1968, p. 41.

[2] *Ibid.*

[3] In order to augment Canada's official holdings of foreign exchange during the crisis, the Bank of Canada entered into a swap with the Federal Reserve System. The Bank of Canada gave the Federal Reserve System $378 million worth of Canadian Government bonds in exchange for a corresponding value of United States dollars. There were no monetary repercussions from this transaction (as you can see by tracing it through the monetary base equation). The swap was made on June 26, 1962, and undone in stages between October 31 and December 26, 1962. A similar transaction occured in early 1968, again in response to a foreign exchange crisis.

[4] See, Bank of Canada, *Annual Report,* 1957, p. 29; 1964, p. 37.

[5] A provision for increases in reserve ratios in a "national emergency" was introduced in 1933, but the Federal Reserve was not granted the authority to vary the ratios at its own discretion until 1935. At present the limits within which the ratios can be varied are:

Demand Deposits	
at country banks	7% - 14%
at reserve city banks	10% - 22%
Time and Savings Deposits	
at all member banks	3% - 10%

[6] The figure of $1,700 million as an upper limit has been calculated using the average required reserve ratio in 1968. From the analysis in the Appendix to Chapter 16, it should be obvious that we cannot know the precise implications of a given increase in the reserve ratios without knowing the impact of the

ensuing monetary contraction on the division of deposits between time deposits and demand deposits, and on the amount of currency in circulation.

7 Cf., M. Friedman, *A Program for Monetary Stability* (New York: Fordham University Press, 1960), pp. 45-50.

8 D. S. Ahearn, *Federal Reserve Policy Reappraised, 1951-1959.* (New York: Columbia University Press, 1963), pp. 145-163.

9 "Record of Policy Actions of the Federal Open Market Committee: Meeting held on April 1st, 1968," in *Federal Reserve Bulletin,* Vol. 55 (July 1969), p. 601.

10 Bank of Canada, *Annual Report,* 1948, p. 7.

11 Bank of Canada, *Annual Report,* 1951, p. 9. It is noted in the Report that the Governor "found the banks in agreement with the suggestion that further expansion of total bank credit was undesirable under existing conditions."

12 Bank of Canada, *Annual Report,* 1956, p. 32.

13 Bank of Canada, *Annual Report,* 1956, p. 34. A similar suggestion to the stock markets that credit for stock market trading should be restricted appears to have met with easier agreement, perhaps reflecting the quasi-regulatory authority of the stock markets in this industry.

14 *Ibid.,* p. 35.

15 Many finance companies have external sources of finance but bank credit remains an essential part of their operations, particularly for the smaller companies. The impact of the credit squeeze was severe, as is testified to by the fact that the iniquity of the 1956 "suggestion" to the banks was a major theme in the Finance Companies' brief to the Royal Commission on Banking and Finance.

16 Bank of Canada, *Annual Report,* 1955, p. 16.

17 Bank of Canada, *Annual Report,* 1957, p. 28.

18 *Ibid.*

19

The Demand for Money

We explored some aspects of the demand for money in Chapters 2 and 5. In those chapters we were concerned with the basic characteristics of money, its role in facilitating the flow of transactions in the economy, and its attributes as an asset which might be selected by an individual assetholder for inclusion in his portfolio. In the present chapter we change our focus. Rather than the individual assetholder's portfolio selection decisions, we are concerned with the aggregate demand for money in the economy as a whole. However, since the aggregate demand for money is comprised of the demands of individual assetholders, the earlier material provides the microeconomic foundations for our macroeconomic analysis. The reader may find it useful to review it briefly.

1/THE TRANSACTIONS DEMAND

Money is an asset designed to be used as a medium of payment. Under normal conditions money is the only generally accepted means by which purchasing power can be transferred from one spending unit to another, and the basic demand for it derives from this fact. It is a demand for money to facilitate transactions — to bridge the gap in time between successive receipts of income and hence to permit a continuing flow of expenditures. We can call this the *transactions demand for money*.

Classical Theory of the Transactions Demand for Money

It is frequently assumed that, given the institutional setting (the frequency with which payrolls are met; the pattern of payments flows among firms; the degree to which payments are made by cheque; the efficiency of the postal service; the speed with which cheques are cleared and collected; etc.), the transactions demand for money depends *only* on the total value of transactions to be effected. Indeed, it is commonly assumed that the relationship between the quantity of money demanded for transactions purposes and the value of transactions to be effected is *linear*. That is, it is assumed that the demand function takes the form:

$$M_t = k\,T. \tag{19.1}$$

In this equation, T is the total value of expenditures or transactions in the economy during a given period of time, a month or a year, perhaps.

This is a *flow variable*. M_t is the quantity of money demanded for transactions purposes by all spending units in the economy. It is a *stock variable*. Thus, in a sense, the two variables are in different time dimensions and to reconcile them M_t must be interpreted as the *average* quantity of money demanded at successive instants during the time period over which T is measured. The coefficient k simply defines the relationship between the stock of money demanded and the flow of transactions. It is the reciprocal of the rate of turnover of the money supply.

We can refer to equation 19.1 as the classical theory of the transactions demand for money. It is depicted graphically in Figure 19-1.

Sometimes, what we have called the classical theory of the transactions demand for money is taken simply as an empirical observation, without any explicit theoretical justification. However, the usual theoretical defence is by analogy with the income-payments cycle of an individual household.

Figure 19-1
Transactions Demand for Money: *Classical Theory*

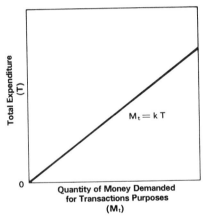

The Income-Payments Cycle and the Household's Demand for Trans actions Balances. Consider a householder who receives a regular monthly salary of, say, $600, all of which is spent on goods and services during the month. For simplicity, suppose he pays all of his salary into a current account with his bank at the beginning of the first day of the month, and spends it in equal daily installments of $20 during the month. The behaviour of his bank balance is described by the step-wise line in Figure 19-2. On the first day of the month it will jump to $600 (the heavy vertical line); by the last day it will be zero. It is easy to demonstrate that the average daily cash balance during each month will be $300. Early in the month it will be greater; late in the month it will be less. However if we define the householder's demand for money for transactions purpose as the average daily cash balance which he holds in anticipation of expenditures to be made before the next regular receipt of income, then it is $300, or half his monthly income.

Figure 19-2
The Income-Payments Cycle of a Household: Daily Cash Balances Assuming a Monthly Income of $600 and Daily Expenditures of $20

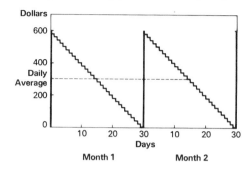

If we can further assume that with a change in his income the householder will not alter the *pattern* of his expenditure within the month but will change the amount of his daily expenditure proportionately (i.e. the "institutional setting" is given) then we can represent his personal transactions demand for money function by the equation:

$$m_t = \tfrac{1}{2}\, y_m \tag{19.2}$$

where m_t is the household's average daily cash balance during each month, and t is the household's total monthly expenditure on goods and services.

The derivation of the equation is demonstrated in Figure 19-3. The right-hand panel duplicates Figure 19-2, with the daily steps straightened out, and with the daily level of cash balances shown for two other levels of monthly income (= expenditure), assuming the same pattern of expenditures during each month (i.e., equal daily expenditures of the entire

Figure 19-3
Derivation of a Household's Transactions Demand for Money Function: Classical Assumptions

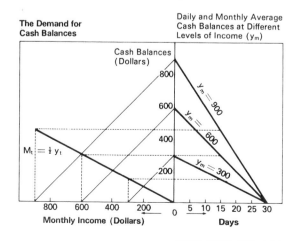

monthly income). The heavy line on the left-hand panel relates the average cash balance during the month (vertical axis) to the total monthly income (= expenditure). This is the household's demand for transactions balances.[1] (Note that on the horizontal axis, monthly income increases to the left.)

Generalizing the Example. This formulation of an individual householder's transactions demand for money, while over-simplified, sets in clear relief the basic idea that money is held as a time-bridge between regular receipts of income, on the assumption that income and expected payments have different time patterns. The example could be made more complicated by modifying it to allow for part of the monthly salary being saved and invested in financial instruments rather than spent, and for more complex time patterns of income and expenditure. Although it is a bit more difficult, the basic concept could also be applied in the analysis of the demand for transactions balances on the part of business firms faced with differing time patterns of cash receipts from sales and cash expenditures. For both household and firms, transactions balances serve as a bridge in time, and as long as the basic pattern of income and expenditures does not change, the demand for transactions balances on the part of each spending unit will be a linear function of the total value of transactions.

The Aggregate Demand Function. Remember, however, that these are microeconomic examples relating to individual households and firms. The notion that the aggregate demand function derived by adding up all of the microeconomic demand functions will have similar properties may be intuitively appealing, but it is far from clear that this is the case. The shape of the aggregate demand function depends not only on the shape of the individual demand functions of individual firms and households, but also on the distribution of transactions among spending units with differing individual demands. Since this information is unobtainable, we cannot be confident of the shape of the aggregate demand function. Nevertheless, the linear function of Figure 19-1 is very convenient, and is a possible implication of the assumptions about household and firm behaviour contained in the examples.

Why hold Transactions Balances in Cash? The classical theory of the demand for transactions balances is plausible at first glance, but considered carefully, it is really far from convincing as a theory of the transactions demand for *money*.

The classical theory demonstrates that a household or a firm with patterns of income and expenditure which are not co-incident in time will have a demand for transactions balances in some form. This is not the same thing as a demand for money because *money is not the only form in which transactions balances can be held,* and it may not be the most desirable form, since it yields no interest income. Hence, why should the household of our example hold money, which it knows will not be spent till the end of the month, when it can invest the idle money in short-term, highly liquid assets, which yield interest income, and can be sold at the very moment that expenditures are to be made. Indeed, why hold any cash at all? At the beginning of the month the householder can invest $580 (his salary minus the first day's expenditure) in a *series* of short term $20 loans or securities, one to mature on each day during the month. This would provide him with cash as needed to meet anticipated expenditures, and would put his money balances to work earning interest income. His demand for *cash* balances on a daily average during the month would approximate zero.

This possibility is not allowed for in the simple classical formulation.

Tranfer Costs and the Transactions Demand for Money

If we lived in a "frictionless" world in which there were no costs involved in buying and selling financial instruments, the rational policy would indeed be to hold no money among transactions balances. As long as there were a positive rate of interest, people would hold money for only an instant before they made an expenditure, and the average cash balance of every spending unit would approach zero.

Thus, the *crucial assumption implicit in the classical theory of the transactions demand for money is that transfer costs are so high that such transfers between money and non-money liquid assets are impracticable. It implies a world of extreme frictions.* Although it is true that the real world is not frictionless, the implicit classical assumption of complete immobility between money and other assets is clearly not valid either.

Transfer Costs. The costs involved in transfers among asset forms were discussed in Chapter 8. These costs proved to be important in explaining the phenomenon of financial intermediation. They are also essential in explaining the nature of the transactions demand for money.

Some transfer costs are quite explicit, such as the fees and commissions of brokers, dealers and investment advisers. Some, however, are implicit, such as the inconvenience of changing habitual arrangements, the time and bother involved in making the detailed calculations necessary for sophisticated decisions, or even the time involved in going to the bank to cash in a savings bond. Transfer costs are incurred both when assets are acquired, and when they are sold. There is also the problem of indivisibilities. Thus the wealth-owner may find that minimum investment requirements force him to hold money until he has accumulated sufficient wealth to purchase a desired asset, e.g., treasury bills with a minimum denomination of $10,000.

The important point is that unlike interest income, these transfer costs normally do not depend directly on the value of the assets or the length of time which they are held. Given the schedule of fees, they depend mainly on the *number of transactions.*

The Inventory Theoretic Model of the Transastions Demand for Money. Given the existence of different time patterns of cash expenditures, a positive interest rate on non-money assets, and transfer costs which depend on the number of transfers between money and other assets, how much money should an individual hold? Because of the interest rate, the classical conclusion that all transactions balances should be held in money is not likely to be optimal. Because of the transfer costs the opposite conclusion that all transactions balances should be held in non-money assets is not likely to be optimal either. What division between money and non-money assets will maximize the net return on the transactions balances?

This problem in economic theory was explored independently in two pioneering articles by William Baumol[2] and James Tobin.[3] Because of its affinity to the problem faced by the retailer or manufacturer in deciding on the appropriate level of inventories to be held, their approach to the problem has been labelled the "inventory-theoretic" model of the transactions demand for money. We will not explore the formal mathematics of the inventory-theoretic model of the transactions demand for money. However, the basic argument should be intuitively obvious.

It is assumed that a household with an income-payments cycle like that examined in the earlier example seeks to maximize the net yield on its transactions balances. This depends on finding the optimum combination of money and earning assets in which to hold the transactions balances. If too much money is held, the loss of interest income will reduce the yield. If too little money is held, the transfer costs between earning assets and money will more than offset the additional interest income, thus reducing the net yield. It turns out that given the level of transfer costs, the interest rate on earning assets, and the total value of transactions, that there is a definite optimum level of cash balances. What is important, however, is that for an individual household or firm:

(1) *The optimum level of money balances increases with the total value of expenditures* to be made during the period. However, the relationship is quite complex. The optimum level of cash balances for a household increases as the square root of total expenditures.

(2) *The optimum level of money balances increases with the level of transfer costs* between money and non-money assets.

(3) *The optimum level of money balances varies inversely with the level of interest rates* on non-money assets.

The first of these three conclusions has a familiar ring. However, it should be noted that in the Baumol-Tobin analysis, the optimum level of cash balances does not increase in proportion to the total value of expenditures as classical theory implies. Rather, it increases much less than proportionately, implying economies of scale in individual transactions demands for cash (i.e., a doubling of the level of income and expenditure for a household will not double the optimum level of cash balances).

The second and third conclusions, taken together, show that: "when the yield disadvantage of cash is slight, (i.e., when interest rates are low) the costs of frequent transactions will deter the holding of other assets, and average cash holdings will be large. However, when the yield disadvantage of cash is great, it is worthwhile to incur large transactions costs and keep average cash holdings low."[4] That is, the transactions demand for money on the part of individual households and firms — and hence the aggregate transactions demand for money — will display some interest elasticity. The higher the level of interest rates, the lower the average cash holdings. However, the existence of transfer costs will induce people to hold some transactions balances even at relatively high interest rates.

Baumol and Tobin both conclude that the advantages of such sophisticated management of cash holdings may be negligible for the average spending unit. We should not expect to find a high degree of interest elasticity with their cash holdings. However, for spending units with a large cash flow, such as corporations or municipal and provincial governments, the advantages from efficient cash management would be substantial. It is with their cash balances that we would expect to find substantial elasticity with respect to changes in interest rates.

The Interest Elasticity of the Aggregate Transactions Demand for Money. The Baumol-Tobin model, strictly speaking, applies to individual households and firms. What does it tell us about the nature of the aggregate demand for cash balances?

Again, consider the aggregation problem which we noted earlier in connection with the classical theory of the transactions demand for money. The information necessary to draw any firm conclusions about the aggregate demand for cash balances from such general microeconomic information is totally unobtainable.

However, one conclusion at least seems warranted. It is highly probable that the aggregate transactions demand for money has some negative interest elasticity.[5]

This suggests that we must revise our earlier formulation of the aggregate transactions demand for money. Using the common mathematical notation for a *general* functional relationship (i.e., a mathematical statement that one variable depends on another, without specifying the exact nature of this dependence) we can express the relationship between the transactions demand for money, the aggregate value of expenditures (T), and the level of interest rates (r) (taking the level of transactions costs as given), as follows:

$$M_t = T' (T, r) \qquad\qquad (19.3)$$

While we do not know the exact shape of the relationships (e.g., if they are linear or not), we are confident that the demand for cash balances varies directly with the value of expenditures, and inversely with the level of interest rates.

Income and the Transactions Demand

The economic theory underlying both the classical and the inventory-theoretic models relates the transactions demand for money to the value of total expenditures during a given period of time. However, in most modern formulations, the aggregate transactions demand is related to the level of income rather than the value of total expenditures. Although the latter will normally be several times the former (remember all of the double counting which has to be eliminated in deriving an estimate of national income from the flow of total expenditures), it is generally thought that this substitution is acceptable (to be perfect substitutes the relation between the two would have to be constant over time and we cannot be certain of that). Most transactions occur in connection with the generation of income, i.e., in the process of producing and distributing goods and services. Hence, the level of income should be highly correlated with the aggregate value of transactions. Either variable can be used as an index of the impact of the level of economic activity on the demand for money.

Moreover, the use of an income variable in the demand for money has a major advantage. A demand-for-money equation is seldom desired for its own sake. Whether in theoretical or empirical analysis, it is normally wanted as one equation in a macroeconomic model (a mathematical description of the economy in terms of the interaction among highly aggregative variables). Such a model may be relatively simple, involving only a few equations, or may be very detailed, involving a hundred or more equations. In either case, it is helpful to express the demand for money in terms of variables which are explained in the model. Income is normally such a variable; the aggregate value of transactions is not.

With this substitution in mind, we can then rewrite our aggregate transactions demand for money function as follows:

$$M_t = T(Y, r) \qquad (19.4)$$

where Y is an index of aggregate income, such as the gross national product.

These assumptions about the aggregate transactions demand for money are incorporated in Figure 19-4. The demand for money is shown to increase with the level of aggregate income, and at each level of income to vary inversely with the level of interest rates. At any level of income

Figure 19-4
The Transactions Demand for Money: Interest Rate and Income Effects

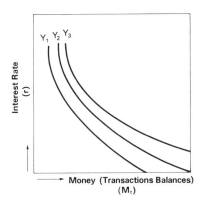

there should be a maximum quantity of money demanded for transactions purposes (i.e., when the interest rate is so low that all transactions
balances are held in money form), but the existence of transfer costs
should guarantee that the demand for money will never be zero at
"reasonable" levels of the interest rate.

2/ASSET DEMANDS FOR MONEY

We introduced this chapter with the observation that money is an
asset which has been specially designed as a medium of exchange. But
this means that to its holders money must be the most liquid of assets.
Our analysis of the portfolio balance decision in Chapter 5 demonstrated
that assetholders have reasons for holding liquid assets in their portfolios
in addition to the accommodation of specific expenditures plans in the
near future (i.e., in addition to a generalized "transactions motive.") In
particular, the provision of a *hedge against uncertainty and speculation
on changes in interest rates* were suggested as important motives for holding liquid assets. But if money is the most liquid of assets, does this
mean that there will be corresponding "precautionary" and "speculative"
demands for money in addition to what we have called the transactions
demand?

We will not repeat the analysis of uncertainty and speculation from
Chapter 5. We take as proven the proposition that they can give rise to
demands for liquid assets. Because of uncertainty about the future course
of income and expenditures, each assetholder will want to hold part
of his portfolio in liquid form. Likewise, in periods when interest rates
are expected to rise, assetholders can be expected to shift out of long-
term securities and into short-term instruments, giving rise to additional
demands for liquid assets. Conversely, when interest rates are expected
to fall, holdings of liquid assets will be abnormally reduced, as assetholders shift into longer-term securities in anticipation of capital gains.

The Demand for Liquid Assets Versus the Demand for Money. In
his famous book, *The General Theory of Employment Interest and
Money*, J. M. Keynes came to the conclusion that the very facts of uncertainty and speculation on interest rate changes were by themselves
sufficient to explain the existence of asset demands for money.[6] However,
Keynes derived this conclusion from a model in which the assetholder's
range of choice is limited to two financial instruments, money and long
term bonds. Money is the only possible hedge against uncertainty, and
money is the only possible vehicle for speculation on a rise in interest
rates.

But again, we must remind ourselves that while money may be the
most liquid of assets, it is not the only highly liquid asset. Normally the
range of alternatives is wide, including short-term claims on governments,
financial intermediaries, and private businesses, and including claims payable on demand or with as little notice as one day. Given a wide range
of non-money liquid assets, all of which yield interest income, we might

well ask Keynes himself his famous question: "Why would anyone outside a lunatic asylum wish to use money as a store of wealth?"[7] Surely it is more attractive to hold precautionary balances in the form of earning assets than in the form of non-interest bearing money, and surely it is attractive to supplement possible speculative capital gains with the interest earned on short-term investment of the speculative balances.

Transfer Costs. But what the foregoing discussion ignores is that the expected interest income must be sufficient to offset the probable costs of maintaining precautionary and speculative balances in non-money form for this to be worthwhile. If there are speculative or precautionary demands for money on the part of assetholders — and particularly those with relatively large portfolios — they must be explained by these economic frictions.

Wealth, Interest Rates and the Asset Demands for Money. If there is an asset demand for money, then it is positively related to total asset holdings (although the relationship may not be linear), and inversely related to the level of interest rates. That is;

$$M_a = A (A, r) \tag{19.5}$$

where M_a is the asset demand for money, A is the total value of asset holdings, and r is the level of interest rates.

The aggregate demand for money, then, is a combination of the transactions demand and the asset demands for money. That is:

$$M = M'(A, Y, r) \tag{19.6}$$

However, the precise formulation of the aggregate demand function is a matter of controversy. While we have suggested that the asset demand for money is essentially a question of the composition of asset portfolios, at the aggregate level the asset demand is commonly related to wealth rather than total asset holdings. The central issue in the controversy is whether wealth, or income, or both should be included in the demand function — with some advocates of the wealth formulation arguing that the interest rate variable should be omitted as of negligible importance.

We will return to these issues below. However, our preference should be clear from what has gone before. We regard the transactions demand for money as paramount; and therefore conclude on *a priori* grounds that the income and interest rate variables are both essential. The importance of the wealth variable is moot. These are conclusions based on theoretical speculation. They may be wrong. Clearly, we have here issues which can only be resolved by subjecting the alternative theories to empirical tests. Unfortunately the empirical tests to date are not conclusive.

In any case, in the short run we can take wealth or total asset holdings as given. The important point for our subsequent analysis is that there are sound theoretical reasons for believing that the aggregate demand for money has a positive association with the level of income and a negative association with the level of interest rates. In other words, *taking wealth as given*,

$$M = M(Y, r) \qquad (19.7)$$

In this context, the main effect of including asset demands for money is to make the demand function somewhat more elastic with respect to the rate of interest, particularly at lower levels of the interest rate. Our assumptions regarding the aggregate demand for money are depicted in Figure 19-5, showing both the negative elasticity with respect to the interest rate and the positive elasticity with respect to the level of income.

Figure 19-5
The Demand for Money: Income and Interest Rate Effects

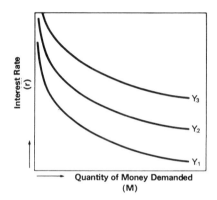

Interest Elasticity of the Income Velocity of Circulation. We introduced the concept of the velocity of circulation of money earlier in the book (Chapter 2). One variant of this concept is the income velocity of circulation, a measure of the intensity with which money is used in the generation of income. We define the income velocity as the ratio of aggregate income to the stock of money,

$$V_y = \frac{Y}{M} \qquad (19.8)$$

Our conclusions regarding the demand for money can be summarized succinctly using this concept.

If the demand for money depends on both the level of income and the level of interest rates, then *the velocity of circulation — the ratio of income to money — will be directly related to the level of interest rates.* At relatively high interest rates, households and firms economize on their money holdings, increasing the velocity of circulation of money. At relatively low levels of interest rates, the opportunity cost of holding money is less, and the velocity of circulation correspondingly falls. Is there any evidence in support of such a proposition?

Figure 19-6 is a "scatter diagram" showing the relationship between the income velocity of money and the yield on treasury bills in Canada for each year from 1948 through 1968. Each point on the chart represents the velocity of circulation of money (vertical axis) and the yield on treasury bills (horizontal axis) prevailing in the indicated year.[8]

Figure 19-6
Interest Rates and the Income Velocity of Money*: Canada, 1948-1968

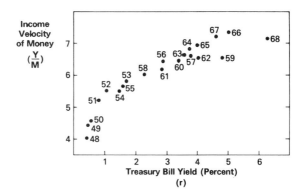

*Money = demand deposits adjusted for float – currency in circulation outside banks.
Income = gross national product.

While the correlation between the two variables is far from perfect, *there is an obvious positive association between the interest rate and the velocity of circulation in Canada in this period.* Years with high interest rates also had relatively high income velocities, and *vice versa.* While this is very crude evidence, it does provide some justification for our theoretical conclusion that the interest rate is a significant factor in the demand for money function.

3/PRICES AND THE DEMAND FOR MONEY

Up to this point we have discussed the demand for money on the implicit assumption that the general level of prices was stable. In the real world, such an assumption is hardly reasonable. Inflation seems to be an ever-present phenomenon, and at times in some countries the rate of change of the price level has been so great as to merit the sobriquet "hyper-inflation". As we noted in Chapter 5, changes in the price level can be an important consideration in portfolio selection decisions. It follows that they should also affect the demand for money.

We must distinguish two different effects of the price level on the demand for money: the *direct impact* of a change in the price level, and the impact of *expectations* of continuing price level changes.

Direct Impact. An increase in the general level of prices involves a decline in the real value of anything whose nominal value is fixed in terms of the unit of account. Money is such an item. For this reason, economists find it necessary to distinguish between the "nominal money supply" and the "real money supply". The former is simply the money supply as we would conventionally measure it — the number of dollars (currency plus chequable bank deposits) in circulation. The real money supply is the nominal money supply adjusted for changes in its real purchasing power. That is, we define the real money supply (M_r) as:

$$M_r = \frac{M}{P} \tag{19.9}$$

where M is the nominal money supply and P is an index of the general level of prices.

As long as we made the implicit assumption of a stable price level, this distinction between real and nominal values was not relevant. However, when we allow for the possibility that the price level may change, it should be clear that the demand for money function, 19.8 should be written in real terms. That is, the aggregate demand for money should be:

$$\frac{M}{P} = M\left(\frac{Y}{P}, r\right) \tag{19.10}$$

What then is the direct impact of a rise in the price level? At any given level of output and employment, i.e., with the level of real income given, a rise in the price level, by increasing the nominal level of income, increases the nominal amount of money demanded at any given interest rate. The demand for real balances has not changed. However, because of the rise in the price level proportionally more dollars are required to do the same work in the economy. In terms of the demand functions for nominal money balances plotted in Figure 19-5, the direct impact of a once-over rise in the price level is equivalent to that of a rise in income — except that the shift of the demand function will leave the ratio $\frac{M}{Y}$ constant at any given level of the interest rate (something which is not necessarily true when the increase in income is entirely real).

The impact of expectations of continuing increases in the price level are somewhat different.

Expectations of Price Level Changes. As we saw in Chapter 5, expected increases in the price level in the future must be taken into account in assessing the probable yield on financial instruments and real assets. In this sense, the expected rate of inflation must be taken as an adjustment to the nominal yield in order to obtain the real yield. Applied to money, the expectation of inflation is equivalent to a negative interest rate on money balances. It should produce the same effect on the demand for money as an increase in interest rates by the amount of the expected rate of inflation. That is, it should reduce the quantity of money demanded at each nominal interest rate.

This effect is illustrated in Figure 19-7. The dotted line is the demand for money in the absence of expectations of inflation. The solid line is the demand for money when inflation is expected at the rate of 100e% per annum.

Figure 19-7
The Demand for Money with Expectations of Inflation

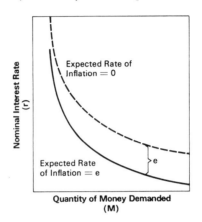

Clearly, the expectation of a very high rate of inflation would shift the demand curve very far to the left — virtually driving money out of circulation. Such is the common observation in periods of "hyper-inflation". Studies of the demand for money under conditions of hyper-inflation have shown clearly that the rate of change of the price level is an important explanatory variable, although little success has been achieved in finding such an effect under conditions in which the changes in the price level were more gentle.[9]

4/SOME UNRESOLVED ISSUES

Although we have hinted at the existence of some points of controversy, we have presented a theory of the demand for money as though there remained few really serious points of disagreement among economists on this matter. Such an implication is far from the truth. While we cannot attempt to explore every nuance of every debate, it is important that students of monetary economics at least have their attention drawn to the major points of controversy.

Empirical Research on the Demand for Money

Like most controversies in economics today, the basic issues are empirical. They can only be settled by confronting theory with fact — by attempting to measure each proposed demand for money function statistically and then subjecting the competing theories to a quantitative test of their relative predictive ability.

Empirical work in this field requires the application of sophisticated analysis, using either cross-sectional or time series data to estimate the demand for money function. To report in detail on each of the various pieces of empirical research that has been undertaken would require a capsule course in econometric techniques, which is not the function of a text on money and banking. Accordingly we can do little more than note our interpretation of the conclusions to be drawn from the various tests that have been undertaken and what further controversies remain to be explored.

Before doing so, it is important to note that not all stastical studies define money in the same way. Some of the studies use the concept of money in the way in which we have, i.e., money is narrowly defined as payments money. In other studies, money is defined more broadly to include some "near monies", most commonly time deposits at commercial banks. (Remember: most studies were done on United States data, and in the United States such deposits are not chequable.) In a few studies money is defined very broadly indeed, to include virtually all short-term highly liquid assets.

It should not be surprising, therefore, that the results are often contradictory. *The broader the definition of money, the more the interest rate substitutions between payments money and other liquid assets will be obscured.*

Is the Demand for Money Interest-Elastic?

We have tried to present cogent reasons why we would *expect* the demand for money to have some degree of elasticity with respect to the level of interest rates. As we shall see, this is an important issue when it comes to identifying how changes in the money supply affect the level of economic activity. It is at the centre of the major debates in monetary economics today.

A distinct negative relationship between aggregate holdings of cash balances and an interest rate was found in the earliest modern statistical studies of the demand for money, such as those by Tobin and Latané.[10] In subsequent more sophisticated and more detailed studies, using different forms for the demand functions, different types of data, and different definitions of money, this relationship has been fairly consistently confirmed.

The major critic is Professor Milton Friedman of the University of Chicago. He has questioned the validity of these findings, contending that using observed interest rates and observed money holdings was improper since the behaviour of both of these variables was in turn explained by other more basic factors. Using a long series of historical data and using cyclical average rather than observed values for the money supply he found that the interest rate was not an important variable in explaining the demand for money. Rather he found that "permanent income" was almost the only significant variable.[11] Recent work by Brunner and Meltzer and Laidler,[12] using Friedman's data and various measures of interest rates, found opposite results, i.e., the inclusion of the interest rate did improve the predictive ability of Friedman's demand function. We will examine Friedman's studies further, later in this chapter.

Aside from the contrary results of Friedman, the evidence appears to be strong that the interest rate is an important determinant in the demand for money. Indeed, one leading student in this field has gone so far as to state that "Of all of the issues in monetary economics, this is the one that appears to have been settled most decisively."[13]

Is There a Liquidity Trap?

The division of the demand for money into transactions demand, precautionary demand, and speculative demand is due to J. M. Keynes, whose work in this field has already been noted. Whereas we have pushed the transactions demand to the fore, Keynes argued that the asset demands and particularly the speculative demand, had the more potent impact on the economy. In this connection, it must be remembered that Keynes was particularly concerned with the behaviour of the demand for money at very low interest rates such as those prevailing during a severe depression.

In the two-asset world of Keynes' model, interest rates which were widely believed to be abnormally low would give rise to strong speculative demands for money. This was the main Keynesian explanation of the negative interest elasticity of the demand for money. However, in the Keynesian literature, the proposition has been pushed farther. It is argued that as the interest rate falls, the elasticity of the demand for money will increase. Indeed, some followers of Keynes argued that at some low rate of interest the demand for money would become infinite and when this occurred we would be in what was called the "liquidity trap". Interest rates would not decline further since all wealth-owners would prefer to hold money rather than alternative assets. The use of monetary expansion to lower interest rates and stimulate economic activity would be useless. Monetary policy would be paralyzed as an instrument of economic policy. Such a demand for money function is depicted in Figure 19-8.

The Keynesian liquidity trap hypothesis has been attacked on various grounds, both theoretical and empirical. We have already noted that in a multi-asset world, a strong speculative demand for money is unlikely to exist at any positive interest rate on short-term securities. This would not necessarily be true, of course, if speculation or general economic conditions led to a sharp reduction in the supply of short-term instruments, reducing the short-term interest rate to near zero (e.g., at some time during the depression of the 1930's banks were reported to be refusing to accept corporate time deposits, and the yield on treasury bills declined to less than $\frac{1}{2}\%$ per annum). Under these extreme circumstances, money might be virtually the only highly liquid asset.

However, critics have also argued that the expectational assumptions of the liquidity trap hypothesis are implausible: that a prolonged period of low interest rates would lead to expectations that such low rates were "normal". Widespread expectations of a rise in rates would not exist.

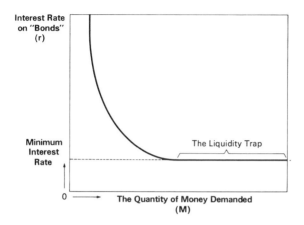

Figure 19-8
The Keynesian Liquidity Trap

Most economists would regard the question of the existence or non-existence of a liquidity trap one to be resolved by confronting theory with fact. Several empirical studies have done just that, notably those by Bronfenner and Mayer, Laidler, and Brunner and Meltzer.[14] While their results were consistent with the proposition that there is a negative relationship between the level of interest rates and the demand for money, their attempts to establish that the *elasticity of the demand for money increases* at low levels of interest rates generally produced negative results. Most of these tests used historical data for the United States during various periods in the twentieth century. It was anticipated that in the depths of the depression of the 1930's, when interest rates reached all-time lows, the liquidity trap would be found. Yet in various tests that were undertaken, no matter how money was defined — whether interest rates used were long or short term and whether wealth or income was included in the function — the existence of a liquidity trap in this sense could not be clearly established. It is always very difficult to prove a negative proposition like "the liquidity trap does not exist", and many economists remain unconvinced by the evidence. However, we must accept that the available studies cast significant doubt on the importance of the Keynesian liquidity trap concept.

Is Wealth or Income the Appropriate Variable in the Demand Function?

At various points in our discussion of the demand for money, we have mentioned the work of Professor Milton Friedman. Friedman's analysis plays such a prominent role in contemporary controversies in monetary economics that it merits a somewhat fuller exposition.[15]

The starting point of Friedman's analysis is essentially the same as ours. That is, he starts with the proposition that money is an asset, a form in which wealth may be held. To the business firm it is a capital good, a source of productive services which add to the productivity of the enterprise. The holding of money yields utility directly to the household. Thus, to the household, money is a durable consumer good, a source of implicit income in the form of consumable services. The nature of the service yielded by money, to both households and firms, is that which we have already identified. It permits the separation in time of expenditures from the receipt of income.

Where, then, does Friedman's analysis differ from that which we have presented? In brief, *Friedman employs a broader concept of money, minimizes the importance of interest-rate-induced substitution effects and of the current income variable in the demand function, and places particular stress on a very general concept of wealth as the main explanatory variable for the demand for money.*

Friedman chooses a broader definition of money than our "payments money" concept on the empirical grounds that better statistical results are obtained with a definition which includes non-chequable time deposits at commercial banks (but which does not include comparable deposits at other financial intermediaries, or other highly liquid assets.) He notes, however, that the appropriate definition is not a point of major importance. He finds almost as good results with a narrower definition.

Consider first the demand by households for money. The household's wealth, to Friedman, is the present value of all expected future income, regardless of the source or the form of the income (i.e., whether it is received in money or in the form of intangible services). Thus, his analysis includes human as well as non-human sources of income. Each source of wealth is an asset, with a measureable yield, and to maximize the utility derived from its portfolio each household must so arrange the composition of its portfolio as to equate the expected yields at the margin. In the process, each household elects to hold some portion of its wealth in the form of money. Firms, for whom money is a capital good, will engage in a similar balancing process, equating the marginal productivity of all factors of production, including money, at the margin.

A crucial problem in the empirical application of this approach is the measurement of wealth. Friedman surmounts this problem by substituting a summary measure of the stream of expected future income from which the concept of wealth is derived, i.e., the concept of *permanent income* which we encountered in Chapter 4 in our discussion of the saving decision. Assuming peoples' expectations are heavily influenced by developments in the recent past, Friedman estimates permanent income on the basis of a weighted average of past incomes, with most recent income weighted most heavily. This measure is used in the demand for money function as a proxy for wealth.

On the basis of a large body of empirical research, Friedman concludes that permanent income is the single most important determinant of the aggregate demand for money. Current income is only significant as one of the components of permanent income. While he does not deny that interest rates may play some role in the demand function — as we have seen, his theoretical formulation involves the balancing of rates of return on all assets at the margin — he argues that the interest elasticity of the demand for money is sufficiently low that this factor can be virtually ignored. Cyclical fluctuations in the velocity of money circulation are not explained by the influence of interest rates. Rather, they are explained by fluctuations of current income around permanent income. For example, in periods of boom, income tends to rise relative to the stock of money. However, this rise in the income velocity of money, conventionally measured as the ratio $\dfrac{Y}{M}$, does not reflect interest-rate-induced substitutions of other liquid assets for money in asset portfolios. Rather, it simply reflects the fact that current income has risen relative to permanent income. The quantity of money demanded is relatively stable not because interest rates have increased but because permanent income is relatively stable. Indeed, the main conclusion which Friedman draws from his work is that providing the price level is relatively stable, *the demand for money is a relatively stable function of permanent income*. This proposition, together with the theoretical analysis underlying it, is commonly known as the *new quantity theory of money*. We will return to it in the next chapter.

Figure 19-9 describes this relationship graphically, in a simplified way. Y represents current income, which is increasing over time, but at a fluctuating rate. Y_p represents permanent income, the rate of growth of which is relatively more stable. Since the quantity of money demanded (M_d) is a constant function of permanent income, it follows a growth path like that of permanent income. Parenthetically, we might note that Friedman finds that money is a luxury good. That is, the demand for money increases somewhat more rapidly than permanent income.

Figure 19-9
Income, Permanent Income and the Demand for Money

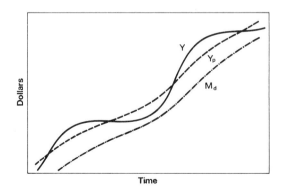

Friedman's analysis thus has similar roots to that which we have presented, but comes to rather different conclusions. In part this is because of a different definition of money, but in part too, it reflects a different interpretation of the evidence. Unfortunately, the evidence is far from conclusive either way. There is substantial evidence that Friedman has underestimated the importance of interest rates in the demand for money function — even on his own formulation of that function. However, there is also some evidence that wealth or permanent income performs better in statistical demand functions than does the current income variable which we stress. This is an area of continuing research and we can only refer the serious student to the ever-expanding literature.

5/THE DEMAND FOR MONEY: CONCLUSIONS

The demand for money is the basic concept of monetary economics but, as we have tried to make clear, this is not an area in economics in which there is a universally accepted doctrine. It is a field in turmoil, stirred up by theoretical disputes and contradictory empirical results.

We have attempted to present a perspective on the demand for money which emphasizes the role of money as a medium of exchange, and which directs attention to the role of transfer costs in explaining the otherwise apparently irrational habit of holding money as an asset.

Our approach seems to stand in opposition to approaches which stress that the demand for money reflects a process of choosing the form in which wealth is to be held. That is far from our intention. In fact we agree that this is the nature of the demand for money. The point at issue is: What objective factors bear on the decision on the portion of wealth which will be held in the form of money? We argue that it depends on the value of transactions to be effected with money and the relationship between the interest rate (adjusted for expectations of price level changes) and transfer costs, while others argue that the ratio of money to wealth is relatively constant (meaning that wealth itself is the main determinant of the demand for money), modified only slightly by such factors as interest rates. Still others, notably Friedman, argue that wealth is the principal determinant, and that money is a luxury good.

All agree, however, that the concept of a demand for money is meaningful: it can be measured statistically, appears to be relatively stable over time, and, as we shall see in the next chapter, has powerful economic implications.

FOOTNOTES

[1] In this equation we have used small letters to signify that it relates to an individual rather than the aggregate.

If we substitute the householder's annual income for his monthly income in equation 19.2, it becomes:

$$m_t = 1/24 \ y_a$$

This assumes that the salary continues to be paid in monthly installments, and that expenditures are made on exactly the same pattern. Then the average *daily* cash balance is unchanged; the only change is that the income variable is inflated by a factor of 12.

It can be readily seen that if several large payments are made early in the month, the average cash balance will be less than $\frac{1}{2} y_m$. In the extreme, if the entire monthly income is paid out in a single lump sum payment during the first day, the average cash balance will approximate o. Likewise, if few payments are made early in the month, with the bulk spent in several large payments late in the month, the average cash balance will be greater than $\frac{1}{2}y_m$. In the extreme, if only one large lump sum payment were made at the end of the month, the average cash balance would approximate y_m.

[2] W. J. Baumol, "The Transactions Demand for Cash: An Inventory Theoretic Approach," in *The Quarterly Journal of Economics*, Vol. 56 (Nov. 1952), pp. 545-556.

[3] James Tobin, "The Interest Elasticity of Transactions Demand for Cash," in *The Review of Economics and Statistics*, Vol. 37, (Aug. 1956) pp. 241-247.

[4] Tobin, *op. cit.*, p. 242.

[5] The macroeconomic implications of the square root rule are particularly hard to interpret. The usual problem of relating to the distribution of income and expenditures among households arises, of course. However, even ignoring that, we cannot tell whether the fact that the optimum level of cash balances for *each household* varies with the square root of the household's expenditures also implies that the *aggregate demand* for cash balances varies with the square root of total expenditures. Clearly, if the increase in total expenditures is spread over a larger number of firms and households (with no individual household's expenditures increasing) the square root rule would not apply. Without solid empirical evidence to the contrary, perhaps the classical linear assumption is most useful at the aggregate level.

[6] J. M. Keynes, *The General Theory of Employment, Interest and Money* (London: Macmillan, 1936), p. 168.

[7] *Ibid.*, p. 216.

[8] In constructing this chart we have chosen a narrow definition of money, i.e., demand deposits (adjusted for bank float) plus currency in circulation outside banks. This corresponds to a payments money concept, including those money forms which are most actively used in making payments. A broader definition of money would yield similar conclusions, as is shown, for example, in A. Breton, "A Stable Velocity Function for Canada?", in *Economica*, Vol. N.S. 35 (Nov. 1968), pp. 451-453. We have used gross national product as the measure of aggregate income.

[9] The most widely quoted study is Philip Cagan, "The Monetary Dynamics of Hyperinflation," in M. Friedman, ed., *Studies in the Quantity Theory of Money* (Chicago: University of Chicago Press, 1956), pp. 25-120. The literature is reviewed in D. Laidler, *The Demand for Money: Theories and Evidence* (Scranton: International Textbook Co., 1969), pp. 104-106.

[10] J. Tobin, "Liquidity Preference and Monetary Policy," in *Review of Economic Statistics*, Vol. 29 (May, 1947), pp. 124-131; H. A. Latané, "Cash Balances and the Interest Rate — A pragmatic Approach" in *Review of Economics and Statistics*, Vol. 36 (Nov. 1954), pp. 456-460.

[11] Friedman in fact tested the importance of interest rates in an indirect way. He hypothesized that the demand for money was a function of a calculated figure for permanent income (see Chapter 4). He then compared the residual, i.e., the difference between observed and predicted values for the demand for money with various interest rates. On the basis of a *visual* correlation of the residuals and the various measures for interest rates he could find no consistent pattern and therefore concluded that interest rates were not a primary determinant of the demand for money. See Milton Friedman, "The Demand for Money: Some theoretical and empirical results," in *Journal of Political Economy*, Vol. 67 (Aug. 1959), pp. 327-51.

[12] K. Brunner and A. H. Meltzer, "Predicting Velocity: Implications for Theory and Policy," in *Journal of Finance*, Vol. 18 (May 1963), pp. 319-354; D. Laidler, "The Rate of Interest and the Demand for Money — Some Empirical Evidence," in *Journal of Political Economy*, Vol. 74 (Dec. 1966), pp. 545-555.

[13] Laidler, *The Demand for Money*, p. 97.

[14] M. Bronfenbrenner and T. Mayer, "Liquidity Functions in the American Economy," in *Econometrica*, Vol. 28 (Oct. 1960), pp. 810-834; D. Laidler, "The Rate of Interest and the Demand for Money — Some Empirical Evidence," in *Journal of Political Economy*, Vol. 74 (Dec. 1966), pp. 545-555; Brunner and Meltzer, *op. cit.*

[15] Some of Professor Friedman's basic works in this field have been collected in the volume, M. Friedman, *The Optimum Quantity of Money and Other Essays* (Chicago: Aldine, 1969). The essays, "The Quantity Theory of Money: A Restatement," (pp. 51-68); "The Demand for Money: Some Theoretical and Empirical Results," (pp. 111-140); and "Interest Rates and the Demand for Money," (pp. 141-156) are particularly important.

20

The Theory of Monetary Policy

Monetary policy involves the manipulation of the supplies of money and credit by the central bank, with the objective of influencing certain macroeconomic results of economic activity. Various objectives are important from time to time, but three will figure most prominently in our discussion: the level of income and employment, the general level of prices, and the stability of the foreign exchange rate. This chapter attempts to discover the channels through which the monetary actions of the central bank may affect economic activity and hence influence the levels of income, employment and prices. In the next chapter we will explore the international dimensions of monetary policy, and in Chapter 23 review several studies of the quantitative impact of monetary actions. It is important to keep this program in mind as you read this chapter. We are concerned only with the direction of the impact of monetary actions, not with their magnitude.

We saw in the last chapter that at any point in time there is a definable demand for money which depends, *inter alia*, on the level of income and the level of interest rates. In Chapters 16 and 17 we saw how the central bank could manipulate the money supply — primarily through open market operations which change the size of the monetary base. The question before us, then, is: Given the demand for money, what happens when the central bank changes the supply?

We can divide the repercussions into two interrelated categories: financial adjustments and real adjustments. By *financial adjustments* we mean the changes which occur in portfolios of financial instruments held by all types of assetholders. By *real adjustments* we mean changes which occur in the level of aggregate demand for goods and services, and hence in the general levels of production, employment and perhaps prices. The link between the financial adjustments and real adjustments, whose nature is a subject of controversy among monetary economists, is a major concern of monetary theory.

1/ FINANCIAL ADJUSTMENTS

The direct impact of central bank monetary actions is to produce disequilibrium in asset portfolios throughout the economy. The repercussions which follow result from assetholders' adjustments in the face of portfolio disequilibrium.

Portfolio Disequilibrium Within the Banking System

Consider first the financial repercussions of central bank measures to expand the money supply. As you will recall, such actions would normally take the form of purchases of government securities in the open market, although a variety of other expansionary techniques are also available to a central bank.

Bond Prices and Yields. The central bank cannot purchase government securities in the open market without raising their prices and hence somewhat depressing their yields. However, we will leave that aspect of the matter aside for the moment. As we shall see, the direct impact of the central bank on government bond yields becomes swallowed up in the larger effects resulting from private portfolio adjustments.

Excess Bank Reserves. The major initial impact of the central bank's open market purchases is to produce disequilibrium in the asset portfolios of commercial banks. The banks have a larger proportion of cash reserves among their assets than they would like, given the existing levels of interest rates. As we saw in Chapter 16, in this situation the profit motive will induce the banks to acquire additional earning assets. This has three important financial repercussions.

First, to some extent the banks will satisfy their demand for earning assets by purchasing securities, probably short-term government bonds, in the open market. Like the initial purchase by the central bank, this will tend to *raise the price and hence lower the yield on government securities.* Secondly, the banks will probably demonstrate increased willingness to extend loans. That is, at any given level of interest rates, they will be willing to extend more credit. The supply curve for bank loans shifts outward. Depending on the competitive environment, this should lead to some reduction of interest rates and an easing of other terms for bank loans. In the jargon of central banking, there will follow *a reduction in the cost and an increase in the "availability" of bank credit.* Third, on the other side of the balance sheet, the increase in the banks' earning assets will be matched by *an increase of the money supply.*

These are all familiar propositions, developed in detail in Chapter 16. What then happens outside the banking system?

Portfolio Disequilibrium Among Other Assetholders

We now have three developments which combine to produce disequilibrium conditions within the portfolios of private assetholders other than banks: they are holding a larger than normal amount of money; the yields on government bonds have declined somewhat; and bank credit is available on more favourable terms. Together, these factors will induce private assetholders to rearrange their portfolios.

Excess Supply of Money. Perhaps the most important effect, and certainly the one most stressed in traditional monetary theory, is the increase in private holdings of money. This money was put into the hands of individuals when they responded to offers from the central bank or the commercial banks for securities in their possession at marginally favourable prices, or through the extension of loans by the commercial banks. In general, for the private assetholders, the new money is a temporary repository of purchasing power between the sale of one asset and the purchase of another. Given the levels of income and interest rates they have no reason to hold the additional money itself. The new assets which they seek to acquire may be securities, or — and this is important as a link to the "real" side of the adjustment process — they may be real assets, capital goods or consumer durables.

The Level of Interest Rates. We can leave aside the effects on demands for real assets for the moment. In the market for securities, the attempts of private assetholders to purchase securities in exchange for the money which they do not want to hold will add to the upward pressure on security prices and hence to the decline in yields initiated by the central bank and aggravated by the portfolio adjustments of the commercial banks. Note also that through private portfolio adjustments, the decline of government bond yields will be generalized to securities of all types and all maturities. Assetholders will attempt to dispose of any securities whose yield has been abnormally depressed and attempt to purchase securities which still have relatively favourable yields. Given that the supply of each security is temporarily fixed, all that can happen as a result of such trading is a change in relative prices. Through the market adjustment, yields will tend to be equalized (allowing for risk and liquidity, of course) at new lower levels. In other words, *the end result is a decline in the general level of interest rates.* Indeed, *if* there were no real adjustments, *the level of interest rates would have to fall until private assetholders were content to hold the enlarged money supply.* (Remember: as we demonstrated in Chapter 16, there is no way that private assetholders can reduce the size of the money supply. They can only pass the unwanted money among themselves, until interest rates are bid down sufficiently that some assetholders are willing to hold the money in their portfolios.)

This is an important "if". There may be repercussions on real economic activity, and, as we shall see, these real repercussions also serve to adjust the demand for money to the expanded supply of money.

Linkages to Aggregate Demand

The Real Balance Effect. We have already identified one direct link between monetary expansion and aggregate demand. The simple fact that people are holding more money than they desire at the existing levels of income, interest rates, and prices means that they now have more real assets than before the open market purchase. With increased real money balances they will be inclined to purchase other assets including, perhaps, real assets. This direct effect of the increase of money holdings on demands for goods and services is called the *real balance effect*. It plays a central role in some monetary theories.

Substitution Effects. The reduction of the general level of interest rates (and the associated increase in the availability of bank credit) also induces *substitution effects.* Remember that, while the yields on financial instruments have fallen as a result of the expansion of the monetary base, yields on fixed capital assets have not changed. Thus, lower yields on financial assets will increase the *relative* attractiveness of real assets. Rational assetholders will attempt to increase the share of real assets in their portfolios, some of them simply adjusting the composition of their existing asset portfolios, selling financial assets to acquire capital goods or consumer durables, and others, motivated by the lower cost and increased availability of credit, borrowing funds to acquire additional real capital. The overall result is an increase in the demand for goods and services.

This is the major link to aggregate demand which we have been seeking. *Monetary expansion, by reducing the yield on financial instruments relative to that on real capital, creates an incentive to invest in real assets, thus tending to increase the aggregate demand for goods and services.*

The Yield on Real Assets. A crucial concept in this analysis is the yield, or the rate of return, on real assets. Is this a meaningful concept?

We have already examined the concept of "yield" in some depth in Chapter 5 and its Appendix. We discovered that it is simply the rate of interest implicit in the relationship between the market price of an asset and the stream of future income produced by that asset. We can apply the same concept to any piece of capital equipment. The stream of future income is the net addition to the revenues of the firm resulting from the employment of that piece of equipment (net after allowing for the cost of all cooperating factors). This stream may have a long or a short life; and it may be relatively certain or very uncertain. The market price of the asset is simply the cost of acquiring and installing the capital goods whether they are purchased from another firm or constructed on the spot. Given a stream of future income with a finite length, and a market price for the asset producing the income, we can calculate the expected yield in the manner discussed in the Appendix to Chapter 5. The yield on new real capital goods is commonly called the *marginal efficiency of capital.*

For industrial equipment and buildings, then, the concept of yield has a clear meaning. What about consumer durables?

Consumer durables can be thought of as producing a stream of future income — not in a financial sense, but in "real" terms, as a flow of intangible services which yield utility directly to the consumer and which have an implicit market value. In principle, then, we can also calculate the yield on durable consumer goods. While such calculations are difficult in practice, the yield on consumer durables is a meaningful concept for theoretical analysis.

The Saving Decision. There is also another type of substitution effect which might be induced by the general decline in the level of interest rates — *a substitution of present consumption for future consumption.* We discussed the saving decision at some length in Chapter 4, and noted that among other things the division of income between current consumption and saving might be influenced by the yield on financial assets. Although the direction of the effect is not absolutely certain, it is generally assumed that lower interest rates will induce more consumption and less saving. If so, we have another link between monetary expansion and the aggregate demand for goods and services.

Summary. In short, the linkages between the financial adjustments and aggregate demand are complex. They involve in part the substitution of real assets for financial assets in portfolios, borrowing to finance the expansion of some portfolios, and the substitution of current consumption for future consumption. Many individual decisions will be involved as each assetholder reassesses his portfolio in light of the new set of relative yields. As a result, the links may be highly diffused, and perhaps difficult to identify. They are not necessarily confined to the market for industrial capital goods. They may involve the market for consumer durable goods, and indeed for non-durable consumer goods and services.

Reaction to Monetary Restriction

All of our discussion of the financial repercussions of monetary policy has been in terms of the responses of assetholders to an *expansion* of the monetary base. Their reactions to a *restriction* would simply be the reverse of those which we have discussed. However, perhaps we should briefly outline these reactions before proceeding with our analysis of the real impact of monetary policy on income, employment and price levels.

A restriction of the monetary base, as we know, is effected by the sale of government bonds by the central bank. This will create some upward pressure on bond yields, and, by creating a cash reserve deficiency in the banking system, will lead to higher cost and restricted availability of bank credit. As the banks seek to deal with their reserve deficiency further upward pressure on bond yields will occur, and this, coupled with the restriction of bank credit, will induce portfolio adjustments on the part of private assetholders. The rise in bond yields will be generalized to a general rise in the level of interest rates, reducing incentives to invest in real assets. Through the various substitution effects which we discussed above, the incentives for businesses to purchase capital equipment, and for households to purchase consumer durables will be reduced, and there may be some incentive to increase the rate of saving out of current income. All considered, there should be a restriction in the aggregate demand for goods and services.

Monetary Policy and Debt Management Policy

Monetary Policy as Debt Management. Our discussions of monetary policy has focused on changes in the monetary base and hence in the money supply. However, as we noted earlier, the monetary base is but one form of government debt. It has peculiar characteristics as debt in that it can be used as a medium of exchange, has the shortest possible term to maturity (payable on demand), and is non-interest bearing. However, the very fact that it is government debt suggests an alternative perspective on monetary policy. It can be regarded as an aspect of *debt management policy*, i.e., governmental policy with respect to the composition, and particularly the term structure, of the outstanding government debt.

In this context, an expansion of the monetary base through open market purchases of government securities by the central bank can be considered as a reduction in the average term-to-maturity of the public debt, without any change in the size of the debt. The central bank has issued demand debt to replace dept in public hands with a longer term-to-maturity. Similarly, a contraction of the monetary base through open market sales of bonds by the central bank increases the average term-to-maturity of the public debt without altering the size of the debt. The central bank issues longer-term securities to replace demand debt in the hands of the general public.

"Conventional" Debt Management. Is the average term-to-maturity of the public debt itself an important macreconomic variable? If it is, this provides the government with an additional instrument for stabilization policy because the government, or the central bank, can always engage in other types of operations in the open market to change the average term-to-maturity of the public debt. For example, the central bank can purchase long-term bonds from the general public issuing treasury bills rather than money in their place, thus reducing the average term-to-maturity. Alternatively, the Bank can issue long-term bonds, retiring treasury bills rather than money, increasing the average term-to-maturity. We can call such operations, involving a change in the term structure of the interest-bearing public debt with no change in either the monetary base or the aggregate size of the public debt, "conventional" debt management operations.

Monetary Effects of Conventional Debt Management. Many economists argue that conventional debt management operations have macreconomic effects which are similar to those of monetary policy.

The principles underlying this argument are those which we developed earlier in our discussion of the demand for financial instruments and equilibrium in financial markets (Chapters 5 and 6). Consider the case of debt management operations to reduce the average term-to-maturity of the public debt. In order to achieve this objective, the government must disturb the pre-existing equilibrium in financial markets. It must sell short-term securities (perhaps treasury bills) which private assetholders do not want to hold at *existing interest rates*, and purchase long-term bonds which private assetholders do not want to sell *at existing interest rates*. In other words, the government must bid down the price, and hence increase the yield, of treasury bills, while it simultaneously bids up the price, and hence lowers the yield, of long-term bonds.

A complex of portfolio adjustments should follow, as private asset-holders and borrowers respond to the new *structure* of interest rates. While we cannot trace through these adjustments in any detail, two probable results are of interest.

First, the general public is holding more treasury bills (a highly liquid substitute for money in some asset portfolios), which should *reduce the demand for money*. The outstanding stock of money is unchanged. As a result, there will be more money in the economy than the public wants to hold under the existing circumstance. As we saw above, the existence of this *excess supply of money* should lead, directly or indirectly, to an increase in the demand for goods and services. In this sense, the debt management operation is the equivalent of an expansionary monetary policy.

Second, the relative decline in the yield on long-term government bonds might induce other *substitution effects* which would tend to expand aggregate demand. Because of this change in the yield on long-term government bonds other less liquid assets, including real assets (and perhaps current consumption), will become somewhat more attractive to private assetholders. They should make some marginal adjustments in their portfolios, leading to some expansion of aggregate demand. Thus, the substitution effects reinforce the effects of the reduction of the demand for money.

A lengthening of the average term to maturity of the government debt would presumably have opposite effects, increasing the demand for money and increasing the attractiveness of long-term government bonds as opposed to real assets for inclusion in private asset portfolios. The combined effect should be a contraction of aggregate demand for goods and services.

Monetary Policy versus Debt Management Policy. While conventional debt management operations can have effects which are similar to those of monetary policy, there is an important difference. We saw in Chapter 16 that an expansion of the monetary base through the purchase of government bonds by the central bank would induce an absolute expansion of the size of the asset holdings of private financial institutions (particularly banks and near banks) several times as great as the expansion of the monetary base. Given present institutional arrangements in Canada, equivalent conventional debt management operations (e.g., an increase in treasury bills outstanding equal to the postulated increase of the monetary base, offset by an equal reduction in long-term bonds outstanding) would not produce corresponding multiplier effects because the monetary base is not affected by the debt management operation. It seems likely, therefore, that the impact of conventional debt management operations on aggregate demand would be smaller than that of equivalent monetary operations.

Stabilization versus Interest Cost. While the strength and reliability of the effects can be questioned (we will consider some evidence in Chapter 23), the arguments which we have just reviewed provide an *a priori* case for the assertion that the term structure of the public debt is an important macroeconomic variable influencing the level of aggregate demand, and hence that conventional debt management operations can play a useful role in stabilization policy. However, it should be noted that the use of debt management operations for this purpose requires that the federal government not behave like the profit-maximizing debtors discussed in Chapter 6. That is, in general, the objective of debt management operations cannot be to minimize the effective interest cost of the public debt.

A moment's reflection should convince you of the potential conflict in debt management operations between the dictates of stabilization policy and the dictates of interest cost minimization. Given the size of the public debt, interest cost minimization requires that the debt be funded into longer-term securities when interest rates are relatively low. By issuing long-term bonds when rates are low the government can keep its interest payments low even though interest rates rise in the future (if the debt was largely short-term, it would mature and have to be refunded at the higher interest rates). However, as we have just seen, an increase of the average term-to-maturity tends to depress aggregate demand — and periods of low interest rates are likely to be precisely those times when the government is seeking to increase aggregate demand.

Exactly the opposite arguments apply to periods of high interest rates. At those times, interest cost minimization dictates that any new securities issued be short-term bonds. If long-term bonds are issued, the high interest rates will be built into the public debt even though interest rates subsequently fall. However, periods of high interest rates are usually periods when the government wants to retard aggregate demand — and, according to the arguments developed above, this calls for a lengthening of the average-term-to-maturity of the debt when interest rates are high.

The Conduct of Monetary Policy. It follows from this line of analysis that, in the implementation of monetary policy, attention should be paid not only to the *magnitude* of the change of the monetary base, but also to the *method* by which the change is effected. An increase of the monetary base resulting from central bank purchases of treasury bills will presumably have a marginally different impact on aggregate demand than will the same increase resulting from central bank purchases of long-term bonds. Unfortunately, however, although there has been considerable criticism of central bankers' preferences for dealing in short-term securities almost exclusively (the so called "bills only" doctrine),[1] there is little factual evidence that the form of the open market operations makes a significant difference. It remains an interesting theoretical proposition.

Conclusion. Although we have barely scratched the surface in our discussion of the management of the public debt, we cannot pursue the topic further here. We will now return to our analysis of the transmission of monetary policy, viewing monetary policy in the traditional framework. However, it is important to realize that we are exploring only one aspect — although a particularly important aspect — of a much broader problem of the management of the public debt.

2/REAL ADJUSTMENTS: QUANTITY THEORY

We now turn to the consideration of what happens on the "real" side of the economy as a result of the financial adjustments induced by monetary policy. Again we start by considering the case of monetary expansion. As we have seen, incentives are created for business firms and households to purchase more goods and services. What are the implications of these incentives in terms of the objectives which we specified for macro-economic policy, i.e., income, employment and the price level?

There are two radically different hypotheses to be considered, each of which contains an important message. We can call the first of these the *quantity theory* and the second the *Keynesian theory*.

The Classical Quantity Theory

A famous economist of the early part of the century, Irving Fisher, declared in his renowned book, *The Purchasing Power of Money*, that "one of the normal effects of an increase in the quantity of money is an exactly proportional increase in the general level of prices".[2]

This is the simplest and most forceful statement of the classical quantity theory of money. What type of model of the economy leads to this conclusion?

Long-run Full Employment. In the first place, this statement is a proposition about the long run. *The Fundamental assumption underlying the classical quantity theory is that in the long run the economy tends to full employment of its productive resources*, and particularly of the labour force. This means that in the long run, the *level of output and employment does not depend on the size of the money supply.* In Fisher's words: "An inflation of the currency cannot increase the product of farms and factories, nor the speed of freight trains or ships. The stream of business depends on natural resources and technical conditions, not on the quantity of money. The whole machinery of production, transportation, and sale is a matter of physical capacities and technique, none of which depend on the quantity of money".[3]

This proposition should not be interpreted as an assumption of *continuous* full employment. Indeed, Fisher recognized that changes in the quantity of money might have temporary, "transitional" effects on levels of output and employment,[4] but these transitional effects are not of primary concern. Rather, attention is directed to the long run, when all of the economic forces inherent in the situation have worked themselves out. The mechanism which guarantees full employment as the "normal" equilibrium state of the economy is the general flexibility of prices. Unemployment implies an excess supply of labour at existing wage rates. Given time, and price flexibility, the relative price of labour (the *real* wage rate) will fall sufficiently that the excess supply will be absorbed into productive employments. Inevitably, full employment will be re-established.

Thus, in Fisher's model, "The price level is normally the one *absolutely passive* element . . . . "[5]

The Demand for Money. We have already discussed the second fundamental assumption of the classical quantity theory of money in Chapter 19. It is that *the demand for money is a stable function of the level of income.*

We can express this assumption in terms of the income velocity of money, a concept which we introduced in our discussion of the demand for money in Chapter 19. Remember, the income velocity of money (v) is defined as the ratio of aggregate income (Y) to the average stock of money (M), i.e.,

$$v = \frac{Y}{M} \tag{20.1}$$

For Fisher's statement of the quantity theory with which we introduced this section to be literally true, the velocity of money would have to be *constant.* Indeed, the classical quantity theory has frequently been interpreted in this way. However, this was not quite the proposition intended by the classical quantity theorists. They were asserting that aside from temporary "transitional" effects, *the velocity of circulations was determined by factors which were independent of the supply of money.* Velocity had a long-run equilibrium value determined by relatively slow-changing technical and institutional factors, by the requirements for money to facilitate the flow of transactions in the economy. Thus, as long as the basic institutional and technical determinants of the demand for money were given, the quantity of money demanded in the economy in the *long run* would depend directly on the level of income. That is,

$$M_d = \left(\frac{1}{v}\right)Y \tag{20.2}$$

where M_d is the quantity of money demanded, and v is the long-run (equilibrium) velocity of money.

The Mechanics of the Quantity Theory. In order to explore the economic process involved in the quantity theory, let us trace through the effects of a sizable increase in the supply of money.

As we have already seen, given the demand for money and given the existing levels of prices and incomes, the initial impact of an increase in the stock of money would be to create an excess supply of money. There would be more money in the economy than was demanded (or required?) under the existing circumstances. Remember, the stock of money is determined primarily by the government and the banking system. While each individual can dispose of money which he does not want to hold by purchasing goods, services or securities, he does so by passing the money on to someone else. Collectively, they cannot reduce the total stock of money. Moreover, under the classical assumption of full employment, the aggregate quantity of goods and services available cannot expand to satisfy the increased demands for goods and services on the part of those holding the excess money. All that can happen is that the general level of prices of goods and services is bid up.

We must now re-introduce the distinction between *nominal* values and *real* values. The classical assumption of full employment is equivalent to the assumption that *real income* is fixed. The increase in the general level of prices implies an increase of income in *nominal* terms. The price level must rise, then, until the level of nominal income is such that the excess supply of money is entirely absorbed. That is, the price level must rise until:

$$M_s = M_d = \left(\frac{1}{v}\right) Y \qquad (20.3)$$

This same proposition is sometimes stated in another way, focusing attention on the real money supply. Let us divide equation 20.2 through by P, the general level of prices, in order to put it in real terms.

$$\left(\frac{M}{P}\right)d = \left(\frac{1}{v}\right) \frac{Y}{P} \qquad (20.4)$$

where $\left(\frac{M}{P}\right)d$ is the quantity of *real money* demanded, and $\left(\frac{Y}{P}\right)$ is the level of real income. This is the demand for money expressed in real terms.

At the initial price level, the increase in the stock of nominal money has the temporary effect of increasing the supply of real money. However, given the basic institutional and technical determinants of velocity, and given the full employment level of real income, equation 20.4 tells us that the demand for real money will not have changed. Thus it follows: *Given an increase in the nominal money supply, equilibrium between demand and supply will only be re-established when the price level rises sufficiently that the real money supply is reduced to its original level. This means that the price level must eventually rise in proportion to the initial increase in the nominal money supply.* You should take careful note of the fact that in this model, *the price level is the one and only variable which adjusts to maintain long-run equilibrium between the demand for and the supply of real money.*

Implications for Monetary Policy. In the simplest possible terms, this is the classical quantity theory of money. It is fundamentally a theory of the demand for money, set in the context of an economy which has an automatic tendency toward full employment. It is a long-run theory — a set of propositions about ultimate equilibrium conditions — in which the price level is a variable, but the levels of income and employment are not.

The implications for monetary policy are quite straightforward. Among our policy objectives, aside from transitional influences, only the general level of prices is amenable to control by the monetary authorities. Stability of the price level can only be achieved if the authorities maintain the stock of money which is demanded at the full employment level of income.

But perhaps we should set this conclusion in the context of a growing economy. In this context, stability of the price level, in the long run, depends simply on the choice of an appropriate rate of growth for the money supply. The growth rate of the nominal money supply should be the rate at which the availability of productive resources and technical advance will permit aggregate output to grow, adjusted, of course, for any changes in the institutional and technical conditions underlying the demand for money function.

The Modern Quantity Theory

We have used the adjective "classical" to identify an early version of the quantity theory of money which has a very long history in the literature of economics, and achieved perhaps its most perfect exposition in the writings of Irving Fisher. As we shall see, this theory was abruptly discarded by the majority of the economics profession in the 1930's and 1940's in favour of the macroeconomic theories derived from the works of J. M. Keynes. However, in recent years a new version of the quantity theory has emerged, primarily from the work of Professor Milton Friedman of the University of Chicago. The modern quantity theory is more subtle and more flexible than its classical counterpart, and has provided a major stimulus to theoretical and empirical work in monetary economics.

The Demand for Money. The major departure of this theory is a more general formulation of the demand for money function. We discussed Professor Friedman's analysis of the demand for money as an asset in Chapter 19 and the major conclusions, you will recall, were that the demand for money was directly related to wealth rather than income, and that for empirical work wealth could be approximated by a variable called permanent income. Other variables may enter the demand for money function, including the rates of return on other assets. However, the dominant variable is always permanent income. Thus, the fundamental assumption of the modern quantity theory of money is that *the demand for money is a stable function of* permanent *income.*

Stability of Velocity. This proposition permits a re-interpretation of the classical statement that in the long run the velocity of money is relatively stable.

One of the commonest criticisms of the classical quantity theory is that, in fact, the velocity of money is not a constant. This is evident in Figure 20-1 which describes the behaviour of the income velocity of money in Canada from 1920-1969. During this period velocity underwent wide fluctuations. As we noted above, such criticisms tend to involve a misinterpretation of the classical theory. It was not argued that velocity was a constant, but that in the long run velocity was *independent* of the money supply. Nonetheless, if velocity is not at least reasonably stable over time periods which are not so long as to be irrelevant for policy purposes, the classical theory loses much of its potential interest. It may not be wrong, but it may be irrelevant.

In this context, the modern quantity theorist argues that it is important to distinguish between *measured velocity* and *permanent velocity.* Measured velocity, the ratio of current income to the stock of money, is subject to short-term fluctuations. *Permanent velocity, the ratio of permanent income to the stock of money, is relatively stable.* Measured velocity (v_m) depends not only on the underlying determinants of the demand for money (i.e., the determinants of permanent velocity, v_p), but also on the relationship between measured income (Y_m) and permanent income (Y_p). That is:[6]

$$v_m = v_p \left(\frac{Y_m}{Y_p} \right) \tag{20.5}$$

Figure 20-1
The Income Velocity of Money in Canada, 1920-1969

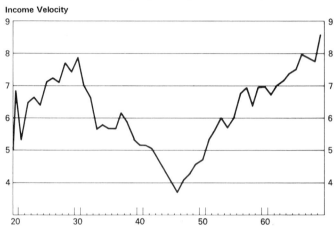

The fluctuations which we observe in the velocity of money, for example in Figure 20-1, are misleading. They do not reflect instability of permanent velocity, and hence of the underlying demand for money, but rather reflect fluctuations of measured income around permanent income. They are a product of the *transitory* component of measured income (see Chapter 4).

Time Lags. It follows, as in the classical theory, that an increase in the supply of money will have a direct and powerful effect on the demand for goods and services. Moreover, in an economy which in the long run tends to full employment, the ultimate adjustment will be in the general level of prices. The price level must rise until the real money supply is again reduced to the quantity appropriate to the existing level of permanent income.[7]

In these respects the real adjustment process involved in the modern quantity theory is to all intents and purposes the same as that involved in the classical theory. However, the modern exponents pay much more attention to frictions and lags in the process of adjustment. In particular, they stress that the lags are both *long* on the average, and highly *variable*. On the basis of past experience it has been argued that *on the average* 12 to 16 months must pass before the maximum effects of a change in the money supply will be felt, but that this period may be as short as six months or as long as 18 months.[8]

Policy Implications. According to this analysis, manipulation of the money supply can be a powerful weapon of economic policy, although the length and variability of the time lags involved also render it a potentially dangerous weapon. The problem is that since the effects of a change in the money supply will not be fully felt until some time in the future, present actions should not be geared to present developments in the economy but to future developments. However, even presuming adequate predictive abilities, if the time lag is highly variable, what is the relevant period in the future to which actions should be geared?

Exponents of the modern quantity theory argue that in the past, attempts to stabilize the economy by manipulating the money supply have actually had a destabilizing effect. For example, monetary actions taken in response to recession have had their major impact on the economy when the recession was passed and the problem was excessive aggregate demand. That is, the major impact was felt when the opposite policies were called for, and in this way monetary policy tended to be a major disturbance to the level of economic activity. Indeed, it has been argued that the attempts of central banks to use their discretionary control over the money supply to counter short-term fluctuations in economic activity are *inherently destabilizing* — they will almost inevitably have a perverse effect. Under these circumstances, the modern quantity theorists argue that it would be much better if the monetary authorities simply followed the classical rule and increased the money supply at approximately the rate of growth of the potential output of the economy. Such a policy would remove the central bank as a major source of disturbances in the economy, and would provide the maximum contribution to economic stability of which monetary management is capable.

3/REAL ADJUSTMENTS: KEYNESIAN THEORY

To many economists of the 1930's and 1940's the classical quantity theory of money, with its assumption of long-run tendencies to full employment, seemed either wrong or utterly irrelevant. Indeed, in the face of massive and prolonged unemployment there was considerable speculation about whether the chronic unemployment of a high proportion of the labour force rather than full employment was the normal equilibrium state of the economy. In this context, the Keynesian model which focused on the level of employment, swept the field in macroeconomic analysis.

The classical quantity theory of money was a theory of long-run equilibrium, in which the price level is the central variable. The economics of "transitional" periods between one long-run equilibrium and another, including the possibility of prolonged, large-scale, involuntary unemployment, received little attention. To Keynes, by contrast, the analysis of this period contained the essence of the macroeconomic policy problem — a point which is underlined by the famous Keynesian aphorism, "In the long run we all are dead". The Keynesian theory is a theory about the short run in which output and employment are the central variables. Indeed, in the extreme version of the Keynesian theory, the price level is presumed to be fixed by institutional rigidities. Let us briefly explore this extreme model.

Some Basic Identities

The central concept in the Keynesian model is aggregate demand. This is a concept which we have used on several occasions. We must now consider it more carefully.

Aggregate Demand. By aggregate demand we mean the aggregate expenditures from all sources during a given period of time for the purchase of goods and services newly produced by factors of production owned by residents of Canada. Note that aggregate demand has a time dimension. It is a flow concept.

Depending on the purpose of the analysis, aggregate demand can be broken down into many categories of expenditure. For most purposes, at least four sources of demand must be recognized: household expenditures for all types of consumer goods and services (commonly called *consumption* and represented by the symbol C) ; business expenditures for new capital goods, machinery, equipment, buildings and inventories (*investment —* I) ; government expenditures for all types of goods and services, but excluding purely transfer payments like unemployment insurance compensation which are not payments for goods or services rendered (*government expenditure* — G) ; and the expenditures of non-residents of Canada to purchase Canadian-produced goods or the services of Canadian productive factors (*exports —* X) . Mention of the foreign sector should remind us that not all expenditures by Canadian households, business firms, and governments constitute demand for the services of Canadian productive factors. Part of this demand is for the importation of foreign-produced goods or the services of foreign-owned productive services (*imports —* Im) . In measuring aggregate demand we must deduct this part of the aggregate expenditures of Canadian spending units.

By this definition,

$$\text{AGGREGATE DEMAND} = D = C + I + G + X - \text{Im} \qquad (20.6)$$

Aggregate Income. Another concept which we have used on several occasions is aggregate income. By this we mean the total income of all types (wages, rent, interest, profits) earned by factors of production owned by residents of Canada during a given period of time. Like aggregate demand, it also is a flow concept.

The owners of factors of production earn income because of the participation of their factors in the production process. Indeed, because we have included profits in the category of income, it should be obvious that if it were not for problems relating to certain taxes, subsidy payments and depreciation accounting,[9] the sum of all incomes earned should equal the value of output produced. All income payments besides profit show on the books of business firms as costs. But the difference between the value of output and costs measured in this sense is profit. Hence, if we add profit to factor costs, we should have a measure of both the value of output (*gross national product* = GNP) and the value of *aggregate income* (Y).[10]

Thus,

$$\begin{matrix} \text{AGGREGATE} \\ \text{INCOME} \end{matrix} = Y = GNP = \begin{matrix} \text{AGGREGATE} \\ \text{OUTPUT} \end{matrix} \qquad (20.7)$$

We also know, however, that the value of aggregate output is the same thing as the value of aggregate expenditures. These two concepts are merely two sides of the same set of market transactions. GNP is the value of what has been produced and sold; D is the value of what has been purchased.

It follows then, that:

$$\begin{matrix} \text{AGGREGATE} \\ \text{INCOME} \end{matrix} = Y = C + I + G + X - Im = \begin{matrix} \text{AGGREGATE} \\ \text{OUTPUT} \end{matrix}$$
$$(20.8)$$

What we have in the middle of this expression is aggregate demand.

Output and Employment. Remember, we are assuming that *the price level is fixed.* Since we can think of gross national product as the price level multiplied by the quantity of output produced, the assumption of a fixed price level means that any change in aggregate demand must involve a proportional change in output.

But, in the short run, given the established techniques of production and existing productive equipment, any change in output will be reflected in a change in the level of employment. For various reasons, the change in employment may not be proportional to the change in aggregate demand, but it will be in the same direction. Thus, a decline in aggregate demand means a drop in the level of output, and it means unemployed labour and idle machinery and factories.

A Simplified Framework. Striving for closer and closer approximations of reality, modern Keynesian models recognize many more sub-categories of aggregate demand. However, our interest in the Keynesian model is very general. We only want to identify the basic principles of how monetary policy is supposed to influence the level of income and employment. We can simplify rather than complicate the model, by delaying consideration of the government sector and the international sector.

The simplified framework which we will consider is as follows:

$$\begin{matrix} \text{AGGREGATE} \\ \text{DEMAND} \end{matrix} = C + I = Y = GNP \qquad (20.9)$$

This equation is an identity. It provides a framework for analysis, but tells us nothing about the economic processes which determine the levels of income and employment. For this we need assumptions about the behaviour of the relevant macroeconomic variables. So far we have made two important assumptions: that the price level is fixed and that the level of employment depends directly on the level of output. What are the other essential assumptions of the Keynesian theory?

The basic distinction between the two categories of aggregate demand in equation 20.9 is between those types of expenditures which are presumed to be directly affected by the current level of income (typified by consumption) and those types of expenditure which are largely independent of the current level of income (typified by investment). While the terminology is not fully appropriate, the latter are sometimes called "autonomous" expenditures. We will consider this category first.

Behavioural Assumptions: The Investment Decision. Investment in the Keynesian model implies a decision to install new capital goods (factories, machinery, equipment), or to increase inventories of goods in process of production or distribution.

The relevant considerations in such a decision are the expected yield on the new capital goods (the marginal efficiency of capital), and the market yields on financial instruments (the level of interest rates). Of these the expected yield on new capital goods must be the dominant, dynamic factor. It involves a projection of earnings into the more or less remote future, an exercise which by its very nature must be speculative, subject to all kinds of psychological influences, and surrounded by uncertainty. For this reason it should not be surprising that among all of the categories of aggregate expenditure, investment is the one which econometricians find is most difficult to "explain" statistically. That is, they find it difficult to establish clear, stable relationships between investment expenditures and other macroeconomic variables.

Interest Rates and Investment Demand. The theoretical role of the yield on financial instruments in the investment decision has already been alluded to. On the one hand, interest rates represent the opportunity cost of using the firm's funds for real investment, and on the other hand (and probably much more important, over all) they represent the cost of borrowing the funds required to finance the purchase and installation of the capital goods. Elementary economic theory tells us that when interest rates are high, business firms will attempt to economize on capital, choosing less capital-intensive techniques of production. At high interest rates many potential investment projects will not be undertaken because they do not offer a sufficiently high yield. But, as the cost of borrowing falls, more and more projects become feasible. As just one elementary example, consider the feasibility of constructing a new subway in a large metropolitan area, a highly capital-intensive project. One question which arises is how far the line should be extended into the suburbs. The lines in the center of the city, with high population density and correspondingly heavy traffic, can be expected to generate large revenues per mile of track. They offer a high yield. However, the farther the lines are pushed into the low population density suburbs, the smaller the revenue per mile of track, and correspondingly the lower the yield on the investment. Considered simply as a commercial venture, the extent of suburban penetration will depend on the level of interest rates. At very high interest rates, only the central city will appear to be a profitable location for a new subway. At very low interest rates, extension into the suburbs will appear profitable. The amount of subway investment, in other words, varies inversely with the interest rate.

The Investment Demand Function. In general, then, *the higher the level of market interest rates, the lower the level of investment expenditures.* This assumption is represented graphically in Figure 20-2, with the flow of investment expenditures planned by firms measured along the base axis, and the level of interest rates along the vertical axis. *This is the investment demand function for any given "state of expectations" relating to the yields of potential new capital projects.* Among other things a change in the economic outlook will shift the function − a buoyant outlook shifting it to the right, and pessimistic expectations shifting it to the left. Similarly, a significant technological revolution might suddenly increase the amount of investment that would be worthwhile at various interest rates.

Figure 20-2
The Investment Demand Function

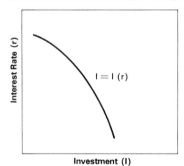

Investment (I)

Behavioural Assumptions: The Consumption Function

We discussed the Keynesian postulate with respect to consumption in Chapter 4. In brief, Keynes asserted that the dominant factor determining the level of consumption expenditures is the level of income, but that consumption increases less than proportionately with the level of income. That is, what he called the marginal propensity to consume has a magnitude less than 1. In linear form, the Keynesian consumption function is:

$$C = C_o + cY \qquad (20.10)$$

where C_o is a constant (that part of consumption which is independent of the level of income − "autonomous" consumption) and c is the marginal propensity to consume, the slope of the consumption function in the top panel of Figure 20-3.

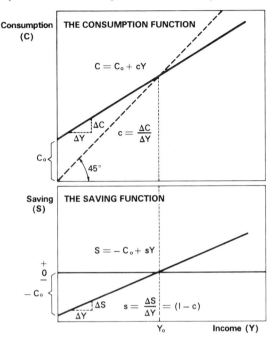

Figure 20-3
"Keynesian" Consumption and Saving Functions

A Saving Function. Applying an identity which we developed in Chapter 4, we also know that:

$$Y = C + S \qquad (20.11)$$

where S is aggregate saving. It follows, then, that:

$$\begin{aligned} S &= Y - C \\ &= Y - (C_0 + cY) \\ &= Y(1-c) - C_0 \end{aligned} \qquad (20.12)$$

In our simplified model, which ignores the government sector and external trade, this is the saving function. If we let s represent the marginal propensity to save, such that:

$$s = (1 - c), \qquad (20.13)$$

we can rewrite equation 20.12,

$$S = -C_0 + sY \qquad (20.14)$$

The saving function is thus derived directly from the consumption function, as is shown in Figure 20-3.[11]

Equilibrium in the "Commodity Market"

An equilibrium level of income is one which does not have an inherent tendency to change. We know from equation 20.9 that aggregate income is the sum of consumption and investment expenditures, and we know from the above discussion that these two components are determined independently. Consumption depends on the level of income, and investment on the state of expectations and the level of interest rates. However, for *any given level* of income to be an equilibrium level, it must be true that the level of investment expenditures which businesses want to undertake is exactly equal to the level of savings which households want to make.

A moment's thought should convince you of the validity of this proposition. If businesses want to invest more than households want to save, at the given level of income, the sum of planned consumption and planned investment will have to exceed that level of income. Income will, of necessity, rise. The opposite is true if investment falls short of the planned savings of households.

Thus we have the equilibrium condition in what we will call the commodity market. *An equilibrium level of income is one at which the planned investment of businesses equals the planned saving of households.*

Indeterminacy of Equilibrium Income. If the level of investment depends on the rate of interest, then there must be many different equilibrium levels of income which are consistent with any given investment and saving functions. Indeed, since there will be a different equilibrium level of income for each possible level of interest rates, we cannot identify a unique equilibrium level of income unless we have determined the level of interest rates. At best, we can draw a curve which shows all of the possible equilibrium levels of income, one for each level of interest rates. Such a curve is commonly called an I-S curve because it shows all of the combinations of interest rates and income levels at which planned Investment equals planned Saving.

Derivation of the I-S Curve. One method of deriving the I-S curve is illustrated in Figure 20-4. This involves what is at first glance a rather complicated geometrical construction, a four-quandrant diagram, with the origin at the center (O) and with the scales on each axis increasing as you move away from the origin. (Note that this is in contrast to the usual four-quadrant diagram of elementary algebra in which movements downward and to the left from the origin have a negative sign.) However, it is basically a simple construct, designed to demonstrate graphically the necessity for equilibrium interest rates and income levels to simultaneously satisfy both the investment demand function and the savings function.

Equilibrium requires that I = S. For any selected interest rate, say r_1, the investment demand function in Quandrant II tells us the associated level of investment, i.e., I_1. Projecting this into Quadrant III, the saving function tells us the only level of income at which saving will equal this level of investment, i.e., Y_1. This is the equilibrium level of income for the interest rate, r_1. We can similarly find the equilibrium level of income for all other possible interest rates. In Figure 20-4 we have done this for two other levels of interest rates, r_2 and r_3.

Figure 20-4
Derivation of the I-S Curve

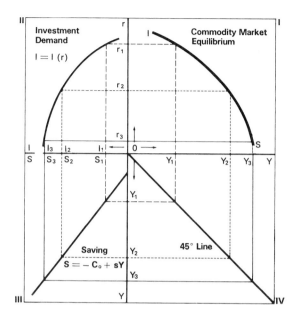

The line in Quadrant IV is simply a geometrical device to project the equilibrium incomes to the base axis of Quadrant I. This line makes a 45° angle with each of the two axes, so that the distance OY_1 in Quadrant I is the same as the distance OY_1 in Quadrant III. The resulting curve in Quadrant I, then, identifies the equilibrium level of income associated with each possible level of interest rates. It is the I-S curve. At any point above the I-S curve, saving will exceed investment, and income will have to fall. Likewise, at any point below the I-S curve investment will exceed saving, and income will have to rise (to demonstrate your understanding of the analysis, you should be able to explain why these statements are true). *The I-S curve is the locus of equilibrium points in the commodity market.*

Position and Shape of the I-S curve. The *position* of the I-S curve depends on the positions of the investment demand and saving functions (and on the size of the marginal propensity to save). An increase in investment demand will shift the I-S function to the right. By contrast, an increase in the demand for saving, in the sense of an increase in saving at every level of income, will shift the I-S function to the *left.*[12] You should be able to demonstrate these propositions.

Likewise, the shape of the I-S function depends on the *shapes* of the investment demand and the saving functions. If investment were very *inelastic* with respect to the rate of interest (if the I function were very steep), the I-S function would likewise be very inelastic. The increase in income for any given drop of the interest rate would be relatievly small. Correspondingly, the smaller the marginal propensity to save (the closer the S function is to the axis), the more elastic will be the I-S function. The increase in income for any given drop of the interest rate will be relatively large.

Equilibrium in the Money Market

This analysis of equilibrium in the "commodity market" makes clear the central variable in the Keynesian model: the level of interest rates. Without specification of the level of interest rates, the equilibrium levels of income and employment are indeterminate. But what determines the level of interest rates?

We cannot answer this question until we have explored the financial side of the Keynesian model. In particular, we have to establish the conditions for equilibrium between the demand for and supply of money. We call this "equilibrium in the money market".

The Demand for Money. As we stated in Chapter 19, Keynes accepted the classical argument that the demand for money depended on the level of income, but argued that the level of interest rates was also a major factor in the demand function. Moreover, Keynes argued that at low interest rates the demand for money would become highly elastic with respect to the interest rate. Indeed, some of Keynes' followers hypothesized, there may be some low interest rate at which the demand for money becomes perfectly elastic: what we called earlier the liquidity trap. Such a demand for money function, at a given level of income, was depicted in Figure 19-8.

Indeterminacy of Equilibrium. In what follows, we take the supply of money as given by the central bank. If the demand for money depends on both the level of income and the level of interest rates, equilibrium in the money market depends on finding *combinations* of income and interest rates at which the demand for money equals the supply of money. As in the commodity market, we cannot identify a unique equilibrium in the money market considered alone. The best we can do is to draw a curve similar in concept to the I-S curve, which describes all possible combinations of income and interest rates which will produce equilibrium in the money market. Such a curve is normally called an L-M curve.[13]

Derivation of the L-M Curve. One method of deriving the L-M curve is presented in Figure 20-5. The graphic technique is similar to that employed in Figure 20-4.

For the purposes of this exercise, it is assumed that the Keynesian demand for money function takes a particular form: i.e., that the interest rate and income effects on the quantity of money demanded are independent of each other, and hence separable. That is, it is assumed that the impact of a given interest rate on the quantity of money demanded is the same regardless of the level of income, and vice versa. This makes it possible to draw a curve showing the interest rate effect (as in Quadrant II) without regard to the level of income,[14] and to add the interest rate effect directly to the income effect (Quadrant IV) to obtain the total quantity of money demanded. We also make the "classical" assumption that the relationship between income and the quantity of money demanded is linear. It must be emphasized that these are very special assumptions, adopted to make the graphic analysis manageable.

Consider Quadrant II first. If the interest rate is r_1, the quantity of money demanded because of the interest rate effect alone is M_1^*. The total supply of money made available by the central bank is M. Therefore, if equilibrium is to exist in the money market, in the sense that the demand for money equals the supply of money, the quantity of money demanded because of the level of income must be $M-M_1^*$. The problem is to identify the level of income which will produce this demand for money.

Figure 20-5
Derivation of the L-M *Curve*

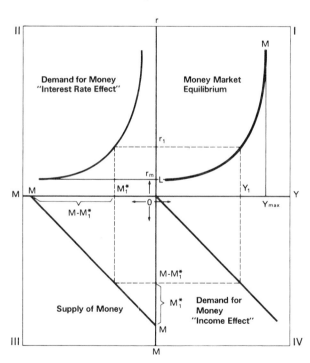

Quadrant III, labelled "The Supply of Money", is the only part of Figure 20-5 which should require special explanation. Again, this contains a special construct, making use of elementary geometry. The line MM makes a 45° angle with each of the axes of Quadrant III. It joins up points indicating the total money supply as measured from the origin along each of these axes. It also serves to reflect the two components of the demand for money from the horizontal axis to the vertical axis of Quadrant III. Thus, because the line MM makes a 45° angle with the vertical axis, the distance from the point M to the point $(M\text{-}M_1^*)$, represents the quantity of money demanded because the level of interest rates is r_1. The remainder of the distance to the origin $O - (M \text{-} M_1^*)$, represents the quantity of money which has to be demanded because of the income effect if equilibrium is to prevail. From the curve in Quadrant IV, which shows the relationship between income alone and the quantity of money demanded, we can identify the level of income which will induce this demand for money. This level of income Y_1, is indicated on the horizontal axis of Quadrants I and IV. Y_1 is the equilibrium level of income, given the interest rate r_1.

This provides us with one point on the L-M curve. By the same process we could find other combinations of interest rates and income levels which would permit equilibrium in the money market. The end result would be a curve like that labelled L-M in Quadrant I.

In order to demonstrate your understanding of the construction of the L-M curve you should be able to show that any point above the L-M curve (i.e., to the left of the curve) implies a combination of income and interest rates at which the quantity of money demanded is less than the available money supply. It cannot be an equilibrium situation. Similarly, you should be able to demonstrate that any point below the L-M curve implies a combination of income and interest rates at which the quantity of money demanded exceeds the quantity supplied by the central bank. *The L-M curve describes the locus of equilibrium points in the money market.*

The L-M Curve and the Money Supply. Note particularly the shape of the L-M curve. It slopes upward to the right, with a virtually horizontal portion at very low interest rates, and a virtually vertical portion at high interest rates. The flat portion of the curve reflects the Keynesian assumption of a liquidity trap. It implies that there is a minimum level of interest rates. The vertical portion implies that there is a maximum level of income for any given money supply.

You should also remember that the L-M curve is drawn for a given money supply. If the money supply is increased (the M-M curve of Quadrant III shifts to the left), the L-M curves will shift to the right. The minimum interest rate may not change (why not?), but the maximum income level will increase. Similarly, a reduction in the money supply will shift the L-M curve to the left.

The L-M Curve and the Price Level. Remember, the Keynesian model assumes a fixed price level. What happens, however, if the price level changes?

In Chapter 19 we noted two different effects of a change in the price level. We can use Figure 20-5 to illustrate the differences between them.

Consider first the impact of a *once-and-forever rise in the price level*: what we called in Chapter 19 the direct impact of a rise in prices. For this purpose we should interpret all of the curves in Figure 20-5 as showing the relationships between *real* magnitudes. That is, the money supply is the real money supply, and the income level is real income. Then, with the *nominal supply of money fixed* by the central bank, a rise in the general level of prices would imply a reduction in the real money supply. The curve MM in Quadrant III would shift to the right, implying higher interest rates and lower real incomes. Neither of the demands for money functions, *expressed in real terms,* would shift.

By contrast, consider the effects of a general *expectation of a continuing rise of the price level* in the future. The opportunity cost of holding money at any given level of market interest rates has increased by the expected rate of inflation. As a result, the demand curve in Quadrant II will shift to the right. That is, at any given market interest rate, a smaller quantity of money would be demanded. The end result would be a higher level of income and a higher level of interest rates. The mere expectation of inflation can have powerful economic effects. (What would be the impact of the expectation of deflation?)

Macroeconomic Equilibrium in the Keynesian System

Macroeconomic equilibrium requires equilibrium simultaneously in both the money market and the commodity market. If one of the markets is in disequilibrium, at least one of the variables in the system, income or the level of interest rates, will change, and when it changes the equilibrium will be disturbed in the other market. Therefore, full equilibrium requires a combination of income and interest rates which simultaneously satisfies both the I-S function and the L-M function, i.e., that combination identified by the intersection of the two curves. Thus, in the upper panel of Figure 20-6, the equilibrium income and interest levels are Y and r_e respectively.

Figure 20-6
Monetary Policy in the Keynesian Model

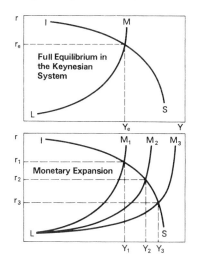

Monetary Policy in the Keynesian System

We are now in a position to use the analytical apparatus of the I-S and L-M curves to examine the effects of monetary policy in the Keynesian model. In particular, let us consider the effects of an expansion of the money supply by the central bank.

We start with the economic system in equilibrium at income level Y_1 in the bottom panel of Figure 20-6. An increase in the money supply shifts the L-M curve outward, from $L-M_1$, to $L-M_2$. At the pre-existing levels of income and interest rate the money market is now in disequilibrium. Asset-holders are holding more money than they want to.

In the usual expositions of the Keynesian model, the complex of portfolio adjustments which we discussed in the first section of this chapter are much circumscribed. The only action which assetholders are permitted to take is to attempt to purchase more "bonds". The excess supply of money does not directly induce them to acquire real assets — there is no real balance effect in either the consumption function or the investment demand function. With the stock of bonds given, all that can happen initially is that the price of bonds is bid up, and hence interest rates reduced. This is the key element in the Keynesian analysis. *It is the level of interest rates which provides the link between the financial sector and the real sector.*

As interest rates fall, the quantity of money demanded increases (Quadrant II, Figure 20-5) and the level of investment expenditures rises (Quadrant II, Figure 20-4). As Figure 20-4 shows, an increase in investment expenditure produces an increase in income. Again, remember that in this model the price level is fixed. The increase of income means an increase in employment.

The system will gravitate toward a new equilibrium, with the levels of income and interest rates at Y_2 and r_2 respectively on the bottom panel of Figure 20-6. A further increase of the money supply would produce a further adjustment in the same direction, perhaps to Y_3, r_3. Of course, a reduction of the money supply would shift the L-M function and hence the equilibrium point in the opposite direction.

The economics of the Keynesian model, with its assumption of a fixed price level, is the economics of an under-employment economy. The problem is to increase the level of income from a level which involves substantial unemployment, to one which implies full employment of the labour force. Is monetary policy always capable of achieving this objective?

Impotent Monetary Policy: The Liquidity Trap. The top panel of Figure 20-7 illustrates one situation in which monetary policy is impotent. This is the Keynesian liquidity trap case. Interest rates are at their minimum level, so that further expansion of the money supply does not increase the level of income.

This diagram also illustrates in an extreme form the Keynesian explanation for short-term fluctuations in the velocity of money, such as those described on Figure 20-1. Because of the interest elasticity of the demand for

Figure 20-7
Impotent Monetary Policy

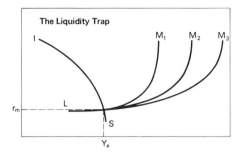

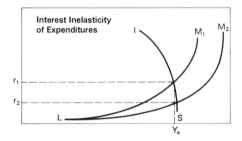

money, variations in income are not proportional to variations in the money supply. Not only will velocity change, but, contrary to the classical quantity theory argument, these *variations in velocity are induced by changes in the money supply*. Indeed, they serve to offset at least part of the impact of monetary policy, since velocity falls as the money supply expands, and rises as the money supply contracts. In the extreme case of an economy caught in the liquidity trap, the money supply can change with no effect on income. In these circumstances, according to the Keynesian model, *there is no limit to the velocity of money*. Indeed, the very concept of velocity is meaningless.

For this reason, it should not be surprising that the Keynesian concept of the liquidity trap has stirred up more controversy than any other concept in the recent history of monetary policy, nor that it has come under particular attack from advocates of the modern quantity theory of money.

As we noted in Chapter 19, empirical studies of the demand for money tend to confirm the hypothesis that the demand for money is sensitive to the interest rate, but cast doubt on the extreme elasticity implied by the liquidity trap. Beyond this, many monetary theorists have invoked the concept of a *real balance effect* to argue that even with a liquidity trap there still exists a mechanism for monetary policy to increase income and employment. Although interest rates are fixed at a minimum level by the liquidity trap, eliminating interest-rate-induced substitution effects, further increases in the money supply will have a direct impact on expenditures. That is, it is argued that the size of the money supply itself is a factor affecting investment and consumption. However, there is little evidence that such a real balance effect caused by a decline in prices or by expansion of the money supply, if it exists, has any great quantitative importance.[15]

Impotent Monetary Policy: Interest Inelasticity of Expenditures. A more important possible reason for the impotence of monetary policy (particularly in the context of attempts to use monetary policy to restrict aggregate demand) is interest inelasticity of expenditures. This problem is illustrated in the bottom panel of Figure 20-7. In this case, because of the steepness of the I-S curve, an increase in the money supply, shifting the L-M curve from L-M$_1$ to L-M$_2$, lowers the level of interest rates, but does not significantly increase the level of investment or income.

Again, there will be a change in velocity. If the increase in the money supply is not accompanied by an increase in income, by definition velocity falls. The converse would be true for a reduction in the money supply in the same range of the I-S curve, for example, a shift of the L-M curve from L-M$_2$ to L-M$_1$.

Clearly, the interest elasticity of expenditures is a crucial consideration in assessing the efficacy of monetary policy. We will review some of the evidence on this mater in Chapter 22.

The Fiscal Policy Alternative

Our discussion of the Keynesian model to this point has focused exclusively on its implications for monetary policy to the neglect of its broader insights into the economics of stabilization policy. Nonetheless, we have discovered one important conclusion: since there is a significant risk that monetary policy will be impotent in periods of large-scale unemployment, the achievement and maintenance of full employment may require other policy measures. Historically, the important result of the Keynesian monetary analysis was to thrust *fiscal policy* to the fore as the primary regulator of economic activity.

The economics of fiscal policy is subject enough for a book in itself. However, since many of the current controversies in monetary economics relate to the relative effectiveness of monetary and fiscal actions, it is important that we review the rudiments of the Keynesian analysis of fiscal policy.

The Nature of Fiscal Policy. By fiscal policy we mean decisions with respect to the levels of revenues and expenditures of the government sector of the economy. It is argued that by varying government expenditures or the level of taxation (or both) the government can have a direct and powerful impact on aggregate demand, and hence, in the short-run (i.e., with a given price level), on production and employment.

Government Expenditures and Aggregate Demand. The impact on aggregate demand of changes in the level of government expenditures on goods and services should be obvious from the aggregate demand equation (20.6). If the government increases its expenditures without doing anything which would induce private spenders to reduce their expenditures (whether consumption, investment or exports), then aggregate demand *must* increase. Indeed, as the early Keynesians emphasized, the resulting increase of income and output might well induce further increases of private expenditures, particularly consumption expenditures which are assumed to depend directly on income, thus reinforcing the initial increase of aggregate demand. This is the familiar "multiplier" process, noted earlier in discussing the shape of the I-S function. A reduction of government expenditures on goods and services would have the opposite effect, i.e., it would reduce the levels of aggregate demand, production and employment.

Taxes, Transfer Payments, and Aggregate Demand. The impact on aggregate demand of changes in the level of taxation is only slightly more complicated. Taxes do not appear directly in the aggregate demand equation, but changes in tax rates should have an indirect effect on aggregate demand because of their impact on expenditures by private spenders (households and firms). Taxes limit the share of earned income which private spenders have available to support their expenditures. A reduction of tax rates thus increases the funds available for other purposes and hence should stimulate private spending. By contrast, an increase in tax rates restricts the funds available in the private sector, and hence should restrict private spending.

There are a great variety of taxes, and hence many possible combinations of changes in tax rates, all of which may have different effects on private expenditures and hence on aggregate demand. The implications of an increase in customs tariffs might be quite different from the implications of an increase in the corporation income tax. However, the analysis is usually couched in terms of the personal income tax, with consumption expenditures the relevant component of aggregate demand which is to be regulated by fiscal policy. An increase in personal income tax rates, by reducing the disposable income of households, is expected to reduce consumption expenditures and aggregate demand. A reduction of personal income tax rates, by increasing disposable income, should increase consumption expenditures.

In this context it is important to distinguish between government expenditures on goods and services and government transfer payments. Transfer payments are typified by family allowances or unemployment compensation. They are payments by the government which are not payments for goods or services rendered to the government. In this sense they are negative taxes. They do not add directly to the aggregate demand for productive services, but they do add to the disposable incomes of private spenders and hence should stimulate private demands for goods and services. In the rest of our analysis we will not consider transfer payments explicitly. Rather we will assume that they are deducted from taxes to obtain "net taxes".

Government Expenditure and Tax Functions. There is an important assymetry in the treatment of government expenditures and tax revenues as instruments of stabilization policy in the standard exposition of the elementary Keynesian model.

It is usually assumed that the *level* of government expenditures on goods and services is a policy variable with respect to which decisions can be made independently of government tax revenues and independently of such other economic variables as the level of income or the level of interest rates. This is not to deny that many categories of government expenditures are substantially affected by economic developments. The government is not a monolithic sector, in which a single set of consistent decisions is made, controlling all expenditures at all levels of government in all parts of the country. Canada is, after all, a federal state. However, it is not necessary for all government expenditures to be a policy instrument. All that is necessary is that the central government have the *potential* to control the *total* of government expenditures — perhaps partly by varying its own expenditures on goods and services, and perhaps partly by influencing expenditures at other levels of government through inter-governmental transfers (grants-in-aide, etc.) .

Therefore, in drawing the government expenditure function as a horizontal line in Figure 20-8 we are assuming that the central government has the potential to control the level of aggregate government expenditures on goods and services as an instrument of fiscal policy.[16]

By contrast, it is generally assumed that the instrument of government policy is not the level of tax revenues but the *rate* of taxation of national income, i.e., that the government establishes a schedule of tax rates as a matter of policy, with the level of tax revenues then depending on variations in the level of income.

The relationship between tax collections and income can be quite complex. It depends partly on the mix of taxes established by the govern-

Figure 20-8
The Government Sector: Expenditure, Tax and Budget Functions

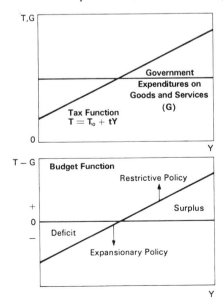

ment (e.g., the relative importance of sales and excise taxes, property taxes, corporation income taxes, personal income taxes, etc., on changes in the composition of economic activity and income (e.g., relative changes in retail sales, or in corporation profits) and partly on the progression of tax rates with income in the personal income tax. For simplicity, we have assumed a familiar linear tax function in Figure 20-8, of the form:

$$T = T_o + tY \qquad (20.15)$$

where $T =$ tax collections and $Y =$ gross national product. The coefficient t is a constant marginal tax rate, the slope of the tax function in Figure 20-8.

A particular fiscal policy, then, implies a decision on both the level of government expenditures and the position and shape of the tax function.

Budgetary Surpluses and Deficits. Figure 20-8 summarizes our assumptions about the government sector, including the balance on the government's budget (lower panel). It is important to note that active use of fiscal measures for economic stabilization implies that the government cannot be concerned with maintaining an exact balance of expenditures and tax revenues. As the lower panel of Figure 20-8 demonstrates, the balance on the government's budget for any given fiscal policy (level of expenditures and tax function) depends on the level of income. At high levels of income, high tax revenues will produce a budget surplus. At low levels of income, low tax revenues will produce a budget deficit. An expansionary policy can be implemented either by increasing government expenditures or by shifting the tax function downwards. The effect is to increase the budget deficit or decrease the budget surplus at each level of national income, or, alternatively, to increase the level of income at which the government's budget is balanced. A restrictive policy can be implemented either by reducing government expenditures or by shifting the tax function upward. The effect is to reduce the budget deficit or increase the surplus at each level of national income, or, alternatively, to reduce the level of national income at which the government's budget is balanced.

In this sense, *the size of the surplus or deficit in the government budget is the central consideration in fiscal policy.* The strong functional relationship between the balance on the government's budget and the level of national income should be noted. This means that the government sector tends to be an automatic stabilizer of economic aggregate demand. A decline in aggregate demand from private sources tends to be cushioned by the combination of stable government expenditures and declining tax collections, and hence by the emergence of a deficit in the government's budget. Similarly, an upsurge of aggregate demand tends to be restrained the full employment deficit or surplus.[17]

The sensitivity of the balance on the government's budget to changes in the level of national income also means that the actual magnitude of the budget deficit or surplus is not an adequate measure of the degree of ease or restrictiveness in fiscal policy. Since a deficit, for example, may emerge from a drop in national income with a given set to fiscal policy (i.e., given government expenditures, given tax schedules), it cannot be evidence of an expansionary policy. An expansionary policy would require a larger deficit than that which would emerge automatically as a result of the level of aggregate demand and income. It is frequently argued that a suitable summary measure of the degree of ease or restrictiveness of fiscal policy is the estimated balance on the budget with present expenditures and tax schedules if the economy were at full employment. This concept is called the full employment deficit or surplus.[17]

The Government Sector and the I-S *Function.* To carry through with the analytical technique which we developed earlier, we must introduce a government sector into the I-S/L-M model. The important result of doing this is to change the shape of the I-S curve. This is illustrated in Figure 20.9.

Figure 20-9
Derivation of the I-S *Curve with a Government Sector*

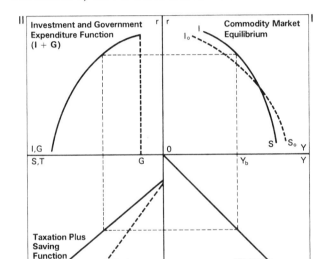

In constructing Figure 20-9 we have simply taken government expenditure and tax functions, such as those discussed above, and superimposed them on the basic I-S model of the commodity market developed in Figure 20-4. In Quadrant II of Figure 20-9 we have added a fixed amount of government expenditures (G) to the original investment demand function. The result is a new investment and government expenditure function (I + G) which lies to the left of the original investment demand function. In Quadrant III, the tax function has been added to the savings function, to obtain a new tax-plus-savings function.[18] *The new equilibrium condition is that the level of investment plus government expenditures must equal the level of tax collections plus savings* (you should be able to demonstrate why this is the new equilibrium condition). In Quadrant IV we have the familiar 45° line, which reflects the equilibrium income levels to the base axis in Quadrant I. The I-S curve, as before, shows those combinations of interest rates and income levels at which equilibrium can be achieved in the commodity market, taking account of both government expenditures and taxes.

As a reference base, we have also plotted the original I-S curve from Figure 20-4 in Quadrant I of Figure 20-9 (the line I_o-S_o). The change in shape as a result of the introduction of the government sector should be obvious. At relatively low levels of income, the new I-S curve lies outside the old curve. Because of the assumed shape of the tax function, the income-generating effects of the given level of government expenditures outweigh the restrictive effects of taxation. As a result, the effect of government fiscal operations is to raise the equilibrium level of income associated with each possible level of interest rates in this range.

As we move down the I-S curve, the restrictive effects of increasing tax revenues eventually offset and overwhelm the expansionary effects of the given level of government expenditures (this phenomenon has come to be known as "fiscal drag"). At relatively high levels of income, the new I-S curve lies inside the old curve. In this range, the effect of government fiscal operations is to lower the equilibrium level of income associated with each possible level of interest rates.

The basic conclusion, then, is that the introduction of the government sector makes the I-S curve steeper. The equilibrium level of income is less sensitive to changes in interest rates, or, in other words, to shifts in the L-M curve.

The level of income at which the government sector's budget is balanced (tax collections=government expenditures) is indicated at Y_b by the broken line. It is interesting to note that at this level of income, the new I-S curve lies outside the old. A balanced budget in the government sector is not neutral with respect to the level of income. It has a slight net expansionary effect.[19]

Fiscal Policy. In this framework, fiscal policy — whether implemented through government expenditures or through tax rates — involves a deliberate shift of the *I-S* function. Figure 20-10 illustrates the impact of a restrictive fiscal policy implemented through an increase of tax rates. In Quadrant III, the original tax-plus-savings function (broken line, T_o+S) has been shifted to the left, with an increased slope. The effect is to shift the I-S function inward (from I_o-S_o), and to make it steeper. At each possible level of interest rates, the equilibrium level of income has decreased.

Figure 20-11 illustrates an expansionary fiscal policy implemented through an increase of government expenditures. The investment-plus-government-expenditures function in Quadrant I has been shifted to the left by the amount of the increased expenditures, with the result that the I-S curve is shifted outward. At each possible level of interest rates, the equilibrium level of income has increased.

The possibilities for an expansionary fiscal policy in a situation in which monetary policy is impotent — what many economists would call the pure Keynesian case, involving a liquidity trap — are illustrated in

Figure 20-10
Restrictive Fiscal Policy and the I-S Curve: Increase in Tax Rates

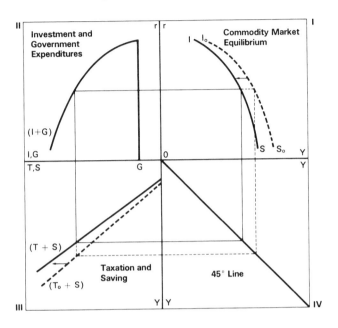

Figure 20-11
Expansionary Fiscal Policy and the I-S Curve:
Increase in Government Expenditures on Goods and Services

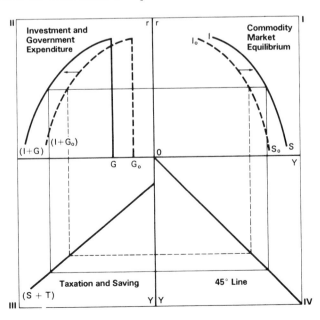

Figure 20-12. We saw in Figure 20-7 that in this situation, with a horizontal L-M function, monetary expansion could not lower interest rates below the minimum level, r_m, and therefore could not raise the level of income toward full employment. The analysis of Figure 20-12 demonstrates that by shifting the I-S function, an expansionary fiscal policy can raise the level of income (in this case from Y_0 to Y), even though interest rates are frozen at some minimum level, r_m, by the operation of the liquidity trap. The same analysis applies for the case in which investment expenditures are sufficiently insensitive to interest rates as to make monetary expansion impotent.

Figure 20-12
Expansionary Fiscal Policy when Monetary Policy is Impotent:
The Case of the Liquidity Trap

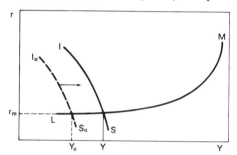

Coordination of Monetary and Fiscal Policies. Normally, both monetary and fiscal policies, used independently, will have some impact on aggregate demand. *Coordinated* monetary and fiscal actions will have an even more powerful impact on aggregate demand than either instrument used (in the same degree) independently. This point is illustrated in Figure 20-13.

In this figure we have drawn I-S and L-M curves which have elasticity enough that both monetary and fiscal policies would be individually effective in raising national income. Starting with the initial curves, I_0-S_0 and L_0-M_0, and with the initial equilibrium level of national income, Y_0, we can trace through the independent effects of monetary expansion (shifting the L-M curve to L_1-M_1) and fiscal expansion (shifting the I-S curve to I_1-S_1). Monetary expansion alone will raise income from Y_0 to Y_m. Fiscal expansion alone will raise income from Y_0 to Y_f. The combination of the same monetary expansion and the same fiscal expansion, however, will raise income to Y_{m+f}. This is the traditional argument for the coordination of monetary and fiscal policies. By parallel analysis, you should be able to show how conflicting monetary and fiscal policies can neutralize each other.

Impotent Fiscal Policy. There is one other situation which merits brief attention. The Keynesian model suggests one case in which fiscal policy would be impotent, which is illustrated in Figure 20-14.

Figure 20-13
Coordinated Monetary and Fiscal Policies

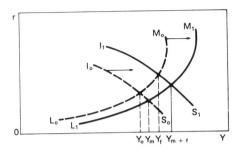

Figure 20-14
Impotent Fiscal Policy

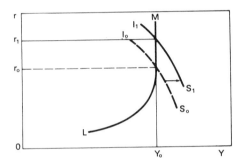

In this case, fiscal expansion is incapable of raising the level of national income, output and employment, because at the existing level of income, the L-M curve is perfectly inelastic with respect to the level of interest rates. An expansionary fiscal policy could only drive up the interest rate until private investment expenditures are reduced sufficiently to make room for the additional government expenditures (or for the additional consumption made possible by tax cuts).

Such an extreme situation could only arise if there was no interest elasticity in the demand for money. There could be no substitutes for money as an asset. Indeed, money would have to be perfectly complementary to economic activity, such that any increase in income and output would absolutely *require* an expansion of the money supply. For this reason, this is generally referred to as the pure classical case. It should be noted, however, that if the I-S curve is also highly interest inelastic, monetary expansion will not be *sufficient* to increase the level of income. Although monetary expansion is *necessary*, *both* monetary and fiscal expansion would be required.

In general, neither the extreme Keynesian case (liquidity trap) nor the extreme classical case seems likely to be a common occurence. However, in some degree, the lesson of the classical case is important. Fiscal expansion may be largely reflected in interest rates rather than income growth, unless it is supported by appropriate monetary policies.

Financing the Deficit. In our discussion of fiscal policy, we have studiously avoided discussing the methods to be used to finance any government budgetary deficit (or alternatively, to discuss what would be done with a budgetary surplus). But as we have seen, an expansionary fiscal policy implies a budgetary deficit, an excess of government expenditures over revenues, and that deficit must somehow be financed. Our elementary accounting identities tell us that the net government debt, in one form or another, must expand. Correspondingly a restrictive fiscal policy implies a surplus in the government's budget, an excess of revenues over expenditures. The net government debt must contract. We have considered only the impact of government revenues and expenditures on aggregate demand. Must we not also take into account the separate effects of changes in the government debt outstanding? If so, will this not seriously alter our basic conclusions on the impact of fiscal policy?

Such an argument has been advanced vigourously by some advocates of the new quantity theory of money.[20] In particular, it has been argued that, used independently (i.e., without coordinated monetary policy), fiscal policy is almost always ineffective. The financing of a government deficit will absorb funds which would otherwise be available to finance the investment expenditures of firms. Private expenditures will be depressed sufficiently to offset the impact of increased government expenditures or of reduced taxation. Correspondingly, a government surplus, involving the retirement of government debt, will indirectly provide funds to finance private expenditures, and these expenditures will expand sufficiently to offset the restrictive effects of reduced government expenditures or increased taxation.

There is one possible technique of financing the government deficit which we can dispose of quickly. It is always possible to provide the required funds to the government by expanding the money supply. For example, the central bank could make advances directly to the government, or it could purchase government bonds in the open market, thus "making room" for new issues of government bonds. However, this does not answer the quantity theorists' argument. This is not a case of "pure fiscal policy". It is precisely the case depicted in Figure 20-13 — that of coordinated monetary and fiscal expansion. Rather than offsetting the impact of fiscal policy, this method of financing the deficit reinforces the impact of fiscal policy. Financing the deficit by creating money ensures the maximum possible impact from an expansionary fiscal policy, and conversely, using the funds generated by a budgetary surplus to retire part of the money supply ensures the maximum possible contractionary effects from a restrictive fiscal policy.

But that case tells us nothing about the basic proposition that fiscal policy alone is ineffective. What about the case in which there is a budgetary deficit and no monetary expansion? Then, the government must sell bonds to finance the deficit, and private assetholders must be persuaded to purchase these bonds. Will it not require higher interest rates on government bonds to induce private assetholders to purchase them, and will not interest rates on other bonds rise correspondingly as the private assetholders sell them to make room for more government bonds? And will not the higher interest rates in turn restrict private spending?

The Keynesian answer is that this argument assumes that private asset portfolios are fixed in size. To the contrary, it is argued, an expansionary fiscal policy will generate additional income, which will in turn induce more saving, thus providing the required additional demand for government bonds to be held as financial assets. Remember the earlier discussion of the consumption function and the saving function. A rise in income implies higher levels of *both* consumption and saving. Remember, also, one of the lessons of Chapter 4: saving is a demand for wealth and, in this context ,a demand for financial instruments. As income and savings expand, private asset portfolios expand, thus creating the demand for the bonds which the government must issue in order to finance its deficit.[21] Indeed, one way to state the condition for a new equilibrium to be established in the commodity market is that income must rise to the point at which sufficient savings are forthcoming to absorb the increases in the government debt.

In other words, in the pure Keynesian case, the problem of financing the deficit is not a limitation on the effectiveness of fiscal policy. If a constraint arises, it is because assetholders demand to hold part of their expanding asset portfolios in the form of the one asset which is in absolutely limited supply, i.e., money, and the restriction will be greater the less willing are the assetholders to substitute other financial assets for money. That is, it will be the interest elasticity of the demand for money function and hence the L-M function which limits the effectiveness of fiscal policy in raising aggregate demand and income. We are right back where we started. Taking into account the problem of financing the government's deficit does not suggest any new conclusions; it simply provides a different perspective on the same analysis.[22]

Exactly the same analysis applies in reverse to the problem of disposing of the surplus created by a restrictive fiscal policy. We will leave it to you to trace through the analysis yourself.

Conclusions. Keynesian theory suggests that fiscal policy is a powerful instrument for economic stabilization even when monetary policy is rendered impotent by a liquidity trap or the insensitivity of private expenditures to monetary variables. In general, the analysis suggests that monetary and fiscal measures should be used in conjunction with each other. Coordinated monetary and fiscal policies are much more powerful than either policy used alone.[23]

The Keynesian Model of the Economy vs. the Quantity Theory Model

Perhaps it would be useful before we go on, to briefly highlight the essential differences which we see between the two leading models of the response of the economy to monetary policy.

The fundamental issue is quite simple. How is a central-bank-contrived disequilibrium between the demand for and supply of money resolved? We have distinguished between financial adjustments and real adjustments. Let us consider the financial adjustments first.

In terms of financial responses to monetary policy, there is very little difference between the two theories on the level of general principles. Underlying both theories is the notion that private assetholders strive to re-establish "balance" in their portfolios. However, to insist on this general similarity between the theories is to miss the essential issue. In both cases, the discussion of portfolio adjustments is greatly simplified, such that only the demand for money function receives careful, explicit attention. The Keynesian theory stresses the interest elasticity of the demand for money, with the elasticity increasing at low interest rates, producing the "liquidity trap". The quantity theory minimizes the importance of interest rates in the demand for money, stressing instead the stability of the relationship between the demand for money and (permanent) income.

There are corresponding differences in the assumed links between the financial adjustments and real economic activity. The Keynesian theory emphasizes the role of interest rates in regulating capital expenditures, and, between the interest elasticity of the demand for money and possible interest insensitivity of capital expenditures, admits the possibility of little or no real response to monetary policy. The quantity theory envisages the linkage as much more complex, involving many types of expenditure and direct real balance effects. There may be long and variable time lags, but the eventual impact of monetary policy on aggregate demand is powerful and certain.

It is in terms of the real adjustments themselves that the contrasts between the theories are most sharply drawn. The Keynesian theory takes the price level as determined independently in the short-run by institutional factors. If there are any real repercussions from monetary policy (which, it is argued, there may not be) it is real income and employment which must adjust. By contrast, the quantity theory assumes price flexibility. Since it is assumed that the economy automatically tends to full employment (at least if the money supply is managed properly, i.e., is kept from being a source of frequent, erratic disturbances), and the demand for money is a stable function of income, the only factor which can adjust to eliminate the monetary disequilibrium is the price level. Indeed, without the assumption of price level flexibility, the quantity theory differs from the Keynesian analysis only in terms of the financial responses to monetary policy, and hence in its prediction of the strength and certainty of the impact of monetary policy on aggregate demand.

In the analysis of real adjustments in the economy, there is, predictably, a middle ground between the two extreme theories. Many economists – and much empirical evidence – would argue that the assumptions of neither theory, with respect to the essential issue of price flexibility, are 'reasonable". A third view has emerged, which is perhaps closer to Keynes than to the classicists. It does not take the price level as given, but does accept that prices are "sticky". For reasons which will become obvious, we label this the "trade-off theory".

4/REAL ADJUSTMENT: TRADE-OFF THEORY

A literal interpretation of the Keynesian assumption of a fixed price level is, of course, untenable. Price levels do change, and at times rather dramatically. The appropriate interpretation of the Keynesian price level assumption is that the price level does not change in the short run in response to changes in aggregate demand. However, even in this less rigid form, the assumption seems to be in conflict with the evidence.

The "Phillips Curve" and the Price Level-Employment Trade-Off Function

The extreme version of the Keynesian model which we developed above obviously could *only* apply to an economy operating at less than full employment. When full employment is reached, output and employment cannot expand, and hence any further increases in aggregate demand must result in proportional increases in the price level. Ignoring differences in the financial sector, the Keynesian theory merges with the quantity theory.

But this implies a dramatic break in the macroeconomic performance of the economy at some magic point called "full employment". The trade-off theory is based on empirical analysis of this transition. It has been demonstrated that rather than an abrupt shift from a regime in which output is the sole adjuster to a regime in which the price level is the sole adjuster, what actually happens is a *gradual transition* from a regime in which output is the primary but not exclusive adjuster to a regime in which the price level is the primary but not exclusive adjuster. That is, empirical research has discovered a negative relationship between the *level* of unemployment and the *rate of change* of wage rates, a particularly crucial set of prices. This relationship is apparently relatively *stable*, and, at least over the limited range of unemployment levels observed in the 1950's and 1960's, is *continuous*. A curve describing this relationship is called a "Phillips Curve", because of the pioneering contribution of an Australian economist, Professor A. W. Phillips.[24]

One estimate of a Phillips curve for Canada is presented in Figure 20-15.[25] A corresponding curve showing the relationship between the level of unemployment and the rate of change of the level of prices of consumable goods and services can be called the "price level-employment trade-off function", or simply the "trade-off function". While there is not a one-to-one relationship between rates of change of wages and prices, the Phillips curve and the trade-off function have broadly similar characteristics. A trade-off function for Canada is presented in Figure 20-16.

The Theory of the Trade-Off Function

In terms of the nature of the real adjustments in the face of changes in aggregate demand, the trade-off function provides a middle ground between the extreme version of the quantity theory and the extreme version of the Keynesian theory. It is based on strong, although not undisputed empirical evidence for many countries and many time periods.[26] Unfortun

Figure 20-15
Estimate of a Phillips Curve for Canada

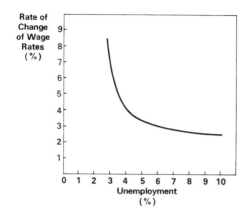

Figure 20-16
Estimate of a Price Level-Employment Trade-Off Function for Canada*

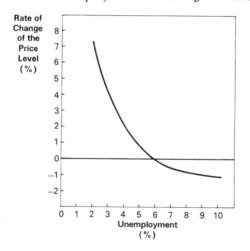

* Price level = consumer price index.

ıtely, it does not have an equally clear and consistent theoretical explanation. Rather, theories of the trade-off function tend to be based on ıd hoc assumptions about the nature of the pricing mechanism in imperfect markets. The first problem is to explain the Phillips curve since the trade-ıff function is derived from it.

The Phillips Curve. The common rationale for the existence of a Phillips curve is based on institutional information about price setting and ırice adjustments in labour markets. The theory of markets and price formation developed in most elementary economics courses is equilibrium theory. It asks the question: at what price will the quantity demanded equal the quantity supplied? or, what is the new equilibrium price, given a change in demand, or a change in supply? The common theory of the Phillips curve, by contrast, focuses attention on the situation when demand does not equal supply — when markets are in disequilibrium. In this sense, the theory underlying the Phillips curve is *disequilibrium theory*.

In the classical analysis of markets, as presented in most elementary textbooks, no constraints are placed on the adjustability of prices. When markets are in disequilibrium, prices change rapidly, thereby adjusting the quantity supplied and the quantity demanded until a new equilibrium price is established. Observers of labour markets note, however, that wage rates are not that flexible. Wage rates are established in a process of collective bargaining, and are subject to contracts of varying length. Thus, underlying the market is a pricing process which occurs at discrete intervals, not continuously. This does not mean that effective wage rates cannot change between contract dates. Contracts are sometimes opened for re-negotiation, special bonuses are sometimes permitted, workers may be re-classified into different wage categories (even though the tasks performed do not change), and variable amounts of overtime work at premium wage rates will introduce variability into hourly earnings even with a fixed scale of wage rates. The essential point is, however, that the institutions of the market make the wage rate "sticky". It does not adjust quickly or smoothly in the face of excess demand or excess supply in the labour market. As Keynesian theory suggests, a change of demand is likely to be reflected initially in a change in the level of employment rather than in a change of the wage rate.

However, this does not mean that wage rates are established arbitrarily, or that they do not respond to market forces. Rather, it is argued that the adjustment of wage rates to new market conditions takes time, and that the *speed of the adjustment* is a variable which also depends on market conditions. Very strong excess demand for labour will induce rapid wage rate increases. Modest excess demand will induce slow wage adjustments. Thus, it is argued, the rate of change in the wage rate depends on the degree of excess demand (+ or −) in labour markets.

In this argument, the level of unemployment is taken as a measure of the degree of excess demand in labour markets in the aggregate. However, the relationship between the level of unemployment and the level of excess demand is not clear. Since there is always some "frictional" unemployment (workers who are between jobs) and some "unemployables" in the labour force, "full employment" in the sense of zero excess demand for labour cannot mean literally 100% of the labour force employed. Moreover, all individual labour markets are not subject to exactly the same conditions of excess demand at the same point in time. As a result, there may be some unemployment which is a product of structural imbalance in labour demand and supply. For these reasons, it is argued, substantial upward pressure on wage rates may ex t even though employment is less than 100% of the measured labour force.

The Trade-Off Function. Given the Phillips curve, the trade-off function follows because of the importance of wage rates in total costs of production. In competitive markets, higher wage rates mean higher marginal costs, and hence higher prices. In oligopolistic markets, where "mark-up" pricing is common, higher wage rates mean higher average costs, and hence higher prices. In either case, a relationship between unemployment and the rate of change of wage rates implies a relationship between unemployment and the rate of change of prices.

The exact relationship between wage rates and costs of production depends on the rate of change of labour productivity. However, studies show that while the rate of productivity advance has a slight cyclical pattern, it depends primarily on longer term considerations and can be reasonably represented by a steady long-run trend. Under these circumstances, the unemployment/wage-rate relationship provides the main short-run domestic explanation for the rate of the price level advance.

Policy Implications

The trade-off theory is clearly much closer to the Keynesian theory than to the classical quantity theory. Indeed, one might characterize it as an important variation on the basic Keynesian model. The significant point is that is suggests that manipulation of aggregate demand through monetary policy (or fiscal policy) can normally be expected to have both price level and employment effects. Without additional policy instruments capable of shifting the Phillips curve or of changing its shape, the authorities cannot decide on price level and employment objectives separately. They must think in terms of *combinations* of objectives; trading-off price level stability against employment to achieve the preferred combination.

The study from which Figure 20-9 is derived suggests that stability of the consumer price level in Canada is probably inconsistent with aggregate unemployment of anything less than 4.5% of the labour force. Significantly lower levels of unemployment seem to imply very rapid rates of inflation.

Recent studies of trade-off functions have identified other factors affecting the rate of change in the price level as well as the level of unemployment.[27] Among these, the rate of change of import prices is the most important. For Canada, this means that the rate of change of prices in the United States has an important direct impact on the rate of change of Canadian prices, a point to which we will return in Chapter 21.

The trade-off hypothesis suggests another possible dimension for stabilization policy, measures to shift the trade-off function so as to improve the trade-offs between unemployment and inflation. Partly with this in mind, the Economic Council of Canada has vigourously urged that aggregate demand policies be complemented by "supply policies", including:

> manpower and other supply policies to improve resource allocation and open economic bottlenecks, policies to stabilize the growth of construction expenditure and so reduce the pockets of excess demand which periodically develop in that sector, policies to achieve better coordination of expenditure

planning and fiscal policy by all three levels of government, the laying of a groundwork for a fresh policy approach to the problem of market power, policies to improve productivity growth and facilitate adjustment to technological and other change, and policies relating to the government's increasingly important role as an employer and as a participant in collective bargaining.[28]

Supply policies are presumed to remove some of the inflexibilities in markets in the economy which may contribute to the Phillips curve phenomenon.

Another course of action which is commonly advocated is an "incomes policy". This may involve non-compulsory guidelines for wage and price increases (backed by the "moral suasion" of the government) or formal price and wage controls. In Canada, such proposals resulted in the establishment of a temporary Prices and Incomes Commission in 1969. This Commission has no legal power to control wage and price decisions, but it has attempted to exert moral suasion over business pricing and labour wage demands. It is too early to assess the impact of the Canadian incomes policy, and evidence on foreign experience is conflicting.[29] It has been argued, however, that an incomes policy cannot be effective in the Canadian context, particularly given the openness of the economy and the decentralization of decision-making on wage rates and prices.[30] It is also worth noting that to the extent that such a Commission is effective, its operations are subject to the criticisms of direct controls which we explored in Chapter 18.[31]

5/THEORIES OF MONETARY POLICY: AN OVERVIEW

We can briefly summarize the discussion in this chapter by posing and answering two questions.

1. Monetary policy implies manipulation of the money supply in order to affect real economic activity. If the central bank creates an excess supply of money, does this necessarily create an excess demand for goods and services?

According to the Keynesian model, the answer is "not necessarily". The total impact may be absorbed in the financial system.

According to the quantity theory, the answer is unquestionably "yes". The impact of monetary policy may filter out through many devious channels and with long and variable time lags, but it is reliable and strong.

2. Presuming that there is some impact on the aggregate demand for goods and services, does this imply a change in the volume of output and employment? of the price level? or both?

According to the Keynesian model, output and employment are affected. According to the quantity theory, the price level is affected, "in the long run". According to the trade-off theory, both will be affected in some degree, depending on the existing level of unemployment.

You should note the key role which the demand for money plays in the analysis. If monetary policy is to be a useful tool of policy there must be a stable demand for money function, such that the effects of a change of the money supply can be predicted with reasonable certainty. You should also note that the major issues in controversies among monetary economists are empirical. In principle they are answerable by reference to "the facts". Unfortunately, as we have seen in Chapter 19 with respect to the demand for money, and as we shall see again in Chapter 23 in a broader context, "the facts" are not always certain.

FOOTNOTES

[1] The "bills only" doctrine is explained and defended in W. Reifler, "Open Market Operations in Long-Term Securities", in *Federal Reserve Bulletin*, Vol. 44 (Nov. 1958), pp. 1260-1274. For a critical analysis see D. Luckett, " 'Bills Only': A Critical Appraisal", in *Review of Economics and Statistics*, Vol. 42 (Aug. 1960), pp. 301-306.

[2] Irving Fisher, *The Purchasing Power of Money* (New York: Macmillan, 1911), p. 183.

[3] *Ibid.*, p. 155.

[4] *Ibid.*, pp. 55-73; pp. 159-161.

[5] *Ibid.*, p. 172.

[6] Current or measured income (Y_m) is defined as the sum of permanent income (Y_p) and transitory income (Y_t). That is:

$$Y_m = Y_p + Y_t \tag{a}$$

The two concepts of velocity are then:

$$\text{(permanent velocity)} \quad v_p = \frac{Y_p}{M} \tag{b}$$

and:

$$\text{(measured velocity)} \quad v_m = \frac{Y_m}{M}$$

$$= \frac{Y_p + Y_t}{M} = v_p + \frac{Y_t}{M} \tag{c}$$

Using (a) we can rewrite (c):

$$v_m = v_p + \frac{Y_m - Y_p}{M} \tag{d}$$

From (b) we know that:

$$M = \frac{Y_p}{v_p} \tag{e}$$

Substituting (e) in (d):

$$v_m = v_p + \frac{(Y_m - Y_p) v_p}{Y_p}$$

$$= v_p + \frac{Y_p}{Y_m} \tag{f}$$

[7] Perhaps because of the danger of misinterpretation, the modern quantity theorists seldom make the strong theoretical assertion of proportionality between money and the price level which was the hallmark of the classical quantity theory. More common is a guarded empirically based statement of the type: "To my knowledge there is no instance in which a substantial change in the stock of money per unit of output has occurred without a substantial change in the level of prices

in the same direction. Conversely, I know of no instance in which there has been a substantial change in the level of prices without a substantial change in the stock of money per unit of output in the same direction." M. Friedman, "The Supply of Money and Changes in Prices and Output," reprinted in *The Optimum Quantity of Money* (Chicago: Aldine, 1969), p. 173.

[8] Friedman, *op. cit.*, pp. 180-181.

[9] The student who is not familiar with elementary national income accounting should review the relevant section of any standard principles of economics textbook.

The problem arises because in the conventional methods of accounting there are certain "costs" involved in the production of output which do not directly accrue as income to any factor of production. Primary among these is the capital consumption or depreciation allowance. It is because it is included in the measure of output that this measure is called the "gross" national product. Indirect taxes have the same effect. To the business firm they are costs; but they do not accrue as income to any factor of production. (Note that income taxes are different. As long as we measure income received before income tax is paid, the same problem does not arise.) Government subsidies to businesses are in effect negative indirect taxes.

It must also be remembered in this context that inter-firm sales of semi-processed goods net out in measuring aggregate income. That is, only the value added at each stage is included in the measure of aggregate output; and it is this figure which is equal to aggregate income (measured gross of depreciation and indirect taxes).

[10] Again, remember, both income and output must be measured in the same way: either net or gross of depreciation, indirect taxes, and subsidies.

[11] The dotted line in the top panel is drawn at a 45° angle to the base axis. Where this line crosses the consumption function, income and consumption are equal, and savings are zero. This point has been projected onto the lower panel. At all levels of income lower than Y_0, consumption exceeds income and saving is negative. Householders are drawing on their accumulated savings or are borrowing to finance consumption in excess of their income. At all income levels higher than Y_0 consumption is less than income and savings is positive. The saving function measures the vertical distance between the consumption function and the 450° line.

[12] A larger marginal propensity to save will also shift the I-S curve to the left, and a smaller *marginal* propensity to save will shift it to the right. Why? (Hint: review the discussion of the investment-income multiplier, usually just called "the multiplier", from your principles of economics course.)

[13] Keynes called his demand for money function the "liquidity preference function". Thus, the L-M function connects points at which (L)iquidity preference=the (M)oney supply.

[14] This point is tricky. Remember that the direct effect of income on the demand for money is otherwise allowed for. What is depicted in Quadrant II is the effect of the interest rate pure and simple. It is to be added to the effect of income.

If our assumption did not hold, we would have to draw a different curve in Quadrant II for each level of income. Curves for successively higher levels of income might lie inside or outside the given curve, and might have a different shape. This would complicate the analysis unnecessarily.

[15] The real balance effect is usually invoked as an argument to explain why a decline in the price level in an economy stuck in the liquidity trap would stimulate the level of income and employment. Remember, a decline in the price level — providing it does not provoke expectations of a continuing decline — is the equivalent of an increase in the money supply. It produces an increase of the relevant magnitude, the *real money supply*.

In assessing the significance of the real balance effect with a fixed price level, remember that in acquiring the new money each assetholder has either sold securities which he previously held, or borrowed from the bank. As a result, the increase in the money supply does not increase any assetholder's wealth. It seems unlikely that the change in the composition of his portfolio alone will create a powerful incentive to acquire real assets.

Where the real balance effect arises because of a drop in the price level, the situation is not fundamentally different. Not only is the real value of the money supply increased; so is the real value of all debts. In the aggregate: These effects offset each other such that aggregate real wealth does not change (except, perhaps, for claims on outsiders, which many economists take to include the government, on grounds that no one thinks of the public debt as his personal liability, subject to repayment in higher-real-value dollars).

[16] In some macroeconomic models of the economy, total government expenditures are considered an exogenous policy instrument. Cf., J. F. Helliwell, L. H. Officer, H. T. Shapiro and I. A. Stewart, *The Structure of RDXI*, Bank of Canada, Staff Research Studies, No. 3, (Ottawa, 1969); J. F. Helliwell, R. G. Evans, F. W. Gorbet, R. F. S. Jarrett, and D. R. Stephenson, *Government Sector Equations for Macroeconomic Models*, Bank of Canada, Staff Research Studies, No. 4, (Ottawa, 1969).

In some other macroeconomic models, the expenditures of junior governments are endogenous. Separate equations are included to "explain" their behaviour. Only the expenditures of the central government are considered an exogenous policy instrument. Cf., F. de Leeuw and E. Gramlich, "The Federal Reserve — M.I.T. Econometric Model," in *Federal Reserve Bulletin*, Vol 54 (Jan. 1968), pp. 11-40.

[17] The concept of the full employment budget as the guide to fiscal policy has been developed and applied by the Council of Economic Advisers in the United States. A relevant excerpt from their 1962 *Annual Report* is reprinted in W. L. Smith and R. L. Teigen, *Readings in Money, National Income and Stabilization Policy* (Homewood, Illinois: Richard D. Irwin, 1965), pp. 281-284. A similar approach to the analysis of fiscal policy has been urged in Canada by the Economic Council of Canada. See their *First Annual Review, Economic Goals for Canada to 1970* (Ottawa: Queen's Printer, 1964), pp. 197-198; *Second Annual Review, Towards Sustained and Balanced Economic Growth* (Ottawa: Queen's Printer, 1965), pp. 160-167. The concept is also explored at some length by the Royal Commission on Taxation, *Report, Volume 2, The Use of the Tax System to Achieve Economic and Social Objectives* (Ottawa: Queen's Printer, 1966), pp. 67-85.

[18] The savings function in Figure 20-9 is different from that in Figure 20-4. In constructing Figure 20-4 it was not necessary to distinguish between earned income and disposable (or after-tax) income. There was no government sector to collect taxes. In constructing Figure 20-9, however, this distinction is essential. We assume that the income concept which is relevant for private saving and consumption decisions is disposable income. Thus, if there is a linear consumption function such as that developed in Figure 20-3, it is a relationship between consumption and disposable income. The income concept in Figure 20-9 is gross national income. Disposable income is less than national income. The saving function in Quadrant III, then, shows the effects of both the relationship between disposable income and national income, and the saving decision out of disposable income. We assume that the existence of government reduces the level of private saving at each level of gross national income. The saving function in Figure 20-9 is closer to the vertical axis than that in Figure 20-4.

[19] This is the proposition commonly called the "balanced budget multiplier". The mathematics of it are developed in most textbooks on macroeconomic theory. The common sense of the argument is as follows:

There is a systematic quantitative difference in the *immediate impact* of government expenditures and tax collections on aggregate demand. Government expenditures have a direct, dollar for dollar impact, increasing aggregate demand. Taxation has the opposite direct dollar for dollar impact on *disposable income*. However, people react to the reduction of their disposable income partly by reducing consumption expenditures, and partly by reducing saving. The impact on aggregate demand (via reduced consumption expenditures) is less than the total amount of the tax collections. Therefore, a balanced budget, in which government expenditures equal tax collections, has a net expansionary effect on aggregate demand. The reduction of consumption is less than the increase of government expenditures.

[20] Perhaps the clearest and most explicit statement is that of M. Friedman in M. Friedman and W. Heller, *Monetary and Fiscal Policy: A Dialogue* (New York: W. W. Norton & Co., 1969) , pp. 43-62, 71-80.

[21] Changes in the relative supply of government bonds (increased) and private bonds (unchanged) may well have some effect on relative interest rates on the securities. Thus, the government may find that interest rates on the public debt have risen *relative* to rates on private debt.

[22] We have ignored the problem of time lags in this discussion of fiscal policy. If there are very long time lags in the effects of fiscal measures on aggregate income, then the initial effects of a deficit in the government budget may fall heavily on interest rates. The total effect, then, is very complex, depending as it will on the time lags in the impact of interest rates on private spending as well as the time lags in the impact of fiscal measures on aggregate demand.

[23] It is sometimes argued that monetary and fiscal measures should not be co-ordinated in this sense, i.e., they should not be used to achieve the same objective. From time to time, economists have argued that monetary policy should be geared to keeping interest rates low in order to stimulate investment and economic growth, with fiscal policy used to stabilize aggregate demand in the short-run. Similarly, it is sometimes argued that monetary policy should be used to maintain equilibrium in the balance of international payments, while fiscal measures are used for domestic stabilization. We will return to the latter argument in the next chapter.

[24] A. W. Phillips, "The Relation Between Unemployment and the Rate of Change of Money Wage Rates in the United Kingdom, 1861-1957," in *Economica*, N. S., Vol. 25 (Nov. 1958) , pp. 283-299.

[25] R. G. Bodkin, E. P. Bond, G. L. Reuber and T. R. Robinson, *Price Stability and High Employment: The Options for Canadian Policy*, Economic Council of Canada, Special Study No. 5 (Ottawa, 1966) .

[26] *Ibid.*, pp. 31-81; pp. 193-277.

[27] The trade-off function in Figure 20-9 is drawn on the assumption that corporate profits are "average"; that import prices are stable; and that wage rates in the United States are increasing at 3.2% per annum (a widely quoted guideline for "non-inflationary" wage rate increases in the United States) .

[28] Economic Council of Canada, *Third Annual Review, Prices, Productivity and Employment* (Ottawa: Queen's Printer, 1966) , pp. 168-169.

[29] David C. Smith, *Incomes Policies: Some Foreign Experiences and their Relevance for Canada*, Special Study No. 4 for the Economic Council of Canada (Ottawa: Queen's Printer, 1966) .

[30] Economic Council of Canada, *Third Annual Review*, pp. 158-163.

[31] A particularly powerful statement of this argument is presented in M. Friedman, "What Price Guideposts," in G. Shultz and R. Aliber, *Guidelines, Informal Controls and the Market Place* (Chicago: University of Chicago Press, 1966) .

21

The International Constraint on Monetary Policy, Part 1:

The Balance of International Payments and

Macroeconomic Equilibrium

Our discussion of the theory of monetary policy in Chapter 20 ignored one crucial dimension of the problem in assuming that the central bank had complete freedom to manipulate the money supply. Such freedom implies no significant constraints on the level of interest rates, other than those imposed in the market by the behaviour of assetholders. This is not always the case.

For example, in discussing the theory of central bank control of the supply of money (Chapter 17), we referred in passing to one situation in which the central bank did not have this freedom, i.e., during and after World War II when the government had adopted a policy of stabilizing government bond yields at low levels. Under postwar inflationary conditions, a policy of pegging interest rates was inconsistent with the vigorous use of monetary policy to restrain aggregate demand. The Bank of Canada was virtually powerless to restrain the inflationary pressures.

In the contemporary context, there is an equally powerful "external" constraint on independent monetary action by the central bank which arises from the freedom of international capital flows in a world of fixed exchange rates. This international constraint on Canadian monetary policy is the subject of this chapter.

Like other parts of our macroeconomic analysis, the foundations for the analysis of this chapter were laid earlier in the book. In Chapter 7 we explored the international connections of Canadian financial markets, focusing on the international dimensions of the portfolio selection decisions of individual assetholders and on their implications for equilibrium in Canadian financial markets. The task now is to extract certain implications for macroeconomic policy from that analysis.

1/THE INTERNATIONAL MONETARY CONSTITUTION

As will become evident, the nature of the interaction between domestic stabilization policy and international financial markets depends on the process by which the foreign exchange rate is determined. In this sense, the foreign exchange rate is the central variable in our analysis in this and the subsequent chapter.

The Foreign Exchange Rate

You will recall from Chapter 7 that the foreign exchange rate is simply *a price* — the Canadian dollar price of one unit of foreign currency. Of course, there are many foreign currencies, and in this sense many foreign exchange rates. However, given the key role which the United States dollar plays in international finance in general, and in the Canadian foreign exchange market in particular, we use the expression *the* foreign exchange rate to mean the Canadian dollar price of one United States dollar.

Although it is simply a price, in most respects just like the price of any other financial instrument which is determined in the market place by the interaction of supply and demand forces, the foreign exchange rate has one rather unusual and, for our purposes, crucial characteristic. It is the central concern of an international agreement, the Articles of Agreement of the International Monetary Fund, which amounts to an international monetary constitution. This agreement spells out the basic rules of the international money game. These rules are commonly called "the Bretton Woods System" because the original agreement was negotiated and signed at an international conference at Bretton Woods, New Hampshire, in 1944.

The Bretton Woods rules are not inviolable. National governments have been unwilling to make the surrender of their national monetary sovereignty which would be required by slavish and unquestioning adherence to these rules, and many countries have made major or minor violations from time to time. Among industrialized countries, Canada is a prime example. From October 1950 through May 1962 Canada had a flexible exchange rate in defiance of the Bretton Woods rules, and again on May 31, 1970 reverted to the flexible exchange rate, although the Canadian government promised "to resume the fulfilment of its obligations under the Articles of Agreement of the IMF as soon as circumstances permit." Thus, during the first 23 years of the Bretton Woods System (March 1947 – March 1970), Canada was in violation of the basic rules of the game almost half of the time!

Nonetheless, the Bretton Woods rules are the established order in international monetary affairs. The fact of serious violations of the rules, and particularly those by Canada, should not be taken as evidence that the rules are irrelevant. Rather, they are evidence that rigid application of the rules gives rise from time to time to serious stresses and strains within the international financial system. From our point of view, the underlying problem is that the Bretton Woods rules impose severe constraints on domestic stabilization policies. Indeed, policies required by the international rules of the game occasionally stand in stark conflict with policies required to achieve important domestic objectives. Our task in this and the subsequent chapter is to examine the economics of monetary and fiscal policies in the context of an international financial system operating according to the Bretton Woods rules. Only then will we be able to understand both the conduct of monetary policy in Canada and the nature of the problems which give rise to urgent proposals for reform of the international financial system.

There have been many proposals for the reform of international monetary arrangements, some involving changes in existing institutional arrangements in order to make the Bretton Woods system work better, and some to alter the underlying rules of the game. However, the reforms which have been adopted to date have been of the first sort. More drastic changes may occur in the near future, but at the moment the Bretton Woods rules remain essentially unchanged.

What are the most important rules of the game?

The Pegged Exchange Rate

The basic obligation assumed by governments under the international monetary constitution is to declare an official "par" rate of exchange, and to ensure that the actual foreign exchange rate at which transactions are consummated in the foreign exchange market does not depart from the par rate by more than 1%. Until it was withdrawn on May 31, 1970, the official par rate on the U.S. dollar was $1.08.[1] The government was then obliged to ensure that the forces of supply and demand in the foreign exchange market did not drive the foreign exchange rate above approximately $1.09, or below approximately $1.07.

The Adjustable Peg. Adjustments of the official par rate of exchange are not ruled out, although such changes are to be *infrequent,* subject to *international consultation and approval,* and only in response to *exceptional and intractable balance of payments pressures.* A flexible exchange rate, which, in response to demand and supply pressures, fluctuates over a wider range than 1% on either side of par, is a clear violation of the letter and the spirit of the constitution.

As we shall see, it is the requirement of a pegged exchange rate which imposes severe international constraints on the freedom of national monetary authorities. Under certain circumstances, the stability of the foreign exchange rate must be the overriding concern of central bank policy. The independent use of monetary controls to help achieve domestic price level or employment objectives may be rendered impossible.

Avoidance of Direct Controls

There is frequently an "easy" way out of the dilemma posed by a conflict between the domestic and the external objectives of monetary policy through the use of direct foreign exchange controls. Thus, for example, when the problem is excess demand for foreign exchange at the maximum permitted foreign exchange rate, it is possible to maintain stability of the foreign exchange rate by substituting official rationing of the restricted supply of foreign exchange for rationing by the price mechanism. By giving itself the power to approve or disapprove applications for foreign exchange, the government adds another weapon to its policy armoury, making it possible to keep the foreign exchange market in a continuous state of disequilibrium (i.e., with demand in excess of supply at the pegged exchange rate). Since it is then unnecessary to use monetary policy to maintain equilibrium in the foreign exchange market, monetary policy is freed from the international constraint, at least in the short run.

As we saw in Chapter 17, direct controls involve arbitrary interference with the allocation of resources in the economy. In general, they impair microeconomic efficiency. In any case, aside from exceptional circumstances, direct foreign exchange controls are prohibited by the rules of the game. Thus, the constitutional provision in this area is more accurately stated as *the maintenance of the foreign exchange rate within 1% of an agreed official par rate, without resort to direct foreign exchange controls.*

In the event of excess demand or excess supply pressures in the foreign exchange market, the government has two courses of action open to it if it is to maintain the stability of the foreign exchange rate without resort to direct foreign exchange controls. We can call these "direct intervention" and "indirect intervention".

Direct Intervention

The government can intervene directly in the foreign exchange market, buying foreign exchange when there is an excess supply at the minimum permitted exchange rate, and selling foreign exchange when there is excess demand at the maximum permitted foreign exchange rate. For this purpose, the government requires a stock of foreign exchange which can be augmented or drawn upon as necessary to permit direct intervention in the market. Most of Canada's foreign exchange reserves are held in the "Exchange Fund Account" (see Chapter 17) although both the Bank of Canada and other government agencies hold other working balances in foreign exchange, and the Government has large drawing rights with the International Monetary Fund which are normally counted as part of official reserves. We will consider these further in Chapter 22.

Indirect Intervention

Alternatively, the government can attempt to regulate the underlying private demands for or supplies of, foreign exchange. Thus, for example, if the problem is excess demand for foreign exchange, the government can attempt to reduce private demands for foreign exchange, or to increase the flow of foreign exchange from private sources onto the foreign exchange market. Part of our problem is to show how the government can do this, and particularly how monetary policy can be used to regulate the demand for and supply of foreign exchange.

The main concern of this chapter is the analysis of these two modes of governmental intervention in the foreign exchange market. However, before turning to this analysis it is useful to have before us a brief sketch of the foreign exchange market.

2/THE FOREIGN EXCHANGE MARKET

The term "foreign exchange market" is alternatively used in a broad sense to encompass all transactions involving the exchange of foreign currencies against Canadian dollars, and in a narrow sense to refer to a highly organized component of the broad market, the centralized interbank market in foreign exchange. In what follows, we use the term in the broader sense, which encompasses all transactions in which foreign exchange is exchanged against Canadian dollars, *whether those transactions occur in Canada or abroad.* It should also be noted that the definition encompasses both *spot* and *forward* exchange transactions. However, since they are normally closely related to each other (see Chapter 7), throughout most of the discussion we will not distinguish between the spot and forward exchange rates.

The Canadian "Retail" Market

The chartered banks are the heart of the foreign exchange market within Canada. As a part of their function of providing payments facilities for the economy, the banks "deal" in foreign exchange. That is, they buy and sell foreign exchange to meet the needs of their customers, be they businesses, households, or governments.

If the banks are to be able to satisfy the requirements of their customers immediately and without question, they must hold an inventory of foreign exchange. To this end, the banks hold some foreign currency in the vaults of their branches, and maintain deposits with foreign correspondents. These are the banks' "working balances". Foreign exchange purchased through the branch network is added to the working balances, and foreign exchange sold through the branch network is drawn out of the working balances.

However, both profit maximization and the ever-present foreign exchange risk dictate that working balances should be no larger than is necessary for efficiency in foreign exchange operations. This means that the banks must have an efficient mechanism for the quick disposal of excess foreign exchange acquired through their branches, and for the quick acquisition of foreign exchange to replenish working balances should they be depleted as a result of the activities of the branches. Such a mechanism is provided by the interbank market.

The Interbank Market

The interbank market in Canada is physically located in Montreal and Toronto, with Montreal more important in terms of the volume of trading. There is a foreign exchange brokerage office in each city which is owned and operated by the Canadian Bankers' Association and to which only members of the Association and the Bank of Canada have access. Banks with excess foreign exchange offer it for sale to other banks through the intermediary of the brokers. Similarly, banks which find themselves deficient in foreign exchange submit bids, through the brokers, for the required amounts. When a transaction is arranged — when the broker manages to find a buyer and a seller who can agree on an amount and a price — both the amount and the price (but not the identities of the principals) are reported to all participants in the market, thus providing them with continuous, current information on the state of the market.

The foreign exchange rate established in the interbank market — shall we call it the "wholesale rate"? — is the key rate. It is the one reported in official statistics of the foreign exchange rate. To the banks it represents the cost of acquiring foreign exchange for their retail operations. Accordingly, they use it, with an appropriate mark-up, as the basis for setting their "retail" rate.

Changes in the exchange rate established in the interbank market reflect the balance of supply and demand pressures in the whole Canadian banking system. However, the foreign exchange rate is not established in the Canadian interbank market in isolation. There is a necessary international dimension to interbank foreign exchange transactions, and hence to the foreign exchange market.

International Arbitrage. In Chapter 7 we defined the external value of the Canadian dollar as the reciprocal of the foreign exchange rate. In this sense, the external value of the Canadian dollar can be said to be established in trading in Montreal. However, an interbank foreign exchange market also exists in New York (and in other financial centers throughout the world), where Canadian dollars as well as other currencies are bought and sold. Clearly, the price of a Canadian dollar as established in New York must be the same as the external value of a Canadian dollar as established in Montreal (making due allowance for the cost of transactions, of course), or it will be profitable to purchase exchange in one market for sale in the other.

For example, suppose the price of one United States dollar established in trading in Montreal was $1.08, giving an external value of the Canadian dollar of U.S. $0.926. If the price of the Canadian dollar in New York was $0.930 it would be profitable to exchange Canadian dollars for United States dollars in New York, and then to sell the United States dollars in Montreal. The gross profit (from which we must deduct transactions costs) would be $0.004 per dollar transferred. On a large volume of funds, this could be an attractive proposition.

Transactions of this type, involving buying in one market for immediate resale in another, are called *arbitrage* (we encountered similar concepts in the discussion of nation-wide security markets in Chapter 3 and in the discussion of the theory of forward exchange rates in Chapter 7). Arbitrage may involve more than two foreign exchange markets, and it may be conducted by professional arbitrageurs who are alert to "disorderly cross-rates" of exchange, or by the normal participants in the market. Perhaps most important as a continuing force in the market are the operation of banks buying the foreign exchange which they require in the cheapest market, and selling their excess foreign exchange in the dearest market. The banks are well organized to do this, being in instantaneous contact with their agencies in New York and other major international financial centers.

An International Market. The important point is that arbitrage will occur as long as the rates in the two markets are out of line with each other, and this arbitrage will have the effect of bringing the rates into line. In this way, arbitrage ties the foreign exchange markets in all countries together into a single international foreign exchange market. In this market, what appears to Canadians as a demand for foreign exchange appears to the rest of the world as a supply of Canadian dollars. Similarly, what is from the Canadian point of view a supply of foreign exchange, is, from the non-resident's point of view, a demand for Canadian dollars. It does not matter whether a given exchange of Canadian dollars for United States dollars occurs in Montreal or in New York; arbitrage will ensure that it has the same effect on the foreign exchange rate.

Supply and Demand in the Foreign Exchange Market

So much for the institutions of the foreign exchange market. They simply provide the framework within which the forces of supply and demand work themselves out. If we are to understand the policy dilemmas posed by a policy of pegging the foreign exchange rate we must look beyond the institutions of the market and examine the nature of the underlying supply and demand forces themselves.

Demands to exchange Canadian dollars for foreign exchange can originate either inside Canada or abroad, and can be for many different purposes, including a simple desire to hold foreign money in place of Canadian money as an asset, perhaps for speculation on changes in the exchange rate. However, in a general way we can think of the demand for foreign exchange as arising out of the desires of Canadian residents to make payments abroad, for the purchase of goods and services from non-residents, to make gifts, to purchase equities or bonds from non-residents, to make other investments abroad. Similarly, the supply of foreign exchange arises out of the desires of non-residents to make payments in Canada, either for the purchase of goods and services from residents of Canada, to make gifts to Canadian residents, for the purchase of equities or bonds, or to make other types of investments in Canada.

The analysis of supply and demand in the foreign exchange market must start with these flows of international payments — with Canada's balance of international payments.

3/THE BALANCE OF INTERNATIONAL PAYMENTS

The balance of international payments is a statistical summary of the actual flow of economic transactions between residents of Canada and residents of the rest of the world during a given period of time. Statistics on Canada's balance of international payments for the year 1969 are presented in Table 21-1.

Table 21-1
Canada's Balance of International Payments, 1969

(Millions of Dollars)

I. CURRENT ACCOUNT

Receipts		Payments	
Merchandise Exports	14,982	Merchandise Imports	13,987
Non-Merchandise Exports		Non-Merchandise Imports	
Travel	1,074	Travel	1,292
Freight and Shipping	936	Freight and Shipping	991
Interest and Dividends	414	Interest and Dividends	1,345
Other Services	1,062	Other Services	1,588
TOTAL: GOODS AND SERVICES	18,468	TOTAL: GOODS AND SERVICES	19,203
International Transfers		International Transfers	
Inheritances, Immigrants' Funds		Inheritances, Emigrants' Funds	
and other Private Remittances	454	and other Private Remittances	366
		Official Contributions	144
TOTAL: CURRENT RECEIPTS	18,922	TOTAL: CURRENT PAYMENTS	19,713

NET BALANCE ON
CURRENT ACCOUNT   −791

II. CAPITAL ACCOUNT

Direct Investment	
Foreign Direct Investment in Canada	655
Canadian Direct Investment Abroad	−255
Portfolio Investment: Long Term Forms	
Canadian Securities:	
Trade in Outstanding Issues	55
New Issues	2,067
Retirements	−396
Foreign Securities	106
Other Long-Term Capital Flows	25
Portfolio Investment: Short Term Forms	
Resident Holdings of Foreign Bank Balances	−1,604
Non-Resident Holdings of Canadian:	
Bank Deposits	60
Money Market Instruments	332
Other Short-Term Capital Transactions (net)	−189
NET BALANCE ON CAPITAL ACCOUNT	+856

III. OFFICIAL RESERVE ACCOUNT

Net Change in Official International Reserves	65

IV. RECONCILIATION

Net Balance on Current Account	−791
Net Balance on Capital Account	856
Net Change in Official Reserve Account	65

SOURCE: D.B.S., *Quarterly Estimates of the Canadian Balance of International Payments,* Second Quarter, 1970 (Ottawa: 1970).

The Accounts

For the purposes of balance of payments accounting, international transactions are divided into two major categories. Transactions involving payments for goods and services and recurring international gifts are recorded in the *current account*. Transactions involving payments for equities, bonds or other types of international investments are recorded in the *capital accounts*.

Current Account. In statistics of the current account of the balance of international payments it is customary to distinguish between the value of commodities traded and the value of services. This distinction has been incorporated in the presentation of the current account in Table 21-1. It should be noted that while new foreign investments in Canada are recorded in the capital account, payments for the services of foreign-owned capital employed in Canada — interest and dividends — are recorded in the current account.

It is also useful to distinguish between the commercial transactions recorded in the current account and the relatively small value of public and private gifts and migrants' funds also reported in the current account. While in principle they are different from regular commodity trade — they involve international "transfer payments" — they are customarily recorded in the current account because of their regular, recurring nature.

In recent years Canada has typically had a deficit in the current account of the balance of international payments. That is, current payments have exceeded current receipts. This deficit is made up of a surplus on account of merchandise trade, and a large deficit on account of transactions in services, in which the net payments of interest and dividends looms particularly large. However, the overall current account deficit has been far from stable. Fluctuations in the current account have important implications for the macroeconomic performance of the economy, a matter which we will later examine further.

If we ignore the small amount of international transfer payments recorded in the current account, current account transactions involve demands for and disposition of *aggregate output*. Thus, as we saw in Chapter 20, what we call here the current account also appears as "exports" and "imports" in the national income accounts and in the aggregate demand equation.

The analysis of the macro-behaviour of the current account is therefore an aspect of the analysis of aggregate demand, income and employment. By contrast, transactions recorded in the capital account involve the purchase and sale of *financial assets*. The analysis of the behaviour of the capital account, therefore, must involve the analysis of the accumulation of wealth and portfolio balance decisions.

Capital Account. The capital account reports the *flow* of international transactions in financial instruments during a given *period of time* (in Table 21-1 the period is one year, 1969). This should not be confused with the stock of international indebtedness outstanding at any *point in* *time.* The two magnitudes are related, of course, in the same way that saving and wealth are related. The capital account of the balance of international payments shows the international transactions which produce a change in the size and composition of the stock of international indebtedness.[2] It should not be surprising that the annual capital flows are small relative to the total stock of international debt oustanding. For purposes of comparison, Canada's balance of international indebtedness as of December 31, 1967 (the most recent date for which data are available) is presented in Table 21-.2.

Table 21-2
Canada's Balance of International Indebtedness, December 31, 1967

(Billions of Dollars)

I. LIABILITIES (Foreign Capital Invested in Canada)

Direct Investment	20.7
Government and Municipal Bonds	5.8
Other Portfolio Investments	5.8
Miscellaneous Long-Term Investments	2.4
Total Long-Term	34.7
Other Investments, including short-term*	5.5
TOTAL GROSS LIABILITIES	40.2

II. ASSETS (Canadian Capital Invested Abroad)

Direct Investment	4.0
Portfolio Investments	2.6
Government of Canada Loans, etc.	1.6
Miscellaneous Long-Term Investments	0.7
Total Long-Term	8.9
Short-Term Assets†	6.2
TOTAL GROSS ASSETS	15.0

III. NET LIABILITIES

* Includes non-resident equity in Canadian assets abroad.
† Includes official foreign exchange reserves.

International investment transactions can be classified in many different ways. In Table 21-1 we have chosen to highlight the differences between direct and portfolio investment, and within the category of portfolio investment between investments in long-term securities and in short-term securities.

Direct Investment is associated with non-resident control of corporations: non-residents invest funds in business firms which are operating in Canada but which are effectively controlled by non-residents. Typically, this involves a foreign corporation investing funds in the expansion of a Canadian subsidiary firm. Similarly, Canadian direct investment abroad involves Canadian residents investing funds in firms which operate in other countries but which are controlled by residents of Canada.

Portfolio investment, by contrast, implies international investment in securities without any implication of foreign control. It may involve transactions in Canadian or foreign equities or bonds, including securities issued by business firms, financial intermediaries, local and national governments, and international organizations. The gross flow of funds includes the placement of new issues of securities, the retirement of outstanding issues, and the secondary trading of securities in the open market. Transactions in short-term securities include such transactions as the placement of funds in foreign currency bank accounts, the purchase or sale of money market instruments, bank loans and changes in international accounts receivable and payable (which are included in the account "other short term capital movements").

Official Reserve Account. We have not yet mentioned one major account in the balance of international payments, what is called in Table 21-1 the Official Reserve Account. Changes in official foreign exchange reserves — whether in the holdings of the Bank of Canada, in the Exchange Fund Account, or in Canada's position with the International Monetary Fund — are recorded in this account. Since foreign exchange reserves are properly regarded as international assets (and hence recorded in the balance of international indebtedness, Table 21-2), transactions reported in this account are also international capital flows. However, they have a peculiar role in the foreign exchange market, relating to direct governmental intervention to stabilize the foreign exchange rate, and for this reason it is important to segregate them from the rest of the international capital flows.

The Balance of Payments Identity

A basic principle of balance of payments accounting is that the sum of the net balance on current account and the net balance on capital account must equal the net change in official reserves. We can express this as an identity:

$$
\begin{bmatrix} \text{EXPORTS OF} \\ \text{GOODS AND} \\ \text{SERVICES} \end{bmatrix} - \begin{bmatrix} \text{IMPORTS OF} \\ \text{GOODS AND} \\ \text{SERVICES} \end{bmatrix} + \begin{bmatrix} \text{CAPITAL} \\ \\ \text{IMPORTS} \end{bmatrix} - \begin{bmatrix} \text{CAPITAL} \\ \\ \text{EXPORTS} \end{bmatrix}
$$

$$
= \text{NET CHANGES IN} \qquad (21.2)
$$
$$
\text{OFFICIAL RESERVES}
$$

In this equation the expression "capital imports" refers to the inflow of funds in payment for securities sold to non-residents (including the inflow of funds for direct investment in Canada). *A capital import involves either an increase in Canada's external liabilities* (in any form, including nonresident equity in Canadian firms), *or a reduction in Canada's external assets.* Similarly, the expression "capital export" refers to the outflow of funds in payment for securities purchased from non-residents. *A capital export involves either a reduction in Canada's external liabilities or an increase in Canada's external assets.*

The validity of the balance of payments identity should be intuitively obvious. However, to demonstrate the point, consider the situation in which there is a negative balance of $100,000 in the current account (i.e., imports of goods and services exceed exports of goods and services by $100,000). One way of looking at the current account is to say that the export of goods and services provides the foreign exchange to finance the import of goods and services. In the present case, exports will not pay for the full value of imports. How is the deficit to be financed?

If you think about it, there are a strictly limited number of possibilities. It is possible that residents of Canada will draw down their holdings of foreign exchange, or perhaps will sell foreign securities, providing foreign exchange through the foreign exchange market to importers, permitting them to pay for the extra $100,000 worth of goods and services. But this reduction in Canada's external assets is a capital import. The current account deficit is financed by a capital import, and the balance of payments identity holds.

Alternatively, the foreign vendors of the goods and services might extend credit, or non-residents might decide to purchase Canadian securities or indeed to increase their holdings of Canadian money, thus making the necessary foreign exchange available through the foreign exchange market. However, any of these occurences imply an increase in Canada's external liabilities, and hence a capital import. Again, the current account deficit is financed by a capital import, and the balance of payments identity holds.

All of these capital account transactions depend on a fortuitous coincidence of circumstances.[3] Suppose that under the existing conditions in Canadian and foreign financial markets no Canadian holder of foreign currency assets chooses to dispose of part of his holdings and no foreign assetholder is willing to take additional Canadian dollar assets into his portfolio. Then, *either the government must provide the foreign exchange out of its holdings, or the current account deficit cannot occur.* There are no other possibilities. *A current account deficit must be financed either by a private capital inflow or an official capital inflow.*

Exactly the opposite propositions hold true for a current account surplus.

The Policy Alternatives Again. The balance of payments identity thus provides another, more explicit, statement of the policy alternatives set out earlier. That is, if the free choices of Canadian and foreign assetholders do not provide international capital flows which are consistent with the net current account balance, the authorities have only two alternatives if they are to maintain the stability of the foreign exchange rate without resort to direct controls. On the one hand, they may finance any net deficit by drawing down official reserves, or absorb any net surplus by building up official reserves. This is what we called *direct intervention.* Alternatively, they may change the basic conditions which govern the flows of international payments on current or capital accounts. This is what we called *indirect intervention.*

Posing the possibility of indirect intervention raises several obvious questions. What are the major determinants of the flow of payments on current account? Can the authorities intervene to regulate these flows (without resort to direct controls, of course) ? What are the major determinants of the flow of payments on capital account? Can the authorities intervene to regulate these flows? What is the significance of all of this for monetary policy in Canada?

4/THE CURRENT ACCOUNT IN THE KEYNESIAN MODEL

A major concern of the pure theory of international trade is to explain the level and composition of imports and exports in the long run in a fully employed economy. The analysis usually assumes national economies which have different endowments with factors of production, and explains mutually advantageous trade flows between these economies in terms of the principle of comparative advantage. However, this is a long-run theory which deals with a range of analytical problems which are not of concern to us in the present context. We will take the structure of comparative advantage as given, and will focus exclusively on short-run fluctuations in the aggregate levels of imports and exports, in an economy which is not necessarily at full employment. For this purpose, the appropriate framework is the theory of aggregate demand, income, employment and price levels set out in Chapter 20.

Remember, we are assuming the foreign exchange rate to be fixed within very narrow limits. Moreover, as in our discussion of the basic Keynesian model, we take the level of prices, in Canada and abroad, as given. We will also revert to the terminology employed in respect to international trade in the discussion of aggregate demand in Chapter 20: the term "exports" will refer to all current account receipts from the sale of goods and services abroad, and the term "imports" will refer to all current account payments for the purchase of goods and services from abroad. In each case we are implicitly omitting international transfer payments from the current account.

Imports, Exports and Aggregate Demand

We saw in Chapter 20 that exports add to aggregate demand, whereas imports are a leakage from aggregate demand. Ignoring the government sector again, we can write the basic aggregate demand identity:

$$\begin{matrix} \text{AGGREGATE} \\ \text{INCOME} \end{matrix} = D = C + I + (X - Im) = Y = \begin{matrix} \text{AGGREGATE} \\ \text{DEMAND} \end{matrix}$$

$$(21.1)$$

This identity provides a framework for our analysis. We carry over the assumption which we made earlier regarding the behaviour of investment, consumption and saving. What we need now are assumptions about the short-run behaviour of aggregate imports and aggregate exports.

The Import Demand Function. Our basic assumption is that in the short run, with other things being equal (i.e., the level of prices, the foreign exchange rate, and the long-run determinants of the structure of comparative advantage), *the level of imports and hence the demand for foreign exchange on current account, depends directly on the level of aggregate demand.* As aggregate demand rises, the demand for imports rises. As aggregate demand falls, the demand for imports falls.

In contemporary Canada, the magnitudes involved in this relationship between imports and aggregate expenditures are not small. Thus, in recent years imports have ranged between 22% and 24% of gross national expenditure. It is also important to note that some components of aggregate demand have a stronger impact on imports than others. Thus, it has been estimated that almost one-third of all investment expenditures in Canada directly or indirectly involve the purchase of imported goods and services. The corresponding figures for other categories of expenditure are significantly less: 20% for consumption, 15% for exports and 11% for government expenditures.[4] It follows that the demand for imports depends not only on the level but also on the *composition* of aggregate demand. A rise in investment expenditures will have a particularly strong impact on the demand for imports. A corresponding increase in government expenditures will have a significantly smaller effect.

We can incorporate both of these assumptions into an import demand function distinguishing between imports which depend on investment expenditures (Im_1) and imports which depend on consumption expenditures (Im_2).[5] That is,

$$Im = Im_1 + Im_2 \qquad (21.2)$$

For simplicity we will assume that in each case imports are proportional to the relevant expenditures.

$$Im = m_1 I + m_2 C \qquad (21.3)$$

The coefficients m_1 and m_2 are not necessarily equal (in the example considered below we assume that m_1 is greater than m_2, in accordance with the information noted above).

Equation 21.3, then, is our import demand function. It tells us that *imports depend on the level of consumption expenditures and the level of investment expenditures.*

Exports. In the same way that Canada's imports depend on the level of aggregate demand in Canada, so Canada's exports depend on the level of aggregate demand in the rest of the world, and particularly in the United States. Exports help determine the level of income and employment in Canada, but they are not in turn determined by the levels of income and employment in Canada.[6] In this sense, given the assumptions of the Keynesian model, exports are an exogenous variable – a variable whose magnitude is determined by external factors. In our analysis we simply take the value of exports as given.

The Current Account and the I-S Curve

The addition of an exogenous export variable and an import demand function such as equation 21.3 makes no difference in principle to the "real" side of the basic Keynesian model. In terms of the concepts which we developed in the previous chapter, they simply alter the *position* and *elasticity* of the I-S function. Figure 21-1 is a demonstration of this, using the now familiar four-quadrant diagram.

In discussing the significance of external trade for macroeconomic equilibrium it is useful to distinguish between the effects of autonomous exports and the effects of the import demand function.

Exports as "Autonomous" Expenditures. When we first constructed the I-S curve, in Figure 20-4, we had only one category of expenditures which we assumed to be independent of the level of income, i.e., invest-ment expenditures. In the present case we have two types of "autonomous" expenditures, investment and exports. Moreover, exports, unlike investment, are independent of the level of interest rates.

In quadrant II of Figure 21-1, the given value of exports is indicated by the distance OX. In deriving what we might call the "autonomous expenditure function" of that quadrant, we have simply added the given magnitude of exports to investment (derived from the original investment demand function of Figure 20-4) at each level of interest rates. That is,

$$A = I + X \qquad\qquad (21.4)$$

The effect on conditions for commodity market equilibrium is the same as if investment expenditures had increased at every level of interest rates. That is, the I-S curve will be shifted to the right. *The effect of including exogenous exports in the Keynesian model is simply to increase the equilib-rium level of income at each possible level of interest rates.*

Figure 21-1
Commodity Market Equilibrium with International Trade

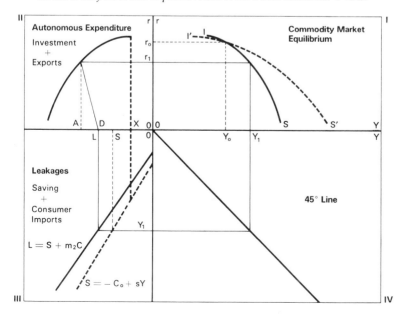

The Demand for Imports as "External Leakage". The effects of adding an import demand function of the type which we have specified to the Keynesian model is somewhat more complex. In general, the effects of imports is the opposite of the effects of exports. They reduce the equilibrium level of income for each level of interest rates, shifting the I-S curve to the left. However, the fact that imports vary directly with investment and consumption expenditures also has an important effect on the *shape* of the I-S curve. *By limiting the increase in domestic consumption expenditures consequent on any given increase of investment expenditures, imports reduce the interest-elasticity of the I-S function.*

An important part of the impact of imports on the I-S curve arises because that portion of investment expenditures which is devoted to the purchase of imports is irrelevant to the process of income generation in Canada. The import content of investment is an "external leakage" which must be deducted from income generating "autonomous" expenditures. In Quadrant II of Figure 21-1 we show the effect of this adjustment for the arbitrarily selected level of interest rates, r_1. At this level of interest rates, autonomous expenditures $(X + I)$ would be OA. However, from this must be deducted the import content of investment expenditures, leaving OD as the domestic component of autonomous expenditures. It is this magnitude -- the sum of exports and the *domestic component* of investment expenditures -- which is projected into Quadrant III at each level of interest rates.[7]

The second part of the import demand function, the import content of consumption expenditures (m_2C), has the same effect on the I-S curve as would an increase in the marginal propensity to save. It increases the share of any increment to income which is diverted away from income-generating consumption expenditures, and thus limits the total increase of income which can result from a given increase of autonomous expenditures. Accordingly, in Quadrant III we have added the import content of consumption (m_2C) to the original saving function from Figure 20-4, (the broken line in Quadrant III), to obtain the total leakage function,

$$L = S + m_2C \qquad\qquad (21.5)$$

This function is represented by the solid line in Quadrant III.

Equilibrium in the Commodity Market with International Trade. You will recall from Chapter 20 that equilibrium in the commodity market at any level of interest rates requires a level of income such that the (income-depressing) planned savings of households exactly offset the (income-generating) planned investment expenditures of business firms. With the introduction of international trade we have to re-define the conditions for equilibrium. Investment can exceed saving without pushing up income providing the excess of investment over saving is just offset by net inflow of goods from abroad. The income-generating effects of excess investment are just offset by the net leakage of aggregate demand through the current account. The opposite is also true. That is, an excess of saving over investment is also consistent with equilibrium in the commodity market providing it is offset by an excess of exports over imports. The income-depressing effects of excess saving are just offset by the income-generating effects of excess exports.

We can state our new equilibrium conditions as:

$$X + I = Im + S$$
$$= m_2C + m_1I + S \qquad (21.6)$$

Rearranging the terms:

$$X + I - m_1I = m_2C + S \qquad (21.7)$$

or:

$$A - m_1I = m_2C + S \qquad (21.8)$$

In Quadrant III we see that the equilibrium level of income, given interest rate r_1, is Y_1. At this level of income, leakages $(S + m_2C = OL)$ equal the domestic component of autonomous expenditures $(A - m_1I = OD)$. By a similar process we could find equilibrium levels of income for all other possible levels of interest rates.

The I-S Curve. The line in Quadrant IV is the now familiar 45° line, used to reflect equilibrium levels of income from the vertical axis of Quadrant III to the horizontal axis of Quadrant I. Since investment depends on the levels of interest rates, there will be a different equilibrium level of income for each possible level of interest rates. As usual, the I-S curve, the solid line in Quadrant I, is the locus of all combinations of interest rates and income levels which are consistent with equilibrium in the commodity market.

The broken line, I'-S', in Quadrant I is the original I-S curve from Figure 20-4, drawn on the assumption of the same investment and saving functions, but no international trade. It provides a convenient reference base for identifying the effects of introducing the international trade into the Keynesian model.

The two I-S curves have one point in common: that combination of interest rate (I_o) and income (Y_o) at which imports equal exports. This tells us that *international trade makes no difference to the macroeconomic equilibrium in the economy if the current account is in balance.* In our model, the level of income at which the current account is in balance depends on the level of exports. The larger the value of exports, the higher will be the level of income at which exports will equal imports, and the farther to the right will be the intersection of the two I-S curves.

In general, however, imports and exports are not equal, and whenever the current account is not in balance the presence of international trade affects the combinations of interest rates and income levels at which the commodity market will be in equilibrium. Thus, to the left of the intersection of the two I-S curves in Quadrant I, exports exceed imports. Because of this fillip to income, the new I-S curve lies above the old. *International trade will limit the decline of income and employment which would be the normal consequence of a rise in the level of interest rates.*

To the right of the point of interesection, the new I-S curve lies below the old. Imports exceed exports. Because of the import content of both investment and consumption expenditures, *international trade limits the increase of income and employment which would be the normal consequence of reduction of interest rates.*

Implications for Monetary Policy. These conclusions on the significance of international trade for macroeconomic equilibrium (with fixed prices and a fixed exchange rate) do not introduce any new principles into our analysis of monetary policy. However, they do provide additional reasons for thinking that the I-S curve may be relatively interest *inelastic,* and this is an important matter. As we saw in Chapter 20, the lower the elasticity of the I-S function, the less is the likelihood of a strong macroeconomic response to monetary policy.

There is also another dimension to the macroeconomic implications of international trade which we have glossed over. One conclusion which can be drawn from our analysis is that, given the level of exports, the behaviour of imports tends to stabilize the level of income and employment in Canada. It tends to dampen any increase of income, and to limit any decline of income, consequent on any given change of autonomous expenditures. However, international trade also exposes the Canadian economy to another source of instability, through fluctuations in the level of exports. Any change in exports will shift the I-S function in the same direction, and hence will alter the equilibrium levels of income and employment. To the extent that exports depend on aggregate demand in the rest of the world, and particularly in the United States, this provides a strong link between income and employment in Canada and economic activity abroad. If the I-S function were relatively inelastic, it would be difficult to counteract external effects on Canadian income and employment through monetary action alone.

5/THE CAPITAL ACCOUNT IN THE KEYNESIAN MODEL

In our analysis of the role of international trade in the Keynesian macroeconomic model, we imposed no constraints on the current account balance. We implicitly assumed that there was no limit to the magnitude of the current account deficit or surplus which could be induced by a rise or fall in the level of aggregate demand. However, our earlier discussion of the balance of payments identity revealed that current account deficit *must* be matched by an equal surplus in the capital account, or else official foreign exchange reserves *must* be drawn down. Similarly, any current account surplus *must* be matched by an equal capital account deficit, or else official foreign exchange reserves *must* increase. Do these facts not affect the extent to which current account deficits or surpluses can be incurred?

The answer is "yes". As a result, in analyzing the conditions for macroeconomic equilibrium in the Canadian economy, we cannot consider the current account in isolation. We must consider it in relation to international capital flows and possible changes in official foreign reserves.

The role of official foreign exchange reserves in this context poses special problems which are better deferred for separate treatment. What regulates private international capital flows?

The Determinants of International Capital Flows

We have already considered the international investment decision in some detail in Chapter 7. There is no need to repeat that discussion here. If we regard international capital flows of all types — direct investment as well as portfolio investment — simply as international transactions in financial instruments (in the broad way in which we have defined the concept of a financial instrument), then what is involved in international capital flows are the portfolio balance decisions of Canadian and foreign asset-holders and debtors. Thus, capital outflows result when Canadian asset-holders choose to take foreign securities into their portfolios, when foreign assetholders choose to reduce their holdings of Canadian securities, or when Canadian debtors decide to retire foreign-held debt. Similarly, capital inflows result when foreign assetholders choose to take Canadian securities into their portfolios, when Canadian assetholders choose to reduce their holdings of foreign securities, or when foreign debtors decide to retire Canadian-held debt.

Many types of financial instruments, many different assetholders and debtors, and hence many individual decisions are involved in the aggregate of international capital flows in any given year. Each decision calls for the weighing of a variety of considerations, some economic, some political; some long-term, some short-term. However, the central consideration in most of these decisions — whether they relate to direct investment or portfolio investment — must be the *expected yield* on the investment (considered relative to risk and liquidity, of course). Foreign capital will be attracted to Canada by relatively high expected yields on Canadian investments. Canadian capital will be attracted abroad by relatively high expected yields on foreign investments.

Interest Rates and Capital Flows. This line of argument suggests that there should be a direct link between Canadian monetary policy and international capital flows. A tight money policy, as we have seen, implies higher interest rates in Canada. Given interest rates prevailing abroad, this should induce foreign assetholders to purchase relatively higher-yielding Canadian securities, and should induce Canadian borrowers to raise more funds from foreign banks and financial intermediaries. The net result should be an enlarged inflow of capital to Canada. Similarly, an easy money policy implies lower interest rates in Canada. Given the interest rates prevailing abroad, this should reduce the incentive for foreign assetholders to hold Canadian securities and the incentive for Canadian borrowers to raise funds abroad. Indeed, a sufficient reduction of Canadian interest rates could induce substantial foreign borrowing in Canada. The end result of an easy money policy should be a reduction of the capital inflow, and perhaps a net capital outflow.

Not all international capital flows are highly sensitive to international interest rate differentials. For example, empirical researchers have found little statistical evidence of a strong response of direct investment to interest rates. However, there is substantial evidence of high interest-elasticity of portfolio investment, in both long-term and short-term forms.[8] This effect is sufficiently strong to have a decisive impact on the balance of payments and the foreign exchange market should Canadian interest rates depart significantly from those prevailing in the United States.

The Net Capital Flow Function. These basic assumptions about the dependence of international capital flows on the level of Canadian interest rates are incorporated in the net capital flow function presented in Figure 21-2.

Figure 21-2
The Net Capital Flow Function

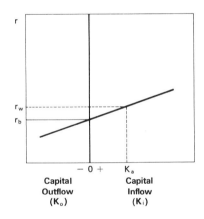

We assume that international capital flows are highly sensitive to international interest rate differentials, and hence we have drawn the line with a relatively low slope. However, we have not adopted the extreme assumption of perfect international capital mobility which is sometimes employed in the analysis of this problem. Such an assumption would produce a perfectly horizontal line at the world interest rate (or perhaps at the world rate plus a small "risk premium"). Furthermore, we have drawn the net capital flow function as a straight line purely for convenience.

The level of interest rates in Canada (r) is meaured along the vertical axis, and the net international flow of capital along the horizontal axis. At interest rate r_w, the level of interest rates in Canada is the same as that in the rest of the world (i.e., for all practical purposes, in the United States). That is, the international differential between yields on comparable securities is zero. We have assumed that at this level of interest rates there is still a net inflow of capital into Canada (K_a). We might call this the "autonomous" capital inflow. It may take the form largely of direct investment.

At higher levels of interest rates in Canada, a greater net inflow of capital (K_1) will occur. At lower levels of interest rates there will be a smaller net inflow, until, at interest rates lower than r_b, a net capital outflow (K_o) from Canada results.

Balance of Payments Equilibrium

The important new concept, balance of payments equilibrium, can be defined as *a condition in which normal market forces tend to keep the foreign exchange rate within the permitted range about the official par rate, without direct controls and without direct intervention by the government.* Balance of payments equilibrium requires that the international capital flows resulting from the free choices of Canadian and foreign asset-holders and debtors are just sufficient to offset the net balance on current account at the pegged rate of exchange. No change in official reserves is required to achieve a balance of international payments.

The conditions for balance of payments equilibrium thus depend partly on the behaviour of the capital account, and partly on the behaviour of the current account. We have a function, the net capital flow function, which describes the behaviour of international capital flows in response to Canadian interest rates. What we require to complete our analysis is a companion function describing the behaviour of the current account.

The Current Account Balance Function. The required current account balance function can be derived directly from our earlier analysis of the determinants of imports and exports, and particularly from Figure 21-1. You will recall that we assumed that the value of exports was exogenous, determined by factors external to Canada, and that the value of imports depended separately on the levels of investment expenditures and consumption expenditures in Canada. On these assumptions, the current account balance depends on the level of income in Canada in the manner indicated in Figure 21-3.[9]

At one particular level of income, Y_o, imports will equal exports and the current account will balance. At higher levels of income, imports will be larger, and hence there will be a negative balance in the current account. At lower levels of income, imports will be smaller, producing a surplus in the current account.

The B-K Function. Balance of payments equilibrium, then, must depend on the level of interest rates and the level of income in Canada. At any given level of income, there will be a unique level of interest rates which will induce a capital inflow equal to the current account deficit associated with that level of income (or a capital outflow equal to the current account surplus). Thus, balance of payments equilibrium requires a different level of interest rates for each possible level of income, and we can derive a function, similar in concept to the I-S and L-M functions,

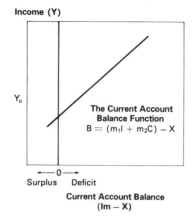

Figure 21-3
The Current Account Balance Function

Income (Y)

Y₀

The Current Account
Balance Function
B = (m₁I + m₂C) – X

←—0—→
Surplus   Deficit

Current Account Balance
(Im – X)

which identifies all possible combinations of interest rates and income levels consistent with balance of payments (or foreign exchange market) equilibrium. We call such a curve a B-K function.[10]

The derivation of the B-K curve from the net capital flow function of Figure 21-2 and the current account balance function of Figure 21-3 is demonstrated in Figure 21-4. The technique is the same as that employed earlier, and should require no explanation. The net capital flow function is in Quadrant II, with the net international flow of capital measured along the base axis and interest rates along the vertical axis. The current account balance function is in Quadrant III, with the current account balance measured along the base axis, and the level of income measured in a downward direction along the vertical axis. We can use these two curves to find combinations of interest rates and income at which the net capital flow and the current account balance are equal. Equilibrium income levels for each level of interest rates are projected from the vertical axis of Quadrant III to the base axis of Quadrant I, using the 45° line of Quadrant IV. The result is the balance of payments equilibrium line, B-K, described by the solid line in Quadrant I.

At points above the B-K function the level of interest rates is too high relative to the level of income. The net inflow of capital from abroad will exceed the current account deficit (in order to demonstrate your understanding of the B-K function you should be able to show that this is the case). Excess supply in the foreign exchange market will put downward pressure on the foreign exchange rate. If such a condition is to exist, in the absence of direct controls and without a change in the foreign exchange rate, the excess supply must be absorbed by an increase of official foreign exchange reserves.

At points below the B-K function, the level of interest rates is too low relative to the level of income. The net inflow of capital will fall short of the current account deficit, and excess demand in the foreign exchange market will put upward pressure on the foreign exchange rate. If such a

Figure 21-4
Derivation of the Balance of Payments Equilibrium Function (B-K)

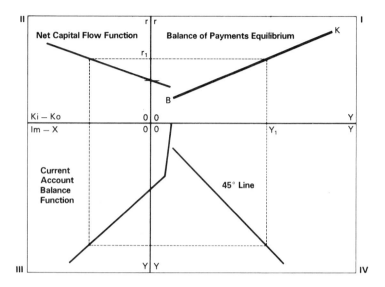

condition is to exist, official foreign exchange reserves must be drawn down to satisfy the excess demand at the maximum permitted ($+ 1\%$ of par) foreign exchange rate.

You should note that according to our assumptions, at higher levels of income, balance of payments equilibrium requires higher levels of interest rates. The more sensitive are international capital flows to interest rate differentials, the flatter this line will be. In the extreme case of perfect international capital mobility, the B-K line will be horizontal at the world level of interest rates, r_w.

6/MACROECONOMIC EQUILIBRIUM WITH INTERNATIONAL TRADE AND INTERNATIONAL CAPITAL FLOWS

We are now in a position to incorporate international trade in goods and services and international capital flows into our analysis of macroeconomic equilibrium.

Macroeonomic Equilibrium

We discovered in Chapter 20 that full macroeconomic equilibrium in a *closed economy* requires that equilibrium be achieved simultaneously in the money market and the commodity market. In an *open economy* we add a third condition: equilibrium must be achieved simultaneously not only in the commodity and money markets, but also in the balance of international payments. That is, *full macroeconomic equilibrium in an open economy requires a combination of interest rates and income levels which will simultaneously satisfy the I-S function, the L-M function, and the B-K function.*

A state of full macroeconomic equilibrium is illustrated in Figure 21-5. At any combination of income and interest rates other than Y_e and r_e at least two of the three markets must be in disequilibrium (and with many conceivable combinations, all three markets will be in disequilibrium). For example, at the levels of interest rates and income indicated by r_1 and Y_1 equilibrium would be achieved in the commodity market. However, given the money supply, the money market would not be in equilibrium (the supply of money would exceed the demand, creating downward pressure on interest rates) and given the foreign exchange rate and foreign interest rates, the balance of payments would not be in equilibrium (the inflow of capital would exceed the current account deficit, creating downward pressure on the foreign exchange rate). At levels of interest rates and income represented by r_2 and Y_2 the commodity market would again be in equilibrium, but there would be excess demand in both the money market and the foreign exchange market. Full macroeconomic equilibrium would not exist. (To demonstrate your understanding of this discussion you should be able to explain the nature of the disequilibrium conditions represented by other combinations of interest rates and income.)

Figure 21-5
Full Macroeconomic Equilibrium in an Open Economy

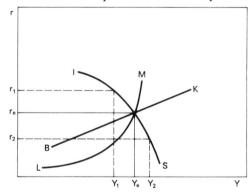

In the conditions depicted in Figure 21-5, full macroeconomic equilibrium is possible. Indeed, any departure from equilibrium income and interest rates would eventually be corrected. Thus at points like r_1 Y_1, downward pressure on interest rates resulting from the excess supply of money and the excess capital inflows would increase investment, income and imports, and would tend to move the system toward equilibrium at r_e Y_e. Similarly, at points like r_2 Y_2, upward pressure on interest rates would move the system toward equilibrium at r_e Y_e.

The Impossibility of Equilibrium

However, the tendency of the economy toward general macroeconomic equilibrium as depicted in Figure 21-5 is an *accident* – a product of the way in which we have drawn the three curves. Given the underlying be-havioural functions (i.e., the demand for money function, the investment function, the import demand function, etc.), and given any arbitrarily selected money supply and foreign exchange rate, *general macroeconomic equilibrium may be impossible.* That is, *given the money supply and the foreign exchange rate, there may be no combination of interest rates and income which will simultaneously satisfy the* I-S *function, the* L-M *function, and the* B-K *function.*[11]

An example of a situation in which general macroeconomic equilib-rium is impossible is depicted in Figure 21-6. The three functions do not have a common point of intersection. In this situation, with interest rates and income at r_1 and Y_1 respectively, the money and commodity markets will be in equilibrium but the balance of international payments will be in surplus. The economy can only be maintained in this condition if official foreign exchange reserves increase in each time period by the amount of the balance of payments surplus (which we have ruled out by our definition of equilibrium).

Figure 21-6
Macroeconomic Equilibrium Impossible
Domestic Equilibrium: Balance of Payments Surplus

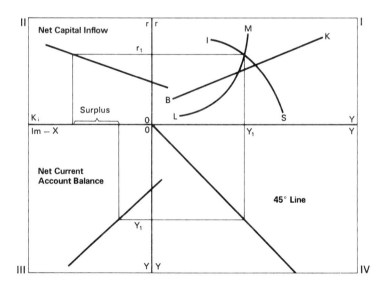

The opposite situation is depicted in Figure 21-7. At the level of interest rates and income $(r_2 \ Y_2)$ which produces equilibrium in the com-modity and money markets, the balance of payments is in deficit. The economy can only be maintained in this condition if official foreign ex-change reserves are drawn down in each time period by the amount of the balance of payments deficit (ruled out by our definition of equilib-rium).

Figure 21-7
Macroeconomic Equilibrium Impossible
Domestic Equilibrium: Balance of Payments Deficit

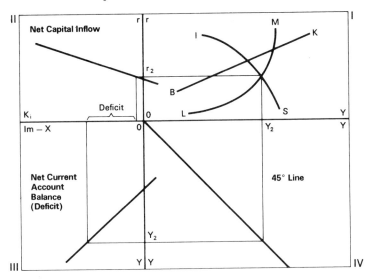

It should also be noted that if macroeconomic equilibrium is achieved, as in Figure 21-5, it will be a fragile condition. Underlying each of the functions in Figure 21-5 is a great variety of variables and behaviour patterns, some domestic and some external, each of which is subject to substantial change over short periods of time. A significant change in any major macroeconomic variables will disturb the equilibrium. Thus, for example, a rise in investment demand will shift the I-S function; a decline in exports will shift the B-K function; and an increase in the demand for money will shift the L-M function. Moreover, a shift in any one of these functions will convert a condition of full equilibrium into a condition (such as Figures 21-6 or 21-7) in which equilibrium may be impossible without further intervention on the part of the government.

Implications for Monetary Policy

Let us continue our earlier assumption that the level of official foreign exchange reserves must not change significantly (as we shall see in the next section, this is not an unreasonable assumption). What, then, are the implications of this analysis for monetary policy?

Governmental Policy and Macroeconomic Equilibrium. The important point to be derived from this analysis is not that under certain plausible conditions macroeconomic equilibrium may be impossible in an open economy, but rather that *the achievement of equilibrium may require* *a particular set of governmental policies.* In this regard, we must remember that the position of the L-M curve is a matter of governmental policy. It depends on the size of the money supply. Thus, in a situation typified by Figure 21-6, full equilibrium is only impossible if the government insists on restricting the money supply to the level which produces the indicated L-M curve. Full macroeconomic equilibrium can always be achieved in this situation through monetary expansion, shifting the L-M curve to the right until it intersects the I-S and B-K curves. There is some money supply which is compatible with full macroeconomic equilibrium — but that money supply implies a lower level of interest rates and a higher level of aggregate demand in the economy.

Similarly, in situations like that depicted in Figure 21-7, full equilibrium can always be obtained by the appropriate monetary policy. In this case, the money supply must be restricted, shifting the L-M curve to the left until it intersects with the I-S curve and B-K curves. Full equilibrium implies a higher level of interest rates and a lower level of aggregate demand.

This discussion suggests a very important conclusion. *In a relatively small, open economy, with a pegged exchange rate and with official foreign exchange reserves which cannot undergo major fluctuations, the central bank does not have the power to determine independently the course of monetary policy. Rather, monetary policy is dictated by the necessity of finding a money supply which is compatible with equilibrium in both the commodity market (the* I-S *curve) and the balance of payments (the* B-K *curve).* Indeed, the very purpose of monetary policy ceases to be the regulation of domestic aggregate demand in the interests of employment and price level stabilization in the fashion discussed in Chapter 20. Monetary policy becomes a tool for the harmonization of the balance of payments and domestic aggregate demand in the interests of macroeconomic equilibrium.

In principle, macroeconomic equilibrium can also be achieved through fiscal policies designed to shift the I-S curve. However, for short-run adjustments, this is seldom a practical alternative. The very flexibility of monetary policy normally throws the bulk of the shorter term adjustments on it. Nonethless, the potential use of fiscal policy for this purpose — and particularly for the solution of longer term problems — should not be overlooked.

Conflicts Between Domestic and External Policy. This new perspective on monetary policy has another important implication. In Chapter 20 we discovered several reasons, within the Keynesian framework, why monetary policy might be relatively impotent as a tool for achieving domestic macroeconomic objectives like full employment and price level stability. The balance of international payments obviously imposes another constraint on the effectiveness of monetary policy for domestic economic stabilization. Indeed, *under certain circumstances, the balance of payments constraint may actually dictate monetary policies which are perverse from a domestic point of view.*

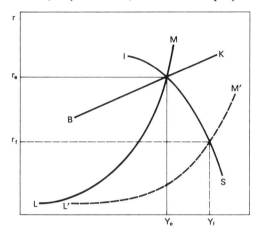

Two important cases must be considered. The first is represented in Figure 21-8. In this situation, the equilibrium level of income (Y_e) falls short of the level required to maintain full employment in the economy (Y_f). (Remember that we are dealing with a Keynesian economy, in which the price level is fixed.) Domestic considerations call for monetary expansion, shifting the L-M curve to L'-M', inducing lower interest rates and increased credit availability, and higher levels of investment, income and employment. Balance of payments considerations prevent this. Equilibrium can only be maintained in the foreign exchange market at the pegged exchange rate with high interest rates. There is a clear conflict between the use of monetary policy for domestic objectives and for external objectives. Overriding balance of payments considerations render monetary policy *perverse* from a domestic point of view.

That is not to say that full employment and balance of payments equilibrium cannot be achieved simultaneously in this situation. As noted above, fiscal policy can be used to move the I-S curve. What would be required in this situation would be expansionary fiscal policy (lower taxes, higher government expenditures) to move the economy toward full employment, coupled with a restrictive monetary policy to maintain balance of payments equilibrium.

Another case of conflict in the use of monetary policy is illustrated in Figure 21-9. The equilibrium level of income (Y_e) is greater than the full employment level of income (Y_f). Full equilibrium calls for a larger money supply (L-M) than that which is required for full employment (L'-M'), and the lower interest rates and larger level of aggregate demand are inconsistent with price level stability. The monetary policy required to maintain stability of the foreign exchange rate in the absence of substantial increases in official foreign exchange reserves is an inflationary monetary policy.

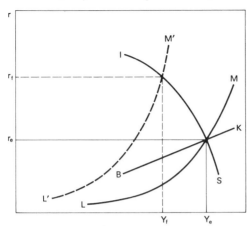

Again, harmonization of the domestic and external objectives is possible in principle through the combined use of monetary and fiscal policies.
As in the previous case, monetary and fiscal policies must be used in the
opposite directions.

Figure 21-10
Conflicts Between Policy Objectives
Agreement on Direction of Policy: Conflict on Intensity of Expansion

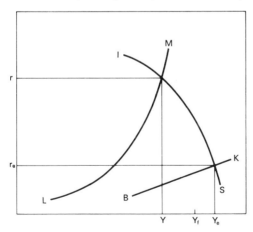

Conflicts between external and internal objectives are not inevitable,
of course. In the case illustrated by Figure 21-10, at the existing level of
income, (Y), there is neither full employment nor full macroeconomic
equilibrium (the combination B-Y lies above the B-K function, and hence

the balance of payments is in surplus). The achievement of full employment and macroeconomic equilibrium both call for monetary expansion.
There is no conflict on the *direction* of policy.

It should be noted, however, that in such a situation, the degree of
monetary expansion appropriate to each objective may be different. This
is also illustrated in Figure 21-10. Thus, once full employment is achieved
(Y_f) further monetary expansion is still called for to eliminate the balance
of payments surplus. The conflict between internal and external objectives
re-emerges at full employment.

Obviously, examples of this sort can be multiplied *ad nauseam.* However, the manipulation of graphs is only useful if it produces important
conclusions about the functioning of the economy. Have we discovered
anything of significance?

An Important Conclusion. The results of our analysis to this point are
very important. They demonstrate that *in an economy like Canada's there
is little scope for a vigorous, independent monetary policy designed to
regulate domestic aggregate demand if the foreign exchange rate is pegged,
and if official foreign exchange reserves cannot undergo short-term fluctuations.*

Surely this is a powerful conclusion, at least if we accept the two
caveats. We know that the international monetary constitution calls for
pegged exchange rates. But what about official foreign exchange reserves?

Can they not be used to reconcile the domestic and external objectives
of monetary policy? That is, can the official foreign exchange reserves not
be increased to absorb any surplus in the foreign exchange market, or
drawn down to finance any deficit in the foreign exchange market, resulting from the use of monetary policy for purely domestic purposes? What
is the function of official foreign exchange reserves in the financial system?

7/OFFICIAL FOREIGN EXCHANGE RESERVES

Official foreign exchange reserves are a pool of foreign exchange
and other foreign currency assets which can be readily converted into
foreign exchange, in the hands of the government and its agencies, and
available to finance governmental direct intervention in the foreign exchange market. These reserves can be held in various forms, and the nature
and composition of foreign exchange reserves raises a number of interesting and important economic issues. (We will sketch out some of the
major points in Chapter 22.) We must be concerned with the role of
foreign exchange reserves in ameliorating the potential conflict between
domestic and external objectives of monetary policy, and for this purpose
it is the overall size rather than the composition of foreign exchange
reserves which is the vital concern.

Foreign Exchange Reserves and Balance of Payments Deficits

Let us first consider the case illustrated by Figure 21-8. This is a
situation in which full employment calls for monetary expansion, but

monetary expansion implies excess demand for foreign exchange at the maximum permissible foreign exchange rate. There is a clear conflict between the domestic and the external objectives of policy. Full employment implies a balance of payments deficit.

Foreign Exchange Reserves as a Buffer Stock. The conflict is more apparent than real if the implied balance of payments deficit can be financed readily by drawing down official foreign exchange reserves. In this sense, official foreign exchange reserves can serve as a buffer stock, absorbing the balance of payments consequences of domestic economic policies (or, alternatively, shielding domestic policy from adverse developments in the balance of payments). Indeed, this *is* the economic function of official foreign exchange reserves. They are supposed to make the government's commitment to maintain the pegged exchange rate credible, without imposing continuous tyranny of the balance of payments over domestic monetary and fiscal policies.

If foreign exchange reserves are to perform this function they must be large relative to potential balance of payments deficits. Remember that at any point in time official foreign exchange reserves are a *stock* of finite magnitude. A balance of payments deficit (a *flow*) during any period will reduce the level of reserves available to finance a deficit in the following period. A continuing deficit will deplete the stock of reserves more or less rapidly, depending on the size of the deficit relative to the stock of reserves. Thus, Canada's foreign exchange reserves of just over $3 billion at the beginning of 1970 would last only 30 months in the face of a steady monthly deficit of $100 million, or 15 months in the face of a steady monthly deficit of $200 million.

This seems to imply that the independence of domestic monetary and fiscal policy from the balance of payments constraint is simply a matter of having adequate foreign exchange reserves. The larger the stock of reserves, the greater the scope for independent action in pursuit of domestic full employment, unhampered by concern over potential balance of payments deficits.

There is an important element of truth in this proposition. Large reserves will finance larger or more prolonged deficits than will small reserves. However, the degree of independence provided by even quite large reserves can be illusory. A simple comparison of the size of the reserves with the size of probable deficits which will result from vigorous pursuit of a domestic full employment policy neglects the effect of the vital force of speculation in the foreign exchange market.

Speculation in the Foreign Exchange Market. We referred briefly to the possibility of speculative demands for foreign exchange in anticipation of a rise in the foreign exchange rate in Chapter 7. From time to time in recent years, such speculation has proven to be a powerful, and at times decisive, force in foreign exchange markets. We cannot discuss the role of official foreign exchange reserves as a buffer stock between the balance of payments and domestic policy without considering the possibility that a drop in foreign exchange reserves will incite speculative activity.

The contemporary foreign exchange rate system is peculiarly vulnerable to speculative activity. While exchange rates are pegged, unlike the situation under the classical gold standard, they are not sacrosanct. Periodic adjustments are permissible, and have occurred with reasonable frequency in recent years, even for major currencies. However, with few exceptions (Canada in 1950; Germany in 1969) such changes occur in sudden, discrete jumps of relatively large magnitude (e.g., 10% to 15%). The basis for speculation is not removed by gradual, continuous adjustments of the exchange rate such as might occur if it were a flexible price.

In this environment, with the exchange rate pressed against the ceiling and foreign exchange reserves falling, speculators may see a possibility for large gains *with virtually no risk of a major loss.* If a rise in the par rate of exchange occurs, they stand to make a substantial gain. Under the circumstances, there is virtually no possibility that the par rate of exchange will be reduced. As a result, the worst they can expect is a small decline in the market rate away from the ceiling. Given the very one-sided risk, this is a speculation which might even appeal to "risk averters". Indeed, much speculative activity (in the sense of a transfer of funds in anticipation of a change in the exchange rate) is undertaken by conservative corporate treasurers who argue that they are not seeking speculative gains, but are seeking to protect the financial position of the corporation.[12] It should not be surprising, therefore, that a country which is losing foreign exchange reserves with the exchange rate pressed against the ceiling should find its currency under intense speculative attack.

The important point is that the government must make available all of the foreign exchange which the speculators demand if it is to prevent the exchange rate from rising above the ceiling. In other words, speculation induced by a drop in the level of official foreign exchange reserves will accelerate the decline of those reserves — and further declines will intensify the speculative activity. From the point of view of the monetary authorities, it is a vicious circle. Experience in several countries has demonstrated that the pressures of speculation can be overwhelming.

It is not necessary that the speculative attack culminate in a change in the par rate of exchange for it to be relevant and important. Whether or not it alters the exchange rate, in the face of intense speculation the government will be forced to adjust domestic monetary and fiscal policies to take the pressure of the balance of payments, if it is to avoid resort to direct foreign exchange controls. Indeed, the balance of payments crisis may dictate temporarily more severe domestic restraint than would have been necessary otherwise.

Intervention in the Forward Exchange Market. It is unlikely that speculation will be confined to the spot exchange market. Anticipations of a rise in the foreign exchange rate are also likely to lead to speculative demands for *forward exchange* (Chapter 7). Indeed, from the point of view of the speculator, forward exchange has an advantage over spot exchange as a vehicle for speculation in that it does not call for immediate payment. Payment will not occur until the contract expires and the actual delivery of foreign exchange occurs (at which time the speculator will presumably immediately sell the foreign exchange, taking his gains or losses). Because it involves no immediate payment, speculation in forward exchange might seem irrelevant to the problem of maintaining adequate foreign exchange reserves. If there is no immediate delivery of spot exchange, speculation in forward exchange cannot directly constitute a drain on the official foreign exchange reserves.

However, speculation in forward exchange will put upward pressure on the forward exchange rate, and this has two important consequences. First, by providing a clear signal that "the market" expects the spot rate to rise in the near future, a significant rise in the forward rate might intensify speculation in the spot market. Second, as we saw in Chapter 7, given the levels of short-term interest rates in Canada and abroad, a rise in the forward exchange rate will create an incentive to move funds out of Canada on a covered interest-arbitrage basis. Thus, speculation in forward exchange will *indirectly* induce a capital outflow, add to the balance of payments deficit, and accelerate the drain of foreign exchange reserves.

For these reasons the government will probably find it expedient to intervene in the forward exchange market as well as in the spot market. The Exchange Fund will offer to "sell" forward exchange in order to stabilize the forward exchange rate. That is, the Fund will enter into contracts to deliver foreign exchange at some specified date in the future at a price agreed upon now. At times, the Canadian Exchange Fund has been called upon to take a very large position in forward exchange.

Do Forward Sales Reduce Foreign Exchange Reserves? When it "sells" forward exchange, the Exchange Fund has entered into a contract to deliver part of the nation's foreign exchange reserves to speculators at some future date. It can be argued, therefore, that the Fund's forward exchange position ought to be taken into account in computing the nation's foreign exchange reserves. That is, the Fund's forward sales contracts ought to be deducted from the published holdings of spot foreign exchange in order to obtain the nation's *net foreign exchange reserves* (and likewise the Fund's forward purchases ought to be added to reserves).

This is not done. Indeed, the Fund's forward position is normally not published until long after the event. Moreover, some economists would argue that the two should be kept quite separate: that regardless of its holdings of spot exchange, in the face of speculative buying of forward exchange, the Fund can enter into almost unlimited forward exchange contracts without prejudicing the nation's underlying foreign exchange position. If the forward contracts are truly speculative, the purchaser has no intention of actually taking the funds out of the country. He will be happy to sell back the foreign exchange to which he is entitled after the anticipated change in the exchange rate has occurred, or at any time that he is convinced that no change will occur. Thus, it is argued, there is no real risk that the Exchange Fund will ever be called upon to deliver the foreign exchange which it has sold forward; and there is nothing to stop it from taking a very large position in forward exchange, perhaps selling forward substantially more foreign exchange than it actually has in its spot reserves.

The proposition can be pushed a step further. It is sometimes argued that in the face of a strong speculative attack, the government ought to intervene vigorously in the forward market, taking as large a position as necessary to drive the forward exchange rate *down*, producing an inflow of funds on an interest-arbitrage basis, and perhaps breaching the solid front of expectations underlying the wave of speculation. Adapting the concepts introduced in Chapter 17 to describe central bank operations, it is argued that intervention in the forward exchange market can be used as a dynamic instrument of policy rather than simply as a defensive measure.

While aggressive action in the forward exchange market sometimes plays an important role in central banking operations, central bankers generally argue that extreme policies such as those sketched above are not practical. The risks to the Exchange Fund involved in a very large forward position are too great to be regarded with the equanimity displayed by economic theoreticians.

Inter-Central Bank Credits: Another Buffer. Finally, before we leave the general topic of governmental measures to stabilize the foreign exchange rate in the face of a balance of payments deficit, we must relax the assumption that at any point in time official foreign exchange reserves are absolutely fixed in amount. In addition to its *explicit* reserves in the form of gold, foreign exchange and drawing rights at the International Monetary Fund available for immediate use at any time, Canada has a second line of defence which is *implicit* in the Bank of Canada's close cooperation with the central banks of other industrialized nations, and in Canada's membership in the International Monetary Fund. In effect, Canada belongs to an international mutual assistance society of central bankers, and Canada, like other members, can normally rely upon substantial credits being extended by the International Monetary Fund, the Bank for International Settlements[13] and other central banks in time of emergency, providing additional foreign currency assets to support the government's intervention in the foreign exchange market.

Credits which are potentially available in this way are commonly called *conditional reserves* because the extension of credit is conditional on the lenders being convinced that the borrowing government will implement effective monetary and fiscal policies which assign top priority to the correction of the balance of payments problem. While conditional reserves have proven to be a valuable and flexible device for combatting waves of speculation, and for the stabilization of exchange rates, they are not designed to liberate domestic monetary and fiscal policy from the discipline of the balance of payments.

Conclusions: The Significance of Speculation. Speculation, whether in the spot market or the forward market, is a powerful force which cannot be ignored in assessing the adequacy of foreign exchange reserves as a buffer between domestic monetary and fiscal policy and the balance of international payments. The "adjustable peg" system of foreign exchange rates is peculiarly vulnerable to speculation, and periodic speculative attacks on one currency or another have become almost commonplace in international finance. From our point of view, the important point is not that speculative attacks occasionally force a change in par rates of exchange. Rather, it is that speculation, or the threat of speculation, forces monetary and fiscal authorities to assign a higher priority to the balance of payments in deciding on policy than might seem desirable on other grounds or than might seem necessary given the magnitude of the buffer stock apparently provided by official holdings of foreign exchange. The presence of conditional reserves eases the problem of coping with a speculative attack, but it does little to modify the primacy which must be assigned to balance-of-payments equilibrium in policy deliberations.

Of course, it would be a mistake to imply that all speculative activity is initiated by attempts to pursue domestic policies which are inconsistent with balance of payments equilibrium at the pegged exchange rate. Any development which can be interpreted as a threat to the stability of the exchange rate is capable of inducing speculation, whether it be the nature of domestic monetary and fiscal policies, adverse developments in major export markets, political uncertainty, threats of war, or natural disasters. In recent years, for example, the Canadian dollar has been threatened, at times mildly, at times severely, by domestic political developments (1960-62), devaluation and associated restrictive monetary policies abroad (1967), and by American measures to control international capital flows in order to correct their own balance of payments problem (1963 and 1968).

An Example: Speculation Against the Canadian Dollar, January-March 1968. While we have asserted that speculation can move large sums of money across national boundaries in very short periods of time, we have not provided any evidence that this is true. We cannot survey all of the recent examples of intense speculation in foreign exchange markets, but it may be useful to consider one case from recent Canadian history.

At the end of 1967 Canada had what might be considered a very comfortable foreign exchange reserve position. Including Canada's automatic drawing rights at the International Monetary Fund, foreign exchange reserves totalled U.S. $2,700 million. On January 1, 1968, the United States government announced a severe intensification of measures designed to restrict the outflow of capital from that country. Although Canada was partially exempted from these regulations, there was widespread concern that there would be a sharp reduction in the flow of American capital into Canada, and perhaps some repatriation of United States funds already here. The obvious balance of payments implications of such developments induced intense speculation against the Canadian dollar.

The issue was not decisively settled until March, 1968, when the United States government issued an unequivocal public statement that Canada was exempt from the new regulations. In the meantime, to prevent the speculative pressures from pushing the exchange rate through the upper limit, the government was called upon to provide U.S. $707 million to the spot exchange market and U.S. $471 million to the forward exchange market (see Table 21-3 and Figure 21-11). Thus, the gross drain of spot exchange in the short period of three months amounted to over a quarter of the nation's total foreign exchange reserves at the outset of the period, and the combined spot and forward sales amounted to well over 40%.

It is interesting to note that the actual net decline in the most publicized component of foreign exchange reserves, official holdings of gold and foreign exchange, was very small over the period as a whole (there were some significant fluctuations within the period, however). In part, this is because over a third of the sales of spot exchange were offset by credits extended by the Federal Reserve System (an example of the mutual protection society at work). The remaining two-thirds of the gross drain was withdrawn from Canada's position at the International Monetary Fund. In the course of the crisis, Canada negotiated additional lines of credit amounting to U.S. $900 million with other central banks, but found it unnecessary to draw on them. Domestically, the government pursued a restrictive monetary policy, led by a jump in the Bank Rate to what was then a record height (see Figure 17-3), and announced a set of fiscal measures designed to restrain aggregate demand.[14]

That was an example of speculation incited by developments outside Canada. However, on another occasion it could just as easily arise from the incompatibility of domestic monetary and fiscal policies and balance of payments equilibrium. The real point of the example is its demonstra-

Table 21-3
Apparent Drain from Canada's Foreign Exchange Reserves
December 31, 1967—March 31, 1968

(Millions of U.S. Dollars)	
Foreign Exchange Reserves, December 31, 1967	
Gold and Foreign Exchange (Spot)	2,267.8
Automatic Drawing Rights at I.M.F.	433.4
TOTAL	2,701.2
Foreign Exchange Reserves, March 31, 1968	
Gold and Foreign Exchange	2,244.4
Automatic Drawing Rights at I.M.F.	0.1
TOTAL	2,244.5
Net Decline in Spot Reserves	456.7
Borrowings from the Federal Reserve System	250.0
GROSS LOSS OF SPOT EXCHANGE	706.7
Forward Position of the Exchange Fund*	
December 31, 1967	+ 16.8
March 31, 1968	−454.5
APPARENT NET SALES OF FORWARD EXCHANGE	471.3
TOTAL NET SALES: SPOT + FORWARD	1,178.0

* Excluding forward contracts with the Bank of Canada.

Figure 21-11
The 1968 Foreign Exchange Crisis

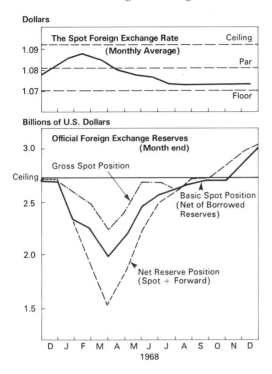

tion of the power of speculation to drain a large quantity of foreign exchange in a short period of time. Speculation is a powerful discipline on the monetary and fiscal authorities — a discipline which is reinforced by the terms on which international financial assistance is available.

Foreign Exchange Reserves and Balance of Payments Surplus

So far, our discussion of the role of foreign exchange reserves as a buffer between domestic policy and the balance of international payments has been cast in terms of coping with balance of payments deficits in a period of less than full employment. Before we leave the subject, however, we must refer briefly to the opposite case, in which the balance of payments is in surplus when the economy is at full employment.[15] This is the situation depicted in Figure 21-9. Monetary expansion would eliminate the balance of payments surplus, but monetary expansion would be inflationary.

Foreign Exchange Reserves as a Buffer Stock. Again, foreign exchange reserves appear in the role of a buffer stock. The balance of payments surplus can, in principle, be added to the official foreign exchange reserves and stored up to be used subsequently in times of balance of payments deficit.

However, the accumulation of foreign exchange reserves is not without its problems. In this case, the problem is to finance the acquisition of reserves in a manner which is not inconsistent with domestic policy objectives.

The Monetary Effects of Changes in the Level of Foreign Exchange Reserves. We discussed the monetary implications of changes in foreign exchange reserves in some detail in Chapter 17. The central point to emerge from that analysis was that operations of the Exchange Fund have no necessary direct effect on the monetary base. Monetary repercussions, if any, depend on the financial adjustments which are made to accommodate the change in the Exchange Fund. Thus, purchases of foreign exchange by the Exchange Fund will expand the monetary base if they are financed, directly or indirectly, by the Bank of Canada. However, if the government simply draws on its cash balances with the chartered banks to pay for the foreign exchange acquired by the Exchange Fund the monetary base will be unaffected. (What will happen to the publicly owned money supply?) In general, the government does not have large excess cash balances. Thus, if there is a sustained surplus in the balance of payments the government can only avoid monetary expansion if it can generate a budgetary surplus (by raising taxes or reducing other government expenditures), or if it can borrow the required funds in the Canadian capital market. What has to happen is a diversion of part of the income of the nation from the acquisition of consumer and capital goods to the acquisition of gold and foreign exchange. The nation must be induced to accumulate wealth in the form of official foreign exchange reserves (although it is far from evident that the yield on official foreign exchange reserves is sufficiently great to justify the diversion of resources from alternative uses, whether in consumption or in real capital formation). If it borrows heavily, the government may force up interest rates on government bonds, and indeed may aggravate the balance of payments problem by attracting more foreign capital. If it raises taxes to finance the accumulation of foreign exchange reserves, the government may meet strong political resistance. In principle, it should be possible to finance the accumulation of foreign exchange reserves in a non-inflationary manner: in fact the technical and political problems of doing so may be very great. The problem of coping with a balance of payments surplus in a fully employed economy will obviously be aggravated if there is a wave of speculation that the exchange rate will have to be reduced.

The problem of avoiding inflation in the face of a substantial balance of payments surplus in a fully employed economy are clearly illustrated in the cases of Canada in 1950 and in 1967-69 and Germany in 1968-69. While we will not examine them here, these examples are well worth investigation on the part of the student of monetary economics.

A Ceiling on Foreign Exchange Reserves: The Special Problem of Canada, 1963-1968

Before we leave the general topic of the role of foreign exchange reserves as a buffer stock between domestic monetary and fiscal policies and the balance of international payments, we must draw attention to the peculiar problem which faced the Canadian authorities from 1963 through 1968.

In 1963, as a measure to restrict the outflow of capital and hence to reduce their balance of payments deficit, the United States imposed a special tax (interest equalization tax) on new issues of foreign securities in the United States capital markets. Because of Canada's heavy dependence on the American capital market, Canadian securities were exempted from the tax, providing certain conditions were satisfied. The United States government was particularly concerned about both the growth of United States short-term, liquid liabilities to foreigners, and the continuing drain of gold from the United States' government's official hoard.[16] As a consequence, Canada's exemption from the interest equalization tax was made conditional on an agreement by the Canadian government to restrict the accumulation of foreign exchange reserves (which are largely United States dollars and gold).

In effect, this meant that there was a ceiling on Canada's foreign exchange reserves. Given that the danger of speculation limited the extent to which foreign exchange reserves could be run down in a short period of time, the interest equalization tax agreement meant that the effectiveness of foreign exchange reserves as a buffer between domestic policy and the balance of payments was much impaired. Canada came close to being a literal example of the case discussed earlier of a small country with a pegged exchange rate and fixed foreign exchange reserves. In such a situation, domestic policy is a slave to the balance of payments.

The initial "target" level for Canada's foreign exchange reserves was U.S. $2,700 million, approximately the actual level of reserves on June 20, 1963, just before the agreement was concluded. As can be seen in Figure 21-12, this was an effective ceiling on Canada's holdings of gold and United States dollars until the end of 1965. In late 1965, because of unusual strength in the Canadian balance of payments (as a result of a large sale of wheat to the Soviet Union), Canada accumulated a large "net creditor" position at the International Monetary Fund,[17] although official holdings of gold and U.S. dollars did not exceed the target "level". At the same time, the United States balance of payments deteriorated, and in December new controls over capital exports were announced. Again, Canada was granted a partial exemption, but only on condition that the "target" level reserves be lowered to U.S. $2,550 million, *including* the "net creditor" position at the International Monetary Fund. As is evident in Figure 21-12, the Canadian government had to sharply reduce its holdings of foreign exchange in early 1966 to come under the new ceiling (the broken line shows foreign exchange reserves including the net creditor position at the I.M.F.).[18]

Aside from the effects of the foreign exchange crisis of early 1968, Canada's foreign exchange reserves remained pressed against the ceiling until late 1968. At that time, the United States agreed to a more flexible foreign exchange reserve policy for Canada "in order to accommodate the adaptation of monetary policy to the changing needs of the domestic economy, seasonal factors, and other influences of a temporary nature."[19]

Figure 21-12
Foreign Exchange Reserves: Actual and Target Levels, 1963-1968

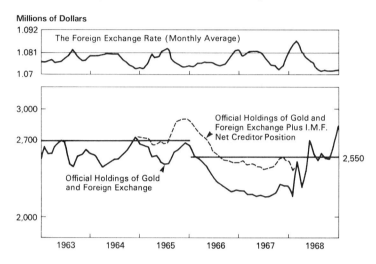

Conclusions: Foreign Exchange Reserves
and the Independence of Monetary Policy

With a fixed foreign exchange rate, the independence of monetary policy depends on the existence of foreign exchange reserves as a buffer stock between domestic policy and the balance of payments. Large foreign exchange reserves are important, but it should be obvious from our discussion of speculation that the independence of domestic monetary and fiscal policies does not depend on the size of reserves alone. The essential question is whether the government can tolerate wide swings in the level of reserves in a short time period. As the Governor of the Bank of Canada observed in his testimony before the Royal Commission on Banking and Finance,[20]

> with a structure of international transactions as large as ours, and containing as many potentially volatile elements, it must be expected that from time to time the changes in the level of our reserves will be very large, and we must be prepared therefore to accommodate them.

If the system is to work,

> Canadian public opinion must prepare itself to accept large fluctuations in our reserves . . . . It will militate against the smooth operation of the fixed [exchange] rate system if, instead of focusing on the underlying posi-

tion of the country's balance of payments, public attention should be pre-occupied to an exaggerated degree with short-term changes in reserves . . . .

If sharp changes in exchange reserves engender strong speculation, foreign exchange reserves are more likely to be useful in financing relatively small balance of payments deficits of relatively short duration, rather than relatively large, persistent deficits. This is surely a slim reed on which to tie the independence of domestic monetary policy.

FOOTNOTES

[1] In principle, members of the International Monetary Fund declare their par values in terms of gold since the United States *gold dollar* of 1944 is specified in the Articles of Agreement as the unit of account for the International Monetary Fund. In practice, however, this means that par values are declared and maintained in terms of the United States dollar (the legal "gold content" of which has not changed since 1944).

[2] However, the capital account of the balance of international payments excludes an important factor in the change in international indebtedness — the re-investment of retained earnings by non-resident controlled corporations. Many economists would argue that the re-investment of profits ought to be recorded in the balance of payments, both as an additional outflow of dividends in the current account and as an inflow of capital in the capital account. While in a sense this creates two artificial transactions, it does serve to remind us of the understatement of the investment of foreign-owned funds in Canada during any given year.

[3] In the long run, the coincidence of capital imports and current account deficits is not fortuitous. There are a complex of adjustment mechanisms which tend to produce this equality. They are analyzed in books on international economics under the general heading of the "transfer problem". We will not explore them here.

[4] T. R. Robinson, "The Foreign Trade Sector and Domestic Stability: The Canadian Case," in *Yale Economic Essays* Vol. 9 (Spring 1969), pp. 46-87.

[5] For simplicity we are again ignoring the government sector, and we are implicitly assuming that exported goods and services have no import content.

[6] This is not strictly correct. A rise in Canadian income will increase Canada's imports from abroad. But this rise in the rest of the world's exports to Canada will increase income in the rest of the world, and hence imports from Canada (=Canadian exports). We are assuming that any "reflex" effect of this sort is so small that it can be ignored.

There is also a possibility that there is an offsetting "supply effect". A rise in Canadian income increasing the demand for all types of goods and services, may also increase the share of exportable goods which is absorbed within Canada. The supply available for export will accordingly be reduced. These are complexities which we can safely ignore in our analysis.

[7] Remember, we are ignoring the fact that exports may also have some import content. OX in Figure 21-1 should be interpreted as exports net of the value of any imported materials or component parts used in the production of those exports.

[8] Some of the evidence is reviewed in R. E. Caves and G. L. Reuber, *Canadian Economic Policy and the Impact of International Capital Flows* (Toronto: University of Toronto Press for the Private Planning Association of Canada, 1969), pp. 11-18.

[9] Our assumptions also imply that the current account balance will depend on the *composition* of aggregate demand, since the import content of investment and consumption expenditures, in general, will be different. However, with given investment demand and consumption function, the composition of aggregate

demand is also given for any particular level of income. For this reason, we can ignore this complication to the analysis.

[10] It shows combinations of interest rates and income at which the Current Account (B)alance equals the Net (K)apital Inflow.

[11] The student with some algebra will note that the basic problem is that we have only two variables but three equations which must be solved simultaneously. It is only by accident that a solution will be found.

[12] Speculation occurs whenever someone takes an "open" position in foreign exchange (see Chapter 7) or when one covers what would otherwise have been an open position, because he anticipates a rise in the exchange rate. Thus, a corporate treasurer who purchases foreign exchange now, whether spot or forward, knowing that the corporation will need it in the future and anticipating a rise in the exchange rate, is speculating. Similarly, a corporate treasurer who buys forward exchange to cover short-term foreign currency liabilities, when he would not normally do so, is speculating. In each case the treasurer would argue that he is merely protecting the financial position of the corporation against a reasonably foreseeable risk, and in this argument he is correct. Nonetheless, he has the same impact on the foreign exchange market as a professional speculator. To say that the corporation is speculating in foreign exchange is not to say that it is doing anything illegal or immoral. On the importance of corporations as speculators in foreign exchange, see Royal Commission on Banking and Finance, *Report* (Ottawa, 1964), pp. 297-299; J. H. Young and J. F. Helliwell, "The Effects of Monetary Policy on Corporations," in Royal Commission on Banking and Finance, *Appendix Volume* (Ottawa: Queen's Printer, 1964), pp. 419-426.

[13] We will discuss the International Monetary Fund and the Bank for International Settlements further in the next chapter.

[14] These events are discussed at some length in the Bank of Canada, *Annual Report, 1968* (Ottawa, 1969).

[15] Remember that there is no conflict when there is unemployment and the balance of payments is in surplus, or when there are inflationary pressures and the balance of payments is in deficit. In either case, the *direction* of the policies required to achieve domestic objectives and balance of payments equilibrium is the same. As we noted earlier, however, the *degree* of ease or restriction called for by domestic and external considerations may be different. At some point, conflict may re-emerge.

[16] See Chapter 22, pp. 575-7.

[17] Canada's net creditor position at the I.M.F. is the excess of Canada's quota (discussed in the next chapter) over the I.M.F.'s holdings of Canadian dollars. In effect, it represents foreign exchange which Canada has directly or indirectly lent to the I.M.F. Canada's net creditor position will be reduced if Canada draws foreign exchange from the Fund, and will be increased if Canada repays earlier drawings or if other nations draw Canadian dollars from the Fund. Under the General Agreement to Borrow, Canada has also agreed on occasion to lend foreign exchange to the Fund directly. Any such credits are also added to Canada's net creditor position.

[18] In Figure 21-11 a different ceiling is indicated, corresponding to a different measure of foreign exchange reserve (i.e., including Canada's automatic drawing rights at the I.M.F., which are slightly larger than Canada's net creditor position).

[19] "Letter" from H. Fowler, Secretary of the Treasury of the United States to E. J. Benson, Minister of Finance, Canada, December 16, 1968. Reprinted in Bank of Canada, *Annual Report, 1968*, p. 67.

[20] Bank of Canada, *Evidence of the Governor before the Royal Commission on Banking and Finance* (Ottawa, 1964), p. 11.

22

The International Constraint on

Monetary Policy, Part 2:

Price Levels, Exchange Rates and the

International Liquidity Problem

1/THE PRICE LEVEL AND THE BALANCE OF PAYMENTS

In the preceding chapter we explored the theoretical relationships between monetary policy and the balance of payments within a strict Keynesian framework. That is, we assumed not only that the exchange rate was pegged, but also that the price level was fixed. However, in our earlier analysis of the economics of monetary policy we discovered that the assumption of a fixed price level was at best only a crude approximation to reality. Fluctuations in aggregate demand, whether induced by exogenous developments or by monetary and fiscal policies, will normally have an impact on the price level as well as income and employment. What are the implications of this fact for our analysis of macroeconomic equilibrium in an open economy?

World Prices and the Canadian Price Level

Our discussion of changes in the price level in Chapter 20 implicitly assumed that the prices of goods and services consumed in Canada are determined within Canada. This is only partly true. With a pegged foreign exchange rate, there are many prices determined in world markets, not in Canadian markets, i.e., the prices of goods and services entering Canada's international trade, whether as imports or exports.

It is true that for the items in question, Canadian demand and supply are components of total world demand and supply, and hence contribute to the determination of price in world markets. However, for most of the products in question, Canadian consumption or production is very small relative to the aggregate market. Indeed, for most imports and many exports we can safely consider Canadians as "price-takers'"— they buy and sell at prices determined in world markets without having a significant influence on those prices.

To the extent that this is true, it means that some part of the Canadian price level is beyond control by domestic monetary and fiscal policies as long as the foreign exchange rate is pegged. A rise in world prices — and particularly a rise in United States' prices — will produce some rise in the Canadian price level. In this way, Canada can directly import inflation. Similarly, a decline of prices in the United States will produce some decline in the Canadian price level.

The direct impact of United States' prices on the Canadian price level has been clearly demonstrated in empirical studies.[1]

World Prices and the Structure of Prices in Canada. The fact that the prices of some goods and services entering into the Canadian price level are determined in markets outside the country also means that the Phillips Curve analysis developed in Chapter 20 can only apply to part of the price level. You will recall that this analysis was based on an empirically observed relationship between the rate of change of money wage rates and the level of unemployment, which has been explained by *ad hoc* theorizing about the process of wage rate adjustment in labour markets. Lower levels of unemployment imply increasingly rapid rates of increase of money wage rates, and higher wage rates, by increasing costs of production, imply higher prices. The relationship between unemployment and wage rates presumably affects all labour markets in Canada. However, the impact on prices only applies to goods and services which do not enter into international trade at given world prices.

Thus, with a pegged exchange rate and a given level of world prices, a rise in the level of aggregate demand and the consequent fall in the level of unemployment implies not only a rise in the general *level* of prices, but also a change in the *structure* of prices. Costs of production will rise in Canada relative to the rest of the world; and the prices of goods and services produced in Canada for domestic consumption will rise relative to the prices of internationally traded goods. The opposite would happen in the face of a decline in Canadian aggregate demand. These changes in the structure of prices have important implications for international trade and the balance of payments.

International Substitution Effects. One of the basic propositions of elementary economic theory is that a change in relative prices will induce substitution effects among the goods in question. Exactly the same thing will happen if the prices of Canadian-produced goods and services change relative to the prices of goods and services produced in the rest of the world. *A rise in the Canadian price level will induce international substitution effects.*

These effects will show up in various ways. Domestic consumers will be induced to purchase more imported goods as substitutes for the relatively more expensive Canadian-produced goods. Domestic producers of very close substitutes for imported goods will find that they cannot raise prices without losing many customers — but with rising costs they will find it much less profitable to produce these goods for sale at the given world prices. Their output will fall, as imports take over a larger share of the market. Similarly domestic producers of goods for export, faced with higher labour costs, will find it less profitable to produce for sale in world markets at the given world prices. Their exports will fall. Indeed, even those exporters who are not price-takers (i.e., who have some monopoly power in world markets, either individually or collectively) will find that at higher prices their sales will be reduced.

The extent of the impact on the flow of international trade will depend on the magnitude of the change in prices and the relevant elasticities of demand and supply. However, the general effect of a rise in Canadian costs and prices relative to world prices will be some decline in exports and some rise in imports, reducing a surplus or increasing a deficit in the current account of the balance of payments. A decline in Canadian prices relative to world prices would have the opposite effects. That is, it would tend to increase exports and reduce imports, increasing a surplus or reducing a deficit in the current account of the balance of payments.

This effect of changes in the price level on international trade introduces an important new consideration into our analysis of the relationship between domestic monetary and fiscal policies and the balance of international payments.

The Price Level, Domestic Policy Objectives, and the Balance of Payments Constraint. In the previous chapter we explore the relationship between domestic monetary and fiscal policies and the balance of international payments on the assumption that the domestic objective of policy was very simple: the achievement of that unique level of aggregate demand which would provide "full employment" without inflation. If instead of a unique "full employment" level of income the authorities are faced with a "trade-off function", a negative association between the level of unemployment and the rate of change of the price level, the objective of domestic policy is necessarily more complicated. The choice of an objective involves an important subjective consideration. The government must balance the undesirable consequences of higher rates of inflation against the undesirable consequences of higher levels of unemployment in order to find what they consider to be the socially least undesirable combination of unemployment and inflation. The objective of domestic policy, then, is the point on the trade-off function which the government considers to be most preferable. It is not necessarily a point of "full employment," nor is it necessarily a point of price stability. Let us briefly reconsider the problem of reconciling the *domestic* and *external* objectives of monetary and fiscal policies in this context.

The Trade-Off Function and Policy Conflicts. In our previous analysis we considered the domestic and external objectives of policy to have been achieved simultaneously if the balance of payments was in equilibrium at "full employment". When we introduce the trade-off function, the comparable condition might seem to be that the balance of payments be in equilibrium at the point on the trade-off function selected by the government, i.e., at the combination of inflation and unemployment which is preferred on domestic social and political grounds.

Unfortunately, the equilibrium of the balance of payments may be fleeting. The rate of price level change selected by the government may have continuing effects on the balance of payments which will eventually disrupt the equilibrium.

For example, suppose the rate of inflation chosen by the government for domestic reasons is higher than that prevailing in the rest of the world. Even though the balance of payments is initially in equilibrium,[2] *if Canadian prices rise more rapidly than prices in the rest of the world, international substitution effects will gradually worsen the current account balance, and a deficit will emerge in the balance of payments.* The exchange rate will be driven to the ceiling, and exchange reserves will begin to fall, with all of the attendant problems discussed in the previous section. *What appeared initially to be a condition of harmony between the domestic and the external objectives of policy will be turned into a condition of conflict.*

Something has to give. There are only two possibilities (unless the government resorts to direct controls) : the exchange rate or the domestic policy objectives. If the exchange rate is to remain pegged at its original par, the balance of payments must be brought into equilibrium, and that means that domestic policy will have to be modified in order to accept a lower rate of inflation and a higher level of unemployment than the government would otherwise find most desirable on social grounds. In effect, domestic policy formation is faced with a price level constraint. *If the balance of payments is to be kept in equilibrium, the country will have to move toward the same rate of inflation as that obtaining in the rest of the world.*

The problems which arise because of balance of payments deficits are always dramatic. However, as we have already seen, continuous balance of payments surpluses can also be troublesome to a nation determined to maintain a pegged exchange rate.

With this in mind, consider what happens if the government chooses a rate of inflation which is less than that prevailing in the rest of the world. In this case, international substitution effects will tend to produce an improvement in the current account, and although the balance of payments is initially in equilibrium, a balance of payments surplus will eventually emerge.[3] The exchange rate will fall, and the government will be forced to accumulate foreign exchange reserves.

Again, somthing will have to give. The government cannot go on accumulating foreign exchange reserves indefinitely. Even if the financial problems associated with the accumulation of reserves do not directly produce inflationary pressures, the government will eventually have to modify its domestic objectives and accept the higher, world rate of inflation, if it is going to maintain the pegged exchange rate.

Conclusion: The Price Level Constraint. The conclusion of this analysis is important. While there is always some room for manoeuvre inherent in the imperfect operations of markets and in time lags in the adjustment of production, consumption and trade, *with a pegged exchange rate the government of a small country does not have the freedom to choose any rate of inflation which it desires,* even though that rate of inflation may initially be consistent with balance of payments equilibrium. There is a price level constraint on domestic policy. Although this constraint is not instantaneous, *the government will be forced eventually to adapt its policies to the world rate of inflation* — accepting the implications of the trade-off function for the domestic level of unemployment. Attempts to achieve any other combination of inflation and unemployment will mean a chronic balance of payments problem.

But all of this presumes that the exchange rate is pegged. What happens if we make the ultimate relaxation of our assumptions and allow the exchange rate to vary? Can the world economy and the world financial system function with flexible exchange rates?

2/THE ECONOMICS OF FLEXIBLE EXCHANGE RATES

A change in Canadian prices relative to prices in the rest of the world can have a powerful impact on the Canadian balance of international payments. However, it is not necessary to change the Canadian price level in order to produce these effects. They can be achieved equally well by changing the foreign exchange rate.

Changes in the Exchange Rate Versus Changes in Price Levels

A rise in the price of foreign exchange (= a *fall* in the external value of the Canadian dollar) raises the delivered price of foreign goods to Canadian buyers just as effectively as a rise in foreign price level itself. Thus it will tend to restrict Canadian imports. Similarly, a rise in the foreign exchange rate lowers the delivered price of Canadian goods to foreign markets just as effectively as a decline in the Canadian price level. It will tend to increase Canadian exports. Taking the two effects together, a rise in the foreign exchange rate will improve the current account balance, and hence will tend to increase a balance of payments surplus or reduce a balance of payments deficit. In terms of its impact on the balance of payments, *a rise in the foreign exchange rate is a substitute for a fall in the Canadian price level or for a rise in the world price level.*

The opposite arguments hold for a fall in the foreign exchange rate (= a rise in the external value of the Canadian dollar). By making Canadian goods more expensive for foreign buyers, it will tend to restrict exports. By making foreign goods less expensive for Canadian buyers, it will tend to increase imports. Thus, a fall in the foreign exchange rate will tend to worsen the balance on current account, and hence will tend to reduce a balance of payments surplus or increase a balance of payments deficit. In terms of its impact on the balance of payments, *a fall in the foreign exchange rate is a substitute for a rise in the Canadian price level or a fall in the world price level.*

The Exchange Rate and Contradictions Among Policy Objectives. It follows that changes in the exchange rate can be used to resolve balance of payments problems which would otherwise force a drastic change in domestic monetary and fiscal policies. Thus, a balance of payments deficit (whatever its cause), can be removed by an appropriate rise in the foreign exchange rate; and a balance of payments surplus can be removed by an appropriate drop in the foreign exchange rate.

However, these are once-over changes. If domestic policy involves a rate of price level change which is different from that in the rest of the world, balance of payments equilibrium will require *continuous adjustment* of the exchange rate. A more rapid rate of inflation in Canada than in the rest of the world is only consistent with balance of payments equilibrium if the exchange rate continuously rises. A slower rate of inflation in Canada than in the rest of the world would call for a continuous fall in the exchange rate.

In other words, the independence of domestic policy from external constraints is only possible if the exchange rate can be adjusted continuously to changing pressures in the foreign exchange market.

Flexible Exchange Rates. As we noted earlier, the foreign exchange rate is simply a price – the price of foreign money – and as such is determined by the interaction of supply and demand in the foreign exchange market. However, under the pegged exchange rate system, that price is only allowed to vary within very narrow limits about the official par rate, (unless, of course, a decision is taken to alter the par rate). With a flexible exchange rate, there would be no such constraint on the movement of the exchange rate.[4] A flexible exchange rate is free to adjust continuously to changing pressures of supply and demand in the foreign exchange market.

Flexible Exchange Rates and Monetary Policy

Flexibility of the exchange rate creates a fundamentally different environment for monetary and fiscal policy from that provided by the present international monetary constitution. We examined the implications of the Bretton Woods rules for domestic stabilization policy in the previous chapter. Let us now briefly explore some of the implications of a flexible exchange rate system.

The Exchange Rate and Balance of Payments Equilibrium. The crucial difference between the fixed and the flexible exchange rate systems is the mechanism for establishing equilibrium in the balance of international payments.

As we saw in Chapter 21, with a fixed exchange rate the maintenance of equilibrium in the balance of payments must be the responsibility of *government policy,* and particularly of monetary policy. Unless there is considerable flexibility in the levels of wages and prices, there is no automatic mechanism to ensure the equilibration of demand and supply forces in the foreign exchange market in the short run. With a flexible exchange rate, by contrast, the *foreign exchange rate* can be expected to adjust automatically to maintain equilibrium in the balance of payments.

Consider the case in which the balance of payments is in deficit, perhaps because the deficit on current account is greater than the surplus on capital account. There will be excess demand for foreign exchange at the existing exchange rate. It is this pressure of excess demand which will tend to increase the foreign exchange rate, and in the absence of an official constraint on the rate, the rate will rise.

Will the increase of the exchange rate tend to eliminate the balance of payments deficit?

The Current Account. As we noted above, a rise of the foreign exchange rate is equivalent to a rise in the world price level relative to prices and wage rates in Canada. As a result, there should be substitution effects in the current account of the balance of payments. Exports, which are now relatively cheaper to the rest of the world, should increase, and imports, which are now relatively more expensive to Canadians, should fall. The current account should adjust so as to eliminate the excess demand for foreign exchange.

The Capital Account. The behaviour of the capital account is more problematic. As we saw in Chapter 7, the *level* of the foreign exchange rate *per se* should not be relevant to international portfolio investment decisions. As long as the investor *expects* to bring his funds back at the same exchange rate at which he takes them out of the country, the level of the foreign exchange rate will not be a factor in his calculations. This should be obvious from the examples explored in Chapter 7 (e.g., Example 7-1). If the investor expects the exchange rate to be the same when he brings his funds home as when he sends them out, the exchange rates applicable to the two foreign exchange transactions (out — in) simply cancel each other out. All that is relevant to the calculation of the expected net return is the difference in interest rates (although the *risk* of change in the exchange rate will be relevant to the investment decision, of course).

It is different if the investor has reason to expect a change in the foreign exchange rate. Any increase of the foreign exchange rate will give an added premium to Canadian investments in foreign securities, and will impose a penalty on non-residents' investments in Canadian securities. Similarly, a reduction of the exchange rate will impose a penalty on non-residents' investment in Canadian securities, and will add a premium to Canadian investments in foreign securities.

To know what will happen in the capital account as the exchange rate rises, then, we must know what happens to investors' expectations about the future course of the exchange rate. If they expect a continuing rise in exchange rate there will be an incentive for more Canadian investment abroad and less non-resident investment in Canada. Capital outflows should be increased or capital inflows reduced. However, if investors feels that the rise is temporary, and that the rate will eventually subside, there will be an incentive for less Canadian investment abroad and more non-resident investment in Canada. Capital inflows should be increased or capital outflows restricted. If, by contrast, they expect the exchange rate to be unchanged at any particular level established at any particular time, then capital inflows and outflows will be unaffected by the change in the exchange rate. In other words, if the net capital inflow does not increase or decrease it will stay the same!

The crucial consideration is that of investors' expectations of future changes in the exchange rate, not the present level of the exchange rate. Unfortunatly, we know very little about the determinants of these expectations. With this in mind, perhaps it is best to first consider the case in which we can ignore expectations. That is, we will assume that investors take the existing exchange rate to be the best estimate of what future exchange rates will be, regardless of the present level or the past history of the exchange rate. In this case, the entire adjustment in the balance of payments occurs in the current account. The net capital inflow will be unaffected by the rise in the exchange rate: imports must fall and exports rise until the current account deficit is tailored to the net capital inflow. Exactly the opposite arguments would apply if we had chosen a case of balance of payments surplus. What are the implications of these balance of payments adjustments for monetary policy?

To explore this matter, we return again to the IS-LM model of the open enconomy developed in Chapter 21. What modifications have to be introduced to allow for the flexibility of exchange rates?

The Balance of Payments Constraint on Monetary Policy. The first important point is that the B-K curve (the locus of combinations of interest rates and income levels which are consistent with equilibrium in the balance of payments) is no longer a useful concept. Balance of payments equilibrium will be maintained continuously by adjustments in the foreign exchange rate.

To see this, consider again how we constructed the B-K curve. We started with the *net capital flow function* (Figure 21-3), reflecting the sensitivity of international capital flows to international differences in interest rates. If we can ignore expectations of future changes in the exchange rate, this function will be unchanged under a regime of flexible exchange rates.

The second component of the B-K curve was the *current account balances function,* which we built up on the assumption that exports were given and imports depended on the levels of investment and consumption expenditures. However, with a flexible exchange rate, both imports and exports depend directly on the level of the foreign exchange rate. Moreover, since the foreign exchange rate will always rise when there is an excess demand for foreign exchange (e.g., the current account deficit exceeds the capital account surplus) and fall when there is an excess supply of foreign exchange (e.g., the current account deficit is less than the capital account surplus), the exchange rate will always adjust until the current account balance is equal in size and opposite in direction to the capital account balance.

It should be emphasized that this could require wide fluctuations in the exchange rate from time to time, depending on the sensitivity of import and export demands to change in the exchange rate.

With a flexible exchange rate, then, the current account balance is a residual, determined by the capital account balance. The current account balance function is the mirror image of the net capital flow function. The sole determinant of the aggregate current account balance will be the level of Canadian interest rates relative to world interest rates.

This is illustrated in Figure 22-1. In this figure, the net capital flow function (K) is the same as that developed earlier (Figure 21-2). However, the current account balance function (B_f) is based on the assumption that the flexible exchange rate will adjust until the current account balance is just equal in size and opposite in direction to the capital account balance. At high levels of interest rates in Canada (r_1), there will be a net capital inflow. However, as a result of the automatic adjustment

Figure 22-1
The Current Account, the Capital Account and the Balance of Payments:
with Flexible Exchange Rates

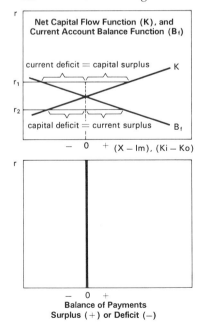

of the exchange rate, the surplus in the capital account will be exactly offset by an equal deficit in the current account. At low levels of interest rates in Canada (r_2), there will be a net capital outflow. However, as a result of the automatic adjustment of the exchange rate, the deficit in the capital account will be exactly offset by an equal surplus in the current account. The net balance of payments surplus or deficit (lower panel) will always be zero, regardless of the level of interest rates in Canada (and hence, by implication, regardless of the level of income and output in Canada). *A flexible exchange rate will ensure that the balance of payments is always in equilibrium.*

This points to our first important conclusion. *If the government is willing and able to ignore wide fluctuations of the foreign exchange rate, a flexible exchange rate frees domestic monetary policy from the balance of payments constraint.*

This is not the only implication of flexibility in the foreign exchange rate, however. A flexible exchange rate, coupled with highly interest-elastic international capital flows, will reinforce the impact of monetary policy on domestic income and output.

Effectiveness of Monetary Policy. The implications of flexible exchange rates for the domestic impact of monetary policy should be obvious if you keep in mind that both exports and imports are factors determining the level of aggregate demand.

We have seen that restrictive monetary policy which raises Canadian interest rates relative to interest rates in the rest of the world will induce capital inflows and thus, by creating an excess supply of foreign exchange, will depress the foreign exchange rate. The exchange rate will have to fall until the combination of increased imports and reduced exports produces a current account deficit large enough to offset the capital inflow. But remember: both the increase in imports and the reduction of exports depress aggregate demand. These exchange-rate-induced effects on aggregate demand are in addition to any effects which might result from the direct impact of tight money on investment expenditures. In other words, the flexibility of the exchange rate, coupled with the sensitivity of international capital flows to Canadian interest rates has strengthened the restrictive impact of a tight money policy.

You should be able to trace through a similar analysis for the case of an expansionary monetary policy under a regime of flexible exchange rates. The conclusion is the same: flexibility of exchange rates reinforces the impact of an expansionary monetary policy.

The IS-LM Model Again. These arguments are illustrated in Figure 22-2, which is another adaptation of the much used four-quadrant diagram. First consider Quadrant II. The investment demand function, the broken line, I_o-I_o, is the same as that used in the diagrams of Chapters 20 and 21. In the present analysis, however, instead of showing the individual components of the current account balance, as in Figure 21-1, we have adopted the conclusion of the previous section that, in a regime of flexible exchange rates, the current account balance will be determined simply by the net capital inflow. Accordingly, we have deducted the current account balance function of Figure 22-1 from the investment demand function in Quadrant II, to obtain what might be called the *investment — trade balance function* (I-T). It plays the same role in the analysis as the *autonomous expenditure function* of Figure 21-1.

The construction of the I-T curve should be obvious. At high levels of interest rates there will be heavy capital inflows. As a result, exports must fall and imports must rise, producing a negative trade balance. This negative trade balance is a deduction from aggregate demand, and accordingly we have deducted it from the investment function to obtain the relevant point on the I-T curve. By contrast, at very low levels of interest rates there will be strong capital outflows. Exports will have to rise and imports fall until there is an equally large trade surplus. This trade surplus is an addition to aggregate demand, and accordingly it has to be added to the investment demand function to obtain the relevant point on the I-T curve.

In Quadrant III we now have only the saving function of our earlier analysis. We do not have to include induced imports in this Quadrant, as we did in Figure 21-2, since total imports are allowed for in the construction of the I-T curve.

The new equilibrium condition is that the level of investment expenditures plus the net trade balance (= the net capital flow) must equal gross saving. (You should be able to explain why this is the equilibrium condition.) In Quadrant IV we have the 45° line which is used to reflect the equilibrium levels of income to the base axis of Quadrant I.

Figure 22-2
Commodity Market Equilbrium with Flexible Exchange Rates

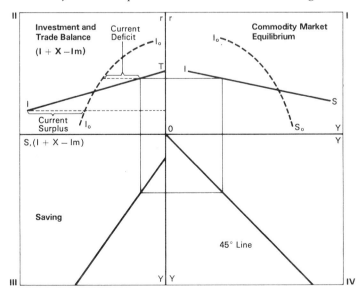

Taking these together with the associated interest rates, we can trace out the I-S curve for the flexible exchange rate case.

We have also plotted the original I-S curve for the fixed exchange rate case (broken line, I_o-S_o) in Quadrant I as a reference base. The important point to note is that in the flexible exchange rate case the I-S curve is much more elastic with respect to the interest rate. A given increase in the money supply, shifting the L-M curve, will have a much more powerful impact on income and employment than in the fixed exchange rate case.

A *flexible exchange rate not only frees monetary policy from the international constraint, it also increases the effectiveness of monetary policy as an instrument for manipulating aggregate demand.*

A Classical Case. The elasticity of the I-S function in the flexible exchange rate case depends directly on the elasticity of the net capital flow function. In the extreme, we might conceive of a net capital flow function which is perfectly elastic with respect to Canadian interest rates. That is, any deviation of Canadian interest rates from some given level (world interest rates, or world interest rates plus a risk premium) would induce a massive movement of capital either in or out of the country. In such a situation, the level of interest rates in Canada would be rigidly tied to the world level of interest rates, and the I-S curve would also be perfectly interest-elastic at this level of interest rates.

In this case, the level of income depends simply on the demand for and supply of money (i.e., on the position of the L-M function). Monetary policy would be all powerful, while fiscal policy would have absolutely no impact. An increase in government expenditures, for example, would tend to increase income. But with a given money supply, this would imply higher interest rates. The resulting flood of capital flowing into the country would prevent interest rates from rising, but it would induce a drop in the foreign exchange rate. The result would be an offsetting deficit in the current account of the balance of payments. There could be no net change in the level of income and output unless there was a sympathetic increase in the money supply. With a perfectly elastic net capital flow function, and flexible exchange rates, we are back in the world envisioned by the classical quantity theorists.

Exchange Rate Expectations. In this analysis of the economics of flexible exchange rates we have ignored what we said earlier was a crucial consideration in international capital flows — investors' expectations of future changes in the exchange rate. What modifications of the analysis are necessary if we drop the assumption that investors always expect the existing exchange rate to continue into the relevant future? ·

Let us consider the case in which an expansionary monetary policy initiates a rise in the flexible exchange rate. Aside from the assumption about exchange rate expectations which we have already explored, there are two possibilities. Either the rate is expected to continue to rise, or it is expected to fall back toward a more "normal" level.

Expectations of future rises in the exchange rate will induce speculative capital movements. Capital outflows will increase and capital inflows will be retarded. The net capital flow function of Figure 22-1 will shift outward to the right (larger capital outflows or smaller capital inflows at each possible level of interest rates) and the current account will have to respond. The I-T curve of Quadrant II, Figure 22-2 will shift to the right, inducing a similar shift in the I-S curve of Quadrant I. The impact of the expansionary monetary policy which initiated the whole process will be accentuated.

This is not the end of the story, however. If rises in the exchange rate induce expectations of further rises, the whole process could become cumulative. The exploration of the possible interactions between expectations and adjustments in the exchange rate requires a class of dynamic models which are well beyond the scope of an elementary money and banking textbook. It should be clear, however, that if a rise in the exchange rate induces strong expectations of a continuing rise in the future, there is a serious danger of severe instability in the foreign exchange market.

Expectations of a continuing rise in the exchange rate will reinforce the impact of monetary policy in a regime of flexible exchange rates. The opposite is true if the rate is expected to fall back to "normal" in the near future.

If a rise in the exchange rate induces expectations of a return to a lower, more "normal" level, the effects will be the opposite of those discussed above. The net capital flow function will be shifted to the left (smaller capital outflows or larger capital inflows at each possible level of interest rates) as speculators seek to avoid losses on holdings of foreign currency assets. As a result the I-T curve and the I-S curve will also be shifted to the left. The rise of the exchange rate will be dampened, and the overall effectiveness of the expansionary monetary policy will be reduced.

As we noted earlier, little is known about the determinants of expectations of changes in the foreign exchange rate. However, students of Canada's experience with flexible exchange rates between 1950 and 1962 have generally concluded that the second type of behaviour was most characteristic: that is, expectations of a return to "normal" tended to dampen fluctuations in the exchange rate. The full benefits of a flexible exchange rate regime could not be attained.

The Controversy Over Flexible Exchange Rate

Considered from the point of view of the effectiveness of domestic monetary policy, flexible exchange rates appear to have a major advantage over pegged exchange rates. Yet flexible exchange rates are anathema to most central bankers (who are charged with the implementation of monetary policy) and to many economists who specialize in international financial economics. As a result, proposals for the adoption of a system of flexible exchange rates are surrounded by sharp controversy. Two main charges are commonly directed against flexible exchange rates.

Instability and Uncertainty. It is argued that flexible exchange rates are inherently highly unstable. This amounts to an assumption that the dominant pattern of expectations is of the first type discussed earlier: that a change in the exchange rate will generate expectations of future changes in the same direction. Flexibility of the exchange rate, it is argued, provides excessive scope for speculators, and their activities may generate wide and purposeless fluctuations in exchange rate. Experience in the 1920's and 1930's is commonly cited as evidence that this is a real and serious problem.[6]

Promotion of Nationalist Economic Policies. The second argument is the primary argument in favour of flexible exchange rates, converted to an argument against flexibility.

Again, experience of the 1920's and 1930's is invoked in support of an argument that flexible exchange rates promote nationalist economic policies rather than internationalist policies. Manipulation of a flexible exchange rate can be used instead of tariffs to protect domestic industries, and, more particularly, to promote production in periods of recession. Thus, a country may use the flexible exchange rate to "export" its own unemployment problems.

We have seen that a pegged exchange rate imposes severe constraints on domestic monetary policy as long as the government is determined to maintain the par rate. The choice of a price level objective is particularly circumscribed. It is increasingly argued that in the contemporary context, world-wide inflation is a serious threat, and that pegged exchange rates are an essential source of "financial discipline" on inflation-prone national governments. Flexible exchange rates would remove that discipline. Thus, it is argued, the adoption of flexible exchange rates would result in an accentuation of inflationary pressures throughout the world. In effect, this is an argument that national governments cannot be trusted with responsibility for the formulation of monetary and fiscal policies in the international – and, indeed, in the national – interest.

The Case for Flexibility.[7] The case for flexibility is largely an assertion of national sovereignty in the formulation and implementation of monetary and fiscal policies – including the right to make disastrous mistakes – and the denial of the relevance or validity of each of the points raised above. Far from disrupting the international economy, it is argued, flexible exchange rates would further international development by providing an automatic solution to the international liquidity crises which have periodically beset, at times with devastating effect, the pegged exchange rate system.

First, the relevance of evidence drawn from the experiences of several countries with flexible exchange rates in the 1920's and 1930's is disputed, largely on grounds of the peculiar economic and political environment of the time. Indeed, most of the evils commonly ascribed to flexible exchange rates are asserted to have been a result of attempts to maintain or establish inappropriate par rates of exchange, or of the social, political and economic turmoil of the time. They could hardly be blamed on the flexibility of exchange rates. Other historical evidence — such as the Canadian experience from 1950-1962 — is commonly cited to demonstrate that flexible exchange rates have existed without the supposed deleterious effects to the international economy. The Canadian exchange rate was not turned into an instrument of nationalist economic policies; was not a harbinger of inflation; and while flexible, was remarkably stable.[8] The Canadian experience is commonly cited as evidence that in an otherwise stable environment, expectations may tend to stabilize the exchange rate rather to induce pointless fluctuations (thus somewhat reducing the effectiveness of a flexible exchange rate as a tool of nationalistic economic policies).

Indeed, it is argued that proponents of the present international monetary constitution have the economics of speculation backwards. We have already seen that the adjustable peg system is not only peculiarly vulnerable to speculation, but also tends to incite speculation. Speculation is turned into a one-way gamble, and as a result the official limits to exchange rate fluctuations become dams behind which tremendous speculative pressures can build up. With a flexible exchange rate, by contrast, speculators are faced with greater risks, and adjustments of the exchange rate in response to small amounts of speculative activity will quickly remove the basis for continued speculation. Speculation could actually be *less intense* than under the Bretton Woods system, and such speculation as did occur would perform the desirable economic function of speeding adjustment to new, more appropriate levels of the exchange rate. Thus, it is argued, speculation is a problem in attempting to maintain stability under an adjustable peg system, not under a flexible exchange rate system.

The associated proposition that flexible exchange rates increase the uncertainty surrounding all international investment decisions has also been disputed by proponents of flexibility. With respect to decisions on longer-term projects, there can be no certainty regarding the level of the exchange rate, even under the Bretton Woods system. Major re-alignments of par rates of exchange can and do occur. A flexible rate system would simply make the transition to new levels easier. With respect to short-term uncertainty, the forward exchange mechanism is capable of providing fully adequate hedges against the relevant risks.

Furthermore, it is argued, the pegged exchange rate system has not been successful in preventing countries from pursuing inflationary financial policies if they so choose. All it does is associate such policies with periodic financial crises, or with direct controls. More fundamentally, attempts to impose "'financial discipline" from outside is a significant infringement on national sovereignty. It is a denial of the right of a national government to choose its own policy objectives.

Thus, proponents of flexible exchange rates argue that the present pegged exchange rate system is the worst of all worlds. It does not provide the certainty and the pressure for the international integration of economic and financial policies which would follow from immutable exchange rates, nor does it provide the freedom in domestic policy formation that is associated with flexible exchange rates. Indeed, it is calculated to maximize policy conflicts and purposeless speculation.

Conclusions. The economics of flexible exchange rates is a broad topic, requiring historical as well as theoretical and statistical analysis. We have barely scratched the surface. However, the important point has been made: flexible exchange rates provide a type of flexibility in domestic policy formation which is absent with a pegged exchange rate system. There is good reason to believe that flexible exchange rates are viable, but there is strong opinion to the contrary. In any case, there is little likelihood of widespread resort to flexible exchange rates in the near future. Perhaps the practical problem for the immediate future is to make the Bretton Woods system less vulnerable to periodic crises. This requires, among other things, a solution to the international liquidity problem.

3/THE INTERNATIONAL LIQUIDITY PROBLEM

The key role of official foreign exchange reserves in the functioning of an international monetary system based on both fixed exchange rates and a commitment to avoid direct controls over international trade and payments, should be obvious from what has gone before. But how large a stock of reserves is needed? Is the rate of growth of existing reserves adequate?

This is an urgent question, which calls for a quantitative answer. Unfortunately it is also a very complicated question to which no convincing quantitative answer has yet been given. Over the past two decades there have been many qualitative judgments that the stock of foreign exchange reserves was inadequate, but no one has produced an acceptable measure of the deficiency. Indeed, the expanding literature on the topic reveals that economists are not even agreed on how to define an optimum stock of foreign exchange reserves in theory, let alone how to measure it.[9] The best we can do is suggest some relevant considerations.

To begin with, it is useful to distinguish between two inter-related concepts: the demand for foreign exchange reserves on the part of a single national government, and the optimum stock (or rate of growth) of foreign exchange reserves in the world as a whole.

The Nation's Demand for Foreign Exchange Reserves

The Benefits. We have seen that from any government's point of view, the attraction of large foreign exchange reserves is that they provide a buffer between domestic macroeconomic policies and the balance of payments. With this in mind, one can think of a variety of factors which ought to enter into deliberations over the "target" level of reserves. Clearly, the government ought to be concerned with the risk that its domestic policy objectives will require policies inimicable to balance of payments equilibrium. But it should be equally concerned with the risks of balance of payments deficits resulting from internal or external developments over which it has no control: such things as sudden shifts in "autonomous" capital flows, unanticipated demands for imports, adverse developments in major export markets, changes in the economic policies of other governments, crop failures, civil strife, war or natural disasters. The exchange market repercussions of any such developments could force sharp deflationary monetary and fiscal policies or else resort to direct controls unless the government has sufficient foreign exchange reserves to finance large-scale direct intervention in the market.

The Cost. Risk aversion might seem to dictate a very high target level of reserves. However, it must also be recognized that from the nation's point of view the accumulation of foreign exchange reserves has opportunity costs against which benefits must be weighed. Foreign exchange reserves involve a national investment in idle international purchasing power which could easily be used for other purposes.[10] The rate of return on alternative .investments ought to enter the calculation of the optimum level of reserves.

Presumably, the government should also take into account the availability and cost of reserves on short notice from other sources. This includes not only the possibility of borrowing reserves from other governments and international institutions, but also the possibilities for attracting short-term capital through the international capital market with moderate interest-rate or forward exchange rate inducements.

The Problem of Quantification. The preparation of such a list of factors which might be relevant to decisions on a target level of foreign exchange reserves is not a difficult exercise. However, it is merely a preliminary to the real analysis of the problem. It is a long step from there to the discovery of a technique for quantifying the various considerations listed, and a further long step to their use in calculating the optimum level of reserve holdings for a particular country at a particular time. Without these steps, the listing of considerations is almost trivial. These steps have not been taken. Economics has yet to make a significant contribution to the government's problem of actually choosing a target level of foreign exchange reserves.

Preferences Among Adjustment Techniques. Moreover, if we consider foreign exchange reserves to be a buffer between domestic policy and the balance of payments, then the nation's demand for foreign exchange must depend not only on such objective factors as the risk of balance of payments deficits, but also on such subjective considerations as the intensity of the government's aversion to risks, and its willingness to resort to domestic deflation, exchange controls or a change in the exchange rate in times of balance of payments pressure. If the government has a firm commitment to full employment, free international payments, and the existing exchange rate, it should have a strong preference for large foreign exchange reserves. If the government has few compuctions about invoking direct controls, changing the exchange rate, or deflating the domestic economy at the first sign of a deficit, it will probably have little demand for foreign exchange reserves even though its balance of payments is vulnerable.

Inevitably, the government's target level of foreign exchange reserves must be a matter of judgement and practical experience. Perhaps, as Professor Machlup has argued, governments' demands for foreign exchange reserves cannot be explained by economic analysis, since they are based on a mixture of "rational theories, irrational myths, and traditional principles".[11] Perhaps this explains the bewildering differences in reserve policies among nations, which seem to defy explanation in terms of the usual economic variables.[12]

The International Optimum

Although each nation's demand for foreign exchange reserves may not be explainable in terms of rational economic principles, the fact that they exist is sufficient to raise another question: is the supply of reserve assets in the world as a whole sufficient to meet the demands of all national governments? As we shall see, the crucial issue is a judgement on what macroeconomic policies national governments ought to pursue.

Real vs. Nominal Reserves. By analogy with the demand for money, we can assume that governments are concerned with the level of their foreign exchange reserves in *real* terms rather than in *nominal* terms. A doubling of the world price level, with nominal foreign exchange reserves given, will impair a nation's foreign exchange reserve position just as effectively as the loss of half of its reserves at a given price level. But it can be argued that in the long run, the quantity of *real* foreign exchange reserves supplied will always adjust *automatically* to the quantity of *real* foreign exchange reserves demanded, *regardless of what happens to the nominal quantity of reserves.* This is suggested by an extension of the quantity theory of money: equilibrium will be maintained in the long run through adjustment of the world price level.

A Quantity Theory Adjustment. Suppose, for example, that the stock of foreign exchange reserves in the hands of national governments was frozen at its present level, but that aggregate demands for reserves continued to grow. Faced with a shortfall of reserves, governments would tend to pursue restrictive policies, either through tight domestic monetary and fiscal policies or through direct restrictions on international trade and capital flows. For one country considered in isolation, these are effective policies for accumulating foreign exchange reserves. They serve to redistribute the available stock of reserves among nations. However, when all (or most) countries pursue the same policies, the ultimate effect will be a depression of demand, income and price levels throughout the world. But, given the nominal stock of reserves, a reduction in the world price level means a larger stock of *real* foreign exchange reserves. Ultimately, the supply of real reserves will be equated to the demand.

It also follows from this line of argument that a very rapid rate of growth of foreign exchange reserves could be inflationary. If an international agency existed which could create new supplies of reserve assets, to be distributed freely to national governments, it could expand the stock of reserves at a faster rate than the aggregate of demands for reserves to be held. Attempts of all nations simultaneously to reduce the level of their reserves would create upward pressures on the world price level, and the rise in the price level would adjust the real quantity of reserve assets to the quantity demanded.

Mrs. Machlup's Wardrobe. If such an automatic adjustment mechanism exists, why should we be concerned about the rate of growth of foreign exchange reserves in the world as a whole?

Professor Machlup has likened this issue to his wife's demand for dresses. While he cannot explain his wife's ambitions in terms of rational economic principles, the important thing is that she has strong desires for dresses, and if they are not satisfied,

> she will fuss and fret, and if I were to keep her from getting additional clothes, she would impose restrictions and controls affecting my home life and our external relations with friends and acquaintances. I conclude that the right amount of clothes owned by my wife is that which keeps her from fussing and fretting and spares me the danger of unpleasant restrictions.[13]

The desires of the central bankers should be considered in the same light. Although their ambitions in terms of reserve holdings may defy economic analysis, the important point is that they exist:

> I conclude that the "need" for reserves is determined by the ambitions of the monetary authorities. I submit we ought to see to it that they get foreign reserves in amounts sufficient to be happy and satisfied; in amounts, that is, that will keep them from urging or condoning policies restricting imports or capital movements.[14]

In other words, the problem with inadequate growth of (nominal) foreign exchange reserves is not that desired levels of real reserves cannot be achieved in the long run by some combination of policies. Rather, it is that the alternatives to adequate growth of nominal reserves — worldwide deflation and widespread restrictions of trade and capital flows — are unpalatable. They imply unemployment, reduced levels of economic efficiency and hence of real income, and lower rates of economic growth. The excessive growth of foreign exchange reserves on the other hand, creates the danger of worldwide inflation.

The Problem of Adequate Reserve Growth. The optimum rate of growth of the world's foreign exchange reserves is an elusive concept. We know very little about the determinants of national demands for foreign exchange reserves. However, even if we did understand these completely, to define the optimum rate of growth we would still be left with the question: what macroeconomic policies should national governments pursue? What degree of independence should they have from balance of payments constraints in formulating their domestic policies?

Although we cannot explain the nature of national demands for foreign exchange reserves, they seem certain to grow in the future. If the supply of reserve assets does not grow accordingly, governments may pursue unfortunate, restrictive policies. If we are concerned to avoid such policies, we must be concerned with the rate of growth of the supply of reserve assets. The informed judgement of most people in this field is that the growth rate has not been adequate in this sense in recent years. Why? What controls the rate of growth of reserve assets?

The Nature and Composition of Foreign Exchange Reserves

As a first step in the analysis of the control of the supply of foreign exchange reserves, we must be clear about their nature and composition. Summary data on the reserve holdings of all countries other than China, the U.S.S.R. and the countries of eastern Europe (for which no data are available) at the end of 1968 are shown in Table 22-1. The postwar evolution of the present composition of reserve holdings is shown in Figure 22-3.

Gold. For all countries taken together, gold is clearly the single most important reserve asset, accounting for over half of all foreign exchange

Table 22-1
The Composition of Official Foreign Exchange Reserves, January 1, 1970

(Millions of U.S. Dollars)

I. ALL COUNTRIES*	Dollars	Percent
Gold	39,125	51
U.S. Dollars	16,038	21
Other Convertible Currencies	15,037	20
Drawing Rights at I.M.F.	6,726	9
TOTAL	76,920	100
II. ALL COUNTRIES, EXCLUDING U.S.A.*		
Gold	27,266	46
U.S. Dollars	16,038	27
Other Convertible Currencies	12,256	20
Drawing Rights at I.M.F.	4,402	7
TOTAL	59,956	100

* Excluding China, U.S.S.R. and Eastern Europe.
SOURCE: International Monetary Fund, *International Financial Statistics*, March 1970.

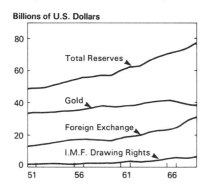

Figure 22-3
The Changing Composition of Foreign Exchange Reserves, 1950-1970
(billions of U.S. dollars)

SOURCE: I.M.F., *International Financial Statistics,* various issues.

eserves at the beginning of 1970. However, the relative importance of gold las been declining steadily. In the late 1930's gold accounted for over ♦0% of holdings of reserve assets. By 1949 this ratio had declined to ⁷0%, and by 1960 to 60%.[15]

Foreign Exchange. As the importance of gold has declined, the im-
ɔortance of foreign currency assets has increased. In principle, reserves
ould be held in any convertible currency, i.e., any currency for which
here is an active, unrestricted, international market. In practice, however,
wo currencies dominate as reserve assets: the pound sterling and the U.S.
dollar.

In the nineteenth and early twentieth centuries London was the world's
ɪnancial and banking center, and the pound sterling was the dominant
ʼurrency in international finance. As New York replaced London at the
ʼenter of the world's financial system, the relative importance of the pound
ɪeclined and the importance of the dollar increased. Since World War II,
ɪse of the pound in international payments and as a reserve asset has
ɔeen virtually confined to the so-called Sterling Area, a group of coun-
ɪries with close historical and economic ties to the United Kingdom
vhich effectively peg their exchange rates to the pound sterling.[16]

Outside the Sterling Area, and a similar but smaller Franc Area,[17]
he United States dollar dominates the scene. The U.S. dollar has become
he "working currency" of international trade and finance, and since all
ʼurrencies are effectively pegged to the U.S. dollar, it is the "vehicle
ʼurrency" in which all countries conduct direct intervention in the foreign
ɪxchange market to maintain the pegged exchange rate. While gold retains
ɪts traditional status as an international reserve asset, all countries hold
ɪt least working balances in U.S. dollars, and some countries, like Canada
(Table 22-2), hold a much larger portion of their reserves in this form.

Table 22-2
The Composition of Canada's Official Foreign Exchange Reserves
January 1, 1970

	Millions of U.S. Dollars	Percent
Gold	872.3	28.1
United States Dollar Assets	1,743.6	56.2
Other Foreign Currency Assets	12.3	0.4
Drawing Rights at the International Monetary Fund*	478.1	15.4
TOTAL	3,106.3	100.0

* Excludes the special drawing rights (U.S. $124.3) which were assigned to Canada on January 1, 1970.
SOURCE: Bank of Canada *Statistical Summary*.

I.M.F. Drawing Rights. Unconditional drawing rights at the International Monetary Fund account for a small but growing share of aggregate reserves. Moreover, the fact that such drawing rights accounted for only 9% of aggregate reserves at the beginning of 1970 significantly understate the importance of the International Monetary Fund in the international monetary system.

Conditional Reserves. Our measure of foreign exchange reserves doe not include conditional reserves, such as credits extended by the I.M.F beyond the basic, unconditional drawing right. Such reserves are significant although there is no effective way to measure the aggregate sum potentially available. We will return to a discussion of the I.M.F. later.

The Structure of the International Monetary System

Gold, U.S. dollars, and (to a lesser extent) pounds sterling and I.M.F drawing rights are thus the basic reserve assets. If we are to understand the mechanism regulating their supply we must have a rudimentary knowledge of the institutional structure of the international monetary system. It is particularly important to establish the role of gold in this system.

In the discussion in this section we confine attention to the system as it existed up to early 1968. We will turn to the forces which produced the crisis of 1967-68 and to the subsequent changes in institutional arrangements later.

The Classical Gold Standard.[18] Historically, gold was money *par excellence*. Indeed, during the nineteenth century, most industrial countries were formally on the gold standard. Gold coinage was in active circulation and gold was the "standard money" into which other types of money were convertible on demand, for both domestic and international payments.

The necessity for convertibility into gold imposed severe constraint on the management of the domestic money supply. While the ratio of old to the domestic money supply was not rigid, any substantial loss of gold through the settlement of international payments necessarily implied domestic monetary contraction, and any substantial inflow of gold generally implied domestic monetary expansion. There was no real question of a conflict between domestic and external objectives of monetary policy. In principle they were the same: convertibility into gold at a fixed exchange rate. Since excessive domestic monetary and credit expansion would result in a balance of payments deficit and an outflow of gold, governments could not pursue widely divergent monetary policies without precipitating a crisis. Thus, the very fear of gold drains was sufficient to maintain monetary discipline (except on the peripheries of the world economy, such as in North and South America, where suspensions of gold convertibility were not uncommon).

The classical gold standard was suspended during World War I, but the economic reconstruction of the postwar period included a painful, if short-lived, return to gold. In the economic disruptions of the great depression and World War II the direct link between gold and domestic monetary management was again severed as country after country abandoned the gold standard and restricted the rights of its citizens to own or trade in gold. Gold stocks in the hands of private citizens and commercial banks were expropriated and turned over to central banks or exchange stabilization funds. For varying periods of time, the world's major currencies were allowed to float freely in the foreign exchange markets, but eventually new pegged rates were established. There was an alignment of nations into "currency blocks" and widespread resort to exchange controls, made very rigid during World War II. However, while it had lost its domestic monetary functions and it could not be traded legally among private citizens, gold was still universally recognized as "international money", at least for official settlement purposes. As it turned out, the gold standard had not been abandoned. Through the nationalization of the gold stock, it had merely been transformed.

Remnants of the Gold Standard. New gold standard principles were formally incorporated into the reconstruction of international monetary arrangements agreed to at the Bretton Woods Conference of 1944. On the symbolic level, the 1944 gold dollar became the unit of account for the new International Monetary Fund, and all members were required to declare par rate of exchange in terms of this gold dollar. Part of each country's initial subscription to the Fund had to be in gold, or in currencies convertible into gold. The I.M.F. accumulated a large stock of gold, and members were obliged to exchange their currencies for gold in the hands of the Fund if necessary, at the par rate of exchange. As is evident in Figure 21-3, although the United States dollar emerged as the practical currency for international payments, central banks continued to accumulate a major portion of their foreign exchange reserves in gold.

The keystone of the Bretton Woods financial structure was the relationship between the United States dollar and gold. Although the United States government had terminated its formal obligation to convert private holdings of United States dollars into gold in the early 1930's (and residents of the United States were prohibited from owning or trading in gold, other than for artistic, industrial and numismatic purposes), the government continued to guarantee the convertibility of dollars in the hands of foreign governments "for legitimate monetary purposes" and to purchase all gold offered to it at the official price of $35 per ounce.[19] The United States gold stock, which, at the end of World War II, amounted to almost three quarters of the gold in monetary reserves in the western world, became in effect the central gold reserve for the world monetary system.

The London Gold Market.[20]   Although not a part of the formal structure of the monetary system agreed to at Bretton Woods, a set of institutions which had a vital impact on the functioning of that system was an international network of gold markets, which, from 1954 on, had the London gold market as its hub.

As we noted earlier, many countries imposed severe restrictions on the ownership and trading of gold before and during World War II. In an environment of monetary instability and rampant inflation, black markets for gold, a traditional and relatively durable international store of value, flourished nonetheless. Although there were some important exceptions (notably the United States and the United Kingdom), most countries relaxed or abolished restrictions on gold ownership and trading in the early 1950's and even those countries which maintained rigid controls found it almost impossible to eliminate large-scale illegal transactions. In 1954, after a period of stability in free gold markets, the London gold market was opened for trading among non-residents through the intermediary of British brokers (British citizens were still prohibited from owning or trading gold). It quickly became the dominant wholesale market.

The basic stock-in-trade of the London gold market and its satellite markets throughout the world was the annual output of the western world's gold mines, which ranged between $1,000 million and $1,500 million in the late 1950's and the 1960's, augmented by periodic Russian gold sales, which reached $550 million in 1965. From time to time various central banks also sold gold in the free market to gain foreign exchange. As long as the free market price was above the U.S. treasury's buying price ($34.9125 per ounce) suppliers of gold would offer it for sale in the market. If the price dropped below this, gold would flow into the United States' stock. As a result, the U.S. treasury's buying price set an effective floor under the free market price.

On the demand side, the market serviced a regular flow of private demands, amounting to approximately $500 million in the mid-1950's and rising to much higher levels in later years. Some of this demand was for normal artistic and industrial purposes. However, there was a continuing undercurrent of demands for private hoarding and, particularly in later years, for short-term speculation on the price of gold. The latter, as we shall see, eventually became a decisive factor disrupting the system.

European central banks also satisfied a large part of their demands for gold through purchases in the London gold market. Because they had the option of dealing directly with the U.S. treasury, these central banks provided a bridge between the gold market and the United States' gold reserve. If they could satisfy their demands for gold in the open market at a price less than the U.S. Treasury's selling price ($35.0875) they would do so. If the open market price rose above this, they would switch their demands to the U.S. treasury. This put an effective ceiling on the market price — unless private demands exceeded the flow of gold onto the market.[21]

In October 1961 this happened for the first time since the London gold market opened in 1954. Private speculation drove the market price to over $40 per ounce. Fearing that price instability would aggravate speculative pressures, the United States government intervened, supplying gold to the market through the Bank of England to stabilize the price close to the official price. In 1961 and 1962, in a series of agreements with major European central banks,[22] the Federal Reserve System organized joint intervention as necessary to keep the market price close to the official price. The United States agreed to provide half of the gold required by the so-called Gold Pool, but of course the U.S. commitment to supply gold to central banks meant that in the long run a drain out of the Gold Pool was a drain out of the U.S. reserve.

In this way, given the flow of gold onto the market, private demands for gold determined the rate of growth of aggregate stock of official gold reserves; and the sum of private demands and the demands of other central banks determined the rate of change of the United States' gold stock. This proved to be a vulnerable situation which eventually rendered the entire monetary structure unstable. We will return to the analysis of the problem when we have completed our sketch of the structure of the international monetary system.

The International Monetary Fund. One of the important financial institutions to be established as a result of the Bretton Woods Conference was the International Monetary Fund. In a sense it was to be a central bank for the international monetary system, but initially it was denied the basic power of a central bank. It could not issue liabilities which would be accepted as international money.

From a financial point of view, the International Monetary Fund is simply a pool of gold and national currencies. When the Fund was established, each member was assigned a quota, 25% of which had to be subscribed in gold (the so-called gold tranche) and the balance in its own currency. As a result of new members joining the Fund and across-the-board increases of all quotas in 1959 and 1968, the aggregate value of all quotas increased from U.S. $8.8 billion in 1947 to U.S. $21.3 billion at the beginning of 1970. The Fund can also augment its holdings of currencies by borrowing directly from members. Under the General Arrangements to Borrow, the Fund had formal lines of credit with ten members totalling almost $6 billion at the beginning of 1970 (and at that time, under the G.A.B. and other arrangements the Fund had outstanding borrowings from these ten members of almost U.S. $1 billion).

Each member's rights and obligations *vis à vis* the Fund depend on the Fund's holdings of the member's currency relative to the member's quota. Members are permitted to purchase foreign exchange from the

Fund in exchange for their own currency (such transactions are usually called drawings) under certain specified conditions. Each member has the right to draw foreign exchange from the Fund virtually without question providing that the drawing does not increase the Fund's holding of the member's currency above its quota. This sum is the unconditional drawing right which we have included in our measure of foreign exchange reserves.

Drawings which will increase the Fund's holdings of the member's currency in excess of its quota are "conditional". That is, they are governed by a complicated set of rules limiting both the amount which can be borrowed and the timing of the drawings (all of which can be waived by the Fund), and they require "substantial justification" on the part of the member. Indeed, for very large drawings, the Fund normally requires the member to make a formal "declaration of intent" regarding domestic policies which will be undertaken to solve the balance of payments problem. Given an acceptable declaration of intent, the Fund will frequently make a standby arrangement, permitting virtually automatic drawings as necessary up to a specified sum within a specified period of time. Such an arrangement is sometimes a powerful psychological weapon to counter speculative pressures.

Each drawing from the Fund simultaneously reduces the Fund's holdings of other currencies (thus increasing other member's drawing rights from the Fund) and increases the Fund's holdings of the drawing member's currency. Drawings which increase the Fund's holdings of the member's currency above 75% of its quota creates an obligation to repurchase. The amount and timing of the repurchase is governed by another complicated set of rules, but all repurchases must be made with gold or convertible foreign exchange. Interest is charged on the fund's excess holdings of a member's currency as an inducement to early repayment, the interest rate increasing with both the magnitude of the excess and the time that it is outstanding. Thus, drawings on the Fund are appropriately regarded as short-term loans.

An Example: Canada and the I.M.F. in 1968. Canada's transactions with the I.M.F. in 1968 are set out in Example 22-1, to help clarify some of the complexities of the operations of the International Monetary Fund.

Canada's quota in the International Monetary Fund is U.S. $740 million. At the end of December, 1967, the Fund held U.S. $341.6 million worth of Canadian dollars. Thus, Canada's basic drawing right was U.S. $399.6 million. However, Canada also had outstanding loans of Canadian dollars to the I.M.F. under the General Arrangements to borrow equivalent to U.S. $35 million, which the I.M.F. was obliged to repay if Canada was forced to borrow from the Fund. Since repayment of the G.A.B. loan would reduce the Fund's holdings of Canadian dollars, the loan in effect augmented Canada's I.M.F. quota. As a result, Canada's unconditional drawing right at that time amounted to U.S. $433.4 million.

In the early part of 1968 other members of the I.M.F. repaid outstanding debts to the Fund in Canadian dollars. This increased the Fund's

Example 22-1
Canada's Transactions with the International Monetary Fund, 1968
(Millions of U.S. Dollars)

December 31, 1967

Canada's Qutoa	740.0
Outstanding Loans under the G.A.B.	35.0
Augmented Quota	775.0
I.M.F. Holdings of Canadian Dollars	341.6
Unconditional Drawing Right	433.4

January 1, – February 29, 1968

Transactions Affecting I.M.F. Holdings of Canadian Dollars	
Third Country Repayments in Canadian Dollars	+ 7.3
Canadian Drawing of Foreign Exchange	+426.0
I.M.F. Repayment of G.A.B. Loan	− 35.0
Net Change in Fund Holdings of Canadian Dollars	+398.3

February 29, 1968

Canada's Quota	740.0
I.M.F. Holdings of Canadian Dollars (341.6 + 398.3)	739.9
Unconditional Drawing Right	0.1
Canada's Obligation to Repurchase [739.9 − (0.75 x 740)]	184.9

March 1 – December 31, 1968

Transactions Affecting I.M.F. Holdings of Canadian Dollars	
Third Country Drawings of Canadian Dollars	−138.5
Canadian Repurchase of Canadian Dollars	− 67.6
Net Change in Fund Holdings of Canadian Dollars	−206.1

December 31, 1968

Canada's Quota	740.0
I.M.F. Holdings of Canadian Dollars (739.9 − 206.1)	533.8
Unconditional Drawing Right	206.2

holdings of Canadian dollars by U.S. $7.3 million, and reduced Canada's unconditional drawing right by the same amount. During the foreign exchange crisis of early 1968 Canada drew U.S. $426 from the Fund, and the Fund repaid the outstanding G.A.B. loan. As a result of these transactions, the Fund's holdings of Canadian dollars increased by U.S. $398.3, to U.S. $739.9 or 100% of Canada's quota. Canada had exhausted her unconditional drawing right, and, since the Fund's holdings of Canadian dollars exceeded 75% of Canada's quota, had created an obligation to repurchase from the Fund. Further Canadian borrowing would normally be conditional on the presentation of an acceptable program for correction of the balance of payments problem.

During the balance of the year other countries borrowed Canadian dollars from the Fund, and Canada repaid part of her earlier borrowings. Both sets of transactions reduced the Fund's holdings of Canadian dollars, and by year-end, unconditional drawing rights had been re-established to the extent of U.S. $206.2 million.

This example should make clear the relationship between Canada's quota, the I.M.F.'s holdings of Canadian dollars, and Canada's drawing rights. It also illustrates how Canada's position at the I.M.F. can be affected by the transactions of third countries with the Fund.

The I.M.F. and International Credit Creation. In the International Monetary Fund, member governments have established an international agency with authority to create inter-governmental credit, under fairly carefully defined circumstances and in strictly limited amounts. When a member draws on his gold tranche, it is drawing gold and foreign exchange which it had previously accumulated through its own national efforts and subscribed to the Fund. Thus, the gold tranche is simply the nation's gold reserves held in a different form. However, when a member draws foreign exchange in excess of this — in what are called the "credit tranches" — *new reserves are created.* The drawing member comes into possession of foreign exchange which was previously not counted as part of any nation's foreign exchange reserves, and it is free to use this foreign exchange. Other members have in effect extended credit in their own currencies through the intermediary of the I.M.F., and thus they temporarily help finance the drawing member's balance of payments deficit. In this way, the existence of the Fund makes a net addition to international liquidity.

How much credit can the International Monetary Fund extend to members? At first glance, the answer might seem to be the sum of all member's quotas and the Fund's lines of credit under the General Agreements to Borrow, less the gold tranche. At the end of 1968 this was in excess of U.S. $20 billion, a net addition of over 25% to the explicit reserves of the western world. However, such a calculation implies that all currencies in the I.M.F. pool are equally useful, which is not the case.

Members draw from the Fund in order to obtain currencies which they can use for direct intervention in the foreign exchange market. For this purpose they normally require United States dollars. This does not mean that they will only draw U.S. dollars from the Fund. However, it does mean that any currencies drawn from the Fund will normally be converted into U.S. dollars, usually in a direct transaction with the foreign exchange authorities of the country whose currency is drawn. This means at present that the usable currencies in the International Monetary Fund are those of only a few member countries with relatively strong foreign exchange reserve positions.

This is reflected in the pattern of drawings from the I.M.F. From 1947 through 1960, some 87% of all drawings from the Fund were of one currency, the U.S. dollar. With the economic recovery of Western Europe, more currencies became convertible and hence potentially useful to the Fund. However, the pattern of drawings from the Fund remained highly concentrated. Thus, from 1960 through 1968, the currencies of five industrialized countries[23] accounted for 72% of all drawings. By adding five more industrialized nations to the list[24] we can account for 93% of all drawings. Yet, at the end of 1968 almost 35% of the Fund's holdings of gold and national currencies took the form of the currencies of less developed nations or smaller developed countries, most of which were not convertible.

The contribution of the International Monetary Fund to international liquidity is thus greater than the gold tranche, but much less than the sum of all quotas and lines of credit under the General Agreements to Borrow.

Inter-Central Bank Credit. The International Monetary Fund is not the only source of international credit to supplement foreign exchange reserves. As we noted earlier, the central banks of major industrialized nations extend credit *directly* to each other in time of need. Thus, each serious foreign exchange crisis has involved close consultation among the central banks, frequently leading to a large "package" of assistance. For example, during the 1968 Canadian crisis, some U.S. $900 million in credits were extended by other central banks, although the Bank of Canada did not find it necessary to draw on them.[25] At the end of 1968 outstanding *ad hoc* lines of credit of this sort totalled U.S. $9,263.

In addition to such *ad hoc* arrangements, the Federal Reserve System has developed an extensive network of explicit reciprocal lines of credit with other central banks. By the end of 1968, this "swap network" involved 14 central banks and the Bank for International Settlements, and amounted to U.S. $10.5 billion, two and a half times the United States' quota at the I.M.F. The "swap network" has been used extensively both by the United States and by the other participants. Canada's line of credit at the end of 1968 was U.S. $1 billion. During the 1968 crisis Canada drew on its line of credit to the extent of U.S. $250 million.

The major participants in this reciprocal credit network are the central banks of the ten countries participating in the General Arrangements to Borrow (the "Group of Ten") and Switzerland, a non-member of the I.M.F. Thus, membership in the reciprocal credit network interlocks with the International Monetary Fund, but *the arrangements were deliberately made outside the framework of the I.M.F.*[26] A general increase of I.M.F. quotas, a possible alternative, would have increased credit facilities on a global basis. The reciprocal credit network, by contrast, could be confined to industrialized nations. It is argued that the liquidity problem among industrialized nations is of a different order than the chronic reserve problems of less developed nations. The latter is in fact a problem of capital deficiency for economic development, and should be handled as such. Moreover, it is argued, the rapid evolution of international financial problems among industrialized nations requires a much more flexible instrument of policy than that provided by the International Monetary Fund. The end result, however, is an exclusive — some would say unseemly — rich nation's monetary club, and a bifurcation of the international monetary system.

The Bank for International Settlements. At the center of the reciprocal credit network, administering and effectively presiding over it, is another increasingly important but little known international financial institution, the Bank for International Settlements.

This bank, with its headquarters in Basle, Switzerland, is controlled by a group of Western European central banks. It was established in 1930 to handle the collection and distribution of reparations payments from Germany under the ill-fated Young Plan of 1929. This function was short-lived, but the bank proved to be a convenient and flexible vehicle for inter-central bank consultations and co-operation, and hence it survived the quick demise of its initial rationale. In the period after World War II it found a useful role administering various Western European financial arrangements, including the European Payments Union and its successor, the European Monetary Agreement (a sort of Western European clearinghouse). The bank does not do a regular banking business with the general public. Its funds are derived primarily from the deposits of central banks, and are invested primarily in government securities and time deposits with banks (much of the latter in the Euro-Dollar market).

From our present point of view, the important thing about the Bank for International Settlements is that it has provided the forum for consultations, negotiations and agreements among the central banks of industrialized nations, particularly following what has been called the Basle Agreement of 1961, under which central banks agreed to cooperate in the mutual defense of their currencies from speculative attacks in the foreign exchange market.[27] Consultations are almost continuous in that all members of the Group of Ten regularly attend the monthly meetings of the Board of Directors of the B.I.S., even though not all are on the Board. From time to time they are joined by representatives of other central banks.

The flexibility of the Bank for International Settlements has also permitted it to take on other functions of importance for the stability of the international monetary system. For example, from time to time it has intervened in the gold market, and in recent years it has become a sort of central banker to the Euro-Dollar market.

We encountered the Euro-Dollar market in our analysis of the business of Canadian Chartered Banks (see Chapter 8). It is an international market for U.S. dollar balances, normally on short-term deposit. It has developed rapidly since the mid-1950's, and has contributed significantly to the international mobility of capital. However, from time to time very large-scale movements of funds have threatened the stability of the market. Given the crucial role of the U.S. dollar in the international financial system, the possible instability of the Euro-Dollar market became a matter of official concern. As a result, the Bank for International Settlements, supported by a line of credit with the Federal Reserve System, agreed to intervene directly for the purpose of stabilizing the market.

Since the Basle agreement, the Bank for International Settlements and the network of inter-central bank credits surrounding it have grown rapidly. The result is an international credit system rivalling the International Monetary Fund in size, but oriented specifically to the international liquidity problems of the industrialized nations of the world. It is impossible to put a number on the magnitude of inter-central bank credits which *could* be negotiated in time of crisis. However, some idea of the relative importance of the I.M.F. and the Basle network is suggested by Table 22-3.

Table 22-3
Two Systems of International Liquidity

(Millions of U.S. Dollars)			
	1961	1964	1968
THE INTERNATIONAL MONETARY FUND			
Aggregate Quotas	15,043	15,850	21,198
THE BASLE NETWORK			
The General Arrangements to Borrow*	—	6,200	6,057
The Federal Reserve System's Swap Network	575	2,350	10,505
Ad Hoc Credit Facilities	1,132	4,380	9,263
	1,707	12,930	25,825
THE BANK FOR INTERNATIONAL SETTLEMENTS			
Total Assets	1,295	1,890	3,940

SOURCES: International Monetary Fund, *Annual Report*, 1969; *International Financial Statistics*; Bank for International Settlements, *Annual Report*.

The Structure of the International Monetary System: An Overview. These, then, were the basic institutional monetary systems prior to the changes introduced in 1968 and 1969. It is perhaps useful to pull the main points together in a brief summary before we go on to consider the process of reserve asset creation.

The foundation of the Bretton Woods system was firmly planted in the stock of monetary gold. Gold was one of the two major reserve assets; and the other, the U.S. dollar, was fully convertible into gold at a fixed price for both official and private holders. The explicit reserve holdings of national governments were supplemented by an elaborate network of inter-governmental lines of credit. In part these went through the intermediary of the International Monetary Fund, but in major part they by-passed the Fund and were organized around the Bank for International Settlements.

This system proved to be unstable in the long run. The inevitable crisis occurred in 1967 and 1968, forcing immediate reforms. What was the root of the problem?

The Instability of the International Monetary Structure

The important point to keep in mind is that there were two types of international reserve money, gold and U.S. dollars, which were convertible into each other on demand at a fixed price, but which were not regarded as perfect substitutes by the world's central bankers, and which had very different aggregate supply conditions. In this combination of circumstances lay the inherent instability of the international monetary system.

International Financial Intermediation. The role of the United States in the world financial system has been likened to that of an international financial intermediary. At the same time that the United States was issuing *monetary liabilities* to the rest of the world, i.e., borrowing on short-term liquid claims, it was acquiring less liquid long-term and short-term claims on the rest of the world (as well as exporting capital in the form of official gifts). This pattern is evident in the balance of payments data presented in Figure 22-4. Through the 1950's and 1960's the United States ran a substantial current account surplus, exporting capital on a massive scale on both public and private account. Part of the capital outflow was offset, however, by foreign borrowing on short-term — through the export of gold and liquid U.S. dollar liabilities.

Figure 22-4
The United States' Balance of International Payments
and the International Liquidity Drain, 1950-1970
(billions of U.S. dollars)

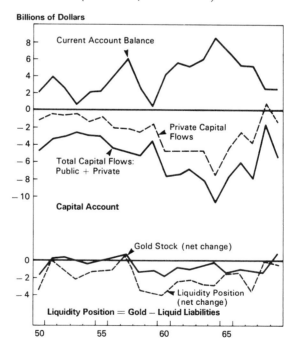

SOURCE: *Federal Reserve Bulletin*, various issues.

As we saw in Chapters 8 to 10, borrowing on short-term liquid instruments and lending on long-term and less liquid instruments is the classic pattern of a bank-type financial intermediary. In general, there is no reason to think that such an arrangement would be impractical in the long-run, providing the world's central bankers were willing to accept the U.S. dollar as the exclusive international money. Indeed, the adoption of an international "dollar standard", with the U.S. dollar as the exclusive, inconvertible international money has many proponents.[28]

However, the Bretton Woods System had *two* types of international money — U.S. dollars and gold. This proved to be a fatal flaw. Some central bankers displayed a strong preference for gold among their foreign exchange reserves. Given the rate of growth of foreign exchange reserves in the rest of the world, the required gold could only be provided by drawing down the United States gold stock. Eventually, the United States was placed in the position of a banker faced with a precipitous decline in his cash reserves. And the U.S. responded as a banker would, by restricting the extension of credit. Traditional monetary policies to curb the capital outflow were supplemented by various types of direct controls over capital exports.[29] However, as long as the U.S. dollar was the basic international money, measures which seemed necessary to the Americans to protect their own international liquidity position could only be effective if they curbed the rate of growth of reserves in the rest of the world, and hence if they aggravated the international liquidity problem of the rest of the world.

International Redistribution of Gold Reserves. In the immediate postwar period the role of the United States as banker to the new international gold standard seemed quite viable. As we noted earlier, the United States had emerged from World War II with almost three-quarters of the world's stock of monetary gold, more than ample to guarantee the convertibility of dollar balances in foreign official hands (in 1950 the U.S. gold stock was over $24 billion, while U.S. liquid liabilities were only $8.4 billion of which $4.9 billion were in official hands). Moreover, the economic disruptions produced by the war had left Europe with a seemingly chronic balance of payments deficit vis à vis the United States. Even under the tightly controlled conditions which prevailed, official foreign exchange reserves increased only very slowly.

By the mid-1950's, however, the situation began to change. With economic recovery and, in some cases, important monetary reforms, the balance of payments of continental western European countries improved dramatically. This was accompanied by large-scale accumulations of foreign exchange reserves, almost two-thirds of which were held in gold, with the balance largely in United States dollars. From 1950 through 1966 the accumulation of gold in the foreign exchange reserves of the industrialized countries of Western Europe alone was almost double the increase in the western world's total reserves of monetary gold (Table 22-4). Other developed countries (principally Spain, Portugal, Canada, South Africa and Japan) also accumulated gold, although in much lesser amounts. The overall effect was a vast redistribution of gold from the two reserve centers, and particularly from the United States, to other developed nations. As the reserves of the rest of the world increased, those of the United States declined (Figure 22-5) setting the scene for the gold crisis of 1967-68.

Table 22-4
Gold and Foreign Exchange Reserves, 1950-1966

(Millions of U.S. Dollars)

	I. TOTAL MONETARY GOLD STOCK*	II. RESERVE CENTERS UNITED STATES		UNITED KINGDOM	
		Total Reserves	Gold	Total Reserves	Gold
1950	35,300	24,265	22,820	3,443	2,862
1966	43,185	14,881	13,235	3,100	1,940
Net Change 1950-1966	7,885	−9,384	−9,585	−343	−922

	III. OTHER COUNTRIES				
	INDUSTRIAL EUROPE		OTHER DEVELOPED COUNTRIES		LESS DEVELOPED COUNTRIES
	Total Reserves	Gold	Total Reserves	Gold	Total Reserves	Gold
1950	5,160	3,510	5,520	1,522	9,715	3,045
1966	31,287	19,076	11,057	4,095	11,655	2,555
Net Change 1950-1966	26,127	15,566	5,537	2,573	1,940	−490

* Excludes U.S.S.R., China, Eastern Europe. Includes holdings of international institutions not listed separately in the Table.

Figure 22-5
The Redistribution of Foreign Exchange Reserves
Foreign Exchange Reserves of the Reserve Centers and the Rest of the World, 1950-1969
(billions of U.S. dollars)

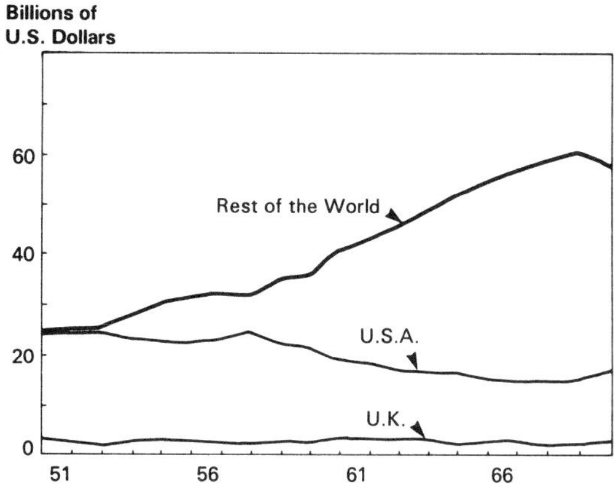

Only a much more rapid rate of increase in the supply of monetary gold could have staved off the crisis by permitting the European central banks to increase their gold reserves without impairing the reserve position of the United States. What governed the rate of increase of the aggregate stock of monetary gold?

Gold Production. Gold mining is a peculiar industry. The price of gold has been fixed at U.S. $35 per ounce since 1935, but costs of production have increased inexorably, partly as a result of the general rise of prices and wage rates, and partly as a result of the exhaustion of the richest and most accessible deposits of ore. The implications for the profitability of gold mining are obvious. In spite of subsidies to gold mining in several countries (including Canada), the production of new gold outside South Africa has been declining steadily over the past two decades.

In South Africa, the situation was different, but only by accident. Major new gold fields were brought into production beginning in 1953, and as a result total South African output increased substantially for several years. Whereas in 1953 South African mines accounted for half of the world's output of new gold, by the mid-1960's they were producing three-quarters of the total. However, the entire increase in output in this period occurred in the new mine fields. Output from the old fields fell off as rapidly as in the rest of the world. By 1966 the output from the new fields began to level off also. Apparently this fillip to the base of the world's monetary system had run its course, and the underlying long-run retardation of gold production had re-asserted itself.

Russian Sales and Private Demand. Although the production of new gold increased steadily from 1950 to 1966, net additions to the world's monetary stock were much more erratic (see Figure 22-6). On the one hand, new production was augmented by periodic Russian sales of gold (partly to finance purchases of Canadian wheat), and on the other hand the supply available to the monetary authorities was reduced by highly variable private demands for gold.

Although modest in amount at the outset, from their inception in 1953 through 1965, Russian gold sales accounted for almost half of the increase in the monetary gold stocks of the west. In the last three years alone, Russian sales amounted to over 85% of the total increase in official gold holdings. The abrupt tremination of these sales in 1965 produced a radical change in the supply situation.

Private demand was even less stable than Russian sales. As we noted earlier, part of the private demand for gold was for normal industrial and artistic purposes. While there are no very good statistics on the purchase of gold for these purposes, available estimates suggest a steady increase in demand, from around 25% of annual output in the late 1950's to between 40% and 50% in recent years (Figure 22-6). Part of the acceleration of purchases by industrial users in 1967 and 1968, however, reflected hedging against a possible rise in the price of gold, and hence should be counted as speculation.

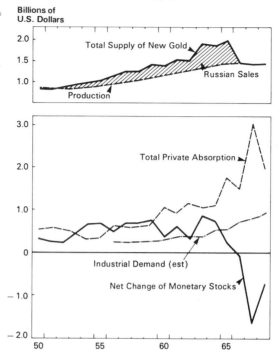

Figure 22-6
The Gold Market: Supply and Demand

Private hoarding of gold was a highly volatile factor in the total demand for gold. There had been a continuing demand for gold to be held as a store of value throughout the postwar period, presumably on the part of individuals who did not have confidence in their domestic money. The crucial factor in later years was shorter-term speculation on a rise in the price of gold. The continuing decline of the United States gold stock, coupled with the continuing rise in U.S. liquid international liabilities and the lack of agreement among central banks on the nature of appropriate reforms to the international monetary system, raised serious doubts that the existing gold price could be continued. As is evident in Figure 22-6, from 1960 through 1967 successive waves of speculation increased in intensity until they overwhelmed the market. In 1967, for the first time in the postwar period, total monetary stocks of gold experienced a major decline. The vulnerability of an international monetary system tied to gold was laid bare for all to see. Reform was urgent.

Reform of the International Monetary Structure

Proposals for the reform of the international monetary system are legion. They range from proposals to create a true international central bank with power to create an international fiat money, to proposals to return to a more classical version of the gold standard. These proposals have been surveyed in several excellent and readily accessible publications.[30] It is important to briefly review the reforms implemented in 1968 and 1969. These involved two interrelated measures: a sharp distinction between private gold and official gold, and the introduction of a new international reserve credit facility, Special Drawing Rights at the International Monetary Fund.

Bifurcation of the Gold Stock. The initial response of the members of the Gold Pool to the crisis in the gold market which followed the devaluation of the pound sterling in the fall of 1967, was a vigorous re-affirmation of the two policies of pegged exchange rates and a fixed price for gold. However, the steady drain of gold from the Pool under continuing speculative pressure led to an emergency meeting of the seven members of the Pool in March, 1968, following which a new gold policy was announced.[31] It introduced a sharp distinction between private gold and monetary gold.

The basic decision was to cease the *de facto* pegging of the price of gold in the free market. The members of the Pool announced that they would no longer sell gold to the free market nor buy gold from the free market, and that they would not supply gold to other central banks to replace gold sold in private markets. At the same time, gold then in the hands of central banks would continue to be treated as a reserve asset. The United States would still buy and sell gold "for legitimate monetary purposes" at $35 per ounce, and all would feel free to use gold for official international settlements. Other central banks were invited to subscribe to the new principles, and most, but not all, did.

Under the new "two-tier" policy for gold, the existing monetary stock of gold became, in effect, expensive yellow tokens, with a fixed nominal value of $35 per ounce, usable only for inter-central bank clearings. Private gold could be traded freely in the open market at a price determined by the interaction of supply and demand. The initial response of the free market was a sharp rise in the price of gold. However, if the agreement were rigidly adhered to, a significant decline of the price of gold seemed probable. This is evident from the balance of supply and demand in the market at the pegged price of $35 (Figure 22-6). Thus, in 1964, the last reasonably "normal" year before the final speculative spasm, industrial purchases of gold were only half the annual output. Even allowing for some continuing private hoarding, a substantial expansion in industrial demand would be required to clear the market. This implied lower prices.

For some time, the price of gold was maintained by South Africa withholding gold from the market. Thus, in the year following the March 1968 announcement, South Africa sold less than half its output of gold, and part of that was to other central banks.[32] South Africa could not continue this policy indefinitely, and as gold sales accelerated in the second half of 1969, the price of gold fell in the free market, and by year-end was under the official price of $35 per ounce.

The demonetization of gold was not complete, however. One interpretation of the Articles of Agreement of the International Monetary Fund implies that any member is entitled to sell gold to the Fund at $35 per ounce in exchange for convertible currencies.[33] When the price in the free market dipped below $35 per ounce, South Africa invoked this principle, and the Fund agreed to a formula for the acquisition of some South African gold. This has probably re-introduced the floor under the gold price, and has guaranteed some continuation of the growth of the monetary stock of gold (since the I.M.F. can always require members to accept gold in exchange for their own currencies). It also means that the growth of the monetary gold stock will be subjected to the vagaries of private demands for gold, although the removal of the ceiling price in the free market removes the private tap to the official gold stock and hence the dam behind which private speculative pressures previously built up relentlessly.

However, the March 1968 agreement did not solve the long-run problem of international liquidity. If adhered to literally by all central banks, it would have frozen the stock of monetary gold, but because of the non-adherence of some central banks, and the role of the I.M.F. in the gold market, it has probably simply retarded the growth of the stock of monetary gold. In any case, it is not clear that the agreement by itself is viable in the long run. Gold was not demonetized. Given deep-seated central bank traditions regarding the share of foreign exchange reserves which should be held in gold, continued growth of world foreign exchange reserves could set up renewed demands for gold among the world's central banks, and, in spite of assertions after the 1968 meeting that the existing monetary gold stock was fully adequate, this could again create uncertainty and doubt about the United States gold reserve position.

The March 1968 agreement contained a clear implication that further increases in aggregate foreign exchange reserves would be neither in gold nor in U.S. dollars, but in a new reserve asset, Special Drawing Rights.

Special Drawing Rights. A 1969 amendment to the Articles of Agreement introduced a new principle into the operations of the International Monetary Fund. It permits the Fund to create a new reserve asset to be held by members in addition to their foreign exchange reserves, without the members subscribing either gold or their own currencies to the Fund. The first Special Drawing Rights were allocated in January 1970, with further allocations to be made in each of the succeeding two years. Total allocations over an initial three-year period will be the equivalent of $9.5 billion.

Special Drawing Rights are simply entries in a new set of books maintained by the I.M.F. These S.D.R.'s are intended to be used in the same way as foreign exchange reserves to finance temporary balance of payments deficits and hence to avoid exchange controls, unnecessary domestic deflation or a change in the exchange rate. To this end, participating members may transfer their S.D.R.'s to other members designated to receive them by the I.M.F., in exchange for convertible foreign currencies. The designated members are obligated to accept the S.D.R.'s, and thus to extend reserve credit to the deficit country. However, there are built-in safeguards. No member may be required to accept additional S.D.R.'s in excess of twice his allocation, and all members are required to maintain their holdings of

S.D.R.'s at 30% of their allocation on the average over a five-year period. The latter provision means that a member drawing down his allocation of S.D.R.'s is obliged to reconstitute his position through purchases of S.D.R.'s with convertible currency from other members or from the I.M.F itself. This ensures that S.D.R.'s will not become a large-scale chronic source of credit from one set of members to another.

Interest is paid on holdings and charged on allocations of S.D.R.'s at the same nominal rate of 1½% per annum. Thus, a member who holds precisely what he is allocated will break even. Members who draw down their holdings will pay interest to the Fund, and members who are required to accept additional S.D.R.'s will receive interest from the Fund. All charges and interest are payable in S.D.R.'s. The rate is so low as to be ineffective as a serious incentive, however.

The provision for annual allocations of S.D.R.'s is designed to allow for the continuing growth of reserves on a global basis. The whole arrangement will be subjected to review at the end of the initial three-year period when new allocations are to be decided. New allocations have to be accepted by members having 85% of the voting rights in the I.M.F., permitting a veto by the larger nations with large quotas. Thus the rate of growth of reserves through the S.D.R. mechanism is not a matter for impartial technical decisions within an international central bank. Rather, it is in the arena of international politics. Since there can be no guarantee of unanimity of opinion on the appropriate rate of growth of reserves in the future, there can be no guarantee that the rate of growth of S.D.R.'s will be in any sense "adequate".

4/MONETARY POLICY, THE BALANCE OF PAYMENTS AND THE INTERNATIONAL LIQUIDITY PROBLEM: CONCLUSIONS

The main objective of the last two chapters was to explore the interrelationships between monetary policy and the balance of international payments in a small country like Canada. We discovered that with international capital movements highly sensitive to changes in interest rates, monetary policy has a powerful impact on the balance of payments. Under a regime of fixed exchange rates, this has two implications. On the one hand, the central bank cannot implement monetary policy without concern for its balance of payments implications, and on the other hand, exogenous developments in the balance of payments may dictate the course of monetary policy. Large foreign exchange reserves are a necessary condition for domestic monetary policy to have any degree of independence; but given the power of speculation to move large sums of money across national boundaries in a short period of time, large foreign exchange reserves may not be sufficient to guarantee independence. Perhaps nothing short of greater flexibility of exchange rates can do that.

All of this implies growing demands for foreign exchange reserves in every country in the western world. With the international monetary system tied to a gold base, a reliable mechanism to provide for the growth of aggregate reserves did not exist. The natural mechanism, U.S. international financial intermediation, was viewed with suspicion in many parts of the world, and was subject to serious constraint in the form of a worsening of the United States' own gold reserve ratio. The system proved unstable, and faced increasingly severe trials until the final crisis of 1967-68. The upshot was a patchwork reform of the system: a partial demonetization of gold, and the introduction of a new reserve asset, Special Drawing Rights. It remains to be seen if the long-run results of the innovations will be as salutary as their proponents have promised.

FOOTNOTES

[1] For example see R. G. Bodkin, E. P. Bond, G. L. Reuber and T. R. Robinson, *Price Stability and High Employment: The Options for Canadian Policy*, Economic Council of Canada, Special Study No. 5, (Ottawa: Queen's Printer, 1966) .

[2] If the balance of payments is not in equilibrium at the preferred combination of inflation and unemployment, then one of two situations must exist.
    a. The balance of payments is in *surplus*. In this case, international substitution effects will move the balance of payments toward equilibrium, reducing exports and increasing imports and hence reducing the surplus. However, if the same domestic policy continues to be pursued, the analysis in the text will begin to apply at this point i.e., the balance of payments will move right through equilibrium and into an ever-increasing deficit) .
    b. The balance of payments is in *deficit*. In this case, the substitution effects will aggravate the deficit, forcing a more rapid re-appraisal of the domestic policy.

[3] If the balance of payments is not in equilibrium at the preferred combination of inflation and unemployment then one of two situations must exist.
    a. The balance of payments is in *deficit*. In this case, international substitution effects will move the balance of payments toward equilibrium, increasing exports and reducing imports and hence reducing the deficit. However, if the same domestic policy is continued, the balance of payments will move right through equilibrium into an ever-increasing surplus.
    b. The balance of payments is in *surplus*. In this case, the substitution effects will aggravate the surplus, forcing a more rapid re-appraisal of domestic policy.

[4] A distinction is sometimes made between a freely fluctuating exchange rate, such as that implied in the text, and a floating exchange rate. In the latter, the government intervenes to modulate sharp movements of the rate. The Canadian experiment of 1950-1962 was of the latter type.

[5] The case against exchange rate flexibility has been concisely stated in the International Monetary Fund, *Annual Report*, 1962, pp. 58-67. The first part of this discussion is a reprint of the Fund's 1951 statement on flexible exchange rates, issued shortly after Canada adopted the flexible exchange rate. The second part is a new statement, emphasizing the inflationary risks inherent in flexible exchange rates, issued shortly after Canada abandoned the flexible exchange rate.

[6] The classic analysis of this period, including a powerful and influential statement of the case for the "adjustable peg" exchange rate system is R. Nurkse, *International Currency Experience: Lessons of the Inter-War Period* (Geneva: League of Nations, 1944) .

[7] A short, vigorous statement of the case for flexible exchange rates is presented by H. G. Johnson, "The Case for Flexible Exchange Rates, 1969," in Federal Reserve Bank of St. Louis, *Review*, Vol. 51 (June 1969) , pp. 12-24. A classic statement is that of M. Friedman, "The Case for Flexible Exchange Rates," in *Essays in Positive Economics* (Chicago: University of Chicago Press, 1953) , pp. 157-201.

[8] The Canadian case has been discussed in many places, including Royal Commission on Banking and Finance, *Report* (Ottawa, 1964) , pp. 479-88; and P. Wonnacott,

The Canadian Dollar 1948-1962 (Toronto: University of Toronto Press, 1965).
[9] A review of some of the conceptual problems is presented by R. Clower and R. Lipsey, "The Present State of International Liquidity Theory," in *American Economic Review*, Vol. 58 (May 1968), pp. 586-595.
[10] Note: the rate of return on foreign exchange reserves is not necessarily zero, but rather depends on the composition of the reserve assets held. Gold bears a negative rate of return in that it is expensive to handle and store. Foreign money *per se*, has a zero return, but typically it is held in relatively small quantities (i.e., working balance). Most "foreign exchange" is held in the form of interest-bearing bank deposits or United States government securities.
[11] F. Machlup, "The Need for Monetary Reserves," in Banca Nazionale del Lavoro, *Quarterly Review*, No. 78 (Sept. 1966). This is more readily available as *Reprint No. 5*, Reprints in International Finance, International Finance Section, Princeton University. Professor Machlup's view is also developed in F. Machlup, *International Payments, Debts and Gold* (New York, Charles Scribner's Sons, 1964), Ch. 13.
[12] Machlup, "The Need for Monetary Reserves," pp. 4-26.
[13] *Ibid.*, p. 26.
[14] *Ibid.*, p. 27.
[15] R. Triffin, *The Evolution of the International Monetary System: Historical Reappraisal and Future Perspectives*, Princeton Studies in International Finance, No. 12 (Princeton: Princeton University Press, 1964), pp. 27-29; pp. 66-71.
[16] The Sterling Area emerged in 1931 when the United Kingdom abandoned the gold standard and a number of countries tied their currencies to the new floating pound. It became consolidated in the exchange controls imposed during and after World War II, which made a significant distinction between transactions with Sterling Area countries and transactions with the rest of the World (and particularly the dollar area). Remnants of such restrictions still apply to international investment transactions. Sterling Area countries hold a major part of their reserves in pounds, use the pound as the normal means of international settlement, and look to the London capital market for finance. Although Sterling Area countries have their own stocks of gold and dollars, the British gold reserve is in effect a central reserve for the whole sterling area.
[17] The Franc Area consists of fourteen former French colonies: Cameroon, Central African Republic, Chad, Congo (Brazzaville) and Gabon, (members of the Monetary Union of Cameroon and the Equatorial African States); Dahomey, Ivory Coast, Mauritania, Niger, Senegal, Togo, and Upper Volta (members of the West African Monetary Union); and the Malagasy Republic. At the end of 1968 the total foreign exchange reserves of the Franc area, almost all held in French Francs, were only U.S. $271 million.
[18] This stylized description hardly does justice to the nature and history of the gold standard. Interesting re-interpretations are presented by A. I. Bloomfield, *Monetary Policy under the International Gold Standard, 1880-1914* (Federal Reserve Bank of New York, 1959); and R. Triffin, *op. cit.*
[19] The U.S. Treasury would actually buy at $34.9125 per ounce, and sell at $35.0875.
[20] The authoritative description of the London market is "The London Gold Market," in Bank of England *Quarterly Bulletin*, Vol. IV (Mar. 1964), pp. 16-21.
[21] The willingness of central banks to purchase in the open market also depended on the *location* of the depository in which they wished to hold the gold. It has been estimated that the cost of transporting gold from New York to London was in the neighbourhood of $0.08 per ounce. Thus, if the gold was to be held in Europe, they would buy in the London market at any price below the range $35.16-$35.20. The latter is generally taken as the ceiling price in the market, and was formally made such by the activities of the Gold Pool, referred to in the next paragraph. Almost half of the gold owned by countries other than the United States is actually held in New York. Gold to be added to this stock, of course, would only be purchased in the free market if the price were below $35 per ounce.
[22] The central banks of England, Belgium, France Germany, Italy, the Netherlands and Switzerland, and the Bank for International Settlements.

[23] Germany the United States, Italy, France, Canada.

[24] Netherlands, the United Kingdom, Belgium, Japan, Sweden.

[25] Credits were extended by the central banks of Italy and Germany, the Bank for International Settlements, and the Export-Import Bank of Washington D.C., an American government agency.

[26] The General Arrangements to Borrow have the same exclusiveness about them, and in a sense are outside the framework of the I.M.F. (in spirit, if not in administration). The I.M.F. cannot borrow under this arrangement to supplement its resources for general use — only to extend credits to other members of the Group of Ten. Also, while Switzerland is not a member of the I.M.F., it participates indirectly in the General Arrangements to Borrow through reciprocal bilateral lines of credit with each member of the Group of Ten. Taken together, these eleven countries are commonly called the "Paris Club".

[27] The occasion for the Basle Agreement was the first serious bout of speculation threatening the stability of the international monetary system, which also produced the Gold Pool in whose operations the B.I.S. was intimately involved. It has been emphasized that there was no *written* agreement at Basle, just a recognition of mutual interests in international monetary stability. See F. Hirsch, *Money International* (London: Penguin Press, 1969), Ch. 12. This is an admirably readable book on the whole subject of international finance.

[28] For example, R. I. McKinnon, *Private and Official International Money: The Case for the Dollar,* Princeton University International Finance Section, Essays in International Finance, No. 74, (Princeton, 1969).

[29] The important measures included the interest equalization tax of 1963 and restrictive "guidelines" for banks and non-bank financial institutions extending credit to non-residents and to firms making direct investments abroad. It was an intensification of such measures which produced the Canadian foreign exchange crisis in 1968.

[30] R. Hawkins, "A Critical Survey of Plans for International Monetary Reform," in *The Bulletin,* New York University, Graduate School of Business Administration, Institute of Finance, No. 36 (New York, 1966); R. Hawkins, "Compendium of Plans for International Monetary Reform," *op. cit.,* No. 37-38 (New York, 1966); F. Machlup, *Plans for the Reform of the International Monetary System,* Special Papers in International Economics, No. 3 (Princeton: International Finance Section, Princeton University, 1962).

[31] "New Procedures in the Gold Market," in *International Financial News Survey,* Vol. XX, (March 22, 1968). France had withdrawn from the Gold Pool in July, 1967, reducing the membership from eight to seven. This was taken as further evidence of the rift between France and the United States on international monetary affairs. France's attitudes toward monetary reform stood in sharp contrast to those of the U.S. and most other countries. France distrusted any departure from gold, excessive reliance on the U.S. dollar as international money, and schemes for credit-based reserve creation, particularly on a global basis. From 1959 through 1966 France alone increased its gold holdings by $3,948 million, 46% of the total increase of gold reserves in industrial Europe (excluding the U.K.). France's holdings of foreign exchange were virtually the same in 1966 as in 1959.

France opposed a generalized form of the General Arrangements to Borrow which would have permitted the I.M.F. to use the borrowed funds in its general operations. She also opposed proposals for large scale increases of I.M.F. quotas, and the implementation of the Special Drawing Rights proposal. On French attitudes toward international financial problems see Hirsch, *op. cit.,* Ch. 14.

[32] South African gold was purchased by some central banks which did not subscribe to the 1968 gold policy (e.g., Portugal). In addition, some countries had drawn South African Rands from the I.M.F. As it is entitled to do under the Articles of Agreement, South Africa paid gold rather than convertible currencies when these Rands were presented for conversion. See U.S. Congress, Joint Economic Committee, *The Pedigreed Gold System: A Good System — Why Spoil It?* (Washington, 1969).

[33] See the "Statement" of the Governor for the Fund from South Africa in the *Proceedings* of the annual meeting of the International Monetary Fund, 1969.

23

The Effectiveness of
Monetary Policy

Our theoretical analysis of the impact of monetary policy was inconclusive. The purpose of monetary policy is to regulate aggregate demand
in order to stabilize income, employment and price levels. However, we
were able to demonstrate cases in which, in theory, monetary policy would
have no significant real repercussions, and cases in which monetary policy
would have a powerful impact. Theory may suggest what we should look
for, but theory alone cannot tell us which of the many possible cases is the
relevant one. What, in fact, is the impact of monetary policy on economic
activity? That is an empirical question. Economists' attempts to answer it
provide the substance for this chapter.

1/THE EVIDENCE AND THE ISSUES

The Evidence

One of the frustrations of contemporary monetary economics is that
while most of the important controversies can only be resolved by empirical
research, empirical studies seldom provide conclusive answers. No important
issue is ever completely closed. The availability of new data, new analytical techniques, or new theoretical insights, evokes new studies and hence an
almost unending stream of new evidence to be digested, evaluated and
weighed against previous work. In many cases the evidence from different
studies on any given point is conflicting, without being conclusive one way
or the other (we saw examples of this in our discussion of the demand for
money in Chapter 14). Occasionally, the *same* evidence is subject to dia-
metrically opposed interpretations by different investigators.

An additional source of frustration for the Canadian student is the
limited amount of Canadian evidence on these points. While there have
been some important Canadian empirical studies — and there is a considerable amount of Canadian research underway — much of the evidence on
several basic points must be based on American studies. Unfortunately
American experience is not always directly applicable to Canada.

For these reasons, we cannot hope to provide definitive empirical
answers to the question which we have posed. At best we can hope to

provide a coherent overview of the evidence, some insights into its limitations, and guidance so that the interested students can pursue the relevant literature on their own. In the footnotes we provide a selective guide to the literature. The student should be warned, however, that much of the literature in this field is highly technical, involving advanced techniques of statistical analysis. In fact, the controversy surrounding any given study frequently relates as much to the techniques of analysis employed as to the results obtained.

The Issues

In this discussion we intend to focus attention on three issues, which we can summarize as three questions:

(1) Is the money supply the appropriate variable for the monetary authorities to control, or does our model of monetary policy take too narrow a perspective on the process?

(2) How sensitive are expenditures to monetary variables, including the level of interest rates?

(3) How long and how stable are the time lags which are involved in the operation of monetary policy?

2/IS THE "MONEY SUPPLY" THE APPROPRIATE CONTROL VARIABLE?

The central variable in the theory of monetary policy developed in the preceding chapters is the "money supply", and the central institutions are the central bank and the chartered banks. Thus, as depicted, the process of monetary control is based on the manipulation of the monetary base by the central bank. The chartered banks respond to changes in their cash reserves by expanding or contracting their total assets and liabilities, producing a change in the stock of money in the hands of the general public. Given a stable demand for money function, there will follow, through various channels, sympathetic changes in the levels of interest rates, aggregate expenditures, income, employment and prices.

It has been argued that this is an inappropriate conceptual framework for the analysis of monetary policy because of the almost exclusive emphasis which it gives to the money supply. In fact, this proposition is the starting point for two different types of criticism. According to one school of thought — which we will call the "credit conditions" school — the basic flaw is that the theoretical framework involves *stock variables* rather than *flow variables*. It is argued that the monetary authorities must be concerned with the *flow of credit* to finance capital expenditures by businesses, governments and households, not the *stock of money* in the hands of those businesses, governments and households. The second school — which we will call the "total liquidity" school — accepts the basic analytical approach which places emphasis on stock variables and adjustments in the composition of asset portfolios, but argues that the "money supply" as we have defined it is not the appropriate stock variable for monetary control. In defining money, it is argued, we have arbitrarily selected a particular group of highly liquid assets from a more general set of highly liquid assets, all of which are very close substitutes for each other. The real variable which the central bank should be concerned with is the total liquidity of the economy.

Let us briefly consider these arguments in turn.

The "Credit Conditions" School

An approach to monetary policy which thrusts the flow of credit into the pivotal role bears the authoritative stamp of practitioners of the art of central banking. It has been argued forcefully by central bankers in Canada, the United States and Great Britain, and has been endorsed by major commissions on monetary policy and banking institutions, including the Canadian Royal Commission on Banking and Finance.

Perhaps the most explicit, most extreme and hence most controversial statement of this position was that of a British commission of inquiry into the working of the financial system, commonly called the Radcliffe Committee.[1] The Committee asserted flatly that in the regulation of aggregate demand, "the supply of money itself is not the critical factor".[2] Because of "the impossibility of limiting the velocity of circulation",[3] "spending is not limited by the amount of money in existence . . ." Rather, "it is related to the amount of money people think they can get hold of . . ."[4] In this regard, the availability of funds from financial institutions is particularly important. Thus, "the level of total demand is influenced by the *lending behaviour* of an indefinitely wide range of financial institutions."[5] It is true that the banks, the major creators of money in the financial system, are of "special interest" to the monetary authorities, but this is because the banks are "key lenders in the system", not because they are "creators of money." Thus,

> It is the level of *bank advances* rather than the level of bank deposits that is the object of this special interest; the behaviour of bank deposits is of interest *only* because it has some bearing, along with other influences, on the behaviour of other lenders.[6]

Emphasis on the flow of credit leads logically to the conclusion that the immediate objective of monetary policy should be the regulation of "credit conditions", which the Bank of Canada has defined as:

> the whole range of terms and conditions affecting borrowing and lending and the purchase and sale of financial assets: the level and structure of securities prices and yields, institutional lending and deposit rates, and the various requirements (over and above the payment of a certain rate of interest) which lenders require of borrowers as a condition of making funds available . . .,[7]

or, in short, "the cost, terms and general availability of credit to borrowers".[8]

Particular emphasis is placed on the "availability" of funds for would-be borrowers as opposed to the "cost" of funds. This implies a rationing of loans by financial institutions on other than a strictly price basis. Because of standards of credit-worthiness, collateral requirements, and various other qualitative aspects of the loan transaction, the funds may not always go to the highest bidder, and because of variations in credit standards, a tightening of credit conditions may not be fully reflected in observed rises in interest rates. Indeed, the American Commission on Money and Credit concluded that "the direct effects of a restrictive monetary policy appear to work mainly through the availability of funds to would-be borrowers,"[9] and in its typically blunter style, the Radcliffe Committee noted that while the effects of interest rate changes on borrowing and expenditures may be overwhelmed by other factors, "if the money for financing the project cannot be got on any tolerable terms at all, that is the end of the matter."[10] However, it is generally agreed that changes in the level of interest rates are an essential aspect of the process. At a minimum, as the Porter Commission argued, changes in interest rates tend to parallel changes in credit availability, even though they may not reflect fully changes in the *intensity* of credit rationing. At a maximum, changes in interest rates play a vital role in affecting financial institutions' willingness to lend, a point much emphasized by both the Federal Reserve System and the Radcliffe Committee. Indeed, because of such indirect effects on the lending behaviour of financial institutions, the Radcliffe Committee concluded that "the authorities . . . have to regard the structure of interest rates rather than the supply of money as the centrepiece of monetary action."[11]

Money Creation versus Credit Creation. We saw in Chapter 16 that banks necessarily create credit at the same time that they create money, since bank assets (credit) and bank liabilities (money) expand (or contract) together. Control of the money supply also implies control of aggregate bank credit.

Moreover, according to the theory of monetary policy which we developed in Chapter 20, given a stable demand-for-money function, the supply of money and the level of interest rates are closely related. By manipulating the money supply, the central bank creates disequilibria in private asset portfolios, inducing substitution among assets, lowering the yield on financial instruments and making investments in real assets relatively more attractive. In this framework, interest rates (the cost of credit) provides the essential link between monetary policy and the real sector of the economy.

Does it not follow, therefore, that apart from a question of what aspect of the process is emphasized, an approach to monetary policy which focuses on the control of the stock of money and an approach which focuses on the flow of credit are for all practical intents and purposes identical?

There is an important element of truth in such a proposition. Indeed, in many respects the true antithesis of the "'credit" position is the strong monetarist position of the modern quantity theorists (which we will consider further below) rather than the modified Keynesian theory of monetary policy which we developed in Chapters 19 and 20. Yet there are some issues of substance involved in the differential emphasis on money and credit.

Stability of the Demand for Money. One basic empirical issue on which the two approaches differ is the stability of the demand for money function. Confidence in the efficacy of management of the money supply must rest on the belief that money is an asset with unique characteristics for which there is a relatively stable demand function. Only then will changes in the money supply have predictable effects. The credit conditions approach rests on the assumption that the demand for money is not stable — and in particular that the relationship between money and the level of income is not predictable. Thus, the Radcliffe Commission concluded that velocity is simply "a statistical concept that tells us nothing directly of the motivation that influences the level of total demand".[12]

We referred to some of the empirical literature on the demand for money in Chapter 19, and will not repeat that discussion here. Suffice it to note that this is a field in which there is an extensive empirical literature and in which there is a large volume of research activity going forward, partly breaking new ground and partly re-assessing old conclusions. There is general agreement among empirical researchers that there is a relatively stable demand for money, but there is an extremely wide range of opinion as to the nature of that demand function. Thus, although a policy of more conscious management of the money supply *per se* is attractive on theoretical grounds, it is difficult to argue that the empirical basis for such a policy is well established.

A Question of Tactics? This conclusion suggests that the credit conditions approach to monetary policy represents an *ad hoc* accommodation by central bankers in the face of uncertainty about the underlying demand for money. However, there are also at issue more fundamental questions about the *tactics* of monetary management.

One of the important points of the credit conditions approach is that it admits of a wide range of credit control policies in addition to, or as alternatives for, management of the money supply, all of which are asserted to be efficacious in regulating the level of aggregate demand.

The Porter Commission and the Radcliffe Committee both placed considerable emphasis on *debt management* as a technique of policy, where debt management is broadly defined as all operations by the government or the central bank to change the *composition* (not the *size*) of the government debt in the hands of the general public. Debt management is an important theme in the total liquidity school's analysis, and we will return to it again in that context. Suffice it to note at this point that the Porter Commission argued that a flexible debt management policy could be used in conjunction with monetary adjustments to spread the effects of monetary policy more quickly, to alter specific strategic interest rates, and to bring about timely adjustments in particular regions of "the whole range of credit conditions".[13] The Radcliffe Committee envisaged an even more aggressive role for debt management operations.

Perhaps even more characteristic of the credit conditions approach is an emphasis on the efficacy of various types of *direct controls* over lending activities, particularly in times of severe inflationary pressures. The Radcliffe Committee frequently referred to the importance of controlling bank advances, and endorsed compulsory liquid asset ratios for banks.[14] It rejected the extension of direct controls over lending activities of other financial institutions, but only on the administrative grounds that they would not work because of the continual emergence of new types of financial intermediaries.[15] Similarly, the Committee rejected selective direct controls over credit as a normal operating procedure, but asserted that "in some circumstances, . . . control of this kind might be preferable to exclusive reliance on monetary measures".[16]

In a similar vein, the Governor of the Bank of Canada argued the merits of moral suasion as a technique of policy for controlling bank loans in his testimony before the Porter Commission.[17] Like the Radcliffe Commission, the Porter Commission rejected such direct controls as normal operating procedure, but recognized that "there may be occasions" when they are valuable.[18] The Commission also endorsed the use of variable secondary reserve ratios as a measure to regulate bank advances, and urged the extension of cash reserve requirements to other lending institutions.[19]

It should be noted that the credit conditions analysis assigns pariicular importance to loans and advances by financial intermediaries as opposed to purchases of securities which are actively traded in the open market. It follows that a change in the *composition* of the asset portfolios of banks and other financial institutions is ascribed important effects, even though the total size of asset holdings (and hence the size of liabilities) does not change. In particular, an increase in bank loans, financed by sales of short-term securities in the open market, is assumed to have an expansionary effect on aggregate demand, even though the total money supply has not increased.

In one sense, then, the difference between the credit conditions and the money supply analysis is simply a difference of perspective in terms of which variables should be controlled directly and which should be treated as a residual. On the one hand, the money supply model argues that the money supply should be controlled, with the structure of interest rates and other aspects of "credit conditions" left to be determined in the market. On the other hand, the extreme version of the credit model argues that various dimensions of "credit conditions" ought to be controlled by whatever means necessary, leaving the money supply to be determined in the market at whatever quantity is demanded at the established set of "credit conditions".

Non-Bank Financial Intermediaries. Finally, it is important to note that the credit conditions approach implies that the lending activities of a broader range of financial institutions than money-creating commercial banks are of direct concern to the central bank. The model provides an *a priori* case for the extension of formal central bank controls (such as compulsory cash reserve requirements) to such institutions, although it has been argued on empirical grounds that such controls are not necessary. We will return to this point below.

The "Total Liquidity" School

What we will call the total liquidity school has certain points in common with the credit conditions school, particularly concern over the implications of the operations of non-bank financial intermediaries, and emphasis on the role of debt management as an instrument of stabilization policy. However, whereas the credit conditions analysis focused attention on the lending behaviour of financial institutions, the liquidity model focuses attention on the portfolio balance decisions of assetholders and the liability side of the balance sheets of financial institutions. In this sense, then, it is simply a more generalized version of the analysis which we developed in Chapters 19 and 20, but it takes explicit account of, and explores more completely the implications of, the existence and creation of close substitutes for money.

Near Money and Near Banks. The problem of distinguishing between money and near money has arisen at various places in our analysis. If we employ a narrow payments definition of money, then all short-term financial assets which are readily convertible into money on short notice and at a certain or almost certain price can be considered near money. This includes short-term, non-monetary claims on banks and other financial intermediaries, and various types of money market instruments, particularly short-term claims on the government and some commercial and finance paper. As we noted earlier, some economists employ broader definitions of money, in which case the definition of near money must be adjusted correspondingly.

Most, but far from all, of the stock of near money takes the form of liabilities of near banks. One of the striking features in the development of the financial systems of both the United States and Canada in the years since World War II has been the much more rapid rate of growth of the stock of near money than of the stock of money. Thus, as we saw in Chapter 9, within the banking system proper, personal savings deposits and time deposits have increased much more rapidly than have demand deposits, and near banks have grown much more rapidly than the banks (see also Chapter 10). It is the implications of these facts for the effectiveness of monetary policy which are the primary concern of the liquidity school.

Near Banks and the Effectiveness of Monetary Policy. In Chapter 20 we explored various cases in which monetary policy would be relatively ineffective. One of these was the case in which the demand for money was highly interest-elastic, with the Keynesian liquidity trap representing the extreme situation. The basic hypothesis of the liquidity school is that *the growth of near banks as suppliers of near money has increased the interest-elasticity of the demand for money sufficiently to seriously impair the effectiveness of control over the money supply as a technique for regulating aggregate demand.*

This hypothesis rests on two basic propositions: (1) that there is a very high degree of substitutability between money and near money in asset portfolios, such that near monies are much closer substitutes for money than are other financial or real assets, and (2) that there is a high elasticity of supply of near monies. With respect to the second proposition, much emphasis is placed on the activities of the near banks.

It is argued that the rise in interest rates associated with a restrictive monetary policy will increase the profitability of financial intermediation. Unhampered by high, legally enforced cash reserve requirements, near banks will be induced to compete more aggressively for deposits. As we saw in Chapter 16, an expansion of deposits at near banks can occur without any loss of deposits by the banks, and the net effect will be an expansion of the total stock of highly liquid deposits. The banks may well respond, offering more attractive rates on savings and time deposits, and hence participating in the growth of the stock of near money, although savings and time deposits at banks are subject to cash reserve requirements and both in Canada and the United States for many years there were official limits on the interest rates which banks could charge on loans (Canada) or pay on deposits (United States), both of which limited the extent to which the banks could profitably meet the competition of the near banks. In any case, a restrictive monetary policy should make near money a more attractive liquid asset than (non-interest-bearing) money. The stock of near money should expand relative to the stock of money, and near banks should expand relative to banks.

Thus it is argued that the creation of near money makes it possible for assetholders to economize on holdings of money without seriously impairing the liquidity of their portfolios. The higher rates of interest earned on near money overcomes the inconvenience and transactions costs associated with smaller money balances. The effect will be to increase the velocity of circulation of money. Money previously held idle as an asset is replaced by near money, and the money is placed in active circulation through the lending operations of the banks and near banks. A larger flow of transactions and hence higher levels of expenditures, income, employment and prices can be achieved with the same stock of money. To this extent the impact of restrictive monetary policy has been muted.[20]

This hypothesis can also be interpreted in terms of the credit conditions framework. An increase in deposits at near banks simultaneously increases their lending capacity. To the extent that any reduction in the flow of credit from the banks is offset by an increased flow of credit from the near banks, the aggregate effects of monetary policy will be weakened.

Implications for Policy. An extreme version of the liquidity hypothesis is represented by the Radcliffe Committee's assertion that there is no limit to the velocity of circulation of money.[21] This implies that assetholders regard money and near money as perfect substitutes, and that there is no constraint on the ability of near banks to expand their asset and liability holdings. In such circumstances, control of the money supply is futile, since money is but one part of a homogeneous mass of liquid assets. To limit the money supply is like squeezing a balloon: air (liquidity) which is forced out of one area of the balloon reappears elsewhere. The *entire* impact of the restriction of the money supply is absorbed within the financial system. Monetary policy is useless. What is required is a policy of regulating the aggregate stock of liquid assets.

In a less extreme version of the liquidity hypothesis, money and near money are very close, but less than perfect substitutes: a restriction of the money supply will be only *partially offset* by the expansion of the supply of near money. This suggests that the creation of near monies increases the intensity with which monetary restraint must be imposed to achieve any given real effects. However, in either case the efficiency of monetary policy would be improved by controlling the stock of liquid assets rather than the money supply. This means that near banks should be brought within the same framework of central bank controls (e.g., cash reserve requirements) as the banks. It also means that debt management operations may be an effective instrument of stabilization policy.

We defined debt management operations as transactions to alter the composition (as opposed to the size) of the government debt in the hands of general public, for example, swapping longer-term bonds for short-term securities. Such operations can be conducted by the treasury, issuing new securities and retiring outstanding issues, or by the central bank, simultaneously buying and selling securities out of its portfolio. As we pointed out earlier, monetary policy is simply an aspect of debt management, at least when it is effected through open market operations. The central bank simply exchanges non-interest-bearing, demand debts of the government (currency or bank reserves) for longer-term interest-bearing debt. Remember, however, that the expression "debt management" is usually used in the narrower sense to refer to changes in the composition of the interest-bearing (i.e., non-monetary) government debt.

Short-term government securities rank among the important liquid assets in the economy. It is argued, therefore, that the overall liquidity of the economy will be reduced if the government increases the average term-to-maturity of the public debt, selling long-term securities and retiring short-term securities, and that this will have a restrictive effect on the level of economic activity. Similarly, the liquidity of the economy can be increased by reducing the average term-to-maturity of the public debt (increasing the proportion of the debt which is in short-term forms) and this will have a stimulating effect on economic activity.[22]

The liquidity model suggests that debt management operations can have a powerful impact on aggregate demand and on economic activity, and hence that debt management operations ought to be coordinated with traditional monetary policies in an overall policy to regulate the liquidity of the economy. Indeed, the Radcliffe Committee, in advocating a version of the "whole liquidity" model, asserted that "we find control of the supply of money to be no more than an important facet of debt management."[23]

Clearly, the liquidity model is an important hypothesis which merits careful empirical investigation.

Empirical Evidence. As in other aspects of the empirical evidence which we have surveyed, the evidence on this point is mixed and uncertain, and most of it relates to experience in the United States.

We have already seen (Chapter 20), that the velocity of money in Canada has displayed a pronounced cyclical pattern, rising in periods of rising economic activity and restrictive monetary policy, and falling in periods of declining activity and easier monetary policy. As is evident in Figure 20-1, this pattern overlays an apparent upward trend in velocity in recent years. Similar behaviour of velocity is evident in the United States.

However, to what extent are these changes in velocity a result of the activities of near banks and to what extent are they a result of more general portfolio adjustments, of which the substitution of money for near money is only one aspect?

There have been two types of relevant studies. Some investigators have attempted to estimate directly the degree of substitutability between money and near money, and others to examine the responses of near banks to changes in monetary policy.

The degree of substitutability between money and near money can be measured by the elasticity of the demand for money with respect to the rate of interest on near monies. We saw in Chapter 19 that there is fairly strong evidence that the demand for money has some sensitivity to interest rates. The relevant questions, then, are: is there any empirical evidence that near monies are closer substitutes for money than are other financial assets, and if so, is the indicated elasticity of demand for money sufficiently great to provide substantial justification for the liquidity school's concerns?

On the first point, the evidence is contradictory. A well-known study by M. J. Hamburger, using U.S. data, showed that yields on near monies had no greater effect on household's demands for money than did yields on other financial instruments.[24] By contrast, studies by T. H. Lee, also using U.S. data, came to exactly the opposite conclusion.[25] That is, they showed a significantly higher elasticity of demand for money with respect to interest rates on near money than on any other class of financial instruments. A subsequent interchange between Hamburger and Lee did not fully resolve the issue, although it did suggest a balance of present evidence in Lee's favour.[26]

However, and this is a vitally important point, even if we accept Lee's conclusion that near monies are *better* substitutes for money than are other financial assets, the indicated interest elasticity of demand is not so high as to come anywhere near supporting the extreme liquidity school position. It is true that money and near money are substitutes, but they are clearly not perfect substitutes. Far from approximating infinity, the cross-elasticity of demand suggested by Lee's study is in the neighbourhood of −0.6.[27]

The second group of studies focused attention on the cyclical characteristics of the flow of funds to near banks. In the United States, studies by I. Friend[28] and A. R. Benavie[29] found no evidence that near banks gained funds systematically and significantly at the expense of banks in periods of monetary restraint. Indeed, Benavie found evidence that in periods of monetary restraint, near banks lost deposits, thus reinforcing the impact of monetary policy, not weakening it. With respect to Canadian near banks, the Porter Commission came to essentially the same conclusion, although they did express some concern about the behaviour of sales finance and consumer loan companies.[30] However, the Commission did argue that on equity grounds and to increase the certainty of the impact of monetary policy, near banks ought to be subject to the same reserve requirements as chartered banks.

By and large, the impact of debt management operations on aggregate demand remains a matter of theoretical speculation. Little empirical work has been done which would justify some of the extreme claims for the power of changes in the average term-to-maturity of the public debt. Beginning in 1961, a notable experiment in the use of debt management techniques was conducted in the United States. Commonly called "operation twist", this was an attempt to "twist" the term structure of interest rates to help reconcile the domestic and the international objectives of policy. It was thought that higher short-term interest rates would attract foreign capital and thus help solve the balance of payments problem, whereas lower long-term interest rates were necessary to achieve appropriate domestic economic expansion. Two attempts to evaluate the impact on interest rates arrived at contradictory conclusions. A study by Modigliani and Sutch found that the behaviour of the term structure of interest rates at this time could be adequately explained by developments other than operation twist.[31] However, in another econometric study, using a different specification of the equations which determine the levels of long-term and short-term interest rates, T. Holland found evidence that operation twist had in fact raised the short-term rate without lowering the long-term rate, thus partially achieving the immediate objective of the policy.[32] Holland did not explore the ultimate impact on either the balance of international payments or domestic expenditures.

Canadian debt management experience is dominated by the Conversion Loan of 1958. In one operation, almost 60% of the outstanding public debt of Canada was refunded into longer-term securities, increasing the average term-to-maturity from 6 years and 4 months to 10 years and 6 months. We still lack a full assessment of the impact of the Conversion Loan (as distinct from all of the other developments at this time), but some evidence has been presented to suggest that it did have a significant restrictive effect on aggregate demand. Indeed, one Canadian economist, C. Barber, has argued that the Conversion Loan was the primary cause of subsequent deflationary pressures in the Canadian economy.[33] The Porter Commission did not fully subscribe to Barber's conclusion, but did agree that the Conversion Loan and a few other significant changes in the term-structure of the Canadian public debt had some repercussions on economic activity.[34]

In a slightly different vein, A. Breton found that the average term to maturity of the public debt was an important determinant of the velocity of circulation of money in Canada during the period 1935-59.[35] Increases in the average term to maturity were associated with lower velocity. Breton's hypothesis was that the reduction in the liquidity of the economy associated with the lengthening of the average term of the public debt increased the quantity of money demanded at any given level of income, or, alternatively, reduced the level of income which could be supported on any given supply of money.

These bits of evidence are far too sketchy to make a conclusive case. Perhaps all we can safely conclude is that there is limited empirical support for some aspects of a moderate version of the total liquidity hypothesis, but that much more research is necessary before we can place much confidence in the theoretical speculations of extreme versions of this position.

3/HOW SENSITIVE IS AGGREGATE DEMAND TO MONETARY VARIABLES?

Our theoretical analysis in Chapter 20 suggested a second dimension to the determinants of the effectiveness of monetary policy — the sensitivity of real expenditures to monetary variables, whether these variables be defined as the money supply, the total liquidity position of the economy, the level of interest rates, or credit conditions. As we shall see, studies of the real impact of monetary policy fall into two groups, those in the Keynesian tradition which attempt to measure the impact on specific categories of expenditure, and those in the quantity theory tradition which attempt to measure a much more general impact on economic activity. Both sets of studies have been concerned with two closely related but separable aspects of the real impact of monetary policy, magnitude and timing. In this section we will be concerned with the question of magnitudes. In the next section we will review the evidence on time lags.

Nature of the Evidence

The evidence relating to the sensitivity of expenditures to changes in monetary variables is of three basic types: surveys of decision-makers, partial econometric studies of the determinants of expenditures, and complete econometric models of the economy.

Surveys. The basic approach of the survey technique is to ask decision-makers, in a written questionnaire or, preferably, in an interview, about the factors affecting their expenditure decisions, and particularly about the role of such monetary variables as interest rates and the availability of credit. Such surveys have been used to study both consumption and investment decisions, but it is the investment studies which have received most attention in the literature on monetary policy.

Surveys have been criticized on various grounds, some highly specific to the survey in question (the nature of the sample selected, the framing of the questions, failure to follow up non-responses to mail questionnaires, etc.), and some relating to the technique in general.[36] It is argued that in a large, complex firm, there is always a problem of finding the man (or men) actually responsible for making the relevant decisions; that investment decisions are always very complex, and affected by so many considerations that respondents have difficulty in isolating the specific effects of one variable, like interest rates; that answers to hypothetical questions ("what would you do if . . .") are inherently unreliable, and answers to questions about actual decisions suffer from the fact that the relevant events are always in the past and memories fade quickly so that the "facts" of the decisions get distorted; that respondents may lack the motivation to reply accurately since they are busy, may not take the problem seriously, may be already satiated by form-filling required by governments and others, and may fear that the information may be used in a way which is inimicable to the interests of the firm; that attention is almost inevitably focused on major decisions with the result that many minor decisions, which add up to a considerable effect, may be overlooked; and that indirect effects, working through the impact of monetary policy on their customers and hence on the demand for their product and their own investment decisions, for example, may not be understood by the respondents themselves. All things considered, it is widely argued that such surveys tend to be biased in the direction of finding little response to monetary policy.

Perhaps the most comprehensive and most intensive survey of the reaction of businesses to monetary policy, and the one with the fewest technical faults, was that conducted by J. H. Young and J. F. Helliwell for the Royal Commission on Banking and Finance.[37] However, even its results have been criticized as understating the impact of monetary restraint on business investment.[38]

Partial Econometric Studies. Econometric studies approach the problem through the application of advanced statistical techniques, in the attempt to find the equation which best "explains" the behaviour of some economic variable like investment or consumption in terms of a set of explanatory variables like interest rates or national income. What we call "partial" studies focus on one category of expenditures (the "dependent variable") in isolation from all others, taking the explanatory variables in the equation as "predetermined" or "exogenous" for the problem at hand.

Econometrics involves the joint application of statistical methods and economic theory.[39] Thus, while such studies typically test various combinations of explanatory variables to find that combination which explains the largest part of the observed variation of the dependent variable, a statistical procedure, the variables selected for testing in this way are those suggested by economic theory. Moreover, for a variable to be included in the final version of the equation, its co-efficient must pass two tests, one statistical and one theoretical.

The statistical test is that the coefficient of the variable must be "statistically significant". Statistical methods of estimating equations involve the application of probability theory. Thus, the coefficients estimated by econometric procedures are taken as probabilistic estimates of the true coefficient. The true magnitude of the coefficient may be different from the estimated magnitude. Indeed, even though the equation provides an estimate of the coefficient, the true magnitude of that coefficient may be zero (indicating that that variable plays no role in explaining the behaviour of the dependent variable). However, the statistical procedure also assigns probabilities to possible variations of the true magnitude from the estimated magnitude. If a coefficient is statistically significant, the estimated probability that the true value is in fact zero must be so low that the investigator feels he can safely ignore that possibility.

If a coefficient is statistically significant, it must also satisfy a theoretical test before it can be accepted as an estimate of the effects of the variable in question. It must have the "right sign" ($+$ or $-$). That is, the direction of the effect of the variable must be that predicted by economic theory in those cases where theory provides an unambiguous prediction of the direction of the effect. For example, it frequently happens that interest rates are statistically significant in equations explaining investment behaviour, but the coefficient has a positive sign (investment expenditures increase if interest rates rise) rather than the negative sign predicted by theory. In such circumstances the investigator usually concludes that something is wrong with the equation: that for some reason the statistical procedure is assigning to interest rates the effects of some other, unknown variables which have not been included in the equation. In these circumstances, the estimate is usually rejected.

Like surveys, partial econometric studies also suffer from faults which are specific to the individual studies (e.g., failure to use the best data, inappropriate specification of the equation, etc.) and from problems which are endemic to the type of analysis. The lack of fully appropriate data is a common complaint. Econometric studies usually have to make do with statistics describing the historical record, and recorded for many diverse other purposes. Thus the econometrician has to take his observations as given by recorded history: he cannot experiment like the scientist in his laboratory, and he cannot go back to correct the errors of those who initially recorded the "facts". This gives rise to a common technical problem, the inability of the statistical method to distinguish between the effects of two variables which, in the historical record, are highly correlated with each other (a condition technically known as multicollinearity). This problem commonly plagues monetary variables like interest rates, making it particularly difficult to isolate the impact of monetary policy.

Perhaps an even more fundamental problem, however, is inherent in the fact that the studies in question are partial analyses: they focus on a single equation in isolation. To do so, the econometrician must take as "given", variables which are in fact partially determined by the process which he is studying. Thus, in attempting to estimate the effects of interest rates on the level of investment expenditures, he takes the record of interest rate changes as an independent determinant of investment decisions and assumes that the line of causation runs simply from interest rates to investment. In fact, however, the behaviour of investment expenditures will, directly or indirectly, partly determine the behaviour of interest rates (as is evident from the theoretical discussion of Chapter 20). Thus, an increase in investment as a result of other developments will produce a rise in interest rates which will then be detected by the statistical procedure as partly determining the rise in investment.

This problem — commonly called the simultaneous equation bias — plagues single equation studies in varying degrees. In general, it is suspected that simultaneous equation bias tends to produce under-estimates of the impact of monetary variables like interest rates. The advantage of complete econometric models is that, at least in principle, they provide a method of surmounting this particular problem.

Econometric Models. An econometric model is a description of an economy, or part of an economy, in terms of a set of equations. Unlike the partial econometric studies, a complete econometric model allows for the complex pattern of interdependencies among variables in the economic system. Thus, to take a simple example, interest rates are allowed to influence investment, and investment to influence interest rates, and the coefficients in the various equations are estimated so as to allow for both types of effects simultaneously. In principle, this should make it possible to identify each of the effects separately, and hence more accurately assess the impact of monetary policy.

A complete econometric model describes the structure of an economic system. It is then possible to take the set of structural equations, change a single variable like the money supply, and trace its effects through the system. In general, the effects will be very complex, but we can focus attention on the few key variables like gross national product, employment, prices or the state of the balance of payments in which we have particular interest. Such exercises are called *simulation experiments.* Using this technique, we can not only assess the impact of monetary policy, but also assess the effects of alternative policy instruments, including the differential effects of monetary and fiscal policy.

Econometric model building is also plagued by problems of faulty data and multicollinearity of variables. It should also be noted that the estimation of econometric models is a very expensive and time-consuming process. The computational problems alone are staggering, particularly when many different estimations have to be attempted to find the "best fit". The whole procedure would be impossible without large-capacity, high-speed electronic computers.

In addition to the technical problems of estimation with faulty data, the basic problem with econometric models is a product of their chief virtue — the explicit recognition of interdependence in the economic system. Because of the complex pattern of interdependence among the equations of the model, errors in any single equation can have magnified effects throughout the model.

Almost every model has perplexing, sometimes anomalous, results in some equations. The danger exists that these will seriously bias the results of simulation experiments. Again, because of the very high degree of interdependence between monetary variables and other sectors of the economy, the monetary relationships in which we are interested may be particularly vulnerable to this risk.

A Word of Warning. In this section we have tried to emphasize the general limitations of the available evidence on the impact of monetary policy. All of the findings to date must be regarded as tentative. However, it is important that the results not be dismissed out of hand because of the very obvious difficulties in the research procedures. As time passes, and as the evidence of many careful studies accumulates, a reliable picture of the impact of monetary policy is emerging. The faults of earlier studies should be taken as a challenge, not as a basis for rejection of all research in the area.

The Empirical Evidence

Early Studies: Monetary Pessimism. The tone of professional opinion on the impact of monetary policy for two decades was set by a survey of business investment decision-making by a team of economists at Oxford University in the mid-1930's.[40] They discovered that, contrary to received theory, interest rates appeared to play a minor role in investment decisions, and they concluded that investment expenditures would be insensitive to monetary policy actions.

This early study was criticized, partly on technical grounds relating to the composition of the sample, the importance of non-respondents, and the interpretation of responses, and partly because it reflected decisions taken in the abnormal circumstances of the great depression, with interest rates pegged at low levels. However, postwar studies, both surveys and econometric studies, seemed to confirm the Oxford results, and indeed to generalize them to include expenditures by consumers and by state and local governments as well as business capital expenditures and investments in inventories. That is not to say that the studies were unanimous. Indications of some response to monetary variables were found in some studies, but the indicated response was usually weak, and was frequently contradicted in other studies using somewhat different specifications for the equations or somewhat different data. The results, therefore were inconsistent and inconclusive. The only category of expenditure for which strong monetary effects were found consistently was residential construction – and in this case the response was usually attributed to governmental controls over interest rates which induced financial institutions to restrict the availability of mortgage funds in times of rising interest rates, rather than to decisions of house buyers.[41]

From a Canadian point of view, the epitome of the pessimistic post-war empirical position is to be found in research work done for the Royal Commission on Banking and Finance. The Commission sponsored both econometric and survey research on the impact of monetary policy.

Very much in the postwar vein, H. G. Johnson and J. Winder, the authors of the Commission's major econometric study (involving partial analysis), concluded:

> We have had little success – more accurately no greater success than the vast majority of previous econometric research on the effects of monetary policy – in determining any influence of monetary policy on the variables important for economic policy, those that determine the level of employment and activity. On the other hand, . . . our results certainly do not prove that monetary policy has no, or a negligible effect on economic activity: we have detected traces of such influence in certain specific areas, . . . notably new residential construction . . . and of a general influence of money on activity . . .[42]

Most of the Commission's research on the economics of monetary policy focused on Canada during the period of the floating exchange rate.

Monetary policy could be expected to influence the exchange rate through its impact on international capital flows, and changes in the exchange rate could be expected to affect international trade in goods and services. A restrictive monetary policy should have attracted capital, depressed the exchange rate, encouraged imports and discouraged exports, and hence supplemented the domestic effects of monetary policy in restraining aggregate demand. An expansionary monetary policy should have had the opposite effects. In a partial econometric study, R. Shearer found that there were indeed significant effects of monetary policy through this international channel, but like the direct domestic effects explored by Johnson and Winder, the overall impact was very limited in magnitude.[43]

The Commission's major research effort was the survey of the impact of monetary policy on investment decisions referred to earlier. This was an intensive study, involving interviews with responsible officials in almost every major corporation in Canada, and a combination of a mail questionnaire and partial interview survey of a large sample of smaller businesses.[44] Rather than hypothetical events, the focus of attention was on actual periods of restrictive monetary policy in the recent past, and particularly in 1959-1960 (the survey was conducted in 1962-63). The Commission also conducted an ambitious survey of a sample of urban consumers, but with less useful results, and a less formal survey of provincial and municipal decision-making. Largely on the basis of this survey evidence, the Commission concluded that with respect to monetary policy:

> aside from the substantial effects which have on occasion resulted from sharp alterations in the availability of National Housing Act mortgage funds, the domestic effects have been quite limited in the short run.[45]

The Quantity Theory Tradition: Strong Monetarism

Throughout most of the postwar period, nagging criticisms of this pessimistic empirical position were advanced by the few economists who peristed in the quantity theory tradition. Early empirical observations in this vein tended to be rather casual, such as the statement quoted earlier that

> to my knowledge there is no instance in which a substantial change in the stock of money per unit of output has occurred without a substantial change in the level of prices in the same direction.[46]

However, in 1963 two major studies were published which were designed to provide empirical substance to the quantity theory position. One of these was a monumental monetary history of the United States by Friedman and Schwartz,[47] and the other econometric study by Friedman and Meiselman, designed to demonstrate that a simple quantity theory model produced better predictions of changes in the level of economic activity than did a simple Keynesian model.[48]

The Friedman-Meiselman study has been sharply criticized on a number of grounds, some related to the statistical methodology employed, and some related to the specification of the models to be tested. However, the study has been immensely influential in reviving faith in the power of monetary policy, and it has stimulated a spate of other empirical studies.

Some of these studies have been designed to refute the Friedman-Meiselman conclusions for the United States.[49] Others extended the Friedman-Meiselman analysis to other countries, with mixed results. In an early study, G. Macesich found that Canadian experience in the period 1926-1958 tended to confirm the Friedman-Meiselman conclusions on the superiority of the quantity theory formulation.[50] However, in a subsequent note, he reports that when more recent years are included (1959-1965) and slightly different specifications of the Keynesian model are tested, the superiority of the quantity theory model is less clear-cut. Indeed, with some specifications of the Keynesian model, it proved to be superior to the quantity theory model. [51] A. A. Walters and C. R. Barrett report even less success in duplicating the Friedman-Meiselman results for the United Kingdom. They found a mixed pattern, with the quantity theory superior prior to World War I, the Keynesian theory in the inter-war period, and neither model yielding sensible results in the post-World War II period.[52]

Other studies have extended the analysis as an explicit defence of the strength of monetary policy in comparison with Keynesian-inspired fiscal policies. A study of this sort by Anderson and Jordan has attracted much attention.[53] Using much the same methodology as the earlier Friedman studies, but allowing for time lags, they seem to demonstrate a clear superiority of monetary measures over fiscal measures in regulating the level of aggregate demand in the United States. In a similar study for the United Kingdom, Artis and Nobay came to the opposite conclusion.[54]

One of the strong points made by the modern quantity theory school is that the impact of monetary policy on individual sectors of the economy may be relatively small and hence difficult to identify with standard statistical tools, but the effects on individual sectors may add up to a substantial aggregate effect on economic activity. If so, sector by sector studies, such as those referred to above, may seriously under-estimate the overall impact of monetary policy. It is argued, therefore, that it is necessary to seek the impact of monetary actions on a much more general level. It is perhaps significant in this regard that the Johnson-Winder study, referred to above, found little impact of monetary policy in individual sectors (aside from housing), but did find a significant aggregate effect by applying Friedman-style analysis.[55]

Many of the correlations presented by the new quantity theory school are impressive, and the power of their theoretical arguments are frequently persuasive. However, it is difficult to believe that their simple formulations of the empirical analysis really capture the subtleties of the interaction of complex forces in the economy. As in the partial econometric studies referred to earlier, an essential assumption of the analytical methods of the quantity theory models is that the monetary variable, in this case the money supply, is truly an independent variable. If, as seems likely, the growth of the money supply is partly the reaction of the authorities to the growth of the economy, the Friedman method will grossly exaggerate the impact of monetary changes. It will attribute to money responsibility for increases in economic activity which have resulted from other developments, and which have in fact induced the expansion of the money supply. We must regard this analysis also as highly suggestive but inconclusive.

Recent Econometric Models: Renewed Optimism? The strong conclusions of the modern quantity theory school on the effectiveness of monetary policy have begun to receive tentative support from recent attempts to construct elaborate econometric models of whole economies and to use them for simulation experiments tracing the effects of changes in key monetary variables. Econometric model building is not a new art. Several models were developed in the late 1950's and early 1960's, some of which achieved quite remarkable success in economic forecasting.[56] However, the early models were relatively small, did not have well-developed financial sectors (indeed, frequently omitted financial variables), and by and large did not demonstrate substantial monetary effects. An important exception, from the Canadian point of view, was a model by R. Rhomberg published in 1964, which focused on financial variables, including international capital flows, and detected strong monetary effects on investment.[57]

Improvements in computing facilities and econometric techniques have permitted the estimation of larger and more complex models in recent years. So far, preliminary versions of three such models have been reported, the Brookings Institution and the Federal Reserve-M.I.T. models of the United States economy, and the Bank of Canada's model ("RDXI") of the Canadian economy.

The Brookings model, with over 400 equations, is the largest-scale effort of its kind yet to be attempted.[58] Work is continuing to correct certain defects in the model, but interesting simulation experiments have been conducted using a condensed version (176 equations) of the preliminary model. The model identified significant interest rate effects on housing and business investment, and the simulations suggest that, given time, "monetary policy is powerful".[59] Indeed, it would appear that the level of gross national product is more sensitive to changes in the monetary base than to equi-proportionate changes in either the level of government expenditures or personal income taxes.

The Federal Reserve-M.I.T. model is considerably smaller than the Brookings model, but it involves a much more intensive exploration of the financial sector of the economy and of the links between financial variables and real economic activity. Simulation experiments using a preliminary version of this model show even stronger fiscal and monetary effects than those detected by the Brookings model, and also suggest that the monetary effects are stronger than the fiscal effects.[60]

Both of these large-scale models relate to the economy of the United States. However, a preliminary version of a model of the Canadian economy has been published recently by the Research Department of the Bank of Canada,[61] and the results of some early simulation experiments have been reported.[62] This model shows significant interest rate effects on household expenditures on consumer durables and on residential and non-residential construction (and, significantly, on international capital flows and hence on the nation's foreign exchange reserves). Unlike the American models it did not identify such effects on business investment in machinery and equipment. Because the type of simulation experiments reported for the Canadian model differ from those reported for the two American models, it is difficult to compare their implications precisely. However, overall, the model implies that Canadian monetary policy, taken alone, has weaker effects on aggregate demand than those suggested for the United States by the Brookings and Federal Reserve-M.I.T. models. It is highly significant, however, that when Canadian policy is accompanied by a parallel change in American interest rates, the direct impact on Canadian aggregate demand is much increased (and, for many purposes equally significant, the adverse effect of Canadian monetary policy on foreign exchange reserves is much reduced).[63]

It is important to emphasize that the results from these three models are highly tentative. The models themselves are recognized by their builders as preliminary and imperfect, and hence the results of the simulation experiments can only be taken as suggestive. In the Canadian model, in particular, the financial sector is not well developed (it is little more than an examination of some aspects of bank portfolios), and the linkages between monetary variables and real economic activity have not been adequately explored. However, the early results show that econometric model building is a promising new approach to the evaluation of the aggregate impact of monetary policy.

Conclusions: It is difficult to draw any firm, quantitative conclusions from this evidence on the sensitivity of aggregate demand to monetary policy. The trend in the evidence seems to be in the direction of a rejection of the extreme pessimistic position of the early postwar years. The results of recent attempts at large-scale model building suggest stronger effects than anticipated by most economists who rejected research done in the quantity theory tradition. However, given the imperfect nature of these models, it seems likely that the issue will not be definitely settled in the immediate future.

4/HOW LONG ARE THE LAGS IN THE OPERATION OF MONETARY POLICY?

An important subsidiary question in the analysis of the impact of monetary policy relates to the timing of its effects. Granted that monetary policy may have a significant impact on the level of economic activity, it is vitally important to know whether those effects can be achieved in a short period of time or only after a prolonged time lag. If the time lags are short, monetary policy can be a flexible instrument for short-term economic stabilization. If time lags are long, the effective use of monetary policy for such purposes depends on reliable economic forecasting. If monetary policy is powerful but the time lags are long and forecasting is unreliable — and particularly if the time lags are unstable — we may have to abandon the discretionary use of monetary policy for short-term economic stabilization and relate monetary policies to the longer-term growth potentials of the economy. Such an approach to monetary policy has been argued vehemently by some economists, and we will examine it in the next chapter. However, before we turn to it, what is the empirical evidence on time lags in monetary policy?

The Nature of Time Lags

It has become customary in discussions of time lags in monetary policy to distinguish between *inside lags* and *outside lags*. Inside lags reflect time taken in decision-making and implementation by the authorities, i.e., the lapse of time between the emergence of a need for a change in policy (which may only be apparent long after the event) and the taking of action. The authorities make their decisions to alter policy on the basis of their readings of various economic indicators. While some indicators are available with only short delays, e.g., banking statistics, others, such as unemployment figures or statistics of industrial production, are available only after considerable delay. Moreover, all these statistics do not move in unison and as a consequence the authorities initially may be presented with data that paint a conflicting picture of the state of the economy's health. Even once all the indicators or a majority seem to be pointing in a particular direction, the authorities must decide how critical the situation is and what possible moves are required. They may hesitate out of concern to avoid excessive over-reaction which could by itself generate disequilibrium in the economy. In an open economy with a fixed exchange rate, flexible adjustment of monetary policy may also be inhibited by balance of payments considerations.

The outside lag relates to the response of economic activity to the measures taken by the monetary authorities. Part of this lag may occur within the financial system (e.g., in the reaction of the money supply or interest rates to changes in the monetary base), but most attention has been focused on lags in the adjustment of expenditures in response to changes in financial variables. As in the case of the inside lag, the time involved in the recognition of the new situation and in formulating new expenditure plans in light of it, accounts for part of the outside lag. In addition, however, the outside lag has a major technical component. A new construction project, by its very nature, will be spread out over several months (or perhaps years). Time will be required to draft plans, acquire land, call for tenders for equipment and construction, as well as to carry out the actual construction itself. Similarly, a decision to reduce capital expenditures will initially affect only new orders. For some time, the continuing flow of expenditures resulting from past decisions will dominate the statistical record, obscuring the effects of the new decisions.

It is generally accepted that the lags in question will not be *discrete* lags but rather will be *distributed lags*. That is, there will not be a discrete lapse of time between the implementation of policy and the appearance of the effects. Rather, the effects will gradually emerge, building up to a peak and eventually stabilizing (or perhaps tapering off).

The Evidence on Time Lags

Inside Lags. It is generally argued that inside lags are themselves subject to control by the monetary authorities, and hence should not be considered as given data in assessing the potential effectiveness of monetary policy. Improved forecasting techniques, coupled with more decisive decision-making are assumed to be effective in reducing inside lags.[64] However, there have been some attempts to assess the magnitude of the inside lag in the past performance of the monetary authorities. Particularly interesting from a Canadian point of view was Johnson and Winder's study of Canadian monetary policy during the 1950's and early 1960's.[65] They found that on the average there was a lapse of from six to seven months between the end of a cyclical upswing and a change in policy by the central bank, and from seven to nine months between the end of a cyclical downswing and a change in policy. As a result, they concluded that during this period monetary policy in Canada acted in the appropriate direction only one-quarter of the time. However, this startling conclusion must be tempered by the fact that the period which Johnson and Winder studied encompassed a highly abnormal phase in Canadian monetary policy, during which, most economists would agree, Canadian monetary policy was consistently perverse, almost by design (for the years 1958-1961 Johnson and Winder found monetary policy to be in the right direction in only one month out of twelve.) It would be inappropriate to rest the case for the ineffectiveness of monetary policy as stabilization device on evidence drawn from this experience.

Outside Lags. Most of the empirical research on time lags in monetary policy has focused on the outside lags. On these, evidence is gradually accumulating suggesting that the lags are relatively long.

The classic study is that of T. Mayer published in 1958.[66] From an assortment of microeconomic evidence, Mayer concluded:

> a restrictive policy reaches only half its effectiveness five months after the change in credit availability and reaches three-quarters effectiveness only after nine months. An expansionary policy takes even longer — seven months to reach the 50 percent level and ten months to reach the 75 percent level.[67]

Thus, "although a monetary policy itself may be quickly reversed, its effects may not".[68] The persistence of the effects of prior policies can therefore have a serious perverse effect on economic activity.

This theme has been developed vigorously by Professor Milton Friedman and his collaborators in several studies, some of which have already been referred to.[69] From a comparison of changes in the rate of growth of the money supply and cyclical changes in economic activity, Friedman concluded that the average lag in the United States ranged between 12 and 16 months, but that the lag was highly variable. Applying similar analysis to Canadian data, Johnson and Winder discovered a lag which averaged between 5 and 12 months, but also with great variability (e.g., they found lags of up to 20 months).[70]

The Friedman-type analysis of time lags (which involves simply the comparison of turning points in time series) has been severely criticized as involving a grossly simplified and unacceptable methodology. The analysis makes the assumption that the observed fluctuations in economic activity are always caused by prior fluctuations in the rate of growth of the money supply, an assumption which, it is argued, is unwarranted. However, it is interesting that the results of econometric studies tend to confirm Friedman's conclusions.

As we noted earlier, partial econometric studies of expenditures found little evidence of the impact of monetary policy. However, to the extent that such effects were identified, they normally occurred with a time lag of two or three quarters. Similarly, largely on the basis of its survey evidence, the Royal Commission on Banking and Finance concluded that

> a major proportion of the direct effects on employment and output may come within a period ranging from a few weeks to six-nine months, although other effects — both direct and indirect — will extend into later periods.[71]

However, the Commission concluded that these lags were sufficiently short that

> for all but the shortest of cyclical fluctuations the actions of the authorities can play a useful stabilizing role . . .[72]

Recent results from simulation experiments on econometric models, however, suggest even longer lags. Thus, in both the Brookings and Federal Reserve-M.I.T. models of the United States economy, the effects of monetary policy on gross national product are very small initially and only gradually increase to a peak which may be as much as a 6 (Brookings) or 12 (F.R.B.-M.I.T.) *quarters* after the initiation of the policy. Thus, describing the F.R.B.-M.I.T. model, Rasche and Shapiro observe:

> proponents of aggressive monetary policy as an instrument of cyclical stabilization will be disappointed to note that it takes almost two years (7 quarters) for 50 percent of this twelve quarter effect to be realized. Only 17 percent is realized after one year.[73]

The preliminary simulations on the Bank of Canada model, discussed earlier, show a similar pattern of time lags.[74] Using the total effect after 12 quarters as the standard for comparison, 27% of the effect is achieved after one year and 65% after two years. It takes 6 quarters to achieve half of the 12 quarter effect.

Conclusions. For various technical reasons, the measurement of time lags is difficult. Considerable uncertainty must surround the estimates summarized here. However, there is a steadily accumulating body of evidence which suggests that the effects of monetary policy are distributed over an extended period of time, perhaps in excess of two or three years. Moreover, the evidence implies that the effects are very slow to build up to their maximum, much slower, for example, than the effects of various fiscal policies. It has also been argued that the lags are highly variable, a matter which is not resolved by available econometric studies.

Early discussions of the effectiveness of monetary policy tended to focus on the sensitivity of expenditures to such financial variables as interest rates. Evidence of low sensitivity led many economists to reject monetary policy as an effective tool for stabilizing the economy. It was argued by some economists that this pessimism was unwarranted because the degree of sensitivity of expenditures to monetary measures simply told how powerful the monetary measures would have to be to achieve any given real effect. Small sensitivity merely implied massive monetary changes. However, there remained concern about the implications of such massive monetary measures for the stability of the financial system, and we know from our theoretical analysis of Chapter 21 and from the evidence of RDXI that the balance of payments imposes constraints on the degree to which interest rates can be changed independently of changes in the outside world. Thus, the estimated low sensitivity of expenditures to monetary measures remained the basis of earlier monetary pessimism.

Recent studies which suggest much greater sensitivity of aggregate demand to monetary measures partly dispel this earlier pessimism. However, the accumulating evidence that there are long and potentially variable time lags in the operation of monetary policy raises another type of issue regarding the use of monetary policy to stabilize the economy. Will the effects of monetary policy inevitably be perverse? These issues are considered further in the next chapter.

FOOTNOTES

[1] United Kingdom, Committee on the Working of the Monetary System, *Report* (London: H.M.S.O., 1959). Hereafter called the Radcliffe *Report*.

[2] *Ibid.*, p. 133.

[3] *Ibid.*, p. 187.

[4] *Ibid.*, p. 133.

[5] *Ibid.*, p. 134.

[6] *Ibid.*, p. 134.

[7] Bank of Canada, *Evidence of the Governor of the Bank of Canada before the Royal Commission on Banking and Finance* (Ottawa, 1964), p. 119.

[8] Canada, Royal Commission on Banking and Finance, *Report* (Ottawa, 1964), p. 423. Hereafter called the Porter *Report*.

[9] Commission on Money and Credit, *Money and Credit* (Englewood Cliffs, New Jersey: Prentice-Hall, 1961), p. 52. Unlike the British Radcliffe Committee and the Canadian Porter Commission, both of which were appointed by governments, the American Commission on Money and Credit was a private body, established by the Committee for Economic Development, and financed by the Ford Foundation and the Merrill Foundation.

[10] Radcliffe *Report*, p. 131.

[11] *Ibid.*, p. 134. The classic paper setting forth the "availability doctrine" is that of R. Roosa, a long-time official of the Federal Reserve System, "Interest Rates and the Central Bank," in *Money, Trade and Economic Growth, Essays in Honor of J. H. Williams* (New York: Macmillan, 1951), pp. 270-295. Roosa argued that a small change in yields on government bonds would be sufficient to deter financial institutions from selling bonds to make loans. This so-called "locked-in" effect of interest rate changes has been subject to much critical analysis, and has been largely discredited. The availability principle is also evident in the Federal Reserve's insistence on "free reserves" as the indicator of monetary ease or tightness rather than total reserves of the money supply.

[12] Radcliffe *Report*, p. 133.

[13] Porter *Report*, pp. 425-426; 449-450.

[14] Radcliffe *Report*, p. 180.

[15] *Ibid.*, p. 134.

[16] *Ibid.*, p. 184.

[17] Bank of Canada, *Evidence of the Governor*, p. 52.

[18] Porter *Report*, p. 448.

[19] *Ibid.*, pp. 391-393.

[20] The seminal paper in this line of analysis is that of Professors J. G. Gurley and E. H. Shaw, "Financial Aspects of Economic Development," in *American Economic Review*, Vol. 45 (Sept. 1955), pp. 515-538. An explicit statement of the above analysis of velocity is presented in J. G. Gurley, in "Discussion of 'Agenda for a National Monetary Commission'," in *American Economic Review*, Vol. 48 (May 1958), pp. 103-105. More difficult is J. Tobin and W. C. Brainard, "Financial Intermediaries and the Effectiveness of Monetary Controls," in *American Economic Review*, Vol. 53 (May 1963), pp. 383-400.

[21] Inasmuch as we discussed the Radcliffe Committee earlier in connection with the credit conditions model, it may seem strange to re-introduce it in connection with the liquidity analysis. The Radcliffe analysis straddles the two approaches. Thus, at one point, the Committee concludes "It is the *whole liquidity position* that is relevant to spending decisions" (p. 132). Some attention is paid to the liquidity of spending units, with considerable emphasis being placed in this regard on the funds which the spenders *think* are available to them through borrowing. However, the main focus of the Radcliffe analysis is on the liquidity position of financial institutions, and this provides the strong link with the credit conditions analysis.

[22] The standard discussion of the theory of debt management is J. Tobin, "An Essay on the Principles of Debt Management," in Commission on Money and Credit, *Fiscal and Debt Management Policies* (Englewood Cliffs, New Jersey: Prentice-Hall, 1963), pp. 143-218. It is not an easy paper to read, however.

[23] Radcliffe *Report* p. 183. The Porter Commission viewed debt management in a similar framework, but concluded that the impact of debt management operations was somewhat less than that implied by the Radcliffe Committee. Cf., Porter *Report*, pp. 450-456.

[24] M. J. Hamburger, "The Demand for Money by Households, Money Substitutes and Monetary Policy," in *Journal of Political Economy*, Vol. 74 (Dec. 1966), pp. 600-623.

[25] T. H. Lee, "Substitutability of Non-Bank Intermediary Liabilities for Money: The Empirical Evidence," in *Journal of Finance*, Vol. 21 (Sept. 1966), pp. 441-457; "Alternative Interest Rates and the Demand for Money; The Empirical Evidence," in *American Economic Review*, Vol. 57 (Dec. 1967), pp. 1168-1181.

[26] H. Galper, M. J. Hamburger and T. H. Lee, "Alternative Interest Rates and the Demand for Money: Comments and Reply," *American Economic Review*, Vol. 59 (June 1969), pp. 401-407.

[27] Lee presents several different estimates of the elasticity of the demand for money with respect to the rate of interest on near money. Most of these estimates fall in the range −0.4 to −0.7.

[28] I. Friend, "The Effects of Monetary Policies on Non-Monetary Financial Institutions and Capital Markets", in Commission on Money and Credit, *Private Capital Markets* (Englewood Cliffs, New Jersey: Prentice-Hall, 1964), pp. 1-172.

[29] A. Benavie, "Intermediaries and Monetary Policy," in *Michigan Business Reports*, No. 48 (Ann Arbor, Michigan: University of Michigan, Bureau of Business Research, 1965).

[30] Porter *Report*, pp. 216-222.

[31] F. Modigiliani and T. Sutch, "Innovations in Interest Rate Policy," in *American Economic Review*, Vol. 56 (May 1966), pp. 178-197.

[32] T. E. Holland, " 'Operation Twist' and the Movement of Interest Rates and Related Economic Time Series," in *International Economic Review*, Vol. 10 (Oct. 1969), pp. 260-265.

[33] C. L. Barber, *The Canadian Economy in Trouble*: *A Brief to the Royal Commission on Banking and Finance* (Winnipeg, 1962) .

[34] Porter *Report*, pp. 450-456.

[35] A. Breton, "A Stable Velocity Function for Canada?" in *Economica*, New Series, Vol. 35 (Nov. 1968) , pp. 452-453. Similar findings are reported by Johnson and Winder in a study for the Royal Commission on Banking and Finance, H. G. Johnson and J. W. L. Winder, *Lags in the Effects of Monetary Policy*, Working Paper Prepared for the Royal Commission on Banking and Finance (Ottawa: The Queen's Printer, 1964) , pp. 163-168.

[36] See W. H. White, 'Interest Inelasticity of Investment Demand — the Case from Business Attitude Surveys Re-examined," in *American Economic Review*, Vol. 46 (Sept. 1956) , pp. 565-587.

[37] J. H. Young and J. F. Helliwell, "The Impact of Monetary Policy on Corporations," Royal Commission on Banking and Finance, *Appendix Volume*, pp. 305-435.

[38] W. H. White, "The Stronger Effects of Monetary Policy on Corporations," in Economic Council of Canada, *Conference on Stabilization Policies* (Ottawa: Queen's Printer, 1966) . pp. 53-88; J. H. Young and J. F. Helliwell, "Comments", *op. cit.*, pp. 89-97.

[39] Econometrics is a highly technical field, not readily accessible to the beginning student in economics (unless he has had susbtantial background in mathematics and statistics) . A relatively readable introduction, which does not take the subject very far but which, nonetheless, requires attentive study on the part of most students, is provided by A. A. Walters, *An Introduction to Econometrics* (London: Macmillan 1968) .

[40] T. Wilson and P. W. S. Andrews, eds., *Oxford Studies in the Price Mechanism* (Oxford: Clarendon Press, 1951) , pp. 16-31.

[41] A comprehensive survey of the early studies is provided in Congress of the United States, Joint Economic Committee, *Staff Report on Employment, Growth and Price Levels* (Washington, 1959) . Two important survey papers were also published by the Commission on Money and Credit: D. B. Suits, "The Determinants of Consumer Expenditure: A Review of Present Knowledge," Commission on Money and Credit, *Impacts of Monetary Policy* (Englewood Cliffs, New Jersey: Prentice-Hall, 1963) , pp. 1-57; and R. Eisner and R. H. Strotz, "Determinants of Business Investment", *op. cit.*, pp. 60-337. See also R. H. Strotz, "Empirical Evidence on the Impact of Monetary Variables on Aggregate Expenditures," in F. Horwich ed., *Monetary Process and Policy: A Symposium* (Homewood, Illinois: Richard D. Irwin, 1967) , pp. 295-315.

[42] Johnson and Winder, *op cit.*, pp. 241-242.

[43] R. A. Shearer, *The Impact of Monetary Policy on the Current Account of the Balance of International Payments*, Working Paper for the Royal Commission on Banking and Finance (Ottawa: Queen's Printer, 1964) .

[44] One of the principal investigators, J. Helliwell, continued the work under the auspices of the Royal Commission on Taxation, undertaking an intensive exploration of the actual investment decision-making process in eight major Canadian corporations. The results of this investigation are published in J. Helliwell, *Taxation and Investment: A Study of Capital Expenditure Decisions in Large Corporations*, Studies for the Royal Commission on Taxation, No. 3 (Ottawa, 1964) ; and in J. Helliwell, *Public Policies and Private Investment* (Oxford: Clardon Press, 1968) . Chapter 7 of the latter book contains a useful summary of the two studies' findings on the impact of monetary policy on corporations.

[45] Porter *Report*, p. 430.

[46] M. Friedman, "The Supply of Money and Changes in Prices and Output", reprinted in *The Optimum Quantity of Money* (Chicago: Aldine, 1969) , p. 173.

[47] M. Friedman and A. J. Schwartz, *A Monetary History of the United States, 1867-1960* (Princeton: Princeton University Press, 1963) . Another important paper also emerged from this collaboration at this time, "Money and Business Cycles," in *Review of Economics and Statistics*, Vol. 45 (Feb. 1963) , Supplement, reprinted in *The Optimum Quantity of Money*, pp. 189-235.

[48] M. Friedman and D. Meiselman, "The Relative Stability of Monetary Velocity and the Investment Multiplier in the United States (1897-1960," in Commission on Money and Credit, *Stabilization Policies* (Englewood Cliffs: New Jersey, Prentice-Hall, 1963), pp. 165-268.

[49] J. Tobin and C. Swan, "Money and Permanent Income: Some Empirical Results", in *American Economic Review*, Vol. 59 (May 1969), pp. 285-295.

[50] G. Macesich, "The Quantity Theory and the Income Expenditure Theory in an Open Economy: Canada, 1926-1958," in *Canadian Journal of Economics and Political Science*, Vol. 30 (Aug. 1964), pp. 368-390.

[51] G. Macesich, "The Quantity Theory and Income Expenditure Theory in an Open Economy Revisited," in *Canadian Journal of Economics*, Vol. 2 (Aug. 1969), pp. 448-452.

[52] C. R. Barrett and A. A. Walters, "The Stability of Keynesian and Monetary Multipliers in the U.K.," in *Review of Economics and Statistics*, Vol. 48 (Nov. 1966), pp. 395-405. The results are also summarized in A. A. Walters, *Money in Boom and Slump*, Hobart Paper 44 (London: Institute of Economic Affairs, 1969).

[53] L. C. Anderson and J. L. Jordan, "Monetary and Fiscal Actions: A Test of Their Relative Importance in Economic Stabilization," in Federal Reserve Bank of St. Louis, *Review* Vol. 50 (Nov. 1968), pp. 11-24.

[54] M. J. Artis and A. R. Nobay, "Two Aspects of the Monetary Debate", in *National Institute Economic Review*, No. 49 (Aug. 1969), pp. 33-51.

[55] Johnson and Winder, *op cit.*, pp. 227-237.

[56] For example, see D. B. Suits, "Forecasting and Analysis with an Econometric Model", in *American Economic Review* Vol. 52 (Mar. 1962), pp. 104-132.

[57] R. Rhomberg, "A Model of the Canadian Economy under Fixed and Fluctuating Exchange Rates," in *Journal of Political Economy*, Vol. 72 (Feb. 1964), pp. 1-31.

[58] J. S. Duesenberry, G. Fromm, L. R. Klein and E. Kuh, *The Brookings Quarterly Econometric Model of the United States* (Chicago: Rand McNally, 1965).

[59] G. Fromm, "An Evaluation of Monetary Policy Instruments," in J. Duesenberry, G. Fromm, L. R. Klein and E. Kuh, *The Brookings Model: Some Further Results* (Amsterdam: North Holland, 1969), pp. 475-511. Fromm reports the following "elasticities" of gross national product with respect to the three policy instruments: open market operations, 0.346; increase in government expenditures, 0.093; reduction in personal income tax rates, 0.143.

[60] F. de Leeuw and E. Gramlich, "The Federal Reserve–M.I.T. Econometric Model," in *Federal Reserve Bulletin*, Vol. 54 (Jan. 1968), pp. 11-40; R. H. Rasche and H. T. Shapiro, "The F.R.B.–M.I.T. Econometric Model: Its Special Features," in *American Economic Review*, Vol. 58 (May 1968), pp. 123-149.

[61] J. F. Helliwell, L.H. Officer, H. T. Shapiro and I. A. Stewart, *The Structure of RDX1*, Bank of Canada, Staff Research Studies No. 3 (Ottawa, 1969).

[62] J. F. Helliwell, L. H. Officer, H. T. Shapiro and I. A. Stewart, "The Dynamics of RDX1," *Bank of Canada, Staff Research Studies* No. 5 (Ottawa, 1969). This volume contains a useful, detailed flowchart describing the interrelationships among variables and sectors of the model. The results of the simulation runs are also reported in J. F. Helliwell, L. H. Officers, H. T. Shapiro, and I. A. Stewart, "Econometric Analysis of Policy Choices for an Open Economy", in *The Review of Economics and Statistics*, Vol. 51 (Nov. 1969), pp. 383-398.

[63] *The Dynamics of RDX1*, p. 14. It should be noted that this does not include any impact on Canadian economic activity resulting from changes in income and employment in the United States in response to American monetary policy. Rather it reflects only the postulated impact of American interest rates on Canadian interst rates and hence on Canadian expenditures. Investigation of the first type of effect, coming through Canadian exports to the United States, would require the linking together of models of the Canadian and American economies. Some members of the Bank of Canada team are presently engaged in such a project.

[64] In a passage which has the appearance of an attempt to shift responsibility for inside lags away from the central bank, The Porter Commission argued that because of ever-present uncertainty, and the potential cost of serious errors in judgement, the process of policy-making could not be accelerated or made more decisive. Porter *Report*, pp. 465-468.

[65] Johnson and Winder, *op. cit.,* pp. 6-82.

[66] T. Mayer, "The Inflexibility of Monetary Policy," in *Review of Economics and Statistics,* Vol. 40 (Nov. 1958) , pp. 358-374.

[67] *Ibid.,* p. 370.

[68] *Ibid.,* p. 371.

[69] See particularly, M. Friedman, "The Supply of Money and Changes in Prices and Output," and M. Friedman and A. J. Schwartz, "Money and Business Cycles" Friedman has also defended his methodology in an essay "The Lag in Effect of Monetary Policy," in *Journal of Political Economy,* Vol: 69 (Oct. 1961) , pp. 447-466.

[70] Johnson and Winder, *loc. cit.*

[71] Porter *Report,* p. 438. See also Young and Helliwell, *op. cit.,* pp. 405-410.

[72] Porter *Report,* p. 438

[73] Rasche and Shapiro, *op. cit.,* p. 145.

[74] *The Dynamics of RDX1,* pp. 9-17.

24

The Quest for a

Monetary Constitution

Rules Versus Authority in Monetary Policy

The discussion of monetary policy in this book has begged a fundamental question. We have implicitly assumed that the central bank has the
authority to manipulate the money supply on its own discretion, and that
the best contribution which monetary economics can make to the formation
of policy is to provide theoretical and empirical guidance for more timely
and effective intervention on the part of the central bank in its pursuit
of "generally agreed" policy objectives. However, this is a position which
does not command universal support among monetary economists. It has
been vehemently argued that the central bank ought to have no discretion
in the management of the money supply, but ought to be bound to a simple
monetary constitution which involves a fixed rule for changes in the money
supply. In this view, the task of monetary economics is to devise, test and
refine money supply rules. The long-standing debate over this issue has
come to be known as the "rules versus authority" controversy.

1/THE CASE FOR A MONEY SUPPLY RULE

The case for a fixed money supply rule has two roots, one philosophical
and one empirical.

The Philosophy of the Free Market Economy

The foundation of the "rules" position is a philosophy of the appropriate role of government in the economy. It is argued that in general an
economy in which production and distribution are organized and directed
by competitive markets will simultaneously maximize individual freedom
and economic efficiency.[1] This is not to say that the government does not
have a vital role to play in the economy. However, with some exceptions,
the appropriate role of the government is simply "to provide a stable framework of rules within which enterprise and competition may effectively control and direct the production and distribution of goods."[2] Free markets

cannot function efficiently in the face of extreme uncertainty. It is important, therefore, that the rules be simple, comprehensible, and stable.

Production of Money. Control over the creation of money is one of the important exceptions to the general rule that the government should not intervene directly in economic activities. Economic efficiency argues for the use of fiat money rather than commodity money: both perform the same functions, but the former absorbs much less of the scarce real resources of society. However, if money is virtually costless to produce, and hence its value in the market vastly exceeds its costs of production, we cannot rely on profit calculations in competitive markets to produce the optimum quantity of money. In all likelihood, the result would be an explosive inflation. That is, failure of the government to control the money supply would lead to an extreme type of uncertainty, in the face of which competitive markets could not function effectively.

In some early expositions of the argument, this conclusion was followed by the advocacy of "100% reserves" for the banking system.[3] It was argued that if commercial banks were required to maintain 100% cash reserves behind all monetary deposit liabilities, the money supply could be completely divorced from private profitability calculations and placed completely in the hands of the government. Modern advocates of the free market position recognize that 100% reserves are not required for governmental control over the total money supply, even though part of the money supply is produced by private banks. It is sufficient that reserve ratios be relatively stable, or at least predictable, and that the government have direct control over the monetary base.

The Government and Monetary Uncertainty. Lodging control over the money supply in the hands of the government will not necessarily remove monetary uncertainty, unless the actions of the monetary authorities themselves are fully predictable. Thus, in the words of H. C. Simons, an early proponent of the rules philosophy:

> An enterprise system cannot function effectively in the face of extreme uncertainty as to the action of monetary authorities . . . where every business venture becomes largely a speculation on the future of monetary policy . . . [D]efinite, stable, legislative rules of the game as to money are of paramount importance to the survival of a system based on freedom of enterprise.[4]

Simons considered various possible rules, including the fixing of the quantity of money at some arbitrary level. Although he was not completely happy with it, (because it left the central bank with a considerable amount of discretion), he finally settled on one which focused on the *results* of governmental intervention — stability of the price level. That is, he argued that as a simple and comprehensible rule, the central bank ought to be compelled to manage the money supply in such a way as to achieve stability of general index of prices of goods and services.[5]

It is important to note that this "rule" involves an important empirical judgement. It presumes that the central bank can in fact manage the money supply in such a fashion as to achieve stability of the price level. Doubts on the empirical side in recent years have resulted in the advocacy of a different type of rule — one relating to the *form* of central bank intervention rather than the *results*.

The Empirical Basis of the Money Supply Rule

Recent advocates of a rules approach to monetary policy have not doubted Simons' assumption that the money supply affects economic activity, and particularly the price level. Indeed, their position is that of the modern quantity theory, which, as we saw in Chapter 20, and Chapter 23, implies that monetary policy has a very powerful impact. It is the very power of money which makes discretionary monetary policy such a threat to freedom, stability, and efficiency, because *central banks are inherently incapable of harnessing this power to achieve the desired results.*

Time Lags and Discretionary Monetary Policy. The problem is not that central bankers are devious or anti-social in their intentions. They are trapped by the fact that the *timing* of the impact of their actions is uncertain. Thus, time lags come to the fore of the debate. It is not simply that such lags exist and may be distributed over an extended period of time. If that were the only problem, improved techniques of prediction would presumably contain a solution. It is argued, however, that the lags are both long and *irregular,* and it is the latter attribute which causes the trouble.[6] If the timing of the impact cannot be predicted with any degree of accuracy, a discretionary monetary policy is likely to be perverse: imparting contractionary forces when expansion is the order of the day, and imparting expansionary forces when contraction is appropriate. The central bank is as likely to be a source of economic instability as it is to counteract such instability, and the central banker cannot do better because he cannot know when his actions will affect economic activity.[7]

The Money Supply Rule. Given the present state of knowledge, perfection cannot be expected. However, it is argued that the simple rule of *increasing the money supply at a constant rate* would vastly improve the performance of monetary policy. Thus,

> A fixed rate of increase in the stock of money would almost certainly rule out . . . rapid and sizeable fluctuations, though it would not rule out mild cyclical or secular fluctuations [in economic activity], and it would give a firm basis for long range planning on the part of the public.[8]

This raises several technical questions. How should the money supply be defined? What is the appropriate growth rate? What should be done about seasonal, weekly and daily fluctuations in the demand for money?

The central issue is, of course, the growth rate. It is argued that the money supply should be allowed to increase at approximately the same rate as the demand for money would increase, if the general level of prices were constant. In practice this means a rate of growth roughly equal to the long-run rate of growth of productivity in the economy, with perhaps a slight upward adjustment to allow for the empirical finding that money is a "luxury" good, the demand for which increases as per capita income rises (Chapter 19). Precision is not essential. The economy is capable of adjusting to *moderate* upward or downward trends in the general level of prices without any serious loss of efficiency.[9] Thus, Friedman proposes a rate in the range of 3% to 5% per annum.[10] However, what is essential is that the rate, once chosen, be *stable* and hence *predictable*.

In Canada, the major proponent of such a policy has been the Economic Council of Canada. In its Annual Reviews of the performance of the Canadian economy, it has consistently urged a long-run policy of "expanding the money supply roughly in line with growing potential output."[11]

The other questions are technical details. The exact definition of the money supply is not important, as long as it contains the major monetary media, currency and demand deposits (although advocates of the rule usually include time deposits at commercial banks). Seasonal and similar adjustments are appropriate, providing they are to accommodate regular shifts in the demand for money and hence are fully predictable.

It is not argued that this money supply rule will provide the best of all worlds. However, it will protect us from major blunders, and will neutralize the central bank as a source of monetary instability. Thus, the Economic Council of Canada stated in their First Annual Review, that such a policy of expanding the money supply in line with the growth of potential output would, "help both to minimize the dangers of shorter term instability and to assist in the successful attainment of orderly progress towards consistent high standards of performance in the Canadian economy."[12] As experience accrues with the operation of such a rule, our knowledge of the functioning of the monetary system will improve, and we should be able to devise still better rules for controlling the money supply.

2/THE CASE AGAINST A MONEY SUPPLY RULE

Attacks on the proposal for a fixed money supply rule have not been lacking. Thus, the distinguished British scholar of central banking, R. S. Sayers, has asserted:

> We are doomed to disappointment if we look for rules that are applicable to all times and places. We have central banks for the very reason that there are no such rules.[13]

Elsewhere he states that "the essence of central banking is discretionary control of the monetary system."[14]

In a slightly different vein, Professor P. Samuelson has derided the black and white contrast which is drawn between "discretion" and "rules":

> for when men set up a definitive mechanism which is to run forever afterward by itself, that involves a single act of discretion which transcends, both in its arrogance and its capacity for potential harm, any repeated acts of foolish discretion that can be imagined.[15]

In other words, the quest for immutable rules — attractive as they may be — is at best idle dreaming, and at worst highly dangerous.

What analytical content can we put into the objections to a fixed money supply rule?

Stability of the Demand for Money

As we have noted at various points in our exposition of the theory of monetary policy, the key issue is the nature and stability of the demand for money. The critics are in effect arguing that the money supply rule rests too much on one debatable empirical finding: Friedman's conclusion that the demand for money is a stable function of permanent income, and is little affected by the availability of, or yields on, other financial instruments. This gives the demand for money long-run stability, and provides the underpinning for a long-run money supply rule. It is accepted that monetary instability may affect the demand for money, either by engendering extreme uncertainty and hence precautionary demands for money, or by generating expectations of price level changes. But these are not autonomous shifts in the demand for money. They are induced by the behaviour of the money supply. They are a by-product of inappropriate central banking policies.

Whereas the advocates of a money supply rule find the source of all monetary instability on the supply side; i.e., with the central bank itself, the critics are in effect arguing that central bank discretion is essential to offset independent shifts in the demand for money, or to neutralize the effects of substitutions between money and near money. Whereas proponents of the rule emphasize a stable long-run relationship between income and money demanded, critics assert that it is the short-run instability of the ratio which is the central banking problem. We have here an empirical issue on which, as we have seen, the evidence is inconclusive (but perhaps this in itself tips the balance against a money supply rule) .

The Money Supply Rule in the Open Economy. In an economy such as Canada's, the adoption of a fixed money supply rule raises another class of problems. As we saw in Chapter 21, monetary policy in an open economy with a fixed exchange rate will be largely dictated by the balance of international payments. Except by chance, the monetary policy required for balance of payments equilibrium will be inconsistent with any arbitrarily chosen money supply rule. This may even be true if the major external market, the United States, has adopted the same money supply rule because of the possibility of "structural" changes in the flow of trade and investment from time to time. It follows that in an open economy a fixed money supply is inconsistent with a commitment to fixed exchange rates, and it is not by accident that the major exponent of the rules approach to monetary policy is also a major exponent of flexible exchange rates.[16]

It is not by accident either that the major Canadian exponents of a monetary policy oriented to the long run also accept the idea that there must be sufficient short-run flexibility to cope with balance of payments problems unless the exchange rate is allowed to fluctuate freely.[17]

Tests of the Money Supply Rule. It is difficult to devise discriminating empirical tests for the effectiveness of such a sweeping change in the conduct of monetary policy. Since the experiment has not been conducted, history provides no direct evidence. However, several economists have attempted to evaluate the relative effectiveness of rules and discretion, basically by analyzing the behaviour of the money supply in relation to aggregate economic activity (a measure of the degree of monetary ease or tightness) during various time periods, and comparing this behaviour to what would have happened to the relationship under various hypothetical money supply rules. Most of this research has been concerned with American experience, although Johnson and Winder have reported such a study for Canada.

The results of this research are inconclusive. In an early study, E. S. Shaw concluded emphatically that a simple money supply rule (a stable growth rate) would have been in the "right" direction more often than was the Federal Reserve System, over the entire history of that system.[18] In a smaller vein, Johnson and Winder, in a study discussed earlier (Chapter 23), found that Canadian monetary policy had been seriously perverse in the 1950's and early 1960's, and that a money supply rule would have been superior.[19] Bronfenbrenner considered a variety of rules, and reached less clear-cut conclusions. He tentatively accepted the superiority of a modified money supply rule, but agreed that the evidence was not strong.[20] Modigliani, pursuing the Bronfenbrenner study further, came to the opposite conclusion, arguing that the empirical record favoured discretion, providing the monetary authorities use the discretion in the pursuit of clearly defined goals.[21]

This range of empirical findings (a problem to which we should be well conditioned, by now) is disquieting, particularly given the importance of the issues at stake. However in a sense, all of the evidence may be irrelevant. The tests presume that central bankers cannot improve on their past performance. It can be argued, however, that much of the historical record was in fact a learning process. It contains errors in judgement, misconceptions of the nature, purpose and effects of monetary policy, and conflicts (or confusions) over the objectives to be pursued, rather than (or, as well as) inherent defects in discretionary policy emanating from long and variable time lags. Objectives can be clarified and conflicts in priorities resolved, and techniques of central bank decision-making and intervention can be refined.[22] The point is not that perfection is just around the corner, but rather that the historical record may be a poor guide to what can be achieved in the future.

FOOTNOTES

[1] For a highly readable but sophisticated exposition of the general thesis see M. Friedman, *Capitalism and Freedom* (Chicago: University of Chicago Press, 1962). This work is a modern economics classic.

[2] H. C. Simons, "Rules versus Authorities in Monetary Policy," in *Journal of Political Economy*, Vol. 44 (1936), pp. 1-30; p. 1.

[3] H. C. Simons, *op. cit.*, Reprinted in American Economic Association, *Readings in*

Monetary Theory (Philadelphia, 1952), pp. 337-368. Subsequent page references are to the latter publication.

[4] *Ibid.*, pp. 338-339.

[5] *Ibid.*, p. 351.

[6] M. Friedman, "The Supply of Money and Changes in Prices and Output," in *The Optimum Quantity of Money* (Chicago: Aldine, 1969), pp. 171-187.

[7] For an argument along this line with reference to Canada see: D. J. Daly, "The Scope for Monetary Policy—A Synthesis," in *Conference on Stabilization Policies*, Economic Council of Canada, (Ottawa: Queen's Printer, 1966).

[8] M. Friedman, *A Program for Monetary Stability* (New York: Fordham University Press, 1960), p. 92.

[9] M. Friedman, "The Supply of Money and Changes in Prices and Output," p. 186.

[10] M. Friedman, *A Program for Monetary Stability*, p. 91.

[11] Economic Council of Canada. *Towards Sustained and Balanced Economic Growth, Second Annual Review of the Economic Council of Canada*, (Ottawa: Queen's Printer, 1965).

[12] Economic Council of Canada, *Economic Goals for Canada to 1970, First Annual Review of the Economic Council of Canada*, (Ottawa: Queen's Printer, 1964), p. 198.

[13] R. S. Sayers, *Central Banking After Bagehot* (Oxford: Oxford University Press, 1957), p. 7.

[14] *Ibid.*, p. 1.

[15] P. Samuelson, "Reflections on Central Banking," in *National Banking Review*, Vol. 1, (Sept. 1963), p. 16.

[16] M. Friedman, "The Case for Flexible Exchange Rates," in *Essays in Positive Economics* (Chicago: University of Chicago Press, 1953), pp. 157-201.

[17] Economic Council of Canada, *The Canadian Economy From the 1960's to the 1970's, Fourth Annual Review of the Economic Council of Canada* (Ottawa: Queen's Printer, 1967), pp. 255-258.

[18] E. S. Shaw, "Money Supply and Stable Economic Growth," in N. H. Jacoby, ed., *United States Monetary Policy*, rev. ed. (New York: American Assembly, 1964), pp. 73-93.

[19] H. G. Johnson and J. L. Winder, *Lags in the Effects of Monetary Policy*.

[20] M. Bronfenbrenner, "Statistical Tests of Rival Monetary Rules," in *Journal of Political Economy*, Vol. 69 (Feb. 1961), pp. 1-14; "Statistical Tests of Rival Monetary Rules: Quarterly Data Supplement" in *Journal of Political Economy*, Vol. 68 (Dec. 1961), pp. 621-625.

[21] F. Modigliani, "Some Empirical Tests of Monetary Management and Rules Versus Discretion," in *Journal of Political Economy*, Vol. 72 (June 1964), pp. 211-245.

[22] See also H. G. Johnson, "Alternative Guiding Principles of the Use of Monetary Policy," in *Essays in International Finance*, No. 44 (Princeton: Princeton University Press, 1963).

Index

621

E

Econometric models:
Bank of Canada RDXI, 603-604
Brookings, 603-604
defined, 599
and effectiveness of monetary policy,
602-604
Federal Reserve/MIT, 603-604
and simulation experiments, 599
Economic Council of Canada:
and money supply rule, 616
and unemployment and inflation, 495-
496
Economies of scale:
in commercial banking, 322-323
and expansion of US commercial
banking, 295
in portfolio management, 159-163
and role of financial intermediaries,
161-162
Euro-Dollar market, 201, 287, 309n, 398,
572
Exchange economy:
described, 6-7

F

Federal Deposit Insurance Corporation
(*see* Deposit insurance, US)
Federal funds, US:
defined, 286
market for, 286-287, 398
Federal Home Loan Bank System, 307-
308, 310n-311n
Federal Reserve System (*see also* Commercial banks, US)
availability doctrine, 587-588, 608n
and central bank advances, 395-401
and clearing system, 24-28
and competition policy, 300-302, 332
history:
National Monetary Commission, 269
reforms, 299-300
Regulation Q, 308, 332
structure, 25, 298-300
Board of Governors, 300
Open Market Committee, 300
variable cash reserve ratios, 285, 423-
424, 429n

Financial flows:
assets, 57-58, 157-159
defined, 6
Financial Flow Accounts, 120-129,
130n
liabilities, 57-58, 157-159
and real flows, 6
Financial industry (*see* Financial intermediaries and intermediation)
Financial institutions (*see* Financial intermediaries and intermediation;
Financial markets)
Financial instruments:
characteristics, 37-44
defined, 9, 37
demand for, 56-106 (*see also* Portfolio
Balance decision; Saving)
equilibrium price, 117-120
liquidity, 75-81, 96-97
supply of, 13, 107-152
types, 37-55
bills, 40, 100-102
bonds, 38-41, 77-79, 82-84, 86-87,
102-106
commercial and finance paper, 53
money, (*see* Money)
treasury bills, 50-51
variable income securities (stocks),
41-43, 87
Financial intermediaries and intermediation:
banks (*see* Chartered banks; Commercial banks)
caisses populaires (*see* Co-operative
banks)
consumer loan companies (*see* Consumer loan companies)
competition, 246-247, 313-336
and creation of money (*see* Deposit
creation)
credit unions (*see* Co-operative banks)
defined, 2, 12, 153
government lending institutions (*see*
Government lending institutions)
history:
early Canadian development, 248-
260
1800-1830, 249-253
1830-Confederation, 253-256
Confederation-1891, 257-260
1890-1914, 260-263
1914-1920, 261-263
1920-1935, 269-275

Monetary theory (continued)
quantity theory (modern), 447-450, 464-466, 489-491, 497-498n, 601-604, 613-618 (*see also* Quantity theory, modern)
Money:
defined, 5, 14-15
evolution, 15-16
as medium of exchange, 14-16
and payments system, 5, 14-36
substitutes for, 80-81
types, 15-16, 20-22
bank money, 16
commodity, 15-16
currency, 16
fiat, 15-16
legal tender, 16
as unit of account, 43-44
Money, demand for, 431-450
asset, 80, 439-442
empirical research, 444-450
and income, 437-439
and inflation, 442-444
and interest rates, 440-441, 445-446, 451n, 594
and liquidity, 44, 80-81, 439-440
in monetary theory, 338-341, 462, 464, 474, 586-596, 617
and permanent income, 448-450, 451n
and prices, 442-444
theories of:
classical, 338-339, 431-435
Friedman's, 449-450
Keynesian, 439-442, 446-447, 474
transactions demand, 34, 80, 431-439
inventory theoretic model, 435-437
and wealth, 440-441, 447-450
Money, high powered:
defined, 352
and deposit creation, 368, 373
supply, 380-387
Money market:
Bank of Canada advances, 52-53
competition in, 316
and country banking, 53-54
defined, 50
institutional changes, 51, 278, 403
instruments, 50-54
in Keynesian theory, 474-477
role in financial system, 54-55
US, 286
Money multiplier models, 351-352, 373-379

Money supply:
composition of, 16-22, 343
control of (*see* Monetary policy)
creation (*see* Deposit creation)
history, 15-18, 248-280
real vs. nominal, 443
Money supply rule, 613-618
case against, 616-618
case for, 613-616
Mortgage loan companies, 220-221
Multiplier (*see* Balanced budget multiplier)
Mutual funds, 225-230

N

National Bank Act (1863-1864), US, 257, 284, 296-298
Near banks, 205-224 (*see also* Trust companies; Mortgage loan companies; Co-operative banks; Quebec savings banks; Government savings depositories)
access to clearing system, 24, 33
compared to banks, 205-206
defined, 205
and deposit creation, 365-372
deposits (*see* Deposits)
and effectiveness of monetary policy, 591-592, 594
and near money, 365-368, 591
US:
characteristics of, 306-308
competition with banks, 308
types, 304-305
Near money:
defined, 19
Nobay, A. R.:
on effectiveness of monetary policy, 602

O

Oligopoly:
and price competition, 317-318
Open market operations (*see* Monetary policy, instruments)
Operation twist:
and debt management, 595

630

Speculation (continued)
  against Canadian dollar, 1968, 535-537
  and choice among financial instruments, 81-86
  and exchange fund, 533
  and inter-central bank credits, 534
  in stock markets, 85-86
Sterling area:
  and foreign exchange reserves, 563
  history, 583n
Stock exchanges:
  defined, 47-48
  origins, 268
Stock variables:
  defined, 107
Sutch, T.:
  on debt management, 595

T

Taxation:
  and demand for financial instruments, 89
  and fiscal policy, 481-485
Time lags, 465-466, 615
  inside lags, 605-606
  outside lags, 605-606
Tobin, J.:
  on interest elasticity of demand for money, 445
  on inventory theoretic model, 436-437
Trade (see International trade)
Trade-off function (see also Phillips curve)
  policy implications, 495-496
  theory of, 492-496
Transactions costs, 98
  and demand for money, 435-437, 440
Trust companies, 328
  cash reserves, 218
  defined, 215
  estate, trust and agency business, 215-216
  as financial intermediaries, 217-220
  sources of funds, 217
  uses of funds, 216, 218-220

U

Underwriting:
  and competition in financial markets, 316

Underwriting (continued)
  defined, 46
Unemployment:
  classical theory, 461
  Keynesian theory, 466-491
  modern quantity theory, 465, 491
  and Phillips curve, 492
  and rate of change in wages, 492-496
Unit banking system, US, 25, 288

V

Value added:
  in financial industry, 3-4
Variable income securities:
  common stocks, 41-42
  preferred stocks, 42
  yield on, 104-105
Velocity of circulation:
  in classical quantity theory, 462-463
  defined, 34, 441
  and interest rates, 441-442
  in Keynesian system, 478-479
  in modern quantity theory, 464-465
  Radcliffe Committee, 589

W

Wage rates:
  and Phillips curve, 492-495
Walters, A. A.:
  on quantity theory, 602
Wealth:
  defined, 9, 57
  demand for, 57-66
  and demand for money, 440-441, 447-450
Winder, J. W. L.:
  on effectiveness of monetary policy, 600-601
  on money supply rule, 618
  on time lags, 606-607

Y

Yield (see Portfolio balance decision)
Yield curve:
  defined, 75-76
  and liquidity preference, 76-81
  and speculation, 82-84
Young, J. H.:
  on effectiveness of monetary policy, 597